Issues in
Economics Today

Seventh Edition

The McGraw-Hill/Irwin Series in Economics

ESSENTIALS OF ECONOMICS

Brue, McConnell, and Flynn
Essentials of Economics
Third Edition

Mandel
Economics: The Basics
Second Edition

Schiller
Essentials of Economics
Ninth Edition

PRINCIPLES OF ECONOMICS

Colander
Economics, Microeconomics, and Macroeconomics
Ninth Edition

Frank and Bernanke
Principles of Economics, Principles of Microeconomics, and Principles of Macroeconomics
Fifth Edition

Frank and Bernanke
Brief Editions: Principles of Economics, Principles of Microeconomics, and Principles of Macroeconomics
Second Edition

Karlan and Morduch
Economics, Microeconomics, and Macroeconomics
First Edition

McConnell, Brue, and Flynn
Economics, Microeconomics, and Macroeconomics
Twentieth Edition

McConnell, Brue, and Flynn
Brief Editions: Economics, Microeconomics, and Macroeconomics
Second Edition

Miller
Principles of Microeconomics
First Edition

Samuelson and Nordhaus
Economics, Microeconomics, and Macroeconomics
Nineteenth Edition

Schiller
The Economy Today, The Micro Economy Today, and The Macro Economy Today
Thirteenth Edition

Slavin
Economics, Microeconomics, and Macroeconomics
Twelfth Edition

ECONOMICS OF SOCIAL ISSUES

Guell
Issues in Economics Today
Seventh Edition

Sharp, Register, and Grimes
Economics of Social Issues
Twentieth Edition

ECONOMETRICS

Gujarati and Porter
Basic Econometrics
Fifth Edition

Gujarati and Porter
Essentials of Econometrics
Fourth Edition

Hilmer and Hilmer
Practical Econometrics
First Edition

MANAGERIAL ECONOMICS

Baye and Prince
Managerial Economics and Business Strategy
Eighth Edition

Brickley, Smith, and Zimmerman
Managerial Economics and Organizational Architecture
Fifth Edition

Thomas and Maurice
Managerial Economics
Eleventh Edition

INTERMEDIATE ECONOMICS

Bernheim and Whinston
Microeconomics
Second Edition

Dornbusch, Fischer, and Startz
Macroeconomics
Twelfth Edition

Frank
Microeconomics and Behavior
Ninth Edition

ADVANCED ECONOMICS

Romer
Advanced Macroeconomics
Fourth Edition

MONEY AND BANKING

Cecchetti and Schoenholtz
Money, Banking, and Financial Markets
Fourth Edition

URBAN ECONOMICS

O'Sullivan
Urban Economics
Eighth Edition

LABOR ECONOMICS

Borjas
Labor Economics
Sixth Edition

McConnell, Brue, and Macpherson
Contemporary Labor Economics
Tenth Edition

PUBLIC FINANCE

Rosen and Gayer
Public Finance
Tenth Edition

Seidman
Public Finance
First Edition

ENVIRONMENTAL ECONOMICS

Field and Field
Environmental Economics: An Introduction
Sixth Edition

INTERNATIONAL ECONOMICS

Appleyard and Field
International Economics
Eighth Edition

King and King
International Economics, Globalization, and Policy: A Reader
Fifth Edition

Pugel
International Economics
Fifteenth Edition

Issues in Economics Today

Seventh Edition

ROBERT C. GUELL
Indiana State University

ISSUES IN ECONOMICS TODAY, SEVENTH EDITION

Published by McGraw-Hill Education, 2 Penn Plaza, New York, NY 10121. Copyright © 2015 by McGraw-Hill Education. All rights reserved. Printed in the United States of America. Previous editions © 2012, 2010, and 2008. No part of this publication may be reproduced or distributed in any form or by any means, or stored in a database or retrieval system, without the prior written consent of McGraw-Hill Education, including, but not limited to, in any network or other electronic storage or transmission, or broadcast for distance learning.

Some ancillaries, including electronic and print components, may not be available to customers outside the United States.

This book is printed on acid-free paper.

1 2 3 4 5 6 7 8 9 0 DOW/DOW 1 0 9 8 7 6 5 4

ISBN   978-0-07-802181-7
MHID   0-07-802181-2

Senior Vice President, Products & Markets: *Kurt L. Strand*
Vice President, General Manager, Products & Markets: *Michael Ryan*
Vice President, Content Production & Technology Services: *Kimberly Meriwether David*
Managing Director: *Douglas Reiner*
Executive Brand Manager: *Michele Janicek*
Director of Development: *Ann Torbert*
Managing Development Editor: *Christina Kouvelis*
Marketing Manager: *Katie Hoenicke*
Marketing Specialist: *Jennifer M. Jelinski*
Director, Content Production: *Terri Schiesl*
Content Project Manager: *Lisa Bruflodt*
Buyer: *Nichole Birkenholz*
Cover Image: *franckreporter/Getty Images*
Media Project Manager: *Shawn Coenen*
Compositor: *MPS Limited*
Typeface: *10/12 Times*
Printer: *R. R. Donnelley*

All credits appearing on page or at the end of the book are considered to be an extension of the copyright page.

Library of Congress Cataloging-in-Publication Data

Guell, Robert C.
  Issues in economics today / Robert C. Guell, Indiana State University. --
Seventh Edition.
     pages cm. -- (Issues in economics today)
  ISBN 978-0-07-802181-7 (alk. paper)
1. Economics. I. Title.
HB87.G83 2014
330--dc23

                                    2013043696

The Internet addresses listed in the text were accurate at the time of publication. The inclusion of a website does not indicate an endorsement by the authors or McGraw-Hill Education, and McGraw-Hill Education does not guarantee the accuracy of the information presented at these sites.

To Susan, Katie, and Matt

About the **Author**

Dr. Robert C. Guell (pronounced "Gill") is a professor of economics at Indiana State University in Terre Haute, Indiana. He earned a B.A. in statistics and economics in 1986 and an M.S. in economics one year later from the University of Missouri–Columbia. In 1991, he earned a Ph.D. from Syracuse University, where he discovered the thrill of teaching. He has taught courses for freshmen, upper-division undergraduates, and graduate students from the principles level, through public finance, all the way to mathematical economics and econometrics.

Dr. Guell has published numerous peer-reviewed articles in scholarly journals. He has worked extensively in the area of pharmaceutical economics, suggesting that the private market's patent system, while necessary for drug innovation, is unnecessary and inefficient for production.

In 1998, Dr. Guell was the youngest faculty member ever to have been given Indiana State University's Caleb Mills Distinguished Teaching Award. His talent as a champion of quality teaching was recognized again in 2000 when he was named project manager for the Lilly Project to Transform the First-Year Experience, a Lilly Endowment–funded project to raise first-year persistence rates at Indiana State University. He was ISU's Coordinator of First-Year Programs until January 2008, when he happily stepped aside to rejoin his department full time.

Dr. Guell's passion for teaching economics led him to request an assignment with the largest impact. The one-semester general education basic economics course became the vehicle to express that passion. Unsatisfied with the books available for the course, he made it his calling to produce what you have before you today—an all-in-one readable issues-based text.

Brief Contents

1   Economics: The Study of Opportunity Cost   1

2   Supply and Demand   18

3   The Concept of Elasticity and Consumer and Producer Surplus   39

4   Firm Production, Cost, and Revenue   54

5   Perfect Competition, Monopoly, and Economic versus Normal Profit   66

6   Every Macroeconomic Word You Ever Heard: Gross Domestic Product, Inflation, Unemployment, Recession, and Depression   77

7   Interest Rates and Present Value   93

8   Aggregate Demand and Aggregate Supply   102

9   Fiscal Policy   114

10   Monetary Policy   126

11   Federal Spending   139

12   Federal Deficits, Surpluses, and the National Debt   149

13   The Housing Bubble   162

14   The Recession of 2007–2009: Causes and Policy Responses   171

15   Japan's Lost Decade: Could It Happen in the United States?   180

16   Is the (Fiscal) Sky Falling?: An Examination of Unfunded Social Security, Medicare, and State and Local Pension Liabilities   189

17   International Trade: Does It Jeopardize American Jobs?   197

18   International Finance and Exchange Rates   209

19   European Debt Crisis   218

20   Economic Growth and Development   227

21   The Line between Legal and Illegal Goods   234

22   Natural Resources, the Environment, and Climate Change   244

23   Health Care   257

24   Government-Provided Health Insurance: Medicaid, Medicare, and the Child Health Insurance Program   269

25   The Economics of Prescription Drugs   282

26   So You Want to Be a Lawyer: Economics and the Law   290

27   The Economics of Crime   296

28   The Economics of Race and Sex Discrimination   305

29   Income and Wealth Inequality: What's Fair?   317

30   Farm Policy   326

31   Minimum Wage   335

32   Ticket Brokers and Ticket Scalping   343

33   The Economics of K–12 Education   350

34   College and University Education: Why Is It So Expensive?   361

35   Poverty and Welfare   371

36   Social Security   382

37   Personal Income Taxes   393

38   Energy Prices   404

39   If We Build It, Will They Come? And Other Sports Questions   417

40   The Stock Market and Crashes   429

41   Unions   440

42   Walmart: Always Low Prices (and Low Wages)—Always   450

43   The Economic Impact of Casino Gambling   455

Table of **Contents**

Chapter 1

Economics: The Study of Opportunity Cost   1

Economics and Opportunity Cost   1
  Economics Defined   1
  Choices Have Consequences   2
Modeling Opportunity Cost Using the Production
  Possibilities Frontier   2
  The Intuition behind Our First Graph   2
  *The Starting Point for a Production Possibilities
    Frontier   3*
  *Points between the Extremes of a Production Possibilities
    Frontier   3*
Attributes of the Production Possibilities Frontier   5
  Increasing and Constant Opportunity Cost   5
The Big Picture   6
  *Circular Flow Model: A Model That Shows the
    Interactions of All Economic Actors   6*
Thinking Economically   7
  Marginal Analysis   7
  Positive and Normative Analysis   8
  Economic Incentives   8
  Fallacy of Composition   8
  Correlation ≠ Causation   9
Kick It Up a Notch: Demonstrating Constant and
  Increasing Opportunity Cost on a Production
  Possibilities Frontier   10
  Demonstrating Increasing Opportunity Cost   10
  Demonstrating Constant Opportunity Cost   10
Summary   11

Chapter 2

Supply and Demand   18

Supply and Demand Defined   19
  Markets   19
  Quantity Demanded and Quantity Supplied   19
  Ceteris Paribus   21
  Demand and Supply   21
The Supply and Demand Model   21
  Demand   21
  Supply   22
  Equilibrium   23
  Shortages and Surpluses   24

All about Demand   24
  The Law of Demand   24
  Why Does the Law of Demand Make Sense?   24
All about Supply   25
  The Law of Supply   25
  Why Does the Law of Supply Make Sense?   25
Determinants of Demand   26
  Taste   27
  Income   27
  Price of Other Goods   27
  Population of Potential Buyers   28
  Expected Price   28
  Excise Taxes   28
  Subsidies   28
  *The Effect of Changes in the Determinants of Demand
    on the Supply and Demand Model   28*
Determinants of Supply   30
  Price of Inputs   30
  Technology   31
  Price of Other Potential Outputs   31
  Number of Sellers   31
  Expected Price   31
  Excise Taxes   32
  Subsidies   32
  *The Effect of Changes in the Determinants of
    Supply on the Supply and Demand Model   32*
The Effect of Changes in Price Expectations
  on the Supply and Demand Model   34
Kick It Up a Notch: Why the New
  Equilibrium?   34
Summary   36

Chapter 3

**The Concept of Elasticity and Consumer
and Producer Surplus   39**

Elasticity of Demand   40
  Intuition   40
  Definition of Elasticity and Its Formula   40
  Elasticity Labels   41
Alternative Ways to Understand Elasticity   41
  The Graphical Explanation   41
  The Verbal Explanation   42
  Seeing Elasticity through Total Expenditures   43

More on Elasticity   43
   Determinants of Elasticity   43
   Elasticity and the Demand Curve   43
   Elasticity of Supply   45
Consumer and Producer Surplus   47
   Consumer Surplus   47
   Producer Surplus   48
   Market Failure   48
   Categorizing Goods   49
Kick It Up a Notch: Deadweight Loss   49
Summary   50

Chapter 4
Firm Production, Cost, and Revenue   54

Production   55
   Just Words   55
   Graphical Explanation   56
   Numerical Example   56
Costs   57
   Just Words   57
   Numerical Example   58
Revenue   60
   Just Words   60
   Numerical Example   61
Maximizing Profit   62
   Graphical Explanation   62
   Numerical Example   62
Summary   63

Chapter 5
Perfect Competition, Monopoly, and Economic versus Normal Profit   66

From Perfect Competition to Monopoly   67
   Perfect Competition   67
   Monopoly   68
   Monopolistic Competition   68
   Oligopoly   69
   Which Model Fits Reality   69
Supply under Perfect Competition   71
   Normal versus Economic Profit   71
   When and Why Economic Profits Go to Zero   71
   *Why Supply Is Marginal Cost under Perfect
      Competition   71*
   Just Words   72
   Numerical Example   72
   Graphical Explanation   72
Summary   74

Chapter 6
Every Macroeconomic Word You Ever Heard: Gross Domestic Product, Inflation, Unemployment, Recession, and Depression   77

Measuring the Economy   78
   Measuring Nominal Output   78
   Measuring Prices and Inflation   79
   Problems Measuring Inflation   80
Real Gross Domestic Product and Why It Is Not
   Synonymous with Social Welfare   82
   Real Gross Domestic Product   82
   Problems with Real GDP   84
Measuring and Describing Unemployment   85
   Measuring Unemployment   85
   Problems Measuring Unemployment   85
   Types of Unemployment   86
Business Cycles   87
Kick It Up a Notch: National Income and Product
   Accounting   90
Summary   90

Chapter 7
Interest Rates and Present Value   93

Interest Rates   94
   The Market for Money   94
   Nominal Interest Rates versus Real Interest Rates   94
Present Value   95
   Simple Calculations   95
   *Mortgages, Car Payments, and Other Multipayment
      Examples   96*
Future Value   97
Kick It Up a Notch: Risk and Reward   99
Summary   99

Chapter 8
Aggregate Demand and Aggregate Supply   102

Aggregate Demand   103
   Definition   103
   Why Aggregate Demand Is Downward Sloping   103
Aggregate Supply   104
   Definition   104
   *Competing Views of the Shape of
      Aggregate Supply   104*
Shifts in Aggregate Demand and Aggregate
   Supply   105

Variables That Shift Aggregate Demand   105
Variables That Shift Aggregate Supply   108
Causes of Inflation   109
How the Government Can Influence
   (but Probably Not Control) the Economy   109
   Demand-Side Macroeconomics   110
   Supply-Side Macroeconomics   110
Summary   111

Chapter 9
Fiscal Policy   114

Nondiscretionary and
   Discretionary Fiscal Policy   114
   How They Work   114
   Using Aggregate Supply and Aggregate Demand
     to Model Fiscal Policy   115
Using Fiscal Policy to
   Counteract "Shocks"   116
   Aggregate Demand Shocks   116
   Aggregate Supply Shocks   117
Evaluating Fiscal Policy   118
   Nondiscretionary Fiscal Policy   118
   Discretionary Fiscal Policy   118
   The Political Problems with Fiscal Policy   119
   Criticism from the Right and Left   120
   The Rise, Fall, and Rebirth of
     Discretionary Fiscal Policy   120
The Obama Stimulus Plan   121
Kick It Up a Notch: Aggregate
   Supply Shocks   123
Summary   123

Chapter 10
Monetary Policy   126

Goals, Tools, and a Model
   of Monetary Policy   127
   Goals of Monetary Policy   127
   Traditional and Ordinary Tools
     of Monetary Policy   127
   Modeling Monetary Policy   128
   The Monetary Transmission Mechanism   129
   The Additional Tools of Monetary
     Policy Created in 2008   131
Central Bank Independence   132
Modern Monetary Policy   133
   The Last 30 Years   133
Summary   137

Chapter 11
Federal Spending   139

A Primer on the Constitution and Spending
   Money   140
   What the Constitution Says   140
   Shenanigans   140
   Dealing with Disagreements   141
Using Our Understanding
   of Opportunity Cost   142
   Mandatory versus Discretionary Spending   142
   Where the Money Goes   143
Using Our Understanding
   of Marginal Analysis   145
   The Size of the Federal Government   145
   The Distribution of Federal Spending   145
Budgeting for the Future   145
   Baseline versus Current Services Budgeting   145
Summary   146

Chapter 12
Federal Deficits, Surpluses,
and the National Debt   149

Surpluses, Deficits, and the Debt: Definitions and
   History   150
   Definitions   150
   History   150
How Economists See the
   Deficit and the Debt   153
   Operating and Capital Budgets   153
   Cyclical and Structural Deficits   153
   The Debt as a Percentage of GDP   154
   International Comparisons   154
   Generational Accounting   155
Who Owns the Debt?   155
   Externally Held Debt   156
A Balanced-Budget Amendment   157
Projections   158
Summary   159

Chapter 13
The Housing Bubble   162

How Much Is a House Really Worth?   162
Mortgages   163
How to Make a Bubble   166
Pop Goes the Bubble!   167
The Effect on the Overall Economy   168
Summary   169

Chapter 14

The Recession of 2007–2009: Causes and Policy Responses 171

Before It Began 171
Late 2007: The Recession Begins as Do the Initial
  Policy Reactions 174
The Bottom Falls Out in Fall 2008 176
The Obama Stimulus Package 176
Extraordinary Monetary Stimulus 178
Summary 179

Chapter 15

Japan's Lost Decade: Could It Happen in the United States? 180

The Economic Situation in Japan
  Prior to 1990 180
So What Happened in
  Japan to Change All This? 182
  What Did Japan Do (Wrong)? 183
  *How Can This Be Modeled Using the
    Aggregate Supply–Aggregate
    Demand Model?* 185
How Is This Similar to the Current Situation in the
  United States? 185
Summary 187

Chapter 16

Is the (Fiscal) Sky Falling?: An Examination of Unfunded Social Security, Medicare, and State and Local Pension Liabilities 189

What Is the Source of the Problem? 189
How Big Is the Social Security and Medicare
  Problem? 190
How Big Is the State and Local
  Pension Problem? 193
Is It Possible That the Fiscal Sky Isn't About to
  Fall? 195
Summary 195

Chapter 17

International Trade: Does It Jeopardize American Jobs? 197

What We Trade and with Whom 197
The Benefits of International Trade 199

Comparative and Absolute Advantage 199
Demonstrating the Gains from Trade 200
Production Possibilities Frontier Analysis 201
Supply and Demand Analysis 202
Whom Does Trade Harm? 202
Trade Barriers 203
  Reasons for Limiting Trade 203
  Methods of Limiting Trade 204
Trade as a Diplomatic Weapon 205
Kick It Up a Notch: Costs
  of Protectionism 205
Summary 206

Chapter 18

International Finance and Exchange Rates 209

International Financial Transactions 209
Foreign Exchange Markets 211
Alternative Foreign Exchange Systems 213
Determinants of Exchange Rates 215
Summary 216

Chapter 19

European Debt Crisis 218

Introduction 218
In the Beginning There Were 17 Currencies in
  17 Countries 218
The Effect of the Euro 219
Why Couldn't They Pull Themselves Out? The United
  States Did 223
Is It Too Late to Leave the Euro? 225
Where Should Europe Go from Here? 225
Summary 225

Chapter 20

Economic Growth and Development 227

Growth in Already Developed Countries 227
Comparing Developed Countries and Developing
  Countries 229
Fostering (and Inhibiting)
  Development 230
  The Challenges Facing Developing Countries 231
  What Works 232
Summary 232

Chapter 21
The Line between Legal and Illegal Goods 234

An Economic Model of Tobacco, Alcohol, and Illegal
Goods and Services 235
Why Is Regulation Warranted? 235
The Information Problem 235
External Costs 236
Morality Issues 238
Taxes on Tobacco and Alcohol 239
Modeling Taxes 239
The Tobacco Settlement and Why Elasticity Matters 239
Why Are Certain Goods and Services Illegal? 240
*The Impact of Decriminalization
on the Market for the Goods 240*
The External Costs of Decriminalization 241
Summary 241

Chapter 22
Natural Resources, the Environment, and Climate Change 244

Using Natural Resources 245
How Clean Is Clean Enough? 245
The Externalities Approach 246
When the Market Works for Everyone 246
When the Market Does Not Work for Everyone 246
The Property Rights Approach to the Environment
and Natural Resources 248
Why You Do Not Mess Up Your Own Property 248
Why You Do Mess Up Common Property 248
*Natural Resources and the Importance
of Property Rights 248*
Environmental Problems and
Their Economic Solutions 249
Environmental Problems 249
*Economic Solutions: Using Taxes
to Solve Environmental Problems 251*
*Economic Solutions: Using Property Rights
to Solve Environmental Problems 252*
*No Solution: When There Is No
Government to Tax or Regulate 253*
Summary 254

Chapter 23
Health Care 257

Where the Money Goes and Where It Comes
From 257

Insurance in the United States 258
How Insurance Works 258
Varieties of Private Insurance 259
Public Insurance 259
Economic Models of Health Care 260
Why Health Care Is Not Just Another Good 260
Implications of Public Insurance 261
Efficiency Problems with Private Insurance 262
*Major Changes to Insurance
Resulting from PPACA 263*
The Blood and Organ Problem 265
Comparing the United States with the Rest of the
World 265
Summary 267

Chapter 24
Government-Provided Health Insurance: Medicaid, Medicare, and the Child Health Insurance Program 269

Medicaid: What, Who, and How Much 270
Why Medicaid Costs So Much 271
Why Spending Is Greater on the Elderly 272
Cost-Saving Measures in Medicaid 273
Medicare: Public Insurance and the Elderly 273
Why Private Insurance May Not Work 273
Why Medicare's Costs Are High 274
Medicare's Nuts and Bolts 275
Provider Types 275
Part A 275
Part B 276
Prescription Drug Coverage (Part D) 276
Cost Control Provisions in Medicare 277
The Medicare Trust Fund 277
The Relationship between Medicaid and Medicare 279
Child Health Insurance Program 279
Summary 279

Chapter 25
The Economics of Prescription Drugs 282

Profiteers or Benevolent Scientists? 283
Monopoly Power Applied to Drugs 283
Important Questions 285
*Expensive Necessities or Relatively Inexpensive
Godsends? 285*
Price Controls: Are They the Answer? 287
FDA Approval: Too Stringent or Too Lax? 287
Summary 288

Chapter 26
So You Want to Be a Lawyer: Economics and the Law   290

The Government's Role in Protecting Property and Enforcing Contracts   290
Private Property   290
  Intellectual Property   291
  Contracts   291
  *Enforcing Various Property
    Rights and Contracts   291*
  *Negative Consequences of
    Private Property Rights   292*
Bankruptcy   292
Civil Liability   292
Summary   294

Chapter 27
The Economics of Crime   296

Who Commits Crimes and Why   296
The Rational Criminal Model   297
  Crime Falls When Legal Income Rises   297
  *Crime Falls When the Likelihood and Consequences of
    Getting Caught Rise   298*
  Problems with the Rationality Assumption   298
The Costs of Crime   298
  How Much Does an Average Crime Cost?   299
  *How Much Crime Does an Average
    Criminal Commit?   299*
Optimal Spending on Crime Control   300
  What Is the Optimal Amount to Spend?   300
  Is the Money Spent in the Right Way?   301
  Are the Right People in Jail?   301
  What Laws Should We Rigorously Enforce?   301
  What Is the Optimal Sentence?   302
Summary   303

Chapter 28
The Economics of Race and Sex Discrimination   305

The Economic Status of Women and Minorities   305
  Women   305
  Minorities   306
Definitions and Detection of Discrimination   308
  Discrimination, Definitions, and the Law   308
  Detecting and Measuring Discrimination   309
Discrimination in Labor,
  Consumption, and Lending   310

  Labor Market Discrimination   310
  *Consumption Market and Lending
    Market Discrimination   311*
Affirmative Action   312
  The Economics of Affirmative Action   312
  What Is Affirmative Action?   313
  Gradations of Affirmative Action   313
Summary   314

Chapter 29
Income and Wealth Inequality: What's Fair?   317

Introduction   317
Measurement of Inequality   317
  Income Inequality   317
  Wealth Inequality   320
Causes of Household Income and Wealth
  Inequality   321
Costs and Benefits of Income Inequality   322
Summary   324

Chapter 30
Farm Policy   326

Farm Prices Since 1950   326
  Corn and Gasoline   327
Price Variation as a Justification
  for Government Intervention   328
  The Case for Price Supports   328
  The Case against Price Supports   329
Consumer and Producer Surplus Analysis of Price
  Floors   329
  One Floor in One Market   329
  Variable Floors in Multiple Markets   330
  What Would Happen without Price Supports?   330
Price Support Mechanisms and
  Their History   330
  Price Support Mechanisms   330
  History of Price Supports   332
Is There a Bubble on the Farm?   332
Kick It Up a Notch   333
Summary   333

Chapter 31
Minimum Wage   335

Traditional Economic Analysis
  of a Minimum Wage   336

Labor Markets and Consumer and Producer Surplus   336
A Relevant versus an Irrelevant
   Minimum Wage   337
What Is Wrong with a Minimum Wage?   337
Real-World Implications of
   the Minimum Wage   338
Alternatives to the Minimum Wage   338
Rebuttals to the Traditional Analysis   339
The Macroeconomics Argument   339
The Work Effort Argument   339
The Elasticity Argument   340
Where Are Economists Now?   340
Kick It Up a Notch   341
Summary   341

Chapter 32
Ticket Brokers and Ticket Scalping   343

Defining Brokering and Scalping   344
An Economic Model of Ticket Sales   344
Marginal Cost   344
The Promoter as Monopolist   344
The Perfect Arena   345
Why Promoters Charge Less
   Than They Could   346
An Economic Model of Scalping   346
Legitimate Scalpers   347
Summary   348

Chapter 33
The Economics of K–12 Education   350

Investments in Human Capital   351
Present Value Analysis   351
External Benefits   351
Should We Spend More?   352
The Basic Data   352
Cautions about Quick Conclusions   354
Literature on Whether More Money Will Improve
   Educational Outcomes   355
School Reform Issues   356
The Public School Monopoly   356
Merit Pay and Tenure   357
Private versus Public Education   357
School Vouchers   358
Collective Bargaining   358
Summary   359

Chapter 34
College and University Education: Why Is It So Expensive?   361

Introduction   361
Why Are the Costs So High?   361
Why Are College Costs Rising So Fast?   363
Why Have Textbook Costs Risen So Rapidly?   364
What a College Degree Is Worth   366
How Do People Pay for College?   367
Summary   369

Chapter 35
Poverty and Welfare   371

Measuring Poverty   372
The Poverty Line   372
Who's Poor?   372
Poverty through History   373
Problems with Our Measure of Poverty   374
Poverty in the United States versus Europe   375
Programs for the Poor   375
In Kind versus In Cash   375
Why Spend $685 Billion on
   a $91 Billion Problem?   377
Is $685 Billion Even a Lot Compared
   to Other Countries?   377
Incentives, Disincentives, Myths, and Truths   377
Welfare Reform   378
Is There a Solution?   378
Welfare as We Now Know It   379
Is Poverty Necessarily Bad?   379
Summary   379

Chapter 36
Social Security   382

The Basics   382
The Beginning   382
Taxes   383
Benefits   383
Changes over Time   383
Why Do We Need Social Security?   384
Social Security's Effect on the Economy   385
Effect on Work   385
Effect on Saving   385
Whom Is the Program Good For?   386
Will the System Be There for Me?   388
Why Social Security Is in Trouble   388

The Social Security Trust Fund 388
Options for Fixing Social Security 389
Summary 390

Chapter 37
Personal Income Taxes 393

How Income Taxes Work 393
Issues in Income Taxation 398
Horizontal and Vertical Equity 398
Equity versus Simplicity 398
Incentives and the Tax Code 398
Do Taxes Alter Work Decisions? 399
Do Taxes Alter Savings Decisions? 399
Taxes for Social Engineering 399
Who Pays Income Taxes? 399
The Tax Debates of the Last Decade 400
Summary 401

Chapter 38
Energy Prices 404

The Historical View 404
Oil and Gasoline Price History 404
Geopolitical History 405
OPEC 406
What OPEC Does 406
How Cartels Work 407
Why Cartels Are Not Stable 407
Back from the Dead 408
Why Do Prices Change So Fast? 408
Is It All a Conspiracy? 409
From $1 to $4 per Gallon in 10 Years? 409
Electric Utilities 411
Electricity Production 411
Why Are Electric Utilities a
Regulated Monopoly? 412
What Will the Future Hold? 413
Kick It Up a Notch 414
Summary 415

Chapter 39
If We Build It, Will They Come? And Other Sports Questions 417

The Problem for Cities 418
Expansion versus Luring a Team 418
Does a Team Enhance the Local Economy? 419
Why Are Stadiums Publicly Funded? 420

The Problem for Owners 420
To Move or to Stay 420
To Win or to Profit 421
Don't Feel Sorry for Them Just Yet 422
The Sports Labor Market 423
What Owners Will Pay 423
What Players Will Accept 423
The Vocabulary of Sports Economics 423
What a Monopoly Will Do for You 426
Summary 427

Chapter 40
The Stock Market and Crashes 429

Stock Prices 430
How Stock Prices Are
Determined 430
What Stock Markets Do 431
Efficient Markets 432
Stock Market Crashes 432
Bubbles 433
Example of a Crash: NASDAQ 2000 433
The Accounting Scandals of
2001 and 2002 434
Bankruptcy 435
Why Capitalism Needs Bankruptcy Laws 435
The Kmart and Global Crossing Cases 435
What Happened in the Enron Case 436
Why the Enron Case Matters More
Than the Others 437
Rebound of 2006–2007 and
the Drop of 2008–2009 437
Summary 438

Chapter 41
Unions 440

Why Unions Exist 440
The Perfectly Competitive
Labor Market 440
A Reaction to Monopsony 441
A Way to Restrict Competition and
Improve Quality 442
A Reaction to Information Issues 443
A Union as a Monopolist 443
The History of Labor Unions 444
Where Unions Go from Here 447
Kick It Up a Notch 448
Summary 448

Chapter 42

Walmart: Always Low Prices (and Low Wages)—Always   450

The Market Form   450
Who Is Affected?   452
  Most Consumers Stand to
    Gain—Some Lose Options   452
  Workers Probably Lose   452
  Sales Tax Revenues Won't Be Affected Much   453
  Some Businesses Will Get Hurt;
    Others Will Be Helped   453
  Community Effects   453
Summary   453

Chapter 43

The Economic Impact of Casino Gambling   455

The Perceived Impact of Casino Gambling   455
Local Substitution   455
The "Modest" Upside
  of Casino Gambling   456
The Economic Reasons for
  Opposing Casino Gambling   456
Summary   457

Index   459

Web Chapters

NAFTA, CAFTA, GATT, WTO: Are Trade Agreements Good for Us?

The Benefits of Free Trade
Why Do We Need Trade Agreements?
  Strategic Trade
  Special Interests
  What Trade Agreements Prevent
Trade Agreements and Institutions
  Alphabet Soup
  Are They Working?
Economic and Political Impacts of Trade
The Bottom Line

Summary

The International Monetary Fund: Doctor or Witch Doctor?

Before the IMF and Its Birth
Foreign Exchange Markets
Today's IMF
  How the IMF Works
  How IMF Decisions Are Made
The Asian Financial Crisis
  The Cause
  The IMF to the Rescue?
Summary

The Cost of War

Opportunity Cost
Present Value and the Value of a Human Life
Economic versus Accounting Cost
  Personnel, Food, and Supplies
  Cost of Munitions
  Cost of Getting Personnel and Equipment in Position
  Fuel
How GDP Was Affected
Environmental and Cultural Costs
Summary

The Economics of Terrorism

The Economic Impact of September 11th and of
  Terrorism in General
Modeling the Economic Impact of the Attacks
  Insurance Aspects of Terrorism
  Buy Insurance or Self-Protect or Both
Terrorism from the Perspective of the Terrorist
Summary

Rent Control

Rents in a Free Market
Reasons for Controlling Rents
Consequences of Rent Control
Why Does Rent Control Survive?
Summary

Antitrust

What's Wrong with Monopoly?
   High Prices, Low Output, and Deadweight Loss
     Reduced Innovation
Natural Monopolies and Necessary Monopolies
   Natural Monopoly
   Patents, Copyrights, and Other Necessary Monopolies
Monopolies and the Law
   The Sherman Anti-Trust Act
   What Constitutes a Monopoly?
Examples of Antitrust Action
   Standard Oil
   IBM
   Microsoft
   iTunes, iPods, iPhones, and the European Union
Summary

Head Start

Head Start as an Investment
   The Early Invention Premise
   Present Value Analysis
   External Benefits
   The Early Evidence
   The Remaining Doubts
The Head Start Program
The Current Evidence
   Evidence that Head Start Works
   Evidence that Head Start Does Not Work
   More Evidence is Coming and Some is In
The Opportunity Cost of Fully Funding Head Start
Summary

Preface

This book is designed for a one-semester issues-based general education economics course, and its purpose is to interest the nonbusiness, noneconomics major in what the discipline of economics can do. Students of the "issues approach" will master the basic economic theory necessary to explore a variety of real-world issues. If this is the only economics class they ever take, they will at least gain enough insight to be able to intelligently discuss the way economic theory applies to important issues in the world today.

Until the first edition of this book was published, instructors who chose the issues approach to teaching a one-semester general economics course had to compromise in one of the following ways: they could (1) pick a book that presents the issues but that is devoid of economic theory; (2) pick a book that intertwines the issues with the theory; (3) ask students to buy two books; or (4) place a large number of readings on library reserve.

Each of these alternatives presents problems. If the course is based entirely on an issues text, students will leave with the incorrect impression that economics is a nonrigorous discipline that offers opinions devoid of a theoretical basis. A book that intertwines issues and theory implicitly assumes that all the issues are relevant to all students in the course. In fact, some issues are not relevant to some students and others are relevant only when the issue makes news. For example, at Syracuse my students never understood why farm price supports were interesting, whereas at Indiana State no student that I have met has ever lived in a rent-controlled apartment. Other issues are of interest only at particular times. Oil prices were of little consequence to students during the bulk of the 1990s, but students are very interested today. Student interest in Social Security rose during 2005 when President Bush pushed his version of reform but waned as his approval ratings did. Similarly, the minimum wage was of interest to students in 2007 as the new Democratic Congress passed an increase. Finally, some issues are interesting for a time and then fade, like the interest in antitrust statutes as they applied to Microsoft's behavior in the 1990s. The new Seventh Edition does not include the Antitrust chapter nor does it include the chapters on Head Start, Rent Control, the IMF, The Cost of War, or the Economics of Terrorism. These chapters remain on the website (www.mhhe.com/guell7e) and are available for your use. Instead, the new Seventh Edition offers students an ability to access timely material on whether the "Fiscal Sky Is Falling" and whether the "Japan's Lost Decade" could occur in the United States. The Patient Protection and Affordable Care Act are given an entire chapter.

The problem associated with using multiple books is the obvious one of expense. Having multiple reserve readings, still a legitimate option, requires a great deal of time on the part of students, teachers, and librarians, and it is usually not convenient for students. The Seventh Edition of this book meets both student and instructor needs simultaneously. By regularly updating the material, regularly adjusting the portfolio of topics, and using a web platform for "white hot" issues and as an archive of discarded issues, this book allows instructors of economics to keep students interested.

HOW TO USE THIS BOOK

Issues in Economics Today includes 8 intensive core theory chapters and 35 shorter issues chapters. The book is designed to allow faculty flexibility in approach. Some colleagues like to intertwine theory and issues while others like to lay the theoretical foundation first before heading into the issues. Some faculty will choose to set a theme for their course and pick issues consistent with that theme while others will let their students decide what issues interest them. There is no right way to use the book except that **under no circumstances is it imagined that the entire book be covered.**

I believe that an issues-based course must have the virtue of being both timely and flexible. As a result, this book presents a wealth of issues from which instructors or students can pick and choose. This book also has the benefit of having timely web-available chapters that allow students to study issues as they happen. Between the time the first edition went to press and the second edition became available, the accounting scandals of 2002 occurred. During the book's first year the United States went to war in Iraq. Before the third edition hit college bookstores, the housing bubble was of significant concern. It began its deflation as the fourth edition was created. Chapters discussing the economic impact of these events were available within a month of these events. I am committed to providing balanced and timely chapters for the web so that instructors and students have the latest available information.

There are 35 issues chapters that I have divided into the following categories: Macroeconomic Issues (Chapters 9–16), International Issues (Chapters 17–20), Externalities and Market Failure (Chapters 21–22), Health Issues (Chapters 23–25), Government Solutions to Societal Problems (Chapters 26–29), Price Control Issues (Chapters 30–32), and Miscellaneous Markets (Chapters 33–43). These groupings will be helpful as you navigate through the Contents looking for a particular topic. To help you decide which issues chapters to cover, see the table on pages xxvi–xxvii, entitled "Required Theory Table." It shows at a glance which theory chapters need to be covered before pursuing each of the issues chapters. On page xxv, the table entitled "Issues for Different Course Themes" includes my recommendations for courses that focus on social policy, international issues, election year issues, or business.

The format of this book, as well as the tools I've mentioned, are meant to provide you the maximum flexibility in choosing issues chapters for your course.

CHANGES TO THE SEVENTH EDITION

In its Seventh Edition, *Issues in Economics Today* introduces three new chapters that examine the European debt crisis and income and wealth inequality. The health care chapters incorporate and integrate the impact of the Patient Protection and Affordable Care Act and the education and textbook chapters are reorganized into K–12 and college and university education.

All chapters have been evaluated for currency and accuracy. A detailed listing of chapter by chapter changes is provided here for your convenience.

Chapter 1: A more thorough discussion of the importance of constructing a realistic counterfactual when evaluating policy wisdom is offered.

Chapter 2: A thorough reexamination of the presentation is offered in response to specific comments by solicited reviewers.

Chapter 3: A more recent example is used to discuss elasticity regarding energy use.

Chapter 4: The definition of diminishing returns is augmented to offer a reason, fixed capital, for its prevalence in production.

Chapter 5: More modern examples of monopolistic competition and oligopoly are offered.

Chapter 6: Content and data updates have been made as needed to reflect the most current information available. The Keystone pipeline example is offered to illustrate the problem associated with focusing too narrowly on real GDP and the cost of the environment.

Chapter 7: An insert on the use of Microsoft Excel functions and their value is offered.

Chapter 8: An admonition to avoid memorization is offered regarding the understanding of aggregate supply and aggregate demand determinants.

Chapter 9: Content and data updates have been made as needed to reflect the most current information available. A summary and evaluation of the effectiveness of the Obama stimulus is offered.

Chapter 10: Content and data updates have been made as needed to reflect the most current information available. A display of the dramatic transition in the data on excess and required reserves is offered as well as a discussion of the process by which the massive infusion of liquidity will be undone by the Federal Reserve once a decision is made to do so.

Chapter 11: Content and data updates have been made as needed to reflect the most current information available. More modern references are made to logrolling.

Chapter 12: Content and data updates have been made as needed to reflect the most current information available. Reference is made to the 2013 sequester.

Chapter 13: Content and data updates have been made as needed to reflect the most current information available.

Chapter 14: An analysis of the impact of the extraordinary monetary stimulus regarding the housing market is offered.

Chapter 15: No substantial changes made.

Chapters 16–17: Content and data updates have been made as needed to reflect the most current information available.

Chapter 18: Content and data updates have been made as needed to reflect the most current information available. An analysis of the contention that the Chinese are engaging in currency manipulation and the counter-contention that the United States is as well is offered.

Chapter 19: is a new chapter focusing on the European debt crisis.

Chapter 20–21: Content and data updates have been made as needed to reflect the most current information available.

Chapter 22: A thorough reexamination of the presentation is offered in response to specific comments by solicited reviewers.

Chapter 23–25: Content and data updates have been made as needed to reflect the most current information available. A thorough integration of the Patient Protection and Affordable Care Act replaces separate treatment of various health economics issues.

Chapter 26: No substantial changes made.

Chapter 27–28: Content and data updates have been made as needed to reflect the most current information available.

Chapter 29: is a new chapter focusing on the income and wealth inequality.

Chapter 30–31: Content and data updates have been made as needed to reflect the most current information available.

Chapter 32: No substantial changes made.

Chapter 33–34: The chapters are reorganized around K–12 (Chapter 33) education and college and university education (Chapter 34). Content and data updates have been made as needed to reflect the most current information available.

Chapter 35–36: Content and data updates have been made as needed to reflect the most current information available.

Chapter 37: Content and data updates have been made as needed to reflect the most current information available. The impact of the post-2012 election changes to the tax code is included. References are made regarding the creation of a higher marginal tax rate for high incomes and the resolution to the long-standing issue of the alternative minimum tax.

Chapter 38: Content and data updates have been made as needed to reflect the most current information available.

Chapter 39: Content and data updates have been made as needed to reflect the most current information available. References to economic issues exemplified by international soccer leagues are offered.

Chapters 40–43: Content and data updates have been made as needed to reflect the most current information available.

FEATURES

- *A conversational writing style* makes it easier for students not majoring in economics to connect with the material. The book puts students at ease and allows them to feel more confident and open to learning.
- *Chapter Outline and Learning Objectives* set the stage at the beginning of each chapter to let the student see how the chapter is organized and anticipate the concepts that will be covered.
- *Key Terms* are defined in the margins and recapped at the end of the chapters.
- *Summaries* at the end of each chapter reinforce the material that has been covered.
- *Issues Chapters You Are Ready for Now* are found at the end of each theory chapter, so students can go straight to the issues chapters that interest them once they've mastered the necessary theoretical principles.
- *Quiz Yourself* presents questions for self-quizzing at the end of each chapter.
- *Think about This* asks provocative questions that encourage students to think about how economic theories apply to the real world by putting themselves in the economic driver's seat. For example, one Think about This asks, "Suppose you buy a new car. What is the opportunity cost of doing so?" This feature facilitates active learning so that the students will learn the concepts more thoroughly.
- *Talk about This* includes questions designed to trigger discussion.
- *For More Insight See* sends the students to websites and publications to find additional material on a given topic. Since economic issues are particularly time-sensitive, this feature not only helps students learn to do research on the web, but also keeps the course as fresh and current as today's newspaper.

- *Short Answer Questions* are included so that faculty may ask students questions that will help faculty assess student understanding of complex economic phenomena.

SUPPLEMENTS FOR THE INSTRUCTOR

The following ancillaries are available for quick download and convenient access via the online learning center for this book at www.mhhe.com/guell7e and are password-protected for security. Additionally, the Digital Image Library containing all graphs and tables from the text and grading guidelines for the web-based issues questions are also included for your convenience.

Instructor's Manual

In addition to a traditional outline of each chapter's content and updated web references to data sources for each chapter, the Instructor's Manual offers key-point icons to emphasize the importance of particular concepts. Another distinctive feature is that each figure is broken into subfigures with explanations that can be offered at each stage. Solutions to the end of chapter questions are also provided.

Test Bank

The Test Bank includes 80–200 multiple-choice questions for the core theory chapters and 60–100 multiple-choice questions for the issues chapters. These questions test students' knowledge of key terms, key concepts, theory and graph recognition, theory and graph application, and numeracy, as well as questions about different explanations given by economists regarding particular economic phenomena.

PowerPoint Presentations

Narrated PowerPoint Presentations accompany the text, including the web chapters (Are Trade Agreements Good for Us?, the IMF, the Economics of War, the Economics of Terrorism, Antitrust, Head Start, and Rent Control). The Seventh Edition also includes revised complimentary instructor PowerPoints, which can be downloaded from the book's website.

SUPPLEMENTS FOR THE STUDENT

Study Guide

The Study Guide, like the text, is divided into theory chapters and issues chapters, with a slightly different format for each. The theory chapters include the major points of the chapter, a chapter outline, key terms with definitions, and problems. This is followed by a self-test of multiple-choice and true/false questions. The issues chapters include the major points of the chapter, a chapter outline, key terms with definitions, discussion questions, and web-based questions. Additional material to correspond with the Kick It Up a Notch sections is now available. Answers to all problems are included.

Online Learning Center www.mhhe.com/guell7e

A variety of study aids are offered on the student side of the website. These aids include chapter outlines, narrated PowerPoint Presentations, web-based issues questions, and the Study Guide.

ACKNOWLEDGMENTS

This text would not have been possible but for the efforts of a number of people. I thank Indiana State University and its Department of Economics for their continued support of this project. In particular, I thank my chair, John Conant, for his unflagging support, both moral and material. I am indebted to the personnel of McGraw-Hill/Irwin for their work in gathering and compiling peer reviews. Christina Kouvelis, my development editor, and Michele Janicek, my brand manager, were always encouraging and willing to help at every stage. I also thank the Provost of Indiana State University, Jack Maynard, for granting me the time and access to student workers who through the first four editions of this text worked their collective tails off to help me complete each while continuing to coordinate First-Year Programs.

I thank the many participants in McGraw-Hill Symposia who happily offered great insight on the best way to teach interesting issues. Finally, I thank the following peer reviewers whose insight substantially enhanced this book:

Alex Aichinger
Northwestern State University

Thomas Andrews
West Chester University

Michael Araujo
Quinsigamond Community College

Lee Ash
Skagit Valley College

Robert J. Bartelli
Labette Community College

Daria J. Bernard
University of Delaware

Roberta Biby
Grand Valley State University

Ann Marie Callahan
Caldwell College

R. Edward Chatterton
Lock Haven University

Russ Cheatham
Cumberland University

Joab Corey
Florida State University

Ann M. Eike
University of Kentucky

Herb Elliott
All Hancock College

John A. Flanders
Central Methodist University

Holly Fretwell
Montana State University

Neil Garston
CSULA

E B. Gendel
Woodbury College

Glenn Graham
SUNY–Oswego

Abbas P. Grammy
California State University, Bakersfield

Sheryl Hadley
Johnson Community College

Suzanne Hayes
University of Nebraska, Kearney

Rolf Hemmerling
Greenville Technical College

John S. Heywood
University of Wisconsin–Milwaukee

Richard Hoogerwerf
Marian College

Scott Hunt
Columbus State Community College

Hans Isakson
University of Northern Iowa

Debra Israel
Indiana State University

Allan Jenkins
University of Nebraska, Kearney

Dick Johnson
Skagit Valley Community College

Gary Langer
Roosevelt University

Tom Larson
California State University–Los Angeles

Raymond Lee
Benedict College

Gary D. Lemon
DePauw University

Alston Lippert
University of South Carolina

Patrick McMurry
Missouri Western State University

Tom Means
San Jose State University

Kimberly Merritt
Oklahoma Christian University

Daniel Morvey
Piedmont Technical College

Richard Newton
Augusta Technical College

Inge O'Connor
Syracuse University

Nathan Perry
University of Utah

Chris Phillips
Somerset Community College

Patrick Price
University of Louisiana at Lafayette

Taghi Ramin
William Patterson University

Michael Ryan
Western Michigan University

John Sabelhaus
University of Maryland

Sue Lynn Sasser
University of Central Oklahoma

Brenda M. Saunders
Somerset Community College

Robert D. Schuttler
Marian University

Millicent M. Sites
Carson-Newman College

Rebecca Smith
Mississippi State University

Arun K. Srinivasan
Indiana University Southeast

Frank Tenkorang
University of Nebraska, Kearney

Tara Thornberry
Maysville Community and Technical College

Michelle Villinski
DePauw University

Darlene Voeltz
Rochester Community and Technical College

William Walsh
University of St. Thomas

Wendel Weaver
Oklahoma Wesleyan University

Janet L. Wolcutt
Wichita State University

Derek K. Yonai
Campbell University

Ben Young
University of Missouri, Kansas City
Johnson County Community College

Issues for **Different Course Themes**

Social Policy

21. The Line between Legal and Illegal Goods
23. Health Care
24. Government-Provided Health Insurance: Medicaid, Medicare, and the Child Health Insurance Program
25. The Economics of Prescription Drugs
28. The Economics of Race and Sex Discrimination
29. Income and Wealth Inequality: What's Fair?
31. Minimum Wage
33. The Economics of K–12 Education
34. College and University Education: Why Is It So Expensive?
35. Poverty and Welfare
43. The Economic Impact of Casino Gambling

Election Year

9. Fiscal Policy
11. Federal Spending
14. The Recession of 2007–2009: Causes and Policy Responses
16. Is the (Fiscal) Sky Falling? An Examination of Unfunded Social Security, Medicare, and State and Local Pension Liabilities
17. International Trade: Does It Jeopardize American Jobs?
22. Natural Resources, the Environment, and Climate Change
23. Health Care
26. So You Want to Be a Lawyer: Economics and the Law
27. The Economics of Crime
28. The Economics of Race and Sex Discrimination
31. Minimum Wage
34. College and University Education: Why Is It So Expensive?
36. Social Security

International Issues

12. Federal Deficits, Surpluses, and the National Debt
15. Japan's Lost Decade: Could It Happen in the United States?
17. International Trade: Does It Jeopardize American Jobs?
18. International Finance and Exchange Rates
19. European Debt Crisis
20. Economic Growth and Development
21. The Line between Legal and Illegal Goods
22. Natural Resources, the Environment, and Climate Change
30. Farm Policy
38. Energy Prices

Business Issues

10. Monetary Policy
11. Federal Spending
13. The Housing Bubble
14. The Recession of 2007–2009: Causes and Policy Responses
17. International Trade: Does It Jeopardize American Jobs?
23. Health Care
25. The Economics of Prescription Drugs
32. Ticket Brokers and Ticket Scalping
37. Personal Income Taxes
38. Energy Prices
40. The Stock Market and Crashes
41. Unions
42. Walmart: Always Low Prices (and Low Wages)—Always

Required **Theory Table**

Core Theory Required								
1	2	3	4	5	6	7	8	
					X		X	9. Fiscal Policy
					X	X	X	10. Monetary Policy
X								11. Federal Spending
					X		X	12. Federal Deficits, Surpluses, and the National Debt
					X	X	X	13. The Housing Bubble
					X	X	X	14. The Recession of 2007–2009: Causes and Policy Responses
					X	X	X	15. Japan's Lost Decade: Could It Happen in the United States
					X	X	X	16. Is the (Fiscal) Sky Falling? An Examination of Unfunded Social Security, Medicare, and State and Local Pension Liabilities
X	X	X						17. International Trade: Does It Jeopardize American Jobs?
	X							18. International Finance and Exchange Rates
X	X				X	X	X	19. European Debt Crisis
	X				X		X	20. Economic Growth and Development
X	X	X						21. The Line between Legal and Illegal Goods
X	X	X	X	X		X		22. Natural Resources, the Environment, and Climate Change
X	X	X						23. Health Care
X	X	X						24. Government–Provided Health Insurance: Medicaid, Medicare, and the Child Health Insurance Program
X	X	X	X	X				25. The Economics of Prescription Drugs
X	X	X					X	26. So You Want to Be a Lawyer: Economics and the Law
X	X	X						27. The Economics of Crime
	X							28. The Economics of Race and Sex Discrimination
X	X					X		29. Income and Wealth Inequality: What's Fair?
X	X	X						30. Farm Policy
X	X	X						31. Minimum Wage
	X		X	X				32. Ticket Brokers and Ticket Scalping
X						X		33. The Economics of K–12 Education
X	X	X	X	X		X		34. College and University Education: Why Is It So Expensive?
X								35. Poverty and Welfare
						X		36. Social Security
						X		37. Personal Income Taxes

Core Theory Required								
1	**2**	**3**	**4**	**5**	**6**	**7**	**8**	
	X	X						38. Energy Prices
X						X		39. If We Build It, Will They Come? And Other Sports Questions
						X		40. The Stock Market and Crashes
	X	X	X	X				41. Unions
X	X	X	X	X				42. Walmart: Always Low Prices (and Low Wages)—Always
X					X	X	X	43. The Economic Impact of Casino Gambling

CHAPTER ONE

Economics: The Study of Opportunity Cost

Learning Objectives

After reading this chapter you should be able to:

LO1 Define the key terms of economics and opportunity cost and understand how a production possibilities frontier exemplifies the trade-offs that exist in life.

LO2 Distinguish between increasing and constant opportunity cost and understand why each might happen in the real world.

LO3 Analyze an argument by thinking economically, while recognizing and avoiding logical traps.

Chapter Outline

Economics and Opportunity Cost

Modeling Opportunity Cost Using the Production Possibilities Frontier

Attributes of the Production Possibilities Frontier

The Big Picture

Thinking Economically

Kick It Up a Notch: Demonstrating Constant and Increasing Opportunity Cost on a Production Possibilities Frontier

Summary

This chapter lays the foundation for understanding how to think like an economist. It begins by defining the discipline of economics and its most basic concept: opportunity cost. Opportunity cost is modeled and further explained through the use of a diagram called a production possibilities frontier. A road map to the economy and to the remainder of the book is presented in the form of a circular flow diagram. The chapter continues with a discussion of what "thinking economically" means. To understand this concept, we look at why economists use marginal analysis, explore the difference between positive and normative analysis, and examine economic incentives. We conclude by examining logical traps that obstruct our path to such economic thinking.

Economics and Opportunity Cost

Economics Defined

economics
The study of the allocation and use of scarce resources to satisfy unlimited human wants.

Some define **economics** as a hard requirement for general education or a major; others, a "dismal science"; and still others, the study of the allocation and use of scarce resources to satisfy unlimited human wants. The reality is that economics is all three. It deserves its reputation as a difficult course, its practitioners are always disappointing the public by insisting that there is a cost to everything, and it really is a social science dealing with the fact that humans want more than resources are capable of satisfying.

On another level, the study of economics is the application of complicated jargon and graphs to common sense. You already know a lot of economics. You know, for instance, that choices have consequences; that having more money is more fun than having less; and that even though you are rich relative to a starving refugee, you are less rich than you would like to be. Of course, there are many other economic lessons that you learn simply by being alive. What you do not have is a systematic way of thinking about those economic ideas, and that is what this course and this book provide.

In this book all jargon with special meaning to economists will be in **bold,** with its definition, sometimes also in jargon, close by in the text as well as in the margin. If the definition is in "econ-speak" rather than commonsense English, you will also find an English translation nearby. Two terms in our definition of economics need clarification because they have special meaning to economists. First, you find the word "scarce." Something is **scarce** when there is not a freely available and infinite source of it. Second, a **resource** is anything we either consume directly or use to make things that we will ultimately consume.

There are four basic resources that society can allocate: land, labor, capital, and the entrepreneurship of its people. Any other resource, like oil, steel, or corn, is made available to a society when it allocates one or more of the basic resources to uncover, create, or harvest it.

Choices Have Consequences

In this course and with this book you will be faced with a choice: Do you read and study, or do you sleep and party? This choice illustrates the first and most basic concept of economics: opportunity cost. **Opportunity cost** is the forgone alternative of the choice made.

Translated into English, opportunity cost is "what you would have done had you not done what you did." It is important to keep in mind that the "forgone alternative" is the next best choice. It is not all the things "you could have done had you not done what you did," but it is the best of these alternatives because presumably that is "what you would have done."

If, for example, you decide at some point before finishing your assigned reading to put down this book, you will be implicitly saying that you would rather do something other than read this book. In terms of the course you are taking, the "opportunity cost" of such a poor decision could well be the lower grade that results from lost understanding.

Unfortunately, no matter what you do, you cannot escape opportunity cost. If you stay responsible and continue to read your text, the opportunity cost would be what you would do with the time saved. You are giving up the opportunity to watch *American Idol*, play the latest *Call of Duty*, *Halo*, or *Assassin's Creed* game, sleep, or study something else. To you, the preferred one of these would be the opportunity cost of reading the text.

As an aside, professors today see many students trying to avoid opportunity cost by multi-tasking. Scanning your Facebook account, reading your English, texting your significant other, or studying your biology during your economics class may seem like you are simply using time that has no opportunity cost. It is not. Students who attempt it frequently miss details, instructions, or concepts when they are only partially tuned in. The opportunity cost of the multi-tasking attempt is the lost understanding that could have been gained had you focused your attention in class.

Modeling Opportunity Cost Using the Production Possibilities Frontier

The Intuition behind Our First Graph

The concept of opportunity cost can be further illustrated by looking at something called a **production possibilities frontier**. This graph, Figure 1.1, is the first of more than 100 that you will see in this book. It is an example of a **model,** a simplification of the real world that we

scarce
Not freely available and lacking an infinite source.

resource
Anything that is consumed directly or used to make things that will ultimately be consumed.

opportunity cost
The forgone alternative of the choice made.

production possibilities frontier
A graph which relates the amounts of different goods that can be produced in a fully employed society.

model
A simplification of the real world that can be manipulated to explain the real world.

FIGURE 1.1
Production
possibilities frontier:
the starting point.

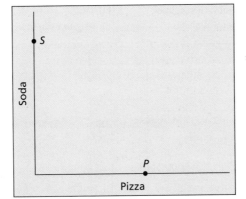

**simplifying
assumption**
An assumption that
may, on its face, be silly
but allows for a clearer
explanation.

can manipulate to explain the real world. This particular one relates the amounts of different goods that can be produced in a fully employed society.

Because chalkboards and book pages have only two dimensions, our explanation is limited. This gives us the first opportunity to introduce something called a **simplifying assumption**. A simplifying assumption is one that may, on its face, be silly but allows for a clearer explanation. A good one also has the characteristic that the conclusions that spring from it are valid in its more complicated scenario. For our production possibilities frontier we will make several simplifying assumptions. We will assume that there are only two goods in the world, that these goods are pizza and soft drinks, and that these goods will be produced with a fixed number of resources and fixed technology.

For another simplification, suppose that there are five types of people in the world: (1) those really good at producing pizza but lousy at producing soda; (2) those pretty good at producing pizza and not so good at producing soda; (3) those sort of OK at both; (4) those good at producing soda and not so good at producing pizza; and (5) those really good at producing soda but lousy at producing pizza.

The Starting Point for a Production Possibilities Frontier

If we imagine that our resource is the time of our workers, it can be consumed directly in the form of their leisure or it can be combined with other resources to produce goods and services. This resource is also scarce because there is not an infinite number of people to work, those people can do only so much work, they will not work without being paid, and there is only so much soda that can be produced—even if all the people on the planet devote their lives to the production of soda. Of course this point also holds if we apply the scarce resource to the production of pizza. There is only so much pizza that can be produced even if everyone on the planet is producing pizza. This notion of scarcity gives us a starting point and an ending point for Figure 1.1.

Point *S* in Figure 1.1 represents the situation where all resources are devoted to the production of soda; point *P* represents the situation where all resources are devoted to the production of pizza. In both cases all the resources in the world are devoted to the production of a specific good and production is still limited. It is limited by the ability of people and by the number of people and machines we have to help those people do their jobs. So that it is clear, remember that the production possibilities frontier is giving us a series of choices. We can pick only one of them. We cannot have both *S* sodas and *P* pizzas; thus, it is an either–or situation.

Points between the Extremes of a Production Possibilities Frontier

We can have some soda and some pizza, so many points between *S* and *P* are possible; we need to determine them. To proceed, assume you want something to eat with your soda, and ask yourself what kind of people you would remove from soda production to foster pizza production. Clearly, you would remove those who are not contributing much to the soda production but would contribute greatly to pizza production. That is, those with the attributes of people in group 1 above: really good at pizza, lousy at soda.

Figure 1.2 shows us what happens if we go ahead and move that group. As you see, this increases pizza production to a respectable level while not costing society much soda. Point *X* in Figure 1.2 represents that new soda–pizza combination. There everyone except those whom

FIGURE 1.2 Production possibilities frontier: moving pizza chefs to their rightful place.

FIGURE 1.3 Production possibilities frontier: moving to even more pizza production.

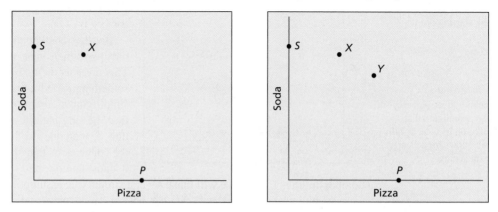

we will call the "pizza chefs" are still making soda, and the pizza chefs are efficiently cranking out as many pizzas as they can on their own. The thing is, though we gained a great deal of pizza production, we lost some soda production. That's why point *X*, while to the right of point *S*, is also lower than point *S*.

If we continue this process further, we are not blessed with a similar effect. The reason is that if we move toward greater pizza production, we do not have those pizza chefs to call on; instead we have our group 2, who are pretty good at pizza and not so good at soda. What that means is that even though pizza production rises, it does not rise as much as it did before. On top of that, our soda production falls more than it had before because when we moved the pizza chefs, they were "lousy" at soda. Now we are moving workers who are simply not so good at soda. Our soda losses are growing at an increasing rate. Thus we have point *Y* in Figure 1.3.

Going further, point *M* in Figure 1.4 results from moving the workers from group 3 (OK at both) from soda to pizza, point *Z* results from moving group 4 workers to pizza, and point *P* results from moving group 5 workers to pizza.

Connecting points like this creates Figure 1.5: a production possibilities frontier. This curve represents the most pizza that can be produced for any given amount of soda or, interpreted differently, the most soda that can be produced for any given amount of pizza.

FIGURE 1.4 All points on a production possibilities frontier.

FIGURE 1.5 A fully labeled production possibilities frontier: the case when people are different.

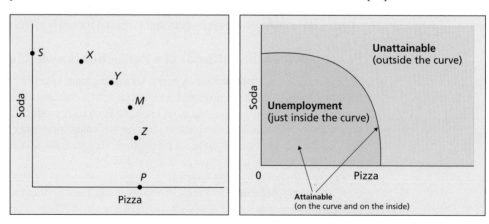

Attributes of the Production Possibilities Frontier

unemployment
A situation that occurs when resources are not being fully utilized.

attainable
Levels of production that are possible with the given resources.

unattainable
Levels of production that are not possible with the given resources.

Of course, if you can produce on the curve, you can produce less than that as well. If you do produce at points inside a production possibilities frontier, there are unemployed resources, or **unemployment** for short. Therefore, all points on or inside the production possibilities frontier are **attainable**.

Conversely, since the production possibilities frontier represents the maximum amount of one good that you can produce for a given level of production of another, those points outside the production possibilities frontier are **unattainable**. This means that currently available resources and technology are insufficient to produce amounts greater than those illustrated on the frontier. On the graph, everything beyond the frontier is unattainable.

The preceding discussion illustrates something you need to be wary of in this book. Words you think you know may mean something entirely different to economists. Thus far we have at least three such words: *unemployment, frontier,* and *good.* You think of unemployment as the condition of someone wanting a job but not having one. Economists do not disagree but expand that definition to resources other than labor. For example, on the interior of the production possibilities frontier there is unemployment, but that unemployment may be of capital. The word "frontier" is used to describe the boundary of production, not a wooded area with bears to avoid. The word "good," to an economist, is a generic term for anything we consume. In the example, soda and pizza are goods.

In the soda and pizza example there were people of different talents at soda and pizza production. The pizza chef had far different skills from the soda master. If, on the other hand, everyone were identical in their soda and pizza production capabilities, then points would fall on the line, as seen in Figure 1.6.

Increasing and Constant Opportunity Cost

Figures 1.5 and 1.6 have important similarities and differences. In both, the points on the production possibilities frontier are the most of one good that can be produced for a given amount of the other good. In both, the points on the curve and inside it are attainable and those

FIGURE 1.6
A fully labeled production possibilities frontier: the case when people are the same.

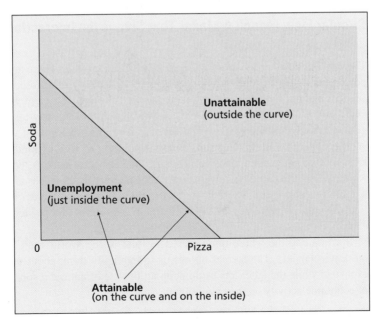

on the outside of it are unattainable. In both, the opportunity cost of moving from one point to another is the amount of one good you have to give up to get another. They differ in one important way, however: whether opportunity cost is increasing or constant.

If the production possibilities frontier is not a line but is bowed out away from the origin, then opportunity cost is increasing. The reason for this is that as we add more resources to the production of pizza, we are using fewer resources to produce soda. Compounding that problem, at each stage as we take the resources away from soda and put them into pizza, we are moving workers who are worse at pizza production and better at soda production than those moved in the previous stage. This means that the increase in pizza production is diminishing and the loss in soda production is increasing. An economist would call this an example of increasing opportunity cost.

If the production possibilities frontier is a straight line that is not bowed out away from the origin, then opportunity cost is constant. If every worker possesses identical skill, though you still have to give up some soda to get pizza, this is not compounded by anything. The resources you put into producing more pizza are just as good as the resources used to get you to that point and the resources taken away from the soda are similarly just as good as the resources used up to that point. An economist would call this an example of constant opportunity cost.

The Big Picture

circular flow model
A model which depicts the interactions of all economic actors.

market
Any mechanism by which buyers and sellers negotiate an exchange.

factor market
A mechanism by which buyers and sellers of labor and financial capital negotiate an exchange.

foreign exchange market
A mechanism by which buyers and sellers of the currencies of various countries negotiate an exchange.

goods and services market
A mechanism by which buyers and sellers of goods and services negotiate an exchange.

Now that we have looked at our first "simplified" model of the economy, it's time to get an idea of the "Big Picture." Think of Figure 1.7 as your road map to the book. This **circular flow model** is designed to put all of the pieces that follow in perspective. It has firms, workers, investors, savers, buyers, and sellers all interacting in markets and dealing with government. It has humanity taking natural resources from the environment, combining them with domestic and foreign financial and human resources to produce goods and services, and then buying and selling those goods and services in domestic and foreign markets.

Circular Flow Model: A Model That Shows the Interactions of All Economic Actors

The ovals in the diagram represent entities of specific kinds: There are households, firms, and governments. Households provide labor for wages. They use those wages to buy goods and services and pay their taxes. They receive services from government. Some save, some borrow, and many do both. Firms provide wages to households and pay taxes to government while getting labor from their workers and services from the government.

The rectangles in the diagram represent **markets** of various kinds: There are factor markets, foreign exchange markets, and goods and services markets. **Factor markets** are where workers and firms, and borrowers and savers interact to set wages and interest rates. **Foreign exchange markets** are where holders of various currencies interact to facilitate international trade. **Goods and services markets** are where consumers and producers interact to negotiate exchange of goods like cars and services like dry cleaning.

Surrounding the whole thing are "The Rest of the World" and "Natural Resources and the Environment." The former allows us to explicitly think about foreign trade and foreign exchange while the latter lets us think about the use of natural resources and the implications of economic activity on the environment.

FIGURE 1.7 The Circular Flow Model.

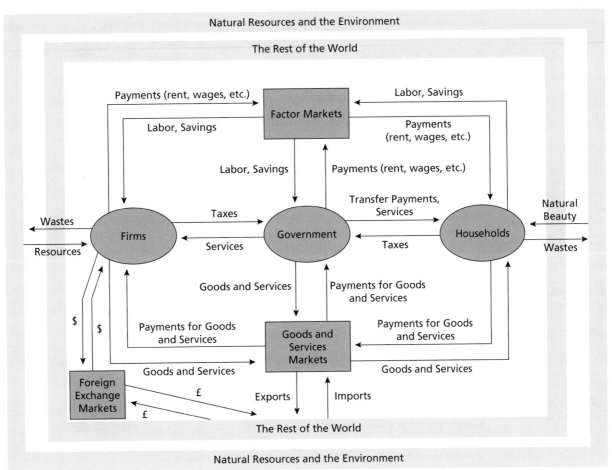

Thinking Economically

Marginal Analysis

optimization assumption
An assumption that suggests that the person in question is trying to maximize some objective.

marginal benefit
The increase in the benefit that results from an action.

marginal cost
The increase in the cost that results from an action.

One of the central tools of economics is marginal analysis. Economists typically look at problems by analyzing the costs and benefits of various solutions. When people buy something, they have to compare the value of what they purchase to the value of what they give up. When companies produce goods for sale, they have to compare the money they generate from sales to the costs they will incur from the production process. When you clean up your dorm room, you weigh the cleanliness gained against the time required to clean it.

Economists generally make an **optimization assumption**. This is an assumption that suggests that the person in question is trying to maximize some objective. For example, consumers are assumed to be making decisions that maximize their happiness subject to a scarce amount of money. Companies are assumed to maximize profits. People are assumed to clean things until the benefits of cleaning more are not worth the time or effort.

Economists see that all of these problems can be looked at using the same framework. Economists compare the **marginal benefit** of an action with its **marginal cost**. Something is worth doing only if the increase in benefits equals or exceeds the increase in costs. If the marginal benefit of an action steadily decreases and the marginal cost of an action steadily increases, then a person maximizes **net benefit** by doing that action until the marginal benefit equals the marginal cost. This is the essence of marginal analysis, and we will see it in action throughout this book.

net benefit
The difference between all benefits and all costs.

Positive and Normative Analysis

When people look at the world they often see things as they are and compare the way things are to the way they think things should be. They see a major league shortstop sign a contract for a quarter of a billion dollars over 10 years while their high school teachers make less than $40,000 a year. Economists, and social scientists in general, distinguish views of "the way things are" from "the way things should be," calling the former **positive analysis** and the latter **normative analysis.** Although there are economists who utilize both forms of analysis, more economists are comfortable explaining why things are the way they are than are comfortable suggesting the way things should be. Some critics look at this as self-delusion on the part of economists, using the argument that we choose which information to weigh more heavily based on normative beliefs.

positive analysis
A form of analysis that seeks to understand the way things are and why they are that way.

normative analysis
A form of analysis that seeks to understand the way things should be.

Economic Incentives

What kinds of choices we make as individuals and as a society depend on our preferences. Returning to the soda and pizza example, whether we like soda or pizza, or in what combinations we most like them, will have an important impact on what we choose to produce and consume. But also high on the list of things that determine what combinations of things we will produce and consume are **incentives.** Something is an incentive if it influences a decision we make. Some incentives are part of a market, like prices. Others are put on by an outside force like a government, and they can positively reinforce behaviors that are desired or deter behaviors that are not. What this means is that you are still able to produce and consume what you want, but something—perhaps a tax or a government regulation—is encouraging a particular choice. For example, by taxing beer and not soda, the government encourages you to steer toward soda and away from beer.

incentives
Something that influences a decision we make.

On a deeper level, an incentive may motivate you to do something you would not ordinarily do. For instance, many incentives are offered in the tax system. Tax credits and deductions for college tuition are considered incentives that will persuade people to get an education. For many people who would go to college anyway, these are not incentives. However, to some people who were perhaps considering college but had not made a decision, any influence these tax benefits would have on the decision would constitute an incentive.

An important and sometimes unfortunate aspect of incentives is that they create unintended consequences. Taxes are an area where some argue that the unintended consequences can be predicted from the incentives that arise out of programs. If welfare payments were reduced when the recipient found part-time employment, some predict the result, that the recipient would not look for part-time employment.

Fallacy of Composition

fallacy of composition
The mistake in logic that suggests that the total economic impact of something is always and simply equal to the sum of the individual parts.

One of the key traps to thinking economically is assuming that the total economic impact of something is always and simply equal to the sum of the individual parts. The **fallacy of composition** is an important logical trap to avoid because invalid economic conclusions will inevitably be drawn.

Outside of economics, cake constitutes a famous illustration of why the fallacy of composition is just that—a fallacy. Imagine a cake. Now imagine the ingredients that go into making the cake. Imagine eating the cake and the satisfaction you get from that. Now compare that level of satisfaction to what you would have if you separately poured flour, sugar, and baking powder down your throat, washed it down with a couple of raw eggs and some cooking oil, and then stuck your head in an oven. The baked combination is obviously better than its individual parts.

As an example within economics, we will learn in Chapter 5 that when many farmers are making high profits, others will want to join in. If they do join in, will all of the old and new farmers be making high profits? We will see that the new farmers' extra production will ultimately drive prices down so far that neither the older nor the newer farmers make money.

What this means is that when we are making economic judgments, we must do so with care. The sums of the individual parts must not be confused with the whole. The two can be, and often are, different.

Correlation ≠ Causation

When people are attempting to think economically, another trap they may fall into is assuming that because two variables changed simultaneously, one caused the other to happen.

direct correlation
A higher level of one variable is associated with a higher level of the other variable.

For instance, if you weighed all people under age 30 and also asked them how many dates they had had in their lifetime, you would find a **direct correlation**, meaning that it appears that the more people weigh, the more dates they have had. This does not imply **causation**. Heavier people do not necessarily get more dates and dating does not make us gain weight. In this case the two variables happen to be correlated with age. People in their twenties weigh more and have had a longer opportunity to have dates than have teens, preteens, and young children.

causation
A change in one variable makes another variable change.

When politicians attempt to take credit for good economic times with the claim that their policies caused the good economic times to happen, we must be suspicious. Of course, we must be equally suspicious if they attempt to pin the blame on their incumbent opponent if bad economic times existed in their opponent's time in office. While their claims may be true, it is perfectly plausible that the policies and the economy were unrelated, or that the economy did well or did poorly despite the policies.

counterfactual
An educated guess as to what would have happened had a policy or an event not occurred.

When economists look at cause and effect, they frequently attempt to generate a **counterfactual**. A counterfactual is an educated guess about what would have happened had a policy or an event not occurred. A well-constructed and convincing counterfactual can help determine whether a policy (like the 2008 Troubled Asset Relief Program or TARP) made things better than they otherwise would have been. It is not enough to say that the economy lost millions of jobs after a policy was passed and therefore the policy was bad. You have to be able to construct a scenario of what would have happened had the policy not been enacted. This is often the reason why economists will disagree and seem absolutely convinced that those with whom they are disagreeing are wrong. Whether the Bush administration's TARP program, the Federal Reserve's lowering of interest rates through unprecedented purchases of long-term debt, or the Obama stimulus package made the economic downturn of the time better than it would have been depends entirely on what your counterfactual is.

inverse correlation
A higher level of one variable is associated with a lower level of the other variable.

Sometimes two variables move in opposite directions. This **inverse correlation** can also be misinterpreted as being causal. If you were to get season tickets to your college's football games and observe the amount of skin (bare arms, legs, and midriffs) showing on the fans and compare that to the amount of hot chocolate sold during the game, you would find that when people show more skin they also consume less hot chocolate. If you came to the conclusion that one caused the other to happen you would, of course, be wrong. Obviously, the weather caused each to occur.

Kick It Up a Notch

DEMONSTRATING CONSTANT AND INCREASING OPPORTUNITY COST ON A PRODUCTION POSSIBILITIES FRONTIER

Economists use the production possibilities frontier to show the concepts of increasing and constant opportunity cost. If we start with no pizza and only soda but then move in increments to change our mix, there is opportunity cost. Just how much depends on whether it is increasing or constant.

Demonstrating Increasing Opportunity Cost

For example, in Figure 1.8, if we go from the point on the graph where we are producing no pizza to the point where we are producing a single unit, a unit whose numbers could be in the billions, our opportunity cost would be characterized by lost units of soda. On Figure 1.8, the opportunity cost of going from 0 units of pizza to 1 unit of pizza is one unit of soda. Moving from 1 unit of pizza to 2 units has an opportunity cost that is 3 units of soda. Similarly, moving from 2 to 3 units of pizza has an opportunity cost of 6 units of soda. As is visually obvious, the opportunity cost of going from 0 to 1 is smaller than going from 2 to 3. This is why we say that the opportunity cost is increasing.

Demonstrating Constant Opportunity Cost

Similarly, we can use Figure 1.9 to show constant opportunity cost. The opportunity cost of moving from producing no pizza to 1 unit is 3 units of soda. Moving from 1 unit to 2 units and from 2 to 3 units also has an opportunity cost of 3 units of soda. In this case the opportunity cost of going from 0 to 1 is the same as going from 2 to 3. This is why we say that the opportunity cost is constant.

What this all means is simple: Choices have consequences. Sometimes those consequences are great and sometimes they are small. If studying for five hours moves you from an F to a B on a test, then the higher grade has a low opportunity cost in terms of lost television watching. Viewed from the other side, the opportunity cost of another five hours of television watching (instead of studying to get a good grade) could be substantial. Opportunity cost is everywhere and is a consequence of every decision you make.

FIGURE 1.8 Illustrating increasing opportunity costs.

FIGURE 1.9 Illustrating constant opportunity costs.

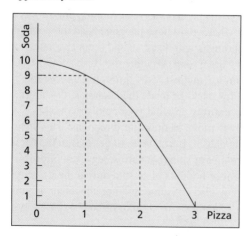

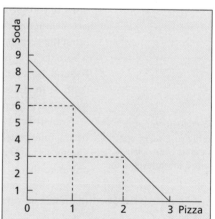

...arned the definition of economics, that choices have consequences, and
...nces are called opportunity cost. We learned how to model choices using a
...bilities frontier. We also learned that, depending on our assumptions, oppor-
...be increasing or constant. We created a road map to the entire economy and to
...s book by creating a circular flow diagram with all the various markets, individu-
...nd governments interacting in society. Last, we explored the meaning of thinking
...ally by examining marginal analysis, positive and normative analysis, incentives,
...flaws of logic that may get in the way of economically accurate thinking.

attainable, 5	incentives, 8	positive analysis, 8
causation, 9	inverse correlation, 9	production possibilities
circular flow model, 6	marginal benefit, 7	frontier, 2
counterfactual, 9	marginal cost, 7	resource, 2
direct correlation, 9	market, 6	scarce, 2
economics, 1	model, 2	simplifying assumption, 3
factor market, 6	net benefit, 8	unattainable, 5
fallacy of composition, 8	normative analysis, 8	unemployment, 5
foreign exchange market, 6	opportunity cost, 2	
goods and services market, 6	optimization assumption, 7	

Issues Chapters You Are Ready for Now

Federal Spending, 139	Poverty and Welfare, 371	If We Build It, Will They Come? And Other Sports Questions, 417

Quiz Yourself

1. Scarcity implies that the allocation scheme chosen by society can
   a. not make more of any one good.
   b. always make more of any good.
   c. typically make more of a good but at the expense of making less of another.
   d. always make more of all goods simultaneously.

2. A production possibilities frontier is a simple model of
   a. scarcity and allocation.
   b. prices and output.
   c. production and costs.
   d. inputs and outputs.

3. The underlying reason that there are unattainable points on a production possibilities frontier diagram is that there
   a. is government.
   b. are always choices that have to be made.
   c. is a scarcity of resources within a fixed level of technology.
   d. is unemployment of resources.

4. The underlying reason production possibilities frontiers are likely to be bowed out (rather than linear) is
   a. choices have consequences.
   b. there are always opportunity costs.
   c. some resources and people can be better used producing one good rather than another.
   d. there is always some level of unemployment.

5. The optimization assumption suggests that people make
   a. irrational decisions.
   b. unpredictable decisions.
   c. decisions to make themselves as well off as possible.
   d. decisions without thinking very hard.

6. Imagine an economist ordering pizza by the slice. When deciding how many slices to order she would pick that number where the enjoyment of the _____ equals the enjoyment she could get from using the money on another good.
   a. first slice
   b. last slice
   c. average slice
   d. total number of slices

7. Of course, all individual students are better off if they get better grades. If you were to conclude that all students would be better off if everyone received an "A" you would
   a. have fallen victim to the fallacy of scarcity.
   b. be right.
   c. have fallen victim to the fallacy of composition.
   d. be mistaking correlation with causation.

8. If you were to conclude, after carefully examining data and using proper evaluation techniques, that a tax credit for attending college benefits the poor more than a tax deduction (of equal total cost to the government) would, you would have engaged in _____ analysis to reach that conclusion.
   a. negative
   b. positive
   c. normative
   d. creative

Short Answer Questions

1. Suppose you buy a new car. What is the opportunity cost of doing so?

2. Suppose you decided to study all last week for this exam instead of doing anything fun. What was the opportunity cost of doing so? Why might the opportunity cost (defined in terms of fun lost) be expected to increase?

3. Suppose you hear a political candidate claim credit or lay blame for an economic outcome. How can you tell whether the candidate is correct? What would you need to know?

4. If you get a 25 percent pay increase, you are better off. Explain why some people would *not* be better off if their employer gave them a 25 percent pay increase.

5. Suppose you were to analyze the state and the economy at the moment. You say to your friends, "The economy has been growing more slowly in the last 10 years than it did in the previous 20 years. The government should cut taxes to stimulate the economy." What portion of that statement is "positive" and what portion of that statement is "normative"?

Think about This

What was your opportunity cost of attending college?

Think about the most expensive thing you have ever purchased. What could you have done with the money? Which outcome would have made you better off—what you did or what you could have done?

Think about the last time you took a series of tests during a short period of time (high school or college finals work here). How did you decide how much time to spend on each subject? How might the study of economics help you make that allocation decision in the future?

Talk about This

Discuss whether you believe people make rational decisions based on the optimization assumption.

Discuss what kinds of noneconomic (something you would normally not think of as an economic decision) trade-offs could be modeled with a production possibilities frontier?

Graphing: Yes, You Can.

Whether you like it or not, graphing is an important part of "getting" economics. If you have ventured to this appendix it is likely that your instructor agrees and wants you to have a firm foundation for what you are about to do. This appendix is geared to the student who never understood what a graph was trying to tell them; to those poor souls who look at a complex diagram and see a bunch of stray lines that have no meaning. In the movie *Jerry Maguire*, Tom Cruise bursts into his home to offer a long heartfelt apology to his wife, who finally interrupts him to say, "You had me at 'Hello.'" Those of us who teach economics have often lost our students at "Hello," or at least at the moment we went to the board, overhead projector, or computer display to draw a graph. Let's get off on the right foot with learning what a graph is and what it can tell us.

CARTESIAN COORDINATES

As the subheading suggests, Cartesian coordinates are named for their inventor, Frenchman René Descartes. As the legend goes, he was staring at the ceiling and began following the path of a fly. He discovered that he could use just two numbers to pinpoint the placement of the fly on the ceiling every time it landed. So lie back for a moment and look at the ceiling.

origin
The point on the graph where both the variables are zero (0,0).

y-axis
The vertical axis.

x-axis
The horizontal axis.

Now pick a corner of the room where the ceiling meets two walls; that will be your reference point. (In math it is called the **origin**.) Assuming the walls are square to one another, call the wall that runs on your left the **y-axis** and the wall on your right the **x-axis**. Now find a spot on the ceiling that stands out; a spider, a small stain, a vent, anything. Draw the shortest possible imaginary line from your spot to the ceiling to the wall on the right. Call that point A. Do the same thing for the wall on the left and call that point B. You can identify that point on the ceiling using just two numbers. The first number is the distance along the x-axis from the corner to A and the second is the distance along the y-axis from the corner to B. In Figure 1A.1 the point that is marked is 9 units along the x-axis and 11 along the y-axis, so it is shown as (9,11)

PLEASE! NOT $Y = MX + B$ . . . SORRY.

slope
The increase in the value of the y-axis variable for a one unit increase in the value of the x-axis variable.

x-intercept
The value of the x-axis variable when the y-axis variable is zero.

y-intercept
The value of the y-axis variable when the x-axis variable is zero.

Whether you want to recall the experience or not, you were first exposed to the **slope, x-intercept,** and **y-intercept** of a line and the dreaded $y = mx + b$ form of the line in your first algebra class. Whether that was in 7th, 8th, 9th, or 10th grade, enough time has passed that a refresher on the ideas is in order. The equation $y = mx + b$ is a line because if you get all of the x, y combinations that come about from plugging in random values of x and computing what you get for y and then graph them, they end up in a line. That line will cross the y-axis at b, because if you plug in 0 for x in the $y = mx + b$ equation, mx is 0 (because anything times 0 is 0), so all you are left with is b. Therefore, b is the y-intercept. It will cross the x-axis at $-b/m$. Therefore, the x-intercept is $-b/m$. As you will (perhaps not so vividly) recall, the slope is the "rise over the run." That means it is the amount by which y rises divided by the amount by which x rises. Suppose we let x start at 3 and rise to 4. If that happens, then y goes from $m3 + b$ to $m4 + b$. y therefore rises by m. The rise is m, the run is 1, so the slope is m. There is nothing magic about the choice of 3; we could have used any number and we would have gotten the same result. The slope is m.

FIGURE 1A.1
Graphing a point.

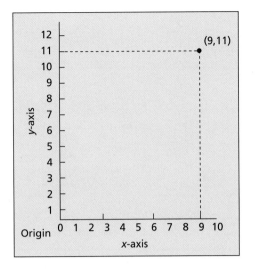

FIGURE 1A.2
Graphing a line
$y = mx + b$
$m > 0, b > 0.$

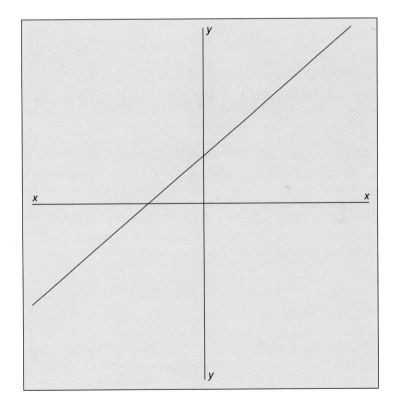

If *m* and *b* are positive, you get a graph like Figure 1A.2. If *m* is positive and *b* is negative, you get something like Figure 1A.3. If *m* is negative and *b* is positive you get a graph like Figure 1A.4, and finally, if they are both negative, you get something like Figure 1A.5. If *m* is large and positive, that means the line is upward sloping and steep; small and positive means that it is upward sloping and relatively flat. If *m* is really negative, then the line is downward sloping and steep, and if it is slightly negative, then the line is downward sloping and flat.

FIGURE 1A.3
Graphing a line
$y = mx + b$
$m > 0, b < 0.$

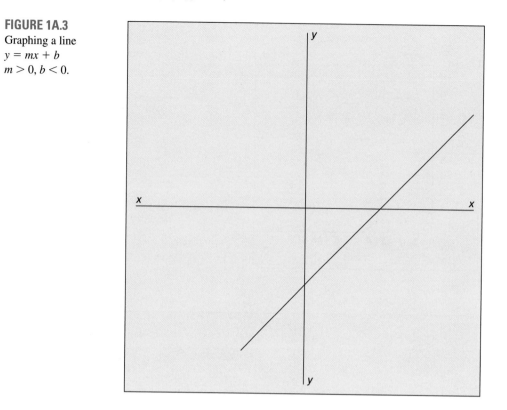

FIGURE 1A.4
Graphing a line
$y = mx + b$
$m < 0, b > 0.$

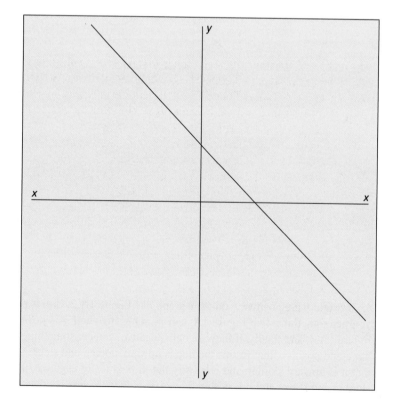

FIGURE 1A.5
Graphing a line
$y = mx + b$
$m < 0, b < 0$.

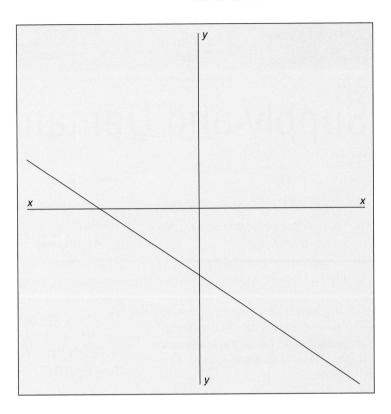

WHAT ON GOD'S GREEN EARTH DOES THIS HAVE TO DO WITH ECONOMICS?

To simplify things some, the only things that matter on our graphs will be those things that happen in the first quadrant (where both *x* and *y* are positive). We will have downward-sloping lines and upward-sloping lines. We will have some lines that are steep and some that are flat. Often, what we graph will not be a line at all but a curve (such as Figures 1.5 and 1.8). That is less important than this: An upward-sloping line or curve means that as the variable on the *x*-axis increases, so does the variable on the *y*-axis; a downward-sloping line or curve means that as the variable on the *x*-axis increases, the variable on the *y*-axis decreases.

This will become apparent when we talk about supply and demand in Chapter 2 and costs of production in Chapter 4. As you will see in Chapter 2, economists put price on the vertical axis (the *y*-axis) and the amount people want to buy or firms want to sell on the horizontal axis (the *x*-axis). The upward-sloping line will be supply and will suggest that companies will produce more stuff if you pay them more for each one, and the downward-sloping line will be demand and will suggest that consumers will buy less stuff when the price per unit rises.

We will also make a big deal out of two lines or curves crossing. When supply crosses demand in Chapter 2, when marginal revenue crosses marginal cost in Chapter 5, and when aggregate demand crosses aggregate supply in Chapter 8, this is going to have particular significance. It is important that when you get there and you don't understand why two lines crossing matters at all . . . **ASK!**

CHAPTER TWO

Supply and Demand

Learning Objectives

After reading this chapter you should be able to:

LO1   Illustrate and explain the economic model of supply and demand.

LO2   Define many terms, including supply, demand, quantity supplied, and quantity demanded.

LO3   Utilize the intuition behind the supply and demand relationships as well as the variables that can change these relationships to manipulate the supply and demand model.

Chapter Outline

Supply and Demand Defined

The Supply and Demand Model

All about Demand

All about Supply

Determinants of Demand

Determinants of Supply

The Effect of Changes in Price Expectations on the Supply and Demand Model

Kick It Up a Notch: Why the New Equilibrium?

Summary

This is the make-or-break chapter of the book: You cannot understand economics without understanding supply and demand. Only if you understand this topic will you be able to read the issue chapters with a good level of comprehension.

You probably are familiar with the words "supply and demand" through television, newspapers, or conversation. The phrase frequently is used by people in a way an economist would not use it. This chapter is intended to show you what economists mean when they use the phrase and how they use the model behind the phrase so you understand the supply and demand model enough that you will be able to use both the model and the jargon correctly when we discuss a variety of economic issues.

Arriving at that level of understanding will take some time. We begin by setting out some of the language we will be using. It may be tempting for you to read too fast, to skim through, figuring that you have heard all the words before. Don't. As we discussed in Chapter 1, the language has precise meaning to economists, and it is not necessarily the same as the meaning you have associated with it before.

Our next move is laying out the supply and demand model itself, starting with brief explanations of the term "demand" and then the term "supply." We then put them together on one graph to form our first look at the model and our first look at what economists call equilibrium. We then step back a moment to examine in detail demand and then supply.

With a rudimentary understanding of the supply and demand model, we explore what happens in it when demand changes and then explore what happens in it when supply changes. Our last step shows why supply or demand changes require a change in the equilibrium.

Supply and Demand Defined

Markets

supply and demand
The name of the most important model in all of economics.

price
The amount of money that must be paid for a unit of output.

output
The good or service produced for sale.

market
Any mechanism by which buyers and sellers negotiate an exchange.

consumers
People in a market who want to exchange money for goods or services.

producers
People in a market who want to exchange goods or services for money.

equilibrium price
The price at which no consumers wish they could have purchased more goods at the price; no producers wish that they could have sold more.

equilibrium quantity
The amount of output exchanged at the equilibrium price.

quantity demanded
The amount consumers are willing and able to buy at a particular price during a particular period of time.

Supply and demand is the name of the most important model in all of economics. Economists use it to provide insight into the movements in **price** and **output**. Remember from Chapter 1 that a model is a simplification of a complicated real-life phenomenon. This model assumes that there is a **market** where buyers and sellers get together to trade. **Consumers** are assumed to bring money to the market, whereas **producers** are assumed to bring goods or services to the market. Consumers want to exchange their money for goods or services while producers want to exchange the goods or services they have for money.

It is important that you understand that the word "market" has a very specific meaning to economists and that it is very different from the business idea of "marketing." A market exists anywhere that buyers and sellers negotiate price and perform an exchange. Therefore, they have to be able to communicate and they have to be able to exchange. Take, as an example, the market for used midsized sedans. There are people who are looking to buy them and people who are looking to sell them. Prior to the Internet, most of the communication was geographically constrained. Buyers went to used-car lots or read ads in the newspaper. People who wanted to unload a car advertised by word of mouth, by newspaper, or sold to a dealer. With the Internet, the market is greatly expanded because communication (autotrader.com; ebay.com, etc.) is easier, but you still are unlikely to buy a car in Seattle if you live in Miami because the cost of getting the car from Seattle is prohibitive. Finally, "marketing" is what the used-car sales staff does to convince you to buy their cars. Try not to confuse the two.

The supply and demand model assumes that there are many consumers and producers, so that no one of them can dictate price. There is a price at which neither consumers nor producers leave with less value than they came with; no consumers wish they could have purchased more goods at the price; no producers wish they could have sold more at that price—in short, everyone is better off for participating. Economists call such a price an **equilibrium price** and the amount that consumers buy from producers an **equilibrium quantity**. The nuts and bolts of this model are the supply and demand curves. The demand curve shows the relationship between the price consumers have to pay and how much they "want to buy," whereas the supply curve shows the relationship between the price firms receive and how much producers "want to sell." Economists refer to the amount that consumers want to buy at any particular price as the *quantity demanded* and the amount that firms want to sell at any particular price as *quantity supplied.*

People participate in markets because markets make their participants better off. Markets evolved because our ancestors recognized that self-sufficiency, though possible, did not allow people to take advantage of their particular skills. A social creation of humans, markets have been shaped by humankind to bring people together to exchange goods and services and, because these exchanges have always been voluntary, participants have always left them content that they have gained from the market's existence. Thus markets have endured as a useful social institution because they continue to advance our individual and societal standard of living.

Quantity Demanded and Quantity Supplied

This is one place where everything you have read, heard, or seen in newspapers, on radio, or on TV will confuse you because economists use these terms very differently from the way they are used outside of economics. Economists insist on highlighting the difference between demand and **quantity demanded.** If you look carefully at the paragraph that is two

MARKETS BOX

capitalist economy
An economic system where markets, in particular markets for financial resources, are free.

socialist economy
An economic system where a significant part (but not all) of the decisions regarding the allocation of financial resources is made by a governmental authority.

communist economy
An economic system where governmental authorities determine the allocation, use, and distribution of financial resources.

Markets exist whether the underlying economic system is capitalist, socialist, or communist. A capitalist economy is so-named because in addition to there being free markets in most goods and services, there are free markets in financial capital. Whether people have money to lend because they have saved it or inherited it, in a capitalist system they control it. The profit that the capital generates goes to the owner of the capital. In a communist system, capital and the profit that it generates are controlled by a government authority. The government authority decides how the money is used. In a socialist system, a significant part of the profit generated by financial capital goes to the government in the form of taxes. The government then uses the tax money to counter the wealth impacts of the distribution of profit. No country is completely capitalist and few (possibly North Korea) are completely communist. Each country exists along a spectrum. The politically conservative Heritage Foundation, in conjunction with the *The Wall Street Journal*, developed an Index of Economic Freedom that measures the degree to which countries have free capital flows, minimal government regulation of business and labor, minimal limits on trade, and a legal system conducive to business. Selected countries are listed in the table below.

It is also worth noting that this is the first, but certainly not the last time that this text will use a source with a political agenda. That usage, however, will be balanced.

Index of Economic Freedom Table

Top 20	Bottom 20	Other Countries and their Rank	
Hong Kong	Angola	Iceland	23
Singapore	Ecuador	Austria	25
Australia	Argentina	Norway	31
New Zealand	Ukraine	South Korea	34
Switzerland	Uzbekistan	Uruguay	36
Canada	Kiribati	Colombia	37
Chile	Chad	Belgium	40
Mauritius	Solomon Islands	Peru	44
Denmark	Timor-Leste	Spain	46
United States	Congo, Rep.	Mexico	50
Ireland	Iran	Israel	51
Bahrain	Turkmenistan	France	62
Estonia	Equatorial Guinea	Saudi Arabia	82
United Kingdom	Congo, Dem. Rep.	Italy	83
Luxembourg	Burma	Brazil	100
Finland	Eritrea	Greece	117
Netherlands	Venezuela	India	119
Sweden	Zimbabwe	China	136
Germany	Cuba	Russia	139
Taiwan	North Korea		

www.heritage.org/index/Ranking

quantity supplied
Amount firms are willing and able to sell at a particular price during a particular period of time.

above, paying particular attention to the last sentence, the quantity demanded is how much consumers are willing and able to buy at a particular price during a particular period of time. Demand, on the other hand, shows how much consumers want to buy at all prices. Demand is a relationship, whereas quantity demanded is a particular point on that relationship. An identical distinction exists with supply. Quantity supplied is how much firms are willing and able to sell at a particular price during a particular period of time, whereas supply alone shows how much firms want to sell at all prices.

Ceteris Paribus

Social scientists in general, and economists in particular, believe in something called the "scientific method," one aspect of which suggests that to isolate the effect of one variable on another you have to separate out the impacts of everything else. Unlike chemistry or biology, though, economists are rarely able to put their subjects (people) into a lab and experiment on them. For instance, economists cannot create a capitalist system in one area of town, a socialist system in another, and a communist system in a third so as to test which economic system serves society best. Economists have to observe in the context of their models. So, even though life does not progress one change at a time, our model allows us to focus on one change at a time. This brings us to the Latin most commonly used by economists: **ceteris paribus,** which means "other things equal." This phrase, when added to a definition or a conclusion, means that though there are many other factors that could affect a phenomenon in real life, this is focusing on the impact of one while holding those other factors constant.

ceteris paribus
Latin for other things equal.

Demand and Supply

For our demand curve we want to know what the relationship is between price and quantity demanded. Determining this relationship is difficult because the relationship depends on such things as whether people are rich or poor, whether the good is in or out of fashion, or how much rival goods cost. To get around this we assume we are looking at the relationship between price and quantity demanded in such a way that none of the other things are changing. Thus, **demand** is the relationship between price and quantity demanded, ceteris paribus.

demand
The relationship between price and quantity demanded, ceteris paribus.

Precisely the same logic applies to supply. There are many things upon which the relationship between price and quantity supplied depends: how much workers must be paid, the cost of materials, or the availability of technology. Again we assume these things do not change, so **supply** is the relationship between price and quantity supplied, ceteris paribus.

supply
The relationship between price and quantity supplied, ceteris paribus.

The Supply and Demand Model

Demand

We have put it off long enough—let's look at the model. To plot a demand curve, let's first tell ourselves a reasonable story and put the relevant information in a table. In many city downtown areas, there are vendors selling food and drink from stands. To simplify the issue, let's suppose we are looking at the market for bottled orange juice sold by these street vendors and that the customers buy the bottles of orange juice from those vendors and consume the juice throughout the day in their downtown offices. There are obviously lots of things that will affect the supply and demand for these bottles of orange juice, but for the moment we are going to assume they are held constant.

We start this inquiry with the price of a bottle of orange juice at zero and ask how many will be wanted. Probably a lot, but not as many as you might think. People get tired of drinking the same thing over and over again and even if they were going to get a bunch to save for later, they still have to carry it to their offices. Suppose, for mathematical simplicity, that there are only 10,000 people in this downtown area and that at a price of zero each person wants only five bottles per day. That would mean that, at a price of zero, there would be a quantity demanded of 50,000 drinks.

Suppose the price were raised to 50 cents per bottle. Each individual would have to weigh whether they wanted a bottle of orange juice or 50 cents. Let's say the average person decides to buy only four per day at that price. As a result of the price increase, the quantity demanded for the market would be 40,000. Suppose another 50-cent increase would decrease the amount

TABLE 2.1
Demand schedule for bottles of orange juice.

Price ($)	Individual Quantity Demanded	Market Quantity Demanded (10,000 people)*
0	5	50,000
0.50	4	40,000
1.00	3	30,000
1.50	2	20,000
2.00	1	10,000
2.50	0	0

*This is ceteris paribus at work, holding the number and type of people constant.

FIGURE 2.1
The demand curve.

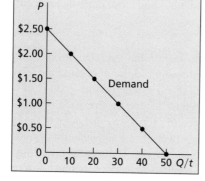

demand schedule
Presentation, in tabular form, of the price and quantity demanded for a good.

wanted by the average person to three. Quantity demanded in the market would fall to 30,000. Without belaboring the point further, price increases would decrease the amount the average person would buy until at $2 per bottle the average person wanted only one, and at $2.50 the average person would buy none. Table 2.1 depicts the options we have just suggested in the form of what is called a **demand schedule**. A demand schedule presents the price and quantity demanded for a good in a tabular form.

This information can also be displayed on a graph. As a matter of fact, that is how you will nearly always see it from now on. Figure 2.1 is a graph of a demand curve. Note that the vertical axis is labeled *P* for price per unit and the horizontal axis is labeled *Q/t* for quantity per unit time. You probably anticipated the first label, but the second may require a short explanation. Quantity per unit time is that number of orange juice bottles that the 10,000 people will want per day. There always has to be a time reference for quantities demanded and for quantities supplied. The dark dots represent the points from our demand schedule, and when we connect the dots we have a demand curve.

Supply

Now, using the same example, let's think about the sellers of orange juice bottles. Suppose for the sake of this example that there are 10 completely independent street vendors selling orange juice bottles, and that there aren't any brand names of the vendors or for the orange juice. Now ask yourself how many orange juice bottles a business would attempt to sell at various prices. Obviously they would not want to give any away, so at a price of zero, quantity supplied would be zero. Even at a very low price, such as 50 cents a bottle, they might not want to sell any because the cost to the vendor of either buying or filling the bottle might be more than the 50 cents per bottle they would get. As prices go up, they would probably be willing to put forth more and more effort to make more and more money. For the sake of this example, we will assume that at $1.00 per bottle each business will sell a bottle to anyone who would come up to them but won't go out of their way to sell more than that. They will station themselves where there are a lot of people and simply sell to them.

Suppose that as the price people are willing to pay rises, the vendors hire people to hawk the orange juice bottles to drum up sales. Let's say that at $1.50 they will each want to hire enough hawkers to sell 2,000 bottles per day and that at $2.00, they will hire enough to sell

TABLE 2.2
Supply schedule for bottles of orange juice.

Price ($)	One Vendor's Quantity Supplied	The Market's Quantity Supplied (all 10 concession vendors)
0	0	0
0.50	0	0
1.00	1,000	10,000
1.50	2,000	20,000
2.00	3,000	30,000
2.50	4,000	40,000

FIGURE 2.2   The supply curve.

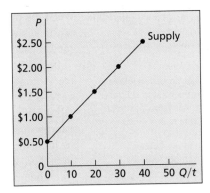

3,000 per day. Finally, suppose that at $2.50 per bottle, they will hire enough hawkers to sell 4,000 per day. Table 2.2 displays this information in what is called a **supply schedule,** which presents in tabular form the price and quantity supplied for a good.

supply schedule
Presentation, in tabular form, of the price and quantity supplied for a good.

This information can also be displayed on a graph. Figure 2.2 shows the supply curve with the axes labeled the same as Figure 2.1: price and quantity over time. Here the dark dots represent the points from our supply schedule. When we connect the dots we have a supply curve.

Equilibrium

Table 2.3 combines the supply schedule and the demand schedule into a single schedule, and Figure 2.3 combines the supply curve and demand curve on one diagram. They both show us that at prices below $1.50 consumers want more orange juice bottles than vendors are willing to provide and that at prices above $1.50 they want fewer bottles than vendors are willing to sell. Where the supply and demand curves cross, the amount that consumers want to buy and the amount firms want to sell are the same. This is called an **equilibrium.**

equilibrium
The point where the amount that consumers want to buy and the amount firms want to sell are the same. This occurs where the supply curve and the demand curve cross.

FIGURE 2.3   The supply and demand model and equilibrium price and quantity.

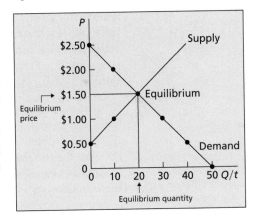

TABLE 2.3   Supply and demand schedules with shortage and surplus.

Price ($)	Individual Quantity Demanded	Market Quantity Demanded	One Vendor's Quantity Supplied	Market Quantity Supplied	Shortage (excess demand)	Surplus (excess supply)
0	5	50,000	0	0	50,000	
0.50	4	40,000	0	0	40,000	
1.00	3	30,000	1,000	10,000	20,000	
1.50	2	20,000	2,000	20,000		
2.00	1	10,000	3,000	30,000		20,000
2.50	0	0	4,000	40,000		40,000

Shortages and Surpluses

shortage
The condition where firms do not want to sell as many goods as consumers want to buy.

surplus
The condition where firms want to sell more goods than consumers want to buy.

excess demand
Another term for shortage.

excess supply
Another term for surplus.

When the price is too low we have a shortage. Firms do not want to sell as many goods as consumers want to buy. When the price is too high we have a surplus. Firms want to sell more goods than consumers want to buy.

Imagine that the vendors start to run out of bottled orange juice. There is an obvious shortage. According to the model of supply and demand, this will have occurred because the price was too low. With long lines of people wanting to buy bottles in front of them, the vendors will see that in the face of a shortage, or excess demand, they can raise the price and still sell their product. The opposite will occur if there is a surplus, or excess supply. If the price is too high, the vendors will want to sell more bottles than consumers will want. Instead of long lines, there will be excess inventory and firms will see that in the face of a surplus they should lower the price to get rid of it.

With self-interested sellers, shortages and surpluses are short-lived. Firms react to changes in inventories by changing the price they charge. They react to shortages with price increases and surpluses with price cuts, and as a result either situation is temporary.

All about Demand

The Law of Demand

law of demand
The statement that the relationship between price and quantity demanded is a negative or inverse one.

We know from this chapter's section on definitions that demand is the relationship between price and quantity demanded, ceteris paribus, and we followed a reasonably believable story about soft drinks at a football game. That story implied that there was a negative relationship between price and quantity demanded. Because of the relationship, the demand curve we drew was downward sloping. The negative relationship between price and quantity demanded is called the law of demand. This "law" is not really a law but is common sense applied to the following rather constant observation: When prices are higher, we tend to buy less.

Why Does the Law of Demand Make Sense?

substitution effect
Purchase of less of a product than originally wanted when its price is high because a lower priced product is available.

real-balances effect
When a price increases, your buying power is decreased, causing you to buy less.

Why do we see this negative relationship so often? There are three distinct reasons. First, when you go to the store and find that the good you want is highly priced, you search for an acceptable substitute that costs less. If you buy something else, you are substituting another good for the one that you originally wanted because its price was too high. Economists say that this is a substitution effect. You buy less of what you originally wanted when its price is high because you use something else instead.

Second, suppose you cannot find an acceptable substitute. In this case, you are stuck buying less of the good because you cannot afford as much. What has happened is that your real buying power has fallen (even though the money you have in your wallet is the same) because prices have risen. This does not necessarily work for all goods (especially basic necessities like water), but generally economists call this a real-balances effect because when a price increases, it decreases your buying power, causing you to buy less.

The third reason we see a negative relationship between price and quantity demanded can be explained with either great detail, or a useful, though not always completely accurate, shortcut. You are in this course and your professor has chosen this book because you do not need the great detail, so you will get the shortcut. It starts from the premise that what you are willing to pay for something depends on how many you have recently had. With this in mind, consider the following very silly but illustrative example. Suppose I give you $10 and I want to know how much you would pay for pizza slices at lunch. Suppose further that as part of this experiment you are given truth serum so you have to honestly tell me two things: (1) on a scale from 1 to 10, how happy your belly is; and (2) how much you valued each slice in terms of money. Starting hungry at a belly happiness index of 1, suppose that you eat one slice and tell me that it was worth $3 and rated a 5 on the belly happiness index. Now you eat another slice and tell me it wasn't worth as much because you were not as hungry, so you say it was worth $2 and your belly happiness index rose to 8. You eat the third slice and tell me that, because you were somewhat full at the time you ate the third slice, your belly happiness index only rose to 9 and the slice was only worth $1.

In this scenario, each time you consume a slice, the value you place on the next slice falls. This means that the value you place on a good depends on how many you have already had. Economists refer to the amount of extra happiness[1] that people get from an additional unit of consumption as **marginal utility** and say that it decreases as you consume more. This **law of diminishing marginal utility** suggests that the amount of additional happiness that you get from an additional unit of consumption falls with each additional unit. Stated more simply, because each additional slice increases your happiness less than the previous slice, the most you would be willing to pay for each additional slice is less than before. The third reason why a demand curve is downward sloping, then, is that for most goods there is diminishing marginal utility.

It is often helpful to view the demand curve as more than a way of finding how much of a good a person wants at a particular price. In addition, you can use it to find out how much a person is "willing to pay" for a particular amount of the good. Whenever you come across this phrase, think "the most they would be willing to pay." Of course you would always want to pay less, but looked at this way the demand curve also represents the most you would be willing to pay for different amounts of the good, ceteris paribus.

marginal utility
The amount of extra happiness that people get from an additional unit of consumption.

law of diminishing marginal utility
The amount of additional happiness that you get from an additional unit of consumption falls with each additional unit.

All about Supply

The Law of Supply

We also know from our section on definitions that supply is the relationship between price and quantity supplied, ceteris paribus, and we followed an equally reasonably believable story about how many orange juice bottles a vendor would want to sell in a city. That story implied that there was a positive relationship between price and quantity supplied. Because of that the supply curve we drew was upward sloping. The positive relationship between price and quantity supplied is called the **law of supply.** Like all other laws in economics, this one isn't a law either but is more like a hypothesis that is supported by nearly all the evidence nearly all the time. Stated more simply: When prices are higher, firms tend to want to sell more.

law of supply
The statement that there is a positive relationship between price and quantity supplied.

Why Does the Law of Supply Make Sense?

Although believable intuitively, the technical reason that a supply curve is upward sloping takes up much of Chapters 4 and 5. What follows is a simplified (though probably not simple) explanation that will be repeated and expanded in Chapters 4 and 5.

Suppose the downtown area where the vendors are selling orange juice bottles has varying areas of population density. It is relatively easy to sell where there are more people, like at a subway exit, and progressively more difficult to sell as you get away from those population centers. As a result, even if vendors hire hawkers to go out and sell orange juice bottles, it is

[1] This is why this discussion has been an intellectual shortcut. Most economists do not believe that you can measure happiness in the same way that you measure distance or temperature. This means that though you can say you are happier in one circumstance than in another, you cannot say how much happier you are. All is not lost, though, because we can get the same idea through the concept of indifference. The reason no one-semester course textbooks explain the downward-sloping nature of demand using the concept of indifference is that it takes too long and gets you no further in your understanding than the last two paragraphs have. Thus the shortcut of marginal utility nets the same result in a lot less time and is judged by most teachers of one-semester economics courses as useful.

going to get harder and harder to sell a lot when they spread out. Even though it is harder to sell, as the price rises, it is still possible and even likely that it would be worth it for vendors to hire hawkers. So even when the last hawkers sent out sell far fewer bottles than the ones sent out originally, the vendors hire them because they make money doing so. So when the price is low, the high-cost sales methods aren't worth it and when the price is high, they are worth it. There might even be a price high enough that the vendors would be willing to deliver individual bottles to individual offices. While this would be very inefficient relative to simply standing at a subway exit, if the vendors have sold all they can this way and the price is high enough, it could still be profitable to the vendors to do so.

What this means, and what Chapters 4 and 5 attempt to demonstrate in detail, is that the reason the supply curve is upward sloping is that it costs more per unit to sell more units. In this example, the orange juice bottles were not any more expensive, but the cost of hawking them or transporting them was higher when we sold to more remote areas.

In addition, when firms decide which good to produce, they will want to produce the one that makes them the most money. Suppose our orange juice vendors have only so much space in the coolers in their carts. In this case, the vendors do not care whether they sell orange juice or water; they simply want to make a profit. If consumers are willing to pay more for bottled water, the vendors will stock their carts with bottled water. What this means is that relative to water, when orange juice prices are higher, the vendor is willing to take water out of the cart and replace it with orange juice. When orange juice prices are lower, the vendor does the opposite.

Determinants of Demand

In the previous section we talked about holding other things constant. Now is the time to consider what happens when things change. As we alluded to in the section on definitions, there are many things that affect the demand relationship for a good. These include how much the good is liked, how much income people have, how much other goods cost, the population of potential buyers, and the expectations of the price in the future. These variables will change how much of the good is wanted as well as how much someone is willing to pay for it. Again "willing to pay" is shorthand for the most someone is willing to pay. If people want more of the good, this also translates into willingness to pay prices that they would not have paid before.

DETERMINANTS OF DEMAND

Taste
Determinant of whether the good is in fashion or whether conditions are right for many people to want the good.

Income
Inferior goods: You buy less of a good when you have more income.
Normal goods: You buy more of a good when you have more income.

Price of other goods
Substitute: Goods used instead of one another.
Complement: Goods that are used together.

Population of potential buyers
The number of people potentially interested in a product.

Expected price
The price that you expect will exist in the future.

Excise taxes
A per unit or percentage tax on a good or service that must be paid by consumers.

Subsidies
A per unit or percentage subsidy for a good or service that is granted to consumers.

Taste

Taste is the word that economists use to describe whether the good is in fashion or whether conditions are right for many people to want the good. A high level of taste means that the good is in fashion or highly desired; a low level of taste means that few people want it. It works on demand in an obvious way: The more people like the good (the higher the taste for the good), the more they are willing to pay higher prices for any particular amount and the more of it they will want. Going back to the orange juice example, the taste for orange juice would rise during cold and flu season as people were trying to boost their immune systems believing that orange juice would aid in keeping viruses at bay.

Income

For most goods, an increase in income will lead to an increase in the amount that consumers want. In cases where you buy more of a good when you have more income, economists call the good normal. If the good is normal and your income rises, you are able to buy more and you want to buy more of the good and you are willing to pay more for it.

How much income people have to buy the good also matters but not always in a positive way. Consider a couple of staples in the college diet, instant ramen noodles and macaroni and cheese. No matter which of these you eat, you can fill your belly for under 50 cents. Now ask yourself how many pouches, boxes, or bags of this stuff you would buy if your grandmother died and left you $25,000. Answer: not many, particularly if you have been eating them because you could not afford other things to eat. This example shows you that it is not always the case that the more you make, the more you buy. In cases where you buy less of a good when you have more income, economists call the good inferior. If the good is inferior and your income rises, you are able to buy more, but you want to buy less of the good and you will need lower prices to induce you to buy any particular quantity.

Returning to our orange juice example, if people consume more bottles of orange juice as their incomes rise, then orange juice is a normal good. If they consume fewer bottles of orange juice when their incomes rise, it is an inferior good.

Price of Other Goods

Similarly, there is no straightforward answer to the question of how you will change your willingness to purchase a good if the price of another good rises. It is possible that if the price of a good like Pepsi rises, you will switch to Coke. In that case, you would be willing to pay more for Coke and want to buy more of it. Likewise, if the price of hot dogs increases, you will decide to buy fewer of them. Since hot dog buns have little good use other than to surround hot dogs, you will need fewer of these too. Economists say that goods used instead of one another (e.g., Coke and Pepsi) are substitutes and that goods that are used together (e.g., hot dogs and hot dog buns) are complements.

Examples of substitutes and complements abound. Peanut butter and jelly are often considered complements because they are typically used together to produce sandwiches. Pepperoni and sausage might be considered substitutes because they are alternative meats for a pizza. To confuse matters, though, goods can be substitutes to some and complements to others. My father-in-law considers peanut butter and jelly to be equally good bagel spreads, so to him they are substitutes. The Meat Lover's Pizza by Pizza Hut includes both sausage and pepperoni, so to people who like this pizza the two may be complements.

Once again, returning to orange juice bottles: Orange juice and grapefruit juice are likely substitutes for one another while orange juice and vodka are likely complements because people (of legal drinking age) may mix them together to form a "screwdriver."

Population of Potential Buyers

The number of people potentially interested in a product will clearly have an impact on the demand for the product. So, as the downtown population rises, more are potentially interested in buying bottles of orange juice. Clearly the larger the city, the more people come downtown to work and shop, and the more people will buy orange juice. Or, for instance, in the dark ages of the 1970s, when there were only a few computer-literate people, only a few people were interested in buying computers. Then schoolchildren, and especially college students, began to rely on computers for their schoolwork, creating a group of potentially interested customers when they graduated. Economists shorten this concept of the number of people potentially interested in a product to call it the population.

Expected Price

When the expected price of a good rises, this induces a stock-up effect. Let's suppose that a winter freeze destroys a large number of the orange groves. Forward-thinking consumers will see the impending increase in orange juice prices and be motivated to stock up now before the price increase takes hold. Similarly, smokers stock up on cigarettes when a tax increase is expected. Frugal drivers buy gas on Wednesdays, before the nearly universal weekend price increase. If there is an expectation that an increase in price is imminent, consumers will be willing to pay more and they will want to buy now rather than later.

Excise Taxes

Sometimes governments want to discourage the consumption of a good and will place a tax on that good. Such a tax would mean that consumers would have to pay more per unit than they otherwise would have to and as a result would decrease the amount that they wished to purchase. Suppose that a city wanted to encourage the recycling of plastic bottles and that consumers had to pay $1 extra per orange juice bottle that they purchased. That would mean that the new demand curve would be $1 lower at every quantity than the old one.

Subsidies

Sometimes governments want to encourage the consumption of a good and will create a subsidy for that good. Such a subsidy would mean that consumers would have to pay less per unit than they otherwise would have to and as a result would increase the amount that they wished to purchase. Suppose that a city in Florida wanted its citizens to be seen by tourists drinking Florida orange juice. To encourage consumers to do so it would allow them to pay $1 less per orange juice bottle that they purchased. That would mean that the new demand curve would be $1 higher at every quantity than the old one.

The Effect of Changes in the Determinants of Demand on the Supply and Demand Model

Tables 2.4 and 2.5 summarize how the determinants of demand work on the supply and demand diagram. Table 2.4 indicates the impact of increases in the variables listed above, whereas Table 2.5 indicates the impact of decreases in those variables. The final column of each table refers to the figure corresponding to the change. Figure 2.4 shows the impact of an increase in demand while Figure 2.5 shows the impact of a decrease in demand. In each figure, the original supply and demand curves are shown in black and the new demand curve is shown in the gold color. The original equilibrium is shown with the big black dot, and the new equilibrium is shown with the big gold-colored dot.

TABLE 2.4   Movements in the demand curve: increases in the values of the determinants.

An Increase in	Causes Demand to	Causes the Demand Curve to Move to the	And Is Shown in Figure
Taste	Increase	Right	2.4
Income, normal good	Increase	Right	2.4
Income, inferior good	Decrease	Left	2.5
Price of other goods, complement	Decrease	Left	2.5
Price of other goods, substitute	Increase	Right	2.4
Population	Increase	Right	2.4
Expected future price	Increase	Right	2.4
Excise Tax	Decrease	Left	2.5
Subsidy	Increase	Right	2.4

TABLE 2.5   Movements in the demand curve: decreases in the values of the determinants.

A Decrease in	Causes Demand to	Causes the Demand Curve to Move to the	And Is Shown in Figure
Taste	Decrease	Left	2.5
Income, normal good	Decrease	Left	2.5
Income, inferior good	Increase	Right	2.4
Price of other goods, complement	Increase	Right	2.4
Price of other goods, substitute	Decrease	Left	2.5
Population	Decrease	Left	2.5
Expected future price	Decrease	Left	2.5
Excise Tax	Increase	Right	2.4
Subsidy	Decrease	Left	2.5

FIGURE 2.4   The effect of an increase in demand on the supply and demand model.

FIGURE 2.5   The effect of a decrease in demand on the supply and demand model.

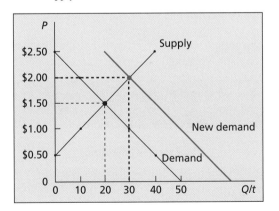

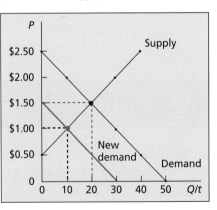

Tables 2.4 and 2.5 as they apply to Figures 2.4 and 2.5 may seduce you into thinking the best way of using this information is to memorize it. As the verb *seduce* suggests, that is a very bad learning strategy. The best use of these tables and figures is to use them as a check against your economic intuition. As an example, suppose you are tasked with drawing a supply and demand diagram for hot dog buns showing the impact of an increase in the price of hot dogs. First, you would recognize hot dogs and hot dog buns as complements and that when

the price of a complement rises, you will consume fewer hot dogs (because the demand for hot dogs is downward sloping) and so you would need fewer hot dog buns. Second, you would recognize that as a decrease in the demand for hot dog buns. Third, you would draw a supply and demand diagram for hot dog buns showing a leftward movement in demand for hot dog buns because a decrease in demand shows up as demand shifting to the left. You would then check that against the information in Table 2.4 (because it is an increase in the price of hot dogs impacting hot dog buns); look down to the "Price of other goods, complement" row, then across to see that your intuition that demand should move left was correct and that the drawing of a figure like Figure 2.5 is correct.

Determinants of Supply

Again, the definitions section alluded to the types of things that can change the supply relationship. They include changes in the price of inputs, technology, price of other potential output, the number of sellers, and expected future price. Again we are assuming that other things are held constant.

Price of Inputs

The price of inputs refers to the costs to firms of all the things necessary to produce output. If an input is used to make a product, then the input costs money and therefore has a price even though its name may change. Obvious examples of inputs are raw material, labor, and equipment. The price of a raw material is simply its price. (Though this sounds like a circular definition, think about our orange juice bottles example. The bottles, the orange juice itself, and coolers to keep the bottles in each have a price.) The price of labor is the wage + benefit cost to employers associated with hiring a person. (Everything that employers pay for that is not paid directly to workers—health insurance, unemployment insurance, worker's compensation, and so on—is defined as benefits.) The price of equipment can affect supply, but just as often, what matters is the rental cost of leased equipment or the interest + depreciation rates that must be paid on the equipment bought with borrowed money. (Interest is the price of borrowed money, and depreciation is the rate at which machines lose value owing to wear and tear.)

DETERMINANTS OF SUPPLY

Price of inputs

Costs to firms of all the things necessary to produce output.

Technology

The ability to turn input into output.

Price of other potential output

When firms have to decide which good to produce, they will want to produce the one that makes them the most money.

Number of sellers

The number of firms competing in the same market.

Expected future price

Firms want to hold back sales to wait for higher prices and unload inventory before prices fall.

Excise taxes

A per unit or percentage tax on a good or service that must be paid by producers.

Subsidies

A per unit or percentage subsidy for a good or service that is granted to producers.

Technology

Within economics, the word *technology* refers to the ability to turn input into output. In our previous example of selling bottles of orange juice in a city, a technological advance that would allow vendors to keep the bottles fresh without ice or refrigeration would reduce costs. This technology would increase output and lower costs. As we are using it here, the technology variable can change because of increases in the ability of employees to work harder and smarter, or it can change because new devices make employees more efficient.

Another example of how increases in technology change markets can be seen in the *very illegal* term-paper business. If you wanted to buy term papers in the 1960s, you would have had to pay people to go to the library to look stuff up in card catalogs of alphabetized index cards and indices of periodicals to find source material. Because access to copy machines was limited, they would have then had to read the material in the library. Finally, they would have had to type the paper on a typewriter, and they would have been able to fix mistakes only with a pasty liquid called Wite-Out®. Paying people to do this would have been expensive.

In the 1970s, all the steps were the same except copy machines would have allowed the people you hired to read source material in their homes. In the 1980s, primitive computers would have allowed them to gather limited quantities of source material on a computer and to write the paper using a hard-to-use, not very flexible word processor. By the 1990s, writers of term papers could look up material on the Internet, print it, read it, and write the paper, all from the comfort of their own bedrooms. In each of these periods, producers of such contraband had to find a way to sell their papers. Often informal networks had to be created and payment had to be in cash. Today, you can go to any number of term-paper sites on the Internet and download a paper by simply entering a credit card number. You, of course, would never do this because your college can easily catch you and throw you out of school. But because it is easier to produce papers in less time than used to be the case, sellers of term papers can charge lower prices and produce more papers.

Price of Other Potential Outputs

The price of other potential output refers to the same idea that we referenced when indicating why the supply curve is upward sloping, except now we focus on what happens to the existing supply curve when the price of the other good changes. As we said, vendors have only so much space in the coolers in their carts. During a hot summer's day they may discover that they sell out of bottles of water and have plenty of leftover bottles of orange juice. If consumers are willing to pay more for bottled water, the vendors will stock their carts with bottled water. They will stock those carts with the combination of water and orange juice that makes them the most money. As the price of water rises, the supply of orange juice will fall because vendors want to stock water.

Number of Sellers

The number of sellers, that is, the number of firms competing in the same market, is important because the more firms there are, the greater is total market production. Using the orange juice example, we assumed that there were 10 different vendors. If these vendors are all making a significant profit, it is likely that other entrepreneurs will want to set up their competing stands. This raises total market supply. Similarly, if there were losses, some of those vendors may quit the business, reducing total market supply.

Expected Price

The expected future price should sound familiar because it is also something that will change demand. In the context of supply, it refers to a firm's desire to hold back sales to wait for higher prices and its desire to sell its goods and thus lower its inventory before prices fall. Firms want to sell their goods when they can make the most money regardless of when that time is. A warning that a hurricane is coming will bid up the current price of gas-powered generators because firms will want to retain those they have in stock to sell at high prices after the hurricane hits. Conversely, if firms figure that the goods they hold will be out of fashion soon, they will want to get rid of them now.

Let's return to the example of the freeze that decimated the orange groves. Not only will buyers of orange juice be motivated to stock up to avoid the increase in price, sellers will know that a price increase is coming and will want to hold on to what they have. As a result, the expected future price not only changes demand for a good, it changes supply as well. Of course, it also works in the other direction. If a bumper orange crop is expected, orange juice prices will be expected to fall and those currently holding orange juice will be motivated to sell their current inventories before the price falls too much.

Excise Taxes

As we indicated in the context of demand, sometimes a government wants to discourage the consumption of a good. In so doing it can tax producers or consumers. If it wants the tax to be collected on the production side, it will place a tax on that good and compel firms to pay the tax. It should be noted here that it doesn't matter whether the tax is on the demand side or the supply side; the impact will be the same and will depend on the Chapter 3 concept of elasticity, not the intention of policy makers. In any event, this tax is modeled by moving the supply curve vertically higher by the amount of the tax. So a city can encourage recycling of plastic bottles by charging firms $1 extra per orange juice bottle that they sell. That would mean that the new supply curve would be $1 higher at every quantity than the old one.

Subsidies

Similarly, subsidies can be applied to the firm producing the good rather than the consumer. A $1 subsidy would be modeled with the new supply curve $1 lower at every quantity than the old one.

The Effect of Changes in the Determinants of Supply on the Supply and Demand Model

Tables 2.6 and 2.7 summarize how determinants of supply work on a supply and demand model. Table 2.6 indicates the impact of increases in the variables listed above, whereas Table 2.7 indicates the impact of decreases in those variables. It is important to understand that on the supply side, an increase in supply is shown by a movement to the right in the supply curve and that a decrease in supply is shown by a movement to the left in the supply curve. As with

TABLE 2.6   Movements in the supply curve: increases in the values of the determinants.

An Increase in	Causes Supply to	Causes the Supply Curve to Move to the	And Is Shown in Figure
Price of inputs	Decrease	Left	2.7
Technology	Increase	Right	2.6
Price of other potential outputs	Decrease	Left	2.7
Number of sellers	Increase	Right	2.6
Expected future price	Decrease	Left	2.7
Excise Tax	Decrease	Left	2.7
Subsidy	Increase	Right	2.6

TABLE 2.7   Movements in the supply curve: decreases in the values of the determinants.

An Decrease in	Causes Supply to	Causes the Supply Curve to Move to the	And Is Shown in Figure
Price of inputs	Increase	Right	2.6
Technology	Decrease	Left	2.7
Price of other potential outputs	Increase	Right	2.6
Number of sellers	Decrease	Left	2.7
Expected price	Increase	Right	2.6
Excise Tax	Increase	Right	2.6
Subsidy	Decrease	Left	2.7

FIGURE 2.6   The effect of an increase in supply on the supply and demand model.

FIGURE 2.7   The effect of a decrease in supply on the supply and demand model.

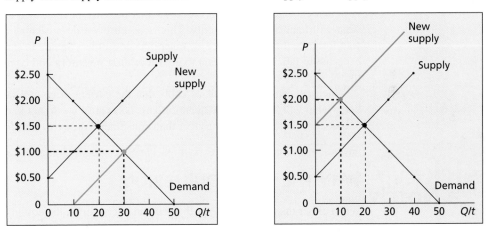

Tables 2.4 and 2.5 the final columns of Tables 2.6 and 2.7 refer to the figures corresponding to the changes. Figure 2.6 shows the impact of an increase in supply while Figure 2.7 shows the impact of a decrease in supply. Just as it was for Tables 2.4 and 2.5 and Figures 2.4 and 2.5, the original supply and demand curves are shown in black and the original equilibrium is shown with the big black dot. This time the new supply curve is shown in the gold color with the new equilibrium shown with the big gold-colored dot.

After having read the admonition against memorizing regarding the demand shifts, you can guess what's next: Don't try to memorize Tables 2.6 and 2.7 as they apply to Figures 2.6 and 2.7. The best use of these tables and figures is to use them as a check against your economic intuition. As an example, suppose you are tasked with drawing a supply and demand diagram for gasoline showing the impact of an increase in the price of crude oil. First, you would recognize that crude oil is the primary input to gasoline so that, when crude oil prices rise, refineries would have to increase their gasoline prices to make up for those higher production costs. Second, you would recognize that as a decrease in the supply of gasoline. Third, you would draw a supply and demand diagram for gasoline showing a leftward movement in supply for gasoline because a decrease in supply shows up as supply shifting to the left. You would then check that against the information in Table 2.6 (because it is an increase in the price of crude impacting gasoline); look down to the "Price of inputs" row, then across to see that your intuition that supply should move left was correct and that the drawing of a figure like Figure 2.7 is correct.

The Effect of Changes in Price Expectations on the Supply and Demand Model

If you have not already noticed, expected future price shows up in both the determinants of demand and the determinants of supply. This means that if the expected future price changes, both the supply and demand curves change as well. If the expected future price rises, consumers will want to stock up, thereby increasing demand. Firms, on the other hand, will want to hold back their inventory to wait for the price increase, thereby decreasing supply. In this case, we do not know what will happen to equilibrium quantity because the demand shift will, by itself, increase quantity, whereas the supply shift will, by itself, decrease quantity. Whether there is a net increase or decrease in equilibrium quantity depends on which shift is greater. On the other hand, the effect on price is known, and it amounts to a self-fulfilling prophecy because a credible prediction of a future price increase will lead to an actual current price increase.

When expected prices rise, we know that the current price will rise, but we do not know what will happen to the quantity. This is because we do not know whether firms' desire to wait for price increases will be stronger than consumers' desire to stock up. When the price is expected to fall, firms will want to get rid of their inventory and consumers will want to wait for the new lower prices.

When expected prices fall we know that the current price will fall, but we again, do not know what will happen to the quantity. This is because we do not know whether firms' desire to unload inventory will be stronger than consumers' desire to wait for lower prices.

Kick It Up a Notch   WHY THE NEW EQUILIBRIUM?

When either the supply curve or the demand curve shifts, the equilibrium has to change. If it does not, one of two things will happen: There will be a shortage where consumers want to buy more than firms want to sell, or there will be a surplus where firms want to sell more than consumers want to buy.

To show that this is the case, imagine that there is an increase in the demand for a good and firms do not increase the price. As shown in Figure 2.8, keeping the price at the old equilibrium would set up a situation where consumers would want more (40) than firms would be willing to sell (20). The resulting shortage would not be eliminated unless there was an increase in the price.

A somewhat different problem would happen if firms did not lower their price in the face of decreased demand. Figure 2.9 shows that keeping the price at the old equilibrium with a decrease in demand would set up a situation where consumers would want fewer (0) than firms would be willing to sell (20). The resulting surplus would not be eliminated unless there was a decrease in the price.

Just as we needed a new equilibrium when there was a change in demand, we need one when there is a change in supply. Figure 2.10 shows that keeping the price at the old equilibrium when supply increases sets up a situation where consumers want fewer (20) than firms are willing to sell (40). The resulting surplus will not be eliminated unless there is a decrease in the price.

Finally, if firms do not raise their prices in the face of decreased supply, there will be a shortage. Figure 2.11 shows that keeping the price at the old equilibrium in the face of decreased supply sets up a situation where consumers want more (20) than firms are willing to sell (0). The resulting shortage will be eliminated unless there is an increase in the price.

FIGURE 2.8 The shortage that is created when demand increases if price and quantity do not.

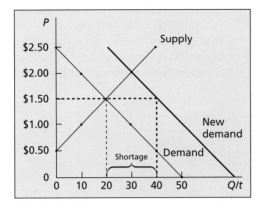

FIGURE 2.9 The surplus that is created when demand decreases if price and quantity do not.

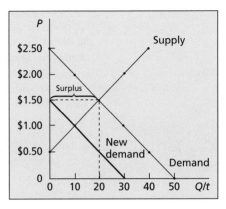

FIGURE 2.10 The surplus that is created when supply increases if price and quantity do not.

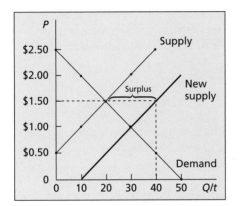

FIGURE 2.11 The shortage that is created when supply decreases if price and quantity do not.

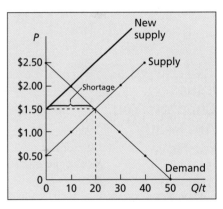

What lesson can you draw from all of this? A change in either the supply or demand curve will change the price at which the quantity consumers want to buy equals the quantity that firms want to sell. If the price does not change, either a surplus or a shortage will ensue.

There are circumstances when a new equilibrium will not be achieved. For instance, **price gouging** is the name given to the situation in which a rapid increase in demand is followed by a rapid increase in price. When demand increases, firms do not have to raise prices to cover costs; they raise prices because they can. Laws preventing price gouging are relatively common.

If you sell ice and have a freezerful to sell, in many states you are not allowed to raise the price of it more than a specified percentage if your community loses electrical power. Economists call the maximum price allowed by law a **price ceiling.** Once the price hits that level, it cannot rise further and you have a shortage for that good. Other examples of price ceilings involve rent control and laws that prevent ticket scalping.

Similarly, equilibrium will not be achieved if there is a **price floor.** This exists when a price may not fall below a certain legally proscribed level. In that circumstance, there is a surplus of the good. Examples of this include farm price supports and the existence of the minimum wage.

Detailed descriptions of the effects of price ceilings and floors are left to their applications in the chapters on rent control, ticket scalping, farm price supports, and the minimum wage.

price gouging
The pejorative term applied to the circumstance when firms raise prices substantially when demand increases unexpectedly.

price ceiling
The level above which a price may not rise.

price floor
Price below which a commodity may not sell.

Summary

The supply and demand model is the single most important model in economics. More than half the issues that you deal with in the latter part of this book will rely on your ability to put an economics problem into the context of this model. In the course of this chapter we explained the supply and demand model by providing all of the language up front. We explained both supply and demand in isolation and then put them together in the form of a coherent model. We then talked about what variables might change demand and then which ones might change supply. We showed that prices and quantities sold would have to change to maintain an equilibrium.

Key Terms

capitalist economy, 20
ceteris paribus, 21
communist economy, 20
consumers, 19
demand, 21
demand schedule, 22
equilibrium, 23
equilibrium price, 19
equilibrium quantity, 19
excess demand, 24
excess supply, 24

law of demand, 24
law of diminishing marginal
  utility, 25
law of supply, 25
marginal utility, 25
market, 19
output, 19
price, 19
price ceiling, 35
price floor, 35
price gouging, 35

producers, 19
quantity demanded, 19
quantity supplied, 20
real-balances effect, 24
shortage, 24
socialist economy, 20
substitution effect, 24
supply, 21
supply and demand, 19
supply schedule, 23
surplus, 24

Issues Chapters You Are Ready for Now

International Finance and
Exchange Rates, 209

The Economics of Race and
Sex Discrimination, 305

Quiz Yourself

1. The supply and demand model examines how prices and quantities are determined
   a. in markets.
   b. by governments.
   c. by churches.
   d. by monopolists.

2. A change in the price of eggs will impact
   a. the demand for eggs.
   b. the supply of eggs.
   c. the quantity demanded and quantity supplied of eggs but neither demand nor supply.
   d. both the supply and demand for eggs.

3. When an economics student draws a supply and demand diagram to model an increase in the income, she is assuming this change happens
   a. semper fidelis.
   b. ceteris paribus.
   c. ipso facto.
   d. de facto.

4. If the supply and demand curves cross at a price of $2, at any price above that there will be
   a. an equilibrium.
   b. a surplus.
   c. a shortage.
   d. a crisis.

5. If the supply and demand curves cross at a quantity of 100, then the price necessary to get firms to sell more than that will have to be _____ equilibrium.
   a. above
   b. at
   c. below
   d. within 10 percent either way of

6. An increase in which of the following determinants of demand will have an ambiguous (uncertain) effect on price?
   a. Taste
   b. Price of a complement
   c. Income
   d. Price of a substitute

7. Which of the following will impact both supply and demand?
   a. A change in price
   b. A change in quantity
   c. A change in expected future price
   d. A change in income

8. An increase in the income of consumers will cause the
   a. supply of all goods to rise.
   b. demand for all goods to rise.
   c. supply of all goods to fall.
   d. the demand for some goods to rise and for others to fall.

9. Without an increase in price, an increase in demand will lead to
   a. a shortage.
   b. a surplus.
   c. socialism.
   d. equilibrium.

10. The underlying reason for the upward-sloping nature of the supply curve is that
    a. the production of most goods comes with increasing marginal benefits.
    b. the production of most goods comes with increasing marginal costs.
    c. the consumption of most goods comes with decreasing marginal utility.
    d. the consumption of most goods comes with increasing marginal utility.

11. If Midwestern grain farmers can plant either soybeans or corn on their land with equal profitability and there is an increase in the price of soybeans, which of the following will result?
    a. A movement to the right in the demand for corn
    b. A movement to the left in the demand for corn
    c. A movement to the right in the supply of corn
    d. A movement to the left in the supply of corn

12. Part of the Patient Protection and Affordable Care Act involved a tax on indoor tanning that tanning salons are required to collect from tanners and send to the federal government. Which of the following would be the predicted result?
    a. A movement to the right in the demand for tanning
    b. A movement to the left in the demand for tanning
    c. A movement to the right in the supply of tanning
    d. A movement to the left in the supply of tanning

13. As the baby boom generation (born between 1946 and 1964) ages, which of the following is a likely outcome?
    a. A movement to the left in the demand for nursing home beds
    b. A movement to the left in the supply of nursing home beds
    c. A movement to the right in the supply of nursing home beds
    d. A movement to the right in the demand for nursing home beds

Short Answer Questions

1. Use your own demand for pizza to illustrate the notion of diminishing marginal utility. Explain why that concept means your demand for pizza-by-the-slice is downward sloping.

2. Suppose you have been given money by your friends and sent to get beverages for a party. Use your demand for those beverages to illustrate why the concept of the "real balance effect" will mean your demand is downward sloping.

3. If there is an alteration to the price of a complement to a good, why is that a change in *demand* when an alteration in the price of the good itself is a change in the *quantity demanded*?

4. If there is an alteration in the price of an input used to produce a good, why is that a change in *supply* when an alteration in the price of the good itself is a change in the *quantity supplied*?

Think about This

Using simple supply and demand analysis, think about the system of allocating human kidneys. The law that forbids the sale of human organs, but allows their voluntary donation, means that there is a bigger shortage of kidneys than there otherwise would be. Does this fact alter your view of the law forbidding the sale of human organs? How about blood?

Talk about This

Are markets always right? List some markets that you think get the production or price of a good wrong. What do these goods have in common?

CHAPTER THREE

The Concept of Elasticity and Consumer and Producer Surplus

Learning Objectives

After reading this chapter you should be able to:

LO1 Define *elasticity* as the responsiveness of quantity to changes in price, recognize its importance in economics, and apply the concept to various real-world goods and services.

LO2 Connect the relationship between the concept of elasticity and the appearance of the demand curve.

LO3 Illustrate that a market equilibrium provides both buyers and sellers with benefits. Consumers pay less than they are willing to pay and producers make a profit. Economists call the former *consumer surplus* and the latter, *producer surplus*.

LO4 Define *deadweight loss* as the measure of inefficiency that exists when prices are too high or too low and apply this to various policies.

Chapter Outline

Elasticity of Demand

Alternative Ways to Understand Elasticity

More on Elasticity

Consumer and Producer Surplus

Kick It Up a Notch: Deadweight Loss

Summary

We now change gears a bit and reconsider the individual supply and demand curves. Our focus here is on the ability of consumers and producers to react to price changes with changes in the amounts they wish to buy or sell. That ability to react, called *elasticity,* will be very important to us as we prepare to use the supply and demand model for issues. We will see how differently shaped demand curves will reflect the degree to which price changes affect quantity.

The last third of the chapter is central in our analysis of several issues. We will see how the supply and demand model can be used to explain why markets are effective in pleasing both consumers and producers. Though we know that consumers long for low prices and producers for high prices, we will see that when a consumer buys something from a producer, both can be pleased with the outcome. We will also see why the net benefit to society is lower when prices are not at equilibrium than it would be if equilibrium were at work.

Elasticity of Demand

Intuition

In the previous chapter, we saw that a change in supply or demand changes the equilibrium price–quantity combination, but we did not discuss which one changes more. For instance, if costs to a firm go up, it is reasonable to ask whether the firm will pass that price increase on to consumers or be willing to accept lower profits. Exploring this question brings in the concept of elasticity.

If the good is one that you need to survive and that has no good substitutes, or if it is one that you spend very little money on, the firm may be able to pass on its increased costs to you in the form of higher prices. On the other hand, if it is a luxury, that is, a good you can do without, if there are many other things that will serve just as well, or if you already spend a lot of your income on it and could not afford a price increase, you may buy a lot fewer. In this case the firm's profits are eaten up.

Definition of Elasticity and Its Formula

elasticity
The responsiveness of quantity to a change in another variable.

price elasticity of demand
The responsiveness of quantity demanded to a change in price.

price elasticity of supply
The responsiveness of quantity supplied to a change in price.

income elasticity of demand
The responsiveness of quantity to a change in income.

cross-price elasticity of demand
The responsiveness of quantity of one good to a change in the price of another good.

There are many kinds of elasticity. In general, elasticity is the responsiveness of quantity to a change in another variable. The two most commonly referred to elasticities are the price elasticity of demand and the price elasticity of supply. Respectively, these are the responsiveness of quantity demanded to a change in price and the responsiveness of quantity supplied to a change in price. Other elasticities include the income elasticity of demand and the cross-price elasticity of demand. The former measures the responsiveness of quantity to changes in income, and the latter measures the responsiveness of quantity to changes in the price of another good.

The price elasticity of demand is measured by looking at how a percentage change in price affects the percentage change in quantity demanded. The formula for elasticity is:

$$\text{Elasticity} = \frac{\%\Delta Q}{\%\Delta P} = \frac{\Delta Q/Q^*}{\Delta P/P^*}$$

where,

$$\% = \text{percent}$$
$$\Delta = \text{change}$$
$$P^* = \text{price (read as ``}P\text{ star'')}$$
$$Q^* = \text{quantity (}Q\text{ star)}$$

The other elasticities are similar in that the percentage change in either quantity demanded or quantity supplied is in the numerator and the percentage change in the price, income, or other price, is in the denominator. Because the bulk of the issues that deal with elasticity deal with price elasticity of demand, we focus here on this particular form of the concept.

From here there are two ways of proceeding: We can explain everything in a great deal of mathematical detail or not. Guessing that the chorus is singing "not," we will skip the math. You will need now to follow the "English" explanations to understand and accept the conclusions about elasticity.

When you use the elasticity of demand formula, you will always get a negative number for it. For our purposes we will simplify things by ignoring the negative sign. The negative sign appears because the demand curve is downward sloping, and an increase in price will therefore cause a decrease in quantity. To illustrate, if a 5 percent increase in price leads to a

elastic
The circumstance when the percentage change in quantity is larger than the percentage change in price.

inelastic
The circumstance when the percentage change in quantity is smaller than the percentage change in price.

unitary elastic
The circumstance when the percentage change in quantity is equal to the percentage change in price.

10 percent decrease in quantity, the elasticity fraction is $-0.10/.05$. Since the important thing about elasticity is the value of the fraction itself, it is acceptable and less complicated for us to ignore the minus sign.

Elasticity Labels

This brings us to an important distinction that will be vital when we look at issues that hinge on whether demand is elastic or inelastic—for example, whether increasing the tax on cigarettes leads to decreases in teen smoking. Economists say that demand is **elastic** when the percentage change in quantity is larger than the percentage change in price and **inelastic** when the percentage change in quantity is smaller than the percentage change in price. Looking at the formula, if the computed elasticity is greater than 1, then demand is elastic; when it is less than 1, then demand is inelastic. When the percentage change in quantity is the same as the percentage change in price (the computed elasticity is exactly 1), demand is **unitary elastic.**

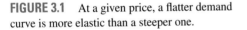

Alternative Ways to Understand Elasticity

To see this more clearly let's look at it using three different thought processes. First we look at elasticity using the graph of our demand curve. Then we look at it using only words. Last, we look at it in terms of how much money is spent on the good.

The Graphical Explanation

We first examine the elasticity phenomenon using graphical skills. Figure 3.1 shows that the flatter the demand curve, the greater the elasticity. This is *not* to say that slope and elasticity are the same thing; it just means that slope matters. To see that slope matters look at Figures 3.1 and 3.2.

FIGURE 3.1   At a given price, a flatter demand curve is more elastic than a steeper one.

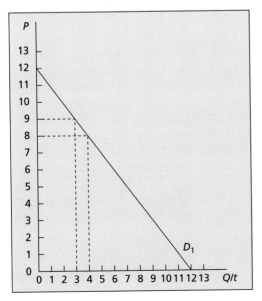

FIGURE 3.2   At a given price, a steeper demand curve is more inelastic than a flatter one.

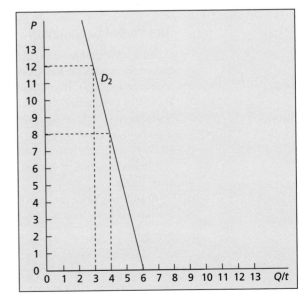

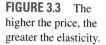

FIGURE 3.3 The higher the price, the greater the elasticity.

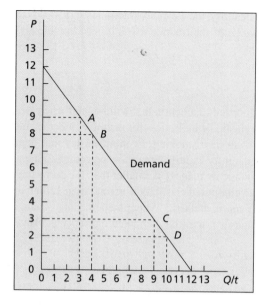

Though they are in separate diagrams, both go through the point $P = \$8$, $Q = 4$. Suppose you were to ask how much price would have to rise in order to induce a reduction in quantity demanded to 3. In Figure 3.1, you can see that it would take an increase to $9, whereas in Figure 3.2 it would require an increase to $12. What that implies is that on the steeper curve (Figure 3.2) demand is less elastic and on the flatter one (Figure 3.1) it is more elastic. In Figure 3.1, a 12.5 percent increase in prices results in a 25 percent reduction in quantity.[1] In Figure 3.2 it takes a 50 percent increase in price to generate a 25 percent decrease in quantity.

Figure 3.3 shows that the higher the price, the greater the elasticity. The price increase from 2 to 3 causes a decrease in quantity from 10 to 9. The same size increase in price from 8 to 9 causes the same size decrease in quantity from 4 to 3. This is because the slope of this demand curve is the same at all those points. Looking at the formula again, we see it is the percentage changes that matter and not just the size of those changes. Even though the price increases and quantity decreases are the same, the percentage changes are very different.

From point D to C the percentage change in price from 2 to 3 is a sizable 50 percent while the percentage change in quantity from 10 to 9 is negligible, only 10 percent. Since the percentage change in the price is greater than the percentage change in the quantity, demand is inelastic here (elasticity is low). On the other hand, from point B to A the percentage change from 8 to 9 is only 12.5 percent, whereas the percentage change in quantity from 4 to 3 is large (25 percent, visually about 33 percent). As a result, demand here is elastic (elasticity is high).

The Verbal Explanation

Although the graphical explanation of elasticity is highly accurate, if it does not make sense to you, it is useless. Recall the original definition of elasticity (the reaction of quantity to a change in price). If you really need a product because there are no good substitutes (like insulin to a diabetic), you will hardly change the amount you buy when the price changes. Thus there is little, if any, reaction of quantity to changes in price. The demand curve for a good you "need" is going to be rather steep. If the good is a luxury item, you are more likely to eliminate it from your budget if it becomes overly expensive. In this case, there is a substantial reaction of quantity to a change in price. The demand curve for a luxury is likely to be flatter.

In addition, price changes for goods that take up little of your income (like drinking water) are not likely to lead to big quantity changes. This is because even if their price increases

---

[1] A price increase from 8 to 9 is a 12.5 percent increase because it is the fraction 1/8. It is a 25 percent decrease in quantity because it went from 4 to 3 (1/4).

DETERMINANTS OF ELASTICITY OF DEMAND

Number and closeness of substitutes

The more alternatives you have, the less likely you are to pay high prices for a good and the more likely you are to settle for an adequate alternative.

Portion of the budget

When a good takes up a significant portion of a consumer's budget, it is more likely to be elastic.

Time

The longer you have to come up with alternatives to paying high prices, the more likely it is you will shift to those alternatives.

greatly, you can easily afford those price increases. Goods that take up a significant portion of your income are more likely to have elastic demand because you are less able to afford large price increases. In this case, goods with low prices are likely to have inelastic demand and goods with high prices are likely to have elastic demand.

Seeing Elasticity through Total Expenditures

total expenditure rule
If the price and the amount you spend both go in the same direction, then demand is inelastic, whereas if they go in opposite directions, demand is elastic.

If we wanted to, we could use math to show that if the price and the amount you spend both go in the same direction, then demand is inelastic. If they go in opposite directions, however, demand is elastic. This **total expenditure rule** of elasticity also allows us to quickly judge whether demand is elastic or inelastic. For instance, when the price of cigarettes goes up, smokers usually have to spend more on them. When the prices of luxuries go up, many of us spend less on them (because we do without them). In this way, we can find out for ourselves whether our demand for a good is elastic or inelastic. All we need to do is to ask ourselves whether a price increase will cause us to spend more on that good.

More on Elasticity

Determinants of Elasticity

Key factors of the three elasticity explanations are important in determining whether a good is elastic or inelastic. The first is the number and closeness of substitutes. When there are many substitutes that all serve nearly as well as the good in question, demand is likely to be more elastic, because price increases induce changes to other goods. Whether price increases can be easily absorbed into a person's budget also matters. If price increases cannot be absorbed—which is likely to be the case if the good takes up a significant portion of the budget of consumers—when they occur, significant quantity reductions will follow. And although timing was not mentioned above, given time, close substitutes can be found or invented, or methods to avoid the price increase will be developed.

Elasticity and the Demand Curve

Elasticity is important because supply changes will have very different results depending on the elasticity of demand. As you can see from the figures on the next page, an identical supply change can affect only price (Figure 3.4), only quantity (Figure 3.5), price much more than quantity (Figure 3.6), or quantity much more than price (Figure 3.7).

FIGURE 3.4   Perfectly inelastic demand.

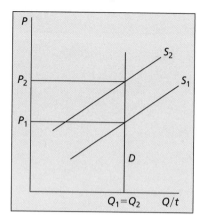

FIGURE 3.5   Perfectly elastic demand.

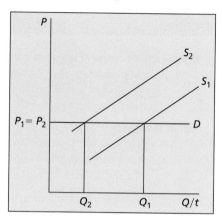

FIGURE 3.6   Inelastic demand.

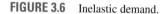
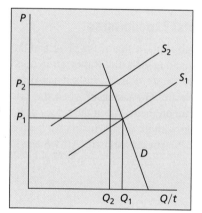

FIGURE 3.7   Elastic demand.

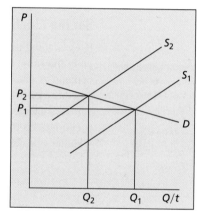

perfectly inelastic
The condition of demand when price changes have no effect on quantity.

perfectly elastic
The condition of demand when price cannot change.

In Figure 3.4 demand curve is **perfectly inelastic** because price changes have no effect on quantity. In Figure 3.5 the demand curve is **perfectly elastic** because price cannot change. As we saw in Figures 3.2 and 3.3, a linear demand curve is elastic at high prices and inelastic at low prices. In Figure 3.6 demand is inelastic over the entire range shown because at every point the percentage change in price is larger than the percentage change in quantity. This will be true when the demand curve is nearly vertical. In Figure 3.7 demand is elastic over the entire range, because at every point the percentage change in price is smaller than the percentage change in quantity. This will be true when the demand curve is nearly horizontal.

If we look back at the elasticity formula, we can use this explanation to compute the appropriate elasticity numbers for each of these elasticity labels. For perfectly elastic demand the computed elasticity is ∞ (infinity), while for perfectly inelastic demand the computed elasticity is 0 (zero). Remembering that unitary elastic demand computes to 1 (one), it makes sense that elastic demand will compute to greater than 1 but less than ∞ and inelastic demand will compute to less than 1 but greater than 0.

ELASTICITY: SOME ILLUSTRATIVE EXAMPLES

Sometimes it is easier to see the importance of elasticity with particular goods. There are economists who spend their days and nights estimating the elasticity of demand for particular goods. This is not because they have nothing else to do. It is because the elasticity of demand for a good is important information to have if you are interested in the impact of a price increase or a tax on that good. For instance, if you take up the chapter on tobacco, alcohol, drugs, and prostitution later in the course, you will find that the question of how much impact a tax on cigarettes will have in decreasing smoking depends greatly on the elasticity of demand for cigarettes.

Consider the goods listed in the following table and their elasticities. You should be able to tell a story about why short-run gasoline demand is less elastic than long-run gasoline demand. You should be able to figure out why demand for foreign travel is quite elastic while demand for food is not. The key to the question of whether a good is elastic or not is whether there is an acceptable substitute.

SAMPLE STORY 1

There are few substitutes to driving to and from work. Though you may or may not be able to take public transportation or car-pool, though you may or may not be able to trade in your SUV for a fuel-efficient car, it would take a substantial change in the price of gasoline to cause you to make the substitution immediately upon seeing an increase in gas prices. This is especially true if you did not anticipate that prices would remain high. On the other hand, if you did see that gasoline prices were going to remain high, you might, over the next year or so, consider trading in the gas guzzler for something more miserly. Similarly, you cannot easily change your electric bill, but over time you can replace an inefficient electric forced air furnace with an efficient heat pump, and you can decide to put electronic

devices that draw electricity even when they look like they are off (such as TVs, coffee pots, and even cell phone chargers) on switches.

Type of Good	Price Elasticity
Inelastic Goods	
Consumer electricity (short-run)	0.13
Eggs	0.06
Food	0.21
Health care services	0.18
Gasoline (short-run)	0.08
Gasoline (long-run)	0.24
Highway and bridge tolls	0.10
Unit Elastic Good (or close to it)	
Shellfish	0.89
Cars	1.14
Elastic Goods	
Luxury car	3.70
Foreign air travel	1.77
Restaurant meals	2.27
Consumer electricity (long-run)	1.89

Sources: Variety of sources combined by author.

SAMPLE STORY 2

Suppose you wanted to take your family on an interesting vacation. Suppose further that your family had narrowed its choices to hiking in the Grand Canyon or seeing the sights in Paris. Given the acceptability of the substitute, a relatively small change in the price of flights and accommodations for the trip to France would have a significant impact on your choice.

Elasticity of Supply

Before moving on, we need to stop and say that nearly everything we have just said about the price elasticity of demand can also be said about the price elasticity of supply. Firms selling goods may be in a situation where they have already brought goods to market that are quite perishable and, therefore, must be sold regardless of their price. We may have other situations where producing more of the goods can be accomplished but only at a sharply increased price. We can imagine a third circumstance where prices do not have to rise much in order to motivate further sales and, finally, it is possible that firms may be willing to produce as many goods as buyers want at the current market price. In the first scenario, the supply curve would be vertical. In the second and third scenarios, the supply curve would be upward sloping, with the second being a steeply sloped supply curve, and the third being a relatively flat one. The final scenario would likely result in a horizontal supply curve. Some examples of goods with

FIGURE 3.8   Perfectly inelastic supply.

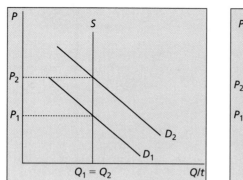

FIGURE 3.9   Inelastic supply.

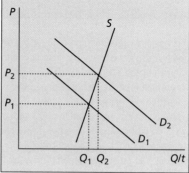

FIGURE 3.10   Elastic supply.

FIGURE 3.11   Perfectly elastic supply.

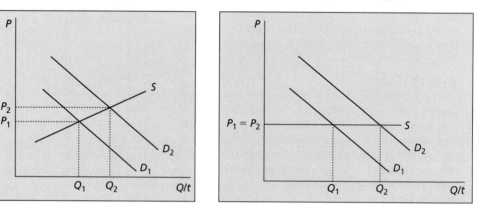

varying elasticities might be helpful here. In the very short run, the elasticity of supply of fresh fruit at a farmers' market is perfectly inelastic as long as the fruit will spoil if it goes unsold. In the relatively short run and in the United States, the supply of gasoline is inelastic because most refineries are not easily capable of expanding or contracting output. They run 24 hours per day, seven days a week, and are brought offline only for maintenance. In the longer run, there are myriad goods where producers can bring new production online. A relatively small increase in the profit margin on a good can motivate significantly greater production. There are very few real-world examples of perfectly elastic supply.

Replicating the idea of Figures 3.4 through 3.7 where we had a constant shift in supply and saw what happened with varying elasticities of demand, Figures 3.8 through 3.11 show what happens when demand shifts with varying elasticities of supply. In Figure 3.8 the supply curve is perfectly inelastic and is vertical. As a result of an increase in demand, price rises greatly, but quantity does not change at all. In Figure 3.9, the supply curve is inelastic and steeply sloped so the change in demand causes prices to rise quite a bit and quantity to rise, albeit not very much. If supply is elastic, such as it is in Figure 3.10, the demand increase causes prices to rise only a little and quantity to rise substantially. Finally, in the case where supply is perfectly elastic, as it is in Figure 3.11, the increase in demand causes only an increase in quantity and no effect is seen on price.

COMPARING THE GAIN TO THE GAINERS WITH THE LOSS TO THE LOSERS

When there are win–win scenarios such as the case outlined, economists generally favor uninhibited exchange. When there are losers, economists look to consumer surplus–producer surplus analysis to weigh the gain to the gainers against the loss to the losers. To you, whether free trade is a good thing or not depends on whether you are a Kia owner who saved several thousand dollars on your car or an unemployed United Auto Workers union member. Whether a new Walmart Supercenter is good for your town depends on whether you are a consumer

paying lower prices for steak or a meat cutter unemployed because the Kroger that you worked for closed. Generally, but by no means universally, economists favor market outcomes because they make the calculation that the gain to the gainers outweighs the loss to the losers. Whether it is trade between the United States and Korea or Walmart outcompeting Kroger, free-trade economists insist that lower prices generate a gain in consumer surplus that is greater than the net loss in producer surplus.

Consumer and Producer Surplus

Consumer Surplus

Most people think that when consumers buy goods, only the firm is better off for the exchange. They do not often acknowledge that consumers are also better off. It turns out that consumers often get much more value than they part with. Look back to "All about Demand" in Chapter 2 and recall that the demand curve represents the marginal utility of the good. This means that the amount each additional unit of the good is worth to the consumer can be read from the demand curve.

Figure 3.12 demonstrates how it is that consumers win in this exchange and provides a measure of the degree to which they win. The value the consumers place on each unit of the good is their marginal benefit for that unit. That is how much they would have paid for that unit. As a result the total value to the consumer is simply the sum of those marginal benefits for each unit and is the area under the demand curve from O to Q^*. It looks like  and is

FIGURE 3.12 Consumer surplus.

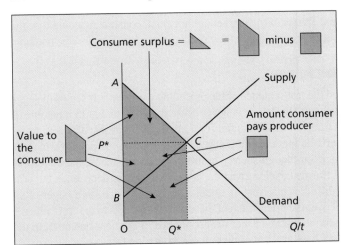

FIGURE 3.13 Producer surplus.

FIGURE 3.14 Net benefit to society.

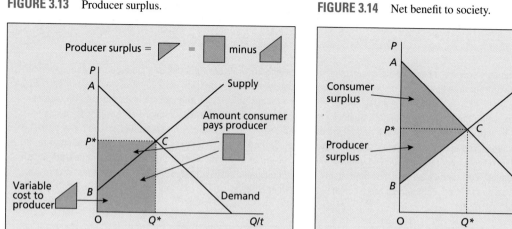

consumer surplus
The value you get that is in excess of what you pay to get it.

bounded by the letters $OACQ^*$. The total amount of money they pay for these goods is the price, P^*, times the amount they buy, Q^*, so it looks like ■ and is bounded by the letters OP^*CQ^*. The difference between the areas is the triangle that represents the value to the consumers minus the amount they pay the producer. Economists call that **consumer surplus**; it looks like ◣ and is bounded by the letters P^*AC.

Producer Surplus

Firms also benefit from exchange. In the Chapter 2 section "All about Supply" the supply curve is upward sloping because it is the marginal cost curve and marginal cost is increasing. Just as we added together marginal benefits to get the value to the consumers in Figure 3.12, we now add together marginal costs for each unit in Figure 3.13 to get the total variable cost to the producer (which is the difference between all its costs and those it needs to start up its business). As a result we can measure the total variable cost as the area under the supply curve from O to Q^*, which looks like ◢ and is bounded by the letters $OBCQ^*$. The amount consumers pay producers is the same OP^*CQ^* rectangle it was in Figure 3.12, ■. The difference is

producer surplus
The money the firm gets that is in excess of its marginal costs.

what economists call **producer surplus**; it looks like ◺ and is bounded by the letters BP^*C.

The net benefit to society, shown in Figure 3.14, is the consumer surplus plus the producer surplus. That is, if the market did not exist, consumers would lose their consumer surplus and the producers would lose their producer surplus. Because the market exists, both are better off.

Market Failure

Reread the last sentence of the preceding paragraph. It seems to suggest that the market works perfectly and that there is never cause for government to intervene. Intuitively you know that is not true. A market can fail for a number of reasons: The actions of a consumer or producer can harm an innocent third party, a good may not be one for which a company can profit from selling even though society profits from its existence, the buyer may not be able to make a well-informed choice given the complexity of the decision, a buyer or a seller may have radi-

market failure
The circumstance where the market outcome is not the economically efficient outcome.

cally different information about a good or service, or a buyer or seller may have too much power over the price. Each of these problems leads to **market failure**—the circumstance where the market outcome is not the economically efficient outcome. In the issue chapters to come, you will explore each of these types of market failures.

When market failure exists, economists use consumer and producer surplus to analyze the degree of the problem as well as to show how the problem can be solved through the proper application of taxes, regulations, or subsidies. Whether this is a tax discouraging the consumption or production of a good, a subsidy designed to encourage its production or consumption, or a regulation against monopoly pricing, economists are not always for or always against these mechanisms. Most economists favor policies that maximize the sum of producer and consumer surplus, however that occurs.

Categorizing Goods

Broadly speaking, goods can be classified into four categories on the basis of the degree to which the consumption of the good can be restricted by a seller to only those who pay for it—called **exclusivity,** and the degree to which one person's consumption reduces the value of the good for the next consumer—called **rivalry.** A slice of pizza has a high degree of both qualities; the pizza joint can easily prevent you from consuming their pizza if you do not pay for it, and once you have eaten a pizza, that particular pizza is not available to others. As a result, economists would label pizza as a **purely private good.** On the other hand, the army protects all citizens from foreign invasion regardless of how much they pay in taxes and their success at doing so is not diminished at all by how many people they have to defend. Economists label national defense as a **purely public good** because it is one for which there is neither rivalry nor exclusivity.

In addition to those extremes, there are goods that have a high degree of one characteristic and a low degree of the other. Cable companies can easily exclude their consumers from getting HBO, but one consumer's viewing of HBO does not affect another's viewing. HBO is excludable, but there is no rivalry. Economists call such goods **excludable public goods.** Similarly, a city street is an example of a good for which it would be nearly impossible to prevent usage by citizens and one for which rivalry is common (think traffic jams).[2] Such goods are what economists call **congestible public goods.**

[2]While you may think license plates allow for exclusivity, they do not serve the entire function in that once you have a licensed car it is very difficult to charge you based on usage. As technology increases, GPS receivers and transmitters may make it possible to charge drivers based on where and when they drive.

exclusivity
The degree to which the consumption of the good can be restricted by a seller to only those who pay for it.

rivalry
The degree to which one person's consumption reduces the value of the good for the next consumer.

purely private good
A good with the characteristics of both exclusivity and rivalry.

purely public good
A good with neither of the characteristics of exclusivity or rivalry.

excludable public good
A good with the characteristic of exclusivity but not of rivalry.

congestible public good
A good with the characteristic of rivalry but not of exclusivity.

Kick It Up a Notch — DEADWEIGHT LOSS

When the market is not at equilibrium, the consumer surplus plus the producer surplus will not be as large. This triangle, *ABC,* is as big as it can be. If consumption is more than Q^*, then consumers are paying more than they think a product is worth, or producers are not meeting their marginal costs, or both. If consumption is less than Q^*, the consumers wish they could buy more (and they would get more consumer surplus), or firms wish they could sell more (and they would get more producer surplus), or both. If the triangle is smaller than *ABC,* then there is **deadweight loss.** This deadweight loss is the measure economists use to discuss the inefficiency of markets when a problem like air pollution exists or when government establishes an impediment to a free floating price, such as the minimum wage.

To see how deadweight loss fits our supply and demand diagram, suppose that for some reason the price cannot be at P^* but is instead at P' (pronounced "P prime"). Figure 3.15 shows the impact of this when P' is greater than P^*, and Figure 3.16 shows the impact when

deadweight loss
The loss in societal welfare associated with production being too little or too great.

FIGURE 3.15 Deadweight loss with a price higher than P^*.

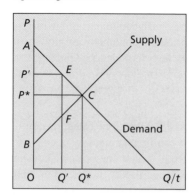

FIGURE 3.16 Deadweight loss with a price lower than P^*.

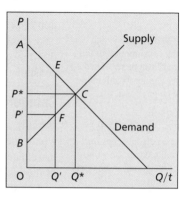

P' is less than P^*. In either circumstance, the new quantity will be less than equilibrium because consumers will not be willing to buy more than Q' (pronounced "Q prime") at the higher P' in Figure 3.15 and producers will not be willing to sell more than Q' in Figure 3.16 at the lower P'.

In Figure 3.15 the price is higher than P^*. At that higher price, though producers will want to sell many more than the previous equilibrium quantity, consumers will want to buy fewer. Unless the consumers are compelled to buy things they do not want, they will buy only Q'.

Given that, we can find the consumer and producer surplus in this market and compare it to what it was in Figure 3.14. The area under the demand curve represents the value to the consumer of Q' goods and this is $OAEQ'$. The price P' times the quantity Q' is the amount of money consumers will pay to get Q', and this is represented by the area $OP'EQ'$. The difference between these, $P'AE$, is the consumer surplus. It costs the producer $OBFQ'$ in terms of variable costs to make these goods. The difference between the money consumers pay them and their costs, $BP'EF$, is the producer surplus. The sum of consumer and producer surplus in this case is $BAEF$, but this is less than ABC, which is what this sum was in Figure 3.14. This means that the area FEC is lost as a result of being at P' instead of P^*, and this is what economists call the deadweight loss of being at P' instead of P^*.

In Figure 3.16 the price is lower than P^*. At that lower price, though, producers will not want to sell as much as they did at the previous equilibrium and consumers will want to buy more. Unless producers are compelled to sell things they do not want to sell, they will produce only Q'. Again we can find the consumer and producer surplus in this market and compare it to what it was in Figure 3.14. The area under the demand curve still represents the value to the consumer of Q' goods and is still $OAEQ'$. The price P' times the quantity Q' is still the amount of money consumers will pay to get Q', but this is now represented by the area $OP'FQ'$. The difference between these, the consumer surplus, is now $P'AEF$. Whereas the costs of the producer, $OBFQ'$, remain the same, the revenue has fallen so the producer surplus falls to $BP'F$. The sum of consumer and producer surplus in this case is also $BAEF$, and this is still less than it was in Figure 3.14. The deadweight loss is again represented by the area FEC.

Summary

This chapter expanded on the supply and demand model by showing the importance of the responsiveness of quantity to changes in price and how the model can be used to show that market exchange results in mutually beneficial results for consumers and producers.

In discussing elasticity we began by introducing the formula, defining the terms *elastic* and *inelastic,* and exploring why demand for some goods may be elastic while others may be inelastic. We then considered how elasticity of demand is determined by the number of close substitutes and the time available to generate them.

To conclude the chapter, we discussed how we could use the supply and demand model to show that consumers and producers each benefit from a market transaction, and we showed how to measure the benefit each gets by defining consumer and producer surplus. Finally, we showed how we measure the inefficiency of being away from equilibrium by defining and illustrating the concept of deadweight loss.

Key Terms

congestible public good, 49
consumer surplus, 48
cross-price elasticity of
  demand, 40
deadweight loss, 49
elastic, 41
elasticity, 40
excludable public good, 49
exclusivity, 49

income elasticity of demand,
  40
inelastic, 41
market failure, 48
perfectly elastic, 44
perfectly inelastic, 44
price elasticity of
  demand, 40

price elasticity of
  supply, 40
producer surplus, 48
purely private good, 49
purely public good, 49
rivalry, 49
total expenditure rule, 43
unitary elastic, 41

Issues Chapters You Are Ready for Now

International Trade: Does
  It Jeopardize American
  Jobs? 197
The Line between Legal and
  Illegal Goods, 234

Health Care, 257
Government-Provided
  Health Insurance, 269
Farm Policy, 326

Minimum Wage, 335

Quiz Yourself

1. The elasticity of demand is related to the slope of the demand curve
   a. and only the slope of the demand curve.
   b. but also the (price, quantity) position on the demand curve.
   c. but also the slope of the supply curve.
   d. and whether the good is normal or inferior.

2. Suppose a firm cannot figure out whether the demand for the good it sells is elastic or inelastic but discovers that every time it raises its price, its total revenue declines. Their
   a. demand is unit elastic.
   b. demand is elastic.
   c. demand is inelastic.
   d. demand is perfectly inelastic.

3. Suppose you observe that minor changes in supply seem to cause dramatic changes in price. You would conclude that
   a. demand is unit elastic.
   b. demand is elastic.
   c. demand is inelastic.
   d. demand is perfectly inelastic.

4. The fact that the demand for eggs is inelastic should not surprise you because
   a. they are a very cheap food.
   b. the demand for nearly all food products is inelastic.

    c. the supply of eggs is inelastic.

    d. they are so expensive.

5. Combined, the consumer surplus and producer surplus at equilibrium is

    a. lower than it would be at prices below equilibrium.

    b. lower than it would be at prices above equilibrium.

    c. typically negative.

    d. as big as it can get.

6. If supply and demand are lines, then at equilibrium both consumer and producer surplus are

    a. equal.

    b. shown as squares.

    c. shown as trapezoids.

    d. shown as triangles.

7. When looking at the impact of a change in trade policy, economists use consumer and producer surplus to look at the winners and losers. Free-trade economists insist that

    a. no one loses.

    b. everyone loses.

    c. there are winners and losers but that the gain to the winners is greater than the loss to the losers.

    d. there are winners and losers but that the loss to the losers is greater than the gain to the winners.

8. When a satellite television company gains a subscriber, there is no impact on existing subscribers. That is, there is no rivalry in the consumption for their service. This is an example of a

    a. purely private good.

    b. purely public good.

    c. congestible public good.

    d. excludable public good.

9. Policy makers have considered putting computer chips in cars that would allow tax collectors to charge people on the basis of how often they drive during rush hours. These policy makers are dealing with the fact that public roads are

    a. purely private goods.

    b. purely public goods.

    c. congestible public goods.

    d. excludable public goods.

Short Answer Questions

1. Give an example of a good that you believe has perfectly inelastic demand for most people. Then explain why you believe that is the case.

2. Give an example of a good that you believe has inelastic demand (not perfectly inelastic) for most people. Then explain why you believe that is the case.

3. Give an example of something you hate to do, and imagine that you could pay someone else to do that thing for you. Explain why both you and the person you pay could end up better off.

4. Give an example of a situation where the government compels you to do something you do not want to do. Why might that be a reasonable requirement? When might it be unreasonable?

5. Suppose you hear the following: "They just increased taxes on cigarettes and on high-priced cigars." Use the concept of elasticity to describe who will be hurt by those taxes. Is a change in the price of the good itself a change in the quantity supplied?

Think about This

Suppose both gasoline supply and demand are highly inelastic. Knowing that a change in the expected price of gasoline will shift both supply and demand, explain how these combined facts can lead you to an understanding of wildly changing gasoline prices.

Talk about This

Talk about your alternative choices for colleges. What schools did you consider? Was tuition a consideration? Does your college's proximity to other schools imply anything about your school's ability to raise revenue by raising tuition?

Behind the Numbers

Hirschman, Ira, Claire McKnight, and John Pucher, "Highway and Bridge Toll Elasticities," *Transportation* 22 (May 1995).

Food Demand and Nutrient Elasticities, www.ers.usda.gov/publications/tb1887/tb1887.pdf

Schaller, Bruce, "Transportation Elasticities," *Transportation* 26 (1999), pp. 283–297.

Gasoline Elasticities: Hughes, Jonathan E., Christopher R. Knittel, and Daniel Sperling. Evidence of a Shift in the Short-Run Price Elasticity of Gasoline Demand (September 5, 2006). Available at SSRN: http://papers.ssrn.com/sol3/papers.cfm?abstract_id=930730

CHAPTER FOUR

Firm Production, Cost, and Revenue

Learning Objectives

After reading this chapter you should be able to:

LO1   Demonstrate the relationship between production and costs and the relationship between sales and revenues.

LO2   Explain that models of production are based on the assumption that firms seek to maximize profit.

LO3   Demonstrate how profit maximization dictates that firms set production so that marginal cost equals marginal revenue.

Chapter Outline

Production

Costs

Revenue

Maximizing Profit

Summary

---

profit
The money that a firm makes: revenue – cost.

cost
The expense that must be incurred to produce goods and services for sale.

revenue
The money that comes into the firm from the sale of goods and services.

economic cost
All costs of a business: those that must be paid as well as those incurred in the form of forgone opportunities.

accounting cost
Only those costs that must be explicitly paid by the owner of a business.

The business of business is making money, and the money business makes is called **profit**. How it makes that profit is by selling its goods for more than it costs to make them. For this chapter (and for most of this book) we make the simplifying assumption that nothing influences business other than maximizing profit. Although this is an exaggeration, it is reasonably close to the truth, and accepting it as the truth simplifies our task considerably. Nothing about this chapter is simple, but you may be comforted by the knowledge that it could be more complicated (of course you may not be).

With the simplifying assumption of myopic profit maximization in place, we can break things down into the cost side and the revenue side. **Cost** is the expense that businesses must incur to produce goods for sale. **Revenue** is the money that comes into the firm from the sale of the goods.

It is important to understand why economists focus on costs that are incurred rather than simply those costs that must be paid. Accountants focus only on expenses that must be paid for a business to produce, but economists also consider the *opportunity cost* of choices. To fully understand the concepts of **economic cost** and **accounting cost**, consider an upstart business whose owner quits a $50,000 a year job and cashes in a $100,000 CD (earning 6 percent) to get it off the ground. An accountant would not consider the $50,000 of forgone job-related income or the $6,000 per year in forgone interest as costs of the business. An economist would. For the remainder of this chapter and all of the next, all costs refer to economic costs.

With that said, since profit is the difference between revenues and costs, we will be able to use what we have developed in these areas to find how much production our profit-maximizing firm will choose. We then explore the production process and the costs that it generates, move on to discuss the revenue side, and then put the two together to show how, under different circumstances, firms choose their production levels. To pull all that off, we carry one example from the beginning of this explication to the end. Let's assume that the industry we are talking about is the computer memory industry, the industry that makes the chips that enable computers to use and quickly access information. Let's suppose that the production of computer memory requires three things: expensive machines, highly trained people, and very inexpensive plastic and metal from which the chips are made. To make things even easier, let's assume that the plastic and metal used to make the chips are free.

So far we have had a section entitled "Kick It Up a Notch" in every chapter. The problem with this chapter is that material presented is already "kicked up" plenty. Complicating matters further, some students need a verbal explanation, some need to "see" it in the form of a graph, while still others can only get their arms around a concrete numerical example. To deal with that, we go through each of them once using just words, once using graphical explanation, and then again with a numerical example.

Production

Just Words

production function
A graph that shows how many resources are needed to produce various amounts of output.

cost function
A graph that shows how much various amounts of production cost.

To get a handle on costs we need to know how much money it takes to produce goods. First we need to know what resources are necessary for production. Then we can construct an input–output relationship called a **production function,** and we will do this in the form of a graph. Our graph will show how many resources we need to produce various amounts of output. From that production function we can find out how much various amounts of production cost. From this resulting **cost function** we will be able to figure out how much each one costs on average and how much each additional one costs.

Of course, this is putting the cart before the horse. Before the firm decides how many to produce, it has to decide what to produce. In our example, the memory chip firm did not decide to make chips for the fun of it. Early computer designers decided that their computers would work better if they had a short-term place to store and quickly retrieve information. Chip-making companies came into existence to provide the computer industry with the parts to make short-term storage of data possible. For the remainder of this section and this chapter we assume that the firm is up and running and is simply trying to figure out how many chips to make at any given time.

fixed inputs
Resources that do not change.

variable inputs
Resources that can be easily changed.

To make any product, you typically have **fixed** and **variable inputs.** That is, you have resources that you cannot change and resources that you can. In our example, the plant and the equipment in the plant are called fixed inputs because they are not easily changed, added to, or subtracted from. On the other hand, the person power to operate those machines is easily changed. You can hire and fire more easily and quickly than you can replace a machine. People and other resources that can be easily changed are called variable inputs.

The first step in our process of figuring out how many memory chips to make is to map out how many resources are needed to produce various numbers of these chips. Of course, without any personnel there is no production. If there are only a few workers, as at point *B* in Figure 4.1, production is not very great because workers are not able to specialize in particular parts of the production process. They waste time moving from one part of the process to another, and they take time to build momentum, working at each stage of production only to find that when they get good at it, it is time to move on to another stage.

division of labor
Workers divide the tasks in such a way that each can build momentum and not have to switch jobs.

The addition of a few more workers solves that problem and production levels increase greatly. Workers divide the tasks in such a way that each can build momentum and does not have to switch jobs. This specialization is called the **division of labor,** and its impact is such that for a small increase in labor we can get a dramatic increase in output.

At some point, though, there are enough workers to get the job done, as at point *D*, and more workers do not add much to production. Some jobs, too, just cannot be easily divided. Although it is usually the case that having more workers increases output, workers find that the existing plant and equipment are too limiting for them to get the most out of new employees. As a result, output increases but not as fast as it had before. This phenomenon, referred to by economists as **diminishing returns,** is a central assumption of this chapter as well as the next.

diminishing returns
The notion that there exists a point where, because there are some fixed inputs like plant and equipment, the addition of resources increases production, but does so at a decreasing rate.

Graphical Explanation

Using the same ideas just presented, let's walk through Figure 4.1. Point *A* begins at the origin because, as was pointed out in the preceding section, if you have no workers you have no output. Where there are too few workers to staff the plant, they have to waste time moving from one stage of production to the next, so the increase in production associated with the first group of workers is relatively low. That gives us point *B*. The curve is bowed to the right between points *A* and *C* because of the division of labor. That is, as you add the same number of workers, you get the benefits from those workers specializing and production increases at an increasing rate. Once you get to point *C*, though, there is not enough plant and equipment to accommodate more workers efficiently. The curve is then bowed to the left because of diminishing returns to the existing plant and equipment.

Numerical Example

Now, let's consider the same concept using the numbers that comprise Table 4.1. Continuing with the memory chips example, suppose the first column represents the groups of workers, the second column represents the total output produced, and the third column represents the extra output added with the inclusion of the group. Because memory chips cannot make themselves, zero labor corresponds to zero output. Suppose that the first group of workers hired initially produces 100 units, but when a second group is added a total of 317 units is produced. That is, the second group adds 217 units to production. Suppose the third group adds somewhat less, 183 units, so that the total becomes 500. If it takes 5 groups of workers to produce

FIGURE 4.1   A production function.

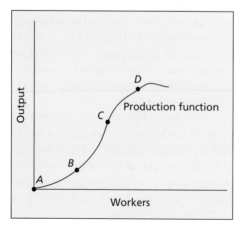

TABLE 4.1   Numerical example: production function.

Labor	Total Output	Extra Output of the Group
0	0	
1	100	100
2	317	217
3	500	183
4	610	110
5	700	90
6	770	70
7	830	60
8	870	40
9	900	30
13	1,000	

700, 9 to produce 900, and 13 to produce 1,000, then we have a story similar to what we saw in the graphical explanation. That is, as we added workers we got more production. The first group of workers was not very efficient because they could not specialize, whereas the second group was efficient because they could. In each case as more groups were added, efficiency waned because the workers were limited by the existing plant and equipment.

We have now explained production in terms of how a varying number of workers can be combined with a fixed amount of plant and equipment to make computer memory chips. We work next on how much it costs to hire those workers and pay for that machinery.

Costs

fixed costs
Costs of production that cannot be changed.

variable costs
Costs of production that can be changed.

marginal cost (MC)
The addition to cost associated with one additional unit of output.

average total cost (ATC)
Total cost divided by output, the cost per unit of production.

average variable cost (AVC)
Total variable cost divided by output, the average variable cost per unit of production.

average fixed cost (AFC)
Total fixed cost divided by output, the average fixed cost per unit of production.

Just Words

Once we know how many workers it takes to produce our memory chips, we can find out how much it costs to make those chips. The first thing to consider is that there are costs of production that we cannot change. In our example these **fixed costs** are the costs of the plant and equipment that we own. Costs that we can change, like the number of workers we hire for our plant, are called **variable costs**. The task now is to compare the number of memory chips we make against the costs of making those chips.

To accomplish this we need four cost concepts: marginal cost, average total cost, average variable cost, and average fixed cost.

Marginal cost (MC) is the increase in cost associated with a one-unit increase in production. Because total cost always rises, marginal cost is always positive. Because total cost rises quickly at low levels of output, marginal cost is high at low levels of output; however, total cost rises much more slowly at moderate levels of output, so marginal cost is much lower there. Last, because a rapid rise in total cost resumes at high levels of output, marginal cost is high in this range. Thus marginal cost starts high, decreases for a while, and then increases again.

Average total cost (ATC) is the per unit cost of production. Because this includes fixed cost, which can be very high, average total cost will be high at low levels of production. It will shrink as production gets more efficient and the fixed costs become spread over greater levels of output. As production rises to higher levels where marginal costs are increasing, these two effects will begin to counteract each other and the drop in average total costs will slow. Eventually the increases in marginal cost will overwhelm the effect of spreading fixed costs over higher levels of output and average total cost will rise again.

The **average variable cost (AVC)** is dictated by the same changes in efficiency that gave us the marginal cost curve. Because it is an average, however, the movements are dampened; the highs are not as high and the lows are not as low.

Average fixed cost (AFC) falls continuously because the fixed costs of production are being spread over greater and greater levels of production. In addition, graphically, average fixed cost is the vertical distance between average total cost and average variable cost.

These cost concepts serve as the basis for much of what follows in this chapter, the next one, and our subsequent study of issues.

Looking back at Figure 4.1, you can see that at point *A* we will not have to pay anything to our workers (because we have no workers to pay), but we still have to pay fixed costs. As a result, point *A* in Figure 4.1 corresponds to point *A* in Figure 4.2. We have workers at point *B* whom we have to pay, and they are not all that productive. Remember that this is not their fault, because there are too few of them to allow specialization. Point *B* in Figure 4.2 is therefore higher than point *A* (because we have to pay them) but not much further to the right (because they are not making that many chips).

FIGURE 4.2 Total cost function.

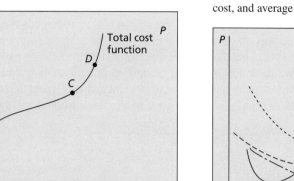

FIGURE 4.3 Marginal cost, average total cost, and average variable cost.

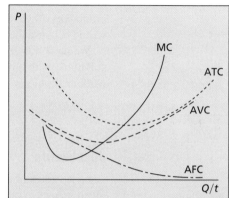

Point *C* in Figure 4.1 indicates that the workers were quite productive; so for the same amount of an increase in our costs we see a significant increase in production. Thus, point *C* in Figure 4.2 is also higher than point *B* but is significantly further to the right. Point *D* in Figure 4.1 shows us where extra workers did not add much to production. Again they cost money, so point *D* in Figure 4.2 is higher than point *C*, but is not that much further to the right. Connecting these points, we have a total cost function. Our graph shows how the function helps us understand and make decisions about the cost of production and the amount produced.

Thus far we have focused on finding the total cost of producing various amounts of output. When we get total revenue, we will be able to find the profit. Before we go there, though, we are going to need four other cost functions: marginal cost, the average variable cost, the average fixed cost, and the average total cost. In higher-level economics courses, students are required to derive these other cost functions from the total cost function. When you derive one function from another, you graphically manipulate the parent function (in this case total cost) to draw its descendants (in this case marginal cost, average variable cost, and average total cost).

Numerical Example

Again we are dealing with concepts that may be easier to comprehend when there are numbers attached. Following the numerical example used in Table 4.1, consider Table 4.2 (on the next page). The first column represents output. The second, Total Variable Cost, is based on the $2,500 per unit of labor from Table 4.1 that is required to produce that output. The third, Total Fixed Cost, is the cost of plant and equipment and is unchanging. The fourth, Total Cost, is the sum of total variable cost and total fixed cost. The fifth, Marginal Cost, is the increase in total cost from each level of production. The sixth, Average Total Cost, is the per unit cost; the seventh, Average Variable Cost, is per unit variable cost; and the eighth, Average Fixed Cost, is per unit fixed cost.

These derivations take economics majors several class periods to understand. We'll skip that but outline why Figure 4.3 looks the way it does. Starting with the easiest one, average fixed cost, it is constantly decreasing because the same costs are being spread over more and more output. Marginal cost, average total cost, and average variable cost all start high, decrease, and then increase. The manner in which they do that, though, is somewhat complicated.

Marginal cost is the increase in costs associated with a one-unit increase in production. That means it is the "rise over the run" in the total cost curve, which means it is the slope of the total cost curve. You can see in Figure 4.2 that total cost rises rapidly at the beginning, flattens out, and then rises rapidly again.

TABLE 4.2   Numerical example: cost functions.

Output	Total Variable Cost	Total Fixed Cost	Total Cost	Marginal Cost*	Average Total Cost	Average Variable Cost	Average Fixed Cost
0	0	8,500	8,500				
100	2,500	8,500	11,000	25	110	25	85
200	3,800	8,500	12,300	13	62	19	43
300	4,800	8,500	13,300	10	44	16	28
400	6,000	8,500	14,500	12	36	15	21
500	7,500	8,500	16,000	15	32	15	17
600	9,500	8,500	18,000	20	30	16	14
700	12,500	8,500	21,000	30	30	18	12
800	17,000	8,500	25,500	45	32	21	10.6
900	22,500	8,500	31,000	55	34	25	9.4
1,000	32,500	8,500	41,000	100	41	32.5	8.5

*Change in total cost/change in output.

Average total cost and average variable cost are both U-shaped because they start high and decrease. The difference between the two curves is average fixed costs. Because average fixed cost diminishes as production increases, the gap between the two curves diminishes. They are both cut from below by the marginal cost curve at their respective minimums. This happens when, because of diminishing returns, marginal costs increase to the point where, first, average variable cost, then average total cost, starts to rise as well.

DRAWING THE ATC-AVC-MC DIAGRAM

If you are inclined to replicate Figure 4.3 yourself (or are required to in your course) try the following:

1. Draw a sweeping check-shaped MC curve.
2. Draw a symmetrical U-shaped AVC curve that bottoms out on MC.

3. Draw an asymmetrical U-shaped ATC curve that also bottoms out on MC (a bit higher than the AVC curve bottoms out) where the vertical distance between ATC and AVC is longer on the left than it is on the right side of the diagram. (For the mathematically inclined among you, this is what you get if you have a cubic total cost function.)

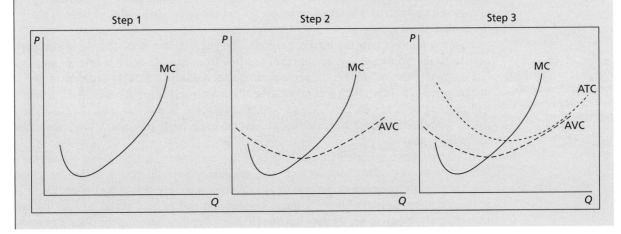

To see how each column in Table 4.2 is computed, let's look at a production increase from 400 to 500. The variable costs associated with producing 400 are $6,000. Variable costs rise to $7,500 when output rises to 500. Fixed costs are $8,500 in both cases. That means that total cost is $14,500 ($6,000 + $8,500) for 400 and rises to $16,000 ($7,500 + $8,500) for 500. The increased cost for the increase of 100 units is $1,500, so each one increased cost by $15, so marginal cost is $15. Average total cost for 400 units is $36 ($14,500/400) and $32 ($16,000/500) for 500 units. The average fixed cost is $21 ($8,500/400) for 400 units and $17 ($8,500/500) for 500 units.

If you plot the last four columns against output, you will see that the curve for marginal cost is indeed check-shaped, that those for average total cost and average variable cost are both U-shaped, and that average fixed cost decreases steadily. You can also see that at 300 units of output marginal cost is at its minimum. Further, you can see that the curve depicting marginal cost cuts average variable cost at its minimum (at 500 units of output) and that the marginal cost curve cuts the average total cost curve at its minimum (at 700 units of output).

Revenue

Just Words

The other side of any production decision is the amount of money that will come in from the sale of the goods. To get a handle on this revenue side we will need to know whether the business has competition and, if so, how much. For instance, if a business faces many other competitors that produce goods like the ones it produces, its behavior will be different from what it would be if it had the market to itself.

In some industries, like agriculture, the price that the firm receives remains unchanged regardless of how much it has to sell. In other industries, like those that supply electric power, the amount sold affects the price. To explore this difference let's first assume our memory chip maker is one of many chip makers. Then we will see what happens when we assume that it is the only one.

If our chip-making firm has many competitors, the price is set in a market that it cannot control. The supply of and the demand for chips determine how much the firm can charge for its chips. To see the futility of trying to set its own price, imagine that it tried to have a price higher than the market price. If it did, computer makers could and would buy all their chips from our firm's competitors. The firm could, of course, set a price lower than the market price. If it did, it would get to sell all it produced. On the other hand, it could do that at the market price. Because our firm wants to maximize profit and because it can always sell as much as it wants at or below the market price, it will always want to charge the market price.

Figure 4.4 shows how the market generates the price for the firm. This price also happens to be the additional revenue the firm receives from the sale of each unit. To see why this **marginal revenue (MR)** is the same as the price, consider a thought experiment. If the market price is 5, how much will revenue be if our firm sells one? Answer: 5. How much will revenue be if it sells two? Answer: 10. The increase in revenue associated with any sale is therefore 5. This is true whether you let the price be 5, 10, or 600; the price is the marginal revenue.

marginal revenue (MR)
Additional revenue the firm receives from the sale of each unit.

If, on the other hand, we are the only ones selling computer chips, computer makers have to buy their memory chips from our firm. This situation is quite different from the case where there were many competitors. Instead of just taking a price given to it by the market, it is setting the price. Instead of being a small, insignificant part of the market, it is the market. Unfortunately, to sell more, the firm has no recourse other than lowering the price it charges.

FIGURE 4.4 Setting the price when there are many competitors.

FIGURE 4.5 Marginal revenue when we have no competitors.

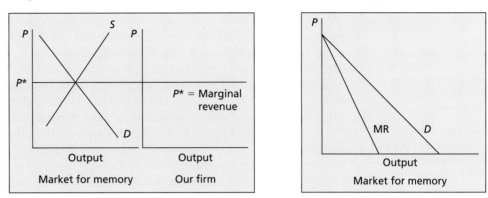

For instance, if it is currently selling 1 million chips a week and it wants to increase its sales to 2 million a week, it must lower the price to everyone, even those who would have bought 1 million at the higher price. This means that in Figure 4.5 the marginal revenue is not graphed with a flat line; it falls as we increase sales.

Numerical Example

Using the same numerical example that we have been using, suppose that our firm is one of many and has no control over price. Suppose further that the price in the market for memory is $45 per unit. This means that the total revenue (TR) increases by $45 for each unit sold and the marginal revenue is thus $45 for each unit sold. This is illustrated in Table 4.3.

If there are no competitors, then the market demand for memory is simply the demand for our firm's memory. This means that our firm must lower its price to induce consumers to buy more memory. Another way of looking at precisely the same thing is to notice that a firm without competition can force the price higher by restricting its output. As before, total revenue is price times quantity, but because price does not remain the same, the marginal revenue falls. This is illustrated in Table 4.4.

TABLE 4.3 Numerical example: revenue when there are many competitors.

Q	Price	TR	MR*
0	45	0	
100	45	4,500	45
200	45	9,000	45
300	45	13,500	45
400	45	18,000	45
500	45	22,500	45
600	45	27,000	45
700	45	31,500	45
800	45	36,000	45
900	45	40,500	45
1,000	45	45,000	45

*Change in total revenue/change in output.

TABLE 4.4 Numerical example: revenue when there are no competitors.

Q	Price	TR	MR*
0	75	0	
100	70	7,000	70
200	65	13,000	60
300	60	18,000	50
400	55	22,000	40
500	50	25,000	30
600	45	27,000	20
700	40	28,000	10
800	35	28,000	0
900	30	27,000	−10
1,000	25	25,000	−20

*Change in total revenue/change in output.

Maximizing Profit

Graphical Explanation

perfect competition
A situation in a market where there are many firms producing the same good.

monopoly
A situation in a market where there is only one firm producing the good.

As mentioned, the level of output for the business that will maximize profit very much depends on whether the business is in **perfect competition**—that is, one of many producing the same thing—or is a **monopoly**—that is, it has no competitors. Regardless of whether it has many competitors or it has the market to itself, we assume firms produce and sell the amount that will make them the most money possible. In economic terms this ends up meaning that every firm should produce an amount such that marginal revenue equals marginal cost (MR = MC). Recall the Chapter 1 concept of marginal analysis; this is our first opportunity to see it at work.

This is not as difficult as it seems. Remember that marginal revenue is the amount the firm brings in from selling one more, and the marginal cost is the amount of money that it costs to produce one more. To illustrate, suppose you start by selling a fixed number, say, 10. If you sell an eleventh and you make money on that sale (MR > MC), you should do it again and sell at least one more. If you sell an eleventh and you lose money on that sale (MR < MC), you should reduce sales by at least one. Since marginal revenue is less than marginal cost for the eleventh chip, you should not have produced it. To maximize profit you could repeat this one-by-one process until you have found the production that makes the most money. On the other hand, you now know that it is only when marginal cost equals marginal revenue that you have exhausted the profit potential on the good you are trying to sell.

Of course it is possible that our entire business is a loser. In the age of word processors and cheap personal computers, the manual typewriter business would be a loser even if ours were the only firm in this industry. The exception to the rule that a firm should produce where marginal cost equals marginal revenue occurs when the best alternative is to do nothing; that is, sometimes the best decision is to shut down the business. This occurs when the amount that you sell a good for is not enough to cover the variable costs that went into the production of the good. The firm should shut down if the price is less than the average variable cost (P < AVC).

Numerical Example

To illustrate profit maximization when there are many competitors, we need to combine the information in Tables 4.1 and 4.3; when there are no competitors, we need to combine the information in Tables 4.3 and 4.4. In either case we need to pick a quantity to maximize profit. This is done where marginal cost equals marginal revenue. Table 4.5 illustrates this for the case where there are many competitors, and Table 4.6 does it for the case where there are no competitors.

THE RULES OF PRODUCTION

- A firm should produce an amount such that marginal revenue equals marginal cost (MR = MC).

- A firm should shut down if the price is less than the average variable cost (P < AVC) at the quantity where marginal revenue equals marginal cost.

TABLE 4.5
Numerical example: profit maximization when there are many competitors.

Q	Price	TR	TC	MR	MC	Profit
0	45	0	8,500	0	0	−8,500
100	45	4,500	11,000	45	25	−6,500
200	45	9,000	12,300	45	13	−3,300
300	45	13,500	13,300	45	10	200
400	45	18,000	14,500	45	12	3,500
500	45	22,500	16,000	45	15	6,500
600	45	27,000	18,000	45	20	9,000
700	45	31,500	21,000	45	30	10,500
800	45	36,000	25,500	45	45	10,500
900	45	40,500	31,000	45	55	9,500
1,000	45	45,000	41,000	45	100	4,000

TABLE 4.6
Numerical example: profit maximization when there are no competitors.

Q	Price	TR	TC	MR	MC	Profit
0	75	0	8,500	0	0	−8,500
100	70	7,000	11,000	70	25	−4,000
200	65	13,000	12,300	60	13	700
300	60	18,000	13,300	50	10	4,700
400	55	22,000	14,500	40	12	7,500
500	50	25,000	16,000	30	15	9,000
600	45	27,000	18,000	20	20	9,000
700	40	28,000	21,000	10	30	7,000
800	35	28,000	25,500	0	45	2,500
900	30	27,000	31,000	−10	55	−4,000
1,000	25	25,000	41,000	−20	100	−16,000

In Table 4.5 we see that the firm that has many competitors has its profit maximized at $10,500, and this happens when the firm produces 800.[1] In Table 4.6 we see that the firm that has no competitors has its profit maximized at $9,000, and this happens when it produces 600.

[1] In the next chapter we will see that firms with many competitors see their profits disappear because new firms enter, thereby increasing market supply and lowering the price.

Summary

This chapter has illustrated production, costs, revenues, and profit maximization. For each concept and relationship, we considered both graphical explanations and numerical examples. We assumed that businesses choose production to maximize profit and that, as a result, they set it where marginal cost equals marginal revenue.

Key Terms

accounting cost, 54
average fixed cost (AFC), 57
average total cost (ATC), 57
average variable cost (AVC), 57
cost, 54
cost function, 55

diminishing returns, 56
division of labor, 56
economic cost, 54
fixed costs, 57
fixed inputs, 55
marginal cost (MC), 57
marginal revenue (MR), 60

monopoly, 62
perfect competition, 62
production function, 55
profit, 54
revenue, 54
variable costs, 57
variable inputs, 55

Quiz Yourself

1. When firms add workers and get more efficient, they are benefiting from
   a. the division of labor.
   b. diminishing returns.
   c. the law of large numbers.
   d. diminishing marginal utility.

2. When firms add workers and find that the additional workers add less to output than their predecessors did, they are experiencing
   a. the division of labor.
   b. diminishing returns.
   c. the law of large numbers.
   d. diminishing marginal utility.

3. Suppose a firm has $1,000,000 in fixed costs and variable costs equal to $100; for every unit they produce,
   a. their marginal costs are decreasing.
   b. their fixed costs are decreasing.
   c. their average costs are decreasing.
   d. the marginal costs are increasing.

4. The average total cost curve will be cut by the marginal cost curve from below as long as
   a. fixed costs are rising.
   b. average costs are decreasing.
   c. marginal costs eventually increase.
   d. marginal costs continually decrease.

5. Whether marginal revenue is constant or decreasing depends on
   a. whether the firm is benefiting from the division of labor.
   b. whether the firm is dealing with diminishing returns.
   c. how much the firm sells.
   d. whether the firm faces competition.

6. When a firm chooses to shut down, it is
   a. making a poor decision because it should always produce where marginal cost equals marginal revenue.
   b. making a poor decision because it should always produce where average costs exceed average revenue.
   c. making a good decision as long as the price it is getting is less than its average costs.
   d. making a good decision as long as the price it is getting is less than its average variable costs.

7. The result that a firm should produce where MC = MR except when the shutdown condition is met is based on the assumption that it is attempting to
   a. maximize profit.
   b. maximize market share.
   c. minimize marginal costs.
   d. minimize average costs.

Short Answer Questions

1. What key assumption for perfect competition would lead you to believe that fast food is not a perfectly competitive industry? Explain why.

2. Suppose your favorite sports team is losing by an insurmountable score. What does the shutdown condition suggest the team should do? Explain why.

3. Does raising the price always increase revenue for the firm raising the price?

4. If your college leadership sought your advice on setting tuition, why would it matter if your college was the only college for miles?

Think about This

Why is it that when a firm has no competition it typically must lower the price to all consumers in order to sell more? What would have to happen for it to be able to lower the price only to new consumers?

Talk about This

We assume that the price to all consumers is the same. List the cases where the price to one person is different from the price to another. Why might a firm do this?

CHAPTER FIVE

Perfect Competition, Monopoly, and Economic versus Normal Profit

Learning Objectives

After reading this chapter you should be able to:

LO1 Distinguish between perfect competition and monopoly and between normal and economic profit.

LO2 Demonstrate and explain why economic profit disappears under perfect competition but not under monopoly.

LO3 Illustrate why, under perfect competition, the supply curve from Chapter 2 is marginal cost.

Chapter Outline

From Perfect Competition to Monopoly

Supply under Perfect Competition

Summary

This chapter builds on Chapter 4 to describe firms in different competitive situations; it shows why, when there are many firms competing against one another, substantial profits are unsustainable; and it concludes by demonstrating why the supply curve from Chapter 2 was upward sloping.

Some firms, such as family farms, are among millions of firms in an industry, whereas other firms completely dominate their industry. In the middle of this continuum are numerous firms with definable sets of competitors. Some industries lend themselves to many competitors while others lend themselves to only a few; we explore examples along this continuum.

In Chapter 4 we operated under the assumption that firms were out to maximize profits. What we want to do now is to determine how well various-sized firms will manage. For instance, we may want to know why it is that family farmers cannot seem to make consistently high profits, whereas Microsoft can. We approach this by separating profit into two categories: the profit that is necessary for firms to stay in business and the profit that is above that level.

Last, we see that the supply curve laid out in Chapter 2 was indeed upward sloping for a reason. We will show that under perfect competition, an upward-sloping supply curve stems from the check-shaped marginal cost curve from Chapter 4.

From Perfect Competition to Monopoly

As we discussed in Chapter 4, the shape of the marginal revenue curve depends on whether there are many competitors or no competitors. Figure 5.1 lays out these extreme cases. On the left, the cost curves from Figure 4.3 are applied to the marginal revenue curve from the case where there are many competitors. On the right, we see the same for the case where there are no competitors. The amount they pick in each case is labeled Q^*. The price they charge is labeled P^*.

Perfect Competition

The key difference between the cases just outlined is the number of competitors. When the number of competitors is large, the firm (e.g., a dairy farm) simply has to take the market price as given but can sell as many goods as it wants at that price. When there are no competitors, the firm (e.g., Microsoft) can set any price it wants but can sell only the number that consumers want to buy at that price. Of course, not every firm is faced with the stark either–or difference. Some firms (e.g., Exxon) have only a few competitors in markets of similar or identical products, and other firms (e.g., McDonald's) have many competitors in markets where each has its own signature brand.

When a firm faces a large number of competitors, such that no one firm can influence the price, when the good a firm sells is indistinguishable from those its competitor sells, when firms have good sales and cost forecasts, and when there is no legal or economic barrier to its entry into or exit from the market, then we have what economists call *perfect competition.* This may seem like an odd name given that the best examples of it are of sellers that do not really "compete" in the way noneconomists normally think of "competition." Whether it is midwestern grain farmers; western ranchers; Florida or California vegetable growers; Wisconsin, New York, or California dairy operations; or Georgia peach growers, the common conception of competition does not seem to apply. As individuals, they do not advertise. A conversation with any of these farmers would reveal that their best friends are their neighbor farmers. When one farm's equipment breaks down or a farmer has a significant health crisis at a critical planting or harvesting time, the neighborhood farmers come to help. That sounds more like cooperation than competition. So why do economists call this "perfect competition" when there does not seem to be any true competition? The reason this is "perfect" goes back to the first characteristic of perfect competition: No one firm has any control over price. No farmers, or any farm product, have any control over the price of their produce when they sell it on the wholesale market.[1]

FIGURE 5.1
Picking the quantity to maximize profit.

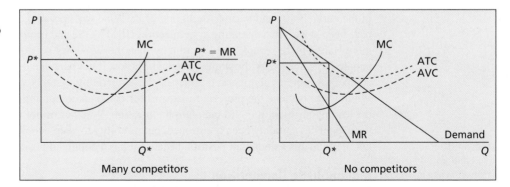

[1] Though they may be able to charge any price they want at a local farmers' market, they are not perfect competitors there. In that setting they are one of a few farmers selling that particular produce.

CHARACTERISTICS OF PERFECT COMPETITION

- A large number of competitors, so that no one firm can influence the price.
- The good a firm sells is indistinguishable from those its competitor sells.

- Firms have good sales and cost forecasts.
- There is no legal or economic barrier to entry into or exit from the market.

Monopoly

Monopolies exist at the other end of the spectrum, when we have markets in which there is only one firm. The important thing to know about the concept of monopoly is that the existence of many firms does not necessarily mean the firms are in competition. For instance, Consolidated Edison was the exclusive provider of residential electrical power to New York City, and Commonwealth Edison still is the exclusive provider of residential electrical power to Chicago. There are hundreds of power companies in the United States but very few of them compete with one another. They are not competitors because they cannot sell in another's area. Another way of looking at this is to say that while there are many power companies, they are not competing in the same market. The reason is that it costs the companies too much to get the electricity to the consumer in the distant market. Just as a cement contractor in Little Rock, Arkansas, is not competing with a cement contractor in Miami for roadwork in south Florida because of transportation costs, electric companies do not compete with one another because they cannot access the same buyers. For monopoly, all that is necessary is that one firm and only one firm sells to the customers in a given market.

Some firms get their monopoly power because the law prevents others from entering the market. An example of a legal barrier to entry is a patent. For example, the manufacturer of Clarinex is the only firm that can produce and sell this drug. On the other hand, some firms get their monopoly power by attaining such a huge size that competing against them is impossible. The frustration that consumers have with monopolies is the lack of choice that results from there being only one seller. While many may understand and accept the lack of choice when the good being sold is a utility with very high fixed costs, and others may understand and accept the need for patents and copyrights to motivate innovation, monopolies where the barriers to entry are simply associated with the size of the one monopolizing company often create anger and frustration. Consider the PC operating system business. Microsoft developed DOS in the early 1980s and various iterations of its Windows operating system after that. There have been at least two operating system genres (IBM's OS2 and Linux) that were considerably more stable, more secure, and less glitchy than the Windows version against which they attempted to compete. Without question, had Microsoft not been the dominant firm when these competitors entered the market, either of these operating systems would have easily beaten Windows to become the preferred platform for personal computing. Because Microsoft had the leading position, it could maintain the position. Whether or not all of Microsoft's tactics were legal has certainly been questioned, but its ability to keep people buying its products has not. It maintains a dominant position because it has a dominant position.

monopolistic competition
A situation in a market where there are many firms producing similar but not identical goods.

Monopolistic Competition

One of the areas of middle ground is **monopolistic competition,** in which many firms sell slightly different products. In the fast-food market there are quite a few firms (McDonald's,

Wendy's, Burger King, etc., in burgers; KFC, Taco Bell, etc., in various niches), but they do not sell exactly the same good. McDonald's has a monopoly on the Big Mac and Happy Meal, but its competitors offer many close substitutes. This means that each firm has a monopoly on its particular menu, but the demand curve for the product is quite elastic. (Remember from Chapter 3 that the number of close substitutes determines elasticity.)

Oligopoly

oligopolistic market
A situation in a market where there are very few discernible competitors.

Another area of middle ground between perfect competition and monopoly is **oligopolistic markets,** in which there are very few discernible competitors. In the cellular telephone business, for example, there are major companies like Cingular/AT&T, Sprint/Nextel, and Verizon Wireless. In the soft drink business there are Coke and Pepsi. In some markets firms sell exactly the same thing, whereas in other markets firms sell close substitutes. In either case, firms are acting in oligopolistic ways and referred to as *oligopolies.*

Which Model Fits Reality

Tables 5.1 and 5.2 summarize these market forms by providing examples and distinguishing characteristics of each type. That does not mean we will spend a great deal of time in the issues chapters worrying about market forms. Recall that in Chapter 2 we implicitly assumed that all markets were perfectly competitive. It turns out that very few markets meet the extreme criteria necessary to be labeled perfect competition. Most of the products that meet the criteria of perfect competition are agricultural; few products outside this area can make that claim. It may strike you, then, as somewhat curious that we will assume that most markets are perfectly competitive when we move into the issues. We do this because the supply and demand model is simple enough so that it can be used to explain and describe most markets where there are several competitors and the products are similar. You should understand that your instructor and I (the author) make this simplifying assumption reluctantly but knowingly.

Finally, you should be prepared for a high level of ambiguity in how particular markets fit into these forms. For instance, long-distance telephone service used to be a monopoly, became an oligopoly in the 1980s, and saw significant expansion in the number of companies offering

TABLE 5.1
Examples of different market forms.

Perfect Competition	Monopolistic Competition	Oligopoly	Monopoly
Agricultural products Lumber	Fast food Clothing	Smartphones Soft drinks	Operating systems Local residential electric power

TABLE 5.2
Distinguishing characteristics between market forms.

Characteristic	Perfect Competition	Monopolistic Competition	Oligopoly	Monopoly
Number of firms	Many (often thousands or even millions)	Several*	Few* (usually two to five)	One
Barriers to entry	None	Few	Substantial	Insurmountable, at least in the short run
Product similarity	Identical	Similar but not identical	Similar or identical	NA

*There is dispute about the line that separates monopolistic competition and oligopoly.

TABLE 5.3 Concentration ratios and Herfindahl-Hirschman indices for various industries, 2007.

Industry Group	Concentration Ratios			
	4 Largest Firms	8 Largest Firms	50 Largest Firms	Herfindahl-Hirschman Index
Breakfast cereals	80.4	91.9	100.0	2,425.5
Ice cream	52.7	66.3	93.6	954.1
Beer	89.5	91.5	96.3	*
Wine	42.3	55.4	75.9	584.0
Clothing	7.9	14.1	39.2	44.0
Computers and peripherals	63.4	71.8	89.3	2,030.7
Furniture	21.2	27.0	53.2	328.7
Automobile manufacturing	67.6	91.3	99.8	1,448.8
Cellular service	80.2	90.7	97.9	**

*This industry is so concentrated that the Census Bureau cannot report exactly how concentrated it is because doing so would provide competing firms with sales information of their individual competitors.
**Not published for service providers.
Source: United States Census Bureau, www.census.gov/econ/concentration.html

service in the 1990s. Perhaps now it fits best under monopolistic competition. The personal computer business is similar in that there was only one firm, IBM, for many years, but today there are a dozen or more selling laptops and desktops. They all sell essentially the same thing but have a monopoly over their brand. The smartphone operating system industry is dominated by Apple and Google, with the device industry being dominated by HTC, Apple, and Samsung. Similarly, if you want to fly from New York to Los Angeles, you have a number of alternatives, perhaps not so many that it would be perfect competition but certainly enough to classify this service as monopolistic competition. On the other hand, if you want to fly directly from Indianapolis to Atlanta, you have two choices for nonstop flights (Air Tran and Delta). If you want to fly directly from Syracuse to Detroit, you have only one choice (Delta). Where airline travel fits depends greatly on to where, and from where, you are traveling. In particular, it depends on who has a hub in the respective airports.

Further, there is no magic line that separates oligopoly from monopolistic competition. Economists who study these things will often look to something called a **concentration ratio** that measures the percentage of total market sales for the top firms (from 4 firms to 100 firms). So even though there are several tobacco companies selling cigarettes, one company, Philip Morris, holds nearly half the market, and the top four hold all but 1 percent of the market. Several equally competitive firms would suggest monopolistic competition, but these concentration ratio data suggest that oligopoly may be a better fit. Table 5.3 presents 4-, 8-, and 50-firm concentration ratios for specific industries.

Another index that economists, particularly those in the antitrust division of the Department of Justice, use is the **Herfindahl-Hirschman Index** (HHI). Instead of just adding together the market shares of the largest firms, this adds the square of the market shares. What that does is distinguish a market where five firms have equal shares from one in which the big firm has a large proportion of sales and the others simply split the rest. If the market share is between 0 and 100 percent and there are N firms, the HHI ranges between 10,000/N and 10,000. A number between 1,000 and 1,800 is considered moderately concentrated while an index value greater than 1,800 is considered highly concentrated. The index value for breakfast cereals is above 2,500 and the one for beer is reported to be above 3,500, but the census bureau (that regularly published the statistics) must suppress the actual number to "protect the identity of any business. . . ." Essentially the industry is so concentrated that reporting how much provides the largest businesses information on others.

concentration ratio
A measure of the market power held by the top firms in an industry. For a specific number of firms (n), it is the percentage of total sales in the industry accounted for by top n firms.

Herfindahl-Hirschman Index
A measure of market concentration developed by adding the sum of squared market shares.

Supply under Perfect Competition

Normal versus Economic Profit

normal profit
The level of profit that business owners could get in their next best alternative investment.

economic profit
Any profit above normal profit.

Let's return to the example we used in Chapter 4: the business of selling memory chips. If we are one of many firms competing in this industry, it stands to reason that making money will be difficult. Because of our assumption of free entry into and exit from this market, any time there are abnormally large profits, other firms will want to start making memory chips. Remember that Chapter 2 presented evidence that an increase in the number of sellers will move the supply curve to the right, thus lowering market price. If that happens, our marginal revenue curve will fall. As a matter of fact, it will fall all the way to where profit is normal. **Normal profit** is the level of profit that business owners could get in their next best alternative investment. The next best alternative would be whatever investment an owner would choose if he or she decided to go out of business. Any profit above normal profit is called **economic profit.**

If business owners do not make their normal profit, they will quit the business and move into another. This means that we might think of normal profit as the salary the business owners pay themselves and, as such, part of the "cost of doing business." If they make less than normal profit, then the salary they can pay themselves is too low to keep them in the industry. On the other hand, if profits are routinely more than that, others will want to enter the industry. This means that in the long run profit will shrink to normal levels.

When and Why Economic Profits Go to Zero

Fortunately for our chip maker, although the firm cannot make long-run economic profits, it is not going to lose money for long either. When firms lose more money than their fixed costs, they shut down. In the short run firms will continue to produce when they lose less than their fixed costs, but as time passes these firms will also want to shut down. So, though our chip maker can make economic profit in the short run and lose money in the short run, the effect of free entry and exit in this market will cause the marginal revenue curve to settle at the minimum of the U-shaped average total cost. What this means in everyday English is that any short-run profit or loss will evaporate in the long run because new competitors will come in or old ones will leave. This will drive the price toward the minimum of average total cost where profit is normal.

Though profit also shrinks to its normal level under monopolistic competition, there is no mechanism for profits to shrink to normal levels under oligopoly or monopoly. This is because the mechanism that shrinks profit is entry. Because entry is almost insurmountable under monopoly and substantially difficult under oligopoly, new firms do not come in to put the pressure on the price to fall.

At this point we need to back off our discussion to define more explicitly what economists mean by short run and long run. To an economist the distinction between the two centers on the ability of a firm to change its fixed inputs. We have assumed all along that we cannot change things like plant and equipment, and this is true in what we call the **short run.** In the **long run** there is enough time to change plant and equipment. We can either buy more plant and more equipment, or we can sell what we have. The distinction is thus not one of time but of flexibility; in the long run we are more flexible and in the short run less flexible.

short run
The period of time where a firm cannot change things like plant and equipment.

long run
The period of time where a firm can change things like plant and equipment.

Why Supply Is Marginal Cost under Perfect Competition

Showing that, under perfect competition, supply and marginal cost are interchangeable is important for several of the issues that follow, but it is also notoriously difficult. That is why we will go back to the three approaches used in Chapter 4. We'll do the "Just Words," and "Numerical Example" approaches first and end with the "Graphical Explanation."

Just Words

In order to see that, under perfect competition, supply and marginal cost are interchangeable, you need to recall two key facts from Chapter 4: (1) All profit-maximizing firms will choose to produce where marginal cost equals marginal revenue (as long as price is greater than average variable cost); and (2) under perfect competition price and marginal revenue are the same. With that in your head, imagine that a firm is trying to decide how much to produce. It will take the price that is given to it by the market (which is also the firm's marginal revenue) and set production where that price equals its marginal cost. If the price rises or falls, it will do the calculation again. In every case, the quantity at which marginal revenue equals marginal cost is the same as the quantity at which price equals marginal cost. That means that in every case the relationship between quantity produced and the marginal cost of producing it (the marginal cost curve) is the same as the relationship between the quantity produced and the price at which it is sold (the supply curve). So, under perfect competition, supply and marginal cost are interchangeable.

Numerical Example

Using the memory chips example again, you can see from Table 4.2 that the average variable cost reaches a minimum at $15 per unit at the quantity of 500 units. This is important because at any price below $15 the firm will choose not to produce. To see that, suppose the price were $12 per unit. Marginal cost equals marginal revenue ($12) at 400 units, but at 400 units the firm's total revenue will be $4,800 ($12 × 400) while its total cost will be $14,500, and it will lose more money ($9,700 = $14,500 − $4,800) than it would if it simply shut down ($8,500).

At every price above $15 the firm either makes money or at least loses less than $8,500, and therefore it makes sense for the firm to produce where marginal cost equals marginal revenue. If the price were exactly $15, the firm would produce 500 units, have $7,500 ($15 × 500) in total revenue, $16,000 in total cost, and lose exactly its fixed costs. If the price were $20, the firm would produce 600 units, bringing $12,000 in revenue while costing $18,000, and the loss is $6,000. The firm would rather lose $6,000 than $8,500, so it produces 600 units.

As the price rises to $30, it produces 700 units, has both revenue and cost of $21,000, and breaks even. At a price of $45 it produces 800 units, has revenue of $36,000, costs of $25,500, and makes a profit. At a price of $55 it produces 900 units, has revenue of $49,500, costs of $31,000, and its profit increases. Finally, at a price of $100, it produces 1,000, has revenue of $100,000, costs of $41,000, and its profit increases further. Putting it all together, the firm's supply curve is its marginal cost curve (out of the minimum of average variable cost) because it sets production by noting the price and using the marginal cost figure to set production. Therefore, the relationship between its marginal cost and its production (its marginal cost curve) is the same as the relationship between the price it will receive and its production (its supply curve).

Graphical Explanation

Figure 5.2 shows our ATC-AVC-MC cost curve diagram with four potential marginal revenue curves. For each, if there is pressure on the price to change in the short run, this is indicated with a short arrow in the direction of the pressure. If there is long-run pressure, this is indicated with a long arrow. At the first price–marginal revenue, MR_1, the loss is so big that firms want to leave in both the short and the long run. This will reduce the number of sellers and the market price will rise in both the short run and the long run. At MR_2 the chip maker is losing money but not enough for it to close down. So, though the firm does not want to shut down in

FIGURE 5.2   In perfect competition the market price is under pressure to move to where economic profit is zero.

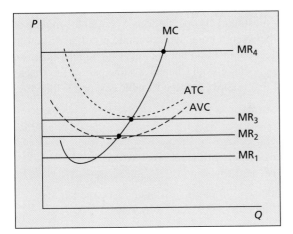

FIGURE 5.3   Points where MC = MR in perfect competition.

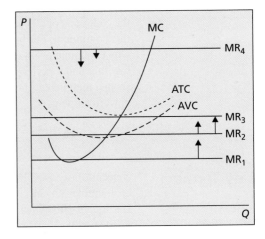

the short run, it will want to shut down rather than invest money in new equipment as the old equipment wears out. Therefore, the long-run pressure is for the price to rise. At MR_4 our chip maker is making an economic profit. If this happens, others will want to join the chip-making industry and there will be short- and long-run pressure for the price to fall. It is only when the price is at MR_3 that there is no pressure on the price.

Now to why under perfect competition a firm's supply curve is its marginal cost curve out of the minimum of its average variable cost. In Figure 5.3 the arrows from Figure 5.2 have been taken away and the points where the firm will produce are indicated by a dot. These points appear where marginal cost crosses marginal revenue, a circumstance that will come about only if firms do not shut down.

In our final manipulation of the figure we get one of the most important implications of perfect competition. Connecting the dots of Figure 5.3 makes clear the relationship between the price of the chips our firm is selling and the number of chips our firm is willing to produce. If that sounds familiar, it is because that is exactly the definition of supply. As a result we now know that supply, under perfect competition, is marginal cost out of the minimum of average variable cost. This, of course, also demonstrates why the supply curve is upward sloping: Marginal cost is increasing.

FIGURE 5.4
Derivation of supply: marginal cost out of the minimum of average variable cost.

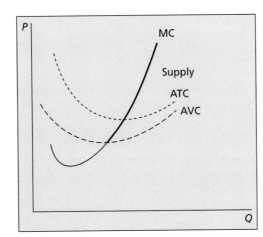

Although more difficult to show than it is worth, it is important to state that there is no supply curve under monopolistic competition, oligopoly, or monopoly. To understand the reason, note that Figure 5.4 generates the supply curve by finding the production levels with a variety of different prices. Recall from Figure 4.4 that these horizontal price lines also represent perfectly elastic demand curves for a particular firm's output. This same derivation does not work for the other market forms because the elasticity of demand for a firm's output is not perfectly elastic and demand curves of different elasticities result in different profit-maximizing firm output.

Summary

This chapter built on the previous one in which costs and revenues were defined and illustrated. We saw the distinction between perfect competition and monopoly and that they are the endpoints of a continuum. We said that most markets operate somewhere in the middle of this continuum. Further, we distinguished between normal and economic profit, and showed why economic profit disappears under perfect competition but not under monopoly. Last, we saw that under perfect competition, the supply curve from Chapter 2 is the part of the check-shaped marginal cost curve from Chapter 4 that is above average variable cost and is therefore upward sloping.

Key Terms

concentration ratio, 70
economic profit, 71
Herfindahl-Hirschman
    Index, 70

long run, 71
monopolistic
    competition, 68

normal profit, 71
oligopolistic market, 69
short run, 71

**Issues
Chapters You
Are Ready
for Now**

The Economics of
    Prescription Drugs, 282
Ticket Brokers and Ticket
    Scalping, 343
The Economics of K–12
    Education, 350

Energy Prices, 404
Unions, 440
Walmart: Always Low
    Prices (and Low
    Wages)—Always, 450

The Economic Impact of
    Casino Gambling, 455

Quiz Yourself

1. An industry in which there are many competitors with specific marketing niches is likely to be characterized by
    a. monopoly.
    b. oligopoly.
    c. monopolistic competition.
    d. perfect competition.

2. An industry in which there are a very limited number of large firms is likely to be characterized by
    a. monopoly.
    b. oligopoly.
    c. monopolistic competition.
    d. perfect competition.

3. Owing to its usefulness and relative simplicity, the supply and demand model is often used
    a. because nearly every major industry in the United States is governed by perfect competition.
    b. because nearly every major industry in the United States is governed by monopoly.
    c. even though, strictly speaking, few industries in the United States are governed by perfect competition.
    d. even though it has no connection to economic reality.

4. Whether a firm stays in business or shuts down depends heavily on the concept of
    a. economic profit.
    b. actual profit.
    c. market share.
    d. concentration ratios.

5. Economic theory would suggest that the profitability of an industry would be
   a. directly related to the number of firms competing in the industry.
   b. inversely related to the number of firms competing in the industry.
   c. unrelated to the number of firms competing in the industry.
   d. zero in the long run, regardless of market structure.

6. Under perfect competition, the supply curve is
   a. the marginal cost curve for all price quantity combinations.
   b. the marginal cost curve, but only that portion that is downward sloping.
   c. the marginal cost curve, but only that portion that is upward sloping.
   d. the marginal cost curve, but only that portion that is above the minimum of average variable cost.

7. An indicator of the degree of competition in an industry is the concentration ratio. It measures
   a. the percentage of sales in the industry by the largest firms.
   b. the percentage of profit in the industry by the smallest firms.
   c. the sales in the industry as a percentage of all consumption in the United States.
   d. the profitability of the industry.

8. Local telephone service was once an area in which consumers had no choices. Many young people no longer use "landlines," preferring instead to use their cellular phones. This means that the market has moved toward
   a. monopoly.
   b. oligopoly.
   c. perfect competition.
   d. monopsony.

9. In a diagram of perfect competition, the marginal revenue line moves up and down when there is exit and entry, respectively, because
   a. the market demand for the good rises and falls when there is exit and entry, respectively.
   b. the market demand for the good rises and falls when there is entry and exit, respectively.
   c. the market supply for the good rises and falls when there is exit and entry, respectively.
   d. the market supply for the good rises and falls when there is entry and exit, respectively.

10. If MR > MC, then when an additional unit is sold, the firm's
    a. profit will be positive.
    b. profit will increase.
    c. profit will be negative.
    d. profit will decrease.

Short Answer Questions

1. Imagine an owner of a firm is thinking about raising prices. Describe the consequences of doing so as a monopolist, oligopolist, monopolistic competitor, and perfect competitor.

2. What are the key difference(s) between monopolistic competition and perfect competition?

3. Describe why there is pressure on the price to fall when P > ATC. Is there a long- and short-run distinction in the answer?

4. Describe why there is pressure on the price to fall when P < ATC. Is there a long- and short-run distinction in the answer?

Think about This

One of the concerns about Walmart's entry into the grocery business in the latter part of the 1990s was that it would set low prices, drive little stores out of business, and then raise prices to monopoly levels when it had no competition. That hasn't happened but that doesn't mean it couldn't happen. Under what conditions, and in what industries, might such a strategy work?

Talk about This

List the monopolies that used to exist when you were growing up that are now facing increased competition. Compare that list to a list provided by your instructor (who is presumably older than you). What current monopolies are likely to be threatened with entry in the future?

Behind the Numbers

Concentration ratios for largest 4, 8, and 50 firms in various industries—www.census.gov/ econ/concentration.html

Every Macroeconomic Word You Ever Heard: Gross Domestic Product, Inflation, Unemployment, Recession, and Depression

Learning Objectives

After reading this chapter you should be able to:

LO1 Define the basic vocabulary of macroeconomics.

LO2 Describe how the economy is measured.

LO3 Describe how gross domestic product, our national measure of output, is calculated.

LO4 Calculate inflation using a price index.

LO5 Describe real gross domestic product as the inflation-adjusted value of economic activity and judge its use as the measure of the economy's health.

LO6 Describe how unemployment is measured and enumerate the types of unemployment that economists recognize.

LO7 Define and apply the vocabulary of the business cycle.

Chapter Outline

Measuring the Economy

Real Gross Domestic Product and Why It Is Not Synonymous with Social Welfare

Measuring and Describing Unemployment

Business Cycles

Kick It Up a Notch: National Income and Product Accounting

Summary

microeconomics
The part of the discipline of economics that deals with individual markets and firms.

We shift gears now to talk about the economy as a whole rather than the consumption or production of specific goods. What we covered in Chapters 2 through 5 is called **microeconomics,** because it deals with individual markets and firms. The prefix *micro*, meaning small, applies here because of the narrow scope of microeconomics. The opposite prefix, *macro,* means large, so **macroeconomics** deals with the economy as a whole. When you read or hear "economic news" you more often than not get macroeconomic news. In that context you hear the same words over and over again. This chapter attempts to define and explain the vocabulary of macroeconomics.

macroeconomics
The part of the discipline of economics that deals with the economy as a whole.

We begin the chapter by examining the methods by which we measure the macroeconomy. In that process we define and explain gross domestic product, inflation, and how and why the gross domestic product is adjusted for inflation. We move from there to explain how unemployment is measured, and we finish with a discussion of the business cycle. You will see that all of these economic measures have flaws that economists recognize and study and that, though real gross domestic product is an accepted measure of the economy's health, it is not a perfect measure of our nation's overall health.

This is by far the most easily understood chapter of all the theory chapters, but you should make sure that you understand the terms and the concepts behind them thoroughly. Chapter 8 and the more macro-oriented issues chapters rely on them heavily.

Measuring the Economy

Measuring Nominal Output

To keep tabs on how well or how poorly the economy is doing, we measure economic activity by adding up the dollar value of all of the goods and services produced for final sale in the United States in a year. The **gross domestic product (GDP)** is the primary measure of the health of the economy, and some important concepts within this definition need to be highlighted:

gross domestic product (GDP)
The dollar value of all of the goods and services produced for final sale in the United States in a year.

1. This measure is a dollar measure that is subject to price variability.
2. Only "final" sales are counted.
3. The goods that are studied must be goods produced within the United States.

The fact that the GDP is influenced by changes in prices must be dealt with at length, but this discussion must be delayed until we explore inflation at length. Moreover, besides inflation, two other fairly straightforward issues should be addressed. The first of these is the issue of double-counting intermediate sales; the second is how to count the production of multinational companies.

To avoid the double-counting of certain economic activity, only final sales are counted. Suppose that you are talking about the production and sale of two loaves of bread. Suppose the first loaf is produced by a woman who grows and grinds the wheat, mixes the dough, bakes the loaf, and sells it all by herself. Suppose another loaf begins with a farmer who grows the wheat and sells it to a miller, who grinds it into flour and sells the flour to a baker, who mixes the dough, bakes the loaf, and sells the loaf to a retailer, who sells the loaf to a customer. If both loaves are of equal quality, then both should be sold for the same price: say, one dollar. Clearly both loaves contribute the same to the amount of bread available to society, so both should count the same when we measure economic activity. If you summed all sales along the way, however, the second loaf would count more than the first.

The other aspect of this measure is that it counts production only if it takes place within the borders of the United States. This means the Fords produced in Mexico are not counted in the U.S. GDP, but the Hondas produced in Ohio are.

The actual computation of the GDP is done in two distinct ways. One way is to count all those things for which people pay money. This is called the *expenditures approach.* The expenditures approach adds up all of the following: consumption, investment, government spending on goods and services, and exports; then it subtracts imports. The other approach, which counts all those ways in which people earn money, is called the *income approach.* This approach adds up employee compensation, interest, rents, profits, and depreciation and then subtracts income earned in other countries and indirect business taxes (such as sales taxes). Both approaches yield the same result because the money that the buyer "spends" is, by definition, the seller's "income." Therefore, adding up everyone's income and everyone's spending yields the same sum.

The sources that the government uses to compute this information are wide and varied. They are known as the National Income and Product Accounts, and compiling them is complicated and time-consuming. For instance, while the government knows quickly and reliably how much it spends on goods and services, nearly every other piece of information included in the GDP has to come from forms that businesses send to the government: tax forms, unemployment insurance forms, reports of sales and sales taxes, and other documentation. It is therefore obvious, but it warrants noting, that trying to produce the final GDP quickly is difficult. What actually happens is that government economists use sampling techniques to produce preliminary estimates that are repeatedly updated as more information is submitted. When all information is in, sometimes more than a year after the first preliminary estimate is made, a final GDP value is published.[1]

Measuring Prices and Inflation

As we said in the previous section, measuring price changes is important. Whether price changes account for changes in the GDP or whether actual production changes account for those changes is vital to the question of whether we are better off in one period than we were in a previous period. A GDP number that increases because prices rise is less desirable than a GDP that increases because people are actually buying products in greater quantities. For instance, let's make the simplifying assumption that there is only one good in society, cheese, we produce 10 trillion tons of cheese in one year, and cheese is sold at a price of $1/ton. That is vastly better than if we produce only one ton of cheese and it is sold at a price of $10 trillion. Clearly, to discuss the value of production we have to discuss how we measure prices.

market basket
Goods that average people buy and the quantities they buy them in.

The way that government economists measure prices is intricate. Under their direction, employees of the Bureau of Labor Statistics (BLS) go shopping for a **market basket** of goods and services in an effort to see if the total cost of that market basket has changed in the current year from what it was in the previous year. To do this they have to establish what should go into that market basket through a process of figuring out what average people buy and in what quantities they buy it. This market basket then makes up a kind of "grocery list" of things that government employees go out and find prices on. With the rapid expansion of available products, the BLS has recently chosen to update the market basket every two years. Their old practice of updating the market basket only every 10 years led to significant problems.[2]

The "list" of items for which government employees go out every month to find prices is very specific, not only indicating what model number or UPC code to look for, but also specifying stores in which the goods need to be located. Frequently, especially with electronic equipment, the item that the employee is supposed to find no longer exists or no longer exists

---

[1] Even then, some components are estimates.

[2] In 1996, the Boskin Commission established that measuring inflation the original way overstated the true inflation rate by 1.1 percentage points. In response to this criticism and in recognition of these problems, the Bureau of Labor Statistics corrected some of these flaws by going to a two-year cycle on market basket updates.

at the specified store. In that case employees must use their best judgment to find a suitable substitute and record key attributes of the good.[3]

base year
Year to which all other prices are compared.

For each month for which the list is in effect, including the first month of the first year, called the **base year,** Bureau of Labor Statistics employees find the prices of everything on the list. When they finish, a national average is computed. The result constitutes the first key piece of information necessary to compute future inflation: It is the national average of the total cost of the market basket. It is called the **price of the market basket in the base year.** In succeeding months a revised national average is generated on the basis of new information on prices.

price of the market basket in the base year
National average of the total cost of the market basket.

To use this information to measure any inflation that may have arisen in any given year, we have to go through three distinct steps:

1. We find the price of the market basket in the relevant years.
2. We compute a price index for the relevant years.
3. We compute the percentage of change in the relevant price indices.

After arriving at the price of the market basket in the base year, we also have to get the price of the market basket in any of the other years in question. For instance, if you ultimately wanted to know the inflation rate for 2012, you would need the price of the market basket in the base year, 1998, the price of the market basket at the beginning of 2012, and finally the price of the market basket at the beginning of 2013.

price index
A device that centers the price of the market basket around 100.

Next, a **price index,** which centers the price of the market basket around 100, is computed for the beginning of 2012 and 2013. For instance, the **consumer price index (CPI)** for 2012 is

$$\text{CPI in 2012} = \frac{\text{Price of the market basket in 2012}}{\text{Price of the market basket in the base year of 1998}} \times 100$$

consumer price index (CPI)
The price index based on what average consumers buy.

This formula can be interpreted to mean that in the base year the CPI is 100. At other times, as prices rise, the CPI will rise above 100. If prices eventually become twice what they were in the base year, the CPI will be 200.

The last step is to compute the percentage change in the price index. To do this, you take the CPI at the beginning of the year and the CPI at the beginning of the next year and plug them into the formula

$$\text{Inflation during 2012} = \frac{\text{CPI on January 1, 2013} - \text{CPI on January 1, 2012}}{\text{CPI on January 1, 2012}} \times 100\%$$

inflation rate
The percentage increase in the consumer price index.

As a practical matter the CPI is important for another reason. For economists it is important because it is used to generate not only an **inflation rate,** the percentage increase in the CPI, but also the **cost-of-living adjustment,** or **COLA.** This adjustment compensates people for the fact that changes in inflation also change the spending power of their income. For social security recipients and others on pensions that pay a COLA, as well as union members with contracts that are tied to a COLA, this represents the extra income they get each year to compensate them for inflation.[4] Table 6.1 presents a historical picture of the CPI.

cost-of-living adjustment (COLA)
A device that compensates people for the fact that changes in inflation change the spending power of their income.

Problems Measuring Inflation

We now have a measure of inflation that gives us helpful information on how the total price of a given market basket changes. For several reasons, however, it does not do a very good job

---

[3] The BLS then constructs a "hedonic price" for these goods. A hedonic price is an educated guess at what the price of the original good would have been given its characteristics. The BLS constructs hedonic prices for clothes dryers, microwave ovens, refrigerators, camcorders, consumer audio products, DVD players, and college textbooks.

[4] Social Security uses the end of June CPI to compute the COLA. By law, Social Security checks to individuals cannot fall, which means that if prices fall, the Social Security Administration simply does not increase benefits until the CPI rises to above its previous higher level. Because the June 2008 to June 2009 CPI fell and because the June 2010 level did not rise to the June 2008 level, Social Security recipients received no COLA for two years.

TABLE 6.1

CPI and inflation in selected years, 1920–2012; base years 1982–1984.

Year	CPI	Inflation Rate (%)	Year	CPI	Inflation Rate (%)	Year	CPI	Inflation Rate (%)
1920	19.4		1987	115.6	4.3	2000	174.6	3.4
1930	16.1		1988	120.7	4.4	2001	177.4	1.6
1940	14.1		1989	126.3	4.6	2002	181.8	2.5
1950	25.0		1990	134.2	6.3	2003	185.5	2.0
1960	29.8		1991	138.2	3.0	2004	191.7	3.3
1970	39.8		1992	142.3	3.0	2005	198.1	3.3
1980	86.4	12.4	1993	146.3	2.8	2006	203.1	2.5
1981	94.1	8.9	1994	150.1	2.6	2007	211.4	4.1
1982	97.7	3.8	1995	153.9	2.5	2008	211.4	0.0
1983	101.4	3.8	1996	159.1	3.4	2009	217.4	2.8
1984	105.5	4.0	1997	161.8	1.7	2010	220.5	1.4
1985	109.5	3.8	1998	164.4	1.6	2011	227.1	3.0
1986	110.8	1.2	1999	168.8	2.7	2012	231.1	1.8

Note: CPI is year-end figure.

Source: Bureau of Labor Statistics, www.bls.gov/cpi/home.htm (Series ID: CUSR000SA0).

in measuring the true impact of inflation. The first way in which the CPI can estimate inflation inaccurately derives from the two-year period between changes in the market basket. Specifically, large price decreases that occur in the first two years after the introduction of a product are ignored. For instance, the iPhone was originally marketed for $600 and two years after its introduction sold for less than $200 at Walmart. When the market basket updates were on a 10-year cycle, VCRs, personal computers, cellular phones, DVD players, iPods, flat-screen TVs, and TiVo boxes/DVRs did not come into the market basket until several years after their introduction. In all of these cases large price decreases and significant quality improvements occurred long before their inclusion. The must-have gadgets of 2010 through 2013, iPads and other tablets, were not included in the CPI market basket until their prices had already fallen. Flat-screen TVs used to be priced at more than $10,000 and can be found now for less than $300. Though the CPI methodology will eventually pick up the final fall in prices once they are included, it will fail to pick up the initial drop in price.

The second way in which the CPI may assess inflation inaccurately relates to quality improvements in electronics, which may occur so quickly that by the end of the final year of the market basket, the good that was originally included no longer exists. The best example of this is the personal computer. Recognizing this, in 2006 the BLS began to adjust for quality improvements in certain goods.

Third, people have significantly changed the places in which they buy goods. For instance, in the 1950s television sets were, by and large, purchased in department stores or small appliance stores. Although the personal service customers received during this period undoubtedly exceeded the level of service we now get at large discount stores or warehouse clubs, the price we pay when we make our purchases at discount stores is also much lower. Today we buy from stores where service is low but prices are also very low. If you remember, the government employees who go looking at prices do so at the specific stores designated at the beginning of the life of the market basket. Because they change the store to match consumer behavior only when they change the market basket, they may fail to capture a significant source of price decreases. In this way, the BLS has lagged behind actual behavior regarding Internet shopping.

Fourth, when prices change dramatically people look for substitutes. Because the market basket is fixed for a two-year period, it is implicitly assumed that people mindlessly buy exactly the same amount of everything, every period, regardless of prices. This is surely a silly assumption for economists to make, given that much of Chapter 2 was devoted to how people

INFLATION'S WINNERS AND LOSERS

An interesting aspect of inflation is that it creates its own set of winners and losers. People living on fixed incomes will be highly sensitive to inflation, and because people who borrow money are paying it back with dollars that are less valuable than the money they borrowed, both they and the lending institutions from whom they borrow will have a stake in the rate of inflation.

Anyone receiving a fixed amount of money per month or per year through an investment or having a fixed amount of cash that they must stretch over a long period of time will be unambiguously hurt by inflation. They will see their buying power drop incrementally over time. To see how important that is, suppose a 65-year-old new retiree sets up an annuity so that she gets $20,000 a year until she dies. If she lives 20 additional years and inflation is running at 5 percent per year, the buying power of that money will be 62 percent lower. Even if inflation is running at a modest 2 percent per year, her buying power will be 33 percent lower. While good financial planners will account for this when setting up such annuities for their clients, retirees who forgo investment advice can get caught in this trap.

In the arena of borrowing and lending there are also winners and losers. Here the important question is not necessarily whether there is inflation but whether inflation is greater than was expected by the respective parties. If inflation is greater than was expected when the interest rate on the loan was established, then borrowers are winners because they are paying the loan back using less valuable dollars than they anticipated. If borrowers are the winners, then lenders are clearly the losers in that they are receiving less valuable dollars in return. Of course, each "dollar" is still worth a dollar, but with inflation running above expectations, each dollar buys less than it was expected to be able to buy when the loan was set up.

On the other hand, if inflation runs less than was expected, the lender is the winner and the borrower is the loser. The borrower is paying the loan back with dollars that have more spending power than they were anticipated to have and the lender is receiving those more valuable dollars.

react to price changes. For an example of how failing to account for substitution can overstate the effects of an increase in the price of one good, consider energy prices. In 2008, gasoline prices climbed from $2 per gallon to more than $4.20 per gallon. Many people sold their SUVs and bought more fuel-efficient cars, or simply drove less.

In response to this criticism and in recognition of these problems, the Bureau of Labor Statistics began an effort to correct some of these flaws. First, as mentioned above, they make an explicit effort to account for the consumer electronics quality problem. Second, they now reestablish the market basket every two years rather than every 10 years. This allows for new goods to enter the market basket much more quickly and have at least a portion of the initial drops in price count. It also allows the BLS to account for substitution between goods when there are long-term changes in prices, such as the increase in gas prices that began in 1998 and culminated in $4.20 gasoline in 2008. This **chain-based index** represents progress as far as economists are concerned.

chain-based index
A price index based on an annually adjusted market basket.

Still, these efforts have not solved the problem entirely. In a summary of the issues, David Lebow and Jeremy Rudd reported that the degree of error in the consumer price index has been cut to less than a percentage point. Though better than before, their 0.8 percentage point estimate for the overstatement is significant. Over the course of 30 years, tax brackets and CPI-adjusted benefits will be overadjusted by 27 percent.

Real Gross Domestic Product and Why It Is Not Synonymous with Social Welfare

Real Gross Domestic Product

Having examined inflation and how it is measured, we can now come back to gross domestic product. As we said, one of the concerns with GDP measurement is that changes in prices can affect the GDP just as easily as changes in output. To cleanse our GDP measure of the

OTHER PRICE INDICES

core CPI
The consumer price index that has had the impact of food and energy costs removed.

core PCE
The Personal Consumption Expenditures deflator that has had the impact of food and energy costs removed.

Personal Consumption Expenditures deflator
A chain-based price index that adjusts for the substitution problem.

Producer Price Index
A price index based on what firms buy.

Because inflation is damaging to an economy and extreme inflation can be very dangerous, the Federal Reserve Board keeps close tabs on it. As we will see in Chapters 8 and 12, the Fed, for short, adjusts short-term interest rates to keep inflation in check. If you look behind the numbers of the CPI you find that it is highly variable. That is why the Fed looks at two more stable price indices. Both are called the core rates because they eliminate the impact of highly volatile food and energy prices. The **core CPI** is based on the traditional CPI, while the **core PCE** strips out the costs of food and energy from a different price index, called the **Personal Consumption Expenditures deflator.** You can see from Figure 6.1 that the core CPI and the core PCE are much more stable than the CPI itself. Because the Fed does not want to overreact to rapid changes in volatile sectors, it focuses its attention on these core measures.

Finally, there is also an index of input items for firms, called the **Producer Price Index.** It is often useful as a look ahead at what inflation will be in a few months as firms turn those inputs into goods that they sell.

FIGURE 6.1 CPI, core CPI, and core PCE.

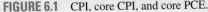

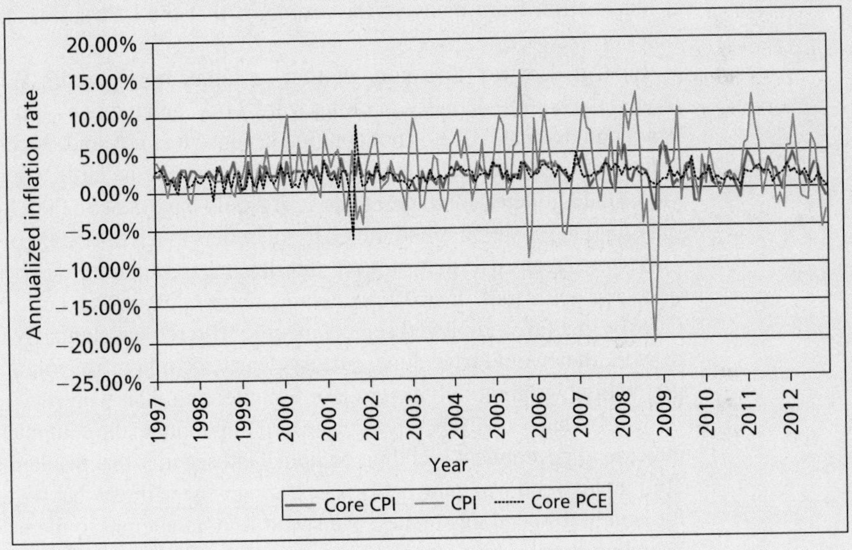

GDP deflator (GDPDEF)
The price index used to adjust GDP for inflation, including all goods rather than a market basket.

real gross domestic product (RGDP)
An inflation-adjusted measure of GDP.

price changes, we use a price index called a **GDP deflator (GDPDEF).** This inflation-adjusted measure of GDP is called the **real gross domestic product (RGDP).** Real GDP is computed by taking current production of goods and services and multiplying those by their previous year prices and then adding these up across different goods and services. The current production of new goods and services is then added to this figure. This process is different from that which creates the CPI in that the market basket changes from year to year so the choice of a base year is somewhat arbitrary. Still, it allows for a comparison of total production from one year to the next while eliminating the effects of inflation. Further, many economists feel more comfortable computing inflation using the GDP deflator approach (which is the annual percentage increase in the GDP deflator) than the CPI approach (which is the annual percentage increase in the CPI). Figure 6.2 shows the trajectory of real GDP since World War II using 2000 as the base year.

FIGURE 6.2

Post–World War II real gross domestic product by quarter, billions of 2005 dollars.

Source: Bureau of Economic Analysis, www.bea.gov

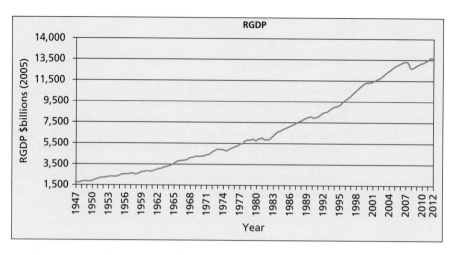

Problems with Real GDP

Even with its adjustments, real GDP does not do everything right. Besides having the GDP deflator suffer from many of the problems that the CPI suffers from, real GDP has several other problems.

First, it does not give your mother or father much credit. When either one does things around the house—laundry, cooking, yard work, and the like—the value created in the process is not counted in GDP. It is not counted because it is not sold. Much work gets done and much value is created without sales. I, for instance, installed a large wooden fence around my back-yard. Had I gotten a contractor to do it, it would have cost $8,000. Since I built it myself, it cost only $3,000 for supplies and the GDP missed as much as $5,000 of the value that was created.

Second, real GDP does not see that leisure is valuable. If we all worked ourselves to the bone and never took days off, we would cause GDP to rise, but we would be worse off for it. Clearly, in a fully employed society, people who retire voluntarily reduce GDP by the amount of work they would have done. Just as clearly, people retire voluntarily because they are happier fishing, golfing, lollygagging, or volunteering than working.

Third, what people buy is not considered important in the computation of GDP. The substantial increase in government spending on homeland security that resulted from the terrorist attacks of 2001 and beyond was quite likely necessary given the threat, but we are not better off as a society for having to spend this money. We spend it in an attempt to recreate the old sense of security. Spending more money on something that used to require less does not make us better off.

Fourth, the population of the United States is always growing. If real GDP does not grow at the rate that the population does, then the per capita real GDP (the inflation-adjusted goods and services going to the average person) will fall.

Fifth, we can sacrifice environmental quality of life for economic gain, but again we would not necessarily be better off. There is untapped crude oil under the coral reefs off the coast of Florida and under the vast tundra of northern Alaska. As the summer of 2010 made clear, drill-ing for oil in environmentally sensitive areas comes at a cost. When the process of "fracking" opened up vast quantities of natural gas for use throughout western Pennsylvania in 2008–2011, GDP was clearly and positively affected. In 2012, President Obama rejected the path of the Keystone pipeline and was criticized by Republicans for doing so. Their argument was that he was constraining GDP. In both cases, both sides are essentially correct. More drilling does increase GDP and reducing that new drilling does decrease GDP, but in both cases those concerned for the environment have a serious point. If the environmental concerns expressed turn out to be valid, this increase in GDP should be offset by the impact on the environment. No one in the government makes this adjustment. We would increase real GDP if we pumped this oil and gas, but the price of doing so would have to include its impact on the environment.

Sixth, just as the laundry and yard work your parents do does not count because the service does not get sold in a market, goods or services sold under the table do not get counted either. The illegal drugs that people buy do not get recorded anywhere. Similarly, if you mowed lawns or babysat as a teenager, it is unlikely you reported any of that income to the government. If you do not report the income on your taxes and your employer does not either, this economic activity does not appear as part of the GDP. This omission is especially important when it comes to the effect of higher tax rates. Studies reflect the obvious: When taxes are higher, people do more of their work under the table.

For all of these reasons, real GDP cannot be considered a perfect measure of social welfare. Still it remains the primary measure of the economic health of the country. Any attempt to account for the problems outlined above would subject the measure to value judgments about the intrinsic worth of certain goods for which there is little agreement. Therefore, economists generally accept real GDP for what it can tell us while remaining aware of its limitations.

Measuring and Describing Unemployment

Measuring Unemployment

Losing one's job is the most traumatic thing that a person can go through short of the loss of a loved one. Economists therefore consider the unemployment rate to be one of the most important indicators both of the economy and of well-being in general. When people who want and need to work cannot find suitable employment, they lose not only income but also self-esteem. The problem for economists is distinguishing in a meaningful way between stay-at-home parents who might work outside the home if they were paid $50,000 a year and unemployed auto workers who refuse to go from $20 an hour assembling cars to the minimum wage flipping burgers. At what point does the lack of a job go from being the economy's fault for not generating good jobs to being the person's fault for not having realistic expectations? This is an important question, but it is nearly impossible to answer.

The government measures unemployment by conducting phone surveys. The first thing the people making the surveys do is to make sure they are speaking to a person 16 or over. (This is because people under 16 are not counted, whether they are working or not.) Second, they ensure that the person they are talking to is not in the military. (Such people are not counted either.) Third, they ask if the person has done work for pay or worked more than 15 hours a week in a family business during the previous week. If the answer to that question is yes, then the person is considered employed. If the answer to that question is no, then the person is asked if he or she looked for work during the week, that is, whether he or she filled out an application or made a job inquiry. If the answer to that question is yes, then the person is considered unemployed.

From those surveys the government creates two numbers, the workforce and the unemployment rate. The **workforce** is generated by adding the employed to the unemployed. The **unemployment rate** is the unemployed divided by the workforce and should be interpreted as the percentage of people in the work force who do not have jobs and are actively seeking them. Both of these numbers are announced on the first Friday of every month.

Problems Measuring Unemployment

This measure of the unemployment rate has some flaws. First, it does not count as unemployed any people who are so discouraged that they stop looking for work. Second, it counts as unemployed those people who are (correctly or incorrectly) encouraged by positive economic news to look for work before there really is any work. Third, it fails to recognize the plight of workers who are working significantly below their skill level or those who would like to work

workforce
All those nonmilitary personnel who are over 16 and are employed or are unemployed and actively seeking employment.

unemployment rate
The percentage of people in the workforce who do not have jobs and are actively seeking them.

FIGURE 6.3

Post–World War II unemployment rates: the civilian unemployment rate (UR) and the rates as they would be if we include discouraged workers (DW) and the underemployed.

Source: Bureau of Labor Statistics, http://data.bls.gov/cgi-bin/srgate

Series: LNS12000000; LNS 14000000; LNS12032194; LNU05026645.

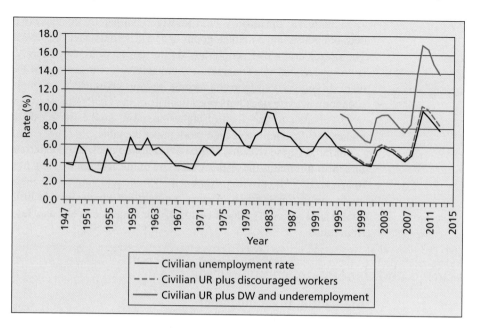

---

underemployment
The state of working significantly below skill level or working fewer hours than desired.

discouraged-worker effect
Bad news induces people to stop looking for work, causing the unemployment rate to fall.

encouraged-worker effect
Good news induces people to start looking for work, causing the unemployment rate to rise (until they succeed in finding work).

cyclical unemployment
State that exists when people lose their jobs because of a temporary downturn in the economy.

seasonal unemployment
State that exists when people lose their jobs predictably every year at the same time.

full time but are stuck in part-time jobs. Those suffering from either of these last two problems are referred to as **underemployed.**

The first two flaws are important because they subject the unemployment rate to incorrect interpretation. For example, if there are 10 people, 8 who work and 2 who are looking, then the unemployment rate is 20 percent. If things turn bad, so that one of the two decides to stop looking, the unemployment rate falls to 11 percent (1/9). Thus bad news in this case causes the unemployment rate to fall. This is called the **discouraged-worker effect,** a process that can be reversed. That is, good news causes people to look for work before there is any, and the unemployment rate rises back to 20 percent. This is called the **encouraged-worker effect.** Figure 6.3 offers a historical perspective on unemployment.

These two effects were prominent during the 2007–2009 recession and beyond. The clearest examples of the discouraged worker effect were in the January and February 2011 reports (for December and January unemployment respectively). During that two-month period, three-quarters of a million people left the labor force, due in large part to the fact that their unemployment compensation had run out. The unemployed are required to look for work while they collect unemployment compensation. Once the benefits ran out, with no opportunities out there, many unemployed simply gave up their search. When they did, the unemployment rate fell dramatically (from 9.6 percent to 9.0 percent).

Toward the end of a long employment dry spell, there is a predictable phenomenon where good news causes a significant increase in job seekers. In May 2003, as the economy started picking up after a slow "jobless" recovery, 500,000 people joined the labor force and only 250,000 got jobs. The result was, although this was a better-than-average month for new job creation, the unemployment rate rose from 6.1 percent to 6.3 percent.

Types of Unemployment

Economists further divide the unemployed by reasons for unemployment. If people lose their jobs because of a temporary downturn in the economy, economists call them **cyclically unemployed.** The **seasonally unemployed** are those people who lose their jobs predictably every year at the same time, like lifeguards in Michigan.

A third type of unemployment is more problematic and permanent. If people lose their jobs because of a change in the economy that makes their particular skill obsolete (either because the industry ceases to exist or because it moves to another country), they are referred to as **structurally unemployed**. These are typically the most difficult people to re-employ because their wage expectations are higher than the positions that remain in the economy that they can fill.

structural unemployment
State that exists when people lose their jobs because of a change in the economy that makes their particular skill obsolete.

Conversely, a fourth type of unemployment often results from good things in the economy. If things are going well and people get better jobs or at least are encouraged to go out and look for better jobs, they sometimes add to the unemployment rate. For instance, if people hear there are better jobs out there and quit their jobs to devote time to looking for them, they might be surveyed when they are unemployed. Still others may be part of a two-earner family where one gets a promotion that requires that the family move to another city and the spouse who does not get promoted quits to find work in the other city. During the time that such people are looking for work, they are categorized as **frictionally unemployed**. These people are unemployed for a short time, but they have skills that employers will want. It just takes time to find the appropriate job. Thus, this type of unemployment exists in any smoothly functioning economy as long as it takes time to find similar or better work.

frictional unemployment
Short-term unemployment during a transition to an equal or better job.

Typically between a quarter and a third of unemployed people are laid off subject to recall (cyclically unemployed), an equal number voluntarily leave their jobs (frictionally unemployed), and the remainder are let go involuntarily without being subject to recall (though not all of this latter group should be referred to as structurally unemployed).

Business Cycles

business cycle
Regular pattern of ups and downs in the economy.

trough
The lowest point in the business cycle.

recovery
The part of the growth period of the business cycle from the trough to the previous peak.

expansion
The part of the growth period of the business cycle from the previous peak to the new peak.

peak
The highest point in the business cycle.

recession
The declining period of at least two consecutive quarters in the business cycle.

Over the years there has been such a regular pattern of ups and downs in the economy that economists have put a name to it: the **business cycle**. Figure 6.4 shows the general pattern of the economy over time. Though the general trend is up, you can see that the path is rarely a straight line. With real gross domestic product on one axis and time on the other, you can see that a business cycle has five main components. The **trough** is the lowest point in the business cycle. The **recovery** is the period of growth in RGDP from the trough to the previous peak, that is, the period where RGDP gets back to where it was before the recession began. The **expansion** is the period of growth in RGDP from the previous peak to the new peak. The **peak** is the period where the growth in RGDP slows and eventually stops. Traditionally, a **recession** has been defined as a period of at least two consecutive quarters when the RGDP falls. This definition has, at times, been ignored as the National Bureau for Economic Research's Business Cycle Dating Committee has attempted a more commonsense approach to establishing the beginning and ending dates for recessions. The 2007–2009 recession, for instance, was determined to have begun in late 2007 despite there being a slightly positive first quarter and significantly positive second quarter of 2008. This was because the downturn clearly started in late 2007 and the first half of 2008 was aided by a stimulus package that provided rebate checks to millions of Americans. By the time those rebates worked their way through the system and the financial crisis of fall 2008 took hold, it was apparent to these economists that the recession began in late 2007.

FIGURE 6.4 The business cycle.

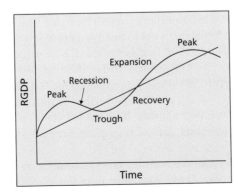

Between 1950 and 2011 there were nine recessions that lasted an average of nine and a half months. Some economists have argued that absent a major precipitating event, such

IF INFLATION IS BAD, HOW CAN DEFLATION BE WORSE?

deflation
A general reduction in prices.

From 1970 through the late 1990s, the predominant concern over prices was their propensity to rise too rapidly. Inflation concerns reached their peak in the late 1970s and early 1980s as prices were rising at or near 10 percent per year. Given that, why would it be a problem for prices to decline? The answer is actually somewhat simple. People delay buying big-ticket items when they are certain it will be cheaper if they are patient.

When inflation is running between 1 and 2 percent per year, it is not in anyone's interest to not buy things in hopes that prices will decline because they won't. On the other hand, if prices are falling, then there is such a motivation. If consumers do not buy goods in anticipation of price declines, then the people who make those goods will see demand fall. They cut costs by cutting wages and benefits, or worse, by laying people off. When profits decline, the value of stocks declines. With less wealth, stockholders spend less on consumer goods. The final straw is when housing prices start to fall. When that happens, people can easily owe more on their house than their house is worth. That results in a dramatic contraction in their willingness to maintain it and the elimination of their ability to borrow money against its equity (since they now have none).

From the late 1980s until 2003 Japan experienced a significant **deflation** in asset prices with the Japanese stock market, as measured by its principal index, the Nikkei 225, falling from nearly 40,000 to less than 8,000. Beginning in 2003 it recovered so that by early 2007 it was above 18,000. During that 13-year period, Japanese real estate values also plummeted. So, though Japan's economy was once the envy of the Western world, its deflation-led economic slump lasted much longer than a typical recession. More recently, the bursting of the housing bubble in the United States in 2007, the demise of the commercial real estate market, and the dramatic drop in world oil prices from mid-2008 through 2009 caused many economists to worry that this same fate would strike the United States.

It was precisely this concern that kept the Federal Reserve focused on ensuring that the fragile recovery of 2010 and 2011 kept going. The Fed's overriding fear was that a deflationary spiral would be nearly impossible to stop. This led the Fed to policies, like the much discussed second round of quantitative easing (dubbed QE2), that under normal circumstances would have been viewed as disastrously inflationary. The goal of these policies was to prevent deflation.

as the September 11 terrorist attacks, the potential for a recession has been lessened by the globalization of the U.S. economy. Typically, a recession is accompanied by a steep rise in the unemployment rate, a moderation in the inflation rate, and a reduction in real gross domestic product in the range of 2 percent to 3 percent. Many times in the last half-century economists wondered whether the business cycle had been "repealed" only to find that it had not. With the possible exception of the recession of 2007–2009, the worst recession since World War II occurred in the early 1980s. At that time the unemployment rate went from around 7 percent to nearly 11 percent and the inflation rate went from 13 percent to less than 4 percent. The recession that occurred in 1990 as a result of Iraq's invasion of Kuwait had muted effects, in that it lasted only eight months. Its effect on unemployment, inflation, and output was not nearly as stark as that of the recession of 1981–1982. The recession of 2001 began with the uncertainty of the 2000 presidential election and ended in November of 2001. At this writing, the length and depth of the recession that began in late 2007 has not yet been determined. However, it clearly ended the string of short and shallow recessions. Figure 6.5 shows the three business cycles from 1981 to 2008.

The potential for a recession has been lessened in some economists' eyes by the globalization of the U.S. economy. Those who argue from this point of view suggest that with

FIGURE 6.5

An example of three business cycles: 1981 to 2008.

Source: Bureau of Economic Analysis, www.bea.gov

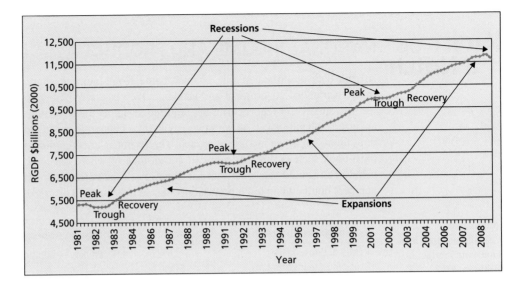

greater international trade, countries moving into recessions are bolstered by international demand for their products. Conversely, countries that are in strong recoveries have that impact dampened because purchases that were once domestic often are made from foreign sources.

On the other hand, other economists warned that the Asian–Russian–Latin American financial crisis of the late 1990s shows how one region's economy can begin a domino effect that is destabilizing. Just as a string of dominoes is more stable when barriers are strategically placed between dominoes, economies may be more stable if the troubles in one country are insulated from the troubles in another. The health of the U.S. economy during the period did, in the end, stabilize the world economy.

Unfortunately, there were few corners of the globe that stood in the way of the 2007–2009 recession. Begun by declining demand in the United States and rapidly increasing world energy prices, it got an unwelcome shot in the arm with the collapse of real estate markets around the world and the subsequent foreclosure-induced financial crisis of late 2008. Whether globalization dampened or amplified the recession will be a matter for future macroeconomic historians to determine.

depression
Severe recession typically resulting in a financial panic and bank closures, unemployment rates exceeding 20 percent, prolonged retrenchment in RGDP on the magnitude of 10 percent or more, and significant deflation.

A phenomenon that has not visited the United States in nearly 60 years is **depression**. Although there is no formal economic distinction between a recession and a depression, there certainly is little doubt that we have not experienced a depression since the 1930s. Depressions are severe recessions usually characterized by any one of the following problems: financial panic and bank closures, unemployment rates exceeding 20 percent, prolonged retrenchment in RGDP on the magnitude of 10 percent or more, and significant deflation.

Lessening the likelihood of depression are the economic and social safety nets (e.g., unemployment insurance, welfare) that exist in most modern economies. The recessions that occur when people lack the confidence to buy things can be prevented from becoming depressions by governments that move to alter interest rates and government spending policies. Further, as things worsen and unemployment rises, unemployment insurance and other policies exist now to lessen the effect. Thus people who are unemployed at the beginning of the twenty-first century have much more spending power than those unemployed at the beginning of the twentieth century. This in turn lessens the likelihood that a recession will turn into a depression.

Kick It Up a Notch   NATIONAL INCOME AND PRODUCT ACCOUNTING

All the data described in this chapter come from multiple sources and can be accessed from a variety of government and academic web pages. Whether from tax reports, sales tax records, surveys, or reports firms are required to supply the government, the data are collected, analyzed, and published. As we saw early in this chapter we can get to GDP using the expenditures approach or the income approach. The formulas are complicated and needlessly tedious for a book such as this, but you can get an idea of what is needed for GDP from the table below. You should also note that for a variety of statistical and methodological reasons the numbers don't add up to be precisely equal, so a "statistical discrepancy" is always present.

Alternative Calculations for Gross Domestic Product in Billions, 2011

Expenditures Approach	Amount	Income Approach	Amount
Personal Consumption	$10,873.8	Employee Compensation	$8,348.1
Gross Private Investment	$1,991.1	All Profits	$3,889.0
Government Consumption and		Indirect Business Taxes	$1,047.1
Investment Expenditures	$3,051.0		
Net Exports	−$594.8	Depreciation	$1,966.6
		Statistical Discrepancy	$70.3
Gross Domestic Product	$15,321.0	Gross Domestic Product	$15,321.0

Expenditures Approach: Table 1.1.5; Income Approach: Table 1.10.
Source: Bureau of Economic Analysis, www.bea.gov

Summary

This chapter presented the basic vocabulary of the macroeconomy and explored many of the measures of it—measures that are not without flaw. We saw that the measure of output is gross domestic product, that prices and inflation are measured using a price index, and that the most frequently referred to price index is the CPI. Moreover, we discussed why GDP is adjusted for inflation to create real GDP and that this, though also flawed, is a key measure of economic health. Further, the chapter explained how unemployment is measured, that this measure is subject to some concern, and that economists divide the unemployed into types depending on how they got that way. We concluded by discussing the language of the business cycle.

Key Terms

base year, 80
business cycle, 87
chain-based index, 82
consumer price index (CPI), 80
core CPI, 83
core PCE, 83
cost-of-living adjustment (COLA), 80
cyclical unemployment, 86
deflation, 88
depression, 89
discouraged-worker effect, 86
encouraged-worker effect, 86
expansion, 87
frictional unemployment, 87
GDP deflator (GDPDEF), 83
gross domestic product (GDP), 78
inflation rate, 80
macroeconomics, 78
market basket, 79
microeconomics, 78
peak, 87
Personal Consumption Expenditures deflator, 83
price index, 80
price of the market basket in the base year, 80
Producer Price Index, 83
real gross domestic product (RGDP), 83
recession, 87
recovery, 87
seasonal unemployment, 86
structural unemployment, 87
trough, 87
underemployment, 86
unemployment rate, 85
workforce, 85

Quiz Yourself

1. In measuring gross domestic product, goods produced by foreign firms in the United States are
   a. counted, and so are goods produced by American firms in foreign countries.
   b. counted, but goods produced by American firms in foreign countries are not counted.
   c. not counted, but goods produced by American firms in foreign countries are counted.
   d. not counted, and goods produced by American firms in foreign countries are also not counted.

2. Gross domestic product is counted using two methods: one which counts all the ways people _____ money and another which counts all the ways people _____ money.
   a. earn, spend
   b. spend, save
   c. earn, save
   d. loan, borrow

3. Inflation is measured using _____ in a price index.
   a. the absolute increase
   b. a multiyear weighted average increase
   c. the percentage year-to-year increase
   d. logarithm adjusted absolute increase

4. In early 2005, inflation increased unexpectedly because of an increase in oil prices. This helped
   a. borrowers.
   b. lenders.
   c. people on fixed incomes.
   d. workers.

5. The consumer price index (CPI) is a heavily criticized measure of inflation because
   a. the government does nothing to fix its known deficiencies.
   b. it consistently understates the increase in the cost of living.
   c. it consistently overstates the increase in the cost of living.
   d. the government constantly makes adjustments in it without warrant.

6. One problem with using real gross domestic product as a measure of social welfare is that
   a. it fails to count home production.
   b. it fails to count services, a growing part of the economy.
   c. it double, triple, and sometimes quadruple counts goods that are produced in stages.
   d. it fails to account for imports, a growing part of the economy.

7. In 2005, General Motors announced a 20 percent reduction in its staffing levels and the closure of many assembly plants. Those laid off as a result would likely be classified as
   a. seasonally unemployed.
   b. cyclically unemployed.
   c. frictionally unemployed.
   d. structurally unemployed.

8. On a graph of real gross domestic product over time, recessions appear as
   a. relatively short and shallow drops on an otherwise increasing path.
   b. long, sharp declines on an otherwise increasing path.
   c. the dips on a path that increases and decreases equally.
   d. the periods where the rate of growth, while still positive, slows.

9. Of these, economists consider this the worst:
   a. inflation of 5 percent.
   b. recession.
   c. deflation of 5 percent.
   d. depression.

Short Answer Questions

1. Explain why an economist would focus on real GDP rather than nominal GDP.

2. Suppose you walked into an unemployment office and found the following people: a laid-off mall Santa Claus, an unemployed auto-industry worker (who is subject to call-back by their company), a woman who lost her job at a manufacturer because the company relocated to Mexico, and a nurse who just moved to town because his wife recently started a new job. Assign the following labels to the people above: cyclically unemployed, frictionally unemployed, structurally unemployed, and seasonally unemployed. Then, explain your assignment of the terms to each person.

Think about This

Economists have argued for many years that the CPI overstates the cost of living. The degree of that overstatement has been the subject for significant economic research. Part of the problem in resolving the agreed-upon problems is that any correction has the effect of reducing Social Security checks and increasing taxes. Should economic measures be subject to political debate?

Talk about This

Economist Joseph Schumpeter once argued that people are too often lulled into an unproductively comfortable state when they have continuous employment. His conclusion was that recessions (more accurately, depressions, in his era) were good because they forced people to be creative and entrepreneurial. He labeled this "creative destruction." Do you agree with the premise of his argument? Do you agree with his conclusion?

For More Insight See

Hausman, Jerry. "Sources of Bias and Solutions to Bias in the Consumer Price Index." *Journal of Economic Perspectives* 17, no. 1, pp. 23–44.

Lebow, David E., and Jeremy B. Rudd. "Measurement Error in the Consumer Price Index: Where Do We Stand?" *Journal of Economic Literature* XLI, pp. 159–201.

"Measuring the Economy"—www.bea.gov/national/pdf/nipa_primer.pdf

Behind the Numbers

U.S. Gross Domestic Product and Recessions—www.bea.gov

CPI and inflation for selected years—ftp://ftp.bls.gov/pub/special.requests/cpi/cpiai.txt

Unemployment rate—www.bls.gov/cps

CHAPTER SEVEN

Interest Rates and Present Value

Learning Objectives

After reading this chapter you should be able to:

LO1 Describe what interest rates are and differentiate nominal from real interest rates.

LO2 Describe the use of present value calculations in determining the value of a payment stream.

LO3 Apply the tool of present value when thinking about economic decisions where the costs and benefits of decisions happen at different times.

Chapter Outline

Interest Rates

Present Value

Future Value

Kick It Up a Notch: Risk and Reward

Summary

Many economic decisions take place over time. That is, the time at which the benefits of a given decision are gained is different from the time the costs are incurred. For instance, when you save money, you put off the ability to buy something now so that you have even more money to spend in the future. When you borrow, you get to consume a good before you have sufficient means to pay for it. Thus we agree to give up a single sum now for a larger amount that we will receive later, or we agree to pay a certain amount per month over a series of months rather than pay a single sum now. In this market, as in any market, there is a price and there is a quantity, and there is a buyer and there is a seller. In this chapter we explore borrowing, lending, investing, and saving decisions.

We begin by exploring interest rates, the price of money, and how they are determined. We look at the importance of anticipated inflation in this decision so as to draw a distinction between nominal and real interest rates, a distinction that is important to economists.

We conclude by looking at financial decisions. We will see that any particular decision to borrow, save, lend, or invest depends on what economists call present value. We will examine scenarios in which we save or borrow a sum of money now in order to get a larger sum of money later. We will also provide more complicated examples in which the payments we make or receive are spread over time.

Interest Rates

interest rate
The percentage, usually expressed in annual terms, of a balance that is paid by a borrower to a lender that is in addition to the original amount borrowed or lent.

The Market for Money

When people lend or borrow money, we call the price at which they do this the **interest rate**. A useful way to think of this market for money is to imagine yourself renting a moving van. When you rent such a vehicle, the owner is letting you use it for a predetermined period of time at a predetermined price. Now, instead of renting a van, think about renting money. The owner of the money is letting you use the money for a period of time at a predetermined price. The period of time is typically denoted per year and so the price is an annual interest rate. This means that when you are borrowing money to buy a car or home or seeking money from investors, you must pay interest.

Of course you could be on the other side and be the owner of money that you put in a bank or use to buy a bond. You are now "renting" the money to someone else. In all cases the rate of interest is an important component in your transaction. In this market that we are discussing, the seller is the one with money and the buyer is the one seeking the money.

Figure 7.1 depicts a market like one we saw in Chapters 2 and 3. Here, though, the price is the interest rate and the quantity is the amount that the lender/saver extends to the borrower. The supply curve is upward sloping because the lender/saver will be motivated to lend more if he or she can get a higher return, and the demand curve is downward sloping because at higher interest rates the borrower will view borrowing as less advantageous. As in any other market, an equilibrium interest rate and amount borrowed or lent will result.

The equilibrium interest rate will depend on a number of factors. For instance, the interest rate for people with good credit histories is typically lower than it is for people with poor ones. The bank interest rate for car loans is usually higher than the interest rate for home loans. Credit card interest rates are very high. The reason for this is the degree of risk. A lender cannot assume that a borrower will pay every loan back in full. Lenders are taking a risk and part of what goes into their decisions is the likelihood that the borrowers will pay back the loans and the consequences if they do not. Credit cards are typically not secured by anything, and, as a result, credit card interest rates are higher than home loans. If a buyer defaults on a home loan, the lender can take possession and ultimately sell the house.

nominal interest rate
The advertised rate of interest.

real interest rate
The rate of interest after inflation expectations are accounted for; the compensation for waiting to consume.

Nominal Interest Rates versus Real Interest Rates

When the interest rate for a certificate of deposit (CD) or car loan is advertised publicly, that is referred to by economists as the **nominal interest rate**. Though this is the rate of interest referred to in Figure 7.1, it is not as interesting to economists as what they refer to as the **real interest rate**. The real interest rate is the rate of interest after inflation expectations have been taken into account. Inflation, which was explained in Chapter 6, is the increase in prices in percentage terms. Inflation matters for our discussion of interest rates because both borrowers and lenders consider the benefits and costs of their decisions in terms of the consumption gained and lost. Since the borrower is presumably going to take the money to buy something now and pay the money back later to a lender who will then buy something with the money, the change in prices is important. Let's consider a concrete example.

Suppose you agree to lend a friend $500 if he agrees to pay you back next year with 10 percent interest. This

FIGURE 7.1
The market for money.

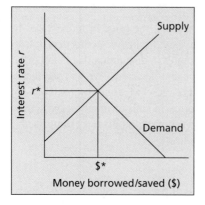

means that next year you will get $550. Suppose that both of you will end up buying iPads with the money and that today it costs exactly $500. If the price of these devices goes up to $600 by the time you get your money, then you have lost out. He got his iPad and you did not have enough for one even after waiting a year to get it. On the other hand, if iPads increased only to $525, then you could afford one when you got your money and would have $25 extra for waiting the year to get it. What this means is that inflation matters in this borrowing/lending decision. This is especially true if we know what the rate of inflation will be.

Although no one knows for sure what inflation will be in the coming year, people are able to use recent experience as a guide. As a result borrowers and lenders form inflation expectations. If you require $25 compensation for waiting a year to buy your iPad and you expect the price to increase by $25, then you will require $550 be paid to you. The first $25 compensates you for the higher prices that will exist when you go to buy yours, and the second $25 compensates you for waiting the year to buy it.

What this means for economists is that the nominal interest rate is equal to the sum of inflation expectations and the real interest rate.[1]

Present Value

present value
The interest-adjusted value of future payment streams.

It is easy to see that $100 is more than $50. It is much more difficult to compare $50 today against $100 six years from now. To put dollar values on an even playing field, we compare monies using a concept called **present value**. Using an appropriate interest rate, though, you can compare money paid at two different times. We say that two amounts paid apart from one another in time are equal in present value if the money paid now could be invested at an appropriate interest rate and generate an amount that turns out to be equal to a higher amount that is paid later.

Simple Calculations

The math required to fully understand present value is somewhat complicated and is displayed below:

$$\text{Present value} = \frac{\text{Payment}}{(1 + r)^n}$$

where

$\qquad$ payment = payment to be received in the future

$\qquad\qquad r$ = interest rate

$\qquad\qquad n$ = number of years before payment is received

Fortunately, the concept and its conclusions are not as complicated as the math. The idea is that the payment in the future needs to be deflated by a factor equal to 1 plus the interest rate for every year that is to pass before the payment is made. If the interest rate is 10 percent and 10 years are to pass, then the payment is deflated 10 times by 1.10.

To use a particular example, consider what $200 paid 10 years from now is worth in present value if the interest rate is 10 percent. To compute this we need to multiply 1.1 by itself 10 times. The result is 2.5937, so the present value is $200/2.5937, or approximately $77.11. This means that if you had $77.11 today, and you invested it at 10 percent interest for 10 years, you would have $200. Stated differently, if 10 years from now you were going to receive $200 and wanted to borrow against it and the going rate was 10 percent, you could borrow only $77.31.

[1] There is a mathematical cross-product term as well, but it is very small when the inflation and real interest rates are low.

	Interest Rate (%)				
Year	**20**	**10**	**5**	**2**	**1**
30	237.38	17.45	4.32	1.81	1.35
10	6.19	2.59	1.63	1.22	1.10
5	2.49	1.61	1.28	1.10	1.05
1	1.20	1.10	1.05	1.02	1.01

As mentioned, the factor 2.5937 was computed by multiplying 1.1 by itself 10 times. Table 7.1 provides factors for several different interest rates for several different periods. The interest rate appears at the top, and the left column indicates the number of years between the time when the borrower gets the money and the time he or she pays it back. The body of the table displays how much money the borrower will have to pay back for every dollar borrowed. For instance, every dollar you borrow on a 20 percent credit card that you fail to pay back within five years costs you $2.49, the original dollar plus $1.49 interest.

Mortgages, Car Payments, and Other Multipayment Examples

We can use this concept to calculate how much house or car we can afford. Here, instead of borrowing a single sum and paying it off with a single payment, we are borrowing a single sum and paying it off in small increments. Of course we could think of situations where we save in small increments to generate a single sum, like saving for a vacation, or situations where we save in small increments to generate other increments, like saving for retirement and getting a monthly check in retirement. These are simply extensions of the same principle.

For each of these examples there is a wonderfully elegant formula that would allow us to plug in various numbers and get results. These formulas, while interesting to those who study financial management issues, are not necessary for us to understand how we might use the present value idea in these other contexts.

For that, let's turn to Table 7.2, where we will try to evaluate whether a particular business deal is a good idea. Suppose that an investment of $100 each year for five years will, starting in the sixth year, return a payout of $100 a year that will continue for the next seven years.

Though the total of benefits is greater than the total of costs, whether this is a good business deal depends on the interest rate. If the interest rate is 5 percent, the present value of benefits is larger than the present value of costs. At 8 percent and 10 percent the present value of benefits is less than the present value of costs. That means that a business whose goal was to maximize profit would go ahead with the investment if interest rates were 5 percent and not if the interest rate was 8 or 10 percent. The interest rate where the present value of costs and benefits are equal is called the **internal rate of return**. In this case it is about 5.8 percent. Generally, when the interest rate that must be paid is less than the internal rate of return, then the present value of benefits exceeds the present value of costs.

internal rate of return
The interest rate where
the present value of
costs and benefits is
equal.

All mortgages and car payments are similarly calculated, though these are somewhat more simple because there is only one up arrow, the value of the house or car loan, and the multiple down arrows, the payments that are required. To give you some perspective on how much you would have to make in monthly payments on a variety of loans, consider Table 7.3, a very abbreviated set of present value factors. Again at the top are the various yearly interest rates and in the left column are the various loan durations. Thus a $1,000 computer purchased on a 20 percent interest credit card will cost the buyer $26.49 every month for five years. This translates into $1,589.63 in total payments over the five-year loan.

TABLE 7.2 Present value of costs and benefits at alternative interest rates.

Year	Cost	Benefit	PV Cost @5%	PV Benefit @5%	PV Cost @8%	PV Benefit @8%	PV Cost @10%	PV Benefit @10%
1	100		100.00		100.00		100.00	
2	100		95.24		92.59		90.91	
3	100		90.70		85.73		82.64	
4	100		86.38		79.38		75.13	
5	100		82.27		73.50		68.30	
6		100		78.35		68.06		62.09
7		100		74.62		63.02		56.45
8		100		71.07		58.35		51.32
9		100		67.68		54.03		46.65
10		100		64.46		50.02		42.41
11		100		61.39		46.32		38.55
12		100		58.47		42.89		35.05
	500	700	454.59	476.04	431.20	382.69	416.98	332.52

TABLE 7.3
Monthly payments required on a $1,000 loan for various interest rates and various loan durations.

	Interest Rate (%)				
Year	20	10	5	2	1
30	16.71	8.78	5.37	3.70	3.22
10	19.33	13.22	10.61	9.20	8.76
5	26.49	21.25	18.87	17.53	17.09
1	92.63	87.92	85.61	84.24	83.79

We can use Table 7.3 to figure out what typical monthly payments will be on purchases that you might make in the coming years. We just saw that if you purchase a $1,000 computer using a typical credit card, you will have to pay $26.49 per month for five years to pay off the loan. If you buy a $30,000 car with a five-year payoff period and get a 10 percent interest bank loan, you will have monthly payments of $637.50 (30 × $21.25). If you buy the same car during a financing promotion when the car company loans you the cost of the car at only 2 percent interest, your payments will be only $525.90 (30 × $17.53) per month. Last, if you purchase a $100,000 home with a 30-year mortgage at 5 percent interest, it will cost you $537 (100 × 5.37) per month.

Future Value

future value
The interest-adjusted value of past payments.

The present value formula can be algebraically rearranged to become a **future value** formula. Future value is the interest-adjusted value of past payments. Using the same variables from the present value formula,

$$\text{Future value} = \text{Payment} \times (1 + r)^n$$

This calculation is useful when you are looking to save an amount now for an expense that will occur at a later time. If, for instance, you had $10,000 and wanted to save it to give to your newborn daughter upon her high school graduation, you might put it in an 18-year certificate of deposit earning 4 percent. If you plug in those numbers ($n = 18, r = .04$), you will find that she could cash it in for $20,258.17.

SPREADSHEETS MAKE COMPLICATED CALCULATIONS QUICK AND EASY

Spreadsheet programs, such as Microsoft's Excel®, allow for quick and easy processing of complicated financial calculations. For instance, the PMT function allows users to calculate the payment that, when made over several periods, will pay off a loan. The PV function allows users to calculate how much they can borrow to buy a home or car when they can afford a particular payment. The FV function allows users to know how much money they will have when they retire or when they are ready to put a child through school if they were to save a particular amount per pay period. The IRR function allows users to calculate the internal rate of return on an investment that takes the form of a flow of uneven payments. The RATE function allows users to calculate the rate of return they are earning on an investment that promises to pay a particular amount in the future should the user save either a fixed amount now or follow a regular savings plan.

Function	Form of the Function	Example Problem	Example solution
Payment (PMT)	@PMT (r,N,PV,FV)	How much would you have to pay per month on a 4-year $30,000 car loan when the bank charges you 5%?	@PMT (.05/12,4*12,30000)
		How much would you have to save per month if you wanted to have $20,000 for a car 5 years from now if you could earn 3% interest?	@PMT (.03/12,5*12,0,20000)
Present Value (PV)	@PV (r,N,PMT,FV)	How much could you borrow if you could afford $500 per month payments on a house on a 30-year 4% mortgage?	@PV (.04/12,30*12,500)
		How much could you borrow at 7% if you were going to receive $10,000 in two years and use that money to pay all of your loan at that time?	@PV (.07,2,0,10000)
Future Value (FV)	@FV (r,N,PMT,PV)	How much would you have in an account in 20 years if you saved $1,000 per month and earned 1% on those savings?	@PV (.01/12,20*12,1000)
		How much would you have in an account in 15 years if you put $15,000 into an account that earned 9%?	@PV (.09,15,0,15000)
Internal Rate of Return (IRR)	@IRR (range on the sheet)	What is the internal rate of return for an investment that costs $100 the first year, $50 the second, but earns $200 in the third year and $40 in the fourth?	

C
-100
-50
200
40
@irr(C1:C4)

Function	Form of the Function	Example Problem	Example solution
	@Rate (N,PMT,PV,FV)	What is the internal rate of return for an investment that costs $10,000 but returns $4,000 for 3 years?	@Rate (4,4000, −10000)
		What is the internal rate of return for an investment that costs $1,000 per year but returns $15,000 after 10 years?	@Rate (10, −1000,0,15000)

Both present value and future value calculations are central to problems in business, the discipline of finance in particular. They require a calculator with a y^x key or a spreadsheet program to make the exponential calculations. Before calculators and computers were common, car dealers and real estate agents used a shortcut, called the **Rule of 72,** which allowed them to estimate these calculations in their head relatively quickly. Note from the preceding calculation that the $10,000 CD roughly doubled when saved at 4 percent for 18 years. The Rule of 72 allows you to estimate the time it would take for an investment to double by dividing 72 by the annual interest rate ($72/4 = 18$).

Rule of 72
A shortcut that allows you to estimate the time it would take for an investment to double by dividing 72 by the annual interest rate.

Kick It Up a Notch

RISK AND REWARD

Investing is risky business. Some investments do not pay off as expected. Economists look at **risk** as the possibility that the investor will not get those anticipated payoffs. There are two basic types of risk, the **default risk,** where the borrower doesn't pay the debts, and **market risk,** where the market value of a stock or bond changes in an unanticipated manner. To compensate the investor, a greater reward is offered. Economists call that greater reward the **risk premium.** Because longer-term predictions are often less accurate than shorter-term ones, there is also a relationship between the reward an investor receives and the length of time the investor must wait to get that reward. Economists call that relationship between reward and the time you have to wait to get it the **yield curve.** A sample yield curve for loaning money to the federal government is shown in Figure 7.2.

risk
The possibility that the investor will not get anticipated payoffs.

default risk
The risk to the investor that the borrower will not pay.

FIGURE 7.2
Yield curve for U.S. treasuries, January 2011, with maturities to 2041.

market risk
The risk that the market value of an asset will change in an unanticipated manner.

risk premium
The reward investors receive for taking greater risk.

yield curve
The relationship between reward and the time until the reward is received.

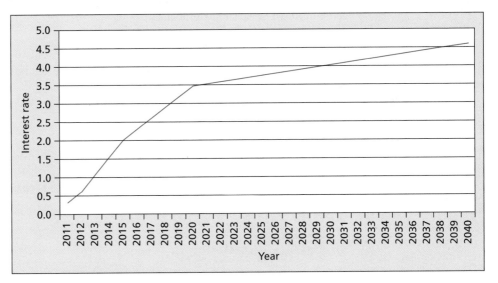

Summary

This chapter introduced the concept of interest rates and showed that the market for money is no different conceptually from the market for any other good. The interest rate was explained as the price of borrowing money. The difference between real and nominal interest rates was explained, highlighting the notion that real interest rates account for anticipated inflation. These concepts were expanded to explain present value and future value and how those concepts can be used to evaluate economic decisions where payments are made or received over a span of time.

Key Terms

default risk, 99
future value, 97
interest rate, 94
internal rate of return, 96

market risk, 99
nominal interest rate, 94
present value, 95
real interest rate, 94

risk, 99
risk premium, 99
Rule of 72, 99
yield curve, 99

Issues Chapters You Are Ready for Now

The Economics of
  Crime, 296
The Economics of K–12
  Education, 350

College and University
  Education: Why Is It So
  Expensive? 361
Social Security, 382

Personal Income Taxes, 393
The Stock Market and
  Crashes, 429

Quiz Yourself

1. When evaluating a business decision, an economist will often resort to the use of present value because
   a. the profits may not be large enough to warrant the time and attention of the investor.
   b. the investment occurs in one time period and the profits in another.
   c. the investment is often in one currency and the profits in another.
   d. the investment is often under one set of managers and the profits under another.

2. In the market for loanable dollars, an increase in the profitability of investments overall will be revealed in
   a. an increase in the supply of loanable dollars.
   b. an increase in the demand for loanable dollars.
   c. a decrease in the supply of loanable dollars.
   d. a decrease in the demand for loanable dollars.

3. When evaluating whether or not to make an investment, one should focus on the _____ because doing so takes into account anticipated inflation.
   a. nominal interest rate
   b. real interest rate
   c. exchange rate
   d. junk bond rate

4. Suppose your grandmother told you (today) that she had set aside an amount of money in a savings account bearing 3 percent interest that was sufficient to give you a $5,000 graduation present in exactly four years. How much would she have had to set aside?
   a. $5,000
   b. $5,000 \times (1.03)^4$
   c. $5,000/(1.03)^4$
   d. $5,000/(1 + 0.034)$

5. Using an interest rate of 5 percent, which figure has the largest present value?
   a. $5,000
   b. $5,050 to be received two years from now
   c. $5,075 to be received three years from now
   d. $5,500 to be received 10 years from now

6. Using an interest rate of 5 percent, which figure has the smallest present value?
   a. $5,000
   b. $5,050 to be received two years from now
   c. $5,075 to be received three years from now
   d. $5,500 to be received 10 years from now

7. The present value of a $1,000 payment received two years from now at 5 percent annual interest will be less than $900 because of
   a. taxes.
   b. compounding.
   c. withholding.
   d. double jeopardy.

8. A 60-month car loan (where no down payment was made) with a 6 percent interest rate and a monthly payment of $500 would allow the borrower to buy a
   a. $35,500 car.
   b. $30,000 car.
   c. $25,863 car.
   d. $28,200 car.

Short Answer Questions

1. Why is the present value of money to be paid in the future less than the amount to be paid, but the future value of money invested now and withdrawn later is greater than the original investment?

2. Why is it that $400 per month paid over five years will not be enough to buy a $24,000 car?

3. Why is there usually a positive relationship between the time a bond will mature (how long the investor has to wait to get her money) and the interest rate on that bond?

Think about This

The amount of principal paid in the early stages of a mortgage is relatively modest. On a $100,000 loan, at 6 percent for 360 months, the first payment is almost exactly $600 with $500 going for interest and $100 going toward principal. Before 2008's financial meltdown, many new homebuyers were getting "interest-only" mortgages. (They paid $500 per month for the first five years and then $644 per month thereafter.) Do you think this was a good idea?

Talk about This

College students and young people generally get themselves into credit problems because they do not fully understand the consequences of borrowing and overestimate their ability to pay loans back. Should your college censor campus bulletin boards and remove credit card offers from mail you receive in residence halls?

Bankruptcy laws prevent people from defaulting on student loans, which means even if you do declare bankruptcy on your credit card debt, you cannot get out from money you owe in student loans. Were you aware of this when you took out a student loan and would that impact your decision to take out a student loan?

CHAPTER EIGHT

Aggregate Demand and Aggregate Supply

Learning Objectives

After reading this chapter you should be able to:

LO1   Apply and manipulate the aggregate supply and aggregate demand model of macroeconomics.

LO2   Explain why the aggregate demand curve is downward sloping and why there is controversy over the shape of the aggregate supply curve.

LO3   List the variables that shift these curves and understand how the shifting translates into price and output impacts.

LO4   Discriminate between demand-pull and cost-push inflation.

LO5   Summarize what is meant by supply-side economics.

Chapter Outline

Aggregate Demand

Aggregate Supply

Shifts in Aggregate Demand and Aggregate Supply

Causes of Inflation

How the Government Can Influence (but Probably Not Control) the Economy

Summary

Now that we have laid out the language of macroeconomics and some of the measurement issues, it is time that we turn our attention to modeling the macroeconomy. Just as we used the supply and demand model in Chapter 2 to help us understand what would happen in a particular industry if certain variables changed, we use the aggregate supply and aggregate demand model to help us understand how other variables affect the economy as a whole.

Remember that models are not perfect. They rest on simplifying assumptions that allow us to boil down the essentials of what we are looking at in a way that clarifies the big picture. In microeconomics, supply and demand is a well-understood and relatively well-accepted framework with which to look at particular industries. Regrettably, in macroeconomics no such comparable model exists.

The closest we come to finding a workable model that is relatively easy to use and that is flexible enough to encompass a variety of differing viewpoints is the aggregate supply and aggregate demand model. It also has the virtue of mirroring the supply and demand model that we studied in Chapter 2, so the concepts are less foreign than they would be with a completely new model.

The reason for caution with regard to macro models is that, unlike microeconomic models, where there is only one market, many interrelated goods and services are combined. Whereas we can readily list five important things that influence the price of apples, we would need more than five pages to list the important things that affect the economy as a whole. The macroeconomy is just much bigger and much more complex than any particular market. With this caution in mind we proceed in this chapter with the aggregate supply–aggregate demand model knowing that, although not perfect, it is reasonably suited to the purpose at hand.

Following the method of presentation in Chapter 2, we explain this model by first examining aggregate demand and aggregate supply individually. Then we look at them together, as part of one model. Just as in Chapter 2, where we then looked at why supply and demand might change, we examine why aggregate supply and aggregate demand might change and what happens when they do. Last, we use the aggregate supply–aggregate demand model to explain, albeit very briefly, supply-side economics.

aggregate demand (AD)
The amounts of real domestic output that domestic consumers, businesses, governments, and foreign buyers collectively will desire to purchase at each possible price level.

Aggregate Demand

Definition

Aggregate demand (AD) is a measure of the amount of goods and services that will be purchased at various prices. It shows the quantities of real domestic output which domestic consumers, businesses, governments, and foreign buyers collectively will desire to purchase at each possible price level. As a practical matter we map this on a graph (Figure 8.1) with our measure of real goods and services sold, real gross domestic product (RGDP), on the horizontal axis and our measure of all prices, the price index (PI), on the vertical axis.

Just as in Chapter 2, when we asserted that the demand curve was downward sloping and then discussed why this makes sense, we do the same now. As shown in Figure 8.1, the aggregate demand curve does, in fact, relate all prices to real output in a negative or inverse manner. This makes sense for three reasons: the real-balances effect, the foreign purchases effect, and the interest rate effect.

real-balances effect
Because higher prices reduce real spending power, prices and output are negatively related.

Why Aggregate Demand Is Downward Sloping

The **real-balances effect** is the idea that any wealth that you may have in the form of cash or securities becomes less valuable as prices rise. Also, if you have less ability to buy real goods and services when prices are higher, then the two are negatively related.

The second reason why the aggregate demand curve is downward sloping is the **foreign purchases effect.** The argument here is that as prices rise in the United States, Americans will be more willing to buy imports and less willing to buy American-made goods. Foreigners will also be less willing to buy U.S. goods, thus reducing our exports to them. If you remember the expenditures approach from Chapter 6, you will recall that any increase in imports reduces U.S. GDP.

foreign purchases effect
When domestic prices are high relative to their imported alternatives, we will export less to foreign buyers and we will import more from foreign producers. Therefore, higher prices lead to less domestic output.

The **interest rate effect** is that higher prices lead to inflation. This in turn leads to less borrowing and a lowering of RGDP. The definition of aggregate demand will help explain the significance of interest rates as they relate to the downward-sloping nature of the aggregate demand curve. Recall from Chapter 6 that, using the expenditure approach, aggregate demand is calculated by adding total consumption, business investment, government spending on goods and services, and exports and then subtracting imports from that sum. Two of those

FIGURE 8.1
Aggregate demand.

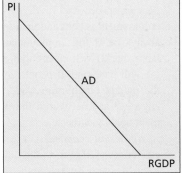

interest rate effect
Higher prices lead to inflation, which leads to less borrowing and a lowering of RGDP.

items, consumption and business investment, are interest-sensitive. When people buy homes, cars, home furnishings, or any good expected to last longer than three years (what economists call *durable goods*), they often do it by borrowing the money. When interest rates are high, the payments people can expect to make on the consumption of these goods will be higher than they are when interest rates are lower. When businesses borrow money to build a new plant or buy new equipment, the payments they must make to their creditors are also determined by the interest rate. Any time the interest rate rises, the volume of both large-dollar-item consumption and business investment will fall because the interest rates have caused costs to be greater. Recall from Chapter 7 that inflation increases interest rates, so if prices rise, inflation rises; if inflation rises, interest rates rise; if interest rates rise, consumption and investment fall; if consumption and investment fall, then RGDP falls.

Aggregate Supply

Definition

aggregate supply (AS)
The level of real domestic output available at each possible price level.

Aggregate supply (AS) is a measure of the level of real domestic output available at each possible price level. The accommodations for differing viewpoints take place in the aggregate supply curve. The differing viewpoints hinge on what is called full employment. Most economists say that full employment exists when cyclical unemployment is zero, so that there are still unemployed people at "full employment." Specifically, the so-called structurally unemployed, the people whose industry has moved or no longer exists, are without work. In addition, the frictionally unemployed, those who quit because they are looking for better jobs or because their spouse found a better job in a new location, are out of work during what is referred to as "full employment." These differences of opinion are displayed in the various ranges of the aggregate supply curve shown in Figure 8.2.

Competing Views of the Shape of Aggregate Supply

We have a serious divergence of opinion among macroeconomists on several important definitions. The following questions separate the two main camps of economists: What constitutes full employment and how are voluntary unemployment and involuntary unemployment defined? While what follows may seem like "airing out dirty laundry in public," it also serves as an excellent "teachable moment" in your general education curriculum. Profound differences of opinion exist in all disciplines, and one of the most profound differences of opinion in macroeconomics centers on these issues. Accepting that there is not a single right answer to every question is an important step in becoming an educated person. So, given that caution. . . .

Classical economists believe in the ability of all markets to generate good outcomes without government involvement. They believe that if minimum-wage jobs are available and unemployed steel workers choose not to take them, they are not involuntarily unemployed, just deluded about their prospects. As a result, they believe that cyclical unemployment is zero and therefore we will, by definition, always be at full employment because changes in the labor market will ensure that each person who wants a job will have one. If people are not willing to work for the market equilibrium wage, then they do not count anyway—at least within the definition of full employment held by classical economists.

Keynesian economists take the opposite view. These economists, followers of the early 20th-century economist John Maynard Keynes, argue that there are always more people willing to work than there are jobs available and

FIGURE 8.2
The aggregate supply curve.

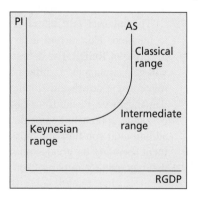

that, as a practical matter, we have never actually reached full employment. To Keynesians the concept of full employment is irrelevant. Thus, however many people are employed, Keynesians argue there could always be more and increases in aggregate demand are needed to employ them.

To depict these differing views on a graph, classical economists believe that the aggregate supply curve is vertical all the time. They believe that prices and wages will constantly equilibrate all markets, so increases in aggregate demand will only bid up prices, and the underlying real gross domestic product will remain unchanged. As an example, recall the memory chip–making firm we studied in Chapters 4 and 5. Suppose it has many competitors that are identical to it. If aggregate demand increases, leading to an increase in demand for computers and therefore memory chips, our firm will want to expand output. Classical economists argue that since all markets are at full employment to begin with, our firm will have to raise the wage it pays to attract more employees to produce those extra chips. Whether or not the firm succeeds in luring away the workers from the competition, total industry output will remain the same, since the total number of workers will not have changed. The only thing that will change if the classical economists are right is that prices will rise.

On the other hand, Keynesian economists believe that prices and wages are rigid and that unemployment results from that fact. The only way to employ these people, so the Keynesians' argument goes, is to increase aggregate demand. Moreover, since prices do not change, the aggregate supply curve should be thought of as horizontal. Again, using our chip maker as an example, if there are many unemployed workers available for hire into the chip-making business, then increasing output to meet increased demand does not require that wages rise.

A reasonable middle ground between these two models is that some industries are at full employment while other industries are not. If this is the case, an increase in aggregate demand may simply bid up prices in some industries and simply increase output in others. Thus, in the aggregate, real GDP rises a little and prices rise a little. If some industries, like computer chip makers, are at full employment and others, like steel, are not, then an increase in aggregate demand that increases demand for these two products will cause only inflation in the chip industry and only an increase in output in the steel industry.

The aggregate supply curve and the differences among economists are shown in Figure 8.2. As you can see, the vertical portion corresponds to what classical economists believe and is so indicated because any increase in aggregate demand will simply increase prices and not output. Similarly, the horizontal region corresponds to what Keynesian economists believe and is labeled as such because any increase in aggregate demand will simply increase output and not prices. The middle ground, labeled the intermediate range, connects the two ideological extremes and does so on the assumption that the classical economists may be right for some industries and the Keynesians for others.

You should understand that the representation of aggregate supply in Figure 8.2 is not one that most economists would embrace as perfect. For our purposes, though, it allows us to deal with the differences of opinion among the major schools of thought within macroeconomics in a way that is as uncomplicated as it can be. (This is not to say that you will necessarily find it to be uncomplicated.)

Shifts in Aggregate Demand and Aggregate Supply

Variables That Shift Aggregate Demand

Just as we saw in Chapter 2, where there were factors that shifted demand, there are factors that will shift aggregate demand. If you look at the elements of aggregate demand, you will find clues to what these might be. Anything that affects people's willingness to consume, government's desire or need to spend money on goods and services, business's desire to invest in new plant and equipment, or net exports (exports minus imports) will affect aggregate demand.

WHY A STRONG DOLLAR ISN'T NECESSARILY GOOD

There is something vaguely unpatriotic about saying there are problems with a "strong dollar." Nevertheless, it is true. As an example take the euro (€)–dollar ($) relationship and apply it to the hypothetical case where a German and an American are car shopping. Suppose each person is looking to buy a mid-sized sedan and each is comparing a German-made car with an American-made alternative. Each, after extensive research, has decided they are of equal quality and overall appeal and that each will simply buy whichever one is cheaper.

Keeping in mind that the euro was created in the 1990s to replace various European currencies and its value was originally pegged to equal one U.S. dollar, then if they are of equal value, the exchange rate is 1–1 (one euro equals one U.S. dollar). That would mean that if each of the cars was equally priced in both the United States and Germany, both cars would cost $30,000 in the United States and both cars would cost 30,000€ in Germany.

Now suppose that American dealers of German cars must buy those cars from Germany for 25,000€ and that German dealers of American cars must buy those cars from the United States for $25,000. That means that American dealers pay $25,000 to a bank to get 25,000€ and German dealers pay 25,000€ to a bank to get $25,000.

If the dollar gets substantially stronger so that the exchange rate moves to 1.00–0.75 (one euro equals 75 cents), then German dealers of American cars would have to pay 33,333€ to a bank to get $25,000 to buy the car from America. To maintain the 5,000€ margin they had been making at the old exchange rate, they would have to raise the price of American cars in Germany to 38,333€. The American dealer of German cars would now need only $18,750 to get the 25,000€ and could therefore

maintain the $5,000 margin by charging a price of $23,750 for German cars. Thus, the American is now more likely to buy the imported (German) car and the German is more likely to buy the domestic (German) car. Thus, a stronger dollar increases imports and decreases exports in the United States.

Before the United States, as well as the rest of the world, plunged into a deep recession in 2007–2009, the dollar was very weak relative to the euro ($1 equaled around 0.64 euros). This was one reason why, until fall 2008, it seemed possible the United States might avoid a recession. American exports were rising at such a rapid pace that it seemed possible that the United States might avoid the deep recession that had already begun in Europe. When the financial crisis of fall 2008 arrived, that hope faded. Though the crisis began with American banks buckling under the weight of massive home foreclosures, the United States was still seen as a safer place to ride out the recession. Foreign investors sought out dollars to invest in United States government bonds. This resulted in a rapid strengthening of the dollar relative to the euro. In the course of 80 days between August and November, the dollar rose to being worth 0.81 euros, a nearly 25 percent appreciation. While this may have been good for American morale, it was not at all helpful to American exporters.

As the recoveries in Europe and the United States plodded along through the first third of the decade, the value of the dollar continued to fluctuate relative to the euro. It fell to as low as $1 equaling .68 euros only to rise to $1 equaling 0.81 euros during the crisis over Greek debt. By the end of 2010, it was between those levels. Each weakening was cheered by American exporters.

For instance, taxes on personal or business income will affect consumption and investment, respectively. With higher tax rates, consumers have less take-home income to spend on things. With higher business or corporate tax rates, prospective business ventures are not as attractive as they might otherwise be. Thus any increase in personal or business taxes will lower aggregate demand, shifting it to the left on the graph, and any decrease will raise it, shifting it to the right on the graph.

Any increase in interest rates will have a similar effect. As we saw in Figure 7.1 and as we described in the previous discussion on the interest rate effect, increases in interest costs diminish individuals' and businesses' willingness to borrow money. The result is that aggregate demand decreases and moves to the left on the graph.

Any increase in business and consumer confidence will be followed by an increase in, and a movement to the right in, aggregate demand. This result occurs because as consumers become more confident in their own financial situation, they are more willing to take on debt to buy durable goods. As businesses have more confidence in their ability to sell their products, they will invest more in their productive capacity. Any reduction in that confidence will, of course, have the opposite effect. It will lessen aggregate demand and move the curve to the left on the graph.

The effect of foreign exchange rates on aggregate demand is complicated by the fact that though exchange rates are widely published, the fashion in which they are published is often confusing. The Japanese yen typically is expressed in terms of how many yen it takes to buy a U.S. dollar, whereas the British pound typically is expressed in terms of how many dollars it takes to buy the pound. It is as if you went into one bakery looking to buy a dozen donuts and they quoted prices in terms of the number of donuts you can buy for a dollar and another bakery quoted prices in terms of the money you needed to buy a single donut. With a bit of arithmetic you can do the comparison; it just takes a minute. This aside, we can say that if the dollar becomes stronger, exports will fall and imports will rise. Thus a strong dollar reduces aggregate demand, moving it to the left on the graph. Of course, a weaker dollar has the opposite impact. Aggregate demand increases and moves the curve to the right on the graph.

The only variable that impacts aggregate demand directly, one that needs little explanation, is government spending. Because government spending on goods and services is a direct part of the addition that makes up aggregate demand, the impact is direct. An increase in government spending causes an increase in aggregate demand, and a decrease in government spending causes a decrease in aggregate demand. Therefore, an increase in government spending will move the aggregate demand curve to the right and a decrease in government spending will move the curve to the left.

These impacts are summarized in Table 8.1. The effect of an increase in aggregate demand is shown in Figure 8.3, and the effect of a decrease in aggregate demand is shown in Figure 8.4.

Recall, if you will, the Chapter 2 admonition against trying to memorize Table 8.1 as it applies to Figures 8.3 and 8.4. Here, as it was in Chapter 2's discussion of supply and demand determinants and curve shifts, the advice is to use these tables and figures as a cross-check against your own intuition and understanding. For example, if you were faced with the problem

TABLE 8.1
Determinants of aggregate demand.

Variable	Part of Aggregate Demand Affected	Effect of an Increase in Variable on the Movement of Aggregate Demand	Effect of a Decrease in the Variable on the Movement of Aggregate Demand
Taxes	Consumption Investment	Decreases AD so curve moves left	Increases AD so curve moves right
Interest rates	Consumption Investment	Decreases AD so curve moves left	Increases AD so curve moves right
Confidence	Consumption Investment	Increases AD so curve moves right	Decreases AD so curve moves left
Strength of the dollar	Exports and imports	Decreases AD so curve moves left	Increases AD so curve moves right
Government spending	Government spending	Increases AD so curve moves right	Decreases AD so curve moves left

FIGURE 8.3 Aggregate demand increases, causing it to move to the right on the graph.

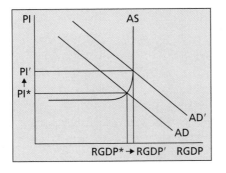

FIGURE 8.4 Aggregate demand decreases, causing it to move to the left on the graph.

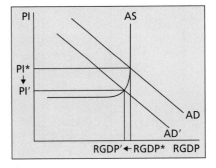

of analyzing a tax increase, you would understand that taxes take money out of the hands of consumers and business and thereby reduce the ability of these groups to buy goods and services. That decreases aggregate demand. An aggregate demand decrease is depicted as leftward movement of aggregate demand. Were you to follow that intuition and understanding, you could check your conclusion against Table 8.1 and Figure 8.4.

Variables That Shift Aggregate Supply

Just as there are factors that will change aggregate demand, there are important factors that will change aggregate supply. These are factors that are important to business. Any change that increases business costs will be important in terms of aggregate supply. Other factors that matter are government regulations and factors affecting productivity.

Any factor that will increase costs of production will hurt aggregate supply. That is, an increase in labor costs or other input costs will decrease aggregate supply and shift the curve to the left, whereas a decrease in those costs will increase aggregate supply and move the curve to the right. Along with any or all other costs of doing business, interest rates also impact the aggregate supply curve in that they affect borrowing costs on lines of credit used to keep cashflow problems at a minimum.

Similarly, if government regulations increase costs of production in some way, then aggregate supply will decrease and the curve will shift to the left. Deregulation will have the opposite impact because firms can eliminate costs of complying with regulations. Last, if firms become more productive perhaps through the use of better technology, then aggregate supply will increase and the curve will shift to the right.

Table 8.2 summarizes these impacts; Figures 8.5 and 8.6 summarize the impacts of these shifts on an aggregate supply–aggregate demand diagram. Figure 8.5 shows the impact of an increase in aggregate supply, and Figure 8.6 shows a decrease in aggregate supply.

TABLE 8.2
Determinants of aggregate supply.

Variable	Effect of an Increase in the Variable on the Movement of Aggregate Supply	Effect of a Decrease in the Variable on the Movement of Aggregate Supply
Input prices	Decreases AS so curve moves left	Increases AS so curve move right
Productivity	Increases AS so curve moves right	Decreases AS so curve moves left
Government regulation	Decreases AS so curve moves left	Increases AS so curve moves right

FIGURE 8.5 Aggregate supply increases causing it to move to the right on the graph.

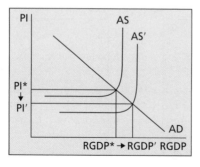

FIGURE 8.6 Aggregate supply decreases causing it to move to the left on the graph.

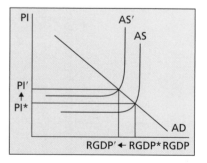

Now apply the admonition against memorization to Table 8.2 as it applies to Figures 8.5 and 8.6. For example, if you were faced with the problem of analyzing a productivity increase, you would understand that productivity increases enhance the ability of firms to produce goods and services. That increases aggregate supply. An aggregate supply increase is depicted as a movement down and to the right for aggregate supply. Were you to follow that intuition and understanding, you could check your conclusion against Table 8.2 and Figure 8.5.

Causes of Inflation

demand-pull inflation
Inflation caused by an increase in aggregate demand.

cost-push inflation
Inflation caused by a decrease in aggregate supply.

As can be seen in Figures 8.3 and 8.6, increases in prices can result from demand-side impacts or supply-side impacts. Anything that causes the aggregate demand curve to move to the right increases prices. Economists refer to the inflation caused for this reason as **demand-pull inflation**. Anything that causes the aggregate supply curve to move to the left also increases prices. Economists refer to the inflation caused for this reason as **cost-push inflation**.

Many of the things that move the aggregate demand curve to the right are things that government manipulates. If government spending is increased or taxes are decreased, aggregate demand is increased and demand-pull inflation occurs. In addition, monetary policy—government decisions about the money supply—purposefully influences interest rates. If the impact of that policy is the lowering of the rates, then the aggregate demand increases as a result of the increase in interest-sensitive consumption and investment.

During the 1960s, when President Lyndon Johnson was simultaneously carrying on the Vietnam War and attempting to wage a war on poverty, there was a substantial concern of demand-pull inflation. Government spending was increasing rapidly, and though taxes during this period also increased, inflation increased from 1 percent in 1965 to 6 percent in 1970.

Input costs are important influences on the aggregate supply curve. For example, an increase in wages that comes about because of either market actions or legislation will move the aggregate supply curve to the left, thereby increasing prices. Increases in such things as oil prices will have a similar effect on the aggregate supply curve.

The inflation of the late 1970s was largely attributable to increases in oil prices. Oil, a significant input to production throughout the economy, increased from $5.21 per barrel in 1973 to $35.15 per barrel in 1981. This, in turn, contributed to inflation rising from 3 percent in 1972 to 18 percent in the first quarter of 1980. Similarly, the short spike in inflation during 2007 through early 2008 was due, in large part, to the tripling of world oil prices during the same period. The impact of the revolutions in the Middle East during early 2011, from Tunisia, Egypt, Libya, and elsewhere caused many to be concerned that oil-related inflation would choke off the slow recoveries taking place in the U.S. and Europe.

How the Government Can Influence (but Probably Not Control) the Economy

In looking at the determinants of aggregate demand and the determinants of aggregate supply, it is clear that government can influence the economy in a number of ways. Taxes, interest rates, the strength of the dollar, and government spending make up four of the five determinants of aggregate demand outlined in Table 8.1, and these are quite clearly areas where the government can exert influence. Input prices and government regulation show up as determinants of aggregate supply in Table 8.2. The latter is quite obviously under the control of government, and there are aspects of the former in which influence is possible.

Demand-Side Macroeconomics

While Chapters 9 and 10 offer more detail on how government policy makers can influence the economy via the demand side, it is worth mentioning here as well. By raising or lowering taxes or by raising or lowering spending, Congress and the president can influence aggregate demand and thereby influence prices and output. Similarly, by raising or lowering target interest rates, the Federal Reserve can influence aggregate demand. To a lesser extent, governments—through their ability to buy or sell world currencies—can influence the value of their own currency. These are the means by which government can steer an economy out of a recession. The rapid reductions in interest rates that occurred between January 2001 and summer 2003, the cut of short-term interest rates to nearly zero in late 2008, the large-scale purchase of mortgage-backed securities by the Federal Reserve in 2008 and again from 2010 into 2013, the tax rebate checks generated in 2001, 2003, and 2008, as well as the Obama-era stimulus plan were all attempts to jumpstart the economy on the demand side.

Supply-Side Macroeconomics

During the late 1970s a new way of thinking about government's ability to influence the economy began to arise. Basically, the new way of thinking involved policy actions that would influence the aggregate supply curve. We have already seen that government spending and interest rate policy influence the aggregate demand curve. Figures 8.3 and 8.4 show that any movement in the aggregate demand curve will either increase RGDP but also increase inflation, or decrease RGDP but also decrease inflation. Movements in the aggregate supply curve to the right have only good consequences: Inflation is reduced and RGDP is increased.

supply-side economics
Government policy intended to influence the economy through aggregate supply by lowering input costs and reducing regulation.

Supply-side economics involves influencing the aggregate supply curve by lowering input costs, reducing regulation, and increasing incentives for hard work and innovation. Though advocates of supply-side economics usually advocate for changes in the tax code, such changes are not necessary. Only some of the actions the Reagan administration (1981–1989) took are properly understood as supply-side actions: Tax cuts aimed at businesses (the investment tax credit and accelerated depreciation schedules), tax code changes that significantly reduced marginal tax rates, attempts at deregulation and lax enforcement of existing regulations, and vetoing of increases in the minimum wage are clearly supply-side policies. These policies, advocates suggest, increased the incentive to innovate, take risks, and work hard by increasing after-tax rewards or by removing impediments. On the other hand, detractors argue, the large part of the tax cuts to individuals that resulted from higher standard deductions, and the even larger defense buildup, are properly thought of as typical aggregate demand-side policy.

The biggest supply-side impact in the 1980s was that the price of a barrel of oil fell from $40 to less than $10. More recently, the tax cuts proposed by President Bush in 2003 to eliminate the taxation of corporate dividends are properly thought of as supply-side economics. The argument he was making was that eliminating the double taxation of corporate dividends would stimulate businesses to invest in productivity increasing assets. Whether or not his logic was on target or flawed, the 2003 tax cut did not eliminate double taxation, though it did reduce the top tax rates on capital gains, an objective of supply-side economists. These tax cuts were a major point of difference between President Obama and Senator McCain during the 2008 campaign and between him and Governor Romney during the 2012 campaign. When Republicans won significant electoral victories in 2010, Obama agreed to extend those cuts through 2012—all because he believed that allowing taxes to rise at that time would have negative supply and demand side impacts. When the president won reelection in 2012, he had his way with tax rate increases for certain high-income earners.

Summary

This chapter introduced the aggregate demand and aggregate supply model that we will use when discussing the macroeconomy and macroeconomic issues. We first examined aggregate demand and aggregate supply in isolation, explaining why aggregate demand is downward sloping. We also looked at the shape of the aggregate supply curve in the context of the differences between classical and Keynesian views of both aggregate supply and full employment. When they were combined as one, we were able to show what happens when certain macroeconomic variables change. In that way we used them to explain the concepts of cost-push and demand-pull inflation and of supply-side economics.

Key Terms

aggregate demand (AD), 103
aggregate supply (AS), 104
cost-push inflation, 109

demand-pull inflation, 109
foreign purchases effect, 103
interest rate effect, 103

real-balances effect, 103
supply-side economics, 110

Issues Chapters You Are Ready for Now

Fiscal Policy, 114
Monetary Policy, 126

Federal Deficits, Surpluses,
   and the National Debt, 149

The Housing Bubble, 162

Quiz Yourself

1. Any event that creates a "crisis in confidence" is likely to lead to
   a. higher aggregate prices.
   b. higher aggregate output.
   c. lower aggregate prices.
   d. inflation.

2. Use the aggregate supply–aggregate demand model to determine which of the following will lead to higher prices.
   a. a tax increase.
   b. a fall in world oil prices.
   c. an increase in interest rates.
   d. an increase in government spending.

3. Use the aggregate supply–aggregate demand model to determine which of the following will lead to higher aggregate output.
   a. a tax increase.
   b. a spike in world oil prices.
   c. a cut in interest rates.
   d. a cut in government spending.

4. Congress and the president have control of the tax system and government spending. As a result, their policies will directly impact
   a. aggregate supply.
   b. aggregate demand.
   c. residual demand.
   d. the demand for loanable dollars.

5. The Federal Reserve has indirect control over short-term interest rates, and, as a result, their ability to control economic activity is through
   a. aggregate supply.
   b. aggregate demand.
   c. residual demand.
   d. the exchange rate.

6. An economist worrying about the economic impact of environmental regulations would model that impact with a
   a. decrease in aggregate supply.
   b. increase in aggregate supply.
   c. decrease in aggregate demand.
   d. increase in aggregate demand.

7. Disagreements about the shape of the aggregate supply curve focus on the degree of _____ in the economy.
   a. unemployment
   b. inflation
   c. fraud
   d. confidence

8. The use of a backward-L–shaped aggregate supply curve allows us to _____ in a way that other shapes would not.
   a. consider various levels of prices
   b. consider different macroeconomic points of view
   c. deal with shifting curves
   d. create an equilibrium

Short Answer Questions

1. Of the reasons that the aggregate demand curve and the demand curve are downward sloping, each has one labeled the "real balance effect." How are they different?

2. If we want our president to "do something" about the economy, what do we usually have in mind? How can we use the aggregate demand–aggregate supply model to show that what we have in mind will work?

3. Suppose a president says: "We are in a crisis and on the verge of another Great Depression. We need to increase government spending to give the economy a boost." What determinant of aggregate demand is the president counting on to keep us out of that depression? What determinant of aggregate demand is the president hoping you do not respond to?

4. Explain the chain of events that connect an overall price increase to a decrease in aggregate demand using the interest rate effect.

5. Define aggregate demand. Then, list and explain the intuitive reasons why aggregate demand is downward sloping.

6. Discuss the shape of the aggregate supply curve by listing and explaining the reasons behind the various ranges.

7. List and explain the three ways that the Federal Reserve controls the money supply (i.e., tools of the monetary authority).

Think about This

President Harry Truman once lamented that he wanted a "one-handed economist" because we economists have a tendency to say "on the one hand . . . but on the other hand. . . ." Economists have never made very good presidential aides because we respect the uncertainty of things; we rarely give straight answers because there are rarely simple, straight answers to give. Macroeconomics generally, and the aggregate supply–aggregate demand model specifically, embrace that uncertainty. If you were a political leader, would you want a "one-handed" economist?

Talk about This

The aggregate supply–aggregate demand model can be useful in predicting macroeconomic consequences of policy actions (like tax cuts, government spending increases, regulatory actions, interest rate adjustments). It does not tell you about the distributional aspects of policy actions. For instance, a regulatory requirement that all employers offer health insurance would shift the aggregate supply curve to the left, increasing prices and decreasing real GDP. Does that make it a bad idea? Would the impact of such a regulation on health care availability counteract these macroeconomic consequences in your mind?

CHAPTER NINE

Fiscal Policy

Learning Objectives

After reading this chapter you should be able to:

LO1 Describe and model discretionary and nondiscretionary fiscal policy using an aggregate supply and aggregate demand diagram.

LO2 Distinguish between aggregate demand and aggregate supply shocks.

LO3 Acknowledge and enumerate the problems associated with discretionary fiscal policy.

LO4 Describe nondiscretionary fiscal policy as the mainstay of our current macroeconomic system.

Chapter Outline

Nondiscretionary and Discretionary Fiscal Policy

Using Fiscal Policy to Counteract "Shocks"

Evaluating Fiscal Policy

The Obama Stimulus Plan

Kick It Up a Notch: Aggregate Supply Shocks

Summary

When you want government to "do something" about the economy, you are typically referring to **fiscal policy,** which was considered a vital tool in macroeconomics at one time. Fiscal policy is the purposeful movements in government spending or tax policy designed to direct an economy. In the United States, fiscal policy is determined by the Congress and the president.

Fiscal policy is not simply one idea; it is really two. **Discretionary fiscal policy** consists of actions taken at the time of a problem to alter the economy of the moment. **Nondiscretionary fiscal policy** is that set of policies that are built into the system to stabilize the economy when growth is either too fast or too slow.

Discretionary and nondiscretionary fiscal policy are described first. Then we consider the benefits of nondiscretionary fiscal policy and explain why some argue that discretionary fiscal

fiscal policy
The purposeful movements in government spending or tax policy designed to direct an economy.

discretionary fiscal policy
Government spending and tax changes enacted at the time of the problem to alter the economy.

nondiscretionary fiscal policy
A set of policies that are built into the system to stabilize the economy.

policy cannot claim similar benefits. We use that discussion to examine why policy makers had abandoned discretionary fiscal policy for many years. We finish by discussing the two Bush tax cuts, and specifically the child-credit rebates, in the context of reviving discretionary fiscal policy.

Nondiscretionary and Discretionary Fiscal Policy

How They Work

The difference between nondiscretionary and discretionary fiscal policy is that one is automatic and the other is not. Nondiscretionary fiscal policy, for example, includes government policies that stimulate the economy when it needs stimulus and dampen it when it needs to be dampened. Under discretionary fiscal policy, Congress and the president agree on a course of action to stimulate or dampen the economy at a specific time.

Nondiscretionary fiscal policy is at work every day as a result of policies enacted years ago. Every time you get a raise, move to a better job, or make a killing in the stock market, the government takes a portion of your improved income in taxes. The effect on your assets becomes more pronounced as you advance in the tax brackets, because when you make more money you pay a higher percentage of that income in taxes. If you happened to have been a welfare recipient and you have found a job, the effect is even greater. Not only is the government now not providing you with money; it is withholding taxes from your pay. In both cases, the effect of nondiscretionary fiscal policy is dampening the increase in your income.

Of course, nondiscretionary fiscal policy can have the opposite effect as well. If you lose your job, get demoted, or lose a lot of money in the market, your tax burden falls. If you lose your job and go back on welfare, the effect is again magnified. The government is not taking money from you but is giving money to you. This stimulates the economy somewhat, and it thus has the effect of helping to counteract the loss you incurred.

Because our progressive income tax system increases the percentage that you pay in taxes as you make more money and because federal and state programs are in place that offer economic assistance when you need it, nondiscretionary fiscal policy is constantly working to stabilize the economy. No one has to use any discretion—that is, make any decisions—to make it work. Therefore, it is called nondiscretionary fiscal policy. Because the actions are built into the system, nondiscretionary fiscal policy is often referred to as a *built-in stabilizer.*

With discretionary fiscal policy, on the other hand, action is required by Congress and the president. When each decides that the economy is in need of a specific action that will properly stimulate or dampen it, the usual actions that they consider involve changes in taxes or spending policies. Historically, fiscal policy has been used to stimulate an economy in recession but rarely to dampen an economy that is running too hot.[1]

The specific policy actions used in the past were tax cuts and funding of public works projects to give jobs to people who were unemployed. In the middle 1970s, for example, President Gerald Ford sought to provide each taxpayer with a tax rebate of $50. During the Great Depression many unemployed workers found jobs in government programs that built roads, dams, and bridges.

During his 2008 campaign, President Barack Obama promised a middle-class tax cut while promising to repeal tax cuts passed during the prior administration that went primarily to those wealthy Americans earning more

than $250,000. President Obama's election in the midst of the financial crisis of fall 2008 was quickly followed by the worst holiday shopping period in 40 years. In this context, the incoming Obama administration spent considerable time during the transition contemplating a fiscal stimulus package. What emerged was a package that included tax cuts for individuals, an extension of and an increase in unemployment benefits, aid to state and local governments both to account for the expected increases in Medicaid enrollment and to forestall the need for significant state and local budget cuts, spending on a series of projects that were priorities for Democrats, and spending on what were called "shovel-ready" infrastructure projects.

The individual tax cuts were structured differently from the 2001, 2003, and 2008 rebates in that they were implemented through short-term changes to withholding tables. The Bush rebates came first with paper checks, then with a combination of paper checks and direct deposits to banks. With each rebate there was a period of time from the passage of the package to the time when the money was in the hands of the consumer. The economists advising President Obama were convinced that there were two significant problems with the Bush-era rebates. They took too long to get into taxpayers' hands and too much of the money was saved rather than spent. They believed that by changing withholding tables they could speed up the process as well as induce more spending by giving average taxpayers smaller amounts per week rather than a large amount at once.

Using Aggregate Supply and Aggregate Demand to Model Fiscal Policy

Our aggregate supply and aggregate demand model is a useful tool for examining the effect of both forms of fiscal policy. Both discretionary and nondiscretionary fiscal policy work to move the aggregate demand curve. Figure 9.1 shows the effect of expansionary fiscal policy and Figure 9.2 shows the effect of contractionary fiscal policy. *Expansionary* fiscal policy options, such as increased government spending and decreases in taxes, are reflected in an aggregate demand curve that moves to the right. *Contractionary* fiscal policy options, including decreased government spending and increases in taxes, are seen in an aggregate demand curve that moves to the left.

It should be noted that there is considerable debate over whether any fiscal policy will have a real impact on the economy. A useful but relatively simplistic way

---

[1]A one-year 10 percent surtax was added to income taxes in the Lyndon Johnson administration. Some justified this action as an effort to combat inflation.

FIGURE 9.1   Expansionary fiscal policy.

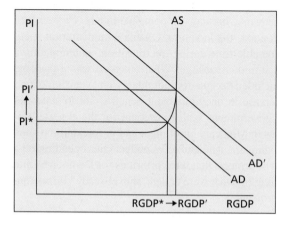

FIGURE 9.2   Contractionary fiscal policy.

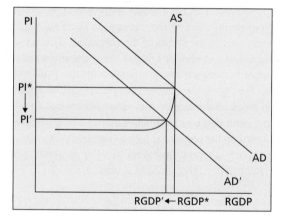

of thinking about this argument is to frame it in terms of where on the aggregate supply curve the economy lies. Those who believe that we are on the vertical portion of the curve argue that any expansionary fiscal policy will be completely ineffective. It will merely create inflation without bolstering output.

It is worth mentioning that the money necessary to engage in expansionary fiscal policy does not come out of thin air. The increased government spending and the reduced tax revenue generate a shortfall that must be made up with either borrowing or printing the requisite money. Economists do not consider the latter option a good one in that inflation is nearly always the result. Thus deficits financed through borrowing money tend to be the result of expansionary fiscal policy.

Using Fiscal Policy to Counteract "Shocks"

Aggregate Demand Shocks

Neither expansionary nor contractionary actions happen in a vacuum. They happen because the economy moves unexpectedly to make RGDP much higher or much lower than policy makers think is healthy. Figures 9.3 and 9.4 show the impact of these **shocks,** or unexpected moves. In each we suppose that aggregate demand is what moves unexpectedly, and in each we start with it at AD_1. Because of a shock it unexpectedly moves to AD_2. If a slump in aggregate demand causes a recession, like Figure 9.3, then the aggregate demand curve moves from AD_1 to AD_2. When people lose their jobs, welfare spending will have

shock
Any unanticipated economic event.

FIGURE 9.3   A negative aggregate demand shock.

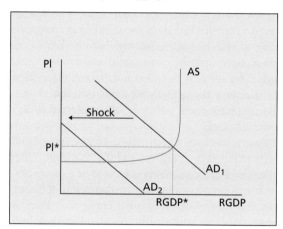

FIGURE 9.4   A positive aggregate demand shock.

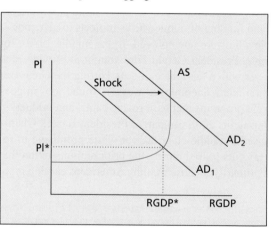

FIGURE 9.5 Nondiscretionary and discretionary fiscal policy as it combats a recession.

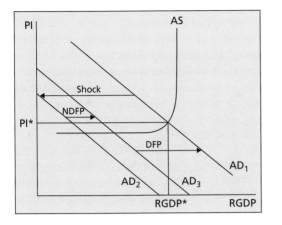

to rise and tax revenue will fall. As Figure 9.5 shows, this nondiscretionary fiscal policy moves the aggregate demand curve partially back to AD₃. Expansionary discretionary fiscal policy (either increases in government spending or decreases in taxes) can move aggregate demand all the way back to AD₁.

If a jump in aggregate demand causes an overheated economy, like Figure 9.4, then the aggregate demand curve moves from AD₁ to AD₂. When people get better jobs or raises, welfare spending will fall and tax revenue will rise. As Figure 9.6 shows, this nondiscretionary fiscal policy moves the aggregate demand curve partially back to AD₃. Contractionary discretionary fiscal policy (either decreases in government spending or increases in taxes) can move aggregate demand all the way back to AD₁.

FIGURE 9.6 Nondiscretionary and discretionary fiscal policy as it combats an overheated economy.

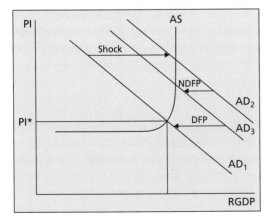

Nondiscretionary fiscal policy (NDFP) moves it back toward AD₁ to AD₃, and discretionary fiscal policy (DFP) can move it all the way back to AD₁ again. In theory, whether the economy experiences a positive demand shock or a negative one, the government can use both discretionary and nondiscretionary fiscal policy to return us to a healthy economy.

We need to ask at this point how it is that aggregate demand can move unexpectedly. There are a number of reasons and each involves the reaction of people to their predictions of the future. If people's positive view of the health of the economy spurs them to buy new cars or furnishings, an aggregate demand curve will move to the right. If the opposite happens and people decide to delay buying these expensive items because of negative feelings

aggregate demand shock
An unexpected event which causes aggregate demand to increase or decrease.

about the economy, the aggregate demand curve will move to the left. Tracking the "feeling" that people have about the economy is not easy and therefore large, unexpected swings can upset the economy. Economists call these swings **aggregate demand shocks.**

Aggregate Supply Shocks

Along with aggregate demand shocks, we must also deal with the problem of aggregate supply shocks. Usu-

aggregate supply shock
An unexpected event that causes aggregate supply to increase or decrease.

ally an **aggregate supply shock** involves an important natural resource. It should come as no surprise that recent supply shocks have all involved the price of oil. During the 1973 Arab–Israeli war, for example, the price of oil climbed dramatically. During the Iran–Iraq war, the price of oil fell dramatically as both sides increased production to pay for war material. The tripling of world oil prices from 2007 to mid-2008 and the dramatic plummeting of those prices from summer 2008 through early 2009 each had dramatic aggregate supply impacts.

Even more recently, the early 2011 uprisings throughout the Middle East illustrated the uncertainty effect of these supply shocks. Crude oil prices, which were below $80 per barrel in January 2011, rose above $100 per barrel with the Libyan uprising, even though Libya itself is a relatively minor producer of oil (3 percent of world production).

Whether drastic changes are positive or negative, policy makers are frequently called upon to do something to counter that aggregate supply shock, and, because they very frequently have little control over the events that cause those shocks, they may wish to use discretionary fiscal policy to mitigate the economic impact.

Evaluating Fiscal Policy

Nondiscretionary Fiscal Policy

Nondiscretionary fiscal policy serves to get output moving back toward the desired level, RGDP*, but it works much better when the shock is to aggregate demand rather than to aggregate supply. In addition, even though previous Congresses and presidents developed tax and spending policies to get the country out of a recession, such discretionary fiscal policy just does not work as well as does nondiscretionary policy.

Since the Great Depression of the 1930s, the U.S. economy has successfully avoided the sorts of boom and bust cycles that plagued the 19th century. The degree to which the built-in stabilizing effect of a welfare state and a progressive tax system generated this state of affairs is debated by economic historians. The two most significant post–World War II recessions, the one in 1982 and the one that extended from late 2007 to mid-2009, were far less onerous than any of the financial panics of the 1800s.

Discretionary Fiscal Policy

You might think that discretionary fiscal policy would work as well. If you did, you would be wrong, but you would be in good company. By the 1950s and 1960s, most economists were confident that discretionary fiscal policy would essentially eliminate the instability of recessions. By 1980 most economists had given up on discretionary fiscal policy. Coincidentally or not, during the 20 years that followed, the United States experienced half the usual number of recessions.

What transformed economists from overconfident discretionary fiscal policy champions in the 1960s to ardent detractors in the 1980s was the very poor performance of these policies during the 1970s. The preceding aggregate demand and aggregate supply analysis is nice to look at, and the nondiscretionary fiscal policy part does work as advertised, but discretionary fiscal policy was more of a fantasy of economists. In the 1950s and 1960s, economists were confident that Congress could know exactly how much stimulus or dampening would be necessary to get the economy back to a desired level of RGDP. Congress would then pass a bill that the president would sign

to implement that policy. As a practical matter, it just did not work in the ways economists predicted it would.

The reasons discretionary fiscal policy does not work as well as advertised (or perhaps at all) are three-fold. First, the failures can be attributed to lags in recognizing, administering, and operating fiscal policy. Second, the failures can result from political motivations overwhelming economic reason, and third, there can be immediate counter-effects with both aggregate demand and aggregate supply, which partially or completely eliminate the positive intent of the policies.

recognition lag
The time it takes to measure the state of the economy.

administrative lag
The time it takes for Congress and the president to agree on a course of action.

operational lag
The time it takes for the full impact of a government program or tax change to have its effect on the economy.

On the issue of the lags, the first of these is the **recognition lag,** which means that the economy in general, and RGDP in particular, is measured with a considerable lag. The second, the **administrative lag,** results because it takes time for Congress and the president to agree on a course of action. The third, the **operational lag,** results because it takes quite a while for the full impact of a government program or tax change to have its effect on the economy.

The recognition lag results from the fact that gross domestic product is not easily and immediately measured. Quarterly GDP is first estimated using reasonably good predictors that are available soon after the end of the quarter. Later, more data are brought to bear and GDP is reestimated. Only after many months is a final GDP figure given. Thus we do not know for sure whether we are in a recession until months after it begins. Similarly, we do not know when we are out of a recession until months after it ends. The problem this creates was highlighted by the 2007–2009 recession. It was late fall 2008 before the National Bureau of Economic Research Business Cycle Dating Committee identified fall 2007 as the beginning of the recession. While it was clear by late summer 2008 that the economy was slowing dramatically, it was a full year after the recession began before it was universally acknowledged. At the end of the 2001 recession, the economy was growing so slowly that it took until summer 2003 for economists to declare the recession had actually ended in the fall of 2001. This meant that by the time they had declared a recession had started, it was almost over and by the time they had declared it over, it had actually been over for a year and a half. The recession of 2007–2009 was not declared to have ended in

June 2009 until September 2010. The stimulus package had not yet spent more than 10 percent of the allocated funds by that time.

The administrative lag results from the inherent inefficiency of American democracy. We have two legislative bodies that must first agree with each other and then must agree with the president. The president, the House, or the Senate can delay or derail fiscal policy. Even if they choose to work on a given problem, Congress never solves a problem without disagreements. They may agree, for example, that we are in a recession but will not be able to decide whether to engage in discretionary fiscal policy through tax cuts or through spending programs. Even when they agree on that, they may argue over the kinds of tax cuts to make, who should get them, what kinds of spending programs would be appropriate, and the congressional districts that should be benefited. By the time they finally agree, of course, more time has passed.

This is quite well illustrated by the political wrangling over the 2008 financial system rescue plan and the 2009 stimulus package. Both presidential candidates were in agreement that the Troubled Asset Relief Program (TARP) was necessary, but it took nearly a month for the plan to pass. Even with significant majorities in both houses and two and a half months from his election to his swearing in, it took President Obama five additional weeks to get a stimulus plan through Congress. Much of the disagreement surrounded the size and composition of the package. Conservative economists and members of Congress were concerned about the budget deficit implications of the package. Liberal economists and members of Congress were concerned that the package would be of insufficient size to have the desired impact. These are perfectly legitimate differences of opinion, but the debate took time.

The operational lag offers the final roadblock to effective discretionary fiscal policy. Even supposing that Congress and the president agree on time that a policy is needed and they agree on the type of policy, it takes months, if not years, for discretionary fiscal policy to have its desired effects.

If the discretionary fiscal policy takes the form of increases in highway construction, a program that increases the numbers of jobs available, federal contracts usually do not pay the entire amount up front. Contractors are paid in the stages of building, and it takes quite a while to go from the beginning of a large construction project to its end. To avoid this delay, the Obama stimulus package hoped to include mostly "shovel-ready" infrastructure plans. The idea was to take plans that had already gone through the design phase. In so doing, the hope was to get these projects started the moment funds became available. It bears repeating that when the recession of 2007–2009 ended in June 2009, less than 10 percent of the stimulus funds from the bill that had passed that February had been spent.

As for the tax aspects of fiscal policy, the vast majority of the money going to taxpayers went to them well after it was needed. The 2001, 2003, and 2008 summer rebate checks and the change to withholding tables in 2009 are evidence that tax cuts can make their way into the economy somewhat more quickly. In the pre-2009 cases, the laws generating the rebates were passed at least six months before the money was fully in the hands of consumers. The downside to these relatively quick tax cuts is that their impacts are often muted by those who use the extra money to save or to pay down existing debt.

The Political Problems with Fiscal Policy

Another argument against discretionary fiscal policy is that even if it worked, vote-obsessed politicians would not use it properly. Aside from the bias toward expansionary fiscal policy alluded to in the introduction, there is the question of who will be affected by any changes in taxation or spending policies. In addition, there is the complication caused by politicians too concerned with re-election. They seek to expand the economy in presidential election years only to act responsibly after the election.

The first of these issues raises questions of political motivation. Whether large-scale, federally funded building projects are needed is one question; where they will go is quite another. For instance, whether the revamped Boston mass transit system, referred to by many as the "big dig," was motivated by purely engineering reasons or because influential members of Congress lived in the area is debatable. Similarly, critics have charged that political influence alone was behind the placement of a majority of highway demonstration projects in the early 1990s in West Virginia. While these are examples of Democrats engaging in steering tax dollars, Republicans too have engaged in such practices. Between 1995 and 2001, the GOP majority leader and the chair of the Senate Appropriations Committee made certain that disproportionate dollars were spent in their home states. The infamous "bridge to nowhere" in Alaska provides an excellent example of politically motivated infrastructure projects. Noted economist James Buchanan and others have suggested that all federal spending, but in particular that spending that is done in the name of fiscal policy, is susceptible to this kind of problem.

TABLE 9.1   Real growth rates by presidential terms.

Source: Bureau of Economic Analysis, www.bea.gov

President	First Year	Second Year	Third Year	Fourth Year
Truman	−0.5	8.7	7.7	3.8
Eisenhower I	4.6	−0.7	7.1	1.9
Eisenhower II	2.0	−1.0	7.1	2.5
Kennedy/Johnson	2.3	6.1	4.4	5.8
Johnson	6.4	6.5	2.5	4.8
Nixon I	3.1	0.2	3.4	5.3
Nixon II/Ford	5.8	−0.5	−0.2	5.3
Carter	4.6	5.6	3.2	0.2
Reagan I	2.5	−1.9	4.5	7.2
Reagan II	4.1	3.5	3.2	4.1
Bush GHW	3.6	1.9	−0.2	3.4
Clinton I	2.9	4.1	2.5	3.7
Clinton II	4.5	4.4	4.8	4.1
Bush GW I	1.1	1.8	2.5	3.5
Bush GW II	3.1	2.7	1.9	−0.3
Obama	−3.1	2.4	1.8	2.2
Average	2.9	2.7	3.5	3.6

There is also the problem of the **political business cycle**. It is suggested that politicians, particularly presidents, will add new spending and tax policies to their pre-election-year budgets to boost the economy in time for their own or their party's reelection. Table 9.1 suggests that this might be the case, given that the average of growth rates in the fourth year of presidential terms of office is slightly higher than that of first-year growth rates.

political business cycle
Politically motivated fiscal policy used for short-term gain just prior to elections.

Criticism from the Right and Left

There were many economists, mainly on the conservative end of the spectrum, who advised against a fiscal stimulus of any kind and then were only too happy to say "I told you so" when, by their calculations, the impact of the 2009 stimulus package was less than the Obama administration had predicted. John Cogan, John Taylor, and others argued that the impact was, if anything, small and temporary, and quite possibly negative. They argued that the only way to truly stimulate consumption and investment is to make long-term structural changes to tax rates in ways that consumers and businesses can confidently predict that their future after-tax income will be higher.

Liberal (and Nobel prize-winning) economist Paul Krugman was just as derisive of the stimulus package as these conservative economists, yet his point of attack was that it was predictably too small to have any of its desired impacts. While dismissing the conservative economists' estimation of the importance of, as he called it, "the confidence fairy," he and others argued as early as December 2008 that policy makers were understating what was necessary by a factor of at least two. Since that time Krugman repeatedly pointed to the fact that total government spending declined in 2010 and 2011 because state and local governments were cutting back on spending by more than the federal government was increasing spending.

The Rise, Fall, and Rebirth of Discretionary Fiscal Policy

In the 1970s it became apparent to policy makers that discretionary fiscal policy was not up to the task of stabilizing the economy. The lags were just too important to ignore, and the recessions of the 1970s had been too short for these recessions to be recognized, laws to be passed, and money spent in time to have any effect on them.

Despite the preceding cautions about the effectiveness of discretionary fiscal policy, its arguments have been used to bolster particular programs. President Clinton used the discretionary fiscal policy argument in 1993 to bolster a $16 billion investment program. Critics defeated his proposal, suggesting that we were already out of the recession and its size was too small to have any impact.

An odd coincidence happened on the way to the grave for discretionary fiscal policy. When the 2001 Bush tax cut passed in May of that year, it was not known then that we were already in a recession. In addition, instead of implementing the tax cut prospectively, it was made retroactive to the beginning of the year, and instead of having taxpayers wait until they filed their tax forms in 2002 to claim their money, rebate checks were sent out in anticipation of those cuts. These checks started arriving in August and September of that year and were nearly fully dispersed when the terrorist attacks of September 11 occurred. Together with a series of interest rate cuts, these tax cuts had the fortunate coincidence of stimulating the economy at precisely the time the stimulus was needed.

When the economy had not picked up much steam through early 2003, President Bush proposed another tax cut. What he proposed was not at all what passed, but what did pass was remarkably similar to what had passed in 2001. Again, rebate checks began arriving in taxpayers' mailboxes in late summer 2003.

The Obama Stimulus Plan

The clearest sign that discretionary fiscal policy was back as a policy tool under active consideration came with the election of Barack Obama as president of the United States. Prior to that, it had been more than 30 years since policy makers actively sought to increase aggregate demand through increases in government spending rather than through tax rebates.

As shown in Table 9.2, the plan itself had four basic elements. The first was to shore up the state-run unemployment, welfare, and Medicaid systems. Though the money had to be appropriated through an act of

TABLE 9.2   The Obama stimulus plan as originally enacted.

Stimulus Plan Element	Amount in $ Millions
Nondiscretionary fiscal policy: Unemployment, welfare, Medicaid	$135,832
Aid to states	53,600
Discretionary fiscal policy: Tax cuts	301,135
Discretionary fiscal policy: Spending increases	300,047

Source: www.recovery.gov/Transparency/fundingoverview/Pages/fundingbreakdown .aspx

Congress, this is best labeled as nondiscretionary fiscal policy as it is a regular part of the federal government's response to economic difficulty. The second element in the plan is not as readily categorized because though it was "discretionary" in that the federal government could have chosen to let states ride out the recession on their own, it was intended to allow states to make it through the 2009 and 2010 fiscal years without having to cut budgets and raise taxes. In essence, this portion was designed to allow states—that often are constitutionally prevented from borrowing—to engage in their own form of nondiscretionary fiscal policy. The remainder was clearly discretionary as it was motivated by a desire to speed a recovery rather than to simply mitigate the impact of it. It remains to be seen whether the stimulus package passed in 2009 was too large, too small, solved the problem, or created other problems. It also remains to be seen, after the 2010 political season when "stimulus" became a dirty word to many across the political spectrum, whether discretionary fiscal policy goes back into the hole it was in between 1980 and 2000.

DID THE OBAMA STIMULUS WORK?

The question of whether the Obama stimulus package worked or not depends entirely on what you assume the counterfactual to be. Recall that a "counterfactual" to a policy is a story associated with what the result would have most likely been had there been no change in policy. Had there been no stimulus package of any kind, had there been no assistance to states to cover higher unemployment and Medicaid claims, had there been no extension of Bush-era tax rates, had there been no "Making Work Pay" credit, had there been no money for shovel-ready

projects, Cash-for-Clunkers, or for alternative energy development, what would have been the result? The judged effectiveness of the stimulus package as a whole, therefore, depends on how you create the counterfactual.

There are, generally speaking, two branches of counterfactuals: Keynesian ones and Ricardian equivalence ones. Keynesian counterfactuals assume that the $787 billion stimulus was all new money being spent and was not displacing any money that would have been spent elsewhere, by someone, even perhaps by another level of government. Ricardian equivalence coun-terfactuals assume that people foresee that current and tempo-rary increases in the deficit will ultimately necessitate future tax increases or spending cuts to pay for it, or that federal grants received by states are offset by reductions in what states would have otherwise borrowed. In this way, currently higher deficits and the private and other level government reactions to those deficits completely wipe out any effect of the policy.

For instance, if you assume that people only bought the cars they did because of the Cash-for-Clunkers program so that all spending on those cars, including the subsidy, was induced by the program, you would, by the evidence, be wrong. In fact, most of the cars purchased during that period were by people who happened to be in the market for a new car anyway and had a "clunker" to trade in. Similarly, if you assume that states would have chosen not to borrow money to provide for Medicaid coverage for those people who were forced on to the program because of their lost jobs, you would count the extra money pro-vided to the states for that purpose by the federal government as extra money that was spent that wouldn't have been. That is probably wrong in some states and correct in others.

However, sometimes the money spent as part of the stim-ulus was clearly new money that resulted from the stimulus. Even the most strident anti-stimulus economists acknowledge that unemployment benefits were extended and made more generous using federal money and that money was available only through the stimulus. The fact that almost all that money was spent by relatively poor recipients has a stimulatory im-pact. Some economists would still quibble with this as stimulus

because they would argue that those who were unemployed and receiving long-term benefits were less likely to accept the reality of lesser jobs at lower wages and that the benefits merely extended their ability to convince or even delude them-selves that their old jobs would reappear at their old wage levels.

The stimulus plan's supporters point to the relatively short period of economic distress in the United States relative to on-going challenges in Europe where there was relatively little ap-petite for stimulus. They argue that the United States emerged from the Great Recession to rates of growth that were, while slow, generally more brisk than did European nations. Detrac-tors simply point to the very slow recovery in real GDP and very slow drop in unemployment in the United States. They point to investments in companies that ultimately went bankrupt or to shovel-ready projects that had little infrastructure-enhancing purpose. They point to large decreases in the percentage of the population working or seeking work, the primary driver for reduced rates of unemployment.

There is no consensus on this topic. Noble prize winners are on both sides of the debate. If the measure to be used to judge its overall effectiveness is the median estimate of its ultimate impact, then the impact was modestly effective. Sev-eral economists have prepared estimates of the impact of the stimulus. A simple summary of the studies done on the topic is included below. Given that the term stimulus became a politi-cal "dirty word" shortly after the package's passage, it appears that academic economists have a greater appetite for discre-tionary fiscal policy than does the public.

Study	Authors	Conclusions
"Did the Stimulus Stimulate? Real Time Estimates of the Effects of the American Recovery and Rein-vestment Act"	James Feyrer, Bruce Sacerdote	Significantly positive
"Does State Fiscal Relief during Recessions In-crease Employment? Evidence from the American Recovery and Reinvestment Act"	Gabriel Chodorow-Reich, Laura Feiveson, Zachary Liscow, and William Gui Woolston	Significantly positive
"Estimated Impact of the American Recovery and Reinvestment Act on Employment and Economic Output from January 2011 through March 2011"	Benjamin Page and Felix Reichling	Mostly Positive
"Targeted Transfers and the Fiscal Response to the Great Recession"	Hyunseung Oh and Ricardo Reis	Mildly Positive
"The American Recovery and Reinvestment Act: Public Sector Jobs Saved, Private Sector Jobs Forestalled"	Timothy Conley and Bill Dupor	No Impact
"An Empirical Analysis of the Revival of Fiscal Activism in the 2000s"	John B. Taylor	No Impact

A more detailed summary of these and other papers can be found at www.washingtonpost.com under the title "Did the Stimulus Work? A Review of the Nine Best Studies on the Subject." It was authored by Dylan Matthews.

Kick It Up a Notch

AGGREGATE SUPPLY SHOCKS

In both Figures 9.7 and 9.8 we start out with AS_1 crossing AD_1 so that prices are at PI* and output is at RGDP*. A hypothetical shock moves aggregate supply to AS_2. If the supply shock is negative and it raises input prices substantially, as in Figure 9.7, people will lose their jobs as RGDP falls. Nondiscretionary fiscal policy will kick in at this point, though, because the loss of jobs will mean an increase in welfare spending and a decrease in taxes. This will cause aggregate demand to shift to the right to AD_2. If the president and Congress then decide to go further with discretionary fiscal policy in an effort to get output back to RGDP*, they will have to cut taxes or raise

spending to do so. The problem is that the shock itself and the nondiscretionary fiscal policy that was implemented have already created high inflation. Discretionary fiscal policy can only serve to worsen the problem.

On the other hand, if the supply shock is that input prices have fallen, as depicted in Figure 9.8, output increases. Nondiscretionary fiscal policy is such that taxes go up and welfare spending goes down. When this happens, aggregate demand falls to AD_2. In this case there is no need for discretionary fiscal policy because, even though there is a shock, it is only for the good. Both the shock and the nondiscretionary fiscal policy also serve to calm inflation.

FIGURE 9.7 Nondiscretionary and discretionary fiscal policy in the wake of a negative aggregate supply shock.

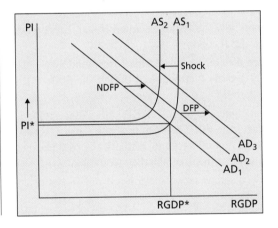

FIGURE 9.8 Nondiscretionary fiscal policy in the wake of a positive aggregate supply shock.

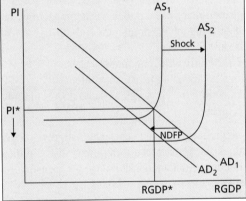

Summary

You now understand the difference between discretionary and nondiscretionary fiscal policy and know how to model them using an aggregate supply and aggregate demand diagram. You understand that different policies are used to counteract aggregate demand and aggregate

supply shocks. You also now understand that though there are considerable problems associated with discretionary fiscal policy, it has seen a recent revival. Still, nondiscretionary fiscal policy remains a mainstay of our current macroeconomic system.

Key Terms

administrative lag, 118
aggregate demand shock, 117
aggregate supply shock, 117
discretionary fiscal policy, 114

fiscal policy, 114
nondiscretionary fiscal policy, 114
operational lag, 118
political business cycle, 120

recognition lag, 118
shock, 116

Quiz Yourself

1. The existence of the federal income tax and the welfare system serve as the primary elements of
   a. discretionary fiscal policy.
   b. nondiscretionary fiscal policy.
   c. monetary policy.
   d. exchange rate policy.

2. Adjustments to tax and spending policies serve as primary elements of
   a. discretionary fiscal policy.
   b. nondiscretionary fiscal policy.
   c. monetary policy.
   d. exchange rate policy.

3. Discretionary fiscal policy is the purview of
   a. Congress only.
   b. the president only.
   c. Congress and the president collectively through law.
   d. the Federal Reserve.

4. Nondiscretionary fiscal policy has its impact by
   a. magnifying the economic ups and downs already occurring.
   b. purposefully adjusting interest rates.
   c. congress focusing its constant attention.
   d. dampening the economic ups and downs already occurring.

5. The aggregate demand–aggregate supply model examines the impact of discretionary fiscal policy and nondiscretionary fiscal policy by focusing on movements of
   a. interest rates.
   b. aggregate supply.
   c. aggregate demand.
   d. regulatory policies.

6. One typical response to a recession for those interested in discretionary fiscal policy is to
   a. raise taxes and cut spending.
   b. lower taxes and cut spending.
   c. raise taxes and increase spending.
   d. lower taxes and increase spending.

7. One typical response to an overheated economy for those interested in discretionary fiscal policy is to
   a. raise taxes and cut spending.
   b. lower taxes and cut spending.
   c. raise taxes and increase spending.
   d. lower taxes and increase spending.

8. Discretionary fiscal policy as a tool for making things better is
   a. universally applauded as being helpful.
   b. universally derided for never being effective.
   c. considered by many to be effective but subject to several concerns over timing and motive.
   d. inconsistent with the aggregate demand–aggregate supply model.

9. The oil price increases of 2002–2005 are an example of a
   a. positive aggregate demand shock.
   b. negative aggregate demand shock.
   c. positive aggregate supply shock.
   d. negative aggregate supply shock.

Short Answer Questions

1. Which lag described in this chapter is the concept of "shovel-ready" intended to combat.

2. Explain how the built-in economic stabilizers work in the U.S. economy.

3. Assign the correct label to the corresponding events/policy actions that occurred during the 2007–2011 time period.
   Events/policy actions: TARP, the 2009 stimulus package, the 2010 extension of the Bush tax cuts, the reduction in taxes most Americans paid because they had less income than they would have had.
   Label: discretionary fiscal policy, nondiscretionary fiscal policy.

Think about This

Concerns over the recognition, administrative, and operational lags as well as the concern that discretionary fiscal policy is subject to political biases have caused some economists to believe Congress and the president should do nothing in the face of a recession. Even if they are correct, is it realistic to expect the public to embrace elected officials who do nothing?

Talk about This

The third and fourth years of presidential terms have higher average rates of real growth than the first and second years. Do you think this is a coincidence or is it a reflection of political reality that politicians are more concerned about reelection than about creating long-run economic growth?

For More Insight See

Journal of Economic Perspectives 14, no. 3 (Summer 2000). See articles written by Alberto Alesina, John B. Taylor, Alan Auerbach, and Daniel Feenberg, and Douglas Elmendorf and Louise Sheiner.

Any textbook entitled *Intermediate Macroeconomics* will have a chapter on fiscal policy.

Behind the Numbers

Gross domestic product.

U.S. Bureau of Economic Analysis; gross domestic product; historical data—www.bea.gov

Early estimates of GD.

U.S. Bureau of Economic Analysis; news release— www.bea.gov/newsreleases/rels.htm

CHAPTER TEN

Monetary Policy

Learning Objectives

After reading this chapter you should be able to:

LO1   Describe the role of the Federal Reserve of the United States.

LO2   Define macroeconomic stability as the Fed's primary goal while noting that controlling inflation has typically been the means by which it has measured its success.

LO3   Integrate an understanding of the tools of monetary policy with their application utilizing an aggregate supply–aggregate demand model.

LO4   Describe the recent history of monetary policy and the Federal Reserve's role in the 2007–2009 recession.

Chapter Outline

Goals, Tools, and a Model of Monetary Policy

Central Bank Independence

Modern Monetary Policy

Summary

Throughout the 2007–2009 recession and beyond, the role of the Federal Reserve—usually called the Fed—in shaping the economy of the United States has grown from mysterious yet important to absolutely central, with politicians, the media, and, on some days, ordinary Americans glued to its actions. No more important aspect of our daily lives is run by people with as little accountability as those who are its executive officers. The Federal Reserve began in 1913 as a response to the boom and bust nature of the financial world of the late 19th and early 20th century. It has become a government institution every bit as important in the lives of people as the three branches of government we learn about in school. In a matter of a couple of hours, one person, the chairman of the Federal Reserve Board, can influence stock prices by 5 percent, cause mortgage interest rates to rise or fall by a full percentage point, and set in place a course of action that will raise or lower the unemployment rate by a point or more. The chairman can do this, moreover, without the approval of or even consultation with any elected person. Fortunately, the chairmen appointed by

presidents and confirmed by the Senate have all been people of impeccable character. Even if their wisdom has been clouded at some points, a hint of corruption in this area of government would be devastating to world financial markets in particular and, by extension, to the whole world economy.

We will use the context of the 2007–2009 recession, and the very slow recovery from it, to explore the goals of monetary policy and then move to discuss the tools the Federal Reserve has to meet those goals. We will begin the discussion of those tools by first focusing on the traditional and ordinary tools of monetary policy and then discuss the extraordinary ones that were first employed in 2008 as the Federal Reserve attempted to stabilize first the financial markets and later the overall economy. As we move through the chapter, we will consider why the Fed exists and why its independence from political winds is important. Next we review some of the history of the pre-2008 use of monetary policy and then move to an examination of Fed policy during and after the 2007–2009 recession.

Goals, Tools, and a Model of Monetary Policy

The Federal Reserve has never had a "tool" that would directly impact the economy. Its goals have to be met using an intermediate target with the hope and expectation that the end result of hitting the intermediate target will be satisfaction of the ultimate goal. What follows then is a description of the goals of monetary policy, the tools of monetary policy that until 2008 were considered adequate to the task of meeting those goals, and a model that explains why the tools work under typical circumstances. We proceed to an explanation of why those tools failed in 2008 and then to a discussion of the extraordinary tools that the Federal Reserve, under Chairman Ben Bernanke, created to deal with the 2007–2009 recession and the tenuous recovery in 2010 and 2011.

Goals of Monetary Policy

The most important historical role for monetary policy and its implementing institution, the Federal Reserve, has been to prevent boom and bust cycles by regulating banks and other financial institutions. While the role of dampening the boom and bust cycle remains an important part of the job, the mechanism has changed dramatically. At first the Fed simply ensured the financial soundness of institutions. Now it also directly manipulates interest rates to change the borrowing habits of banks, businesses, and consumers. In this way it seeks to maintain low levels of inflation and sustainable levels of real GDP growth.

Traditional and Ordinary Tools of Monetary Policy

For the better part of the last 50 years, the Federal Reserve and other similar central banks around the world have been conducting monetary policy by picking an intermediate target variable and utilizing the basic tools at their disposal to hit that target. If the target variable was outside the desired range, the Fed used its tools to nudge the variable back within the range. At times the Fed has had to abandon its target because the policies necessary to stay within the desired range had undesirable effects.

federal funds rate
The rate at which banks borrow from one another to meet reserve requirements.

In the 1970s the target was the **federal funds rate**—the rate at which banks borrow from one another to meet reserve requirements. As inflation heated up in the late 1970s, targeting the federal funds rate proved to be impossible. Keeping the rate down required a continuous increase in the supply of money. As more money chased limited goods, those increases created even greater inflation. This caused interest rates to rise rather than fall. In October 1979, as the rate of inflation continued to rise, the Fed formally gave up on the federal funds rate as its target and shifted to targeting **M2**. M2 is what is known as a **monetary aggregate**. M2 is a broader measure of money because it includes cash, checking accounts, savings accounts, and small certificates of deposit (CDs). **M1** includes only cash and checking accounts.[1] By the summer of 1982, inflation had subsided just as M2 became unstable and too difficult to target. In response the Fed reverted to targeting the federal funds rate.

M2
M1 + saving accounts + small CDs.

monetary aggregate
A measure of the quantity of money in the economy.

M1
Cash + coin + checking accounts.

inflation targeting
A policy whereby a central bank publishes a desired range of a specified inflationary measure and then using the tools of monetary policy to bring that measure of inflation into that desired range.

open-market operations
The buying and selling of bonds, which, respectively, increases or decreases the money supply, thereby influencing interest rates.

The European Central Bank currently targets inflation rather than a monetary aggregate or interest rate. **Inflation targeting** is relatively new as a concept and involves publishing a desired range of a specified inflationary measure and then using the tools of monetary policy to bring that measure of inflation into that desired range. Many argue that from the time Benjamin Bernanke took over as Fed chair in 2006 to the beginning of the financial crisis in the fall of 2007, the Fed engaged in de facto inflation targeting. The Fed made clear through its regular announcements that it was closely monitoring the core PCE deflator described in Chapter 6.

Whatever is targeted, the mechanism by which the Fed keeps day-to-day tabs on the target is **open-market operations.** Open-market operations result when the Fed buys and sells government debt. The Fed owns approximately half a trillion dollars of the national debt, and it sells a portion of that reserve of bonds when it wants to get money out of the system. It buys bonds when it wants to add to the money that is in circulation.

---

[1] In 2006 the Fed abandoned its use of M3 as a useful measure as it was becoming unstable and therefore an unreliable measure.

MONEY CREATION

One of the lessons that economists routinely teach students in courses designed for economics and business majors is the notion of "money creation." The banking system can create more "money" than physically exists in the form of coin and cash. This was implied in our definitions of the monetary aggregates (M1, M2, etc.) because if money were only currency, then there would be no need to add checkable accounts and CDs.

The banking system creates money by a series of loans. To see how, let's assume that there are several people (John, Paul, George, Ringo, Simon, Randy, and Paula) and several banks (1st National, 2nd National, 3rd National, and 4th National [the Midwest is home to an actual bank called "Fifth-Third"]).

Suppose John makes a $1,000 deposit at 1st National, and that bank loans Paul $900 (10 percent, or $100, must be held as part of the required reserve). Suppose Paul buys something from George, who deposits that $900 at 2nd National. Then suppose that Ringo borrows $810 (again 10 percent, or $90, must be held at the Fed) from 2nd National to buy something from Simon, who deposits that money in 3rd National. If Randy borrows $729 (10 percent, or $81, must be held at the Fed) from 3rd National to buy something from Paula and Paula deposits that money in 4th National and.... You get the point—this could go on forever. In the end there are deposits totaling $10,000 ($1,000 + $900 + $810 + $729 + ...) that resulted from that initial $1,000).

Banks can also borrow directly from the Fed rather than borrowing from each other. Banks with sufficient creditworthiness can borrow unlimited amounts from the Fed at the primary credit rate. The **primary credit rate or discount rate** is typically one percentage point higher than the federal funds rate. Banks with lesser credit ratings face higher rates.[2]

primary credit rate or discount rate
The rate at which banks with excellent credit can borrow from the Federal Reserve.

reserve ratio
The percentage of every dollar deposited in a checking account that a bank must maintain at a Federal Reserve branch.

The last way that the Federal Reserve can impact interest rates is by altering the proportion that the bank can lend from the deposits it takes in. The **reserve ratio,** at 10 percent in 2011, requires that a specific percentage of every dollar deposited be placed in a Federal Reserve bank. If the ratio is lowered, the bank has more money to lend, whereas if the ratio is raised, the bank has less money to lend.

Modeling Monetary Policy

The way monetary policy is supposed to work is through what is called the *monetary transmission* mechanism. The Federal Reserve can use any of its tools to impact the left panels of Figures 10.1 and 10.2. That is, through an increase or decrease in the supply of loanable funds, it can have a decisive impact on short-term interest rates. The only real question is whether the causation arrow that connects the left and right panels of these two diagrams is operating.

Let's begin by showing that each of the Fed's tools can impact interest rates. If the Federal Reserve uses open market operations to buy bonds, it increases the amount of money that banks and other financial institutions can loan. This increases the supply of loanable funds in Figure 10.1 and decreases the interest rate in this market. The Fed can just as easily have an opposite desire and want to increase interest rates. The left panel of Figure 10.2 shows what happens when the Fed sells bonds in an effort to increase interest rates. The increase

[2]Prior to 2003 the Federal Reserve utilized another key interest rate to signal its intentions, the discount rate. This was the interest rate at which the Fed itself loaned money to banks usually buying a portion of a bank's loan portfolio. The discount rate was below the federal funds rate, but banks were reticent to use this service too often because it brought with it the potential for extra scrutiny from auditors.

FIGURE 10.1 Expansionary monetary policy: buying bonds, lowering the discount rate, or lowering the reserve ratio.

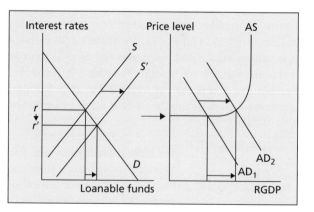

FIGURE 10.2   Contractionary monetary policy: selling bonds, raising the discount rate, or raising the reserve ratio.

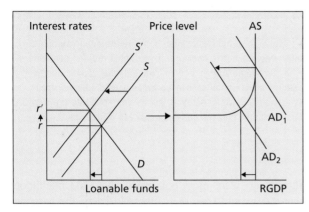

in interest rates is accomplished when the Fed reduces the supply of loanable funds.

Because the federal funds rate is determined by market forces between banks and is not determined directly by the Fed, the way the Fed can influence that rate is by increasing or decreasing the supply of generally available funds for loans. Its rationale is that this action will indirectly influence the federal funds rate. There is enough linkage between the quantity of money that is generally available for loans and the interest rate that banks charge each other so that this seems to work fairly well.

As we noted, the Federal Reserve can impact interest rates by changing the reserve ratio. If the ratio is lowered, the bank has more money to lend and the supply of loanable funds moves to the right, as it does in the left panel of Figure 10.1. If the ratio is raised, the bank has less money to lend and the supply of loanable funds moves to the left, as is indicated in the left panel of Figure 10.2.

As you saw in Chapter 8, one of the determinants of aggregate demand is interest rates. The influence of interest rates stems from the fact that investors want to borrow more to buy plant and equipment when interest rates are lower. In addition, consumers are more willing to buy expensive durable goods like cars and home furnishings when interest rates are lower. For the person who pays cash, the lower interest rate effect is indirect in that buyers sacrifice less interest income when they take money out of savings to buy something. The person who buys a car and gets a shiny new payment book with the shiny new car is more likely to buy that car and more likely to buy a nicer, more expensive car because of the lower interest rate.

A loosening of the money supply or a lowering of the federal funds or discount rate allows banks to make more loans. These are loans that they can make only if they

lower interest rates to ordinary borrowers. The lowering of interest rates causes the aggregate demand curve to rise as a result of increases in investment and interest-sensitive consumption. This is shown in the right panel of Figure 10.1. An identical but opposite story can be told concerning a tightening of the money supply. Less is available for banks to lend, a circumstance that allows them to raise the interest rates they charge to ordinary borrowers. Raising such rates causes a reduction in investment and interest-sensitive consumption. This in turn causes aggregate demand to fall, as is shown in the right panel of Figure 10.2.

The Monetary Transmission Mechanism

Now we get to the question of whether changing short-term interest rates impacts the overall economy in the desired fashion. That is, does the change in the left panel of Figure 10.1 cause the change in the right panel of Figure 10.1, and does the same work for Figure 10.2? The process by which the use of a monetary policy tool impacts the overall economy is called the **monetary transmission** mechanism.

monetary transmission
The process by which the use of a monetary policy tool impacts the overall economy.

Economists disagree about the effectiveness of monetary policy, especially its effectiveness in the long run and in circumstances of extreme economic uncertainty. Let's take the first of these two concerns. Whereas there is some doubt among economists about whether the Fed has the ability to alter short-term economic outcomes in normal economic circumstances, the doubt is much more widely held concerning its long-term ability to increase output through sustained increases in the money supply. The underlying reason for the skepticism is that sustained increases in the money supply will be factored in by investors, who will anticipate that substantial inflation will result from such a policy. Thus, though it may look as if the Fed could use the logic from Figure 10.1 to continuously foster long-run rapid growth, not many economists believe the Fed has this power. As a result, Figures 10.1 and 10.2 should be taken as relevant only in the short term.

The reason conventional monetary policy is less effective in times of extreme economic uncertainty than Figures 10.1 and 10.2 suggest is that borrowers' confidence is so shaken by actual unemployment, the threat of unemployment, or slack demand that any small modifications to borrowing costs are trivial compared to these underlying problems. This was certainly the case during the Great Depression, but you don't have to go back that far for a clear example of what economists call a

THE ROLE OF MONEY

Imagine a world without money. While you may think that would be utopian, it would actually be a pain in the neck. Money allows us to exchange the goods or services we have to offer so that we may get the goods or services we want. Without it we would have to barter. Money allows us to avoid this by serving as a medium of exchange.

Money also holds its value. Suppose the good you had to offer was subject to spoilage. If you could not find someone who had a good you wanted and wanted what you had to offer within a short period of time, your goods would be worthless. With money you can sell your goods and hold onto the cash until such time that you find the goods you want to buy.

liquidity trap
A situation where zero or near zero interest rates do not stimulate borrowing.

liquidity trap. A liquidity trap exists when even zero or near zero interest rates do not stimulate borrowing.

With a global economic slowdown under way in 2008 and 2009, firms had more than adequate capital to produce the significantly reduced volume of goods and services consumers were ready to purchase. As a result, the reduction in interest rates that might have motivated them to borrow money to buy new capital in 2006 and 2007 did not motivate them in the slightest. Furthermore, consumers who might have been persuaded to borrow money to buy cars, homes, or home

furnishings were more concerned about the likelihood that they would keep their jobs. Moreover, the bursting of the housing bubble, which reduced home prices by an average of more than 20 percent, gave many pause when it came to taking on more debt.

The supply side of the liquidity trap can be demonstrated with the help of the data on required and excess reserves of banks (see Figure 10.3). As previously described, large banks are compelled to hold 10 percent of their deposits in the form of required reserves at the Federal Reserve. They can loan the other 90 percent as they see fit. During normal economic times, that is exactly what they do. With the quite obvious and notable

FIGURE 10.3   Proportion of bank reserves held by banks that are required and excess.

Source: Board of Governors of the Federal Reserve System, www.federalreserve.gov/econresdata/statisticsdata.htm

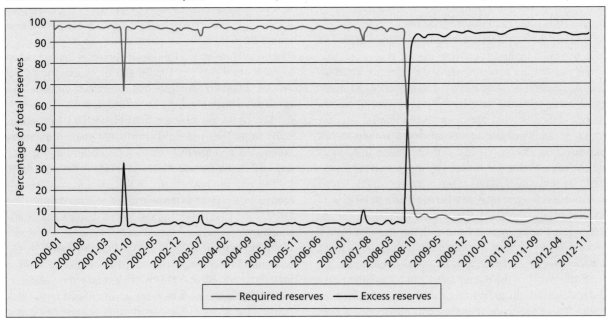

exception of September of 2001, bank reserves were what were required. Upwards of 95 percent of their reserves were required while the remainder were simply viewed as a cushion against unusual daily activity. The excess reserves were loaned overnight in the federal funds market. In late 2008, as the financial crisis hit in full force, the proportion of reserves that were considered "excess" went from 5 percent of the total to 90 percent of the total, and this occurred over a short three-month window. That these proportions did not revert to normal through mid-2013 suggests that, at least from the banks' perspective, the liquidity trap was in full effect. Because the Federal Reserve paid a modest interest rate on these deposits, the risk-adjusted profits the banks could earn by depositing their excess reserves with the Federal Reserve were sufficient to have them do that rather than loaning it to businesses and consumers.

The Additional Tools of Monetary Policy Created in 2008

The Federal Reserve recognized before many the potential severity of the 2008 financial crisis, and well before it became evident to others, the Fed began contemplating other tools it might use to fight a global slowdown. First, it created a new discount window for investment banks and second, it began buying corporate paper, effectively lending money directly to nonbank corporations. Finally, it contemplated buying longer-term debt such as 30-year treasuries and mortgage-backed securities from banks and other institutions in a frantic attempt to lower long-term interest rates and halt the slide of the housing market.

Investment banks were a creation of post–Great Depression policies that sought to separate commercial banks, which took deposits and made loans from those deposits, from investment banks, which simply served as intermediaries to large financial transactions. These investment banks were capitalized with their own equity and their own borrowing and did not take deposits. The discount window that was created for investment banks allowed these entities to borrow money from the Fed in much the same way that commercial banks do through the discount rate or primary credit rate facility. The effort was for naught as the financial crisis of 2008 sent one, Lehman Brothers, into liquidation and threatened the health of the remaining two, Morgan Stanley and Goldman Sachs. In the end, the Federal Reserve needed both entities to become commercial banks so that they could assist the Fed in saving other commercial banks.

Additionally, the Fed began buying corporate paper when even well-capitalized and well-run corporations were having difficulty finding buyers for their short-term debt. **Corporate paper** is the name given to short-term debt offered by large corporations. These corporations routinely borrow billions of dollars for inventory-building purposes or to deal with uneven sales knowing that they will easily be able to pay off the debt with the proceeds of future sales. Without this market, many corporations could not operate. Because the financial system was not working properly in the fall of 2008, the Fed stepped in to make these loans possible.

corporate paper
Short-term debt offered by large corporations.

At times during this 2008–2013 period, the Federal Reserve began buying long-term debt in a process called **quantitative easing**. This process referred to making much more money available to the economy through the purchase of 20- and 30-year United States treasuries and mortgage-backed securities. A **mortgage-backed security** is a financial asset that is the aggregation of mortgages where the holder of the security is paid from the combined mortgage payments of homeowners. This was done to directly impact long-term interest rates to stimulate business investment and to re-ignite the housing market.

quantitative easing
The process by which the Federal Reserve buys long-term securities in order to decrease long-term interest rates to directly stimulate business investment and housing markets.

mortgage-backed security
Financial asset that is the aggregation of mortgages where the holder of the security is paid from the combined mortgage payments of homeowners.

For perspective on the relative importance of the traditional tools and the new tools of monetary policy, consider Figure 10.4. The traditional security holdings of short-term treasuries, the result of open-market operations and the lending to financial institutions via the discount window, constituted the entirety of the $860 billion Federal Reserve holdings. In very late 2008, the Federal Reserve began its still traditional loaning of large amounts to financial institutions, but when that was insufficient to prevent the panic in the financial markets, it followed up only a matter of weeks later with nontraditional purchases of short-term commercial paper. Beginning in 2009, the Federal Reserve tried to overcome the liquidity trap by embracing the nontraditional tools fully. From early 2009 through 2013, it was buying both long-term treasuries and mortgage-back securities in such volume that by March 2013, the total Federal Reserve holdings had nearly tripled. In order to avoid the

FIGURE 10.4   Federal Reserve holdings 2007–2013.

Source: Board of Governors of the Federal Reserve System, www.federalreserve.gov/econresdata/statisticsdata.htm

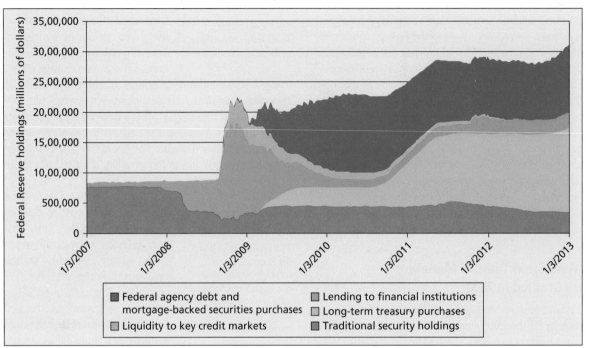

perception that this was simply flooding credit markets with cheap money, "operation twist" was employed during 2011 and 2012 in which the Federal Reserve sold traditional short-term securities while using the proceeds to purchase long-term treasuries. This can be seen clearly in that the bottom two portions of Figure 10.4 total roughly the same amount ($1.6 trillion) from mid-2011 through all of 2012 while the total holdings held steady at $2.75 trillion. The pause was broken in late 2012 when the Fed restarted the purchase of mortgage-back securities in order to keep the economy from sliding back into recession.

Central Bank Independence

The Fed's power over the economy is substantial because it can do what it thinks is best without fear of being contradicted. Its independence from political control gives it awesome power and awesome responsibility to use that power judiciously. The Fed is so independent that it can slow growth or even put the nation into a recession in an effort to stamp out inflation. Economists generally agree that the Fed must be free from political control in order to take the necessary action to fight inflation. Experience across nations in the latter half of the 20th century provides rather powerful evidence that this is true.

Long-run economic growth requires that the financial markets have faith that money invested in a country will not lose value as a result of excessive inflation. When people are concerned about inflation, interest rates increase. Higher interest rates make investments more expensive. Since growth occurs only when investments in the future take place, long-term growth depends on the existence of a believable monetary authority. Monetary authority, by the way, is the general name for institutions like the Federal Reserve. While a politically controlled monetary authority could generate that faith if it never wavered from potentially unpopular policies, experience tells us this does not happen. We know this because those countries with a history of independent monetary authorities have experienced lower inflation rates, lower interest rates, and higher real growth rates than countries without that history of independence. The United States, Germany, Switzerland, Japan, Canada, and the Netherlands are examples of countries with such independence, whereas Spain and Italy are examples of countries without it. For the stability we enjoy, we are willing to accept the risk of having an independent monetary authority.

It is worth a small historical interlude to note that Congress could, by simply passing a law, regain complete control over the Federal Reserve. Article I, Section 8, of the U.S. Constitution gives the Congress control over the power to coin money. It never took the role of monetary policy very seriously, however, and before the Civil War paper money was usually a bank note, typically backed by gold, of an individual private bank. With its authorizing of the printing of money during and after the Civil War, prices fluctuated so fast that three significant financial panics in the span of 60 years convinced Congress to create the Federal Reserve. If Congress became sufficiently motivated, it could return to the business of controlling the supply of money and, indirectly, interest rates. Under ordinary circumstances, the continuous consultations between Federal Reserve Chairman Bernanke, Treasury Secretary Paulson, and then New York Federal Reserve Bank Chairman and Obama Treasury Secretary designate Geithner that occurred in the fall of 2008 would have raised concerns about the degree to which this independence might have been compromised. Clearly, the circumstances were anything but ordinary at the time.

Modern Monetary Policy

The Last 30 Years

The history of monetary policy in the second half of the 20th century is one of increasing importance and self-confidence, and its effect on interest rates can be seen in Figure 10.5. In the late 1970s the Fed attempted to combat the oil-price shocks and a stagnating economy with increases in the money supply. Unfortunately, these efforts served only to add to inflation. In 1981 the Fed changed course with a high-stakes war on inflation. It sent interest rates soaring. Its grip on M2 was such that the federal funds rate went to nearly 20 percent while the discount rate went to 13 percent. By most measures the resulting recession of 1981–1982 was the worst in post–World War II history. The unemployment rate peaked higher, real GDP fell more, and the reduction in inflation was greater than in any of the other post-1946 recessions. It also had the distinction of being the only recession caused intentionally by the Fed.

Since that time the Fed has had a little better luck and has learned from its mistakes. For one thing, since the recession of 1982 it has not had to fight a significant inflation battle. In part this has been because it has been vigilant about not contributing to inflation. After 1984 the highest inflation rate has been 5 percent. Not having to wring out double-digit inflation but only having to keep it under control has made the Fed's job a little easier. In 1988, 1995, and again in 1999 and 2000, the Fed preemptively kept inflation in check by quickly increasing interest rates to slow an economy on the verge of creating inflation. It also worked to prevent a recession in 1994 by quickly pushing interest rates down.

FIGURE 10.5   Key interest rates from 1955 to 2012.

Source: Board of Governors of the Federal Reserve System, www.federalreserve.gov/econresdata/statisticsdata.htm

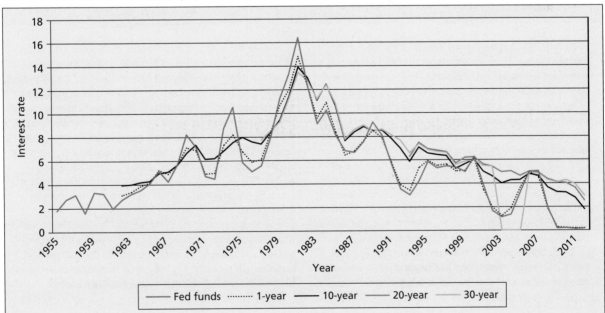

Its response to the 1990 recession was slow, but it was probably forgivably slow. In the months leading up to Iraq's invasion of Kuwait, real GDP growth was slow, inflation was picking up, and consumer indebtedness was starting to peak. On top of that, the Fed was determined to wait for the outcome of a budget deal. At the time, the federal deficit was more than $250 billion, it was headed toward $400 billion, and the Fed wanted to hold President Bush's (George Herbert Walker) and the Democratic leadership in Congress's collective feet to the fire and force them to act.

Unfortunately, Saddam Hussein's Iraq did not wait for the completion of the budget deal. After the invasion of Kuwait, gasoline prices increased sharply, and these circumstances precipitated an equally sharp decline in consumer confidence. Had the Fed acted immediately, it might have had better success keeping the United States out of the 1990–1991 recession, but its focus was on the deficit. It was also wary of duplicating the mistakes of the late 1970s by trying to battle cost-push inflation (inflation caused by movements in aggregate supply to the left) with increases in the money supply.

Whether explicitly or by chance, the Fed simply let the recession happen. It appeared to decide that there was little it could or should do to prevent it. Fortunately, however, the 1990–1991 recession was one of the shortest and the least disruptive recessions on record. Inflation never became a significant problem in part because consumer credit card debt was so high. Thus, except for

a short spike in gas prices, inflation was negligible during this period. Unemployment rose but it came nowhere near 1982's modern record of 11 percent. During the first 18 months of the recovery, from June 1992 through the end of 1993, the economy was so weak, however, that it was unclear at the time whether it was a recovery or just an extension of the recession. In 1992 and 1993 the Fed stepped in with a significant reduction in interest rates, and by the last quarter of 1994 the economy was humming along nicely.

From 1994 on, the Fed kept a vigilant eye on inflation. Where necessary, as in 1995, the Fed let its guard down enough to prevent a slowdown from becoming a recession. By 1998 Fed governors were feeling rather proud of themselves. Unemployment was at a 30-year low, inflation was nowhere in sight, and longtime Fed chairman Alan Greenspan had successfully kept the stock market in check by offering advice against "irrational exuberance." In 1998 the economy was doing fine. It was in no need of increases or decreases in interest rates. Then the Asian financial crisis hit.

The Asian financial crisis resulted from a series of bad loans made in the Pacific Rim nations of Thailand, Malaysia, South Korea, and Indonesia, and from failed attempts by these countries to hold their foreign exchange rates constant.

The Fed's response to the crisis was guarded at first. It wanted to prevent the crisis from spreading but did not

PUBLIC ENEMY #1: INFLATION OR DEFLATION?

In the late 1980s and through the decade of the 1990s, criticism started to be heard from the left and right that the Fed was overly concerned about the reappearance of inflation and not sufficiently concerned about the average person. Whether it has admitted it in public or not, since the late 1970s and early 1980s the Fed had considered inflation public enemy number one. This had been true whether inflation was really a problem, as it was in 1979 and 1980; had the possibility of being a problem, as in 1988, 1995, and 1999–2000; or was just a theoretical threat on the distant horizon.

Only when the country or the world was in trouble and inflation was less than 3 percent, as in the United States in 1993 and 2001 and the world in 1994, has the Federal Reserve relaxed its vigilance against inflation. In being focused on inflation it has cut recoveries short or starved them of sufficient cash to really get going.

In late 2002–early 2003, and again in late 2008 and 2009, a new public enemy number one had begun to come into view: deflation. Recall from Chapter 6 that deflation is the opposite

of inflation but is no less of a concern. Deflation has the effect of encouraging people not to buy now. This is because they know that if they wait, they will save money. This can be self-perpetuating in that by not buying, consumers force businesses to cut prices. This causes profits to fall and layoffs to occur, and buying diminishes even further. Even moderate deflation is worse than inflation in this regard. The Japanese experience with deflation in the late 1980s and 1990s offered very slow growth and stagnant employment. The Fed understood this potential quite well in 2003 when it again began to consider further interest rate cuts. It also understood this well when it drove short-term interest rates to zero in the fall of 2008. We will not know for some time whether it realized the threat too late. The deflation of 2008 was confined mostly to housing (20 percent), energy (60 percent), and to some producer commodities such as corn (40 percent), soybeans (40 percent), and raw metal prices (20 percent to 50 percent). Core PCE did not decrease during the period.

want its action to have the effect of importing the crisis to the United States. Stock prices in the United States did fall 20 percent in three months, and many economists began to predict that a recession would occur in the United States within a year. The Fed lowered interest rates a full percentage point, enough of an action to increase U.S. demand for imported goods. This helped to stabilize Asia. In turn, the dollar got so strong relative to Asian currencies that the relative price of imports purchased by Americans fell enough to offset any domestic price increases.

The recession of 2001 served as another example of monetary policy, its uses and its limitations. Beginning with the ambiguous nature of the 2000 presidential election, the recession of 2001 was met with 12 separate cuts in interest rates by the Federal Reserve. By 2003 the federal funds rate was at its lowest level in more than 40 years. For a time, in the spring of 2003, 30-year fixed mortgage interest rates were below 5 percent for the first time ever.

As can be seen from Figure 10.6, the crowning period of this aggressive monetary policy was between 1999 and 2006. The Federal Reserve Board's Open-Market Committee aggressively moved their federal funds rate target to combat economic circumstances. In mid-1999 the Fed aggressively raised interest rates six separate times to combat what Greenspan termed the "irrational exuberance" of the stock markets. These actions had little impact themselves in stemming the overheated stock

market. The tech-stock bubble burst on its own in 2000, prompting the Fed to begin to lower interest rates.

The Fed was in the process of easing credit conditions in 2001 when the attacks of September 11, 2001, occurred. When stock markets opened the following Monday, it was with a Federal Reserve announcement that it was aggressively moving interest rates lower. With 13 rate cuts in a period of two-and-one-half years, the sluggish economy slowly rebounded through 2002 and picked up considerable steam through 2003 and 2004. In response, the Fed raised interest rates to more normal historical levels in 10 steps through mid-2005. As mentioned repeatedly through this chapter, the Federal Reserve's response to the financial crisis of 2008 was swift, if not entirely effective. It lowered short-term interest rates to nearly zero in an attempt to forestall, or at least dampen, the impact of the recession.

Economists will debate whether these interest rate changes had the desired impact, but consider this: Between June 2003 and June 2004, and again in 2008 and 2009, the Fed was pretty much out of bullets. The Fed can't make businesses borrow money to invest in new plant and equipment and can't make consumers borrow to buy expensive consumer durables. Once the interest rate has been driven to nearly zero, these decisions to borrow money are determined by the confidence that the borrower has in his or her ability to pay the money back.

FIGURE 10.6   Aggressive monetary policy between 1999 and 2012.

Source: Board of Governors of the Federal Reserve System, www.federalreserve.gov/fomc/fundsrate.htm

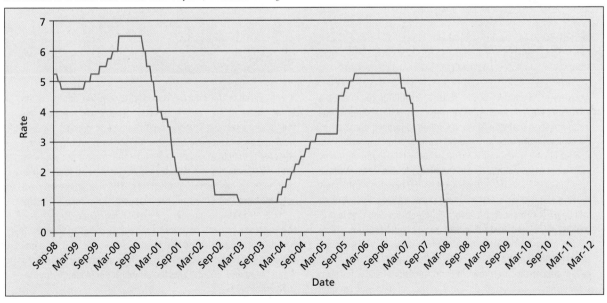

FIGURE 10.7   Selected yield curves on federal funds and U.S. debt.

Source: Board of Governors of the Federal Reserve System, www.federalreserve.gov/econresdata/statisticsdata.htm

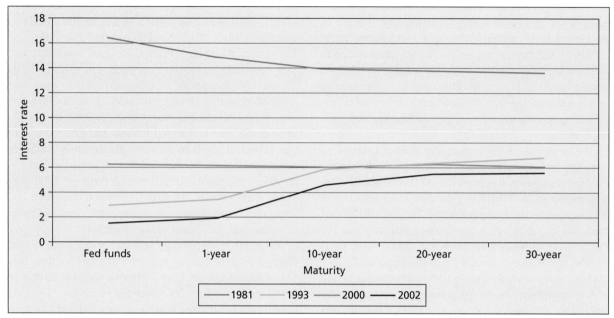

Also worth noting was the Federal Reserve's difficulty in "talking down" skyrocketing home prices and questionable home lending practices in 2005. Fed increases in short-term interest rates during 2005 had little impact on mortgage rates, which remained low during that year.

Though Figure 10.5 makes it look like short- and long-term interest rates move in lockstep, they do not.

Though they typically move together, it's useful to remember Chapter 7's definition of the yield curve. Figure 10.7 notes yield curves from different periods of recent history. What appears is that at times the yield curve is upward sloping (the usual case), while at other times it is flat and at still other times it is downward sloping.

HOW WILL THE FED UNDO THE MASSIVE INCREASE IN MONEY?

At no time in Federal Reserve history has it engaged in such a sustained effort to keep interest rates so low for so long. It has accomplished that through mostly nontraditional means. It has purchased more than $2 trillion in mortgage-backed securities and long-term treasuries. That $2 trillion is now in the economy with most of it in banks and in the hands of investors. With so much loanable money available, when the economy does start moving forward at a robust pace, those banks and investors will begin loaning it aggressively. The problem with that is that it could easily and, in the minds of many economists, inevitably create inflationary pressure. The Federal Reserve's response to that inflationary pressure will likely be two-fold: First, it will begin selling the mortgage-backed securities and long-term treasuries so as to soak up some of that money; and second,

it will increase the interest rate that it pays on deposits that banks make at the Federal Reserve. These two mechanisms will offer banks and investors alternatives to making loans to businesses and consumers. The lower the price the Federal Reserve is willing to sell these assets, the greater the potential return to the banks and investors from purchasing them rather than loaning the money to investors. The higher the interest rate that the Fed offers on bank deposits, the less likely the bank is to loan the money to a riskier borrower. The reason the Federal Reserve's aggressive monetary policy of 2008–2013 has been seen as risky is that the timing is critical. If it begins selling its portfolio too quickly, it could prematurely interrupt a robust recovery, and if it acts too slowly, it could set up double-digit inflation.

Summary

With your newfound wealth of knowledge, you now understand the role of the Federal Reserve of the United States and its primary goal to maintain macroeconomic stability. You see that the Fed's own apparent measure of success in meeting this goal has been the ability to control inflation. You know the tools of monetary policy, understand how they work, and are able to apply that knowledge to an aggregate supply–aggregate demand model. You know the recent history of monetary policy and know how it has shaped the Federal Reserve's current fixation with inflation. Finally, you understand the debate among economists over whether inflation or deflation is a greater concern.

Key Terms

corporate paper, 131
federal funds rate, 127
inflation targeting, 127
liquidity trap, 130
M1, 127

M2, 127
monetary aggregate, 127
monetary transmission, 129
mortgage-backed security, 131
open-market operations, 127

primary credit rate or
   discount rate, 128
quantitative easing, 131
reserve ratio, 128

Quiz Yourself

1. The Constitution of the United States grants to Congress the power of monetary policy in Article 1, Section 8. Since 1913, Congress has
   a. jealously guarded this power.
   b. granted this power to the president.
   c. delegated this power to the Federal Reserve.
   d. ignored this power.

2. When engaging in monetary policy, the impact of expansionary policy on an aggregate demand–aggregate supply model is to
   a. increase aggregate demand.
   b. increase aggregate supply.
   c. decrease aggregate demand.
   d. decrease aggregate supply.

3. The most precise tool of monetary policy is
   a. the adjustment of the federal funds target.
   b. the adjustment of the discount rate.
   c. the adjustment of the reserve requirement.
   d. the use of open-market operations.

4. Federal Reserve independence is
   a. completely fictitious.
   b. totally complete.
   c. subject to Congress's desire to keep it independent.
   d. subject to the Supreme Court's desire to keep it independent.

5. The "creation" of money is
   a. entirely the purview of Congress.
   b. entirely the purview of the Federal Reserve.
   c. formally the purview of the Federal Reserve, constitutionally the purview of Congress, but banks have a practical means of creating money.
   d. entirely subject to the whims of the banking system.

6. During 1999 through 2006, the Federal Reserve
   a. was passive and simply let things happen.
   b. reacted actively to quell potentially inflationary expansions but did nothing to deal with the recession.
   c. reacted actively to deal with the recession but did nothing to quell potentially inflationary expansions.
   d. reacted actively to deal with the recession and to quell potentially inflationary expansions.

7. The ability of the Federal Reserve to control interest rates is
   a. limited almost entirely to short-term rates.
   b. limited almost entirely to long-term rates.
   c. limited almost entirely to intermediate-term rates.
   d. unlimited.

8. Which of the following tools would have likely had the impact of raising short-term interest rates the most?
   a. cutting the federal funds target by one-quarter point.
   b. buying $1 million in bonds.
   c. raising the reserve requirement from 8 percent to 15 percent.
   d. raising personal income tax rates by 1 percentage point each.

Short Answer Questions

1. Explain how open-market operations work.
2. Explain the difference between the discount rate and the federal funds rate.
3. Explain how lowering the reserve ratio affects the economy.
4. Explain how the 2010–2013 quantitative easing through the Federal Reserve purchase of mortgage-backed securities is different in style from what it usually does.

Think about This

Because the chairs of the Federal Reserve Board can have an enormous impact on policy decisions of the Fed and thereby the economy, their selection has been the subject of great political interest. Politically motivated monetary policy could be ruinous economic policy. Previous Fed chairs have understood that their functional independence from congressional interference depends on the apolitical nature of their decisions. What would the economic consequences be if this balance was upset by a president who nominated a Fed chair dedicated to protecting the president's political party?

Talk about This

Presidents tend to nominate Fed chairs on the basis of advice from those working daily in the financial markets.

Who should have an impact on the choice of the Fed chair? Specifically, Fed policy can favor financial interests or the interests of workers. Should unions or others with a claim to represent workers have an impact on the selection of the Fed chair?

For More Insight See

Colander, David, "The Stories We Tell: A Reconsideration of AS/AD Analysis," *Journal of Economic Perspectives* 9, no. 3 (Summer 1995), pp. 169–188.

Ramo, Joshua Cooper, "The Three Marketeers," *Time*, February 15, 1999, pp. 34–42.

Steiger, Douglas, James H. Stock, and Mark W. Watson, "The NAIRU, Unemployment and Monetary Policy," *Journal of Economic Perspectives* 11, no. 1 (Winter 1997), pp. 33–50.

Behind the Numbers

Consumer price index and historical U.S. inflation rates.
Bureau of Labor Statistics—www.bls.gov/cpi

U.S. interest rates 1955–2005.
Federal Reserve Board; statistics: releases and historical data www.federalreserve.gov/econresdata/statisticsdata.htm

CHAPTER ELEVEN

Federal Spending

Learning Objectives

After reading this chapter you should be able to:

LO1 Describe the process that goes into creating the federal budget of the United States.

LO2 Show that mandatory spending—the portion of the budget that is devoted to spending on items for which no annual vote is taken—has steadily increased because of various entitlement programs and interest on the national debt.

LO3 Summarize how 30 percent of the federal budget is allocated almost equally to domestic spending and defense, with a relatively small amount going for foreign aid and for dues to international organizations such as the United Nations.

LO4 Explain how to use marginal analysis when looking at federal spending.

LO5 Distinguish between current-services and baseline budgeting.

LO6 Conclude that the idea of opportunity cost is at the heart of federal spending.

Chapter Outline

A Primer on the Constitution and Spending Money
Using Our Understanding of Opportunity Cost
Using Our Understanding of Marginal Analysis
Budgeting for the Future
Summary

The federal government of the United States of America spends more than $3.8 trillion each year on everything from welfare to national defense. This chapter focuses attention on how the government spends that money, a perfect example of how, in public policy, we use the concept of opportunity cost that was introduced in Chapter 1.

We start with a brief primer on what the Constitution requires before money can be spent. We then discuss the difference between mandatory and discretionary spending and how the balance between the two has shifted over the years. Next we lay out where the money was budgeted in the 2014 fiscal year, how that budget reflects on our priorities, and how the shift in distribution over

the years reflects a shift in priorities. We focus our attention, in particular, on health, Social Security, and defense spending, which make up the bulk of the federal budget. We use the Chapter 1 notion of marginal analysis to discuss both the size of federal spending and the distribution of it among various programs. Finally, we describe baseline and current-services budgeting and use Medicare and defense to discuss the differences.

As can be seen in Figure 11.1, federal spending as a percentage of GDP stayed between 18 percent and 22 percent for 22 years. After peaking in 1952 as a result of the Korean War, this measure trended up from 16 percent in 1955 to a peak at 23.5 percent in 1982 as spending on

FIGURE 11.1   Federal spending as a percentage of GDP.

Source: The Office of Management and Budget, www.whitehouse.gov/omb/budget/Historicals

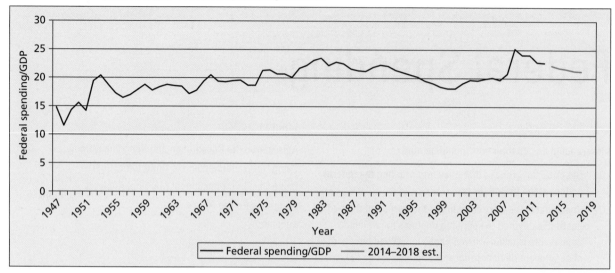

social programs increased. The Reagan years saw a slow decline only to rebound in the George Herbert Walker Bush years as billions were spent in a bailout of failed savings and loan associations. Since that time the size of the federal government, measured as a percentage of GDP, fell to its lowest point in 25 years only to rise again in the wake of the September 11, 2001, attacks, and the subsequent wars in Afghanistan and Iraq. The $750 billion Troubled Asset Relief Program (TARP) passed in October 2008 and the $787 billion Obama stimulus law passed in February 2009 greatly altered this figure. After the Great Recession peak of 25.2 percent, federal spending as a percentage of GDP is projected to decline to approximately 21 percent.

A Primer on the Constitution and Spending Money

What the Constitution Says

According to the Constitution of the United States of America, "No money shall be drawn from the treasury, but in consequence of appropriations made by law." This means that unless Congress passes an appropriations bill and the president either signs it or has a veto overturned, no money can be spent. The president and Congress thus must reach either an agreement or a compromise on spending priorities so that Congress will pass an appropriation bill that the president will sign.

Under normal procedures, the president sends a proposed budget to Congress in late winter or early spring.

The Congress often uses that budget as a blueprint upon which it bases a budget plan of its own. It uses its version as it debates and negotiates with the executive branch of government. When both sides reach agreement on a final budget, Congress passes appropriations bills to actually spend the money that has been budgeted.

All of this work must be completed by October 1 because the government's fiscal year starts then and goes to September 30 of the following year. (So the 2014 fiscal year began October 1, 2013, and ended September 30, 2014.) When these bills are passed and signed by the president, they become law and money can be spent. Otherwise, money cannot be spent.

Shenanigans

This process has a myriad of places for shenanigans. Chief among these are actions taken by the various subcommittee and committee chairs and in the House–Senate conferences. The chairs of the appropriations subcommittees and the chairs of the full committees can and do influence how much gets spent and where it gets spent. Whereas spending on social insurance programs like Medicaid, Medicare, and Social Security cannot be easily altered, highway spending and defense spending are prime targets for spending on items of local rather than national interest. The chair of a subcommittee like the one on highway spending can fund the building of bridges and highways in his or her district much more easily than anyone else can. As with roads and bridges, defense is also an area where the powerful chairs of the subcommittees and the full committees work to ensure that federal money is spent in their districts. Recent history is replete with examples of weapons systems that are not wanted by the military but that are being built anyway because the production facilities are in districts or states of powerful members of Congress.

Even worse, members of the conference committees, who are charged with putting together good compromise bills, have been known to spend significant time making sure money is included for their states or districts and less time making sure the bill is a good one for the country. Members of Congress who have seniority over other members are the ones who are assigned to such committees. Such appointments are considered rewards for years of service. The most egregious products of the conferences are usually found in parts of the final bill that were not in the original House or Senate version of the bill. These are items that conference members knew they could not get passed in their own houses. Knowing they were going to end up on a conference committee, they just waited and made the inclusion of the item they wanted passed a condition of their support for the bill in conference.

Another element of budgetary shenanigans comes when members of Congress agree to support spending programs in each other's districts. This vote trading, called **logrolling** among economists, increases spending in ways that raise eyebrows. A senator from Vermont got his colleagues to declare Lake Champlain a Great Lake so that it would qualify for an environmental program.

logrolling
The trading of votes used to generate sufficient support for projects that are not in the general interest of the country.

The emergency spending legislation approved after the attacks of September 11, 2001, included billions for wholly unrelated items. The infamous Alaskan "bridge to nowhere" was tucked into emergency spending following Hurricane Katrina by then Alaska Senator Ted Stevens. The 2013 Hurricane Sandy relief bill included $33 billion in spending entirely unrelated to the storm. Bridges, roads, university studies, and memorials to obscure local celebrities tend to grow on spending bills in direct proportion to the need to move the legislation quickly as members of Congress take advantage of the situation and agree to spending that would otherwise require extensive review. Promises to quell this type of spending are rarely kept. During the 2006 congressional elections, Democrats promised to hold the line on pet projects only to use these inducements in 2007 to solidify votes on other priorities such as enforcing a deadline for pulling out of Iraq.

Dealing with Disagreements

The appropriations process seldom moves smoothly, and the process is particularly rough when the political party in control of the White House is not in control of Congress. Disagreements abound when this is the case, and rarely can one party "have its way" with the budget. While the Obama administration was elected to office with large majorities in both the House of Representatives and Senate, Senate budget rules required that Obama garner 60 votes for his stimulus package. He could do that only with Republican votes. Even then, he was in a considerably more advantageous position than Presidents Clinton and Bush. Neither could count on his own party to back his budget priorities, and both dealt with periods when Congress was in the hands of the other party. It has been a truly rare circumstance in recent American history where a president had sufficient political party and ideological majorities in Congress to get his way. Thus the usual case for much of the late 20th century featured long and protracted budget debates.

When Congress either does not pass appropriations bills that are acceptable to the president or passes bills the president does not want, there are only four choices:

1. Congress can give in.
2. The president can give in.
3. The government can shut down.
4. Congress can pass a continuing resolution and the president can sign it.

If either side gives in, a bill gets passed. Shutting down the government becomes a battle of chicken until the sides reach compromises. A continuing resolution constitutes an agreement to disagree that lets the government continue functioning.

Specifically, a **continuing resolution** is a bill passed by Congress and signed by the president that allows the government to spend money temporarily in a fashion identical to the previous year. This usually happens

continuing resolution
A bill passed by Congress and signed by the president that allows the government to temporarily spend money in a fashion identical to the previous year.

when Congress does not meet the October 1 deadline. More often than not, it is for only a few of the 13 appropriations bills and for only a few weeks, but in 2013, almost the entire budget was passed as a continuing resolution.

Using Our Understanding of Opportunity Cost

The federal budget of the United States is an object lesson in opportunity cost. Whenever money is spent in one area, it cannot be spent in another. Although more money can be spent in all areas, this also has an opportunity cost. When money is taken from taxpayers, their ability to enjoy private consumption is reduced. Deficit spending is also not without opportunity cost. Interest payments add up into the future and money for private investment is reduced.

Some economists argue that the opportunity cost of government deficit spending is such that for every dollar the federal government borrows and spends, a dollar is removed from private investment. If these economists are correct, this phenomenon, called **crowding out,** is an example of opportunity cost at work: Government cannot just spend money and make everyone better off. In the process, someone is being made worse off. Other econo-

crowding out
The opportunity cost of government deficit spending is that private investment is reduced.

mists suggest that the crowding out is less than complete, which means that for every dollar of government spending something less than a dollar of private spending is lost. In either case there is an opportunity cost to the money spent.

The remainder of this section describes the choices that must be made by Congress and the president when setting out a spending plan.

Mandatory versus Discretionary Spending

Although the actual budget proposal of the president runs to more than 1,000 pages and is incredibly detailed and precise, Figure 11.2 offers its basic distribution of

spending. You can see that the broadest of its distinctions is the difference between mandatory and discretionary spending. **Mandatory spending** delineates those items for which a previously passed law requires that money be spent while **discretionary spending** is subject to annual appropriations decisions. For instance, current law states that people are entitled to certain benefits that must be paid without regard to any other budget details. Future laws could overturn those now in existence, but the benefits that are currently provided through Social Security, Medicare, Medicaid, and welfare are so firmly entrenched in our society that in reality the money spent on them is untouchable. These four areas of the budget are often referred to as **entitlement** spending because the people for whom they are intended are entitled to the money they receive based on their poverty or age. Entitlement spending is a subset of mandatory spending, which also includes interest on the national debt.

mandatory spending
Budget items for which a previously passed law requires that money be spent.

discretionary spending
Budget items for which an annual appropriations bill must be passed so that money can be spent.

entitlement
A program where if people meet certain income or demographic criteria they are automatically eligible to receive benefits.

The appropriations for defense, student loans, the courts, and so on, occur annually. While these budgets rarely change drastically from the previous year, a failure to pass an appropriations bill can significantly affect the operations in these areas.

On the discretionary side of the budget there are three main components: defense, international policy and foreign aid, and everything else (broken out in Table 11.1). The most misunderstood and controversial of these is international policy. Of the $46 billion spent

FIGURE 11.2 Fiscal Year 2014 spending (in billions) and percentage of federal budget.

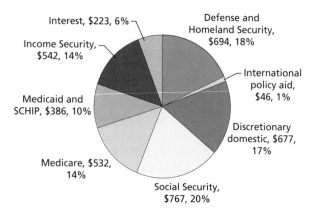

TABLE 11.1 Nondefense domestic discretionary spending, Fiscal Year 2014.

Category of Domestic Discretionary Spending	2014 Spending ($ billions)
Science and space	$ 30.1
Natural resources/environment	40.2
Agriculture	23.5
Transportation	103.8
Education and training	129.0
Veterans	148.2
Justice	58.7

FIGURE 11.3   Mandatory and discretionary spending as a percentage of total federal spending, 1962–2018.

Source: The Office of Management and Budget, www.whitehouse.gov/omb/budget/Historicals

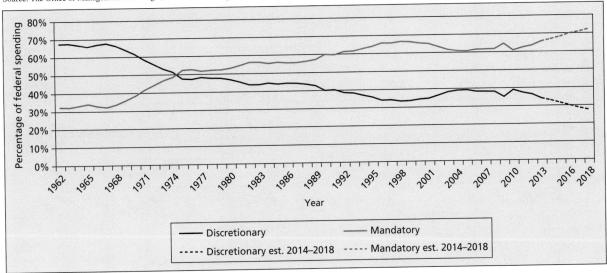

in this area, $15 billion is spent to maintain the State Department and its embassies in other countries and to pay our dues to the UN and other international organizations. The remaining $31 billion goes to other countries in foreign aid.

As you can see from Figure 11.3, the proportion of the budget devoted to discretionary spending has decreased from over 65 percent to under 40 percent, while the proportion devoted to mandatory spending has skyrocketed. This led President Clinton in 1993 to decry the fact that under projections valid at the time, by 2010 Congress would convene each year to debate less than 10 percent of the annual budget. This troublesome trend was halted in the late 1990s, but was on track to resume before the financial crisis of 2008 and coincident recession began. The massive increase in discretionary spending that resulted from the 2009 stimulus plan briefly interrupted this trend. However, aging baby boomers will soon balloon Social Security and Medicare spending, and the massive deficits of 2009 through 2012 and likely beyond will surely increase interest obligations such that President Clinton's prediction may come true, a few years after he thought it would.

This brings us back to the inescapable notion of opportunity cost. Every time a new entitlement program comes on board, such as the prescription drug coverage for Medicare recipients, it not only costs money now and in the future but also reduces the amount of flexibility of future Congresses and presidents as less and less of the budget can be devoted to other priorities.

Where the Money Goes

As you can see from Figure 11.2, defense, Social Security, Medicare, Medicaid, and net interest take up $2.6 trillion of the $3.8 trillion spent each year. The rest is either in the form of other welfare programs such as Temporary Assistance for Needy Families (TANF) or food stamps, or it is spent in the relatively smaller amounts listed in Table 11.1. The biggest of these areas of spending are under the Department of Education and its education and training programs. Of the $129 billion spent on education and training, $22 billion is spent on student loans, grants, and the federal work–study program. The remainder is spent as a supplement to state and local spending on primary and secondary education. With the wars in Iraq and Afghanistan, spending on veterans' benefits has increased to $148 billion. In 2014, transportation spending was budgeted at $104 billion with $59 billion for the federal justice system.

Figure 11.4 indicates that the mix of spending has dramatically changed over the years. Half or more of the federal budget once was devoted to national defense; today the amount is less than 20 percent. While Social Security once took up only 15 percent of the budget, today it is also approximately 20 percent. Net interest paid increased from less than 10 percent to more than

FIGURE 11.4 Composition of federal spending.

Source: The Office of Management and Budget, www.whitehouse.gov/omb/budget/Historicals

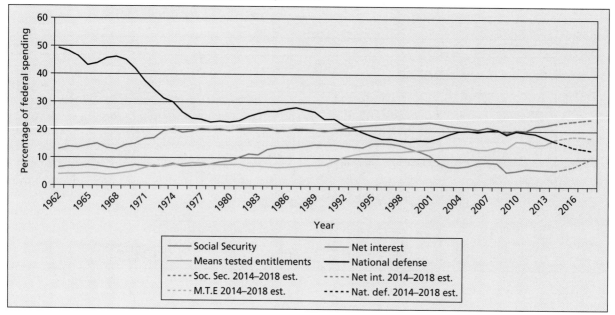

FIGURE 11.5 Real health spending by the federal government, 1962–2018 billions of 2000 dollars.

Source: The Office of Management and Budget, www.whitehouse.gov/omb/budget/Historicals

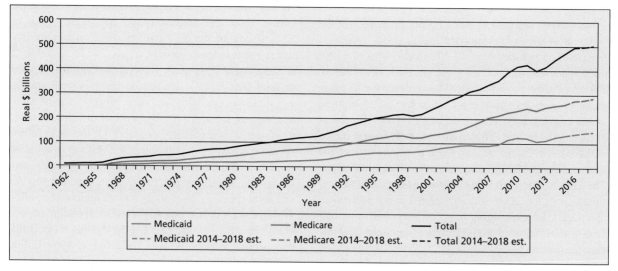

15 percent only to fall to 9 percent as a result of the surpluses of the late 1990s and early 2000s and the historically low interest rates of 2001 through 2004. As deficits grew during 2005–2007 and then exploded during and after the 2007–2009 recession, it is quite likely that interest obligations will soon exceed 10 percent. The only reason it has not already exceeded that amount is that the Federal Reserve has used its power to buy this debt to temporarily reduce the interest rate.

An area of spending that has increased remarkably since 1970 is federal spending in support of health care. As seen in Figure 11.5, adjusted for inflation, federal

TABLE 11.2 International comparisons of defense spending as a percentage of GDP, 2011.

Source: The World Bank, http://data.worldbank.org/indicator/MS.MIL.XPND.GD.ZS

Country	Defense Spending/GDP
United States	4.7
United Kingdom	2.6
France	2.2
Germany	1.3
Japan	1.0

spending on health care has risen 1,000 percent over that time. This is because Medicare and Medicaid spending has risen dramatically. When these programs were introduced in the late 1960s, spending on both was trivial. In the 2014 federal budget more than $304 billion is spent on Medicaid and the State Children's Health Insurance Programs, and $618 billion on Medicare. Together this is more than is spent on any program other than Social Security.

Again we are faced with the fact that there are always trade-offs. The trade-offs that we have made until now have clearly been in favor of entitlements. Social Security, Medicare, Medicaid, and various welfare programs have driven the budget for many years. The combined budget for all nondefense domestic spending, which includes everything from the federal judiciary to student loans, is exceeded by just one program, Social Security. The choice that we have made to ensure that elderly people and persons who are disabled have steady and reliable incomes comes at a cost.

Another choice that we have made is to exercise our military power in other parts of the world. Though some would argue that we had no real choice being the world's only superpower, it does, nonetheless, absorb resources and have an opportunity cost. As can be seen from Table 11.2, we spend a higher percentage of our GDP on military expenditures than our allies.

Using Our Understanding of Marginal Analysis

Federal spending is a prime arena to utilize marginal analysis. We can use this form of thinking to discuss whether the federal government spends too little or too much and whether the distribution of spending on various spending priorities is appropriate. Recall from Chapter 1 that marginal analysis compares the marginal benefit of an action with its marginal cost. In particular, that marginal cost is its opportunity cost.

The Size of the Federal Government

In judging the proper size of the federal government, an economist using marginal analysis would attempt to decide if the benefits resulting from additional tax money would outweigh the benefits that would otherwise accrue to private citizens if they were not taxed that amount. A government that purports to be "of, by and for the people" should seek to take only that money needed to fund programs whose marginal benefit is greater than or equal to their marginal cost. Thus it is not enough to say that we are getting $3.8 trillion in value for our $3.8 trillion; we need to be able to say that we are getting a dollar's worth of value for the last dollar of those $3.8 trillion dollars.

The Distribution of Federal Spending

Just as government should seek to maximize the net benefit to society by picking the optimal size of government, it should ensure that the distribution of spending between various priorities is optimal as well. Once the optimal size is established, the opportunity cost of money spent by one program is that it cannot be spent by another. For instance, the choice to build an aircraft carrier could come at the cost of expanding student grants and loans to cover several thousand more college students. Thus money spent on a program with only modest evidence of success could be viewed as wasteful, even if it is spent with good intentions and does no harm, because the money could be spent elsewhere to greater effect.

Budgeting for the Future

Baseline versus Current Services Budgeting

The yearly budget debate in Washington is replete with claims about who is making what cuts. For instance, during the debate over the 1996 budget, Republicans suggested that spending on Medicare increases yearly at a rate of 9 percent rather than the 14 percent requested by President Clinton. Since another aspect of their program was a broad-based tax cut, they were accused of "cutting Medicare to pay for a tax cut for the rich." This kind of debate is annoying because politicians often redefine simple words such as "cut" or simple phrases such as "broad-based" to suit their argument. It is indisputable that Democrats wanted more money for Medicare and Republicans, less. Moreover, Republicans wanted a reduction in taxes in rough proportion to taxes paid, and Democrats did not.

Had each side used straightforward and agreed-upon definitions, the debate would have been easier to understand. For instance, Democrats often define a broad-based tax cut as one that goes to everyone equally, whereas Republicans define it as one that goes proportionally to those who pay income taxes. Republicans argue that most of a tax cut should go to those making the most money since they pay the most taxes. (See Chapter 37 on personal income tax.) Democrats, on the other hand, define broad-based tax cuts as those that are given to everyone in similar amounts.

The language problem on spending cuts is equally exasperating. The problem is that when you formulate a budget and you compare it to other years' budgets, there is an open question as to how the comparison should be done. If you simply look at last year's budgeted figure and compare it to this year's budgeted figure, you are engaging in what is referred to as **baseline budgeting.** If you are budgeting more than you did last year, that is an increase; if you are budgeting less, that is a decrease. This is a commonsense approach and it is one that Republicans typically take.

baseline budgeting
Using last year's budgeted figure to set this year's budgeted figure.

This approach, however, misses an important point that is vital to interests Democrats support. They wish to ensure that government services are available to everyone who is eligible to receive them. There is no guarantee that baseline budgeting will provide enough money. A reasonable question to ask in budgeting is one that Democrats tend to ask: "How much will it cost to perform services this year in a manner identical to last year?" This is referred to as **current-services budgeting.** Current-services budgeting takes into account such things as overall inflation, inflation in the specific sector, and an increase in the number of people being served. If you want to guarantee enough money to provide identical services in the future, then merely starting with the previous year's baselines may not work. This has been particularly true in the health care field because new, more effective treatments become available. Thus the question is whether the new spending required to meet the old standard of care will be sufficient to meet the new standard.

current-services budgeting
Using an estimate of the costs of providing the same level of services next year as last.

Using current-services budgeting, President Clinton criticized Republicans in 1995 for their plan to "cut Medicare." Republicans countered, using baseline budgeting, that there was no cut at all. By using jargon with technical definitions to further their own positions, each party was telling the truth. In this case the truth depended on the standard that had been set. If the agreed-upon standard had been baseline budgeting, then the Republicans were right; if it had been current services, then the Democrats were right. Because a standard had not been set, they were both right and they were both wrong.

Summary

You now understand the process that goes into creating the federal budget of the United States. You know that in percentage terms a large and increasing part of the budget is devoted to spending on items for which no annual vote is taken. You now see that this mandatory spending goes mostly to Social Security, Medicare, Medicaid, various welfare programs, and the costs of interest on the debt. You understand that the rest goes almost equally to spending on domestic concerns and spending on defense. You see that a relatively small amount goes for foreign aid and other obligations to international organizations such as the United Nations. You understand the difference between current-services and baseline budgeting and why this difference is at the heart of many political debates. Most important, you now understand that the idea of opportunity cost—choices have consequences, and money spent in one area cannot be spent in another—is at the heart of budgeting.

Key Terms

baseline budgeting, 146
continuing resolution, 141
crowding out, 142

current-services budgeting, 146
discretionary spending, 142
entitlement, 142

logrolling, 141
mandatory spending, 142

Quiz Yourself

1. Federal spending is typically _____ percent of GDP.
   a. less than 10
   b. between 18 and 22
   c. between 25 and 30
   d. more than 30

2. The FY 2014 federal budget was around
   a. $3.8 million.
   b. $3.8 billion.
   c. $3.8 trillion.
   d. $3.8 quadrillion.

3. Disagreements between the Congress and the president about the federal budget occur frequently. When they cannot agree on a budget but want to keep the government running, they
   a. use the president's budget.
   b. use Congress's budget.
   c. use a budget created by an independent budget commission.
   d. pass a continuing resolution.

4. Mandatory spending implies spending that is
   a. required by a previously passed set of laws.
   b. required by the U.S. Constitution.
   c. needed more than discretionary spending.
   d. off-limits for any cuts at any time.

5. The largest single item in federal spending is
   a. international aid.
   b. welfare.
   c. interest on the debt.
   d. Social Security.

6. Total federal spending on health care, after adjusting for inflation, has been
   a. growing.
   b. relatively constant.
   c. declining slowly.
   d. declining rapidly.

7. In determining whether the federal government is the right size, an economist would determine whether
   a. the first dollar spent produced $1 worth of social good.
   b. the average dollar spent produced $1 worth of social good.

   c. the last dollar spent produced $1 worth of social good.
   d. $3.8 trillion of social good was created with the $3.8 trillion spent.

8. In determining whether the distribution of federal spending among various agencies was correct, an economist would want to make sure
   a. that each agency manager got what (s)he thought was needed in that area.
   b. that the last dollar spent in each area produced the same amount of social good.
   c. that the average dollar spent in each area produced the same amount of social good.
   d. that the total amount of money spent in each agency produced the same level of social good.

9. If a program's cost rises only with inflation and increases in those that qualify for the program, this represents
   a. an increase in spending using baseline budgeting.
   b. a decrease in spending using current services budgeting.
   c. no increase or decrease in spending using current services budgeting.
   d. *a* and *c* are both correct.

Short Answer Questions

1. Explain how mandatory spending comes about relative to discretionary spending. Then assign the following programs to each: interest payments on the debt, national defense, Social Security, food stamps.

2. In order of magnitude, rank the following spending from greatest to smallest: Social Security, national defense, Medicare, federal support for education, space exploration, and foreign aid.

3. Explain what would transpire for new government expenditures to crowd out other economic activity.

4. One political party believes government spending is too high; another party thinks it is too low. Which party will argue for current-services budgeting as a practice for setting government budgets? Explain why.

Think about This

The Medicare prescription drug benefit passed during 2003 comes at a significant long-term cost (at least $720 billion over 10 years). Consider the opportunity cost of this spending in terms of tax cuts, deficit reduction, or spending on other priorities. Would you have committed the federal government to this spending?

Talk about This

When Congress and the president do not agree on a spending package and cannot agree on a continuing resolution, the government shuts down all but emergency services. What, in your mind, should be considered under the umbrella of "emergency"?

For More Insight See

Lee, Ronald, and Jonathan Skinner, "Will Aging Baby Boomers Bust the Federal Budget?" *Journal of Economic Perspectives* 13, no. 1 (Winter 1999).

Lynch, Thomas, *Public Budgeting in the United States* (Englewood Cliffs, NJ: Prentice Hall, 1979).

Behind the Numbers

Historical data.
    Federal spending.
    Mandatory and discretionary spending.
    Composition of federal spending.
    Federal government health spending.
      Budget of the United States Government. historical tables—www.whitehouse.gov/omb/budget/Historicals
World Bank; data and statistics—http://data.worldbank.org

Federal Deficits, Surpluses, and the National Debt

Learning Objectives

After reading this chapter you should be able to:

LO1 Explain how economists look at the federal budget deficits and surpluses and the national debt.

LO2 Associate significant deficits as resulting from wars and severe recessions/depressions.

LO3 Conclude that economists are interested less in raw numbers than in more sophisticated measures of the burdens that deficits and debt place on us.

LO4 Compare the U.S. national debt-to-GDP ratio relative to U.S. history and to other countries.

LO5 Explain that the federal government owns much of the debt and list what agencies own that debt.

LO6 Summarize the different positions taken by economists on the issue of a balanced-budget amendment to the U.S. Constitution.

LO7 Conclude that the deficit and debt picture has changed substantially since 1990 and articulate why deficit projections are so often wrong.

Chapter Outline

Surpluses, Deficits, and the Debt: Definitions and History

How Economists See the Deficit and the Debt

Who Owns the Debt?

A Balanced-Budget Amendment

Projections

Summary

This chapter could have had a simpler title: "Deficits and the National Debt." That is, except for a brief period in recent history, from 1998 to 2001, the federal government has spent more than it has taken in. The purpose of this chapter is to discuss the history of the deficits, those few surpluses, and the national debt of the U.S. federal government. (Particular attention will be paid to the debts coming out of the 2007–2009 recession and the budgets of President Obama.) After a brief history of these, we discuss the main causes of deficits and debt through time. We examine how economists look at the federal debt and how they compare the current state of affairs with other countries and U.S. history. When we discover who actually owns the federal debt, you will be surprised to see that a significant portion of it is owned by the federal government itself. We discuss whether a balanced-budget amendment to the U.S. Constitution makes sense as economic policy, and we conclude by looking at the rosy projections of surpluses and the national debt made by the Office of Management and Budget and the Congressional Budget Office and comparing them with much less rosy projections made by others.

Surpluses, Deficits, and the Debt: Definitions and History

Definitions

Defining **budget deficit**, **budget surplus**, or **national debt** ought to be simple, but because of the way the federal government does its accounting, the definitions are not as simple as they could be. For instance, you would think that if you did the math, a surplus would result when the total amount of tax revenue that came in was greater than the total amount that you spent. If spending exceeded the revenue, the result would be a deficit, and the debt would be the sum of the deficits minus the sum of the surpluses.

The problem is the usual definitions are not quite right, and it is because the deficit or surplus for a year is the combination of what are referred to as the off- and on-budget deficits and surpluses. Social Security, Medicare, and other parts of the budget that have trust funds attached to them complicate the matter because they are considered **off-budget**. The part of the federal budget that operates from year to year without a trust fund is **on-budget**. So, in 1998, when revenues exceeded expenditures and there was a $60 billion surplus for the total budget, we still added to our national debt because of a deficit in the on-budget part of the equation. Whenever we have an on-budget deficit, we have more debt. Since the off-budget part of the system had a greater surplus than the on-budget part had a deficit, the total budget was in net surplus, yet our debt grew.

budget deficit
The amount by which expenditures exceed revenues.

budget surplus
The amount by which revenues exceed expenditures.

national debt
The total amount owed by the federal government.

off-budget
Parts of the budget designated by Congress as separate from the normal budget. Programs that operate with their own revenue sources and have trust funds; Social Security, Medicare, and the Postal Service are examples.

on-budget
Parts of the budget that rely entirely or mostly on general revenue.

History

The annual budget of the United States is never actually balanced. The closest we ever came to a strictly balanced budget was a $3,800 deficit in 1835. Why is the budget not ever balanced? Congress passes the budget *before* it knows exactly how much money is going to come in. When the United States operated under the Articles of Confederation, before the Constitution was ratified, the country had a considerable debt (more than $75 million) from the American Revolutionary War and no money to pay it off. In fact, because the Continental Congress had no power to tax during the war, almost all of the money necessary to fight and win it was borrowed. In the first 58 years of constitutional government in the United States, from 1791 to 1849, there were more years of surplus (36) than deficit (23), and over that time the country ran a net surplus of $60 million. As a matter of fact, in 1836 the debt had all been repaid and President Andrew Jackson got Congress to give states money. Congress missed the mark and gave away $37,000 too much. The only alternative to giving the money to the states—investing in the private sector—was considered inappropriate.

The American Civil War ended notions that the country would ever again go without a national debt. Two billion dollars was borrowed to fight that war, and even though in the 35 years after the war there were more years with a surplus (21) than a deficit (14), the debt remained at $2 billion by 1900. As a matter of fact, in the first 30 years of the 20th century, there were almost as many years of surplus (13) as deficit (17). The debt during that period grew because the deficits during the two-year U.S. involvement in World War I were twice the size of the combined surplus in the other years. The longest uninterrupted period of debt reduction began just after World War I and lasted until 1930, the first full year of the Great Depression. Surpluses ruled for 11 consecutive years. In general, U.S. economic history prior to the Great Depression can be summarized as one in which the expenses of wars created the debt and steady efforts were made to eliminate the debt when the wars ended.

Since 1930, however, deficits have been more the rule than the exception. During the 82 years from 1930 to 2011, there were only 11 years with surpluses (three years in the 1940s, three in the 1950s, two in the 1960s, two in the 1990s, and two in the 2000s), whereas there were 71 with deficits. Also during that time the national debt grew from $50 billion to $15.5 trillion. Adjusting the deficits and surpluses for inflation, we can compare the relative size of the various years, and this is shown in Figure 12.1.

Figure 12.1 also portrays an important division between the total budget and the off-budget surpluses and deficits. Recall that the total budget is the combination of the on- and off-budget numbers. In recent times, especially after changes in Social Security in 1982 that saw a hefty increase in taxes in anticipation of the large number of retirements among baby boomers, the off-budget surplus has been substantial. In all but 12 of the 80 years

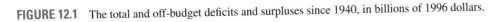

FIGURE 12.1   The total and off-budget deficits and surpluses since 1940, in billions of 1996 dollars.

Source: The Office of Management and Budget, www.whitehouse.gov/omb/budget/Historicals

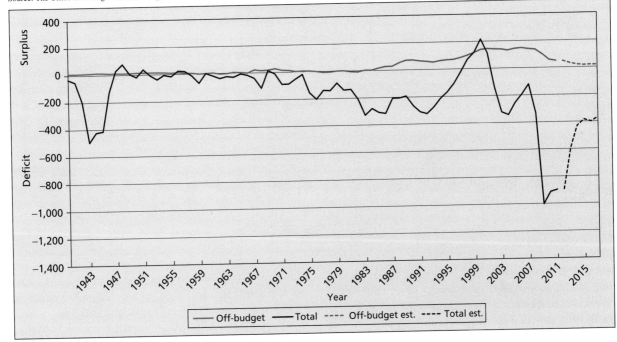

depicted in Figure 12.1, the off-budget part of the system was in surplus, and nine of these were from the late 1970s and early 1980s, before Social Security taxes were raised substantially. This continues to be the case with the surpluses in the Social Security system. These off-budget surpluses masked the severity of budget deficits in the late 1980s and created the illusion of surpluses in the late 1990s. It was only in fiscal years 1999 and 2000 that the on-budget side was showing a surplus. Deficits surged after the Bush-era tax cuts and spending increases resulting from the terrorist attacks of September 11, 2001, and the subsequent wars in Iraq and Afghanistan. The deficits were slated to hover in the $400 billion per year range when, in 2008, the recession and financial collapse took place.

Figure 12.2 displays the trend in deficits as a percentage of GDP. On the left side of the graph, the large annual deficits were for the expenses of war, just as 19th-century deficits were. In addition to all of the other upheaval caused by the Great Depression and World War II, budget deficits, measured in 1996 dollars in Figure 12.1 and measured as a percentage of GDP in Figure 12.2, peaked at more than $400 billion a year, or nearly a third of GDP.

The deficits of the 1980s and 1990s were caused by a confluence of events. In 1981 President Ronald Reagan took office on a platform dedicated to decreasing the size of the federal government and to lessening the threat of communism. Part of this meant that he worked to reduce federal income taxes. Tax rates were slashed and important deductions and exemptions were indexed[1] for inflation to prevent bracket creep[2] from raising taxes later. The part of the equation that focused on quelling communism resulted in an increase in federal spending on national defense from $157 billion in 1980 to $303 billion in 1988. All of this might have meant a budget with historically typical deficits had President Reagan been successful in convincing Congress to cut or even substantially slow the rate of increase in domestic spending. Though the rate of increase in spending on those programs that were on-budget did slow, they did

[1]Recall from Chapter 6 that indexing is adjusting a dollar amount for inflation. It is called indexing because an index, in this case the consumer price index, is used to perform the adjustment.

[2]When inflation occurs and incomes rise exactly in line with inflation, then, unless the tax brackets are adjusted for inflation, people pay a higher percentage of that income in taxes even though the real spending power of their income has remained unchanged. This is called *bracket creep.*

FIGURE 12.2   Deficits as a percentage of GDP: 1940–2017.

Source: The Office of Management and Budget, www.whitehouse.gov/omb/budget/Historicals

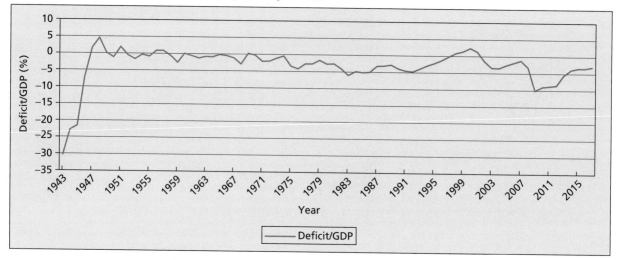

not slow enough. In addition, spending on Social Security and Medicare increased substantially faster than before. While revenues grew quickly despite the cut in income taxes, this growth was insufficient to keep pace with the spending increases. With spending growing in nearly all sectors of the budget and revenues not keeping pace, the deficits during this period were inflation-adjusted, larger than the deficits it took to win World War I but smaller than the deficits it took to win World War II.

Despite incurring the huge deficits, many argue in President Reagan's defense that the victory over the Soviet Union in the Cold War and the **peace dividend** (money that was freed up for other spending priorities when the Cold War was over) that ensued was worth the investment. To back up this position, they claim that the inflation-adjusted military budget in 2000 was smaller than at any other point since World War II and about half of its 1980s peak. If you accept the proposition that the Reagan defense buildup caused, or at least contributed to, a more rapid ending of the Cold War, then those responsible for allowing the deficits of the 1980s are no more to be criticized than those responsible for the deficits from either of the two world wars.

peace dividend
Money that was freed up for other spending priorities when the Cold War was over.

The dramatic turnaround in the deficit picture that occurred between 1996 and 2001 resulted from a nearly 50 percent increase in taxable income. About a third of that increase resulted from a skyrocketing stock market. From 1991 to 2000 taxable capital gains income increased from

just over $100 billion to more than $630 billion. As a result, a deficit that had been approaching $300 billion in 1992 turned into a $236 billion surplus in 2000.

Beginning in 2000, things began to unravel. In March, the stock market reached its peak (12,000 on the Dow Jones and 5,000 on the NASDAQ) and began a two-and-a-half year decline (7,500 on the Dow and 1,200 on the NASDAQ). Taxable capital gains income was cut by more than half in that time. In November of 2000 we had an election where it took a month of court battles to decide who won the presidency. By the time George W. Bush took office, the economy was in recession and unemployment was on the rise. He delivered on a promised tax cut in the spring of 2001 that further diminished revenues. The attacks of September 11 resulted in vast increases in government spending for reconstruction as well as military and domestic security. More tax cuts, undisciplined federal spending unrelated to defense, and the wars in Afghanistan and Iraq further swelled the deficit such that by 2005 the total budget deficit was more than $239 billion.

In 2006 and 2007, the lack of progress in Iraq forced President Bush to choose between withdrawing or increasing forces. His surge strategy, combined with a weakening housing market, caused deficits to rise again. The 2008 tax cuts and weakening economy in early 2008 further exacerbated the deficit, resulting in predictions of $500 to $600 billion deficits that would greet a new president. Then, of course, the bottom dropped out of the financial sector in the fall of 2008. This created four strains on the deficit. First, the weakened state of the economy caused tax revenues to slow. Second, that weakening resulted in increases in unemployment compensation, Medicaid, and other welfare spending. Third, the financial collapse resulted in the appropriation of $750 billion to the Troubled Asset Relief Program (TARP) in an attempt to prevent a global depression. Finally, a month after President Obama was sworn in, he signed a $787 billion stimulus package. Though not all of the money was spent in FY2009, deficits surged past $1 trillion for that year and were on a path not to fall under that level until at least FY2013. The lack of agreement between President Obama and Republicans in Congress resulted in no significant deficit reduction. The tax increases on high-income taxpayers and the sequester (automatic budget cuts) of 2013 had the effect of reducing trillion dollar per year deficits by less than 15 percent.

How Economists See the Deficit and the Debt

As you know by now, economists see things differently from the way many other people see them. Nothing is more emblematic of that different viewpoint than the way economists look at deficits and the national debt. When noneconomists see that we have spent more than we have paid in taxes, they see it as a problem. Only a minority of economists believe that the current U.S. national debt represents a significant threat to current or future economic health. This differs substantially from the position most economists took in the early 1990s when the deficit was large and growing and the debt and its interest obligations were becoming rapidly burdensome. We next examine why economists hold differing views on this matter.

Operating and Capital Budgets

To see things from an economist's perspective, consider first that the debt is made up of a series of budget deficits over time. The next thing to realize about the budget

operating budget
That part of the federal budget devoted to spending on goods and services that will be used in the current year.

capital budget
That part of the federal budget devoted to spending on goods that will last several years.

is that, again from an economist's viewpoint, it is figured all wrong. It should be divided between **operating** and **capital budgets**. Things that are big, expensive, and will last several years ought not be accounted for in the same way as federal purchases of toilet paper. Highways, dams, and buildings are

certainly going to be around for a while, and it makes little economic sense to account for them as though they are going to disappear at the end of the year.

Away from government, what businesses normally do with such large investments is to create a *capital budget*. An investment in an asset with a long life simply has to be able to generate profits over the years that are more than sufficient to make payments on the asset. The expenses of the business that go to pay for items that are used up soon after they are paid for, like labor, paper, and phone calls, go into an *operating budget*. As long as the revenue of the firm is sufficient to cover the operating budget and make the appropriate payments on the capital previously purchased, the business is fine, even if it is carrying a large debt. If big corporations did their accounting the way the federal government does, they would rarely show a profit. When they did show a profit, it would be a great deal smaller than usual.

One problem with separating a capital budget from an operating budget is trying to figure out what spending is an investment that should go into the capital budget and what spending is not. Liberal politicians tend to argue that nearly all social spending should be included in the capital budget. Conservatives, on the other hand, usually say that nearly all military spending should be included in the capital budget. Each would label its spending recommendations as investments in the future and the other's as spending on today. This distinction is important because getting the budget to balance is harder as more goes into the operating side. Moreover, balancing the operating budget is more a political shell game than an exercise grounded in fundamental economic principles.

Cyclical and Structural Deficits

Another way in which economists look at the deficit differently from other people is that we divide it between its structural and cyclical components. In Chapter 6 we broke unemployment into three parts—frictional, cyclical, and structural. We can do a similar thing here. The part of the deficit that is attributable to the

cyclical deficit
That part of the deficit attributable to the economy's not being at full employment.

structural deficit
That part of the deficit that would remain even if the economy were at full employment.

economy's not being at full employment is called the **cyclical deficit,** and the part of the deficit that would remain even if we were at full employment is called a **structural deficit**. If the deficit is large because the economy is not doing well, then the whole economy is the issue, not the deficit. If the deficit is large even when the economy is doing relatively well, then the deficit is a problem. Economists who think deficits can be used to stimulate a lackluster economy consider that part of the deficit attributable to the "stimulus package" useful and label it **functional finance.**

functional finance
That part of the budget attributable to programs designed to get an economy out of a recession.

The Debt as a Percentage of GDP

There are other reasons why most economists did not view the national debt (as it stood during the pre-2008 periods) as all that troubling. Among these was that, as a percentage of national income, the national debt was not anywhere near as high as it had been. If you look at Figure 12.3, you will see that the ratio of national debt to the GDP was greater than 1 after World War II and, while it increased to near .70 in the 1990s, it fell sharply when in the late 1990s deficits turned into surpluses. Of course, that lasted only a short time as burgeoning deficits resumed bringing the debt-to-GDP ratio back near the 70 percent level. With the global economic downturn and the subsequent TARP and stimulus plans all occurring in relatively short order, the debt shot up to near 100 percent of GDP by 2011. Current projections suggest a debt level above 100 percent of GDP will exist through 2020.

Gross domestic product measures what we can afford as a nation, and Figure 12.3 shows that we were in a position that was similar to the average of our recent history; yet with the debt above 100 percent of GDP, a level not seen in quite some time, and with Medicare and

Social Security spending certain to rise much faster than their funding sources, more economists are concerned about the debt picture going forward.

International Comparisons

There is an even more compelling argument that the state of the national debt has changed markedly in the last five years. As can be seen in Table 12.1, the U.S. debt-to-GDP ratio was well within the norms of the rest of the world for the period between 1970 and 2005. Though still nowhere near the levels of Italy and Japan, this debt to GDP ratio that had been significantly better than Canada's and Germany's, and only somewhat worse than that of the United Kingdom, is now noticeably worse than any of those countries. The country that

TABLE 12.1 International comparisons of gross debt-to-GDP ratios.

Source: OECD, www.oecd.org

Year	Canada	U.S.	U.K.	Germany	Italy	Japan
1970	54.1	44.5	78.0	17.5	38.1	10.6
1975	44.9	42.8	62.1	23.1	57.4	20.2
1980	45.6	39.8	54.5	30.2	58.0	47.9
1985	66.3	53.5	59.4	41.6	82.1	64.2
1990	74.5	66.6	33.0	41.5	103.7	68.6
1995	100.3	74.2	52.7	57.2	125.5	87.1
2000	82.1	55.2	45.6	60.4	121.6	136.7
2005	70.3	62.4	46.5	71.1	120.5	177.3
2010	84.4	92.8	81.3	79.9	131.3	198.4
2013	85.5	113.0	110.4	86.2	129.6	224.3

FIGURE 12.3 Debt as a percentage of GDP: 1940–2018.

Source: The Office of Management and Budget, www.whitehouse.gov/omb/budget/Historicals

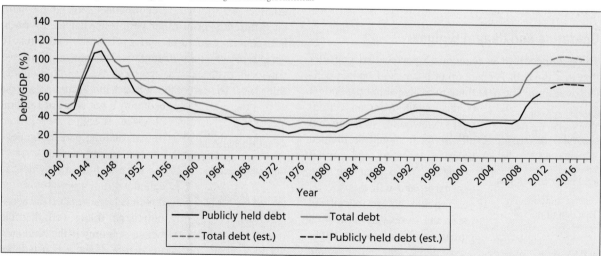

FIGURE 12.4 Who owns our debt? Percentage of the debt held by the public, trust funds, and the Federal Reserve.

Source: The Office of Management and Budget, www.whitehouse.gov/omb/budget/Historicals

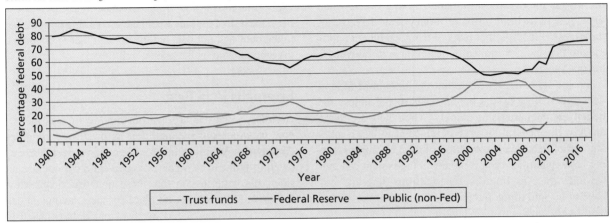

has really begun to tread close to its ability to manage its debt is Japan. Once held up as an example of fiscal rectitude, Japan, has seen its national debt balloon from 10.6 percent of GDP in 1970 to more than 224 percent in 2013. The long stagnant Japanese economy is the subject of Chapter 15.

Generational Accounting

Some economists look at the deficit and surplus in a completely different fashion. These economists, led by Alan Auerbach and Laurence Kotlikoff, argue that, instead of looking at the deficit as a meaningful number, we should look at the "net tax rate" that the current policies imply for future generations. To understand their argument, recall the discussion of present value from Chapter 7. These economists and others argue that if you look at the difference between the present value of what people of different generations pay in taxes and the transfers that they get in government benefits, you can compute a net tax rate. They claim that this number has been getting steadily worse for younger generations, and that future generations will face a terrible tax burden because of the deficits of the 1980s and 1990s and the entitlement crises of Social Security and Medicare.

Who Owns the Debt?

The question of who owns the bonds that a nation sells to finance its debt is an important aspect of any nation's debt. Although this may seem like an irrelevant issue, you may be surprised to know that the U.S. government

owes itself more than a quarter of the debt. That is what separates the "Total" and "Public" debts in Figure 12.3 and is the point of Figure 12.4. There are two ways in which the federal government lends itself money:

1. The Federal Reserve uses federal debt for purposes of open-market operations.
2. The federal trust funds invest their money by lending it to other parts of the federal government.

As you may see in the issue chapter on monetary policy, the Federal Reserve of the United States (the Fed) has three options for moving the economy: open-market operations, changing key interest rates, and changing the reserve ratio. Open-market operations are activities that result in the Fed buying or selling bonds. To get money into the economy, it buys bonds, and to remove money from the system, it sells bonds. Since the role of the Federal Reserve is to keep inflation on an even keel, it must steadily increase the money supply to keep pace with the growth in the economy. Doing so requires that the Fed constantly buys bonds. In this way the federal government owes itself a growing amount of money. If you think that is silly, consider that when the federal government borrows money from itself it also pays itself interest, and, as a matter of fact, in the early 1990s it was borrowing money from itself to pay interest to itself.

The government also owes itself money through the various trust funds it maintains for Social Security, Medicare, highways, airports, and other smaller parts of the government entities. By law, these trust funds are allowed to invest their money in federal bonds only.

Given that these bonds are the safest investment on the planet, this makes sense, but the bonds also return among the lowest interest rates available. In any event, when these programs bring in more money than they spend, the excess is lent to other parts of the government and is money that the government will not have to borrow on the open market.

From Figure 12.4 we see that the amount of federal debt that is held by the public tends to fall unless the deficit and debt are rising quickly. When these are rising quickly, the Federal Reserve is reluctant to buy a great amount of debt in a short period of time because injecting large quantities of new money in the system can create inflation. Any time large deficits are rung up, they have to be sold to the public, and the overall proportion held by the public rises. When the deficit is not large or we have a surplus, the percentage held by the public will fall. It is conceivable that if we ran many years of large surpluses, the bulk of the debt would be owed to the government itself.

On a more dreary note, we should remember that the portion of the debt that the Medicare system owns began to be sold to the public beginning in 2010. That was when the expenses of the hospital portion of Medicare first exceeded the tax payments that fund it. That debt was transferred to the Treasury and then sold to the public. Though the effect was slight at the time, as the process continues, we can expect that the portion of the debt held by the public will rise. Because of the way we do the accounting now, the national debt will not rise, but the amount that is important, the amount held by the public, will.

Externally Held Debt

A concern that has arisen from time to time is the degree to which our national debt is owed to foreigners. At points in American history our national debt has been owed to citizens of other nations. While we could consider this flattering, in that these non-Americans view the United States as a safe place for their savings, it can also be a problem if too much of our debt is owed to foreigners.

Figure 12.5 demonstrates that, in large measure, the Japanese and Chinese have loaned us much of the money we have used to go on the federal spending and tax cut spree of this decade. Our debt to citizens of Japan has more than doubled since 2000 while our debt to Chinese citizens has increased 14-fold. Of the nearly $15 trillion in debt, 55 percent is owed to real people and of that 40 percent is owed to non-U.S. entities.

FIGURE 12.5   U.S. debt owed to foreign entitites.

Source: www.treasury.gov/resource-center/data-chart-center/tic/Documents/mfhhis01.txt

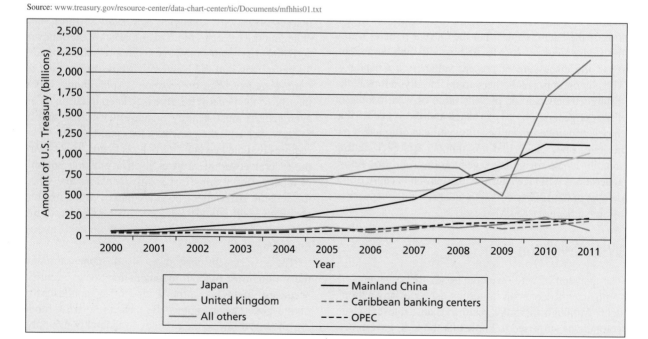

FIGURE 12.6 Built-in stabilizers at work.

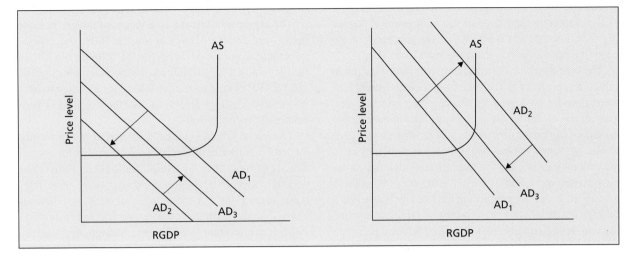

This presents a problem for the future in that eventually these investors will want their money back in the form of goods and services. Foreigners are no different than the rest of us: They save in order to buy something later. When one U.S. citizen owes another U.S. citizen money, the future state of the economy is not necessarily threatened. On the other hand, when the U.S. taxpayer owes money to foreign investors, part of the taxes that we pay in the future will go to pay them interest rather than to pay for schools, defense, or our criminal justice system.

A Balanced-Budget Amendment

One of the important debates of the final quarter of the 20th century was whether we need an amendment to the U.S. Constitution requiring a balanced federal budget. Economists are on both sides of this issue, but the majority believe it is not a good idea. Those who are opposed reason that an inflexible amendment could cause recessions to turn into depressions because the provisions of the amendment would mandate tax increases and spending cuts at precisely the time when just the opposite would be needed. Those in favor of the amendment argue that the politicians' performance in the latter half of the 20th century is evidence of Congress's inability to show the discipline necessary to bring budgets into balance. Balancing the federal budget, it is argued, is necessary to generate low interest rates, which bring about long-term, investment-led growth.

Opponents of balanced budgets and of a constitutional amendment that makes them mandatory offer their best argument against a balanced-budget amendment by appealing to the aggregate supply–aggregate demand model that was explained in Chapter 8. The left panel of Figure 12.6 depicts this model and what would happen if we entered a recession. If aggregate demand were to shrink from AD_1 to AD_2 and a balanced-budget amendment were not required, two things would happen: (1) People would make less money and therefore pay less in taxes, and (2) people would require more assistance from government and spending would have to rise. This would happen without any new laws having to be passed. This nondiscretionary fiscal policy is built into the system and is called a *built-in stabilizer*. This stabilizer would result in aggregate demand's getting a boost back in the direction it came from, perhaps AD_3. If a balanced-budget amendment were in place, we would be without the built-in stabilizer and the movement back to AD_3 would not happen. A recession would thus be worse than it would be if it were to come along now.

Of course the opposite could happen, and the right side of Figure 12.6 depicts that eventuality. Because spending on welfare programs and unemployment benefits would fall and tax revenues would rise, an increase in aggregate demand would result in surpluses. Without a balanced-budget requirement (that might force the money to be spent or taxes cut), aggregate demand would fall back to AD_3. With such a requirement, aggregate demand would not bounce back and the economic boom would be more extensive than otherwise.

procyclical
Situation that renders good times better and bad times worse.

What this means is a balanced-budget amendment would be **procyclical** because good times would be even better and bad times even worse than they would be without such a requirement. This "boom or bust" phenomenon was part of the economic landscape of the 19th century. Avoiding that outcome has been one of the successes of the economics profession in the post–World War II era.

The best argument for mandating a balanced budget in some way, however, is that an elimination of federal borrowing would go a long way to reducing interest rates. The results of the 1990s support the idea that reducing the deficit can create a virtuous cycle in which lower deficits create lower interest rates. With lower interest rates the economy grows, tax revenues increase, the deficit decreases even more, and so on. While this occurred without a balanced-budget amendment in the late 1990s, the 1960s through the early 1990s was a period of extensive borrowing with little fiscal discipline by either political party.

In the 1990s both the Republican and Democratic parties claimed that reducing the federal deficit was important. Both parties, under President Bush (George Herbert Walker) with a Democratic Congress and President Clinton with a mostly Republican Congress, attempted to reduce the deficit. Each did it with means consistent with their own party's philosophy. They were successful because a reduction in the demand for loanable funds by the federal government translated into lower interest rates. In particular, mortgage interest rates were lower during this period than they had been in 30 years. Lower interest rates meant more business investment as well. What ensued was the most dramatic drop in the deficit and the longest peacetime expansion since the end of World War II.

Both proponents and opponents of such an amendment point to the behavior of the states during the 1990s and early 2000s. Opponents note that the fiscal crises the states experienced between 2002 and 2006, and again in 2009 were a direct result of the constitutional requirements to have balanced budgets. Though the constitutions of the states are varied in this regard, they generally suggest that they can spend no more than the revenue for that year plus their built-up reserve. This essentially requires that they have a cyclically balanced budget, one that is in balance over the business cycle. An annual balanced-budget requirement would not let a state create or utilize a reserve. What occurred in many states, though, was that the shortfall in revenues lasted longer than the reserve. Many states raided their state employee pension funds and delayed payments to local school districts and state universities, forcing them to borrow to meet their needs, all in an effort to have a "balanced budget." Opponents argue that governments will resort to these and other "smoke and mirror" tactics when forced to render any balanced-budget amendment meaningless.

The arguments relating to a balanced budget amendment were rendered moot when, in 2008, the federal government borrowed hundreds of billions of dollars for the spring 2008 stimulus and especially after the fall 2008 TARP plan required the federal government to borrow nearly a trillion dollars to save the financial system from meltdown.

The initial Obama budget, curiously if not ironically named "A New Era of Responsibility," called for annual deficits of more than $1 trillion for 2009 and 2010 and deficits above $700 billion for many years after that. It has turned out that the deficit picture was somewhat worse than that with trillion dollar deficits extending into 2012. It is important to understand, though, that the majority of economists would acknowledge that imposing a balanced budget in this period would have seriously diminished the government's ability to stabilize the economy. Economists, even those among a group that might be called deficit "hawks," were not upset by the record deficits of 2009 and 2010. The fear of these economists is that without a serious reduction in the deficit over the course of the next few years, when the large Medicare and Social Security bills due to retiring baby boomers come due, there will be little ability of the federal government to make good on those promises, even with borrowed money.

Economists are all over the map in terms of how and when these deficits should be closed. Some, like Paul Krugman, believe that the real concern is down the road and that tax increases (especially on the wealthy) will be enough to close the deficit to manageable levels. Others, like John Taylor, believe that it should not only be sooner rather than later, but should be accomplished with entitlement reform. Still, almost no economist of any reputation believes that a balanced budget requirement would have been helpful during the 2008–2011 period.

Projections

In the movie *Major League*, a 1989 baseball comedy, the character played by real-life Milwaukee Brewers announcer Bob Uecker suggests that a pitch that ends up in the stands was "juuuuuust a bit outside." In terms of projecting the deficit/surplus picture, the Congressional Budget Office and the Office of Management and Budget have similarly missed the target. In 1990 both were projecting "deficits as far as the eye could see." In 1995 they

FIGURE 12.7   Deficit and surplus projections of the past.

Source: "The Budget and Economic Outlook: An Update," 1985–2011, Congressional Budget Office, www.cbo.gov

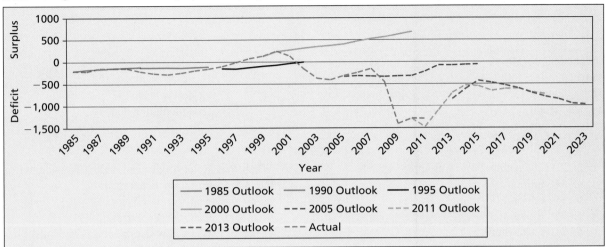

each projected a shrinking deficit. Five years later they projected that "we would be debt free by 2010." Two years after that, it was deficits now, surpluses later.

Figure 12.7 illustrates the rapidly changing projections, but the year 2005, in particular, illustrates the degree of misestimation. In 2000, the prediction for 2005 was that there would be a surplus approaching $402 billion. The year actually came to a close with a deficit of more than $400 billion. As a result, the estimates produced in 2000 missed the mark by $800 billion (or one-third the size of the federal government.)

How could they get it so wrong, so often, and still be given any credibility? In an April 2003 report, the Congressional Budget Office makes a pretty good case that it wasn't their fault. They argue that taking into account the things that occurred during this period, they did a pretty good job in short-term projections. They also argue that longer-term projections are given more weight than they are due.

Consider these factors: No one foresaw that the economy would grow at twice the projected rates in the late 1990s. No one projected that the stock markets would grow as quickly as they did during this period such that taxable capital gains income would increase 700 percent. No one projected that the 2000 presidential election would insert so much uncertainty into the economy and push it into a recession in 2001. They had no way of knowing in 1995 that George W. Bush would take over as president and get a tax cut enacted in 2001 and 2003. They certainly could not have taken into account in 2000 that Al-Qaeda would attack the United States or that we would respond by going to war in Afghanistan and Iraq in 2002 and 2003. Finally, few saw the economy of 2008 and 2009 "falling off a cliff," as Berkshire Hathaway chairman Warren Buffett described it. Still, the "outlook" lines on the graph are all upward sloping, meaning that the OMB and CBO are always projecting a better future when the reality is that there are ups and downs.

Summary

You now understand how economists look at federal budget deficits and surpluses and the national debt. You know that deficits have been more often than not caused by wars and that economists are less interested in the raw numbers of the debt and deficits than in more sophisticated measures of them. You now are aware of U.S. economic history and that comparisons with other countries indicate that the United States had a relatively moderate national debt-to-GDP ratio, but that the deficits of the period from 2008 to 2012 have raised debt concerns dramatically. You know that the federal government actually owns much of the debt, and you should understand why economists are mostly against an amendment to the U.S. Constitution that would mandate that it maintain a balanced budget. Finally, you now see that the deficit-surplus picture changed substantially between 1996 and 2001 and changed again as a result of the 2001 recession, the September 11, 2001, terrorist attacks, the wars in Afghanistan and Iraq, and the recession of 2007–2009.

Key Terms

budget deficit, 150
budget surplus, 150
capital budget, 153
cyclical deficit, 153

functional finance, 154
national debt, 150
off-budget, 150
on-budget, 150

operating budget, 153
peace dividend, 152
procyclical, 157
structural deficit, 153

Quiz Yourself

1. In 2011 the national debt was approximately
   a. $15 million.
   b. $15 billion.
   c. $15 trillion.
   d. $15 quadrillion.
2. The off-budget–on-budget distinction
   a. is important because two large programs, Social Security and Medicare, largely run off-budget.
   b. is a historical fiction.
   c. deals with long-lasting products of government (like roads and bridges).
   d. is important because defense is run off-budget.
3. The U.S. budget
   a. is required to be balanced.
   b. is never truly balanced, but historically surpluses are more common than deficits.
   c. is never truly balanced, but historically surpluses are less common than deficits.
   d. is typically balanced except in time of war.
4. The $400 billion deficits of 2005 were
   a. accurately forecast by the Office of Management and Budget in 2000.
   b. accurately forecast by the Office of Management and Budget in 2002.
   c. accurately forecast by the Office of Management and Budget in 2003.
   d. much higher than any previous Office of Management and Budget forecast.
5. The portion of the national debt owed to citizens of other countries
   a. is economically irrelevant however big it is.
   b. is economically important, but it has been falling in recent years.
   c. is economically important and it has been rising in recent years.
   d. is practically inconsequential because it is so small.

6. When looking at a balanced-budget amendment to the U.S. Constitution, economists
   a. are universally opposed to it.
   b. are universally in favor of it.
   c. are of two minds with opponents concerned about its procyclical nature.
   d. are of two minds with proponents excited about its procyclical nature.
7. By way of international comparison, recent U.S. deficits have increased the ratio of debt to GDP
   a. such that the United States has the highest ratio in the industrialized world.
   b. but every other industrialized nation's ratio is much worse.
   c. but the United States ratio is still lower than that of Germany, Canada, and Japan.
   d. such that only Japan's ratio is worse.

Short Answer Questions

1. If you ranked eras in terms of times in which the national debt was the biggest, what measures could you use and why? How would the measures differ when ranking the deficits of the 1940s, 1980s, and 2010s?
2. Why might you distinguish between borrowing to rebuild roads and bridges and borrowing to increase food stamp allocations?
3. Suppose the deficit were to be $300 billion during normal times, but increases to $500 billion because we are in a recession, then increases again to $600 billion because the government attempts to stimulate the economy. Which of these amounts are the structural deficit and the cyclical deficit and which amount represents functional finance?
4. Explain why to whom a country owes its money matters in terms of the true burden a national debt will have on future generations.

5. Explain why what deficit spending buys matters in terms of the true burden a national debt will have on future generations.

Think about This

The United States and China have had foreign policy disputes in the past. The most problematic situation could arise over the status of Taiwan. Does owing Chinese investors nearly $1 trillion make this problem more or less likely to come to a head? Does economic interdependence promote peace?

Talk about This

What is the opportunity cost of running a high deficit? How might this opportunity cost depend on the shape of the supply curve for loanable funds? What does it tell you about the supply curve for loanable funds when interest rates remained low even while the United States went from a $200 billion surplus to a $1.5 trillion deficit over 15 years?

For More Insight See

Journal of Economic Perspectives 10, no. 1 (Winter 1996). See articles by Alan J. Auerbach, Ronald Lee, Jonathan Skinner, and Douglas Bernheim.

Ronald, Lee, and Jonathan Skinner, "Will Aging Baby Boomers Bust the Federal Budget?" *Journal of Economic Perspectives* 13, no. 1 (Winter 1999).

Behind the Numbers

Total United States off-budget, on-budget and total deficit, surplus, debt, debt sources 1940–2012.
Budget of the United States Government, historical tables—www.whitehouse.gov/omb/budget/Historicals
U.S. GDP 1940–2006.
　　Bureau of Economic Analysis—www.bea.gov
International comparisons of gross debt-to-GDP ratios.
　　Statistical Abstract of the United States; comparative international statistics—www.oecd.org
CBO projections.
Congressional Budget Office; The Budget and Economic Outlook: an update, multiple years—www.cbo.gov

CHAPTER THIRTEEN

The Housing Bubble

Learning Objectives

After reading this chapter you should be able to:

LO1   List the fundamental determinants of housing prices.

LO2   Compare and contrast the components of a traditional mortgage, an interest-only mortgage, and a negative amortization mortgage.

LO3   Discuss how a bubble can be created in a market based on unrealistic expectations.

LO4   Summarize the consequences of a burst housing bubble on the U.S. economy.

Chapter Outline

How Much Is a House Really Worth?

Mortgages

How to Make a Bubble

Pop Goes the Bubble!

The Effect on the Overall Economy

Summary

In this chapter you will learn about the U.S. housing market, mortgages, and lending practices. Specifically, you will learn how, fundamentally, housing prices are determined, and how housing prices are determined in a hot, bubble market. Finally, you will learn how the bursting of such a bubble in 2006 and 2007 was only the first wave of housing foreclosures and how the combination set off the worst economic spiral in at least 27 years.

How Much Is a House Really Worth?

As you can see from Figure 13.1, between 1997 and mid-2006 housing prices in many major urban areas rose much faster than overall inflation (as measured by core PCE) and much faster than housing prices in other areas. This housing price index, created by economists Karl Case and Robert Shiller, has a base year of 2000 and measures the increase in prices in major metropolitan areas. While the price of all goods consumers buy (excluding food and energy) increased about 13 percent between 2000 and 2006, and while home prices in Dallas and Cleveland increased a mere 25 percent, home prices in Miami and Los Angeles had almost tripled. Starting

in mid-2006, the housing market in many metropolitan areas collapsed. Home prices in Phoenix dropped 41 percent, while those in Las Vegas and Miami dropped 39 percent and 38 percent respectively. To understand why this happened, we need to remember some fundamentals from the definition of opportunity cost, from supply and demand, and from interest rates and present value.

The key ingredients in what a house is fundamentally worth pertain to the opportunity cost of the land upon which the home sits, the cost of labor and materials in the community, the characteristics of the home itself, and the income of the likely potential buyers.

Referring back to Figure 13.1, the reason Dallas's home prices never increased at the rate of those in other areas is that buildable land is abundant in North Central Texas. The area is flat, with relatively few alternative uses. Unlike Los Angeles, San Francisco, or Miami, Dallas has almost no physical barriers to expansion. This means that the supply of buildable land is quite elastic. That doesn't mean land is created, but rather land use is changed from ranching to residential use and this can be done very easily. So even if there is a significant increase in the demand for homes, the price of an existing

FIGURE 13.1   Case-Shiller indices.

Source: Federal Reserve Bank of St. Louis, http://research.stlouisfed.org/fred2

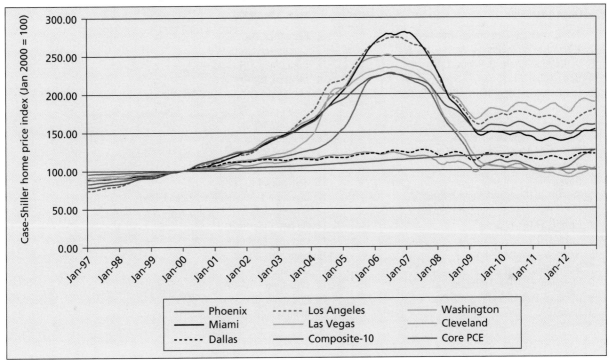

house can, therefore, not increase beyond that of the alternative of building a new one. While building further away from the city center (and there are actually two city centers because Ft. Worth is practically next door) can be inconvenient, resulting from the longer commute, most home buyers would gladly drive 10 to 20 minutes longer per day if they can save tens of thousands of dollars on the price of the home.

The supply of buildable land in Los Angeles, San Francisco, and Miami is quite inelastic because there are oceans, beaches, environmental regulations, and either swamps or mountains that render some land unsuitable for residential building. An increase in demand for homes in these cities will inevitably result in higher prices.

The next biggest factors in explaining home prices are demand side factors such as the characteristics of the home and the income of the buyers. That a home with all modern amenities will sell for more than an older one in need of repair is obvious. Similarly obvious is that the income of a community's potential buyers matters as well. The Department of Housing and Urban Development estimated median family income in San Francisco and Washington D.C. is substantially higher

(nearly $100,000) than median family income in Dallas and Cleveland (about $60,000). Table 13.1 ranks cities on housing affordability using the ratio of median housing prices to median income. Clearly, the cities are not randomly distributed geographically. California has 18 of the top 20 least affordable cities and the Midwest is home to 17 of the top 20 most affordable.

Population growth also figures into the equation. The city of Detroit is the only city in the world to have gone from a population exceeding 2 million to a population of less than 1 million. This means that for every new home that is built, more than one home will go vacant. In growing areas, new neighborhoods spring up constantly. The Atlanta metropolitan area has seen an increase in home prices based almost entirely on its increase in population.

Mortgages

As we learned in Chapter 7's review of present value and interest rates, the mathematics of amortization are relatively straightforward. In determining a car payment or a mortgage payment, you find the monthly payment

TABLE 13.1   Most affordable and least affordable places to live.

Sources: National Association of Home Builders; www.nahb.com

Least Affordable	Most Affordable
1 San Francisco–San Mateo–Redwood City, CA	1 Fairbanks, AK
2 New York–White Plains–Wayne, NY–NJ	2 Cumberland, MD–WV
3 Santa Ana–Anaheim–Irvine, CA	3 Springfield, OH
4 Ocean City, NJ	4 Monroe, MI
5 Los Angeles–Long Beach–Glendale, CA	5 Mansfield, OH
6 Honolulu, HI	6 Carson City, NV
7 San Luis Obispo–Paso Robles, CA	7 Bay City, MI
8 Santa Cruz–Watsonville, CA	8 Elizabethtown, KY
9 San Jose–Sunnyvale–Santa Clara, CA	9 Kokomo, IN
10 Bridgeport–Stamford–Norwalk, CT	10 Rockford, IL
11 Dover, DE	11 Salisbury, MD
12 San Diego–Carlsbad–San Marcos, CA	12 Davenport–Moline–Rock Island, IA–IL
13 Santa Barbara–Santa Maria–Goleta, CA	13 Hagerstown–Martinsburg, MD–WV
14 Laredo, TX	14 Ogden–Clearfield, UT
15 Salinas, CA	15 Lansing–East Lansing, MI
16 Newark–Union, NJ–PA	16 Lima, OH
17 Barnstable Town, MA	17 Dayton, OH
18 Mc Allen–Edinburg–Mission, TX	18 Wheeling, WV–OH
19 Oakland–Fremont–Hayward, CA	19 Pocatello, ID
20 Napa, CA	20 Indianapolis–Carmel, IN

that will pay off the debt, at a particular interest rate, over a particular period of time. A mortgage, besides being a formal piece of paper, is a payment scheme designed to bring the original debt to zero over a period of time. In the good old days, when your grandparents bought a home, mortgages were all structured the same. The home buyer would be required to pay 20 percent of the value of the home, and the bank would loan the remaining 80 percent. On top of that, your grandparents were compelled to provide verifiable documentation of their income, assets, and debts. Even if they had the 20 percent to put down on the home, if their mortgage payment, their estimated annual property taxes, and homeowners insurance were more than 30 percent of the verifiable income, your grandparents' banker would have been reluctant to lend them the money. They would have counseled your grandparents to buy a smaller home. A final aspect of "old-fashioned" mortgages was that your grandparents' banker would have held the mortgage. This meant that if your grandparents defaulted on their mortgage, their hometown bank would take the loss.

To understand how your grandparents' mortgage would work, look at Table 13.2. In a traditional mortgage the payment lasts for 30 years. Though home prices have risen substantially from the time they bought their first home and interest rates have fluctuated between 4.5 percent and 12 percent during that time, to be clear, let's do an apples-to-apples comparison as we compare the old-fashioned mortgage with the newer ones. Let's assume a loan of $250,000, for 30 years, at 5 percent interest. A financial calculator or a spreadsheet program can help you compute the payment to be $1,342 per month. That is $1,342 the first month, the last month, and every month in between.

Now let's turn to the evolutionary and revolutionary changes that have occurred in the mortgage market. The first significant change came in 1968 when Congress spun off the Federal National Mortgage Association (more commonly known as Fannie Mae) and authorized it as a government-sponsored enterprise to buy home mortgages from banks and other financial institutions that wrote them. It would **securitize** them; that is, it bundled those mortgages together and then sold shares of itself to investors. In so doing, it spread the geographic risk of mortgages that resulted from banks holding a significant portion of the portfolios in local markets.

securitize
The process of bundling nonfinancial assets (typically mortgages) together and then reselling them as either shares or as financial instruments to investors.

TABLE 13.2 Traditional, zero-interest, and negative amortization mortgages, 30 years, 5 percent.

Payment Number	Traditional Mortgage			Interest-Only, 5 Years			Interest-Only, 10 Years			Negative-Amortization, 5 Years		
	Payment	Interest	Balance	Payment	Interest	Balance	Payment	Interest	Balance	Payment	Interest	Balance
0			$250,000			$250,000			$250,000			$250,000
1	$1,342	$1,042	249,700	$1,042	$1,042	250,000	$1,042	$1,042	250,000	$ 521	$1,042	250,521
2	1,342	1,040	249,398	1,042	1,042	250,000	1,042	1,042	250,000	522	1,044	251,043
3	1,342	1,039	249,095	1,042	1,042	250,000	1,042	1,042	250,000	523	1,046	251,566
4	1,342	1,038	248,791	1,042	1,042	250,000	1,042	1,042	250,000	524	1,048	252,090
.												
57	1,342	963	230,719	1,042	1,042	250,000	1,042	1,042	250,000	585	1,170	281,487
58	1,342	961	230,338	1,042	1,042	250,000	1,042	1,042	250,000	586	1,173	282,074
59	1,342	960	229,956	1,042	1,042	250,000	1,042	1,042	250,000	588	1,175	282,661
60	1,342	958	229,572	1,042	1,042	250,000	1,042	1,042	250,000	589	1,178	283,250
61	1,342	957	229,186	1,461	1,042	249,580	1,042	1,042	250,000	1,656	1,180	282,775
62	1,342	955	228,799	1,461	1,040	249,159	1,042	1,042	250,000	1,656	1,178	282,297
63	1,342	953	228,410	1,461	1,038	248,735	1,042	1,042	250,000	1,656	1,176	281,817
64	1,342	952	228,020	1,461	1,036	248,310	1,042	1,042	250,000	1,656	1,174	281,336
.												
117	1,342	855	204,827	1,461	932	223,053	1,042	1,042	250,000	1,656	1,056	252,720
118	1,342	853	204,338	1,461	929	222,521	1,042	1,042	250,000	1,656	1,053	252,117
119	1,342	851	203,848	1,461	927	221,987	1,042	1,042	250,000	1,656	1,050	251,512
120	1,342	849	203,355	1,461	925	221,450	1,042	1,042	250,000	1,656	1,048	250,904
121	1,342	847	202,860	1,461	923	220,912	1,650	1,042	249,392	1,656	1,045	250,293
122	1,342	845	202,364	1,461	920	220,371	1,650	1,039	248,781	1,656	1,043	249,680
123	1,342	843	201,865	1,461	918	219,827	1,650	1,037	248,168	1,656	1,040	249,065
.												
358	1,342	17	2,667	1,461	18	2,905	1,650	20	3,279	1,656	21	3,291
359	1,342	11	1,336	1,461	12	1,455	1,650	14	1,643	1,656	14	1,649
360	1,342	6	0	1,461	6	0	1,650	7	0	1,656	7	0

This reduced the risk to any one bank of going bankrupt as a result of a local economic downturn. In so doing, this reduced the risk to investors and thereby reduced home mortgage interest rates. Its sister organization, the Federal Home Loan Mortgage Corporation (commonly known as Freddie Mac), was founded in 1970 and did much the same thing except that it focused on selling these bundled mortgage-backed securities to other investors. Neither the principal nor the profits of either entity was explicitly guaranteed by the federal government, but investors believed there to be an implicit understanding that should these entities have difficulty, the federal government would back them.

Beginning in the late 1980s, mortgages began to spring up where the buyer would have to put down only 5 percent or 10 percent. Though they would have to pay for an insurance policy (that would pay the bank in case of default), this opened up home buying as an option for millions of Americans. In the early part of this decade, zero-down mortgages became common. Only paperwork costs would be charged when the house was sold.

Beginning in 2002, **interest-only mortgages** and even **negative-amortization mortgages** began to spring up. An interest-only mortgage, as the name suggests, has the buyer paying only interest for the first few (typically 5 or 10) years of a mortgage and then paying off the balance over the remainder of the mortgage. A negative-amortization mortgage does much the same thing, except that buyers get to choose how much they want their payment to be in the first few years of the mortgage. These **pick-a-pay mortgages** (also known as pay option adjustable rate mortgages) would typically have the buyer paying about half the interest accrued each month on the mortgage so the outstanding balance on the mortgage would rise over time. After a few years, the mortgage converts to a standard type and the balance is paid off over the remaining years.

Now let's compare the traditional mortgages to the interest-only mortgages and negative-amortization mortgages. Again, comparing apples-to-apples, suppose the homeowner is borrowing $250,000, for 30 years, at 5 percent interest. Looking at Table 13.2 you see that an interest-only mortgage saves the buyer $300 per month for however long the interest-only period lasts, but the payment increases substantially once the mortgage converts to a traditional version. Because with most negative-amortization mortgages, the borrower gets to choose how much to pay during the initial payment period, let's assume they take an option of paying half the interest they owe each month. As a result the outstanding balance rises, so the payment rises, albeit very slowly until the point were it converts to a traditional mortgage and then the payment nearly triples.

These interest-only and negative-amortization mortgages were popular with home buyers because they allowed someone of modest means to get into a home they might otherwise not be able to afford. What is unclear is the degree to which borrowers adequately understood the terms of these mortgages. They may have simply not read their documentation, or they may have been convinced that regardless of how high their mortgage payments rose, the ever increasing value of their home would allow them to take out a second mortgage with a home equity line of credit. Of the interest-only and negative-amortization mortgages issued during 2006 and 2007, approximately half came with built-in home equity lines of credit.

How to Make a Bubble

As NASDAQ investors of the late 1990s discovered, bubbles are created by the expectation of higher prices causing people to buy assets based on that expectation rather than fundamentals. When you are told to "buy now before the price goes up" and you do, you only add to the volume of the bubble. People buy on the expectation that prices will rise faster than their ability to afford those same assets later so they become convinced to buy now. What really gets a bubble going is borrowed money. If you had to put 20 percent down on a home, the increased price would affect your ability to react to that expectation. With the ability to put nothing down, and pay only half the interest, the buyer's ability to continue fueling the bubble is sustained, not diminished.

As NASDAQ bubble-riders remember, bubbles are fun when they go up. Why? Suppose you bought that $250,000 home in Miami in January 2002. Suppose you put nothing down and took out a negative-amortization mortgage. In Miami, from January 2002 to January 2007, the average home more than doubled in value.

interest-only mortgage
A mortgage that allows the buyer to pay only the interest portion of the typical payment for the first few years of a mortgage. The mortgage would reset to a traditional mortgage after that period, typically at a higher payment.

negative-amortization mortgage
A mortgage that allows the buyer to pay less than the interest portion of the typical payment for the first few years of a mortgage. The mortgage would reset to a traditional mortgage after that period, typically at a higher payment.

pick-a-pay mortgage
A variety of negative amortization mortgage that allows the buyer to choose a payment for the first few years of a mortgage.

So you may owe $283,250 on the house you bought for $250,000, but who cares? It's now worth $500,000. Having trouble making the payments that have now increased from $589 per month to $1,656? No problem. You now have $216,750 in equity in that home and since you signed up for a home equity line of credit when you signed up for the mortgage, you can use your home like an ATM. You can even buy an SUV and take a vacation!

While that explains the demand side of the housing bubble, bubbles require calamitous mistakes on both the demand side and the supply side. So you may be asking why banks would lend money to these borrowers. This takes us back to the first of the evolutionary changes in the mortgage market: securitization. While your grandparents' mortgage was owned by their local bank, these mortgages were immediately sold. It was no longer part of the local banker's job to counsel homebuyers against borrowing more than they could afford. Remember that old 30 percent rule? The banker no longer cared that you could not afford the payment because the banker was going to sell the mortgage within days of writing the mortgage. If you defaulted on the mortgage, it was someone else's problem. In addition, about half of negative-amortization mortgages were "liar loans" in that the bankers who wrote the mortgages purposefully did not verify the income or assets of the borrower. They merely consulted the credit agencies. If your credit was good enough that they could sell your mortgage to Fannie Mae or Freddie Mac, they wrote the mortgage and sold it within days.[1]

There is one other aspect of the modern mortgage market that may have contributed to the mess, and that is the noticeable absence of the intimidation involved in the closing process. Your grandparents sat across the table from a banker who went through each piece of paper associated with the mortgage. Your grandparents paid very close attention, in part because they were afraid that if they didn't, somehow the mortgage would not go through. Today, a click here or a phone call there, and you can be approved by a mortgage company with no local interests whatsoever. That means that you get a package of papers that you simply have to take down to a notary public (a designation of a person that certifies that the person signing is indeed the named party) and sign where the "sign here" tabs are located. This eliminates one of the places where a borrower might better understand the features of a mortgage (such as the tripling of the required payment after year 5).

[1] They may still take your payment every month, but they are only servicing it. They send that payment to the true owner.

credit default swap
Insurance on a mortgage-backed security.

Some in the financial system began to openly worry about the impact of a collapse of the mortgage market. This fear created an instrument that, perversely, only added to the bubble. By the middle of the decade, it became more difficult to sell the securitized mortgages because of the growing fear of foreclosures. The same entities that bought the mortgages, securitized them and then sold them to investors, now offered to sell the investors **credit default swaps.** In this case, the credit default swap acted like an insurance policy that promised to pay the holder of the securitized mortgage should the borrowers fail to pay their debts. This satisfied the investors' concern for security and kept the bubble going. The problem was that these insurance policies were not regulated like typical insurance policies. A typical homeowners or auto insurance company is compelled to have sufficient capital to pay claims and is often required to carry reinsurance. Though credit default swaps are, most certainly, insurance policies, those that sold them were not regulated as if they were. Though some in Congress and others in regulatory bodies began to question these practices, the underlying feel-good story of record rates of homeownership and increasing homeowner wealth (at least paper wealth) overwhelmed these voices of concern. This was the now infamous AIG's most profitable line of business for several years prior to its needed bailout by the Federal Reserve.

Pop Goes the Bubble!

What the feel-good story relies upon heavily is the fiction that home prices only go up. Home prices can fall. Imagine this story somewhat differently. Suppose the price of the home falls from $250,000 to $200,000 because the home was only 1,500 square feet to begin with, had few amenities, and was in a relatively unattractive neighborhood. That is, suppose the fundamentals start to take over and the speculative demand to buy a house at any price goes away, meaning that the only reason its price exceeded what was rational for its location was a bubble mentality (like NASDAQ 1999 and 2000). Now the poor homeowner, who paid $250,000 for a home that is worth only $200,000, must pay $1,656 per month because he or she owes $283,250.

What are the options? Not many. First, if the homeowners sell the home they are in, they will owe $83,250 plus real estate fees of approximately $12,000 more, and they will have no home. If they do not have that in savings, they will have to negotiate some other noncollateralized loan to pay off that amount before they can buy another home. Their only option to get out from under the massive debt is bankruptcy. This is a very bad option because they not only lose the home in which they live but they become unable to buy another home for years to come. Of course, they also eliminate their ability to buy cars, furniture, or anything else on time as well. Their ability to go on vacation is quashed by their inability to qualify for credit cards and their ability to pay off their existing credit card debt is eliminated because they no longer have equity in their home.

People who used this form of negative-amortization loan to purchase a home did so either because they believed their income in a few years would be sufficient to cover the increased mortgage payment, or they believed that housing prices would continue to rise, or they believed that a combination of the two would cause everything to turn out in the end. Unfortunately, it didn't "turn out in the end" for many borrowers. Beginning in 2006 foreclosures and near foreclosures (homes more than 30 days in arrears) began to skyrocket. In 2007, foreclosures were up 51 percent, and in 2008 they were up 82 percent. In Nevada in early 2009, 1 in 14 homes was in some sort of foreclosure process. In one month alone, November 2008, 1 in 76 homes in Nevada received foreclosure paperwork. The hardest hit states were California, Nevada, and Florida. It is not hard to see why. Consider Table 13.3 and the ability of the median family, with median income, to buy the median house in those locations we examined in Figure 13.1. Even if they chose a conventional mortgage, their mortgage payments, insurance, and property taxes would be well above 30 percent of their income

in the "bubble" cities. One estimate in 2008 suggested that 1 in 6 households in the United States was above this 30 percent guideline and that 1 in 20 was paying more than half of its income in housing costs. Given that, it is no wonder that home prices stopped rising in 2006.

The Effect on the Overall Economy

At the beginning, the bursting of the housing bubble had a modest impact slowing the rate of growth of the overall economy in 2006 and 2007 by about 1 percent. By late 2007 and into 2008, as foreclosures ballooned, the impact snowballed. It was not until the fall of 2008 that the true impact of the crisis came to light. In order to avoid a massive financial meltdown, the Treasury Department took ownership of both Fannie Mae and Freddie Mac, the Federal Reserve took a significant ownership stake in the insurance giant AIG, and Congress passed the Troubled Assets Relief Program (TARP) to save the nation's largest banks from the consequences of their ill-advised practices.

From September 2008 through the end of that year, credit markets were almost entirely frozen. This meant that institutions that were otherwise healthy could not access credit markets in a normal and necessary fashion. As the news of that fall was almost entirely bad, consumers simply stopped buying anything that was not absolutely necessary. Depending on the automaker, car purchases fell between 40 percent and 67 percent and, by December, GM and Chrysler required TARP funds to survive. The year culminated with the worst Christmas shopping season in more than 40 years.

The final post-mortem has not been written on what the ultimate impact of the housing bubble was. It

TABLE 13.3   Measuring housing affordability in major cities.

	Median Family Income[1]	Median Sale Price of an Existing Single-Family Home[2]	Approximate Annual Mortgage Payments (30 years, 6% interest)	Approximate Homeowners Insurance*	Approximate Property Tax*	Total Annual Housing Costs as a Percentage of Income	Home Costs as a Percentage of Income
Phoenix	$64,200	$257,400	$18,519	$2,000	$4,000	$24,518.92	38.19%
Los Angeles	59,800	589,200	42,391	2,000	4,000	48,390.62	80.92
Washington	97,200	430,800	30,994	2,000	4,000	36,994.36	38.06
Miami	49,200	365,500	26,296	2,000	4,000	32,296.29	65.64
Las Vegas	63,900	297,700	21,418	2,000	4,000	27,418.34	42.91
Cleveland	62,100	130,000	9,353	2,000	4,000	15,352.99	24.72
Dallas	65,000	150,900	10,857	2,000	4,000	16,856.66	25.93

*Author estimate.
[1]Source: HUD Estimated from Home Mortgage Disclosure Act reports.
[2]Source: National Association of Realtors.

certainly caused the steepest decline in economic activity since the Great Depression. It certainly led to relatively modest government deficits obliterating all post–World War II deficit records (whether in real or nominal terms) and states having to cut billions from their own budgets. Because of the timing of many of the ARMs, the ultimate bottom of the housing market did not occur until 2011 or 2012. A look back at Figure 13.1 shows that the recovery in housing, if it has occurred at all, has been very slow. One issue that slowed the process of the housing market finding its "bottom" was the difficulty in selling homes for which more was owed than the home was worth. Part of that problem is that with securitization it is a difficult, time-consuming, and lawyer-filled process to engage in

short sale
A sale of a home where the amount owed is more than the sale price where the seller seeks to have the remaining balance forgiven.

what is called a **short sale**. A short sale involves a buyer and a seller agreeing to a price and the mortgage company agreeing to write off the difference between the price of the home and what is owed on the mortgage. Until all such "underwater" homes are sold we will continue to live with one in seven homes in Nevada, for instance, being vacant.

It will be left to Chapter 14 to review the effectiveness of TARP and the 2009 stimulus package as well as the Federal Reserve's attempt to stabilize markets by buying long-term treasuries and mortgage-backed securities.

Summary

You now understand the fundamental elements that determine housing prices, how homes are typically financed, and that new types of mortgages are replacing traditional 20 percent-down, constant-payment mortgages. You also understand that unrealistic expectations in housing prices can create spiraling price increases and that such bubbles inevitably burst and can have a significant economic impact.

Key Terms

credit default swap, 167
interest-only mortgage, 166

negative-amortization mortgage, 166
pick-a-pay mortgage, 166

securitize, 164
short sale, 169

Quiz Yourself

1. The type of mortgage that allows you to make the lowest possible payment is called a
   a. zero-down mortgage.
   b. a traditional constant-payment, 20 percent-down mortgage.
   c. an interest-only mortgage.
   d. a negative-amortization mortgage.

2. In which type of mortgage do you build equity the fastest?
   a. zero-down mortgage.
   b. a traditional constant-payment, 20 percent-down mortgage.
   c. an interest-only mortgage.
   d. a negative-amortization mortgage.

3. In which type of mortgage do you neither build nor lose equity?
   a. zero-down mortgage.
   b. a traditional constant-payment, 20 percent-down mortgage.
   c. an interest-only mortgage.
   d. a negative-amortization mortgage.

4. Fundamentally, housing prices are a function of the home's
   a. location and amenities.
   b. amenities only.
   c. location only.
   d. interest rates only.

5. A housing bubble occurs when _____ drive(s) prices more than fundamental factors.
   a. the price of gasoline
   b. a home's expected future price
   c. interest rate changes
   d. property tax increases

6. A bursting of a housing bubble could create more problems than the NASDAQ crash in 2000 because the housing bubble involves
   a. assets and NASDAQ was about debts.
   b. risky forms of debt.
   c. more people.
   d. fewer people.

Short Answer Questions

1. Explain how mortgage securitization makes it easier to borrow money to buy a house but harder to deal with when a house is sold for a loss.

2. Explain why securitization contributed to the problem of people buying homes using mortgages for which they did not know all the details (such as the negative amortization mortgages referred to in the text.)

3. Explain why the Federal Reserve felt it necessary to bail out AIG and what result it was attempting to avoid.

4. Explain the role of the credit default swap and why the attempt to make things safer for investors made things worse for everyone.

Think about This

Bubbles are a great deal easier to identify after they burst. Believe it or not there were many who did not believe that the housing market was in a bubble until well into 2008 when it was obvious to everyone. (If you can get your hands on the fourth edition's web chapter on this subject, you can see that I thought it was one, but because prices were stabilizing when I wrote it, I wasn't sure.) The same thing was true with the stock market in 1929 and 2000. Fast forward 30 years and imagine yourself in a position of trying to manage your retirement savings. How are you going to tell if your portfolio is really worth what your 401(k) statements say or whether it is a bubble all over again?

Talk about This

We are in a post-housing bubble world in which millions of families owe substantially more money on their homes than they can sell them for. Recent changes to bankruptcy laws make it more difficult to declare bankruptcy, which leaves many fully employed, hard-working people trapped in their homes with no means of financial escape. As we reconsider financial regulation, should we treat negative-amortization mortgages and interest-only mortgages like cocaine: banned to prevent you from making a lifetime mistake?

The Recession of 2007–2009: Causes and Policy Responses

Learning Objectives

After reading this chapter you should be able to:

LO1   Describe the housing crisis and overall consumer indebtedness as the cause of the 2007–2009 recession.

LO2   Enumerate the consequences of the recession including a record drop in housing prices, a significant increase in the unemployment rate, a substantial drop in real gross domestic product, and a long string of job losses.

LO3   Describe and model the discretionary and nondiscretionary fiscal policy, monetary policy, and TARP program to combat the recession.

LO4   Enumerate and describe the components of the fiscal stimulus package passed in the early days of the Obama administration.

Chapter Outline

Before It Began

Late 2007: The Recession Begins as Do the Initial Policy Reactions

The Bottom Falls Out in Fall 2008

The Obama Stimulus Package

Extraordinary Monetary Stimulus

Summary

The recession of 2007–2009 was one of the most, if not the most, severe recessions in post–World War II history. In terms of peak unemployment, it was the second worst since the Great Depression. In terms of the drop in real GDP and in terms of how long it took for real GDP to recover to its prerecession peak it was the worst. It began in the fall of 2007 looking very much like the short and shallow recessions of 1991 and 2001. Then in the fall of 2008 the bottom fell out as the bursting of the housing bubble and the decimation of the financial sector set off a series of events whose consequences are not yet fully understood.

This chapter will begin with a look at economic activity in 2005 and 2007, discuss the most significant cause of the recession—the bursting housing bubble, the attempts in early 2008 to make it another short and shallow one, the financial sector meltdown of the fall of 2008, and the policy responses from the Federal Reserve, the Congress, as well as Presidents Bush and Obama. The chapter will conclude with a summary of the debate surrounding whether these policies were effective in either shortening or mitigating the impact of the recession.

Before It Began

As can be seen in Figure 14.1, real economic growth was progressing at about the 20-year average (2.7 percent annually) until the final quarter of 2007. As you can see in Figure 14.2, this was despite gasoline prices that had

FIGURE 14.1   Real GDP (billions, 2000) 2005.1–2007.3.

Source: Bureau of Economic Analysis, www.bea.gov/national/xls/gdplev.xls

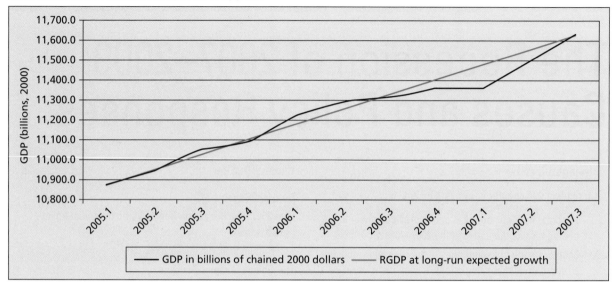

nearly doubled from their early 2005 levels. What was providing the steam behind this growth? Housing.

While a full discussion of how the housing bubble was created (and subsequently how it burst) can be found in Chapter 13, we'll provide a much briefer version here. As can be seen from Figure 14.3, the price of homes (as measured by the Case-Shiller Home Price Index Composite-10) was also increasing at an astonishing rate. While this may have made buying a home difficult under normal circumstances, these were anything but normal circumstances. Lenders were eager to make loans of almost any amount to people wanting to buy a home. This was because between early 2000 and late 2005, the annual rate of appreciation in homes averaged

FIGURE 14.2   Average price of gasoline in cents.

Source: http://tonto.eia.doe.gov/oog/info/twip/twipmgvwall.xls

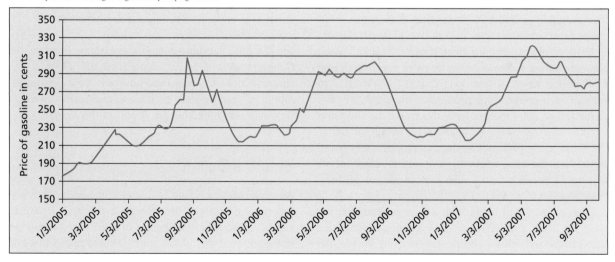

FIGURE 14.3   Case-Shiller Price Index (Composite-10).

Source: www.macromarkets.com/csi_housing/sp_caseshiller.asp

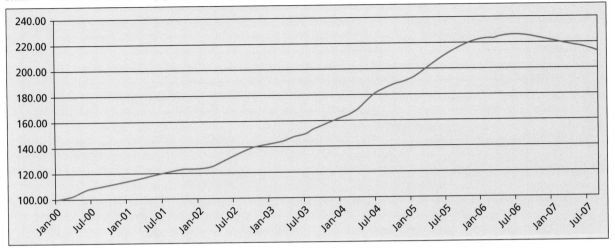

14.2 percent. At that annual increase in prices, it was erroneously thought, even if the borrower defaulted on the loan, the bank would lose no money because they could unload the house for more than the loan value.

This housing price escalation fueled two distinct housing booms: home building and home equity lines of credit. As you can see in Figure 14.4, housing starts, though fluctuating with the weather, steadily increased between 2001 and 2007, and as you can see in

Figure 14.5, nonrevolving credit, which includes home mortgages, home equity lines of credit, and car loans, increased at a 7.1 percent annual clip. Credit card debt increased at a 5.2 percent rate.

During this period the most significant policy concern of the Federal Reserve was the increase in inflation that was resulting from rapidly increasing energy prices and overall increases in demand. As you can see from Figure 14.6, the Federal Reserve increased its targeted

FIGURE 14.4   Single family housing starts.

Source: U.S. Department of Commerce, www.census.gov/const/www/newresconstindex.html

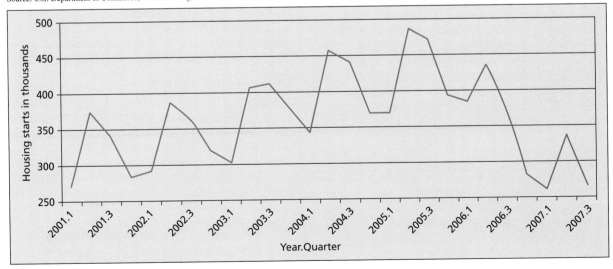

FIGURE 14.5 Revolving and nonrevolving household debt.

Source: Board of Governors of the Federal Reserve System, www.federalreserve.gov/releases/g19/hist

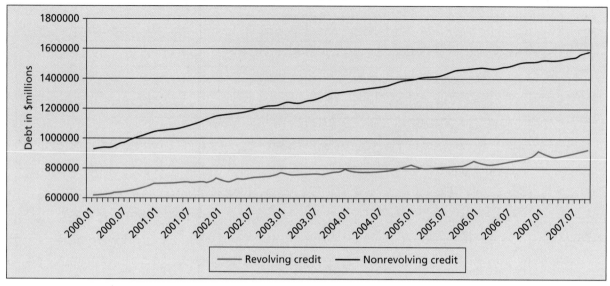

federal funds rate 14 times between June 2004 and June 2006 from 1 percent to 5.25 percent. At one point in January 2006 the concern over inflation was so great the Fed increased the federal funds rate 1.25 percentage points in one step. Given that the vast majority of increases and decreases in the federal funds rate have been limited to one-quarter of a point changes, this was considered a very aggressive action to quell inflation.

Late 2007: The Recession Begins as Do the Initial Policy Reactions

We know now that the National Bureau of Economic Research Business Cycle Dating Committee has pinned the beginning of the recession as late fall 2007. It was evident to policy makers that a slowdown was about to occur in late 2007. As can be seen in Figure 14.7, the

FIGURE 14.6 The federal funds rate.

Source: Board of Governors of the Federal Reserve System, www.federalreserve.gov/fomc/fundsrate.htm

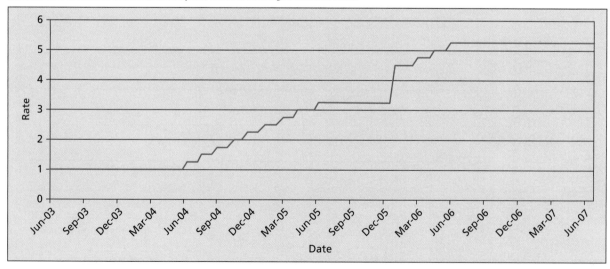

FIGURE 14.7   Federal funds rate September 2007–December 2008.

Source: Board of Governors of the Federal Reserve System, www.federalreserve.gov/releases/h15/data.htm

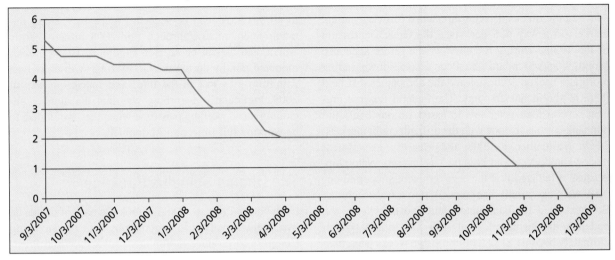

Federal Reserve began cutting its federal funds rate in September 2007 and didn't stop cutting the rate until it was at zero in December 2008.

The Bush administration began lobbying in early 2008 for a stimulus package. Its preferred mechanism was to make its tax cuts of 2003 permanent as well as to provide tax rebates to taxpayers. It failed in securing the former, but succeeded in garnering the latter. By early spring 2008 the rebate plan was enacted and by early summer, millions of Americans received $600 per individual, $1,200 per married couple. For most this money was deposited directly into their checking accounts by early summer. For the rest, rebate checks were mailed before summer was out. If you look at Figure 14.8, you can see that this $158 billion package had a significant short-run impact. Economic growth in the third quarter of 2008 was consistent with a healthy economy, but the economy was not at all healthy. Oil prices were rising to $145 per barrel and home foreclosures were increasing rapidly.

FIGURE 14.8   Real GDP 2007.2 to 2008.3.

Source: Bureau of Economic Analysis, www.bea.gov/national

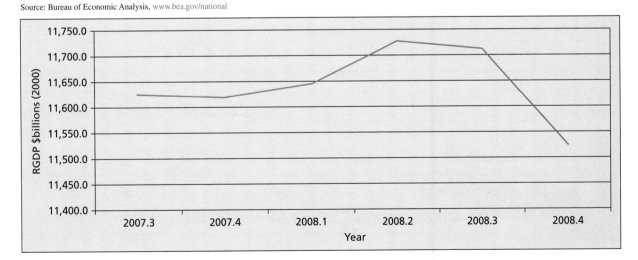

The Bottom Falls Out in Fall 2008

In the late summer and early fall 2008, a crisis of confidence in the financial sector threatened to freeze capital markets in a way not seen since the Great Depression of the 1930s. During the summer the rating agencies, Moody's and Standard and Poor's, were downgrading mortgage-backed securities and the companies that held them in significant amounts. The Federal Reserve created several loan programs to assist various bank and nonbank entities to cope with the difficult credit markets.

On September 7, 2008, the Treasury Department placed Fannie Mae and Freddie Mac in conservatorship, because it realized that these government-supported entities were essentially bankrupt. Within a week Lehman Brothers filed for bankruptcy, and two days later, the Fed lent the insurance giant AIG $85 billion (which ultimately became $182.5 billion). Two weeks later, then Treasury Secretary Paulson and Federal Reserve Chairperson Bernanke went to Congress seeking $700 billion for their planned Troubled Asset Relief Program. Two weeks after that, Wachovia teetered on the edge of bankruptcy and was purchased by Wells Fargo.

Within the span of two months, from Labor Day weekend to election day 2008, the financial system was on the verge of collapse. The terrible news, repeated on a daily basis, produced such a crisis of confidence that Christmas 2008 was the worst holiday shopping season in 40 years. As can be seen in Figure 14.9, a fair unemployment picture through mid-2008 turned sharply worse, and as can be seen in Figure 14.10, job losses mounted rapidly during the fall of 2008 with more than 2 million jobs lost in the third and fourth quarters of 2008. Particularly disturbing was that the number, including those working part-time when they would like to be working full-time, almost doubled.

The Obama Stimulus Package

Even before President Obama took the oath of office, he was deeply involved in negotiations with the incoming Congress to produce a stimulus package. While President Bush had engaged fiscal policy in the form of tax rebates, as the Obama plan emerged, it was not confined to tax changes but included significant spending.

As you can see in Figure 14.11, the aggregate demand–aggregate supply model can be used to model both the recession as well as the built-in and discretionary policy reactions. As the initial crisis of consumer

FIGURE 14.9   Unemployment rates 2006–2009.

Source: Bureau of Labor Statistics, http://data.bls.gov/cgi-bin/srgate
(LNS12032194; LNU05026645; LNS12000000; LNS14000000).

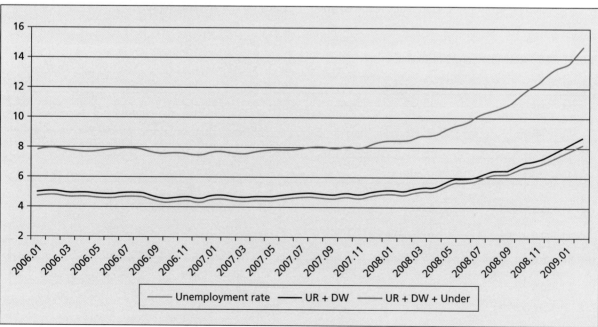

FIGURE 14.10 Net change in employment (2009).

Source: Bureau of Labor Statistics, http://data.bls.gov/cgi-bin/srgate (LNS12000000).

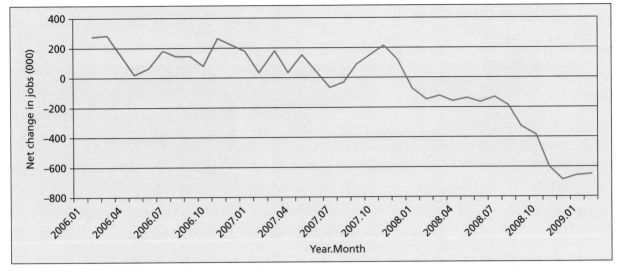

FIGURE 14.11 Modeling the impact of nondiscretionary fiscal policy and the Obama stimulus package (discretionary fiscal policy).

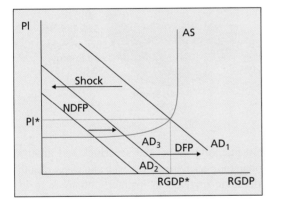

confidence took hold, aggregate demand contracted markedly. As unemployment rose, the welfare state kicked into high gear with substantial increases in unemployment insurance, food stamps, and Medicaid spending. This nondiscretionary fiscal policy (NDFP) dampened the initial impact of the decrease in demand. A stimulus package passed by Congress and signed by the president is, by definition, discretionary and as you read in Chapter 9 is called discretionary fiscal policy (DFP). Whether or not the Obama plan has had or will

have the desired impact will be known only with the passage of time.

The stimulus package passed by Congress and signed by the president was entirely discretionary since they had to pass a law to make it happen. Still, as you read in Chapter 9, a portion of the spending was to shore up the nondiscretionary fiscal policy spending on welfare and unemployment insurance that is typically run through the states. The details of the Obama stimulus plan can be seen in Figure 14.12. As you can see, a roughly equal portion went to tax cuts (38 percent) and spending programs (39 percent) with the remainder going to shore up Medicaid, welfare, and unemployment programs.

You can also see in Figure 14.12 that the bulk of the tax cuts went to individuals, with some additional tax cuts going to energy conservation programs. For instance, in 2009, the purchase of energy efficient appliances was given preferential treatment. About half of the aid to individuals came in the form of money to states to help them provide Medicaid, given the anticipated increase in enrollment caused by the recession. About a quarter of the individual aid went to increase unemployment benefits by $25 per week and to extend benefits beyond the already approved 26 weeks. The final portion of the spending was broken into many pieces for many different priorities of the new administration.

FIGURE 14.12   The Obama stimulus plan in detail.

Source: www.cbo.gov.

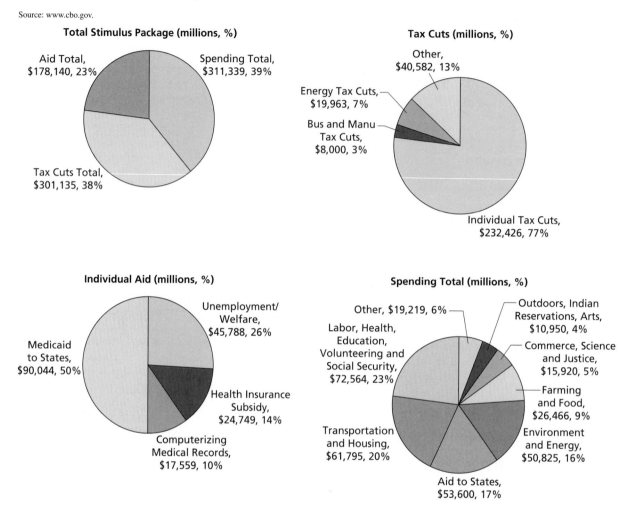

Extraordinary Monetary Stimulus

At the same time the Obama administration was attempting a fiscal stimulus, the Federal Reserve was engaging in the most expansive monetary stimulus in its history. When the fiscal stimulus ended, the monetary stimulus continued. For a detailed look at the monetary stimulus of this period, it would be worth while to read (or reread) Chapter 10's discussion of the "The Additional Tools of Monetary Policy Created during 2008" and to examine Figure 10.4. The short version is this: The Federal Reserve's portfolio of assets nearly tripled between 2008 and 2013, and that tripling meant that there was available to the banking system three times more money in 2013 than there was in 2008. Moreover, the stimulus continued through 2013 as the Federal Reserve was purchasing

$40 billion in mortgage-backed securities and another $40 billion in long-term treasuries each and every month.

This dramatic increase in loanable money kept interest rates extraordinarily low for the whole period. In 2012 and 2013, home mortgage interest rates were below 3 percent for those with good credit. That allowed those who refinanced their mortgages to lower payments or shorten the terms on those mortgages, or in many cases, both.

Whether this monetary stimulus was effective is also open for debate and will likely not be settled among economists until the stimulus has been reversed. As the textbox at the end of Chapter 10 indicates, there were significant risks associated with this policy, that, at this writing in the spring of 2013, have neither been proven or disproven.

Summary

The recession of 2007–2009 was set off by a confluence of events surrounding the bursting of the housing bubble. The housing bubble resulted in dramatic losses in the financial sector and a tightening of credit. This tightening was despite repeated attempts by the Federal Reserve, the Bush administration, and the Obama administration to revive the financial sector. The resulting loss of jobs and shrinking of GDP made this recession quite likely the worst since World War II. The attempts by the Federal Reserve to shore up the financial sector and by the Obama administration to stimulate the economy were breathtaking in their magnitude, though uncertain in their impact.

Quiz Yourself

1. Which of the following was not likely a contributing factor to the recession of 2007–2009?
   a. The bursting of the housing bubble.
   b. The 2008 tax rebates.
   c. The failure of major financial service companies.
   d. The drop in oil prices from $150 to $40 per barrel in late 2008.
2. In the years prior to the recession the economy was growing
   a. at about its typical rate.
   b. at a rate much slower than typical.
   c. at a rate much faster than typical.
3. Gasoline prices _____ in late 2007 through mid-2008.
   a. spiked
   b. increased relatively slowly
   c. remained constant
   d. plunged
4. The Federal Reserve's response to the recession of 2007–2008 was
   a. clearly effective in shortening the recession.
   b. quick but not obviously effective in shortening the recession.
   c. slow and subject to criticism for being rather timid.
   d. procyclical in that it had precisely the opposite impact as intended.
5. The Obama administration's stimulus package was
   a. almost entirely made up of tax cuts.
   b. almost entirely made up of spending on "shovel ready" projects.
   c. a balance between tax cuts, spending on projects, and shoring up the unemployment and welfare systems.
   d. almost entirely spent on welfare programs.
6. The job losses during this recession were
   a. typical of a short recession.
   b. nonexistent.
   c. significant and rapid.

Short Answer Questions

1. Explain each of the following in terms of whether they were discretionary fiscal policy, nondiscretionary fiscal policy, or monetary policy: TARP, the AIG bailout, the 2009 stimulus package, the rapid increase in unemployment compensation spending, the rapid reductions in state sales, and income tax revenues resulting from people having lower incomes.
2. How was "quantitative easing" different from what the Federal Reserve normally does?
3. Which lag described in Chapter 9 did the concept of "shovel-ready" intend to combat?

Think about This

Nobel Prize–winning economist Paul Krugman repeatedly warned through 2008 and 2009 that it was far worse for Congress to be too timid than too aggressive. In retrospect, was he correct? What would have been the result of a $1.5 trillion stimulus package?

Talk about This

What lessons would you draw from the recession of 2007–2009? What could have realistically been attempted in the middle of the housing boom to forestall the bust that came after?

CHAPTER FIFTEEN

Japan's Lost Decade: Could It Happen in the United States?

Learning Objectives

After reading this chapter you should be able to:

LO1 Understand that rates of economic growth, stock market values, and land values in Japan were high and/or growing rapidly between 1955 and 1990.

LO2 Describe the economic collapse that occurred between 1988 and 1990 and compare its causes with those of the U.S. financial markets in 2008.

LO3 Describe the policy attempts of the Japanese government to revive the economy during the 1990s and compare and contrast those with the attempts of U.S. policy makers to mitigate the damage of the 2007–2009 recession.

LO4 Describe the low growth rates of the Japanese economy from 1990 to 2010 and assess the likelihood that the United States will suffer from a similarly extended period of slow economic growth.

Chapter Outline

The Economic Situation in Japan Prior to 1990

So What Happened in Japan to Change All This?

How Is This Similar to the Current Situation in the United States?

Summary

Once upon a time there was a country that went through a period of significant economic expansion, where property values were increasing at an astronomical rate, where borrowing to buy residential and commercial real estate was a relatively easy process, and where stock prices had grown so fast and for so long that it seemed like normal economics didn't apply. That may sound like the United States between 1982 and 2007 or even China of 1980 through 2011, but it is actually a story about Japan. This chapter is only somewhat about Japan and its experience from the early 1990s through the earthquake, tsunami, and nuclear-reactor crisis of 2011 and mostly about the similarities and differences between what the Japanese faced and the policies it employed to recover its economic standing and what the United States faced in

2007–2009, the policies it tried to employ, and whether a "lost decade" is likely going to be the result.

The Economic Situation in Japan Prior to 1990

During the decades of the 1970s and 1980s the story of Japan was one of phenomenal growth in their economy and prestige in the world. After the devastation and humiliation of World War II, Japan rebuilt itself on an ethic of hard work, a focus on education, an impression of loyalty between employees and employers, a very high saving rate, and a dedication to producing quality manufactured goods for export to the United States and

FIGURE 15.1   The Nikkei 225.

Source: WREN Advisers, www.wrenresearch.com.au/downloads

other countries. During this period, Japan surpassed the United Kingdom, Germany, and France to become the second largest economy in the world. It did so producing the types of innovative products that were both inexpensive and well constructed.

Honda, Toyota, Sony, and others became staples of the American consumption bundle. During the 1970s, these products became so good that they threatened the existence of American companies like General Motors, Ford, Chrysler, Phillips, RCA, and others. The result was a rapidly growing Japanese GDP, a massive trade surplus with the United States, a growing stock market, and a rapidly growing price on what the Japanese couldn't produce: land in Japan. As can be seen from Figure 15.1, the Japanese equivalent of the Dow Jones Industrial Average, the Nikkei 225, increased in value from under 2000 in late 1970 to nearly 40,000 in 1988.

Figure 15.2 illustrates the growth in the Japanese economy from 1955 through 1990. Though Japan experienced recessions in 1974 and again in 1980, neither were as deep nor as long as those that were occurring in the United States. The rates of growth during the 1960s, 1970s, and 1980s were among the highest in the world and were 9.0 percent, 4.8 percent,

and 4.5 percent respectively on an annual basis. For comparison, as can be seen in Table 15.1, the rates of growth in the United States during that period were 3.2 percent, 4.2 percent, and 3.05 percent respectively. During this time as well, the Japanese government was the envy of the modern world in terms of fiscal rectitude. If you studied Chapter 12 ("Federal Deficits, Surpluses, and the National Debt"), you may have noticed that the Japanese national debt was around 10 percent of its GDP when at the time other countries had national debts that were 50 percent or more of GDP.

TABLE 15.1   Comparing rates of GDP growth for the leading world economies.

	In Dollars				In Yen
	Japan	**United States**	**China**	**Germany**	
1960s		3.20%			9.00%
1970s		4.20%			4.80%
1980s	4.07%	3.05%	8.88%	1.81%	4.50%
1990s	0.90%	2.98%	9.54%	1.78%	1.28%
2000s	0.43%	1.38%	9.38%	0.51%	0.35%

SHOULD YOU COMPARE COUNTRIES IN TERMS OF THEIR OWN CURRENCIES OR IN TERMS OF ONE CURRENCY?

One of the problems economists face when comparing the economic activity between countries is that while it is tempting to convert everything into one currency so you can compare trillions of dollars of GDP to trillions of dollars of GDP, there are problems associated with any method you use in performing the comparison. For instance, if you simply use the exchange rate between currencies (explained more fully in Chapter 18), you can leave the inaccurate impression that a sharp increase in the rate of growth or a sharp decline in the rate of growth was felt by people in that country. If the exchange rate rises or falls by 5 percent and economic activity in inflation-adjusted terms in that country was 3 percent, this can be reflected as either wildly expansionary growth or similarly draconian contraction. Figures 15.2 and the last column of Table 15.1 express the values of GDP and GDP growth without converting to dollars. Table 15.1's first column expresses Japan's economic growth after the figures were converted to dollars at the exchange rates at the time using a process called purchasing power parity.

So What Happened in Japan to Change All This?

Looking back at Figure 15.1, you can see that in late 1989 the Nikkei average was standing at nearly 39,000. At those levels, stocks were significantly overvalued relative to the profits those firms were generating. If you studied Chapter 7 ("Interest Rates and Present Value") and if you go on to study Chapter 40 ("The Stock Market and Crashes"), you will understand that stock prices fundamentally reflect the present value of future expected profit streams and stock market bubbles occur when the prices of stocks reflect a "me too" or "better buy now before the price goes up" attitude among investors rather than a straightforward analysis of future profits. Like all bubbles before this one and after this one, it burst. The Nikkei average had, within a year, lost half of its value and the losses just continued from there.

FIGURE 15.2 Real GDP in trillions of yen 1955–1990.

Source: Cabinet Office, www.esri.cao.go.jp/en/sna/menu.html

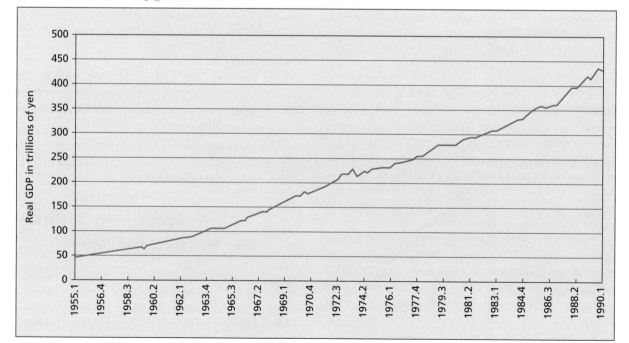

FIGURE 15.3   Real GDP in trillions of yen 1990–2010.

Source: Cabinet Office, www.esri.cao.go.jp/en/sna/menu.html

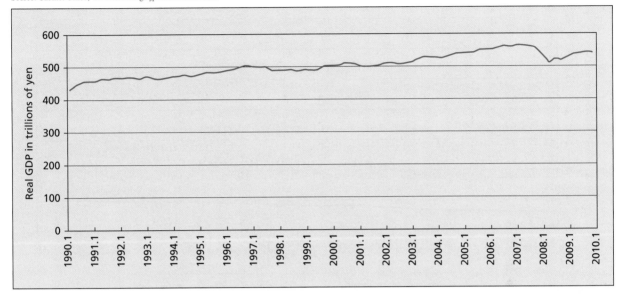

The losses were not confined to stocks. In fact, stock price declines were mirrored throughout the asset markets of Japan. In 1991, according to *The New York Times*, the total value of every plot of real property in Japan was $18 trillion. For a country of roughly the same size as California, that was at the time more than the combined total of all real estate in the United States. Between 1991 and 2005, the total value of all real estate had declined to less than half that. In the United States during the same period, all real estate tripled in value and, though real estate prices in the United States are down from their 2007 peak, they remain much higher than they were in 1991.

The two effects built upon one another. As stock prices were plummeting, those with stock purchased on margin calls had to shed themselves of real estate in order to meet those margin calls. Those who found themselves underwater in their homes had to sell off their stock holdings to pay off the loan amounts that the sale of the land did not cover.

With this massive decline in wealth in Japan, personal and corporate bankruptcies hit record highs. People who thought they had saved sufficiently to retire were now in no position to retire and, paradoxically, raised their rates of savings dramatically. While that may have been a good idea for them as individuals, it was catastrophically bad for the overall economy. By 1990 Japan had slipped into the worst economic period that any post–World War II major economy had experienced.

That stagnation continued much longer than any economist at the time anticipated. As can be seen in Figure 15.3, there was essentially no growth to speak of in real GDP (in yen terms) between 1991 and 1996 and painfully slow growth until 2003.[1] As can be seen in Figure 15.4, where Japan had been a clear number two to the United States during the 1980s and 1990s, China was rapidly challenging that status by 2010 (and is widely reported to have surpassed Japan in 2011).

What Did Japan Do (Wrong)?

To evaluate what the Japanese policy makers did and did wrong, we need to appeal to Chapters 6, 8, 9, and 10. The principal problem that policy makers failed to recognize was, first, the degree to which the real estate bubble was indeed a bubble; their late reaction, and, as it turns out, overreaction to it; their failure to see the interconnections between the real estate bubble that was collapsing and the stock market bubble that was also collapsing; their failure to appreciate the problems of combatting a deflationary spiral; and (to many liberal U.S. economists) their constant underfunding of stimulatory actions while spending those stimulus funds on the wrong types of things. Let's take each of these perceived or real failures one by one.

[1]Note that the scale of the vertical axis does not change from Figure 15.2 to 15.3, which means growth in Japan went from rapid to nonexistent very quickly.

FIGURE 15.4   Real GDP in U.S. dollars.

Source: The World Bank, www.worldbank.org

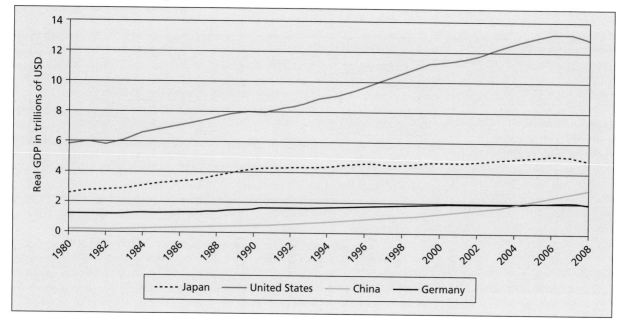

Through the 1980s there was a great deal of pride among the Japanese people and government with regards to the successes of the Japanese economy. They had come out of the ashes of World War II to become the second leading world economy. Their government debt to GDP ratio was the lowest in the industrialized world, and so when real estate and stock prices began accelerating rapidly during the late 1980s, there were many in the banking sector, in the corporate sector, and in the government who simply assumed that this was a rational consequence of the economic vitality they were enjoying. The growth in the Nikkei (from 8,000 to nearly 40,000) was greater than, but not that much greater than, the growth in the Dow Jones (from 800 to 3,500) during a similar time frame. The growth in real estate values was simply a matter of pride. The Ginza (a downtown Tokyo commercial district) had land selling for $90,000 per square meter, which was the most expensive land in the world. The policy makers simply chose not to attempt to counter the joint bubbles.

Until they did. When they did, they reacted by increasing rates of interest and loan regulations with regard to real estate transactions as well as stock transactions in a way that rattled both markets. The overreaction was enough to end both speculative bubbles but not before they had gotten well out of hand, and it was also enough to burst both rather rapidly. The Nikkei lost more than

half its value in 18 months and another quarter of its value in the next 18 months. People who thought they had the equivalent of $1,000,000 in Japanese stock upon which to retire now had $300,000.

The attempts to restore the Japanese economy were constant. Inflation-adjusted government consumption spending increased during the first year of the recession but not by nearly enough to have any substantive impact and then fell to 20 percent below its prerecession levels during much of the period. Public investment in infrastructure increased quite rapidly, increasing by 50 percent through the first half of the 1990s, only to be cut to below prerecession levels.

If you refer to the problems associated with discretionary fiscal policy noted in Chapter 9, the Japanese government committed many of the classic errors in carrying out that policy. Looking at Figure 15.5, you can see that the increase in rapidly impactful spending (the government consumption spending) was small and temporary. The increases in infrastructure spending were significant but, in the era of modern capital driven infrastructure spending, employed relatively few people.

Worse, an expectation of zero inflation or negative inflation created an insurmountable problem of expectations management. As described in Chapter 6, even modest deflation is much more dangerous than moderate inflation. That is because it causes individuals to delay their

FIGURE 15.5   Real government consumption and investment in yen.

Source: Cabinet Office, www.esri.cao.go.jp/en/sna/menu.html

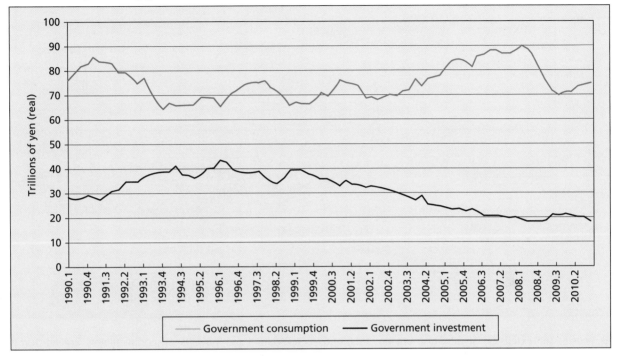

consumption in hopes of receiving lower prices later, finding that when they do wait, they indeed get lower prices, resulting in nearly everyone waiting to buy everything. You can see from Figure 15.6 that inflation (as measured by annualizing the quarterly GDP deflator percentage changes) was negative during much of the period and, with the exception of two oil-related price spikes (in 1998 and 2008), deflation in Japan was the norm.

How Can This Be Modeled Using the Aggregate Supply–Aggregate Demand Model?

The recession in Japan was somewhat unusual in that country's post–World War II history. It had experienced the global recessions of 1974 and 1982 but with nowhere near the severity of the recession in the United States. It was triggered by the shock of the simultaneous collapse of both the stock and real estate markets. Figure 15.7 depicts that as well as the typical nondiscretionary fiscal policy impacts that occur in every country that has a welfare state and a progressive tax system, which Japan has. The attempts by the Japanese government to revive their economy completely with discretionary fiscal policy were, as we can also see, frustrated by the impact of

deflationary expectations that simultaneously countered the attempts at revival. Those economists predisposed to believe these policies would have worked argue that the only way they can work is if they permanently overcome those deflationary expectations, which, as can be seen in Figure 15.6, they never did.

How Is This Similar to the Current Situation in the United States?

The answer to the heading to this section should be "eerily." The setup with a proximate cause being an overly confident set of borrowers and lenders speculating in real estate, when combined with a doubling of stock market values from the year 2000, certainly set the same stage. The bursting of a clear bubble in the real estate sector set off a process that threatened the health of banks both in Japan in the 1990s and the United States in 2008 and 2009.

The policy responses have also been somewhat similar, though here it appears that the United States has been somewhat less tenuous in its stimulatory actions. From the Congress and the president, there was the Troubled Asset Relief Program (TARP), the stimulus package, the extension of the tax cuts within the stimulus package

FIGURE 15.6   GDP deflator based quarterly (annualized) inflation/deflation.

Source: Cabinet Office, www.esri.cao.go.jp/en/sna/menu.html

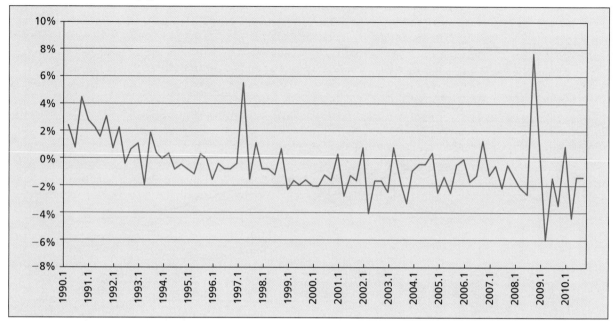

as well as the extension of the Bush-era tax cuts; and from the Federal Reserve there were the first and second rounds of quantitative easing. All of this has made it somewhat less likely that the United States would enter a period like that experienced by the Japanese.

Some economists fear, most notably those on the political left, that the United States is following exactly the Japanese model of being too tenuous in the beginning and too quick to withdraw the stimulus. Paul Krugman, a Nobel laureate economist as well as a notable liberal

FIGURE 15.7   Modeling the Japanese recession of 1990.

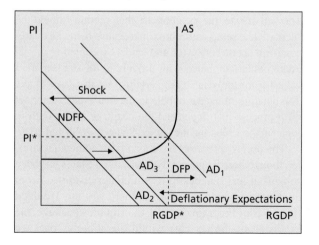

television and newspaper commentator, argued for a $2.5 trillion stimulus when what was passed was $787 billion. He, and others, believed at the time and believe at this writing that when looked at in totality government spending will be reduced far too soon. This is because state and local government spending was cut during 2010 every bit as fast as federal government spending was increased. The election of 2010 also brought into power a series of federal and state politicians more inclined to cut government spending than to raise it.

Other economists, most notably the chairperson of the Federal Reserve, have argued that while it will take time for the issues that resulted from the housing bubble to work their way through the system and they will remain in the economy for a protracted period, the actions taken, with the AIG takeover by the Federal Reserve, the TARP program that saved several leading banks from being declared insolvent by their regulators, and the sustained push by the Federal Reserve to buy long-term federal treasuries and mortgage-backed securities will keep the deflationary pressures at bay. Flip back to Figure 10.4 in Chapter 10 and notice what it shows regarding the remarkable actions taken by the Federal Reserve since the 2007–2009 recession began. From the moment the crisis hit, around Labor Day 2008, the Federal Reserve has injected $2.5 trillion in liquidity into the system. Initially, their actions were to lend financial institutions significant sums to make sure they were sufficiently capitalized to withstand the pressures associated with defaulting loans. As that money has been paid back, they have purchased more than a half trillion dollars in long-term debt and nearly a trillion in the bonds of Fannie Mae and Freddie Mac. In one respect, this has made it easier for the Obama administration to argue for the continuation of trillion dollar deficits to fund the stimulus. The biggest single lender to the government has been the government (through the Federal Reserve).

It is exactly this that makes some conservative economists worried and not particularly sure these programs were at all helpful in restoring economic prosperity. They are not worried that we will repeat the deflation of the Japanese, but they are worried that we will repeat the inflation of the late 1970s or worse. Because the money that is lent in this regard is money in the system that would not otherwise be there (not in paper form but in electronic form, though that hardly matters, these economists argue) and that more money will be chasing the same number of goods, inflation will be the result. It is not the deflationary expectations that are holding back aggregate demand in their minds; it is that businesses lack the confidence they require to invest in future production. This they attribute to the aforementioned uncertainty about inflation, the health care bill passed in 2009 that raises, to an uncertain level, the long-term costs of hiring, and the high levels of government spending and deficits that they fear will ultimately result in large tax increases on those businesses and wealthy individuals that do the hiring.

Summary

You now understand that rates of economic growth, stock market values, and land values in Japan were high and/or growing rapidly between 1955 and 1990, conditions that were mostly repeated in the United States in 2007. You are also able to describe the economic collapse that occurred between 1988 and 1990 in Japan and are able to compare its causes with those that led to the collapse of financial markets in the United States in 2008. Further, you are able to describe and model the policy attempts of the Japanese government to revive the economy during the 1990s and compare and contrast those with the attempts of U.S. policy makers to mitigate the damage of the 2007–2009 recession. Finally, you are now able to describe the low growth rates of the Japanese economy from 1990 to 2010 and can assess the likelihood that the United States will suffer from a similarly extended period of slow economic growth.

Quiz Yourself

1. The Japanese economy was growing rapidly during which period?
   a. the 1940s.
   b. from 1955 to 1990.
   c. from 1990 to 2000.
   d. from 2000 to 2010.

2. The Japanese economy was, from 1970 to 2010,
   a. the largest in the world.
   b. the second largest in the world.
   c. the fifth largest in the world.
   d. the most unstable of the large developed economies.

3. Which of the following triggered the 1990 recession?
   a. a significant drop in land prices.
   b. a significant drop in stock prices.
   c. a significant increase in oil prices.
   d. a and b.

4. The Japanese government's fiscal policy response to the recession of 1990 was
   a. consistently contractionary.
   b. consistently expansionary.
   c. inconsistent.
   d. focused on keeping their debt as low as possible.

5. The fiscal policy of the Japanese government was largely
   a. ineffective because it was inconsistent and never sufficient to overcome deflationary pressures.
   b. ineffective; though it was consistent in the attempt, it was never sufficient to overcome deflationary pressures.
   c. aided by deflationary pressures.
   d. stifled by the inflation it fostered.

6. The Japanese 1990–1996 recession and the U.S. 2007–2009 recession
   a. had very different causes.
   b. had very similar causes with precisely the same policy responses.
   c. had similar causes, similar (but not identical) policy responses with outcomes that may or may not be similar.
   d. were exactly the same in every respect.

Short Answer Questions

1. What are the key similarities between the Japanese 1990 experience and the 2008 U.S. experience?
2. What policy failings did the Japanese commit that the chairperson of the Federal Reserve and President Obama hope to avoid?
3. What are the consequences of deflation in terms of aggregate demand?
4. What did the Federal Reserve do in 2010 and 2011 that the Bank of Japan did not do to quell deflation?

Think about This

Federal Reserve Chairperson Ben Bernanke was, before he became associated with the Federal Reserve, one of the leading academic authorities on the Great Depression and, along with other scholars, had developed hypothetical plans that they would implement in case one were to strike the United States. TARP, the fiscal stimulus packages, the near-zero short-term rates, and purchase of long-term securities were all part of that plan. His current supporters would say the plan worked because we did not go into a second Great Depression. Is that logic sound?

Talk about This

If you had to choose between one long period of very slow economic growth (say 20 years at less than 1 percent per year) or a very deep recession with very high unemployment but one that was followed by a return to normal economic activity if at the end of the 20 years the latter option resulted in a somewhat higher level of GDP, which would you choose?

Behind the Numbers

Japanese Economic Activity—www.esri.cao.go.jp/en/sna/menu.html

World Economic Activity—www.worldbank.org

Japanese Real Estate Values—www.nytimes.com/2005/12/25/business/yourmoney/25japan.html?pagewanted=all

Is the (Fiscal) Sky Falling?: An Examination of Unfunded Social Security, Medicare, and State and Local Pension Liabilities

Learning Objectives

After reading this chapter you should be able to:

LO1 Describe the source of the problem of the largest fiscal challenges facing the federal and state and local governments as those associated with Social Security, Medicare, and pensions for state and local government employees.

LO2 Compare and contrast defined benefit and defined contribution pension plans and explain why defined benefit plans can be unfunded or underfunded but defined contribution plans cannot.

LO3 Describe the scope and degree of underfunding of each of the sources of fiscal problems.

LO4 List and evaluate the likelihood of each of the scenarios in which the underfunding of Social Security, Medicare, and pensions for state and local government employees presents smaller problems than is expected.

Chapter Outline

What Is the Source of the Problem?

How Big Is the Social Security and Medicare Problem?

How Big Is the State and Local Pension Problem?

Is It Possible That the Fiscal Sky Isn't About to Fall?

Summary

The story of "Chicken Little" is one in which the lead character claims that "the sky is falling" though the only thing that fell was an acorn. This chapter examines whether the fiscal sky is falling and uses the concept of present value to consider the question of whether the promises made by politicians of the past with regard to Social Security, Medicare, and defined benefit pensions to employees of state and local governments can be kept.

What Is the Source of the Problem?

As you may go on to read in Chapters 25 and 36, Medicare Part A and Social Security are funded through a system of payroll taxes. Working 40 quarters and paying taxes entitles people to subsidized hospital care as well as a pension based on the highest 35 years of earnings. For many employees of state and local governments, a system similar to Social Security, albeit one in which instead of both employers and employees paying equal shares, states and local governments make most of the investments, provides pension benefits, typically based on the last three to five years of salary.

All three systems are either entitlements or **defined benefit programs** in that if you participate for the required period of time, you get a benefit according to a set of rules and a formula. For instance, defined benefits plans frequently have a rule defining retirement eligibility that is structured around the variable years-of-service + age. When this number exceeds a particular level (often 85), the person is eligible to retire. This is why a teacher who began teaching in a school district at age 25 can retire at full benefits at 55.

defined benefit program
A pension plan that defines eligibility for retirement and benefits according to a set of rules and a formula.

This plan differs from a **defined contribution program.** In a defined contribution program, those enrolled, as well as their employer, contribute to an account according to a formula (which can be 100 percent employee, 100 percent employer, or some mix), and the investment of that account is under the control of the employee. Under defined contribution systems, retirees only get what their account accumulates.

defined contribution program
A pension plan in which those enrolled, as well as their employer, contribute to an account according to a formula, and the investment of that account is under the control of the employee.

Under a defined benefit program, because you pay according to a formula and you receive benefits according to a formula, there is the possibility that the formula will be wrong (on either side), resulting in a surplus (more than enough has been collected to pay the promised benefits) or a deficit (not enough has been collected and invested to pay the benefits). As is probably obvious, politicians would love the former because they can increase benefit payouts, but the latter is more likely. It is the latter that has occurred and now plagues the public pension system. Because you only get to reap what you sow in a defined contribution plan, there are no surpluses or deficits in those programs.

Defined benefit programs used to dominate the world of employee retirement systems, but they quickly fell by the wayside as fewer and fewer workers spent their entire careers with one firm. This is important because under most defined contribution plans there is a minimum years-of-service requirement and people who work 15 years with three different employers

would usually get nothing or at least substantially less in aggregate pensions than they would if they worked 45 years with one employer. Because significantly fewer employees spend their careers with one private employer and because a large number of public employees do stay with their original employer, it is now the norm for employees in the private sector to have defined contribution plans and for public employees to have defined benefit plans.

Defined benefit plans, because they involve employers investing money on the behalf of employees, require either a degree of trust or a degree of regulation. **Employee Retirement Income Security Act of 1974 (ERISA)** provides regulation for defined benefit plans offered by private employers. The rules require that the funds in the accounts meet the actuarial requirements to keep them fully funded. This simply means that, accounting for expected returns on investments, life expectancy of pensioners, and so forth, the assets of the investments must be able to meet the liabilities, which to the fund are the pension payments to retirees. They also must make payments to the Pension Guaranty Trust Corporation, which operates as a public insurance company in cases where the pension fund cannot meets its obligations and the company that is supposed to pay in goes bankrupt. This guarantees pensioners that their defined benefit plans will pay pensions if the company that sponsored them does not survive.

Employee Retirement Income Security Act of 1974 (ERISA)
A regulatory system for defined benefit plans.

Another thing that ERISA requires private companies to do is that when they offer health benefits to retirees, those funds also have to be fully funded. So if a private company, for whatever reason, wants to guarantee its employees that when they retire the company's health insurance will follow them until they get to Medicare eligibility, they have to put enough aside to pay for that.

How Big Is the Social Security and Medicare Problem?

It is important to understand that ERISA applies most stringently to private pensions, and the public pensions, namely Social Security and state and local pensions, do not have to be fully funded. This is the crux of the problem. Social Security is, in present value terms, underfunded by more than $12 trillion dollars, state pension funds are underfunded by $3 trillion, and local government pension funds are underfunded by more than one-half trillion. On top of that, though it is not a pension fund, Medicare is underfunded by another $4 trillion.

Let's begin at the federal level. The Social Security and Medicare system had one gigantic, and perhaps even fatal, operational assumption: Current employees could pay for current retirees. This assumption was necessary so that people could begin collecting benefits when the programs passed. Otherwise, the programs would have been collecting taxes and providing nearly no benefits for several years. Unfortunately for both systems, that mechanism requires that the number of babies born in a year remain roughly stable or grow at a steady rate so that eventually the ratio of workers per retiree can remain roughly constant. With the dearth of babies born between 1931 and 1945, due first to the scarcity of food during the Great Depression, which made many women at least temporarily infertile, and, secondly, World War II, which made young men temporarily scarce, and the subsequent baby boom of the post-war era, that assumption did not hold.

The result was that in 1982 analysts anticipated that beginning in 2008, as the first baby boomers became eligible for early-retirement Social Security benefits, and extending until around 2040, both Social Security and Medicare would have insufficient funds to pay for the anticipated benefits. In that year a compromise was worked out that significantly raised payroll taxes in order to create the Social Security and Medicare trust funds and raised the full-benefit retirement age from 65 to 67.

As of 2011, those accounts remain seriously underfunded. As can be seen in Figure 16.1, the annual deficits in these programs alone will, very soon, reach very high levels. Because these deficits will occur mostly in the future, there are two reasonable ways of looking at them. The first, presented in Figure 16.1 displays them by discounting using the present value methodology of Chapter 7. Using an interest rate associated with long-term U.S. treasuries, 3.4 percent,[1] the annual deficits are discounted and plotted below. The area between the 0-line and the Social Security line is the degree of the problem with regard to that program going out 75 years.[2] It is $27 trillion. Similarly, between the 0-line and the Medicare line is the degree of the deficit in that program, which is $15 trillion. For perspective, at this writing the sum of those two numbers is nearly three times GDP. That means that the total liabilities of the United States are more than $58 trillion (the sum of the national debt and the unfunded liabilities of Social Security and Medicare.)

[1] The zero-coupon bond yield at this chapter's writing (March 2011).
[2] This is the length of time the Social Security and Medicare trustees are required to consider and report upon.

FIGURE 16.1 The present value of the annual Social Security and Medicare deficits: 2011–2088.

Source: www.ssa.gov/oact/TR/2012/tr2012.pdf

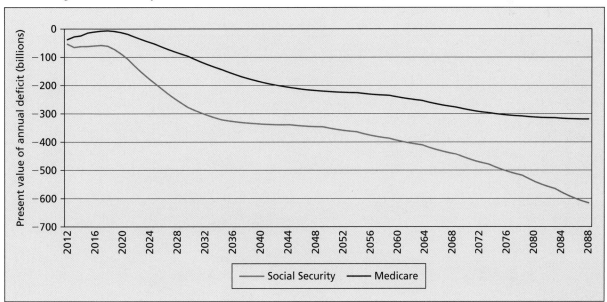

FIGURE 16.2   The dependency ratio: 2010–2090.

Source: www.ssa.gov/oact/TR/2012/tr2012.pdf

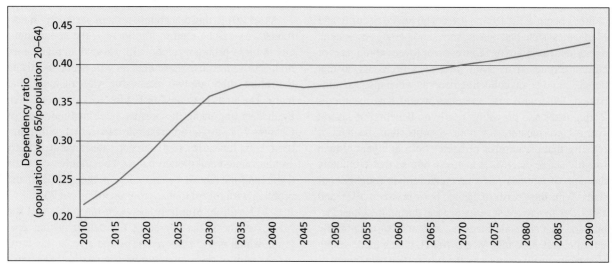

To compound the problem, there will be a decreasing percentage of the population working to pay that enormous bill. As can be seen in Figure 16.2, the dependency ratio, the ratio of the population dependent on others to support them to the population supporting them, will rise from around 22 percent currently to more than 37 percent in the next 20 years and to more than 40 percent within the next 75 years.

The other way of looking at the size of these problems is to consider that the earning capacity of the next generations will be greater than the earning capacity of today's generation, and through immigration and birth, the U.S. population continues to grow, making it somewhat likely that the problem could present less of a burden than these figures imply. In Figure 16.3 we see that we could pay for these deficits with an amount of money equal to around

FIGURE 16.3   Social Security and Medicare deficits as a percentage of projected payroll.

Source: www.ssa.gov/oact/TR/2012/tr2012.pdf

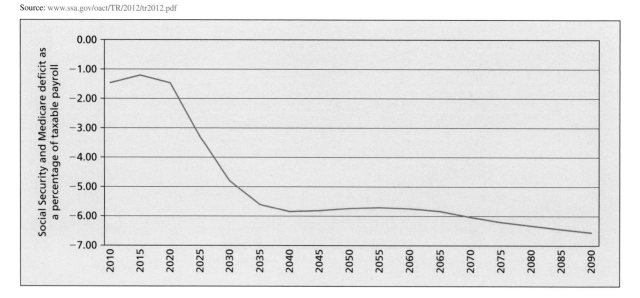

1 percent of payroll over the next decade. Though, by this measure, these deficits as a percentage of payroll rise to 5 percent in rapid order between 2020 and 2035, they only grow by another 1.5 percentage points in the ensuing 40 years.

How Big Is the State and Local Pension Problem?

State and local governments provide their own pensions in addition to Social Security. They do so, by and large, using defined benefit plans. The tumult in Wisconsin in 2011 was in large part due to conflicts between its Republican governor and the public employees. Though the collective bargaining dispute took the headlines, the underfunded pensions were at the heart of the problem there and across the country. You can see the degree to which these unfunded liabilities will affect each state by looking at Table 16.1, a table that was included in a comprehensive study of the subject by Robert Novy-Marx and Joshua Rauh. Under their methodology, they began by looking at the liabilities that these states acknowledge and the assets they claimed, but then made adjustments to the discount rate that these states use to establish those liabilities. Finding those discount rates unreasonably high, they instead chose to use what they determined to be a more reasonable rate—the rate that you would get on U.S. Treasury bonds.[3] What they found was that states have roughly $3 trillion in unfunded liabilities in their state-funded pension plans.

[3] The technical reasons for this consideration are beyond the scope of this text; however, from Chapter 7 you understand that higher rates of discount mean that liabilities far off into the future will have a smaller present value. The authors argue that the discount rates on the liabilities are overstated for political purposes to mask the actual size of the problem.

TABLE 16.1   State pension liabilities.

Source: Robert Novy-Marx and Joshua Rauh, "Public Pension Promises: How Big Are They and What Are They Worth?" *Journal of Finance*, 2011.

State Name	Liabilities, Stated	ABO Liabilities, Treasury Rate	Pension Assets	State Name	Liabilities, Stated	ABO Liabilities, Treasury Rate	Pension Assets
Alabama	42.0	61.8	21.4	Montana	9.1	12.4	5.3
Alaska	15.3	21.7	12.4	Nebraska	8.4	11.6	5.5
Arizona	43.6	73.5	24.8	Nevada	25.4	36.3	18.8
Arkansas	21.5	30.4	14.6	New Hampshire	8.5	12.5	4.3
California	518.1	699.7	329.6	New Jersey	132.8	191.2	67.2
Colorado	57.3	86.2	28.8	New Mexico	28.8	39.8	15.9
Connecticut	45.3	69.1	20.1	New York	239.8	325.7	192.8
Delaware	7.6	10.9	5.8	North Carolina	74.9	101.8	64.0
Florida	136.4	186.3	96.5	North Dakota	4.4	6.3	2.7
Georgia	75.8	110.1	53.1	Ohio	197.5	281.4	114.7
Hawaii	17.5	24.2	8.1	Oklahoma	33.6	45.9	15.8
Idaho	11.7	16.6	8.7	Oregon	57.5	80.7	42.9
Illinois	151.0	233.0	65.7	Pennsylvania	110.6	164.5	64.3
Indiana	37.3	49.8	19.6	Rhode Island	13.9	20.5	6.6
Iowa	26.0	35.0	18.0	South Carolina	42.4	63.5	20.3
Kansas	21.3	30.3	10.2	South Dakota	7.4	10.3	5.6
Kentucky	45.2	63.4	21.1	Tennessee	36.7	49.6	26.4
Louisiana	36.8	54.8	18.4	Texas	191.2	268.4	126.1
Maine	14.4	20.1	8.3	Utah	22.6	31.2	14.7
Maryland	52.7	72.1	28.6	Vermont	4.0	5.7	2.4
Massachusetts	59.7	86.9	32.7	Virginia	69.1	89.6	41.3
Michigan	73.2	103.1	39.5	Washington	62.3	86.4	43.5
Minnesota	60.6	91.0	35.9	West Virginia	13.7	18.3	7.2
Mississippi	31.4	44.2	15.5	Wisconsin	79.7	114.6	58.4
Missouri	53.5	75.2	33.1	Wyoming	7.0	9.8	4.4

These same scholars duplicated this analysis for county and municipal pensions. Using a comprehensive (but not universal) list of cities and counties and their pension plans, they performed similar calculations for those local governments. What they found, as shown in Table 16.2, was that for those counties and cities they could include in their database, there was $383 billion in unfunded liabilities on pensions, and if that was extrapolated to the remaining population of local governments, they have a total of $574 billion in unfunded pension liabilities. Some of those cities had laughably large unfunded liabilities. For instance, the city of Chicago had so many outstanding liabilities that if every household in the city contributed $40,000 to the city, it would still be insufficient to entirely eliminate the gap. Even worse, because the state of Illinois had not contributed anywhere near enough money to its pension funds for state employees (such as teachers, college professors, state highway patrol, prison guards), it would take almost an additional $30,000 to cover those liabilities.

To put a bow on this, imagine a household in Chicago wanted to pay off its share of all unfunded Social Security, Medicare, and pension liabilities (completely ignoring the other portions of the national debt); they would have to come up with more than $215,000, of which one-third would be their state and local liabilities. If this fiscal "sky is falling" prediction is accurate, the fiscal sky will fall in the next 20 to 25 years. That is the period in which the Medicare problem will hit its present-value peak, the state and local pension problem will peak, and the Social Security problem will still be increasing.

TABLE 16.2   County and municipal pension liabilities.

Source: Robert Novy-Marx (University of Rochester and NBER), and Joshua Rauh (Kellogg School of Management and NBER), www.kellogg.northwestern.edu/faculty/rauh/research/nmrlocal20101011.pdf

Name (Number of Plans)	Liabilities, Stated Basis, June 2009 ($B)	Liabilities (ABO), Treasury Rate	Net Pension Assets ($B)	Unfunded Liability ($B)	Unfunded Liability/ Revenue	Unfunded Liability per Household ($)
Chicago	46.3	66.6	21.8	44.8	763%	41,966
New York City	155.8	214.8	92.6	122.2	276	38,886
San Francisco	16.3	22.6	11.9	8.7	306	34,940
Boston	7.4	11.0	3.6	7.5	430	30,901
Detroit	8.1	11.0	4.6	6.4	402	18,643
Los Angeles	34.6	49.3	23.2	26.1	378	18,193
Philadelphia	9.0	13.0	3.4	9.7	290	16,690
Cincinnati	2.2	3.2	1.2	2.0	321	15,681
Baltimore	4.4	6.4	2.7	3.7	260	15,420
Milwaukee	4.4	6.7	3.3	3.4	687	14,853
Fairfax County	8.3	11.1	5.5	5.6	169	14,415
Hartford	1.2	1.6	0.9	0.7	249	14,333
St Paul	1.5	2.2	0.8	1.4	464	13,686
Jacksonville	4.1	6.0	2.0	4.0	278	12,994
Dallas	7.4	10.8	4.6	6.3	298	12,856
Contra Costa County	6.3	8.7	3.7	5.0	425	12,771
Santa Barbara County	2.3	3.3	1.4	1.8	329	11,995
Kern County	4.2	5.6	2.0	3.6	612	11,919
San Jose	5.4	7.5	3.4	4.1	321	11,391
Houston	11.1	16.4	7.2	9.1	356	10,804
Nashville Davidson	2.9	4.1	1.8	2.3	151	10,048
Arlington County	1.5	2.0	1.2	0.8	103	10,000

Is It Possible That the Fiscal Sky Isn't About to Fall?

It is at least plausible that the preceding overstates the actual problem that Americans will face. Optimists point to a number of factors that could make these problems substantially smaller in scope. First, the analysis is predicated on the ability of the authors of the Social Security and Medicare trustees' reports to predict wages, life expectancy, GDP, interest rates, and other economic variables 20, 30, 50, 75 years in advance. Additionally, there are any number of changes that could make the next 20 years only slightly uncomfortable with regard to these underfunded programs. Incomes could grow at a more rapid, but still historically reasonable, rate, or the programs' benefits could be curtailed.

Aside from the possibility that the forecasts are just wrong, consider the most likely and most important source for potential optimism. Taxable incomes could grow at the rate they did in the 1980s and 1990s and do so for a sustained period. Similarly, productivity and/or technological increases could be sufficient to raise real GDP growth expectations from the 2.5 percent to 3.5 percent they have been to 3.5 percent to 4.5 percent. A one percentage point increase in growth would make the U.S. real GDP 28 percent higher in 25 years than it is now projected to be at that time, and that would be more than enough to make the funding of those particular programs substantially less onerous.

Second, programmatic changes could be made, especially to Social Security, that could take the largest part of the long-term problem off the table. For instance, some combination of tax increases (either eliminating the maximum taxable earnings for Social Security, increasing tax rates 1 percent across the board on both employers and employees, or extending Social Security taxes to unearned income) or benefits changes (eliminating the option for taking benefits at 62, raising the retirement age to 70, using price inflation rather than wage inflation to adjust benefits for the cost of living) could be enacted. If these were enacted in the next five years, most of the problem in Social Security could be eliminated.

Whether state and local governments can break the promises they have already made to their teachers, firefighters, police, and other workers is another story. There would certainly be political and even legal challenges to such changes. As governors around the country were seeing in 2011, it is politically difficult to require public workers to contribute (more) to their pensions; so, though there could be a political solution that would require higher contribution levels by the workers themselves, if that does not occur soon, such a solution will not be enough to solve the state and local pension problem. That would leave state and local governments needing to cut benefits to current retirees (which would ignite an even more furious political and legal challenge) or to seek a bailout from higher levels of government.

The biggest challenge to optimists has to be Medicare. Its problems were almost completely ignored within the Obama administration's health care plan. That plan's focus was on expanding eligibility and not on realistic cost control. Second, Medicare's fiscal challenges will be front and center earlier than the other programs.

Summary

Whether or not you believe the "sky is falling" on fiscal issues relating to Social Security, Medicare, and the pensions systems for state and local government workers, you should now understand the source of the problem. Combined, various levels of government have underfunded their programs for retirees by trillions of dollars. You understand that the Medicare challenge will occur first, followed shortly thereafter by the state and local pension challenge. The Social Security shortfall will not become acute until the late 2030s but remains the largest fiscal challenge. You understand that because these liabilities will occur so far in the future that the rate at which you discount them and the rate at which the economy will grow can significantly alter the estimated scope of the problem.

Key Terms

defined benefit program, 190	defined contribution program, 190	ERISA, 190

Quiz Yourself

1. In terms of magnitude, which of the following has the greatest fiscal shortfall?
   a. state pension funds.
   b. local pension funds.
   c. Medicare.
   d. Social Security.

2. In terms of when these fiscal shortfalls are likely to require significant changes to budgets or program rules, which of the following is likely to occur first?
   a. state pension funds.
   b. local pension funds.
   c. Medicare.
   d. Social Security.

3. Using a higher rate of discount
   a. makes no difference when calculating the present value of future liabilities.
   b. raises the present value of future liabilities.
   c. lowers the present value of future liabilities.

4. The dependency ratio in the United States is
   a. growing.
   b. steady.
   c. falling rapidly.
   d. falling slowly.

5. State and local pensions for government employees are usually
   a. defined benefit plans.
   b. defined contribution plans.
   c. entitlements.
   d. determined year to year.

6. Deficits cannot occur in
   a. defined benefit plans.
   b. defined contribution plans.
   c. entitlement budgets.
   d. state and local budgets.

Short Answer Questions

1. Why does the discount rate matter when evaluating the future liabilities of defined benefit pension plans?

2. Why does it matter whether you have a defined contribution plan or a defined benefit plan in terms of whether there is a degree of underfunding that your boss might not be telling you about?

3. Why would a school teacher be a better candidate for a defined benefit pension than a computer programmer?

4. Why would the Pension Guaranty Trust or something like it be necessary in defined benefit plans?

5. Is Social Security closer to a defined benefit plan or a defined contribution plan?

Think about This

When you go into the voting booth, which type of politician appeals to you: the optimistic sort that seeks to assure you that brighter days are ahead or the pessimistic sort that seeks to warn you of impending disaster? Are voters the source of the problem?

Talk about This

Suppose nothing is done about state and local pension issues and state and local governments face a choice of either paying their retired teachers what they were promised in terms of pensions or paying current teachers enough to ensure an adequate education for children. (Suppose for the purpose of this discussion, you are convinced at the state level if you impose a tax increase, too many citizens will leave to go to another state, rendering the tax rate increase ineffective.)

Behind the Numbers

Social Security and Medicare,
    www.ssa.gov/oact/TR/2010/tr2010.pdf

State and local pensions.

Novy-Marx, Robert, and Joshua Rauh, "Public Pension Promises: How Big Are They and What Are They Worth?" *Journal of Finance*, 62, pp. 2123–2167.

Novy-Marx, Robert (University of Rochester and NBER), and Joshua Rauh (Kellogg School of Management and NBER), www.kellogg.northwestern.edu/faculty/rauh/research/nmrlocal20101011.pdf

International Trade: Does It Jeopardize American Jobs?

Learning Objectives

After reading this chapter you should be able to:

LO1   Name the principal trading partners of the United States and the goods that are most often traded.

LO2   Illustrate how international trade benefits both trade partners.

LO3   Define the principles of absolute and comparative advantage and utilize these definitions to prove the benefits from trade.

LO4   Compare and evaluate the reasons given for limiting trade and illustrate the mechanisms for doing so.

LO5   Conclude that limiting trade protects some industries and jobs, but at a very high cost.

LO6   Enumerate attempts to use trade as a diplomatic weapon and evaluate the success of those attempts.

Chapter Outline

What We Trade and with Whom

The Benefits of International Trade

Trade Barriers

Trade as a Diplomatic Weapon

Kick It Up a Notch: Costs of Protectionism

Summary

One of the more important economic developments of the last 35 years is the increased globalization of our economy. Whereas the world used to be made up of more than 150 countries whose economies were mostly independent of one another, nearly all of the economies of the nations of the world now depend heavily on one another.

As you can see from Figure 17.1, in 2009 some 11.1 percent of the U.S. economy was made up of exports. The significant decline in both exports and imports for 2009 was one consequence of the global recession. Exports made up 13.5 percent of U.S. GDP the prior year. You can also see that for the last 30 years the United States has imported more than it has exported. The increasing importance of the international sector has led some to worry about whether this trend is a good one. Are American jobs being unfairly taken by workers from other countries? If so, is this trend toward globalization avoidable?

We address these questions first by explaining why economists generally believe that international trade is good for both parties. Then we discuss the reasons for limiting international trade, distinguishing between reasons that economists embrace and those that they do not. Next we discuss the methods by which trade is limited. To wrap up, we consider whether trade can be used as a tool in political or diplomatic disagreements.

What We Trade and with Whom

Trade in the United States is not only growing; it is also encompassing a diverse area of goods and services, as seen in Table 17.1. We trade in the obvious goods and the not so obvious goods. We import TVs, computers, and other electronics, as well as cars and oil. We export

FIGURE 17.1   Increasing importance of international trade.

Source: United States Census Bureau, www.census.gov/foreign-trade/statistics/index.html

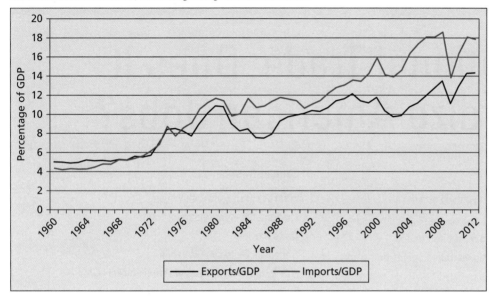

TABLE 17.1   U.S. exports and imports of goods and services.

Sources: International Trade Administration, www.trade.gov; TradeStats Express (TM), http://tse.export.gov

Exports		Imports	
Transportation equipment	247.9	Computer and electronic products	355.2
Computer and electronic products	203.7	Oil & gas	327.0
Chemicals	197.6	Transportation equipment	317.2
Machinery, except electrical	165.7	Chemicals	197.3
Petroleum & coal products	111.6	Machinery, except electrical	148.5
Primary metal mfg.	77.8	Miscellaneous manufactured commodities	102.2
Miscellaneous manufactured commodities	72.0	Primary metal mfg.	101.0
Agricultural products	71.2	Petroleum & coal products	94.4
Food manufactures	64.7	Electrical equipment, appliances, & components	82.3
Electrical equipment, appliances, & components	45.8	Apparel manufacturing products	81.4
Special classification provisions, NESOI	45.7	Fabricated metal products, NESOI	60.7
Services	630.4	Services	434.6
Total	2194.5	Total	2734.0

industrial equipment and airplanes. You probably would have guessed this. We simultaneously export and import large quantities of automobiles, computers (electrical equipment), and services. While that may sound somewhat odd, it is not as strange as it may sound. There are myriad types of cars and we are importing some and exporting others. Similarly, though we export and import computers, this also shows the degree to which many products are made all over the globe.

If you open up any computer, you will find components that were made in a variety of places. The memory comes from one country, the hard drive from another, and the CPU from still another. Your computer may have been assembled in the United States, but it was made from components that could have been produced in 10 other countries. You can see that it is difficult to decide where it was really made. In part this is one reason why the trade deficit we have with China is so high. China is the final assembly point for significant consumer electronics, and it is the final assembly point that gets credit (in our trade data) for their export to us.

There is one good on the list of exports that also may intrigue you—"petroleum and coal products." In this industrial group is coal and the United States is a significant exporter of coal. It also includes refined products, so any oil imported to the United States as crude oil into the refineries around Houston, Texas, and is then sold in Mexico, would show up as an export of a petroleum product of the United States.

The final item in Table 17.1 that also might also seem out of place is the trade in services. It is hard to imagine that we would import babysitting and lawn-mowing services, but it is much more plausible in areas of financial services and, specifically, in insurance. An American insurance company can easily sell life insurance to Canadians, and vice versa. Services make up a large and rapidly growing area of trade, and it is one area where the United States has a substantial trade surplus.

Table 17.2 may also surprise you in that few Americans realize how important Canada is as a U.S. trading partner. In trade it is roughly equal in importance to all of Europe. Figure 17.2 shows the degree to which these deficits continue to burgeon.

TABLE 17.2 U.S. exports, imports, and trade balances of goods with selected countries and regions of the world, 2012.

Source: United States Census Bureau, www.census.gov/foreign-trade

Country	Exports ($ billions)	Imports ($ billions)	Balance ($ billions)
Canada	292.4	324.2	−31.8
Mexico	216.3	277.7	−61.3
Japan	70.0	146.4	−76.3
China	110.6	425.6	−315.1
OPEC	81.9	180.9	−98.9
Europe	328.9	454.8	−125.9
Africa	32.9	66.9	−34.0
World	2194.5	2734.0	−539.5

The Benefits of International Trade

Comparative and Absolute Advantage

To illustrate the benefits of trade it is useful to distinguish between two kinds of "advantages" that people can have. Consider a brain surgeon and her secretary. Suppose that the surgeon worked her way through school by typing papers and that she types faster than her current secretary.

FIGURE 17.2 Trade balances with selected partners.

Source: United States Census Bureau, www.census.gov/foreign-trade

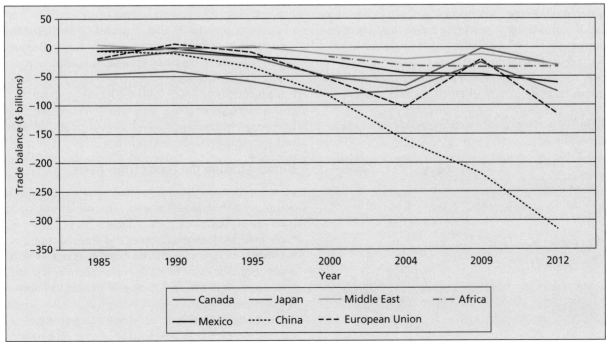

If she is better at both typing and surgery, would it be better for her to do both and fire her secretary? The answer is no; she will be better off having her slow-typing secretary do the typing. Making the decision relies on the notion of opportunity cost that we discussed in Chapter 1.

To review, opportunity cost is what you give up by making the choices that you do. In the case of the secretary and the surgeon, if the surgeon does her own typing, she

absolute advantage
The ability to produce a good better, faster, or more quickly than a competitor.

comparative advantage
The ability to produce a good at a lower opportunity cost of the resources used.

must give up at least some of her lucrative surgeries. On the other hand, if she delegates the typing, she will pay the secretary only a small fraction of the money she would earn doing extra surgeries. In this case she has an **absolute advantage** in both surgery and typing, because she is better at both things than the competition. Her secretary has a **comparative advantage** at typing because the secretary has a lower opportunity cost of doing the typing than does the surgeon.

As a simple example of how this applies to international trade, consider Tables 17.3 and 17.4. We can illustrate comparative and absolute advantage and the benefits from trade for each of two countries by relating their individual production of two goods. We will suppose that the two countries are the United States and Brazil and the two goods are apples and coffee.

In Table 17.3 we will suppose that the United States is better at producing apples than it is at producing coffee and Brazil is better at producing coffee than it is at producing apples. We will assume that a single unit of labor is capable of producing two units of coffee in Brazil but only one unit of apples. In the United States that situation is reversed. A unit of labor produces two units of

TABLE 17.3 Production: Absolute and comparative advantage are the same.

	Coffee	Apples
United States	1	2
Brazil	2	1

TABLE 17.4 Production: Absolute and comparative advantage are not the same.

	Coffee	Apples
United States	3	2
Brazil	2	1

apples but only one of coffee. Clearly, since a unit of labor in the United States can produce more apples than a unit of labor in Brazil, the United States has the absolute advantage in apples. Similarly, it is clear that Brazil has an absolute advantage in coffee.

To analyze comparative advantage we need to measure what is given up when the two countries allocate a unit of labor. For instance, when Americans produce an additional unit of coffee they are giving up two apples. When Brazilians produce an additional unit of coffee they are giving up only one-half a unit of apples. Brazilians therefore have the lower opportunity cost of producing coffee. Similarly, when Americans produce an additional unit of apples they give up one-half a unit of coffee, and when Brazilians do so they give up two units of coffee. As a result Americans have a lower opportunity cost for apples. What this means is that in addition to having an absolute advantage in coffee, Brazilians also have a comparative advantage in coffee. Similarly, Americans have a comparative advantage as well as an absolute advantage in apples.

These advantages need not be in line. Consider Table 17.4, which shows where the Americans are assumed to have an absolute advantage in the production of both goods. A single unit of American labor can produce more apples and more coffee than a single unit of Brazilian labor. As a result, Americans have an absolute advantage in the production of both goods. Comparative advantage is another story. The opportunity cost of an additional unit of coffee to Americans is two-thirds of a unit of apples. For Brazilians the opportunity cost of an additional unit of coffee is only half a unit of apples. Thus Brazilians have the lower opportunity cost of producing coffee and therefore have a comparative advantage in coffee. In apple production the Americans have an opportunity cost of one and a half units of coffee while the Brazilian opportunity cost is two units of coffee. Americans therefore have the lower opportunity cost of apples production and, as a result, the comparative advantage in apples.

Demonstrating the Gains from Trade

In either case the gains from trade can be illustrated. Starting with the situation where the gains from trade are more obvious, look back at Table 17.3. If Americans focus their production on apples and Brazilians on coffee, then for every unit of labor that Americans move to apples and Brazilians move to coffee, there is a worldwide increase in total production of one unit of apples and one unit of coffee.

To see that each is better off with trade than without it, suppose there is a total of 30 units of labor in each country and each prefers apples and coffee in equal amounts. Before trade there will be 10 Americans producing 20 units of apples and 20 Americans producing 20 units of coffee. Similarly there will be 10 Brazilians producing 20 units of coffee and 20 Brazilians producing 20 units of apples.

terms of trade
The amount of a good one country must give up to obtain another good from the other country, usually expressed as a ratio.

To see that trade makes both better off, we need to know how the **terms of trade**, the amount of one good required to get the other, between the two countries will come out. If we suppose that it comes to one unit of apples for one unit of coffee, then we have our answer. The Brazilians will produce only coffee and make a total of 60 units, and the Americans will produce only apples and produce 60 units. The Brazilians will ship 30 units of coffee to the United States in exchange for 30 units of apples, and in the end each will be able to consume 30 units of each and be better off with trade than without it.

Trade is also beneficial when one country has the absolute advantage in both goods. Turning back to Table 17.4 we can show that there are gains from trade here as well. Prior to trade the Brazilian situation is unchanged from the preceding example, but the American situation is such that 12 Americans are producing 36 units of coffee and 18 Americans are producing 36 units of

apples. Again if both focus more on the good for which they have a comparative advantage, coffee for Brazilians and apples for Americans, and the terms of trade adjust appropriately, then the Americans will again ship apples to Brazil for coffee, and both will be better off.

Production Possibilities Frontier Analysis

We can show the gains using our Chapter 1 production possibilities frontier as well. Recall that a production possibilities frontier shows the output combinations that a country can accomplish on its own. If we assume either of the scenarios presented above, then the production possibilities frontiers for the two countries, shown in Figure 17.3, would have different slopes. The Brazilian production possibilities frontier would be flatter and the United States' steeper.

If we again assume the one-for-one terms of trade, perfect specialization would improve the situation for both the Americans and the Brazilians, in that the Americans would now have to give up only one unit of coffee to get a unit of apples instead of the two they had to give up before. The Brazilians would benefit, too. They would have to give up only one unit of apples instead of two to get a unit of coffee.

This is specifically illustrated in the bottom panel of Figure 17.3, which uses the production possibilities

FIGURE 17.3 Increased consumption possibilities with trade.

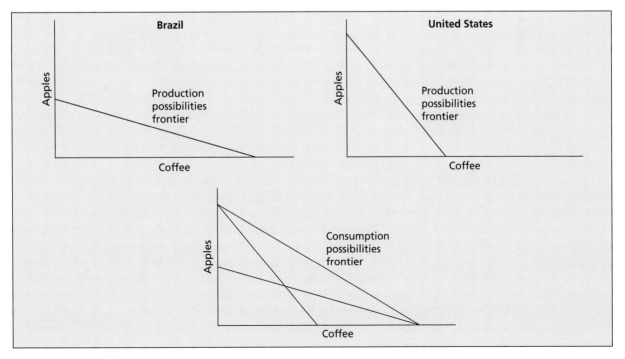

frontier of both to create a new line that shows the consumption possibilities with trade. We saw in Chapter 1 that a production possibilities frontier further away from the origin implies that more production is possible. You can see that the consumption possibilities with trade are greater for both the Brazilians and the Americans than their individual production possibilities without trade. When the Brazilians concentrate on coffee and the Americans concentrate on apples, and they trade, each country is better off. Each produces what it produces best and trades for what it does not produce particularly well.

Supply and Demand Analysis

We can demonstrate the same general conclusion, that Americans are better off because of trade than without it, using supply and demand. Using Figure 17.4, suppose there is a market for domestically produced coffee (from Hawaii perhaps). In a world without trade, the market price of coffee is $P_{domestic}$ and the amount that the domestic industry produces is Q'_d. If there is trade and there is a lower world price of coffee, domestic producers reduce the amount they produce to Q'_s. The domestic producer surplus falls by $P_{domestic}P_{world}CF$. This shows up as lower profits in the domestic coffee business and losses to domestic coffee workers from having to look for other

work. The consumer surplus to domestic coffee consumers rises by $P_{domestic}P_{world}CE$. In the end, the gain to consumers is larger than the loss to producers.

Whom Does Trade Harm?

Even though we have seen that both countries are clearly better off than before, there still are people who would not necessarily like the development of trade. Specifically, American coffee makers and Brazilian apple growers would not necessarily find the idea of trade good. International trade would cause workers in these industries to lose their jobs because the competition would drive their employers out of business. This simple model assumes that the unemployed could find new work in the expanding industries in their respective countries or in other industries generally. This assumption, however, while not bad in the long run, ignores the pain of people losing their jobs and needing to attain new skills. In addition, these displaced workers are likely to get jobs at wages below those they were previously earning.

A relatively recent phenomenon is the development of outsourcing. The term is generally understood by economists to narrowly apply to a firm's use of foreign contractors to perform services that were previously performed within the firm. So, if a computer peripheral company that used to have a technical support line

FIGURE 17.4 Gains from trade.

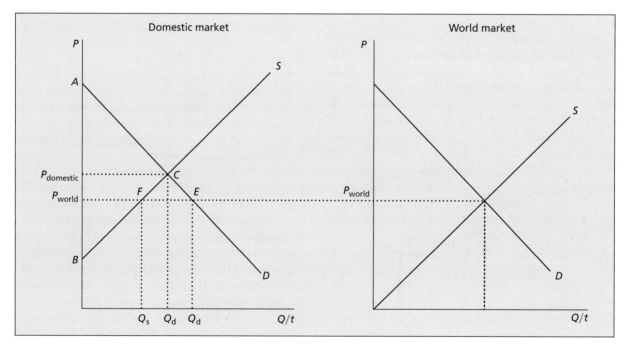

in the United States now contracts to have this service provided by a foreign company, this would be outsourcing. The popular press often refers to anything that used to be done domestically that is now done off-shore as outsourcing. Economists refer to this as off-shoring. An example here would be a manufacturer, like Ford, that used to assemble all of its F-150 pickup truck line in the United States, moving a portion of that operation to Mexico. In either case, the same issue arises. Domestic workers are required to find new jobs.

It is important to note, though, that in a typical non-recession year 30 million of approximately 140 million jobs are eliminated and about 31 million new jobs are created. While some of the 30 million jobs that are eliminated are eliminated because companies engage in outsourcing or off-shoring, more jobs are created than are lost.

Trade Barriers

Reasons for Limiting Trade

Because it is possible that with free trade some businesses go under and some workers lose their jobs, it is useful to summarize some of the questionable and some of the good reasons to limit trade. The questionable reasons begin with protecting jobs within the industries that are being affected by better or cheaper imports. The good reasons are as numerous as they are narrow. We may choose not to trade with other countries in certain goods because those goods may be important to our national security or national identity. Producing such goods at home is therefore important in and of itself. We may choose not to trade with countries that gain their comparative advantage through lax worker safety rules, lax environmental laws, or because they allow businesses to employ child labor.

Though there are clearly short-run costs to free trade, when people lose their jobs to foreign competition and need retraining to get new ones, the long-term benefits usually outweigh these. When labor unions argue against free trade, it is often because the industry that they represent has lost its comparative advantage to other countries. Though this comparative advantage is sometimes lost because of labor or environmental protections, it is usually because the other country has come up with a better or more cost-effective method of producing the good. Protecting an industry in such circumstances is not beneficial for two reasons:

1. For capitalism to work, not only must success be rewarded, but failure must be punished. If companies see that the government will prevent international competition, they will become lax, and they will not produce the best goods for the lowest prices.
2. If other countries see that we protect our firms from competition, they will certainly feel free to do the same. Instead of everyone benefiting from trade, we will return to the days before trade and lose consumption possibilities. We will lose our ability to export our goods to countries where our products are better and cheaper than domestic goods.

The preceding points notwithstanding, there are still good and legitimate reasons for limiting trade even when other countries produce better or cheaper goods. If, for instance, a country other than the United States produced the best and cheapest combat aircraft and it also happened to be a potential wartime enemy of the United States, the United States would be seriously misguided to shut down its own combat aircraft industry and buy planes from the other country. For national security reasons, guaranteed access to war material is important for countries.

Countries also limit trade for reasons that are similar to national defense. If a nation's identity is tied to a particular commodity the way the Japanese identity is tied to rice, for example, it makes sense for the government to limit imports of the commodity so that its domestic producers can survive. Though there is enough productive capacity in the South Central United States to supply the entire rice consumption needs of Japan, and though the Japanese continue to pay more than five times the world market price for rice to maintain a domestic industry, this economically inefficient trade restriction can be justified on two grounds. First, Japan without a rice industry is not Japan; and second, in case of a naval war in the Pacific, it is hard to imagine the United States or any other country devoting significant naval resources to protect rice shipments to Japan. It is not a coincidence that as the Cold War waned, the Japanese began to allow at least limited rice imports.

A final reason for limiting trade is that other countries may get their comparative advantage by using production processes that indirectly harm other countries or that other countries find offensive. If a country lowers its production costs, for example, by polluting in a way that would not be allowed in the United States, the United States might reasonably decide not to let that country sell its products here. This is especially true if the pollution ultimately causes health problems here. The United States might not want to allow the importation of chemicals and other environmentally onerous products from Mexico if, as a by-product of their manufacture, they pollute the Rio Grande.

In addition to environmental objections, countries may find certain labor practices so immoral that they do not allow importation of goods from countries that engage in them. For instance, it is against U.S. law to import any good made with slave labor or with prison labor. Additionally, the United States will not knowingly allow the importation of goods made with forced or indentured child labor, and the U.S. government requires that its contractors certify that no child labor was used in the production of its goods.[1] Several countries allow children as young as eight to work in factories several hours a day. For example, if you own a soccer ball, it was probably made outside the United States, and the production involved at least one child who would not be allowed to work in the United States. The garment industry joins sporting goods in utilizing child labor and engaging in other labor practices that are not legal in the United States. Child labor has existed in nearly every country at some point, and its use is attributable almost entirely to high rates of poverty. In addition, some economists argue that laws outlawing child labor are not necessarily good for the children involved if their only alternative is abject poverty. Despite this, many see the issue less in economic terms and more in moral ones.

Other reasons for limiting trade have appeal to only a limited number of economists. The first of these, the infant-industry argument, says that trade protection is required to give an industry in a country time to get on its feet. In theory, there may be an argument for temporary shelter from competition, but in practice, it often happens that trade is permanently limited.

The second of these limited-appeal arguments is the antidumping argument. **Dumping** occurs when international competitors charge less than their cost in order to drive out competition. The argument is that competitors do this to gain a monopoly in the long run. The problem with this argument is ascertaining the true marginal cost of the international competitor. Inefficient domestic producers' assertions of dumping often hinge on the notion that since they cannot produce at such low costs, it must be impossible. The crux of the dumping argument is the attempt at generating a monopoly, and there are few if any industries in which such a strategy has prevailed.

dumping
The exporting of goods below cost to drive competitors out of business.

[1]See Executive Order 99-06-12, Executive Order on Child Labor, www.fedworld.gov

Methods of Limiting Trade

Once a nation has decided to limit trade, it must choose a method. There are three main methods for limiting trade. A country can put a tax on imported goods, limit the quantity of a good that can be imported, or put regulations on goods that are imported to make it more difficult for the goods to be imported.

The most widely used method for limiting trade is the use of a tax on imports, called a **tariff**. Figure 17.5 shows that if a country wants to limit the amount of a good imported to Q_{limit}, a tax can be put on the good that is sufficient to move the supply curve to where it intersects the demand curve at that output. With such a tariff the price increases to P_{limit}, where domestic producers have a better chance of competing. In addition, the government gets $CP_{limit}AB$ in tax revenue that it can use to retrain workers or to provide other sorts of compensation.

The second method of limiting trade, a **quota**, places a legal restriction on the quantity of a good coming into the country. Also shown in Figure 17.5, this method is popular in that it has the effect of raising the price that domestic producers can charge to P_{limit}. The main difference between a quota and a tariff is that with a quota the government of the importing country receives no tax revenue. Importers get to raise their prices and they get to keep the extra money as profit. Even though it appears this method would seem to be much worse than a tariff for the importing country, quotas sometimes provide political advantages. Often it is less of a diplomatic problem for a country to impose a quota on the imports of another country. Also, as has happened before in the automobile business, it is sometimes

tariff
A tax on imports.

quota
A legal restriction on the amount of a good coming into the country.

FIGURE 17.5 The effect of tariffs and quotas.

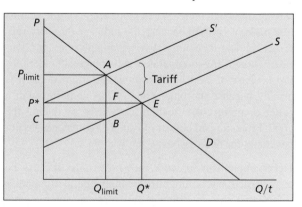

possible to get an exporting country to agree to limit its exports voluntarily. While this operates exactly like a quota, the exporting country retains the power to end the action rather than ceding that power to the importing country. In the early 1980s Japan willingly limited exports of cars to the United States when congressional action was threatened.

The final method by which a country can limit the imports of another country utilizes a recognized right of a country to inspect goods coming in. If you do not want a particular good coming into the country, you can set up rules for its import that effectively make the importation too costly. This method is effective, it is nearly impossible to get around, and it becomes apparent only when the rules become silly. The method is seen mostly with the importation of agricultural products. Although it is perfectly legitimate for a country to want to inspect a shipment to look for certain diseases, bugs, or parasites, countries will sometimes use such inspection as an excuse to limit imports. Because the goods themselves are usually perishable, this can raise the cost to prohibitive levels and effectively prevent any attempts to break into a new market.

Many examples of these **nontariff barriers** exist. Some are perfectly logical; others are dubious. An outbreak of mad cow disease began to affect English herds in 1999, resulting in a ban on English beef sold in Europe. A concern over the potential of allergic reactions in genetically altered corn resulted in a similar European ban on Starlink corn. The European ban on milk from cows that had been given bovine growth hormone (BGH) and the Japanese ban on American apples in the 1980s appear to be examples of the use of nontariff barriers for strictly protectionist reasons.

nontariff barriers
Barriers to trade resulting from regulatory actions.

Trade as a Diplomatic Weapon

There are countless examples in the last 50 years of international trade being used to make a diplomatic point or to solve a diplomatic problem. Since the late 1950s, the United States has imposed trade sanctions against Cuba to destabilize Fidel Castro. In 1979, in response to Iran's refusal to free American diplomats being held hostage in its embassy, the United States made it illegal to trade with Iran. In 1980, in response to the Soviet invasion of Afghanistan, the United States imposed a grain embargo, making it illegal to sell wheat to Russia. In the middle 1980s, in response to a series of terrorist acts by the Libyan government and its surrogates, the United States declared it illegal to buy Libyan oil. In the early 1990s, after Iraq invaded Kuwait, the United Nations imposed economic sanctions against Iraq in hopes that Iraq would retreat. Iraq did not retreat, the Gulf War was fought, and afterward, further economic sanctions were used in attempts to pressure Iraq into giving up its weapons of mass destruction. This too failed.[2] In 2012 and 2013, both Iran and North Korea were sanctioned by the United States and other allies for refusal to give up nuclear weapons. Neither budged.

Manipulating trade simply has not been particularly effective as a method of influencing diplomacy. Castro has outlasted nine U.S. presidents; the Iranians did not buckle to such pressure; the Soviets, the Libyans, and the Iraqis followed their lead. The main reason that cutting off trade has not worked as a diplomatic tool is that it has been impossible to implement adequately. There have always been other avenues that the countries in question could use for trade. The Iranians had never sold much oil to the United States, and they found few problems selling their output to other countries. Argentinean and Australian farmers were only too happy to sell their grain to the Soviets, and the Libyans and the Iraqis had few problems breaking the sanctions imposed on them because many other countries felt free to break them. In theory, the limiting of trade appears to be a powerful diplomatic tool. In reality, it has not been very effective.

[2]Recently released interrogations of Saddam Hussein show that he failed to comply with these UN directives because Iraq had no such weapons after 1995, but that he wanted the Iranians to believe Iraq was stronger militarily than it was.

Kick It Up a Notch   COSTS OF PROTECTIONISM

Reasons and mechanisms for limiting trade are available, but their use incurs substantial economic costs. We can examine those costs using Figure 17.5 and our consumer and producer surplus analysis from Chapter 3. Whatever the mechanism is for limiting trade, if the price of the imported good increases to P_{limit} and the quantity is

TABLE 17.5 Total cost of trade protectionism.

Source: Gary Hufbauer and Kimberly Elliott, *Measuring the Costs of Protection in the United States.* Washington, D.C.: Institute for International Economics, 1994.

Industry	Total Cost to Consumers ($ millions)	Jobs Saved	Cost per Job Saved ($)
Food and beverage	$ 2,947	6,035	$ 488,000
Textiles and light industry	26,443	179,102	148,000
Chemical products	484	514	942,000
Machinery	542	1,556	348,000
Miscellaneous	1,895	4,457	425,000
Total	32,311	191,664	169,000

reduced to Q_{limit}, then there are winners and losers from the protectionist measures. The losers are consumers because their consumer surplus falls by $P*P_{limit} AE$. Domestic producers are winners because they get a higher price, and foreign producers are losers because their sales are limited. The net gain to producers from a quota, or alternatively the net gain to producers plus the tariff revenue to the government, is $CP_{limit} AB - BFE$. In any event there is a net loss to society from the protectionist measures of ABE.

In practice this loss can be very substantial. Table 17.5 illustrates the net loss to the United States from trade protection in certain industries. It also demonstrates the net loss per job that the protectionist measures save. This table clearly shows the efficiency costs to American consumers from tariffs and quotas. We pay a few dollars more for many goods, but these figures add up to more than $32 billion to save 191,664 jobs. At $169,000 per job saved, trade protectionism is one of the worst jobs programs in place.

Summary

You now understand that the United States trades in many goods and with many partners, and that we have a massive trade deficit, but that both we and our trading partners benefit from our international trade. You are now able to use the principles of absolute and comparative advantage as well as a production possibilities frontier to demonstrate why that is the case. You know the reasons for limiting trade and alternative mechanisms for doing so and that limiting trade comes at a very high cost. Last, you now see that the use of trade as a diplomatic weapon has been largely a failure.

Key Terms

absolute advantage, 200
comparative advantage, 200
dumping, 204

nontariff barriers, 205
quota, 204

tariff, 204
terms of trade, 201

Quiz Yourself

1. America's most significant trading partner is
   a. Saudi Arabia.
   b. Canada.
   c. China.
   d. Japan.

2. In 2005, which country had the largest trade surplus with the United States?
   a. Saudi Arabia.
   b. Canada.
   c. China.
   d. Japan.

3. Theoretically speaking, all trade is based on
   a. comparative advantage.
   b. absolute advantage.
   c. numerical advantage.
   d. political advantage.

4. The trends in U.S. international trade are such that
   a. imports are increasing and exports are decreasing.
   b. imports are decreasing and exports are increasing.
   c. both imports and exports are decreasing.
   d. both imports and exports are increasing.

5. Using simple linear production possibilities frontiers in a simple two-good, two-country model, comparative advantage is evident when
   a. one country can make more of both goods than the other.
   b. the slopes of the two production possibilities frontiers are identical.
   c. the slopes of the two production possibilities frontiers are different.
   d. one country is incapable of producing one good.

6. Using simple linear production possibilities frontiers in a simple two-good, two-country model, absolute advantage is evident when
   a. one country can make more of a good than the other country can.
   b. the slopes of the two production possibilities frontiers are identical.
   c. the slopes of the two production possibilities frontiers are different.
   d. one country is incapable of producing one good.

7. Of the following justifications for limiting trade, which one would economists be least likely to endorse? Some goods should not be imported because
   a. they are important for national defense (e.g., tanks, fighter airplanes).
   b. they are important for national identity (e.g., television programs).
   c. their production employs many people (e.g., cars).
   d. other countries use child labor to gain a comparative advantage (e.g., clothing).

8. When choosing to limit trade, a country can impose a tax on imported goods. This is called
   a. an estate tax.
   b. a tariff.
   c. a quota.
   d. a capital gains tax.

9. Economists are concerned about nontariff (regulatory) barriers when they are used to prevent imports when a good
   a. is produced via questionable means (e.g., banning milk produced from cows injected with bovine growth hormone).
   b. is produced via more efficient use of labor.
   c. may spread disease (e.g., banning beef from countries that have experienced Mad Cow disease).
   d. violates local standards for decency.

Short Answer Questions

1. Use the concept of comparative and absolute advantage to illustrate why a fast typing business executive might dictate letters on a digital audio recorder for her secretary to type rather than type them herself.

2. List some reasons why the United States might import and export cars, airplanes, chemicals, and petroleum products.

3. Construct an argument against "energy independence" as a policy goal for the United States using the notion of comparative advantage.

4. Explain why a tariff on imported oil would be better than an import quota as a means by which to achieve energy independence.

Think about This

Today's transportation infrastructure makes international trade more efficient than intra-U.S. trade was 100 years ago. What this means is that it is easier today for a shirt made in China to get to California than it was for a shirt made in Georgia to make it to Missouri in 1900. The U.S. Constitution has always banned states from regulating trade between states. This amounted to a within United States free-trade agreement. Can we use the experience of the United States between 1900 and 2000 to predict what would happen in world trade if there was free trade across the globe?

Talk about This

Simple trade theory suggests that a country should not import and export the same good. It should either import the good or export the good, but not both. Reality is that intraindustry trade is common. What might explain this?

For More Insight See

Journal of Economic Perspectives 12, no. 4 (Fall 1998). See articles by Dani Rodrik; Maurice Obstfeld; and Robert C. Feenstra and Jeffrey G. Williamson, pp. 3–72.

Journal of Economic Perspectives 9, no. 3 (Summer 1995). See articles by J. David Richardson and Adrian Wood, pp. 57–80.

Krugman, Paul R. "Is Free Trade Passe?" *Journal of Economic Perspectives* 1, no. 2 (Fall 1987), pp. 131–144. Any text with a title like *International Economics*.

Behind the Numbers

Country comparisons:
www.census.gov/foreign-trade/balance/index.html

Industry comparisons:
www.trade.gov

CHAPTER EIGHTEEN

International Finance and Exchange Rates

Learning Objectives

After reading this chapter you should be able to:

LO1   Describe the importance of international financial transactions in the global economy.

LO2   Discuss how foreign exchange markets work to facilitate trade.

LO3   List the determinants of foreign exchange rates.

LO4   Analyze how alternative foreign exchange systems operate.

Chapter Outline

International Financial Transactions

Foreign Exchange Markets

Alternative Foreign Exchange Systems

Determinants of Exchange Rates

Summary

If you have studied Chapter 17, "International Trade," you know that globalization is one of the central historical facts of the late 20th and early 21st centuries. In the United States alone, as a percentage of GDP, exports have more than doubled and imports have more than tripled. Since 1970, U.S. investment abroad as a percentage of GDP has increased tenfold and foreign investment in the United States as a percentage of GDP has increased fifteenfold. What the previous two sentences imply is that a massive accumulation of trade deficits has resulted in the transition of the United States from the world's largest creditor nation to the world's largest debtor nation. In addition to discussing the financial implications of increasing trade, increasing American trade deficits, and increasing globalization, this chapter discusses the exchange of the world's currencies.

International Financial Transactions

In order for international trade to occur, international currencies have to be transacted to allow for that trade. There is almost no barter left in the world. Because of that, there is no guarantee that the value of what is imported will equal the value of what is exported. There is also no guarantee that the amount of money Americans invest abroad will equal the amount of money others invest in America. To understand international finance, you have to begin with three basic accounting concepts: balance of trade, current account balances, and capital account balances.

When Americans buy iPads, though the iPad is made by an American-owned company, Apple, it is assembled in China, with components manufactured in several countries. We will wait to talk about currency exchanges until the next section, but we know that the Chinese company needs yuan, the currency of China, in order to pay its employees. Ignoring that detail for the moment, suppose that there is American currency, say $100,000,000, that has left the United States. Whoever ends up with that $100,000,000 can buy things that are made in the United States: They can buy financial assets, like U.S. government debt; they can buy physical assets that remain in the United States, like land, buildings, or manufacturing facilities; or they can simply hold onto the cash. This latter option is rarely chosen unless the holder lives in a country where the dollar is a better form of money than the home currency, or the holder is engaged in an internationally illegal activity where holding cash makes them less traceable. In short, that $100,000,000 has to return to the United States somehow. The "how" is the key question.

balance of payments
The accounting system for how money moves between countries to facilitate the purchase of goods, services, financial instruments, and physical investments.

current account
The portion of the balance of payments accounting that represents the impacts of trade, short-term investment payments, and American payments of foreign taxes, foreign payments of American taxes, and the net transfer of private money.

Table 18.1 lays out the **balance of payments,** the accounting system for how money moves between countries to facilitate the purchase of goods, services, financial instruments, and physical investments. What "balances" with the balance of payments is the current account and the capital account. The **current account** represents the impacts of trade, short-term investment payments, and American payments of foreign taxes, foreign payments of American taxes, and the net transfer of private money. This latter item is most often seen when migrant workers send money home to their families who live outside the United States. As you can see, mostly because of the enormous trade deficit, there is a massive current account deficit of $470 billion.

Over time the current account and the balance of trade mirror one another quite closely. Figure 18.1 maps both as a percentage of GDP from 1960 to 2010. For all but one of the last 33 years, the balance of each has been negative. The exploding trade deficits of the 1990s and the 2000s can be seen as trade and current account deficits that had reached previous records in the middle 1980s and grew to in excess of 5 percent of GDP from 2003 to 2008. Both of these deficits fell rapidly during the recession as Americans cut import demand signficantly.

The **capital account** represents the changes in holding of longer-term financial and physical assets by citizens of one country in another country. The most significant elements of this are the amount of foreign investment in the United States and the amount of investment by Americans in other countries. Recall that when iPads are sold, the holders of dollars have to do something with the money. For the most part, they buy U.S. financial and physical assets. The balance of the capital

capital account
Represents the changes in holding of longer term financial and physical assets by citizens of one country in another country.

TABLE 18.1 Balance of payments, United States, 2012 ($ millions).

Source: Bureau of Economic Analysis, www.bea.gov/international

Major Accounting Item	Sub Accounting Item	Sub Accounting component	Component Amount	Sub Accounting Balance	Balance
Current Account	Balance of trade	Exports	2,936,512	−340,908	−276,378
		Imports	3,277,420		
	Balance of short-term investment income	Income to the United States	742,020	198,606	
		Payments from the United States	543,414		
	Net Transfers (taxes, private payments)			−134,076	
Capital Account	Change in the ownership of assets	U.S.-owned assets abroad	17,918	366,984	276,378
		Foreign-owned assets in the United States	384,902		
	Financial derivatives net			−3,074	
	Statistical discrepancy & net derivatives			−87,532	

FIGURE 18.1 Current Account and Balance of Trade as a Percentage of GDP (1960–2012).

Source: Bureau of Economic Analysis, www.bea.gov/international

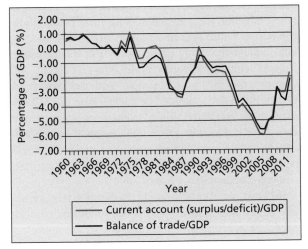

Foreign Exchange Markets

To understand the importance and the complexity of dealing with foreign exchange, consider the simple act of buying a low-end iPad. When you plunk down $500 or so at a local store, the $500 goes several places. The first place it goes is to the store owner, who uses some of it to pay employees and other business expenses, and some to pay Apple. The rest is profit. Apple Inc. contracted with a company in China (Foxconn) to assemble the iPad from parts made all over the world and here is where the issue of foreign exchange comes up. Those in China want to be paid in their own currency called the yuan (to say "yuan," say "u-wan" which is also known by its other name, the "renminbi").

Let's look at this U.S. dollar-for-yuan exchange. Figure 18.3 looks like any ordinary supply and demand diagram except that the labels are more confusing. The confusion stems from the fact that in a typical market you are exchanging a form of currency for a good or a service. Here you are exchanging a form of currency for another form of currency. In this particular case the demand for yuan is also the supply of U.S. dollars, and the demand for U.S. dollars is really the supply of yuan. The price is confusing. Typically the price is quoted in terms of dollars per unit of the good. Here it is U.S. dollars per unit of yuan. It could just as easily be yuan per unit of U.S. dollars. For this reason we have renamed the curves using somewhat roundabout language.

The vertical axis of Figure 18.3 is labeled "Price of yuan in U.S. dollars" because it is the number of U.S. dollars that must be given up to get a quantity of yuan. The horizontal axis is the amount in yuan exchanged. What

account, plus or minus a statistical discrepancy, is the opposite of the balance of the current account.

As can be seen in Figure 18.2, the globalization of asset holding has grown markedly. From less than a percentage point of GDP for much of the 1960s to 10 to 15 times those levels today, the international ownership of financial and physical assets is quite clearly a sign of the times. Figures 18.1 and 18.2 are directly related in that the level of the current account deficit line in Figure 18.1 is the difference between the two lines in Figure 18.2.

FIGURE 18.2 Foreign purchases of U.S. assets and U.S. purchases of foreign assets as a percentage of GDP (1960–2012).

Source: Bureau of Economic Analysis, www.bea.gov/international

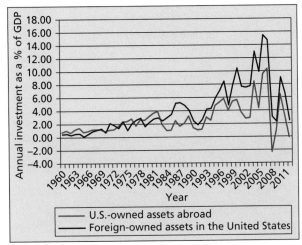

FIGURE 18.3 Yuan to U.S. dollar.

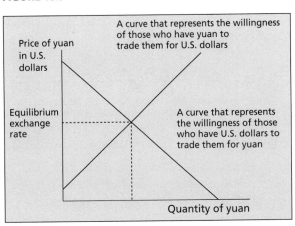

would normally be called a demand curve is the "curve that represents the willingness of those who have U.S. dollars to trade them for yuan." It is downward sloping because people would be less willing to trade their U.S. dollars for yuan if they had to give up more U.S. dollars to do it. What would normally be called a supply curve is the "curve that represents the willingness of those who have yuan to trade them for U.S. dollars." It is upward sloping because people would be more willing to trade their yuan for U.S. dollars if they could get more dollars from them.

Going back to our iPad example, this simple purchase involves a number of different currencies that must be exchanged because the components are produced throughout Asia. If currency exchange is as easy as going to the bank with a $20 bill and asking for 20 $1 bills, then **foreign exchange** is not an obstacle to trade. In most

foreign exchange
The conversion of the currency of one country for the currency of another.

of the Western world, it is a relatively simple proposition for a corporation to get the currencies it needs. There are foreign exchange markets in all large cities that have stock markets. If you need a special permit to exchange currency, however, the transaction is far more cumbersome. Moreover, if that special permit is given only to those who support the ruling party, the ease of trading ranges from difficult to nearly impossible. Who gets hurt by such obstacles to trade? Lots of people. With too many barriers your iPad either will not be manufactured or will cost much more. You will be forced to choose to pay more or to do without it. The store owner will lose profit and the store salesperson will lose commissions. The distributor, Apple, and the Chinese worker will be hurt too; one will not make a sale; the other will not have a job.

In most places in the world, exchange rates are like any freely traded asset. The price, or in this case the exchange rate, changes over time. A look at Figure 18.4

FIGURE 18.4   Exchange rates between the dollar and four major currencies.

Source: Board of Governors of the Federal Reserve System, www.federalreserve.gov/releases/h10/hist

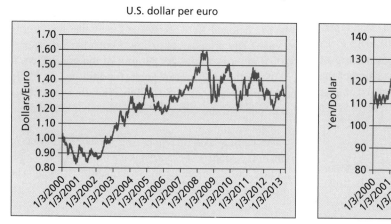

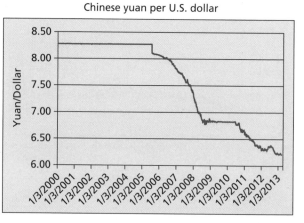

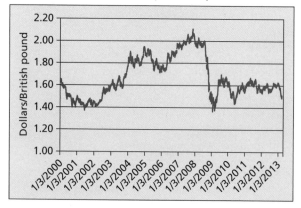

shows the exchange rate between the dollar and other key currencies around the world. As the previous section suggested, any exchange rate between any two currencies can be expressed either as the amount of country A's currency you need to buy one unit of country B's currency, or vice versa. They are commonly expressed in both ways, as they are in Table 18.2, but there are times when a conventional method of expression dominates. For instance, the yen-dollar exchange rate is almost always expressed in terms of the number of yen it takes to get a dollar, whereas the dollar-pound exchange rate is typically expressed the other way. There is no functional difference as one is always the reciprocal of the other.

A strengthening of the dollar relative to the currency in each graph is shown as a decrease in the dollar per other currency line and an increase in the other currency per dollar line. So between July 2008 and November 2008 the dollar strengthened relative to the euro and pound and weakened relative to the yen.

It is important to note that the Chinese government does not let its currency move at the whim of market forces. It was not until 2005 that the Chinese let their currency move, and even then it was only slowly, and not nearly as fast as free market forces would have had it move.

Alternative Foreign Exchange Systems

Throughout modern history, currencies have been exchanged in order to facilitate trade. During that time there have been three models for setting those exchange rates. As suggested by Figure 18.4, most exchange rates are determined by market forces. An increase in the demand for a currency will strengthen it relative to another currency. While this is the system that dominates today, it has not always been that way and as intimated above with reference to the Chinese yuan, market forces can be controlled by governments.

Though we have already discussed the market, let's quickly review the role of the market in determining exchange rates. In a **floating exchange rate system**, there is no government control over exchange rates. The market for various currencies is determined solely by the forces of supply and demand. Shifts in the curves from Figure 18.3 are determined by the factors outlined in the next section. That is, trade imbalances, differences

floating exchange rate system
Foreign exchange rate system where there is no government control over exchange rates.

TABLE 18.2   Exchange rates between several currencies and the U.S. dollar, Friday, March 22, 2013.

Source: X-Rates, www.x-rates.com

Foreign Currency	Amount of Currency Needed to Get $1	Amount of U.S. Dollars Needed to Get One Unit of the Currency
Argentine Peso	5.102992	0.195963
Australian Dollar	0.957003	1.044929
Botswana Pula	8.305648	0.1204
Brazilian Real	2.012116	0.496989
British Pound	0.656532	1.523154
Bruneian Dollar	1.248006	0.801278
Bulgarian Lev	1.510865	0.661872
Canadian Dollar	1.02289	0.977623
Chilean Peso	472.869	0.002115
Chinese Yuan Renminbi	6.211902	0.160981
Colombian Peso	1828.403	0.000547
Croatian Kuna	5.848566	0.170982
Czech Koruna	19.88107	0.050299
Danish Krone	5.740348	0.174205
Euro	0.770168	1.298419
Hong Kong Dollar	7.763435	0.128809
Hungarian Forint	236.129	0.004235
Icelandic Krona	124.0099	0.008064
Indian Rupee	54.34386	0.018401
Israeli Shekel	3.654429	0.273641
Japanese Yen	94.41402	0.010592
Kazakhstani Tenge	150.9464	0.006625
Kuwaiti Dinar	0.28475	3.511855
Latvian Lat	0.540853	1.848931
Libyan Dinar	1.2845	0.778513
Lithuanian Litas	2.659235	0.376048
Malaysian Ringgit	3.112499	0.321285
Mauritian Rupee	31.28493	0.031964
Mexican Peso	12.37608	0.080801
Nepalese Rupee	86.98708	0.011496
New Zealand Dollar	1.196878	0.835507
Norwegian Krone	5.807521	0.17219
Pakistani Rupee	98.25862	0.010177
Romanian New Leu	3.40868	0.293369
Russian Ruble	30.83405	0.032432
Saudi Arabian Riyal	3.75011	0.266659
Singapore Dollar	1.248006	0.801278
South African Rand	9.313914	0.107366
South Korean Won	1118.892	0.000894
Sri Lankan Rupee	126.85	0.007883
Swedish Krona	6.496697	0.153924
Swiss Franc	0.941326	1.062331
Taiwan New Dollar	29.88255	0.033464
Thai Baht	29.29678	0.034133
Trinidadian Dollar	6.414495	0.155897
Turkish Lira	1.815054	0.550948
Venezuelan Bolivar	6.288319	0.159025

in real interest rates, and changes in the relative safety of investments in the two countries will cause changes to exchange rates.

We now turn our attention to the system that was common between World War II and the early 1970s. One of the perceived ills of the exchange rate system of the 1920s and 1930s was that, because it was determined by markets, it created uncertainty for traders. In the days before options markets (where traders could lock in exchange rates for the future), the concern was that uncertain exchange rates dampened trade and that dampened trade was bad for the world economy. As a result, after World War II a **fixed exchange rate system** was enacted. Under a fixed exchange rate system, the country (or group of countries) that wishes exchange rates

fixed exchange rate system
Foreign exchange rate system whereby the country (or group of countries) must stand ready to purchase or sell its currency in exchange for foreign currencies or gold so that any excess demand or excess supply is immediately eliminated.

to be fixed relative to other countries' currencies must stand ready to purchase or sell its currency in exchange for foreign currencies or gold so that any excess demand or excess supply is immediately eliminated. (The gold standard is simply one way in which a country can achieve a fixed exchange rate.) For instance, if you look at the yuan-dollar exchange rate from Figure 18.4, you note that the exchange rate remained constant for an extended period of time. In that system, depicted in graph A of Figure 18.5, an increase in demand for yuan must be met immediately with an increase in the supply of yuan by the Chinese government. That is not difficult for a country to maintain. It can always print more of its own currency. Graph B shows the opposite problem. Were the demand for yuan to decrease, the Chinese government would have to reduce the supply of its own currency. This can be done by its supplying the necessary dollars to buy the yuan, or as graph B shows, pulling yuan out of the system, typically through exchanging other currencies or gold. If, once again, you focus on Figure 18.4

FIGURE 18.5 Alternative exchange rate systems.

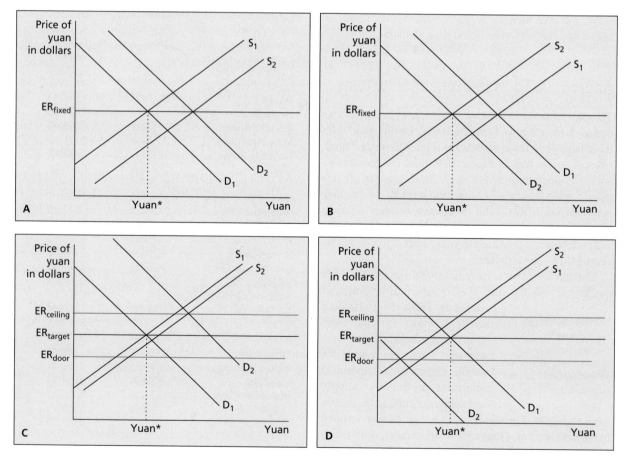

you note that from early 2006 to early 2009, the Chinese government let the yuan strengthen in value from 8 yuan to the dollar to a new set level of 6.8 yuan to the dollar. It has subsequently been allowed to strengthen to 6.5 yuan to the dollar. The Chinese government is clearly engaging in market transactions to ensure that the yuan does not become so strong that it eliminates the cost advantages that Chinese firms have in producing goods for the U.S. market. Many economists would consider this currency manipulation.

The third alternative is a **managed float exchange rate system**. In this system governments decide the range of exchange rates they will allow the market to create, and act only when either the top end or the bottom end of that range is breached. In this circumstance the government need not change the supply of its currency by the amount necessary to bring about the target exchange rate. It must only do enough to bring it back into the desired range. Graphs C and D work exactly like graphs A and B except that the government(s) managing the exchange rate have to increase or decrease the supply of the currency by a smaller amount so as to maintain the desired range.

managed float exchange rate system
Foreign exchange rate system whereby governments decide the range of exchange rates they will allow the market to create, and act only when either the top end or the bottom end of that range is breached.

In post–World War II history the world has seen its major currencies exchanged in all three fashions. As we indicated above, immediately after World War II the fixed exchange rate system dominated. The system became untenable in the early 1970s, and from that point to today, the system has been mostly a floating exchange rate system with periods of managed float when exchange rates changed too markedly for politicians to stomach.

Determinants of Exchange Rates

Recall from our discussion of supply and demand in Chapter 2 and from our discussion of aggregate supply and aggregate demand in Chapter 8, we presented the models and then presented the reasons why each of the curves might shift. We need to replicate that here except that we need to remember that there really is no distinction between supply and demand, so we will look at the factors that will strengthen or weaken an exchange rate. Since each exchange rate applies only to the two countries involved, the factors are expressed relative to one another.

So returning to our discussion of the U.S. dollar and Chinese yuan, the dollar can get stronger or weaker relative to the yuan if either the desire of yuan holders to acquire U.S. dollars changes or the desire of U.S. dollar holders to acquire yuan changes. An increase in the desire of either to have U.S. dollars rather than yuan would strengthen the U.S. dollar, causing the price of yuan—the U.S. dollar-to-yuan exchange rate—to fall. A decrease in the desire of either to have U.S. dollars will weaken the U.S. dollar, causing the price of yuan—the U.S. dollar-to-yuan exchange rate—to rise. So what specific factors determine the desirability of various currencies?

The first and typically most important factor for exchange rates is the trade imbalance between the two countries. The United States has a significant trade deficit relative to China. If the yuan and dollar are determined in markets (and we know from the above discussion of exchange rate systems they are not), the yuan will strengthen relative to the dollar. This is because there will be more dollars in the foreign exchange markets going after yuan.

The second factor influencing exchange rates is the relative real interest rate being offered on investments in the two countries. This combines two ideas, because the real interest rate is the difference between nominal interest and expected inflation. If inflation is expected to be the same in the two countries, because investors will seek the maximum return on their investment regardless of where that happens, they will seek the currency of the country with the highest interest rate. As a result, the currency of the country with the higher interest rate will strengthen relative to the one with the lower interest rate. If the interest rates of the two countries are the same, the country with the lower anticipated rate of inflation will see its currency strengthen relative to the country with the higher anticipated inflation rate.

The third factor is the relative safety of assets held in a particular country. This is why the dollar nearly always strengthens in times of international strife. The U.S. government, though in significant debt, holds the distinction of being the one government that has paid every debt it has ever incurred. Being a haven for international investors seeking safety means that the dollar strengthens even when the strife was triggered in the United States. The dollar strengthened slightly in the wake of 9/11 and strengthened mightily relative to the euro and pound during the fall 2008 financial crisis (which started in, but was not confined to, the United

States). There was also a relatively short-lived strengthening of the dollar during the European sovereign debt crisis of 2010. This occurred despite the United States having its own debt issues because investors were more concerned about the euro-denominated debt of Spain, Greece, and Ireland.

ARE THE CHINESE MANIPULATING THEIR CURRENCY? ARE WE?

During the 2012 presidential election, there was political bombast on several issues, but one of the issues where both sides were in agreement was that "we" needed to get tough on Chinese currency manipulation. Is there evidence that the Chinese manipulate their currency? Of course, there is. That is what happens when you have a fixed exchange rate system. You pick your desired exchange rate and you manipulate the market by buying and selling your currency in exchange for some other currency (or gold) in an attempt to achieve your desired exchange rate. In order to maintain the 6.22 yuan per dollar exchange rate, the Chinese have had to print more of their currency to sell into the market than they would otherwise have to print to maintain a functioning economy.

However, the United States is hardly innocent of the same charge. The United States has weakened its currency relative to every other currency by the unprecedented monetary policy of the Great Recession era (2008–2013). This can be seen most clearly in the upper right graph of Figure 18.4, which maps the value of the dollar relative to the value of the Japanese yen. From its peak in 2008, the dollar had been worth 110 yen. By early 2012, the dollar was only worth 76 yen. This made Japanese exports to the United States much less competitive, and by that time the Japanese had tired of it and began a manipulation to counter the U.S. monetary policy. In so doing, they raised the exchange rate (by weakening the yen) to 96 yen to the dollar by March 2013.

The lesson here is that the charge of currency manipulation can be hurled at many countries, the United States included.

Summary

For foreign trade to exist, currencies must be traded. Whenever trade between two countries is not balanced, the money that is not returned to the country maintaining a trade deficit will have to return eventually and will be used to buy assets in that country. As a result, trade balances, which are augmented by short-term investment flows, will be balanced by longer-term asset ownership exchanges. In this way the current account and capital account balance. The United States runs a large trade deficit and as result runs a large current account deficit. This is balanced by a substantial capital account surplus. The markets in which these currencies are exchanged can be allowed to function freely and without government intervention, or they can be managed by governments to maintain either fixed exchange rates or exchange rates within an acceptable range. Whether a currency is strong or weak typically depends on the trade balance between the two countries, the relative inflation rates, the relative interest rates, and the relative safety of investments in the countries.

Key Terms

balance of payments, 210
capital account, 210
current account, 210

fixed exchange rate system, 214
floating exchange rate system, 213
foreign exchange, 212

managed float exchange rate
  system, 215

Quiz Yourself

1. What two numbers "balance"?
   a. the current account and exports.
   b. the capital account and the current account.
   c. exports and imports.
   d. short-term investment income and short-term investment payments.
2. From one country's perspective a strong currency is
   a. always good.
   b. always bad.
   c. good for some people and bad for others.
3. The dollar to yuan exchange rate will equal
   a. the yuan to dollar exchange rate.
   b. the reciprocal of the yuan to dollar exchange rate.
   c. the yuan to euro exchange rate.
   d. the square of the yuan to dollar exchange rate.
4. If one country determines it wants a fixed exchange rate with another
   a. it can do nothing on its own but must have the cooperation of the other country.
   b. it only needs to announce its desired exchange rate, and that will result.
   c. it must stand ready to purchase or sell its own currency in the market to maintain the exchange rate.
5. An increase in the expected inflation rate in one country will
   a. strengthen its currency.
   b. weaken its currency.
   c. have no impact on the exchange rate between its currency and other currencies.

Short Answer Questions

1. Explain why the current account and the trade balance are so closely aligned.
2. Explain or illustrate why it is that if $1 will buy you .8€ that 1€ must equal $1.25.
3. If you had $1,000 and wanted to get the most for it and you believed that the dollar would get weaker relative to the yen by 10 percent and that you could earn 5 percent in the United States and only 1 percent in Japan, show that you would still want to invest in a yen-denominated asset.
4. If you were a U.S. politician seeking to strengthen the dollar, how might you accomplish that, and what would the consequence be of the attempt?

Behind the Numbers
Exchange rates.
   Current: www.x-rates.com
   Historical: www.federalreserve.gov/releases/h10/hist
Balance of trade, current account, and capital accounts
   www.bea.gov/international

CHAPTER NINETEEN

European Debt Crisis

Learning Objectives

After reading this chapter you should be able to:

LO1 Understand that the creation of the euro integrated monetary policy across member nations without effective integrating fiscal policies.

LO2 Understand that the integration of the monetary systems in the European Union allowed for the influx of relatively cheap capital into poorer European nations.

LO3 Understand that the causes of the Irish and Spanish crises differed markedly from the Italian and Greek crises.

LO4 Understand that the policies that the United States used to mitigate the Great Recession were largely unavailable to those European nations faced with crises.

LO5 Understand that the exit of individual countries from the euro could have set off a Europe-wide banking crisis had it occurred during the crisis.

Chapter Outline

Introduction
In the Beginning There Were 17 Currencies in 17 Countries
The Effect of the Euro
Why Couldn't They Pull Themselves Out? The United States Did
Is It Too Late to Leave the Euro?
Where Should Europe Go from Here?
Summary

Introduction

From late 2008 through all of 2012 (and perhaps beyond), the world economy was either in free fall or recovering at a painfully slow rate. The United States experienced the Great Recession (the subject of Chapters 13 and 14), while China's growth slowed and Europe stumbled from one crisis to the next. In the process, there was a constant threat that Europe's troubles would/could drag the world into another, perhaps even deeper, global recession. This chapter explores the causes of Europe's problems during this period by going back to the scene of the crime—the creation of the euro. The chapter continues with an analysis of the impact of the euro's creation on housing markets in Ireland and Spain and on the borrowing habits of Italy and Greece. The chapter then describes why the

existence of the euro made it very difficult for governments in the most hard-hit countries to recover and why there is so much disagreement over the austerity policies many countries were compelled to employ to secure the help of healthier European economies. The chapter concludes by recognizing that some countries may be better off in the future if they leave the euro, and those countries that remain with that currency may be better off if the weaker ones do leave.

In the Beginning There Were 17 Currencies in 17 Countries

After World War II when country borders were redrawn by the allied powers, each of the countries of Europe reestablished their individual currencies. Germany had the mark; France had the franc; Italy had the lira; Greece had the drachma; and so on. Very quickly it became clear to the various governments that the European economies would recover more quickly with a free-trade union allowing freight to travel between the countries without having to stop at each border crossing. In 1958 the European Union's predecessor, the European Economic Community, was created to establish travel and trade rules throughout the member nations.[1] Through the years, the movement for European integration intensified, culminating in a series of referendum votes in the 1990s approving the Maastricht Treaty that created a common currency for 16 countries.[2] The currency was in use in financial markets only from 1999 to 2001 and has circulated as the currency of the member states since.

By joining the euro, countries gave up a major symbol of their sovereignty, their currency. They also gave up the ability to use monetary policy (described in Chapter 10) as individual countries because they had to cede that authority to the European Central Bank (the counterpart to the United States' Federal Reserve). It was for these reasons that some European Union nations, most notably the United Kingdom, refused to join. The transition process was remarkably smooth. Bank balances were converted from home currencies to euro-denominated balances at specified rates, and actual paper and coin currency was recalled and exchanged. This typically occurred when businesses would deposit their local currency at local banks. At that time they would receive credit for those deposits in euros.

Several other provisions of the Treaty on the Functioning of the European Union were put in place to avoid the kind of economic catastrophe that we have seen in Greece and Spain. One such provision, Article 126, was that countries were required to maintain a deficit to GDP ratio of less than 3 percent and work to a debt to GDP ratio of less than 60 percent. Another, Article 123, stated

that the European Central Bank could not purchase member nation debt. A third, Article 125, prohibited bailouts of one country by the union or by any member state unless it was viewed as necessary to avoid a systemic financial collapse of the entire union.

The Effect of the Euro

The effect of the creation of the euro and these provisions was that the poorer members, some southern European countries, in particular, saw relatively rapid growth. As can be seen in Figure 19.1, growth in Ireland, Spain, and Greece exceeded that of the euro area and the United States from 2001 through 2007.

As can be seen in Figure 19.2, there was and is a considerable discrepancy between the per capita GDP of these countries. With the European Union-27 member nations indexed as 100, the interpretation of the data below is that in 2001 Greece had a per capita GDP 50 percent lower than the Netherlands and Germany. Spain was 15 percent poorer than Germany.

That these countries were growing faster than the richer countries promoted considerable lending to poorer member countries largely because interest rates to poorer member countries converged to the already low rates of the richer member countries. This was because investors believed that a loan to a euro-member country or a financial institution in a euro-member country was largely the same regardless of whether that nation was relatively rich or poor. As can be seen in Figure 19.3, the interest rates on 10-year government debt were, during the period from 2001 to 2007, largely identical across Europe's largest governments.

These low interest rates and the relatively attractive weather of Ireland and Spain generated housing bubbles in those two countries that were even more inflated than those in the United States. Figure 19.4 shows that, between 2000 and 2009 and relative to first quarter 2000, housing prices doubled in the United States, but increased by 125 percent in Spain and by 150 percent in Ireland. The sources of those mortgage loans, however, differed. In the United, Fannie Mae and Freddie Mac bought and securitized mortgages as mortgage-backed securities (MBS). In Europe, the instrument was the "covered bond." In that method, the loans remained with the originating banks (unlike in the United States where the originating bank sold the mortgages within days) and then sold bonds that were backed by those mortgages. As a result, a bank in the

---

[1] Current members: Austria, **Belgium,** Bulgaria, Cyprus, the Czech Republic, Denmark, Estonia, Finland, **France, Germany**, Greece, Hungary, Ireland, **Italy,** Latvia, Lithuania, **Luxembourg,** Malta, the **Netherlands,** Poland, Portugal, Romania, Slovakia, Slovenia, Spain, Sweden, and the United Kingdom. **Bold = original members**

[2] There are now 17 countries that are part of the currency union. They are Austria, Belgium, Cyprus, Estonia, Finland, France, Germany, Greece, Ireland, Italy, Luxembourg, Malta, the Netherlands, Portugal, Slovakia, Slovenia, and Spain. Estonia joined in 2010 and was not part of the original 16. Further, millions more live in countries with currencies whose value is pegged to the euro.

FIGURE 19.1   GDP growth in euro countries and the United States.

Source: European Central Bank, www.ecb.int/stats/html/index.en.html

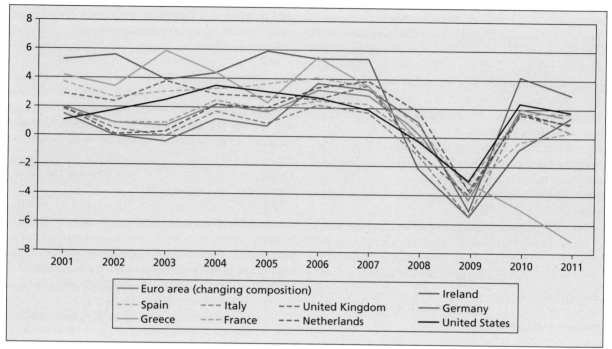

FIGURE 19.2   Per capita GDP across Europe and the United States relative to EU-27.

Source: Eurostat, http://epp.eurostat.ec.europa.eu/portal/page/portal/eurostat/home

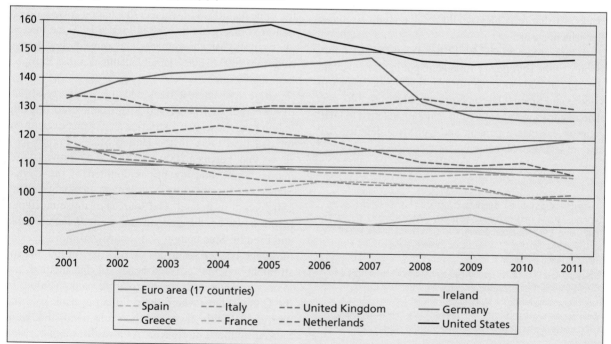

FIGURE 19.3   Long-term interest rates.

Source: European Central Bank, http://sdw.ecb.europa.eu

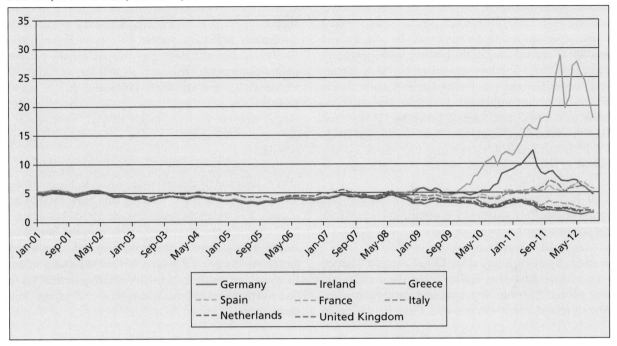

FIGURE 19.4   Housing prices in Spain, Ireland, and the United States.

Source: www.statcentral.ie; www.standardandpoors.com

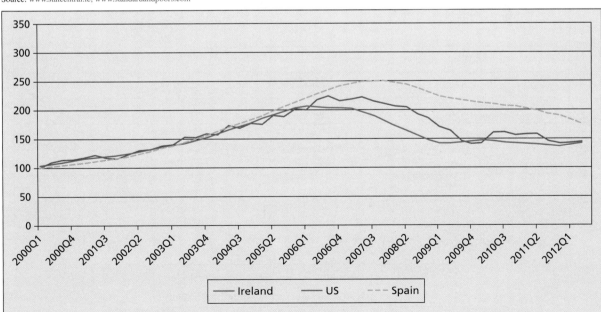

United States that did not purchase MBS for its own portfolio could have largely escaped the housing crisis. In Europe, however, any bank that made the loans and any financial institution that purchased the covered bonds were vulnerable to this crisis. In both Ireland and Spain, the bursting of the housing bubble severely damaged banks in those countries but also threatened larger German and French banks because this is where the money originated. Had there been no covering of the Irish and Spanish bonds by German and French banks, there would have been insufficient funds for Irish and Spanish banks to lend to people buying homes in Ireland and Spain and there would have been no housing bubble.

In Italy, the recession and fiscal crisis had a very different origin. Italy's economy is simply and steadily on the decline and has been for some time. In 2000, its per capita GDP was 18 percent higher than the EU-27 average. By 2010, it was at the EU-27 average. That is, on a relative basis, the Italians spent the decade getting poorer. This has structural and political origins. The structural origin was two-fold. First, Italy is aging

more rapidly than any other major European economy because the birth rate has plummeted for the better part of 40 years. Fewer births translate to fewer workers supporting its pension system. Second, it began with a relatively high debt. As can be seen in Figure 19.5, the Italian national debt was relatively high for the period prior to the crisis, and its deficits, as shown in Figure 19.6, were also high. Politically, Italy's prime minister was a self-aggrandizing, womanizing media mogul with no desire to tackle difficult structural issues such as reforming a pension system for a declining population.

In Greece, the origins were far worse. Its debt was always high and its deficits were worse. If it is possible, they were actually worse than the data show them to be because it is widely believed that the true deficit picture in Greece is worse than they reported to the European Union. This is because tax evasion by individuals and businesses in Greece is so pervasive as to be intractable. Everyone uses as their excuse for cheating on their taxes that others are too and that when others start paying their share, they will too.

FIGURE 19.5 Debt to GDP.

Source: Eurostat, http://epp.eurostat.ec.europa.eu/portal/page/portal/eurostat/home

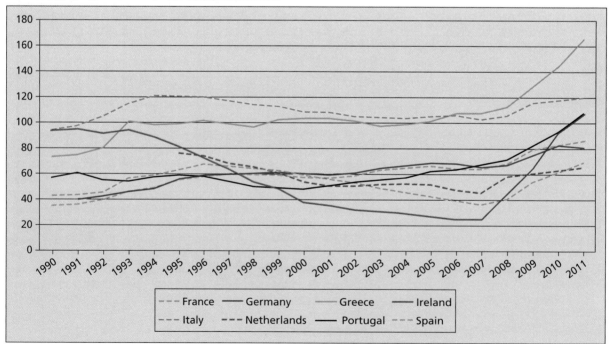

FIGURE 19.6 Deficits to GDP.

Source: Eurostat, http://epp.eurostat.ec.europa.eu/portal/page/portal/eurostat/home

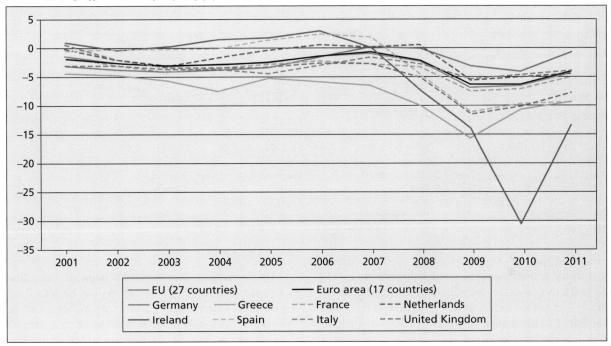

Why Couldn't They Pull Themselves Out? The United States Did

Though the start of the decline in economic activity among powers began in the United Kingdom, it got its first major push in the United States with the collapse of the American housing bubble in late 2008. The United States did three big things to counter the impact of the Great Recession: (1) TARP (the bank bailout), (2) acts of monetary policy on an unprecedented scale, and (3) fiscal policy–induced explosions in deficits in the form of Bush and Obama stimulus packages. The United Kingdom and France did the latter; Germany did not. The deficits in Germany in 2009 and 2010 were on the scale of their 2001–2005 deficits, whereas the deficits in the United States and France were two to three times those levels.

As for monetary policy, as Chapters 10, 13, and 14 noted, the Federal Reserve of the United States created and exercised authority in the area of monetary policy well beyond what any previous Federal Reserve chairperson would recognize. As a result of those actions, interest rates throughout the United States were at or near all-time lows. The Treasury was borrowing money on the short-term market for nearly zero interest. In the long-term market, interest rates were so low that 15-year mortgages were being offered for less than half of previous 1960s era records. These were directly the result of the Federal Reserve's purchasing U.S. debt at record rates.

Why did European nations not do the same thing? Simply put, they couldn't. They couldn't do so individually because interest rates were too high, and they couldn't do so collectively because of the Article 123 provision that prohibited the purchase of membernation debt by the European Central Bank. Italy, Ireland, Greece, and Spain did not have any tools of monetary policy, let alone the expanded ones because, just like the state of Maryland doesn't have its own central bank, neither do individual EU countries.

Further, at its creation, the European Central Bank had one and only one mission—inflation control—and it is governed by the Germans, the Dutch, the French, and the Belgians, who have little interest in generating a threat of inflation for themselves by engaging in monetary policy

FIGURE 19.7 Unemployment rates in Europe.

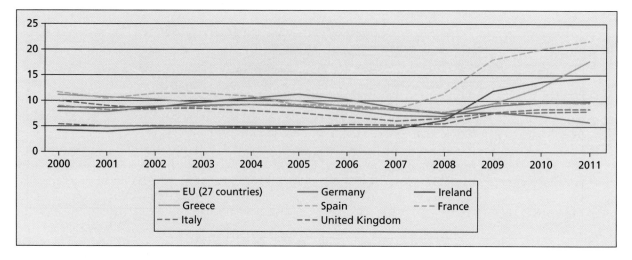

that would help the Greeks, Spanish, Italians, and Irish. To make things worse, the individual country's governments had limited ability at best to engage in their own version of TARP, though the Irish tried. They would have had to borrow the money to do so and, as can be seen by Figure 19.3, the interest rates they faced on borrowing was prohibitive. Further, and for the same reason, they could not engage in fiscal policy to stimulate their economies on their own because, again, they would have to borrow the money to do it. The bottom line is that everything the United States did to minimize the impact of the Great Recession was unavailable to the weaker economies of Europe, largely because they had no control over the value of their currency and had no ability to borrow at reasonable interest rates.

Because there was a growing recognition among the Germans and French that their economies were threatened by the instability of weaker ones, there was a willingness among the Germans and French to help the Greeks, Spaniards, Irish, and Italians. This formal recognition of the threat to the EU, generally, allowed for the cross-national bailouts because the systemic risk clauses of Articles 123 and 125 were invoked. For political and economic purposes, though, the Germans and French insisted that the weaker economies reform their budgets before they received the assistance. In each case the demand was for spending cuts and tax increases. These austerity policies had consequences. Figure 19.7 shows that unemployment rose everywhere but rose more dramatically in these weaker economies. Governments laid off employees, cut pensions, and increased taxes.

From a Keynesian economist's point of view, this is a predictable result of austerity. As can be seen from Figure 19.8, a decrease in government spending and an increase in taxes will result in a decrease in aggregate demand. That will result in a decrease in economic activity and that will result in an increase in unemployment. Austerity could even be self-defeating. The loss of jobs would increase demands on the social safety net and decrease tax revenues. Austerity can ultimately lead to a larger deficit if the austere actions of budget cuts and tax increases plunge the economy into such a poor state that the impacts on the economy generate larger revenue losses than the deficit reductions resulting from the budget cuts and tax increases.

FIGURE 19.8 Result of austerity.

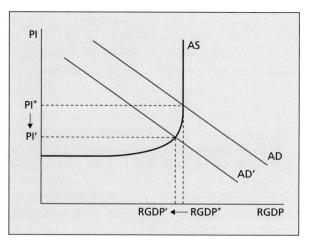

Is It Too Late to Leave the Euro?

For much of 2011 and 2012, speculation was rampant that Greece would leave the euro. The reasons why Greece would want to leave the euro should now be obvious. If you want to regain the ability to print your own currency and engage in monetary policy, you have to have your own currency to do it. Creating their own currency would not be difficult. Getting people to accept it would be difficult. However, if the Greek government were to order all Greek banks to convert euro-denominated accounts into drachma-denominated accounts, the effect would be quick. Though the Greek government could easily issue this order, they would have little power to maintain the value of the drachma, and its value would almost certainly plummet. The inflation in Greece would be dramatic. From some perspectives, that would be a good thing. That's because it would operate as an across-the-board tax on everyone. Your 1,000 euro account would have 1,000 drachmas in it, and then the drachma would lose half its value. You would be able to buy about half as much from the rest of Europe as you had been able to buy, and you would look to Greek providers of the goods or services because their drachma-denominated prices would look relatively more attractive. The attractive aspect of the idea of the "Grexit" (Greek exit from the euro) is that it would fairly quickly stabilize the Greek situation by taxing each Greek by half their wealth as inflation of 100% cuts the buying power of wealth in half.

But, alas, it isn't that easy. Smart Greeks had already anticipated the change. They became convinced that it would eventually happen just this way, so they closed their euro-denominated banks accounts in Greece and took those accounts to other countries. They converted their euros into assets out of the reach of the Greek government. As a result, the only people with any euro-denominated accounts in Greece were those who were either poor (and therefore couldn't afford to do their banking with a foreign bank) or unaware (and therefore vulnerable).

This bankrupted Greek banks because they simply did not have the euros to pay off their depositors. Understand that no American bank could withstand a demand by a large number of its depositors for a cash withdrawal either. Thus the threat of a Greek exit both increased the likelihood of a Greek exit and diminished the viability and desirability of a Greek exit. It also made it harder for the rest of Europe to keep them in. The problem was made worse because if the Greeks left, it would be difficult to contain the concerns of Spaniards that their country would be next. That would jeopardize Spanish banks. Spain would topple Italy and, if Italy was toppled, the euro would be a memory. As a result, as difficult as it was to achieve, the Germans and French felt compelled to keep Greece in the euro. It was a mess that only got better very slowly. It could still collapse, though, at this writing in the spring of 2013, it has not.

Where Should Europe Go from Here?

The irony of the situation is that Greece needed to leave the euro at a time that it could not, and Germany and France needed Greece to be out of the euro but could not allow it to happen out of fear of what the consequences might be. Once stability and growth are achieved, what is possible economically may be even more difficult politically, because those opposed to Greece's exiting the euro will ask why the suffering had to occur to keep them in if the only result was going to be that they would ultimately be out. Perhaps the only likely scenario is that new rules for the EU banking, monetary, and fiscal systems will be put in place to decrease the likelihood of another bubble-created or government-debt fostered threat to the system.

Summary

From late 2008 through all of 2012, the United States experienced and made its way through the Great Recession while Europe stumbled from one economic crisis to the next. The origin of European difficulties was in that they created a currency, the euro, thereby unifying their monetary systems without unifying their fiscal systems. As a result, whether it was Ireland and Spain with housing-bubble-related crises or Italy and Greece with fiscal crises, the challenge for stronger EU countries was how to save the euro without the tools the United States used to weather the Great Recession.

Quiz Yourself

1. The cause of the European financial crisis had its origins in
   a. the creation of the euro.
   b. vast overspending in Germany.
   c. uncompetitive tax collections in Greece.
   d. speculative home buying in Belgium.

2. The proximate cause of the Spanish problem was
   a. vast overspending during the previous decade.
   b. lax tax collections during the previous decade.
   c. a burst housing bubble.
   d. both a and b.

3. The proximate cause of the Greek problem was
   a. vast overspending during the previous decade.
   b. lax tax collections during the previous decade.
   c. a burst housing bubble.
   d. both a and b.

4. The reason the Greeks didn't use a plan similar to TARP to save their banks was that
   a. the Greek Central Bank had no funds.
   b. the interest rates Greece would have had to pay on the loans would have been unaffordable.
   c. banks weren't a problem in Greece.
   d. there was no political will in Greece to borrow that kind of money.

5. The reason the European Central Bank (ECB) didn't engage in the kind of expansionary monetary policy that the Federal Reserve did for the United States was that
   a. the ECB didn't view the problem as serious.
   b. the ECB could not raise the capital.
   c. the provisions of the treaty that created the ECB did not allow for it to buy the debt of member nations unless there was systemic risk.
   d. there was no debt for the ECB to buy.

6. The reason the ECB did not want the Greeks to exit the euro was that
   a. Greece was viewed as a valuable member in temporary distress.
   b. Greece was viewed as so unimportant that it did not want the perception that countries were leaving for any reason.
   c. Greece was a founding member and political friendships were important to the ECB leaders.
   d. Greece was viewed as the first domino in a series of dominos that, if Greece left, it would jeopardize the whole euro system.

Short Answer Questions

1. What should the Maastrict Treaty have included to allow for an adequate response to the various European economic crises?

2. When would be the right time and what would be the correct mechanism for getting a country out of the euro?

3. What would the problems associated with the ECB being allowed to purchase the debt of member nations?

Think about This

For full integration of the European Union, some argue that the nations should be like states of the United States with the central government having limited and enumerated powers. What would those powers be?

If Greece is analogous to Mississippi (relatively poor) and Germany is analogous to New York (relatively rich), what is present in the United States that makes it relatively easy for Mississippi to be in the same country as New York that is absent that makes it relatively hard for Greece and Germany to imagine themselves in the same country.

Talk about This

The bursting of the housing bubble hit Phoenix and Miami much harder than Dallas/Ft.Worth. Why should the taxpayers of Texas have consented to programs that helped only citizens of Phoenix and Miami? Why, then, should Germans care if the Irish housing bubble caused problems in Ireland?

Behind the Numbers

European economic data—http://epp.eurostat.ec.europa
  .eu/portal/page/portal/eurostat/home
European interest rates—http://sdw.ecb.europa.eu

CHAPTER TWENTY

Economic Growth and Development

Learning Objectives

After reading this chapter you should be able to:

LO1   Identify why some already developed countries grow faster than others.

LO2   Explain why creating an environment for economic growth in a developing country is a very different and much harder challenge than fostering growth in an already developed country.

LO3   List what legal, political, and institutional factors have historically limited growth in many developing countries.

Chapter Outline

Growth in Already Developed Countries

Comparing Developed Countries and Developing Countries

Fostering (and Inhibiting) Development

Summary

Economists have been trying to figure out economic growth and development for as long as there have been economists. Why, for instance, does a country such as the United States command nearly one-quarter of the world's yearly economic output while having less than 5 percent of the world's population? Why did the United States grow faster than France during the last decade? Why can't sub-Saharan Africa catch an economic break? Why has politically repressed China grown so rapidly for more than a decade, while India, a democracy for decades, grew much more slowly? Why has South Korea blossomed from a developing country to a developed one? This chapter is a little bit macroeconomics, a little bit international trade, a little bit government policy, and frankly, a little bit guesswork. Economic development is one of the least well-settled areas of economics in part because even the Nobel prize–winning models perform poorly.

Let's start by dividing the question of economic growth and development into two very different questions: Why do already developed countries grow at different rates? Why do underdeveloped countries rarely reach a point where they can emerge from their meager circumstances?

Growth in Already Developed Countries

If we go back to our Chapter 8 aggregate demand–aggregate supply model, we can begin to think about how already developed countries grow. An economy can grow because of sustained increases in aggregate demand but only when there is a simultaneous sustained increase in aggregate supply. To see why, remember the shape of the aggregate supply curve. It starts out flat, begins to slope upward, and finally becomes vertical. If aggregate supply does not grow, then eventually increases in aggregate demand have no impact on real economic growth because sooner or later we will hit the vertical portion of the aggregate supply curve and real GDP growth will stop. We also learned in Chapter 8 that deflation can be a very dangerous economic circumstance, so without

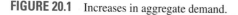

FIGURE 20.1 Increases in aggregate demand.

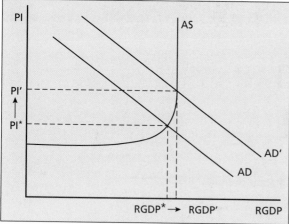

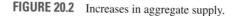

FIGURE 20.2 Increases in aggregate supply.

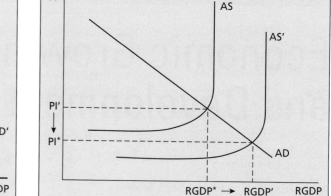

increases in aggregate demand, increases in aggregate supply can conceivably bring a developed economy to a standstill as deflationary pressures diminish people's willingness to buy big-ticket items. What this implies is that economic growth over the long term results from increases in aggregate demand caused by sound fiscal and monetary policy (covered in Chapters 9 and 10, respectively) and sustained increases in aggregate supply.

What fosters increases in aggregate demand? Again Chapter 8 gives us a clue, but a deceptive one. If we just look at the determinants of aggregate demand and what might be done to increase it, we note we can increase government spending, increase consumer confidence, decrease interest rates, decrease taxes, or weaken the dollar. As Figure 20.1 indicates, each will have the desired impact. The problem is you cannot do these in a sustained fashion. First, we cannot continually decrease interest rates or taxes. Zero is an absolute lower bound for each. We cannot continually increase government spending or eventually deficits will drive up interest rates. Consumer confidence is unlikely to grow without bound. This leads us to the conclusion that the ultimate determinant of economic growth in developed countries is likely to come from the aggregate supply side. Increases in aggregate demand simply keep it going.

What fosters increases in aggregate supply? Government regulation can't continuously decrease and neither can wages or other input prices. What can continue to increase without bound is worker productivity. Workers, aligned with the right machines and technology, can always produce more than they produced the previous year

if they work smarter, better, and more efficiently. When they do, we get the results shown in Figure 20.2: more output and lower prices. Note that the word "harder" was not on the previous list of ways to increase productivity over the long run. People can work harder, but at some point you reach the end of human endurance. Getting more output from workers usually requires providing them with the education, tools, and technology to produce more.

What this means is that the economy can grow or contract in the short run for a variety of reasons mostly having to do with changes in aggregate demand, but the ultimate source of long-term growth in already developed countries is increases in worker productivity. As can be seen from Figure 20.3, from 1990 to 2004 developed countries that experienced higher levels of productivity increases also experienced higher GDP increases. The relationship is not one to one but it does exist. For these countries, a one percentage point increase in productivity growth is associated with a 0.3 percent increase in per capita GDP growth. Remember that this does not mean that workers have to work longer hours, or that they have to work at a faster pace, or that we need bosses intolerant of anything but the bottom line. Increases in worker productivity usually come about because of an increase in the education of workers and an improvement in the tools with which they work.

What feeds the worker productivity engine? Worker productivity is driven by policies that contribute to long-term capital formation and worker education and training. If saving is discouraged and consumption is encouraged

FIGURE 20.3   Annual productivity increases and annualized GDP growth rates (1990–2004).

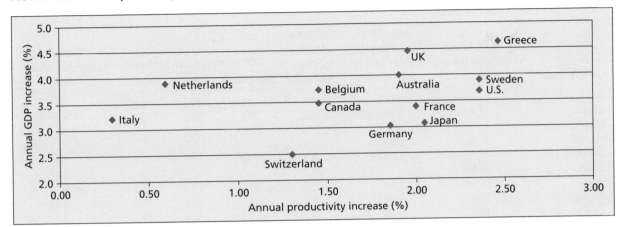

beyond that which is sustainable, there is not a plentiful supply of loanable funds. If the benefits from saving money are exorbitantly taxed, then the motivation to save money is diminished. Growth requires a healthy capital market on the demand side as well. This means that rates of taxation on the gains from that capital must be at levels so that after-tax returns to businesses are sufficiently motivating for investment. A developed and motivated work force is also a prerequisite to economic growth. Workers must be motivated to get the right amount of education and to then productively apply that education in the workforce. With moderate marginal tax rates, rates of interest and inflation, reasonable regulatory policies, a sound education system, and a sound welfare system that does not overly compensate the unemployed, developed economies will continue to grow.

Comparing Developed Countries and Developing Countries

Besides the obvious, income, what is different about rich and poor countries? Table 20.1 brings this all into stark relief. The countries listed on the top of the table have per capita gross national income (GNI)[1] of more than $20,000, while the countries at the bottom of the table have per capita gross national income of less than $2,000. There are some other stark differences that appear on this table. While those at the top of the table generally have a large "middle class," those at the bottom

do not. The **Gini index**, a measure of overall income disparity, is generally higher in poorer countries than richer ones. Those at the top have very little of their GNI coming from agriculture and a significant portion coming from services, while those at the bottom have the reverse. If you go all the way back to Chapter 1's reference to the Heritage Foundation's Index of Economic Freedom, you will also note that those at the top also tend to be the most economically free, while those at the bottom tend to be classified as the most unfree.

Gini index
A measure of overall income disparity.

There is also an accounting issue that we need to discuss. In Chapter 6 we noted that real GDP and social welfare are not synonymous. One of the reasons that is true is the existence of the underground economy. Though the primary example in that discussion was the United States, consider the notion of the underground economy in a developing country like the Sudan. While many people in the United States engage in a little "cash-on-the-side" business (lawn mowing, babysitting, marijuana buying) where the efforts are not counted, most people in the Sudan make their own clothing, grow or raise their own food, or trade one good or service for another. As a result, whereas the underground economy is 10 percent of the U.S. production, as much as half a developing country's economy can be in nonmarket transactions. This is why the comparable figures for each country shown in Table 20.1 are adjusted using the notion of **purchasing power parity**. Economists have estimated what it costs to purchase a similar market basket of goods and services

purchasing power parity
Using the cost of a similar market basket of goods across countries to compare an economic variable like gross national income.

[1]Gross national income modifies gross domestic product by adding in income earned abroad and makes other relatively small adjustments. For the most part GNI is a better number for comparing incomes across development categories.

TABLE 20.1   International comparisons.

Source: The World Bank DataBank, http://databank.worldbank.org

Country Name	2011 Gross National Income per Capita (PPP)	1990–2011 Annualized Rate of per Capita GDP Growth	Distribution of Family Income— Gini Index	GDP—Composition by Sector			Inflation Rate (consumer prices) 2011
				Agriculture	Industry	Services	
Australia	49,130	1.76%	35.2	2.3	19.8	77.9	6.1
Belgium	45,990	1.33%	33.0	0.7	21.7	77.7	2.0
Canada	45,560	1.35%	32.6				3.3
France	42,420	0.99%	28.0				1.3
Germany	44,270	1.39%	28.3	0.9	27.9	71.2	0.8
Greece	24,480	1.21%	34.3				1.0
Japan	44,900	0.69%	38.1	1.2	27.4	71.5	−2.1
Korea, Rep.	20,870	4.30%	35.1	2.6	38.8	58.5	1.7
Netherlands	49,650	1.66%	30.9	2.0	23.9	74.2	1.2
Singapore	42,930	3.65%	42.5	0.0	27.9	72.1	0.5
Spain	30,890	1.48%	34.7	2.7	26.1	71.2	1.0
Switzerland	76,400	0.65%	33.7		25.9		0.2
United States	48,620	1.37%	40.8	1.2	20.0	78.8	2.2
United Kingdom	37,840	1.64%	34.0	0.7	21.6	77.7	2.6
Bangladesh	780	3.60%	30.9	18.3	28.2	53.5	7.5
Congo, Dem. Rep.	190	−3.05%	44.4	45.6	21.8	32.6	13.4
Cote d'Ivoire	1,090	−0.90%	48.4	24.3	30.3	45.4	5.0
Ethiopia	370	2.83%	29.9	46.4	10.5	43.1	24.4
Kenya	820	0.29%	47.7	28.5	17.6	53.9	12.1
Madagascar	420	−0.92%	47.4	29.1	16.0	54.9	8.4
Malawi	360	1.55%	39.0	30.2	19.3	50.5	3.8
Mozambique	470	3.77%	47.1	32.0	24.2	43.8	11.1
Senegal	1,070	0.77%	40.2	15.0	24.0	60.9	3.2
Tanzania	540	2.13%	34.6	27.7	25.1	47.2	9.2
Uganda	510	3.62%	44.2	23.4	25.4	51.1	4.9
Uzbekistan	0	1.78%	35.6	36.1	45.0	15.1	1510.0
Yemen, Rep.	1,160	0.61%	37.7	7.7	29.4	62.9	24.2

in each country and used that to estimate gross national income.

Fostering (and Inhibiting) Development

Modern models of economic development, like the Solow Growth Model, named after its Nobel Prize–winning author, provided the basis for much discussion on this subject of how economies would grow. The central prediction of that model, and of many others that it spawned, was that economies would converge in their levels of economic development. That is, poor countries would grow faster than rich ones to the point where levels of per capita

GDP would not differ substantially. Even a brief look at Table 20.1 shows that this has not been the case.[2]

The remainder of this chapter will focus on how a country might move from below the line in Table 20.1 to above it and what might prevent it from doing so. First, we need to appreciate that the challenges for policy makers in developing countries are substantially different and often substantially more difficult than the challenges of developed countries. Those at the top of the

[2]That is not to say that these models are without value. They provided the basis for much of what we know about economic development, but in all honesty, this is an area of economics for which little consensus exists.

table attempt to use sound fiscal, monetary, and regulatory policies within an overarching democratic political structure to foster long-term increases in labor productivity; low levels of inflation; moderate levels of taxation; and reasonable labor, safety, and environmental regulations. That is difficult enough but all too often, policy makers in countries at the bottom of the table don't typically have a political, governmental, or banking structure to do any of these things. Further, they are faced with choices that go beyond simply future consumption versus present consumption, but of future consumption versus present survival.

The Challenges Facing Developing Countries

To see why developing countries face such challenges, put yourself in the position of an open-minded company manager with a decision to make. Do you locate a manufacturing facility in a developed country or a developing country? Your goal, of course, would be to bring as much profit home to the stockholders as possible. You would probably be enticed by the low cost of labor and land in the developing country. Hourly wages in developed countries are almost always 5 to 10 times higher and at times 20 to 100 times higher than in a developing one. On the other hand, you would also have to recognize the potential pitfalls.

Low Rates of Basic Literacy

It's hard to find a quality labor force in a developing country because, though wages are low, the typical resident has little formal education. They may not be able to read or do rudimentary mathematics. Without the basic ability to follow written instructions, the workers in the developing country will have to be managed much more closely than workers who can read and follow instructions.

Lack of Infrastructure

Second, even if you can adapt your production processes to take advantage of the low-skill, low-wage workers, you still do not have the basic financial, physical, or legal infrastructure in place to keep it going. Local banks are necessary for access to credit, and to transmit profits out of the country. They may not exist or may be constrained in their ability to provide the financial services necessary for your business. Roads, bridges, rail lines, and ports are all necessary to transmit goods around the country and around the world. Without an ability to quickly move your finished products to the rest of the world, any cost advantage you had in wages might evaporate because

of your inability to move your products. Finally, legal protections are necessary for the owners of invested property. Whether those protections are based on social conventions, law enforcement, or trustworthy governments, a social infrastructure protecting investments is necessary for those investments to occur.

Political Instability

Trustworthy governments are hard to find in the developing world. This can be because these government are all too often corrupt, unstable, or both. Take Nigeria, for example. Sitting on one of the largest deposits of oil in the world, its long-standing civil war has prevented it from taking ultimate advantage of its resource. You may be able to get low-wage labor to get the oil out of the ground, but you have to pay bribes to the various warring factions to avoid having your equipment stolen, damaged, or destroyed, and you have to worry about your skilled engineers being kidnapped. Do you locate there or do you attempt to make your money elsewhere?

Corruption

Even when a government is stable, the concern that the political leadership will simply take invested property is paramount. Take Uzbekistan, for example. It is also sitting on significant oil and natural gas reserves, but its political leadership is so corrupt that you never know from one year to the next whether the leadership will nationalize those assets. Countries such as these have a culture that expects and accepts this type of corruption. Managers coming from the cultures of developed economies are not, for the most part, comfortable investing in countries where bribery is common or expected.

Lack of Independent Central Banking

If you look at the list of countries on the top of Table 20.1 and compare them with those at the bottom, you will note that the United States, Europe, and the economically successful countries of East Asia all have systems in place to control inflation. As described in Chapter 10, each has a central bank that sets interest rate policies, and in each case there is a degree of central bank independence from political control. In developing countries these banks are not only not independent, in some cases they do not exist. That means that when there is a central bank, it is often under the control of the ruling party, king, general, or junta. When no central bank exists, banking crises are common. In fact, the United States was without a functional central bank for much of the 1800s and saw several banking crises result.

Without an independent central bank in a developing country, when its ruler wants to print money to build a new palace or to pay soldiers for protection, he or she can and will. There are myriad examples of independent central bankers fighting inflation at the expense of an elected leader's popularity. Leaders in countries with democratic traditions and independent central banks understand that the long-term effect of fighting inflation is far more important than the short-term benefit that is gained from being able to spend newly printed money.

Inability to Repatriate Profits

Your ability to move money out of a country can also be limited by government policies. In many developing countries you can bring as much hard currency (dollars, euros, etc.) into the country as you wish, but you cannot reverse the transaction as easily. So, if you were making a profit in the currency of the host country, you may not be able to convert that into hard currency. This is less of a problem if you are manufacturing in a developing country for sale in a developed country, but it is a problem if you are selling goods in the developing country and wishing to turn those profits into hard currency. Knowing that, you will be less likely to invest in the developing country.

A Need to Focus on the Basics

Developing countries, especially the ones listed in the bottom half of Table 20.1, must focus on the very basic necessities of life. Even a well-meaning government would have a difficult time choosing between expending resources on education or health care or food. The opportunity cost of extra spending on making education more widely available could well be a lack of adequate food or health care for others. With so many people engaged in subsistence agriculture, with so little capital with which to work, and with live births per adult woman

above five, these countries are not in a position to invest in their future because their present is so bleak.

In addition, health concerns in these countries can be overwhelming. The countries on the bottom of Table 20.1 are predominantly from sub-Saharan Africa. These countries have been ravaged by HIV/AIDs to such a degree that notions of long-term economic development became secondary to survival.

What Works

The best examples of countries rising above their 1960s economic status to become newly developed countries are the countries of East Asia. China and South Korea, in particular, have grown at a rather brisk pace for very long. Both got to their present position in different ways. South Korea's success economically coincided with its liberalization politically, while China's success occurred while it was relatively unfree politically. It is not just about natural resources either. Though Saudi Arabia and Kuwait have grown almost entirely as a result of enormous oil wealth, Japan's growth through the 1970s and 1980s was despite the fact that it has no natural resources upon which to build.

The basic building blocks for what works tend to begin with education, a low or manageable level of government corruption, and a level of political and financial stability that creates confidence among foreign investors. Countries that have grown have created political and financial stability, have created physical and social infrastructures that generate confidence, and have predictable, if not democratic, governments. Foreign direct investment in China, for example, continues to grow because investors have some degree of confidence that the government will not confiscate their investments and will let them repatriate profits. South Korea's economy continues to grow because their reaction to the late 1990s Asian financial crisis created confidence among investors that their banking system could adapt to challenges.

Summary

You now understand that economic growth in already developed countries is mostly a function of their ability to increase worker productivity and that economic growth in developing countries is often hampered by the lack of social, political, financial, legal, and economic institutions that are prerequisite to economic growth. You understand the magnitude of the gap between developed and developing countries and that the countries that have moved from developing to developed did not follow a single path.

Key Terms

Gini index, 229   Purchasing power parity, 229

Quiz Yourself

1. For developed economies, sustained increases in aggregate demand, absent increases in aggregate supply, will result in
   a. growth for a while but, ultimately, they will result in only inflation.
   b. continuous economic growth.
   c. deflationary risks.
   d. a boom and bust cycle.

2. For developing economies, sustained increases in aggregate demand, absent increases in aggregate supply, will result in
   a. growth for a while but, ultimately, they will result in only inflation.
   b. continuous economic growth.
   c. deflationary risks.
   d. a boom and bust cycle.

3. In order to sustain economic growth in a developed economy, it is important for
   a. taxes to continuously decrease.
   b. government spending to continually increase.
   c. worker productivity to increase.
   d. worker productivity to decrease.

4. One of the biggest problems for developing countries is that they all too often
   a. are ruled by representative democracies.
   b. are populated by people unwilling to work hard.
   c. lack the financial, physical, and social infrastructure to grow.
   d. indulge in wasteful consumption.

5. For the ruler of a developing country, the opportunity cost of a choice to invest in universal education
   a. is the reduction in health care spending.
   b. does not exist because food is a necessity.
   c. is much lower than a similar choice for the ruler of a developed country.
   d. cannot be measured.

6. Which advantage does a typical developing country have in attempting to draw foreign investment?
   a. very low wages.
   b. poor education.
   c. easy profit repatriation.
   d. independent central banks.

Short Answer Questions

1. What does Mexico have to do in order to grow economically? What does Germany need to do to grow economically? Why are those likely to be different answers?

2. What is the long-term consequence to U.S. economic growth of having an education system that lags behind that of other countries?

3. What issues will China face if it wants to continue to grow?

Think about This

Go to the CIA Factbook web pages cited below and explore the economic statistics of the following countries: Brazil, Egypt, India, Malaysia, and South Africa. Each has a per capita GDP between $3,000 and $15,000 per year. What country in that list do you believe is most likely to move into the class of "developed" countries? That is, which is likely to have its per capita GDP rise the fastest and why?

Talk about This

Suppose you had to decide whether or not to invest in formal education for the masses, but the opportunity cost of doing so was reducing health expenditures for the sick and aged. What choice would you make?

Behind the Numbers

CIA Factbook 2012—www.cia.gov/library/publications/the-world-factbook/index.html

World Bank—http://data.worldbank.org

CHAPTER TWENTY-ONE

The Line between Legal and Illegal Goods

Learning Objectives

After reading this chapter you should be able to:

LO1   Apply the supply and demand model and the concepts of consumer and producer surplus to the markets for tobacco, alcohol, and illegal goods and services.

LO2   Conclude that economists endorse interference in a market for reasons related to the information and costs to innocent third parties.

LO3   Utilize the concept of elasticity of demand to analyze who gets hurt by taxes on tobacco and alcohol.

LO4   Analyze the impact of drug legalization.

Chapter Outline

An Economic Model of Tobacco, Alcohol, and Illegal Goods and Services

Why Is Regulation Warranted?

Taxes on Tobacco and Alcohol

Why Are Certain Goods and Services Illegal?

Summary

Let's face it. No mother wants her child to start smoking or drinking, or to engage in illegal activity. These are not healthy activities. Nevertheless, economists are generally reticent to suggest that a good or service should be banned outright just because it is not good for you. This chapter uses the tools of supply and demand, elasticity, and consumer and producer surplus to look at these particular goods and services and the reason some are regulated, some are taxed, and still others are illegal.

Twenty percent of the American population smokes, and the average American consumes nearly 28 gallons of beer a year. With that much smoking and drinking going on, tobacco and alcohol are obviously important parts of the American economy. The tobacco industry employs 14,800 people a year, and it has annual shipments of $37 billion. The alcohol industry employs 77,200 people, and its annual sales amount to $50.3 billion. Because certain goods and services are illegal, it is impossible to know exactly how much money is spent on them or how many people are employed in their production. What is

known is that nearly half of all adults under 35 have violated the law when it comes to their consumption of an illegal good or service.

Before looking closely at the economics of these goods and services, we will review the fundamentals of supply and demand to remind ourselves of how equilibrium within a market serves the interests of both the consumer and the producer. Then we will turn to reasons why selling and using these goods are regulated, taxed, or banned and why economists might back such restrictions. Along the way, we'll focus not only on secondhand smoke, drunk driving, the spread of disease, and increases in crime but also on the issues of age restrictions, warning labels, and prohibition. After a brief discussion of the importance of elasticity, we'll use the concept within our supply and demand model to indicate who gets hurt by the considerable taxes that are levied on both tobacco and alcohol. Finally, we'll discuss why tobacco and alcohol are legal, why other goods and services are not, and what decriminalization of these goods and services would likely bring.

An Economic Model of Tobacco, Alcohol, and Illegal Goods and Services

We'll use the market that was presented in Chapter 2 as the basis for our analysis of these goods. To be general, we'll just call the good or service in question, "the offending good." You can substitute whatever example you wish because the analysis is exactly the same. As we did with the market in that chapter, we will assume that there are many buyers and sellers, that the demand curve for each is downward sloping, and that the supply curve for each is upward sloping. For the time being, we will pretend that there are no negative consequences to innocent third parties. We will also pretend that all the people who engage in these activities know exactly what they are getting themselves into. While these are fanciful assumptions, the approach gives us a jumping-off point that we can use to look at these markets. To prove that the markets benefit both the consumers and the producers, we have to refer to the consumer and producer surplus analysis that was presented in Chapter 3.

We start with a few facts that are presented in Figure 21.1. Consumers buy $Q*$ goods and pay $P*$ for each. This means that consumers pay producers an amount of money that is simultaneously less than the value the consumers place on the good and more than it cost the producers to provide it. That is, consumers are happier with the good or service than they were with the money they gave up, and producers make a profit. The gain to the consumers is $P*AB$ and is called their consumer surplus. The profit to the producer is $CP*B$ and is called their producer surplus.

As a result of this analysis, we can state that the sale of this offending good makes both consumers and producers better off than they would have been without the sale. The sum of the consumer surplus and the producer surplus is CAB. If it were illegal to buy and sell these goods and services, and if everyone obeyed the law, all of the above-named parties would be worse off. Before you have a fit at this conclusion, though, remember that it was arrived at only after we made some fanciful assumptions.

Why Is Regulation Warranted?

It is now time to recognize reality and to deal with the very real problems of tobacco, alcohol, and illegal goods and services. The goods themselves are very addictive. There are harmful effects to innocent third parties from second-hand smoke, drunk driving, and the spread of disease. In addition, the use of any one of these goods or services negatively affects spouses and children. Their presence has caused experts in public health to persuade legislators to implement restrictions, regulations, taxes, or outright bans.

When people argue for government intervention in a market, they do so from many points of view. Economists, who tend to decry unwarranted intervention, generally categorize reasons into three broad areas. First, they deem it possible for people to suffer from a lack of knowledge or an inability to think clearly. When that is the case, it may be appropriate for the government to step in with information or with warnings of danger. It may even be appropriate for government to make decisions for people. Second, they accept that the good or service may have adverse impacts on people other than the consumer or producer. Those costs, which are ignored in a market, must be taken into account by the government. Last, and least appealing among economists, is that consumption or production of the good may be immoral. That is, even though buying or selling the good may not hurt anybody in a physical sense, its production or consumption hurts society in general.

The Information Problem

For legal goods, advertising is intended to draw people to a product, and advertisers want their ads to be memorable. When the advertising is for products like tobacco and alcohol, we sometimes bemoan the effectiveness of the ads. For children of the 1950s and 1960s, the Marlboro Man™ was the image of health and rugged individualism. For children of the 1980s and 1990s, the R.J. Reynolds' Joe Camel™ was as recognizable as

FIGURE 21.1 Market for an offending good.

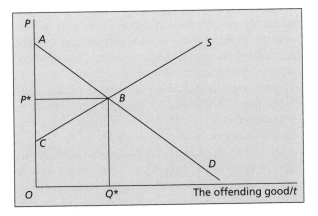

Mickey Mouse. In 1998, tobacco advertising was ended as part of a legal settlement. Still, Anheuser-Busch's series of Budweiser and Bud Light ads have been quite effective with Super Bowl audiences for decades. Though economists recognize the role of advertising in markets for goods that are legal, they debate the usefulness of advertising bans when the goods are legal for only a specified group.

For illegal goods, advertising is not an issue; the real "information" problem is the degree to which people do not adequately weigh the likelihood or impact of addiction. Government's reaction to this can be one of education, one of restriction, or one of prohibition. In the United States we use education to dissuade young people from using drugs and reinforce that with prohibition. In all but certain counties in Nevada, the government's response to prostitution is simply one of prohibition.

The addiction argument clearly applies to cocaine, ecstacy, and methamphetamine. The reasoning is that potential users may not know or fully comprehend that these drugs can be addictive and what the impact of that addiction will be on users. The argument as it applies to prostitution is somewhat different. When prostitutes get started in the sex business, they may not fully realize the consequences of their actions. Some advocacy groups that seek to maintain and strengthen the ban on prostitution, for instance, claim that prostitutes generally begin their trade as children. Estimates place the number of U.S. prostitutes under the age of 18 at between 300,000 and 600,000. People engaged in prostitution, especially at an early age, might not realize that sex workers are sexually assaulted on a regular basis or that the illegal drugs provided to them when they get started are used as a means to keep them under control and dependent. Further, there is widespread concern of a growing market for sexual slaves. The girls caught up in this horrific practice are not convinced to participate but are either abducted or told that they have been chosen to live in the West because of their academic potential or because there is a market for live-in child care workers. Only after their arrival in the West do they learn their fate. Finally, these groups also make the point that more than 80 percent of prostitutes are the victims of childhood incest and that the sex industry capitalizes on this sense of degradation.

In general, then, economists suggest that the information problem can be dealt with using education, age restrictions, or prohibition. The appropriate tool depends on the degree of the problem. For example, the government requires that packages of cigarettes and bottles of alcohol display warning labels that describe the consequences of smoking and drinking. Thus, requiring warning labels and banning tobacco or alcohol advertising on the grounds that these promotions serve only to cloud the judgment of consumers is acceptable to economists. We take the "providing knowledge" a step further when we ensure that every new generation knows the addictive nature of smoking and drinking through programs in the schools.

Of course, there are times when we simply do not trust young people to make good decisions, even when they have all the information. In these cases we either make it illegal to buy the goods or services or we require that people reach a certain age before they can buy them. Economists are not at all uncomfortable forbidding children from consuming tobacco products for two reasons. First, the vast majority of smokers began their nicotine addictions well before becoming adults. Second, there is evidence that the tobacco companies aided their becoming addicted through their marketing efforts. Because only a tiny fraction of smokers began smoking as adults, preventing children from having ready access to cigarettes is in society's interest and in the child's long-term interest.

Ultimately, the reason many economists embrace the prohibition of cocaine, ecstasy, and methamphetamine is that for these the addiction problem is often permanent.

External Costs

Few economists object when government interferes in a market in which someone other than the consumer or producer is hurt by the consumption or production of a good. These externalities are important considerations for market regulation because the point of market efficiency is that everyone either benefits from, or is left unaffected by, a transaction. If that does not happen, then standing by and allowing the market to take care of itself is not always acceptable.

The externalities that result from the use of tobacco are the illnesses and deaths associated with second-hand smoke and the increased health care expenditures incurred by people who do not smoke but must pay increased premiums for health insurance to cover the expenses of smokers. It is not the concern of most economists that (knowledgeable) smokers hurt themselves by smoking. It is the concern of economists that those smokers tend to pass on costs to others.

The sale of drugs often affects someone other than the buyer or seller of the drug. As a result, at least some of the costs of that market are not being accounted for by the buyer or seller. If addicts are more likely to commit crime

EXAMINING THE EXTERNALITIES

There are a few facts on crime that we ought to consider when dealing with drugs in particular. First, 24 percent of all violent crimes (30 percent for rapes) are committed while the perpetrator is on drugs. Second, 55 percent of inmates in jail, detention, or prison used drugs during the month leading up to their arrest. Last, we spend $3.7 billion on drug interdiction at the federal level, another $12 billion in other drug control expenses, and $74 billion on incarceration in this country every year. One-quarter of those incarcerated now are there for drug-related offenses. What effect would legalization have on these statistics? We would save a lot of money—one-quarter of the incarceration costs and all of the interdiction costs. If overall use increased, as it probably would, violent crime would increase as those who were not addicts before legalization became addicts after legalization and, once addicted, became violent.

BATTLING NEGATIVE EXTERNALITIES WHILE CREATING OTHER PROBLEMS

Solving the externalities associated with a good by enforcing a prohibition strategy creates a problem. Sometimes the solution can be worse than the problem it was intended to solve. Much drug violence exists only because of laws criminalizing drug use. If cocaine, methamphetamine, and marijuana were legal and inexpensive, there would be less of a need for addicts to rob in order to get money to buy them. There would be no drive-by shootings to protect turf. There would be no need for the hundreds of thousands of prison beds devoted to drug offenders. It is for this reason that you find a significant number of economists, even very conservative economists, favoring drug legalization. They appreciate that drugs carry with them externalities but see the solution as worse than the problem.

than nonaddicts, then neither the addict nor the dealer is accounting for the rising number of innocent victims when they sell their goods. Similarly, if a person gets a venereal disease from a visit to a prostitute and passes that disease on to an unsuspecting third party, then there is an external cost. Someone who is not part of the original transaction is being affected because of the transaction.

Establishing who should be counted as an innocent victim, though, is not as easy as it might sound. Children clearly are innocent victims, but are nonsmoking spouses? Some economists suggest that as part of the give and take of a marriage, smokers and their nonsmoking partners negotiate the rules for smoking in a household. If they decide it is all right for one to smoke and the other to be negatively affected, then smoking and its implications do not constitute an externality; it is simply one of the costs of the marriage. Other economists disagree. They suggest that regulations are needed to protect any people who are not consumers themselves.[1]

However you decide the issue of who is an innocent victim, those who are subjected to secondhand smoke have higher rates of lung-related illness than exist in the general population. Children in the presence of smokers are much more likely to die from sudden infant death syndrome (SIDS), asthma, and other lung illnesses. Airline cabin crews, servers in restaurants, bartenders, and

a variety of others who have been exposed to others' smoke also report rates of lung illness that are not only higher but beyond those that might have occurred by chance. The costs of treating these innocent victims are ignored by both smokers and tobacco companies. Economists abhor ignored costs. Whether economists support corrective actions when there are such costs depends on the degree of those costs and whether eliminating them is worth the loss of private benefits. In addition, there are more smokers on Medicaid than their proportion within the general population warrants. They, of course, produce some rather substantial costs to the program. If they were not smoking, Medicaid would cost taxpayers less. Here the innocent victim is the taxpayer.

Externalities also exist in less likely places. Since smokers typically die 5 to 10 years earlier than comparable nonsmokers, if they have group life insurance policies whose rates are the same for both smokers and nonsmokers, the expected net payout for smokers' beneficiaries is more than for nonsmokers' beneficiaries. Life insurance rates are therefore higher for nonsmokers than they should be and the rates for smokers are lower than they should be.[2]

These facts combine to suggest that when smokers buy cigarettes, the full cost of their smoking not only is not paid at the cash register but is not even fully incurred

---

[1] This is the same argument that some economists use to suggest that government need not regulate workplace safety. Risk takers must be compensated adequately or they would not take the risk.

[2] This externality is avoided when life insurance companies differentiate their premiums for smokers and nonsmokers. The degree of the employer subsidy would have to depend on this as well.

by the smoker. Most estimates of the external expenses that are paid by the general public come to around a dollar per pack of cigarettes.

This is not to say that economists hold unanimous opinions in these matters. Some suggest that there is a benefit to nonsmokers when other people smoke. These benefits come from two separate but related aspects of smoking. First, as mentioned previously, people who smoke for long periods of time die several years earlier than comparable people who never smoked. Smokers and nonsmokers pay into Social Security and other pension plans, but nonsmokers have some of their retirement essentially subsidized by smokers, because the smokers die before they have collected the benefits to which they were entitled.

A second form of subsidy that smokers grant nonsmokers is that not only do they die early, but they die more suddenly than nonsmokers. When smokers over the age of 60 become ill, their lifetime of smoking has so depressed their immune systems that they die of illnesses that nonsmokers are more likely to survive. They also succumb to those illnesses much faster and less is spent attempting to save them. Even though the money is spent sooner, it is much less. It is grimly ironic then that by dying more quickly than nonsmokers, smokers sometimes cost the health system less than do nonsmokers. By dying early and quickly, smokers avoid expenses that nonsmokers eventually need to pay. Because more than half of Medicare expenses are incurred during the last year of elderly people's lives, hastening their deaths saves money. If this gruesome fact is taken into account, the net external costs of smoking become negligible in the eyes of some economists.

Though there is a morbid economic upside to smoking, there is no such benefit to drunk driving. There are more than 1 million arrests a year for driving under the influence of alcohol. While that number has come down substantially over the last decade, it is still more than high enough to represent a significant problem. Of the roughly 31,000 accidents that result in 33,808 traffic fatalities each year, 32 percent involve at least one person whose blood alcohol level is over the legal limit. Another 5 percent involves someone who has a legal, but still measurable, blood alcohol content. Even when someone does not die, alcohol is a contributing factor in nearly a half million automobile accidents a year.

Despite these troubling statistics, it is time to try to look at the issue from a dispassionate viewpoint. To model the problem of the externalities that are associated

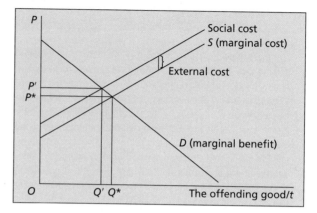

FIGURE 21.2 Modeling externalities.

with people who drive under the influence of alcohol, we need to alter our supply and demand diagram to account for the extra costs for which their behavior is responsible. To understand Figure 21.2, you need to recall that under perfect competition the supply curve is the marginal cost curve to the firms in the business. Any costs that are borne by neither the seller nor the buyer must be added to these costs to create the social cost of the good. On the assumption that the only people who benefit from the consumption of the good are the consumers themselves, the demand curve is the social benefit curve. So instead of coming to the market solution of a price–quantity combination P^*–Q^*, the socially optimal combination is P–Q'. That is, if there is a market for a good where some of the costs spill over to others, then the market will produce too much of the good and charge too little for it.

Morality Issues

We have looked now at the first two circumstances under which economists consider it acceptable for government to intervene in the market. Besides lack of information and externalities in which innocent people may be harmed, a final reason why government might regulate a free market is that the market may be for a good or service that is considered to be immoral. For believers in certain major world religions, alcohol, tobacco, drugs, and prostitution are accorded this status. While appeals to righteousness are not particularly meaningful to economists on an academic level, they are certainly important to many other people. Many religions consider drinking a sin and a few feel the same way about smoking.

WHERE DID MY SUDAFED GO?

One consequence of the national battle against methamphetamine has been that over-the-counter cold medications are no longer simple to purchase. The manufacturers had to decide whether to alter their formulas or put those medications behind the pharmacy counter. Those manufacturers that chose to keep the key ingredient that could be extracted to produce methamphetamine lost sales because consumers were required to provide identification to pharmacists. Others changed their products to include ingredients that are somewhat less effective. Externalities occur all over.

Taxes on Tobacco and Alcohol

Modeling Taxes

To correct an externality, we can tax the offending good, we can limit its use, and we can forbid its use. Of these options, taxes are the most appealing to economists, as they allow people who are willing to pay all of the costs of their consumption to go ahead and consume. Using taxes in this way has the positive effect of discouraging those people who are not willing to pay the costs from becoming consumers of the undesirable or unhealthy good.

The taxes that the United States imposes on tobacco and alcohol are a $1.01 per pack tax on cigarettes and a 32-cent per six-pack tax on beer. The federal taxes on tobacco raise approximately $16 billion a year, while the taxes on alcohol raise $9.5 billion. States also tax these goods, collecting $18 billion in tobacco taxes and nearly $6 billion in alcohol taxes.

Figure 21.3 shows that the effect of the federal taxation on cigarettes and alcohol is to raise the price from $P*$ to P' and to lower consumption from $Q*$ to Q'. An important thing to notice about this effect is that smoking and drinking do not stop. This means that the deleterious effects of secondhand smoke and drunk driving do not

FIGURE 21.3 Modeling taxes.

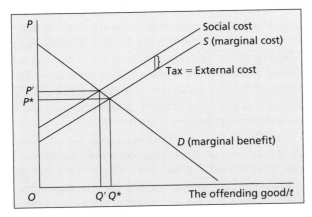

stop either. They are simply reduced. If the tax is set equal to the dollar value of such externalities, then in theory the tax revenue raised is sufficient to cover the costs of the externalities. One problem, though, is that the tax hits the considerate and rude alike. Smokers who light up alone do not cause secondhand smoke, whereas smokers who blow it in your face do. A per-pack tax hits both equally.

In any event, a policy short of prohibition implies that there are an economically acceptable number of expected drunk driving deaths and of childhood secondhand-smoke-induced illnesses. The idea is that as long as we have an adequate sum of money available to compensate the people who are affected, it is acceptable for smokers to smoke, for drinkers to drink, and for people to be influenced in negative ways by their behavior.

People who are not economists have a very difficult time with the "acceptability" of deaths and illnesses. The basic idea is that people drink and smoke because they enjoy doing so. If we take taxing and regulating too far, the reduction in enjoyment by users would outweigh the effect of the reduction on innocent victims.

The notion of acceptable deaths is a difficult one for many to accept. Consider this though: The Brain Injury Association reports that approximately 15 children die each year on playgrounds as a result of falls and other injuries. We continue to send our children out on recess because we weigh what is to be gained with what is to be lost and judge the risk of injury or even death to be tolerable. We drive to work because we see that what is gained—income—is greater than what is lost—a small risk of injury or death.

The Tobacco Settlement and Why Elasticity Matters

For quite some time legislators have given particular consideration to raising the taxes on tobacco. The settlement between several states and the big tobacco companies that was reached in 1998 requires that the companies pay

FIGURE 21.4   Tax on tobacco with inelastic demand.

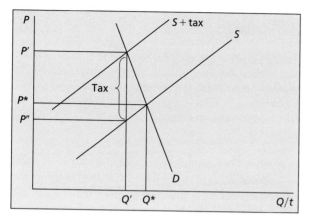

the states more than $250 billion over 20 years to compensate them for Medicaid expenses the states paid that were created by smoking. The companies will then pass on those taxes to the smokers who buy their products. To see how a sequence like this works, we need to look at the supply and demand curve for tobacco.

First, it should be remembered that when someone is addicted to a product, as smokers are to cigarettes, the demand curve for the good is highly inelastic. If you look at Figure 21.4, you see that a tax will again raise the price from P^* to P'. If you compare the size of the tax (P'' to P') to the amount of the price increase, you see that smokers will be paying for most of this tax increase and that tobacco companies will pay comparatively less (P^* to P' versus P^* to P''). Since smokers are far poorer than the average of the general population, this tax is as regressive as any tax we can imagine. Since consumption falls only from Q^* to Q', it is also disturbing that the tax will not have a significant influence on how much people smoke either.

When you look at teen smoking, the picture is not quite so bleak. Because the habit of smoking takes up a much larger portion of teenagers' than adults' incomes, the elasticity of demand for cigarettes by young people is much greater. That is, demand is more elastic and the demand curve is flatter. If you were to draw such a demand curve, you would see that the burden of the tax would still fall mainly on consumers. You would also see that tobacco companies would be paying a greater proportion of the amount of compensation. Further smoking, at least teen smoking, would be reduced by more. Still, economists' best estimates are that elasticities for cigarettes are as low as .2 for adults and as high as .5 for children. This means that an increase of a dollar in cigarette

prices would diminish adult smoking by 10 percent, but it would diminish smoking by children by 25 percent. A study of the elasticity of demand for beer put it at 0.53, which suggests a tax that adds 10 percent to the price of a six-pack would reduce consumption by 5.3 percent.

Why Are Certain Goods and Services Illegal?

The debate over whether drugs and prostitution should be legal usually comes down to a comparison of the negative consequences of what is currently legal, tobacco and alcohol, with what is currently illegal. Clearly a case can be made that the aggregate impact of tobacco and alcohol is much greater than the aggregate impact of illegal drugs and prostitution. As you can tell by now, economists are less interested in "aggregate" impacts than "marginal" ones. Here, the case can be made that the negative externalities associated with one person purchasing one more unit of the illegal goods are greater than the negative externalities associated with one person purchasing one unit of a legal good. The other argument that could be made to justify the current state of the law is that the unknown or underestimated consequences to the consumer of using drugs or engaging in prostitution are substantially greater than those with regard to alcohol. Of course, the opposite case could be made as well.

The Impact of Decriminalization on the Market for the Goods

Given the previous discussion, suppose a good or service is currently illegal. What would result from making it legal? The first thing that would likely happen as a result of making a good legal is that the concerns of both consumers and producers about getting caught would evaporate. Because getting caught would not be a problem any longer, any shift to the left of supply that resulted from clandestine operation would cease to exist. Similarly, any shift to the left in the demand curve by those who might have wanted to partake of the illicit good but did not because it was illegal would cease to exist. The net result of legalizing a previously illegal activity would be a movement in the demand curve to the right and a movement in the supply curve to the right.

Another impact of decriminalization would occur on the elasticity of demand and, to a lesser degree, supply. When a good is illegal, it is often the case that the consumers of the good are addicted to it in some sense. The demand curve for a good for which a consumer is

FIGURE 21.5 Making an illegal good legal or vice versa.

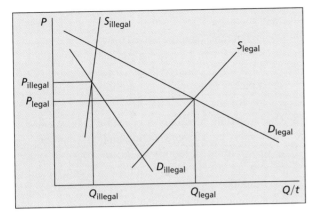

Thus, the direction of a price change as a result of decriminalization depends on whether the reduction in risk to dealers or prostitutes is greater than the increase in interest by consumers. Because the conventional wisdom is that legalization would lower the price, conventional wisdom is just that: The supply curve shift will be greater than the demand curve shift.

The External Costs of Decriminalization

Ultimately, whether legalization makes sense to you depends on whether you believe the external costs of these activities are significant enough to pay the significant costs of punishing users and dealers. One potential solution that many pro-legalizers suggest is that we tax and regulate drug sales and prostitution in order to take into account and pay for the externalities.

Looking back to Figure 21.3, you see that we simply added a tax equal to the external cost that was examined in Figure 21.2 to get the P', Q' result. That is, a proper taxation scheme can make up for the problems of an externality. There is money to educate against the use of the illicit good or to compensate victims of users of the questionable good.

The problem is that if the external costs are very great, the tax will have to be very high. If the tax is very high, there will be a motivation to have a black market in untaxed goods. As evidence of this, consider that in Canada a prohibitively high tax created a black market for cigarettes. In this case people drove to the United States, bought cigarettes, took them back to Canada, and sold them. In another similar case, while prostitution is legal in Nevada, it is highly regulated. That regulation leads to prostitutes' avoiding regulation by working on their own outside the regulated brothels. Whenever a tax is too high or regulation too severe, a black market will exist beside a legal market.

addicted is likely to be very inelastic. Similarly, once people have made the decision to become a seller of an illicit good, the price they sell it for is not usually a stimulus to sell it in great quantities. This is because the risks of getting caught may prevent sellers from expanding their operation quickly as prices rise. Therefore, from either side, the supply and demand curves are less elastic when the good or service is illegal than when it is legal. The net result here is that both curves flatten out when the good is made legal. Figure 21.5 depicts the effect of legalizing a previously illegal good. The demand curve flattens and moves right, and the supply curve flattens and moves right. If the supply curve movement is more than the demand curve movement, as it is in Figure 21.5, the net result is a lowering of price. Not shown, but equally plausible, is the case where the demand curve movement is greater than the supply curve movement and the price rises.

Summary

You now understand how we can apply a supply and demand model and the concepts of consumer and producer surplus to tobacco, alcohol, drugs, and prostitution. You understand that there are reasons that economists endorse interference in a market, reasons that have to do with information and costs to innocent third parties. You have seen how the question of who gets hurt by taxes on tobacco and alcohol is dependent on the elasticity of demand for these goods. Finally, you have seen the argument for the current state of the law with regard to the treatment of these goods and the economic consequences of decriminalization.

Quiz Yourself

1. When examining the question of tobacco taxes, economists focus almost entirely on
   a. the cost to cigarette companies of production.
   b. the cost to cigarette smokers for the cigarettes themselves.
   c. the cost to cigarette smokers for their extra health care expenses.
   d. the costs to nonsmokers (like secondhand smoke).

2. When discussing an addictive drug, an economist is likely to focus on
   a. both the external costs and the "information problem" associated with addiction.
   b. the moral costs totally.
   c. the cost of the drug to the user.
   d. the costs of production.

3. If you became convinced that marijuana was neither addictive nor contributed to externalities, then banning it creates
   a. a social benefit without social cost.
   b. what economists call deadweight loss.
   c. what economists call a vacuum.
   d. a social benefit with an exact countering social cost.

4. Decriminalizing a drug is likely to lead to a price decrease if
   a. the anticipated supply effect is greater than the anticipated demand effect.
   b. the anticipated demand effect is greater than the anticipated supply effect.
   c. the anticipated demand effect is exactly equal to the anticipated supply effect.
   d. both demand and supply decrease.

5. Compared to a recreational user of a drug, an addicted user's elasticity of demand is
   a. much more elastic.
   b. much less elastic.
   c. much less.
   d. flatter.

6. If policy makers were to attempt to set a tax equal to the external costs of alcohol, one would have to evaluate
   a. the cost of production.
   b. the price paid by consumers.
   c. the value of innocent lives lost to drunk driving.
   d. the value of the shortened lives of alcoholics.

7. When examining the "right tax" on a good that produces an externality, the tax should be such that
   a. it is greater than the externality.
   b. it is less than the externality.
   c. it is exactly equal to the externality.
   d. it makes consumption prohibitively expensive for anyone.

8. One unsettling consequence of setting a tax on tobacco sufficiently high to reduce consumption would be
   a. it would likely reduce Medicare costs.
   b. it would likely increase tobacco revenues to farmers.
   c. it would likely increase tobacco company profits.
   d. it would make Social Security's financial outlook worse.

Short Answer Questions

1. If the United States is able to continue reducing the incidence of children smoking, how might that end up costing more in the long run in terms of health-related expenses?

2. If the United States were to legalize marijuana production, what might the negative externalities be and what current negative externalities might be lessened?

3. If the United States were to eliminate the drinking age, what might you predict the outcome to be in terms of externalities?

4. What does the "legalize and tax" method of dealing with currently illegal drugs imply about how proponents of this approach view the ability to put a dollar value on human life?

Think about This
There are considerate smokers and inconsiderate smokers. Secondhand smoke is not an issue when smokers are considerate (in that they smoke where no one is around to breathe it). Should these smokers be taxed when they are producing no harm to society?

Talk about This
As unsavory as it sounds, there are travel agents who book "sex tours" in parts of Asia. Travelers visit prostitutes in various locations. While some of the brothel operators mandate "safe" practices, others allow the patrons to pay extra if they wish to participate in "unsafe" practices. Should you be able to pay someone to risk their lives in this manner?

For More Insight See

Grossman, Michael, Jody Sindelar, John Mullahy, and Richard Anderson, "Alcohol and Cigarette Taxes," *Journal of Economic Perspectives* 7, no. 4 (1993), pp. 211–222.

Thorton, Mark, *The Economics of Prohibition* (Salt Lake City: University of Utah Press, 1991).

Behind the Numbers

State and local taxes on tobacco and alcohol.
Tax Policy Center of the Urban Institute and Brookings Institution.
Tobacco—www.taxpolicycenter.org/taxfacts/displayafact.cfm?Docid=403
Alcohol—www.taxpolicycenter.org/taxfacts/displayafact.cfm?Docid=399&Topic2id=80
Receipts—www.taxpolicycenter.org/taxfacts/displayafact.cfm?Docid=74&Topic2id=80

Employment and value of shipments.
Survey of manufacturers—www.census.gov/manufacturing/asm/index.html
Violent crimes and drug use.
U.S. Dept. of Justice; Criminal Victimization in the U.S., 2008; statistical tables—http://bjs.gov/content/pub/pdf/cvus08.pdf
Federal spending on crime control.
Federal drug control spending, 2011.
Office of National Drug Control Policy; drug control funding tables—www.whitehousedrugpolicy.gov/publications/policy/11budget/fy11budget.pdf
Traffic fatality and blood alcohol statistics, 2009—www.nhtsa.dot.gov
Incarceration statistics—http://bjs.gov/content/pub/pdf/p11.pdf

Natural Resources, the Environment, and Climate Change

Learning Objectives

After reading this chapter you should be able to:

LO1 Apply the principles of present value to natural resource development.

LO2 Apply marginal analysis to answer the question of how clean is clean enough.

LO3 Apply the concept of externalities to explain why pollution warrants government intervention in the market.

LO4 Demonstrate why pollution is much more likely to occur on publicly owned property than on private property.

LO5 Summarize the variety of environmental problems that exist in the world as well as the economic solutions that exist to address these problems.

Chapter Outline

Using Natural Resources

How Clean Is Clean Enough?

The Externalities Approach

The Property Rights Approach to the Environment and Natural Resources

Environmental Problems and Their Economic Solutions

Summary

Maintaining a stewardship over the natural resources of the country and protecting the environment are increasingly popular positions for politicians to take. On the surface the solution to the first of these is to create a system of usage that leaves resources for the next generation, while the solution to the second problem seems rather simple: Stop polluting. For an economist, though, not only is the problem more complicated, but so also is its solution. The environmental problems of modern society are substantial and varied: unsustainable usage of natural resources, pollution of the water and air, the potential extinction of 1,371 species of plants and animals, acid rain that puts forests and fish in jeopardy, and greenhouse effects that are probably responsible for rapidly rising global temperatures.

To most environmentalists solving these problems involves strict questions of right and wrong. Economists, on the other hand, want to look also at costs and benefits. Economics may be central to solving environmental problems because in dealing with the environment we will need to reallocate our resources in directions that generally move from consuming and growing in positive economic ways to preserving and living with economic slowdowns. Where economics can be particularly helpful is in the area of efficiency. Coming up with a plan that reduces pollution is not difficult, but it is hard to come up with a plan that reduces pollution in a way that will minimize the economic costs. That is what economists bring to the discussion.

Using Natural Resources

The earth is a bounty of **limited natural resources** such as land, oil, natural gas, coal, mineral ores (iron, copper,

limited natural resources
Resources that cannot be replaced.

renewable natural resources
Resources that can be replaced.

stewardship
The management of resources in a fashion that weighs their value through time.

etc.), and **renewable natural resources** such as fresh water, wood, and wildlife. The question for a society is how to deploy those resources in such a way that maximizes their long-run usefulness. For a society to do that, it must weigh the value of those resources to those who are living now against the value of those natural resources to generations to come. The issue can be summarized as one of

stewardship, which is the management of resources in a fashion that weighs their value through time.

In the simplest sense, suppose you have a resource that you can use now or you can leave unused and preserve it for later. Suppose you also know what people will pay for it now and you have a good estimate of what they will pay for it in the future. In order to determine whether you should use it now or leave it until another time, you have to use the Chapter 7 concept of present value. To keep things simple, suppose the resource is costless to find, extract, and process and produces a constant value per unit in each time and that there are a fixed number of units. Any positive interest rate will yield a

sustainability
The idea that you should only use renewable resources at the rate at which they can be replaced.

conclusion that you should use it all now—the exact opposite of **sustainability**. Sustainability is the idea that you should only use renewable resources at the rate at which they can be replaced, and it means that you use lim-

ited natural resources at the lowest possible rate in order to preserve them for future generations.

However, the simple introduction of a downward-sloping demand curve for that resource brings about the result that there is a trade-off between present use and future use that will result in a motivation among resource owners to conserve even with a positive discount rate. The downward-sloping demand curve accomplishes this because increasing the present use decreases its marginal benefit.

Suppose, for the purpose of illustration, the resource is oil and that oil is used to produce gasoline. Recall from Chapter 2 and Chapter 3 that the demand for gasoline

represents its marginal benefit to its user. If an additional unit of oil is going to be utilized now, it has a decreasing marginal benefit to the refiner because there is a decreasing marginal utility for gasoline among consumers. The refiner must reduce the price to sell the extra gasoline. The question for the oil company is whether it is worth it to drill for oil now and refine more gasoline now when doing so requires that you reduce your price of gasoline now. In doing so, you give up the opportunity to wait and sell that gasoline later at a price that is likely higher. Though those later profits will have to be discounted, they can well outweigh the profits from producing and selling now.

An upward-sloping supply curve can also aid in motivating conservation. Continuing with the example of oil, the shale oil of the North Dakota area has been known to exist for half a century and yet went largely untapped even when oil prices peaked in 1980 and again in 2008. That is because it is very expensive to tap. The marginal cost of producing more oil, if that oil is from a location such as that is very high and so few companies tried to extract it until recently. As a result there is conservation of difficult to extract resources, because the marginal costs are greater than the marginal revenues.

What this means is that market forces, both on the demand and supply side, will lead to some degree of conservation. The greater the discount rate, the lesser will be the degree of conservation and the lower the discount rate, the greater will be the degree of conservation. This leads some environmentalists to conclude the morally correct discount rate is zero. Economists typically would not go so far as to say that. Economists would more frequently assert that the rate of utilization should be socially optimal for everyone involved, those present and those in the future. These economists would suggest, in the case of oil, that the rate of utilization should also factor in the likelihood that with greater scarcity of oil, alternatives to oil will become more profitable to develop and that history tells us that when society requires an alternative, prices adjust so that an alternative becomes profitable.

How Clean Is Clean Enough?

For many of you, when you were 10, your bedroom was a wreck. When asked whether a room is clean, a 10-year-old will respond with a reply that is pure economics: "clean enough." With that reply, 10-year-olds are saying that to them, further cleaning is simply not worth the effort. In the language of economics, children are saying that the

FIGURE 22.1   Clean enough.

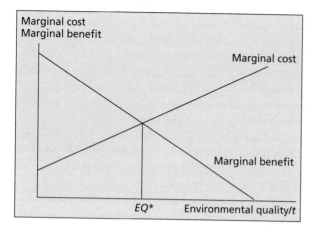

marginal benefit of cleaning more (the value they place on additional cleanliness) is less than the marginal cost of cleaning more (the value they place on Facebook time).

Economists apply the same standard to environmental issues—merely on a larger scale than a child's bedroom. The opportunity cost of a cleaner environment is lost economic satisfaction. We can use marginal cost–marginal benefit analysis to look at this problem, but only if we make some simplifying assumptions.

Let's assume for the moment that we have a generally accepted measure of environmental quality. Let's further assume that the really dirty stuff is relatively easy to clean up but that achieving higher levels of cleanliness is harder and harder. Using the dirty room analogy, you know that the quickest way to make your room look cleaner is to pick up the dirty clothes, which can be done in seconds. Once you get down to straightening and dusting the knick-knack shelves, the benefits are slight and the time required is great. What this implies is that the marginal cost of achieving greater cleanliness is increasing while at the same time its marginal benefit is decreasing. As shown in Figure 22.1, this means that the maximum net benefit of environmental cleanup is *EQ**, where the marginal benefit equals the marginal cost.

The Externalities Approach

We created many environmental problems in the first place when we produced and consumed goods and were concerned only with the costs and benefits that directly affected us. As we saw in Chapters 2 and 3, doing this is usually fine, but problems often arise when the actions

we take impose costs on or present benefits to others. Economists call costs or benefits that are incurred by someone other than the producer or consumer **externalities**. We begin this chapter by reviewing why a market without externalities serves everyone. We then explore why there is a problem with markets when externalities are present. After that, we examine the specific environmental problems discussed above. We conclude with a look at what economics can offer in the way of solutions.

externalities
Effects of a transaction that hurt or help people who are not a part of that transaction.

When the Market Works for Everyone

As we learned in Chapter 3, a market works very well in a world where all the costs and benefits of production are confined to producers and consumers. Figure 22.2 depicts in graphical form that the market price–quantity combination, *P*–Q**, provides benefits to consumers, *OABQ**, at a cost to them of *OP*BQ**. The difference, *P*AB*, is called *consumer surplus,* that is, what consumers get in net benefits. Similarly, for the producer, the variable costs of production, *OCBQ**, are lower than revenue generated from sales, *OP*BQ**. The difference, *CP*B*, is called the *producer surplus.* Thus when the market does not generate costs or benefits to anyone other than consumers and producers, both benefit and no one loses.

When the Market Does Not Work for Everyone

The main problem with the model just described is that it does not take into account that there are nearly always indirect costs to others in either the production or consumption of a good. There are, for example, very few

FIGURE 22.2   When the market works.

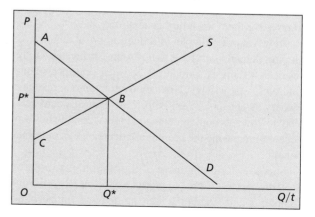

goods that do not require some form of energy for their production. Whether that energy is generated from the direct combustion of a steel mill's smelting facility or electricity generated from burning coal, some fossil fuel is used in nearly all production. Even when the power is hydroelectric, nuclear, wind, or solar, there are environmental and possibly aesthetic costs that are not always considered.

Using fossil fuels like oil or coal creates a number of environmental problems from beginning to end. In each of the stages of getting energy to the user, people or animals are affected. In extraction, land is either temporarily or permanently altered. The 2010 oil spill in the Gulf of Mexico clearly points out that extraction creates a negative externality. Transporting oil, natural gas, and coal consumes energy. Transporting the first two carries with it the potential for an environmental catastrophe like the rupturing of the *Exxon Valdez* disaster and the resulting massive oil spill in Alaska's Prince William Sound. By far the greatest problem, though, is created when fossil fuels are burned. Particulate matter creates breathing problems that are unpleasant for some and life-threatening for others. Burning coal releases sulfur into the air and it produces acid rain. If current scientific predictions of the United Nations Intergovernmental Panel on Climate Change are found to be true, greenhouse gases will cause significant changes in the world's climate.

You may believe that alternatives like hydroelectric, wind, or solar power offer externality-free energy, but, like fossil fuels, each has its own problems. As the Japanese experience of 2011 points out, though nuclear power is potentially clean, it is also potentially disastrous and even accounting for disasters ignores the problem of how to store nuclear waste. Hydroelectric power requires the destruction of river valleys, eliminating habitat as rivers flood the area behind the dams. While wind and solar power are clean in that they do not pollute the air or water, the sheer number of collectors needed to produce an amount of electricity that is equal to the amount produced by coal at the present time is vast. Therefore, this option has the potential of destroying thousands upon thousands of acres of land that we now consider to have great scenic beauty.

Figure 22.3 depicts the problem as an economist would see it. Whereas firms pay attention to the costs of production of their goods, unless forced to, they tend to ignore the environmental costs of their production. Similarly, consumers pay attention to how much a good costs them, but it often serves their purposes to ignore the costs to those around them. Costs to people other than

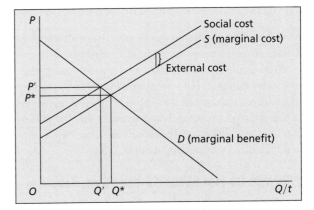

FIGURE 22.3 When a market does not work.

the producers and consumers are considered to be unaccounted for costs in the market. The existence of such costs is unacceptable to an economist. The fundamental flaw with the market is that unless all costs are accounted for, it will produce too much and charge too little. To find the true cost of production and consumption of a good that includes the effects on innocent bystanders, called the **social cost**, you need to add the external cost to the private costs (measured on the supply curve). When these costs are accounted for, the price is to be P' rather than P^*, and the amount produced is Q' rather than Q^*.

social cost
The true cost of production and consumption of a good that includes the effects on innocent bystanders.

Unless you believe that a pristine environment is a matter of right and wrong, allowing no compromises to your position, you will have to accept the existence of some environmental problems even when you account for all the costs. For example, Figure 22.2 does not display a thoroughly clean environment, but it does show how the costs of pollution are weighed against the benefits of consumption. We may decide, for instance, that even though some pesticides threaten certain species, they so enhance food production that using them is worth the cost. The species are still threatened, but at least the cost is recognized. Similarly, we may decide that reformulating gasoline to reduce emissions by 80 percent is worth 20 cents per gallon but that reducing it another 10 percent is not worth the dollar a gallon it would take to accomplish that level of reduction. Here the costs of pollution are weighed, but so are the benefits of consumption. There are substances for which the optimal level is zero. This occurs when the marginal benefit of the production or use of even one drop of the good is less than its social cost.

The Property Rights Approach to the Environment and Natural Resources

A Nobel Prize–winning economist by the name of Ronald Coase came up with a completely different method of dealing with pollution. His widely cited theorem states that markets with externalities can be made to be efficient. This can be done by simply assigning rights to the polluted property, but it requires that bargaining costs not be prohibitive. To see why this is so, we need to first look at why ownership matters.

Why You Do Not Mess Up Your Own Property

Consider a relatively simple problem. Why is it that you are much more willing to litter in a park than you are to litter in your own residence hall, apartment, or house? The reason is that you have property rights in the place you live and you make your own place less valuable when you litter in it. You do not own the park. Though your littering diminishes the value of the park, it does not diminish your own wealth.

This explains why people treat many forms of common property worse than they treat their own. If you have ever lived on a cul-de-sac, you will have noted that the circle of grass in the center of the turn-around was in demonstrably worse shape (or at least less well landscaped) than the surrounding lawns. People tend to treat their own property better than they do public property.

Why You Do Mess Up Common Property

Common property is property that is without a discernible individual owner. This property is usually owned by the government, a neighborhood association, or some other collective group. The problem with common property is that even though it may be worth a great deal to the group, the benefits of treating the property well are not worth the costs to any one individual. Economists refer to this as the "tragedy of the commons."

common property
Property that is not owned by any individual but is owned by government or has some other collective ownership.

Consider again the problem of a neighborhood park. Suppose that a city agrees to pay the up-front costs of a park for a neighborhood of 100 homes. It buys the playground equipment, plants trees and grass, but then turns the park over to the neighborhood. What happens when the grass needs to be cut, a tree falls and needs to be taken out, or the surface under the playground equipment needs to be rejuvenated? While each neighbor may

consider the individual benefit to be worth one one-hundredth of the cost of this regular maintenance, often no one will view maintenance for the entire neighborhood as worth the time or money. The ultimate problem is that no one owns the property. As a result, while the social benefit of the maintenance is greater than its cost, the benefit to an individual is much lower than its cost to that individual.

Natural Resources and the Importance of Property Rights

Economists use many of the same tools to explore the use of natural resources as we use when dealing with pollution. Whether the resource in question is mineral, timber, energy, or the oceans' bounty, economists note that the extraction, cutting, removal, or harvesting imposes costs on someone other than the producer or consumer. It doesn't matter whether this results from the fact that the land is owned by the government or not owned by anyone at all, or because the process of garnering the resource is itself polluting. What matters is that all of the costs must be acknowledged.

Economists also bring another element to the table: the notion of present value. The value of an untapped resource to its owner is the present value of the profit associated with exploiting it over a period of time. In this way there is an optimal rate of exploitation, which is the rate that maximizes the present value. Suppose you owned a resource such as a forest of timber. You could clear-cut it and sell all of it at once. Then you would have to plant new trees, wait for the trees to grow tall enough to harvest, and repeat the cycle. On the other hand, you could cut only those trees that had achieved an optimal height and leave the rest for another year. In this way you would have a few trees to cut every year. An economist would look at this and say that whichever rate of exploitation maximizes the present value of the profit emanating from that timber would be the optimal exploitation rate. Assuming that no timber company can influence prices, then there is no value to waiting to harvest trees unless some are relatively immature. The motivation to wait comes from the fact that trees grow, and thereby grow more valuable. If the interest rate is high (and exceeds the rate of tree growth), then that favors the cut-it-now rate, while if the interest rate is low, that favors the let-them-grow rate.

The problem comes when no one owns the resources that are being harvested. For instance, the oceans are notoriously overfished because there is no value to leaving the fish to grow bigger. Similarly, when logging companies buy the right to harvest trees on federal land, those contracts need to be well specified and well enforced or the company will have no motivation to leave the smaller trees for a later date, especially if the contract expires before the trees grow to maturity. This is much less of a problem on private property because the owner must weigh the present value of the profit from taking an immature tree against the present value of the profit from taking it a few years later. It is often the case that the logging company that owns the property it is working on will leave the smaller trees because it is in its interest to do so.

Environmental Problems and Their Economic Solutions

Environmental Problems

We face many environmental problems, some obvious and others not so obvious. Specific problems include water and air pollution, plant and animal species that face extinction, the effects of acid rain, landfills that are overflowing, limited natural resources that are being used up, and global warming. In this section we look briefly at each.

When humans are affected by the economic activity of other humans, the problem is relatively easy to solve. People complain when they are being hurt. When producers pollute the air or water, there are concerned people who have to breathe the affected air or want to drink or swim in the affected water. They will lobby their representatives for pollution regulations. In fact, the Environmental Protection Agency was created in 1969 in response to pleas that environmental regulations be enforced. The Clean Air Act of 1970 and the Clean Water Act of 1972 were additional responses to people's perceptions that problems existed and their desire to have them addressed.

By most measures, these laws have been effective. The nation's air and water are much cleaner than they were 40 years ago. Air pollution has been addressed with regulations that range from requirements that smokestack emissions be "scrubbed" before being released to requirements that cars have catalytic converters and burn unleaded gasoline. Since the Clean Air Act's inception the amount of sulfur dioxide in the air has been reduced by 25 percent, carbon monoxide by 60 percent, particulate matter by 13 percent, and lead by 94 percent. As can be seen in Figure 22.4, even since 1980, the Clean Air Act has resulted in significant reductions in all measured forms of air pollution.

FIGURE 22.4   Pollutant Concentrations.

Source: Environmental Protection Agency, www.epa.gov

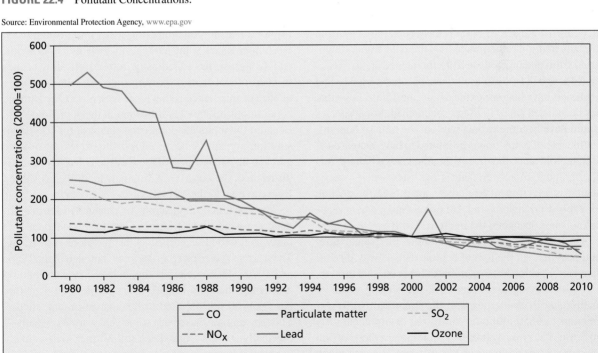

In the area of water pollution, municipal wastewater facilities now have to return untreated water to rivers and streams in nearly drinkable form. Companies can no longer discharge waste materials into rivers or lakes, either. Though some of the damage to these bodies of water is permanent, most are improving. Classic examples of this include the Cuyahoga River near Cleveland, Ohio, which was so polluted that it once actually caught fire. Now it is clean enough that people can eat its fish. Other areas, though, have not yet fared as well. On the bottom of Onondaga Lake in Syracuse, New York, for example, there remains several feet of toxic sludge, and, on the official map of the city, there is a piece of shoreline labeled the "Allied Waste Beds," where Allied Chemical simply dumped its toxic waste.

When air and water are unacceptably dirty, the problem is fairly obvious. However, it is more difficult to see damage to wildlife and it is harder to address the problem. Plants and animals do not object as they become extinct. Fortunately for them there are scientists who monitor their health. To illustrate the difficulty of convincing people of problems with wildlife, though, it took threatening of our national symbol, the bald eagle, to bring about legislative action. The Endangered Species Act of 1973 has resulted in lists of plants and animals that are either threatened or, more serious, endangered. Currently there are in the United States alone 71 threatened and 450 endangered animal species, as well as 149 threatened and 667 endangered plant species. Since the inception of the act, 21 species have been removed from the lists and a number, including the bald eagle, downlisted from endangered status to threatened status.

Although 34 North American species of birds and mammals have become extinct since the 1500s, none that has been listed since 1973 has succumbed. Some species would have become extinct without the help of humans, but the rate of extinction is estimated to have increased at least tenfold since the time of the first known human. It is discouraging, moreover, that for the listed species whose habitat is government land, there are 1.5 on the decline for every 1 on the rebound. On private land, where regulation is less stringent, the figure is 9 to 1.

The key to keeping plant and animal life from extinction is to prevent the loss of habitat. This is why the Endangered Species Act is a problem for economic growth. The lost logging associated with preserving a single mating pair of spotted owls in the American Northwest amounts to $650 million. While strict environmentalists push for the preservation of species, regardless of the economic costs of doing so, the costs are foremost in the minds of the people whose livelihoods are threatened by this law's requirements.

A piece of environmental legislation that combines protections for both wildlife and habitat is the Clean Air Act of 1990. In this legislation, the targeted problem is acid rain. Acid rain is created when power plants burn high-sulfur coal and the sulfur dioxide (SO_2) emissions from that burning combine in the atmosphere with various nitrogen oxides (NO_2, NO_3, etc.) to create a dilute form of sulfuric acid. In particular, the coal that is burned in the Midwest creates an acid that travels to the northeastern states in clouds, and the rain that subsequently forms has caused trees to die and lakes to become deadly for fish.

The legislation limits the quantity of sulfur that industry can put into the air. To comply with the law's provisions, firms can buy more expensive low-sulfur coal, they can buy equipment to clean up the emissions, or they can buy another firm's pollution permits. Offering options like the trading of pollution permits is considered to be very innovative. It allows companies to clean up the environment in the cheapest way possible, and, as we will discuss later, this innovative way of dealing with pollution has earned economists a place at the table in discussing environmental problems.

An additional environmental problem is that landfill space is being used up faster than new space is created. The problem here is less an environmental problem than a location problem. Modern landfills are required to prove that no contamination leaks into groundwater. No homeowners want garbage in their neighborhoods, and Congress has steadfastly refused to allow states to keep others from exporting their garbage. A consequence of this stance is that more New York City garbage is put in out-of-state landfills than in those in New York. Because the interstate commerce clause of the U.S. Constitution prevents states from refusing to let out-of-state garbage in, and because of the way the U.S. population is distributed, the burden of siting new landfills has shifted from the East to the Midwest.

The economic implications of changes in Earth's climate are what we will discuss last in this chapter. It is fairly well settled scientific fact that the globe is warming. The warmest years on record are concentrated in the 1980s and 1990s. The problem is that unless they were told by a scientist that this is bad, most people would neither have noticed nor objected to the change in temperature. Though summers have been somewhat warmer, winters—especially at night—have been still warmer. Who is likely to object if winter weather is milder than usual?

Meteorologists tell us that the earth's temperature has risen about 1.5° Fahrenheit in the entire 20th century. The average, though, is 2.5° higher in 1999 than it was in 1970. It is a change that is simply too small for the typical person to detect. Over time, however, the problems with global warming will become more obvious. With temperatures that are anywhere from 5° to 10° higher by the end of the 21st century, several things may happen. The bad things include a thawing of the polar ice caps, which scientists say will be accompanied by a flooding of coastal cities and islands. Soils may become dry, making it more difficult to grow grains. People will use more refrigerants for air conditioning. Warm-weather diseases like malaria and yellow fever may proliferate, and certain areas of the world will become deserts, in a process labeled with the frightening word "desertification." Going further, the particularly active hurricane seasons of 2004 and 2005 were blamed by some meteorologists on uncharacteristically warm water in the Atlantic and Caribbean. If these scientists are correct, and these were at least partially related to global warming, then our global consumption of energy and its effect on the environment has a tremendous dollar-denominated cost. Taken together, 2004's hurricanes Ivan, Charlie, and Frances, and 2005's Katrina and Wilma represent five of the top six costliest storms ever.

On the other hand, some good things will happen if global temperatures rise. Growing seasons will lengthen in northern climates, less energy will be needed to heat homes and businesses in those areas, and the impact of cold-weather diseases like colds and the flu will diminish. A good way of imagining the positive impact is to realize that though there will be places where the climate will get "too hot," some places that were once "too cold" will now be "just right."

This is not to suggest that there will necessarily be an even-up trade by any means. While temperature zones will change relatively quickly, forests can move only extremely slowly. Thus some forests whose trees require a specific temperature band to be healthy will die out long before new ones appear. There is also new research suggesting that only about half of the increased carbon dioxide, which may be good for some species of plant life, can be absorbed.

Economic Solutions: Using Taxes to Solve Environmental Problems

To solve the environmental problems that we face, we have to encourage or require clean behaviors, or we must discourage unclean behaviors or render them illegal. To varying degrees, all these methods work. America's history of environmental regulations clearly indicates that we have been moving successfully from forms of regulation that concentrate on punishing people to forms where we provide incentives that make clean behavior profitable.

Most environmental regulation still prohibits certain actions that damage the air, water, or wildlife. For instance, the Clean Water Act prohibits dumping of untreated industrial waste into a river. Mandating that the environment be protected, however, is not necessarily the best way to deal with all environmental issues. For instance, it is hypothetically possible that production of a cure for a terrible disease may turn out to be very dirty. In such a case it might be in society's best interest to sacrifice the environment. Instead of an outright ban, a polluting activity could be heavily taxed. Activities that were sufficiently profitable to cover whatever tax was levied could continue.

A tax could conceivably be used to discourage any polluting activity, including the creation of garbage or the use of fossil fuels. As Figure 22.5 indicates, a tax would be set that was equal to the external cost, that is, the dollar-denominated value of the pollution. Production of the good would fall to Q', its socially optimal level, and the price would increase to P'. There would be enough tax revenue to compensate those affected by the pollution resulting from a garbage dump or, perhaps, to fund research on nonpolluting technologies. Assuming a connection between energy use and global warming and between global warming and hurricane flooding, such a fund might also be used to deal with flood relief from hurricanes.

FIGURE 22.5   Solving the problem with a pollution tax.

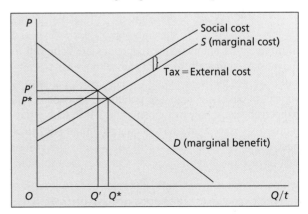

Economic Solutions: Using Property Rights to Solve Environmental Problems

Coase's theorem holds that it does not matter if you grant the property right to the polluter or the victim of the pollution. If you say that people have a right to clean air, then Coase suggests that the polluter would buy the right to pollute from the people; if you say that polluters have the right to do what they want, then Coase suggests that the people will pay polluters to be cleaner. Either way, the right amount of production and pollution will result.

An interesting adaptation of Coase's ideas was the Clean Air Act of 1990 and its use of effluent[1] permits. The law provides that each emitter of certain restricted pollutants can be granted a fixed number of permits ceding the right to pollute a specific amount. In 1990, the quota of polluted emissions was slightly less than the historical levels of pollution. Any firm that polluted less than that amount could sell its remaining rights to pollute to those that polluted more than their permits allowed. In 2000, in the second phase of the Clean Air Act of 1990, emission rights were reduced further, and when the act is reauthorized, it is likely that further reductions will be required. In this way pollution is reduced over time, while polluters have options that allow them flexibility in meeting the reductions.

In 2008, the Supreme Court compelled the EPA to regulate greenhouse gasses (GHG) as pollutants and though the outgoing Bush administration chose not to rush into this area, the Obama administration was quite willing to jump in. Its preferred method was to use this same **cap-and-trade** method. Cap-and-trade gets its name from the process by which the government sets a "cap" on the level of pollution that is allowable, and then allows polluters to "trade" the right to pollute. By giving the rights away each year, and in diminishing amounts, the reductions are achieved in the most economically efficient manner possible. Specifically, we get the most output (usually electrical power) subject to our societal goal of pollution reductions. This happens because power companies have different opportunity costs associated with reducing pollution. Those that have a high opportunity cost will buy permits from those that have a low opportunity cost. Consider the following

cap-and-trade
The method of reducing a pollutant whereby the government gives to polluters, or auctions, a capped amount of pollution permits and then allows those permits to be sold in a market.

uncomplicated example. Suppose there are only two electrical companies and both have older coal-powered generators that generate a great deal of pollution. Each one will have to reduce pollution slightly unless it wishes to buy permits from the other. Suppose one is close to a natural gas pipeline, but the costs of switching to cleaner-burning natural gas have been heretofore just beyond what would have made economic sense for the firm. Suppose the options to the other are much more prohibitive. Suppose, finally, that electrical power demand is increasing, so each will be expected to produce more electricity and will therefore generate more pollution in the future. Because they cannot both increase pollution, the firm that has the lower cost option of reducing pollution will do so and be compensated for doing so by selling its permits to the firm with the higher cost option. In this way, society's goal of both meeting the increase in electrical demand and reducing pollution is furthered.

For the purposes of acid rain reduction under the 1990 Clean Air Act, each permit grants its holder approximately a ton of sulfur dioxide (SO_2) emissions. Total emissions of SO_2 over the life of this provision of the 1990 act have been cut nearly in half, to 5.3 million tons per year. Surprising as it may seem, the price of those emission permits was falling through the 1990s and mid-2000s from $200 to $100. Though those prices spiked in 2006 at more than $1,500, today they are less than $3. At first this was because power companies have found it a profitable sideline to find ways to reduce pollution. And though the reduction in the number of available permits and the increase in electrical power demand put pressure on the permit prices to rise, electric utilities are using new, cleaner technologies either to reduce the number of permits they have to buy or to make money selling their rights. More recently, though, the biggest driver in clearing the air of SO_2 and nitric oxides has been the reduction in natural gas prices. A brief look at Figure 22.6 shows that after 2008 it became much less expensive to operate a natural-gas-fired electrical peaking plant, and as a result utilities began converting from coal to natural gas for those facilities. Natural gas, being a much cleaner burning fuel, allowed utilities to reduce their purchases of permits substantially. Thus the pressure on the price of these permits to decrease that has resulted from this innovation has greatly outweighed the pressure to rise.

Though the cap-and-trade idea was originally one created by economic conservatives in the 1980s as a way to use market forces to deal with environmental challenges, it became a useful political target in 2010. Dubbed "cap and tax," the policy option designed by conservatives in

[1]Effluent is the general term for the stuff that comes out of a smokestack.

FIGURE 22.6 Price of Natural Gas.

Source: U.S. Energy Information Administration, www.eia.gov/dnav/ng/ng_pri_sum_dcu_nus_m.htm

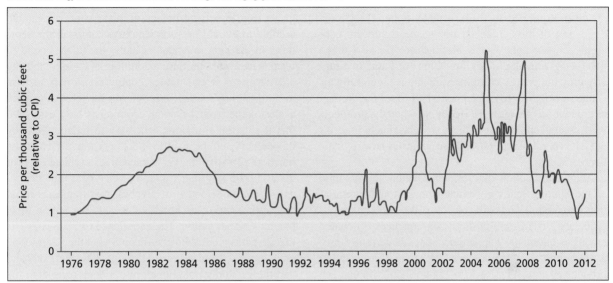

the 1980s to avoid inflexible regulatory frameworks, instead became something conservatives could pin on political opponents in 2010. It worked so well that even with a 60 to 40 majority in the U.S. Senate, Democrats were unable to muster the votes to pass cap and trade as part of their energy bill, which subsequently stalled as a result.

The reasons conservatives opposed cap-and-trade were not all purely political. The acid-rain producing pollutants were clearly identifiable as to their source—specifically, power plants and other large combustion units with obvious smokestacks. The problem with using cap-and-trade for CO_2 and other greenhouse gases (GHG) is that there are many more polluters to monitor and regulate. It is relatively simple to monitor the two gases that overwhelmingly come from a few sources. It would be impossible to accurately monitor GHGs emanating from every car, home, business, and farm.

Another area where economists use the property right idea to help with air pollution is with the offset. Cars pollute, and old cars pollute much worse than newer ones. In California, polluters can either reduce their direct pollution or they can buy enough old cars and get those off the road. Similarly, across the United States, there are foundations that seek to reduce air pollution by buying emission permits so that they cannot be used by a business planning to pollute.

In 2009, as the Obama administration was pushing to reduce pollution, decrease U.S. dependence on foreign oil, and breathe life into the auto industry, it introduced an adaptation of this idea. Called "cash-for-clunkers," the program paid auto dealers up to $4,500 per car as long as they agreed to destroy them rather than resell them in the used car market. As long as the car was registered to the same owner in the previous two years, and as long as a new car was purchased that got 10 mpg more than the one traded in, this $4,500 meant that an old car that might have been worth only a $1,000 in trade, became worth substantially more. Though economists debate how many of the used cars would have been junked anyway and how many of the newly purchased cars would have been purchased anyway, there was likely some modest, pollution-reducing effect. Economists influence environmental regulations and legislation precisely because we offer suggestions like cap-and-trade and cash-for-clunkers, thus aligning self-interest with environmentalism.

No Solution: When There Is No Government to Tax or Regulate

Let's assume that the problems of global warming exceed the benefits. What can be done? When an environmental problem is confined to one jurisdiction, the government, whether it be local, state, or national, can enact legislation to tackle the problem. When the problem is international, such as with global warming, there is no government to impose a regulatory or tax-based solution.

The Kyoto Protocol is a treaty to which the United States is a signatory. Such treaties require U.S. Senate approval, so President Clinton's signature was pointless from the start because there were not 20 votes for ratification and he knew that when he signed it. Shortly after his election, President Bush formally pulled the United States out of the agreement noting the significant economic impact compliance would have. He also noted that the agreement did not limit China or India, two rapidly growing energy consumers, in any meaningful way. China now produces two and one-half times the amount of greenhouse gasses (GHG) as it did when the protocols were created and India produces twice as much. In terms of GHGs per dollar of GDP, these countries now rival the United States.

With the election of President Obama, the position of the United States government toward GHG regulation changed. There will, of course be economic consequences. The extent of those consequences is debated among economists. The United States is currently producing about 25 percent more GHG than it promised to produce. If you refer back to Figure 22.5, you can see how economists might propose to deal with the issue. A tax would need to be placed on the production of GHG sufficient to reduce the amount produced by a quarter. Energy usage would have to either become more efficient, become less prevalent, or come from nonemitting sources such as wind, hydroelectric, solar, or nuclear.

The rapid increase in gasoline prices during 2008 can aid us in figuring out how much that tax would need to be; this is where elasticity comes into play. If the only thing we could do was reduce energy usage, we could estimate the tax on energy using the elasticity of demand for carbon-based energy. Clearly energy demand is inelastic. As the price of gasoline spiked in 2008, increasing 75 percent, gasoline consumption fell 6 percent. This suggests a short-run elasticity of .08. Studies of the long-run elasticity of demand for gasoline suggest it is 0.24. Extrapolation would imply that the price of carbon-based energy would have to quadruple in order to get that 25 percent reduction in the short run though a doubling would be sufficient to accomplish the same thing in the long run. That is likely the upper bound of what is necessary because a doubling of carbon-emitting energy prices would induce energy consumers to look to nonemitting sources. Accounting for the substitution to these other sources, some economists have estimated that the tax on emissions necessary to reduce GHG by 25 percent could be as little as $25 per ton of GHG to as much as $200 per ton. For perspective, a typical car produces a little less than 1 pound of GHG per mile driven, and if you do a bunch of algebra, that translates to an appropriate tax of as little as 25 cents per gallon to as much as $2 per gallon. The experience of 2008 suggests that 25 cents wouldn't be sufficient. Had the $2 gasoline price increase been sustained through 2008 and 2009 and had the economy not slipped into a deep recession, the shift from large SUVs to small cars would likely have been sufficient to have a significant long-run impact on U.S. GHG production.

Regardless of who is right, the issue illustrates the difficulty in dealing with international environmental problems. There is little economic motivation for a single country to impose high costs on itself, and there is no world government to impose those high costs on everyone. So while the politics in the United States have changed with regard to American participation in the Kyoto GHG reduction process, neither the Chinese nor the Indian governments have changed their views. As a result, if those warning of the consequences of global warming are correct, this could be one of the more calamitous examples of the Chapter 3 notion of market failure.

Summary

You now understand how to use the concept of externalities to explain why pollution warrants government intervention in the market. You understand why pollution is much more likely to occur on publicly owned property than on private property and you have a cursory understanding of the variety of environmental problems that exist in the world. You now also have an understanding of some economic solutions to these problems.

Key Terms

cap-and-trade, 252
common property, 248
externalities, 246

limited natural resource, 245
renewable natural resource, 245
social cost, 247

stewardship, 245
sustainability, 245

Quiz Yourself

1. The notion of "clean enough" is
   a. appealing to an economist thinking about average benefit and average cost.
   b. appealing to an economist thinking about marginal benefit and marginal cost.
   c. appealing to an economist thinking about total benefit and total cost.
   d. completely rejected as a concept by an economist.

2. If a chemical does environmental damage but is used in the production of a good that provides satisfaction to the consumer and profit to the producer, an economist
   a. will insist that the market be left alone.
   b. will insist that the chemical be completely banned.
   c. will seek to impose a tax on the good so that the net benefit to society (including the environmental damage) is maximized.
   d. will suggest that consumers voluntarily cut back their consumption.

3. An example of an externality that we see every day is
   a. people paying high prices for gasoline.
   b. people enjoying their ability to drive to work.
   c. oil companies making record profits.
   d. the emissions from a car's tailpipe.

4. When tackling local environmental problems, taxes and regulations can be useful. The reason that global problems (like global warming) are more difficult to control is
   a. it is in every countries' aggregate interest to ignore the problem.
   b. it is in no country's interest to address the problem.
   c. there is no ability to enforce those taxes or regulations.
   d. the "marginal" country is unknown.

5. Overfishing certain parts of the ocean and certain species of fish has been a problem for centuries with countries actually going to war over fishing disputes. Ronald Coase would suggest that there would be no problem if
   a. someone owned (and could control) the ocean.
   b. people stopped eating fish.
   c. people reacted according to the golden rule.
   d. countries agreed to voluntary restrictions on fishing.

6. The evidence on most environmental pollutants (lead in the air and water, sulfur in the air, etc.) is that
   a. they are not nearly as harmful as once thought.
   b. they are increasing at an alarming rate.
   c. they have decreased substantially in the last 20 years.
   d. they have stabilized in the air at their all-time high.

7. An environmental economist would likely recommend which of the following policies?
   a. Eliminate fossil fuel consumption.
   b. A tax on gasoline equal to the environmental damage caused by a gallon of gasoline.
   c. A tax on gasoline greater than the environmental damage caused by a gallon of gasoline.
   d. Voluntary limits on driving.

Short Answer Questions

1. Why would an increasing marginal cost of producing oil lead to a more spread-out utilization plan?

2. Why would saving some species be worth the cost of saving them while another species might not be?

3. Why would "cap-and-trade" be more aligned with those who wish to use private market innovations to solve environmental problems than a regulatory based environmental system?

Think about This

Fossil fuels were the "clean" alternative to wood burning and overcame wood as a source of fuel only when it became cheaper to use than wood. If left unchecked, this will happen to fossil fuels as well because this limited resource will eventually become more scarce than its alternatives (solar-, wind-, hydroelectric-, or biomass-generated power). Should we just wait it out?

Talk about This

Every power source entails some environmental consequence. Nuclear power leaves behind waste that is dangerous for thousands of years. Hydroelectric power destroys the habitat of valley-dwelling animals. Wind and solar power require vast spaces for collection devices. Combustible fuels typically leave a heat-trapping gas. Currently, the dominant U.S. fuel sources are fossil based (coal, oil, natural gas). While other countries have turned toward nuclear power, we have not. Given that our power needs are continuously growing, what are your solutions?

For More Insight See

Joskow, Paul L., A. Denny Ellerman, Richard Schmalensee, Juan Pablo Montero, and Elizabeth

M. Bailey, *Markets for Clean Air: The U.S. Acid Rain Program* (Cambridge, U.K.: Cambridge University Press, 2000).

Journal of Economic Perspectives 12, no. 3 (Summer 1998). See articles by Gardner M. Brown, Jr., and Jason F. Shogren; Andrew Metrick and Martin Weitzman; Robert Innes, Stephen Polasky, and John Tschirhart; and Richard Schmalensee, pp. 1–88.

Journal of Economic Perspectives 9, no. 4 (Fall 1995). See articles by Michael E. Porter and Claas van der Linde; Karen Palmer, Wallace E. Oates, and Paul R. Portney, pp. 97–132.

Journal of Economic Perspectives 7, no. 4 (Fall 1993). See articles by Richard Schmalensee; William D. Nordhaus; John P. Weyant; James M. Poteba and Gacielka Chichilinsky; and Geoffrey Heal, pp. 3–86.

Any environmental economics textbook, for instance, *Economics and the Enviroment* by Eban Goodstein.

Behind the Numbers

Air quality and emissions data.
  Outdoor air pollution.
    Environmental Protection Agency; environmental indicators—www.epa.gov/Envindicators/roe/pdf/tdAir.pdf
  Emissions prices and trading.
    Environmental Protection Agency; clean air markets—www.epa.gov/airmarkets

Global temperatures.
  History and projections.
    Environmental Protection Agency; global warming—www.epa.gov
  Average surface temperature.
    World Meteorological Organization—www.wmo.int

Threatened, endangered, and delisted species.
    U.S. Fish and Wildlife Service; publications—www.fws.gov/endangered

Hurricane costs—www.nhc.noaa.gov/gifs/table3a.gif

Health Care

Learning Objectives

After reading this chapter you should be able to:

LO1 Summarize how the system of health care finance seriously alters the market for health care services.

LO2 Conclude that in the United States 52 percent of the health care tab is picked up by the taxpayer with the remainder being paid either directly by patients or by their insurance companies.

LO3 Analyze the health care industry using the supply and demand model and discuss the limitations of the model when applied to this industry.

LO4 Demonstrate that both private insurance and taxpayer-financed health care systems increase the overall price of health care.

LO5 Compare and contrast privately financed and single-payer, taxpayer-financed health care systems by noting their respective advantages and disadvantages.

Chapter Outline

Where the Money Goes and Where It Comes From

Insurance in the United States

Economic Models of Health Care

Comparing the United States with the Rest of the World

Summary

Health care in the United States has two characteristics that seem to be fundamentally inconsistent. No other country on earth can match the United States in terms of the quality of care that is available, but no developed country has our infant mortality rate. Additionally, in no other country are doctors as skilled, and in no other country are doctors as highly paid. In no other country is the quality of care as high, but in no other developed country is care denied so often because patients are unable to pay for it. At its root, the problem of having high-quality care that is not available to everyone who needs it is attributed only to the way we finance health care.

In this chapter we explain health care in the United States by first detailing the money spent and by whom it is spent. We discuss how private and public insurance work in the United States and discuss the problems associated with each. We then turn to why the economics

of health care differs so much from the economics of any other good. Along the way we compare our health care financing system with the model used in most other developed countries and hit the high points of the Patient Protection and Affordable Care Act, (PPACA).

Where the Money Goes and Where It Comes From

In defeating the health care plan that the Clinton administration attempted to implement, Republicans claimed that Democrats were trying to take over one-sixth of the economy. Indeed, while in 2011 one-sixth of the gross domestic product (2.7 trillion of 15.1 trillion) was spent on health-related goods and services, the government's portion was already half (51.8 percent, or 1.4 trillion) of health care expenditures. President Clinton and his

Democratic supporters were merely attempting to federalize the private portion of health care expenditure.

Of the $1.4 trillion that government spent on health care in the United States in 2011, some $554 billion was spent on **Medicare** (the government health insurance program for the elderly) and $408 billion was spent on **Medicaid** (the government health insurance program for the poor). The remainder was spent by all levels of government on local, state, and veterans' hospitals and in support of medical research.

Medicare
Public health insurance in the United States which covers those over age 65.

Medicaid
Public health insurance in the United States that covers the poor.

Of the $1.3 trillion that was spent on health care in the private sector in 2011, some $896 billion came from premiums paid to insurance companies and by the money that insurance companies realized from their investments. People paid an additional $308 billion in out-of-pocket expenditures, and the remainder was spent by private medical research companies.

In general, of the $2.7 trillion spent on health care in the United States in 2011, $851 billion went to hospitals and $541 billion went to doctors. Drugs accounted for $263 billion and medical research spending accounted for $50 billion.

Insurance in the United States

Most people in the United States are covered by some form of health insurance for at least part of the year. In 2011, for example, 76 percent of the 308 million people in the United States had coverage all year, another 8 percent had coverage for part of the year, and 16 percent had no coverage at all. The coverage during that year came from a variety of sources. The largest group, 170 million people, was covered by group insurance policies, 30 million had individual policies, 48 million were on Medicare, 51 million were on Medicaid,[1] and of those 9 million were on both.

How Insurance Works

Whether we are discussing health insurance, life insurance, or auto insurance, private insurance of any kind works like this. There is a small chance that something bad will happen to you, and there is a large chance that nothing

bad will happen to you. You spend a little money on insurance that will cushion the effects of the bad prospect, should it occur. In other words, you pay a premium so that if the bad thing happens, the insurance provider (whether it be the government or an insurance company) will pay to make things better. In the case of health insurance, people pay premiums so that when they get sick their provider pays most of the expense of dealing with their illnesses.

It is perfectly rational to buy insurance even when the average expense you would face is less than the cost of the insurance. The reason is that most people are **risk averse:** They prefer to be guaranteed a particular outcome, even when the odds are that for the average person, over an average lifetime, insurance is more expensive than the problem they are insuring themselves against. As an example, suppose there is a 1 percent chance that you will have a major health-related expense of $100,000 and a 99 percent chance that you will have only $1,000 of typical health expenses. A **risk-neutral** person would look at the expected expense, $1,990,[2] and not be willing to pay any more than that for full insurance coverage. People who are risk averse, on the other hand, would be willing to pay more than that to guarantee themselves that they would not have to pay any more.

risk averse
A characteristic of a person who would pay extra to guarantee the expected outcome.

risk neutral
A characteristic of a person who would not pay extra to guarantee the expected outcome.

Nearly all private health insurance plans have a number of characteristics in common. You owe a premium that, for most Americans, is paid partly by you and partly by your employer.[3] Insurance companies use premiums for three things: (1) to pay doctor and hospital bills of their patients, (2) to cover administrative expenses, and (3) to provide profit for the owners (usually shareholders) of the insurance company.

If you get sick and have a health expense, it is usually the case that both you and your insurance company will pay part of the bill. There are four key pieces of vocabulary that determine who pays how much. The **deductible** is the amount of health spending a year that you have to pay before the insurance

deductible
The amount of health spending a year that you have to pay before the insurance company pays anything.

---

[1]Because Medicaid's enrollment is fluid, as many as 70 million have Medicaid at some point during the year.

[2]$.99 \times 1,000 + .01 \times 100,000 = 1,990$.

[3]This aspect is actually an artifact of World War II. Because of inflation fears during that time, it was against the law to raise wages to attract workers. Instead, companies increased benefits in the form of group insurance subsidies, and the practice survived the war.

company pays anything. This very much depends on the type of plan you have but can be as low as nothing and as high as several thousand dollars. Typically, the deductible for a plan is between $200 and $300 per person and between $600 and $1,000 per family per year. For instance, if you have an insurance plan with a $200 deductible and you have a covered medical expense that totals $500, you will have to pay $200 before your insurance company pays anything.

co-payment
Either a set amount or the percentage of the bill after the deductible has been taken out that you have to pay.

maximum out of pocket
The most that a person or family will have to pay over a year for all covered health expenses.

mini-med
Low premium health insurance with a low annual maximum.

The **co-payment** is either a set amount or the percentage of the bill, after the deductible has been taken out, that you have to pay. This also has a wide range. Some plans have no copayment; others as much as 30 percent. The **maximum out of pocket** is the most that a person or family will have to pay over a year for all covered health expenses. This means that a $500,000 health expense will not bankrupt the typical person because the maximum out of pocket is usually between $2,000 and $6,000 a year.

Some companies offer what are called **mini-meds**. Mini-med insurance policies are usually only offered to young people, have fairly low premiums and, as one of the features, have low (usually no more than $10,000) annual maximum amounts that the insurance company will pay. These limits are illegal, in general, but these policies serve a niche market that the Obama administration did not want to harm when they banned the general practice of capping health insurance company liability. The fear was that by outlawing all mini-meds, they would reduce health insurance coverage for many young people in their first jobs.

Varieties of Private Insurance

There are several types of private insurance plans out there, but they boil down to three large groups: (1) fee for service, (2) health maintenance, and (3) preferred provider. A fee-for-service provider allows sick people to go to any doctor they want, wherever they want, for whatever ails them. The doctor then bills the insurance company, the insurance company pays its share, and the doctor bills the patient for the remainder. Because there are few controls on spending in a system like this, it is very costly. Patients and doctors, however, have few complaints.

A health maintenance organization (HMO) requires that people see specific doctors at the beginning of any problem. These doctors are referred to as **primary care physicians (PCP)** or, familiarly, as *gatekeepers*. Patients can see specialists only after their primary care physician makes a referral, and the PCP, or gatekeeper, has the job of making sure that his or her patients get the appropriate care as inexpensively as possible. Usually HMO PCPs receive a fixed fee for every patient assigned, and specialists are either salaried or also have fixed fees for every referral. Patients and doctors complain about the controls on spending in HMOs, but these serve to keep costs down.

primary care physician (PCP)
Physician in managed care operations charged with making the initial diagnosis and making referrals. Also called a *gatekeeper.*

A preferred provider organization (PPO) is somewhat of a hybrid. People can choose the doctor they want from a list of doctors. The doctors agree to charge a specific amount per procedure or disease, and they take a lower fee than usual in order to be guaranteed a large number of potential patients.

Table 23.1 outlines the advantages and disadvantages of each of these private insurance options from the patient's standpoint.

Public Insurance

Public insurance, provided by the government, is divided into three main programs: Medicare, Medicaid, and the Children's Health Insurance Program. Medicare is available to eligible citizens who are 65 years old and older. It works very much like a generous fee-for-service health insurance plan, except that the burden for high premiums is placed on the taxpayer rather than the patient or the patient's employer. The tax that funds Medicare appears on your paycheck in the same place your Social Security tax does; they are both under FICA (Federal Insurance Contributions Act). The portion that is used for Medicare is 1.45 percent of your salary, wages, and tips; you and your employer each pay that rate. For part of Medicare, money is also taken from the general tax revenues of the government.

Medicare is generous in the following sense: By private health care standards its premiums are very low, and the co-payments and the deductibles are also low. In truth Medicare is really two programs, a compulsory program that covers hospital-related expenses and a voluntary program that covers doctors' charges. In 2013, those who were eligible for the compulsory version,

TABLE 23.1 Advantages and disadvantages to patients of different forms of private insurance.

Source: Medicare, www.medicare.gov

Insurance Type	Advantages	Disadvantages
Fee for service	Maximum physician choice Little insurance company meddling in doctors' decisions	Highest premiums, deductibles, and co-payment rates because of little control over expensive and unnecessary procedures
HMO	Maximum control over expensive and unnecessary procedures so premiums, deductibles, and co-payment rates are low	Minimal physician choice Significant meddling in physician decisions, especially when differing procedures have significant cost differences
PPO	Some physician choice Moderate premiums, deductibles, and co-payment rates Some control over expensive procedures Minor meddling in physician decisions	

Medicare Part A, and worked between 30 and 39 quarters paid a $243 monthly premium. Those who worked less than 30 quarters paid $441 per month, and for those who worked more than 40 quarters, it was free. The voluntary version, Medicare Part B, cost beneficiaries between $104.90 and $335.70 per month depending on their 2011 income, and covered doctor-related expenses. Elderly people who are eligible for the primary welfare program for the old and poor, Supplemental Security Income, have Medicaid pick up the Part A premium and often the Part B premium as well.

In contrast with Medicare, Medicaid is a no-premium, no-deductible, very low or no co-payment health plan for the poor.[4] Under Medicaid, doctors are reimbursed at rates that are low relative to what Medicare pays and extremely low relative to what private insurance pays. Hospitals and doctors can and do refuse to treat Medicaid patients when they judge the reimbursement rates to be too low.

In 2011 there were 49 million Americans who survived, at least part of the year, without any health insurance at all. Many of these are people who move from one job to another and whose insurance runs out while they are unemployed.[5] On the other hand, a 1994 study by Katherine Swartz indicated that 21 million Americans were without any health insurance for more than a year. Of the uninsured, 18 million are between the ages of 18 and 34. Their lack of insurance may be voluntary in the sense that they may be able to afford insurance but are healthy and therefore choose not to purchase it. A recently emerging group of people without health insurance is those who retire early and are waiting for Medicare to kick in when they turn 65.

Among the uninsured for at least some portion of the year are the nearly 12 million who are under 18. It was in reaction to more than 16 million children living without health insurance that the Children's Health Insurance Program was created in the 1990s. Its function is like that of Medicaid, but it is focused, as the name suggests, on children who live in families where the breadwinners do not have insurance through their employer and do not make enough to purchase it themselves.

Economic Models of Health Care

We can use our supply and demand model to look at what happens when the good in question is not something tangible, like an apple, but intangible, like health care. Additionally, in the context of this model, we can explore how the health care finance system alters people's behavior.

Why Health Care Is Not Just Another Good

Health care is not like any other good. You can look at an apple grown in 1998 and say that it is comparable to an apple grown in 1995 or 1885. An apple is pretty much the

---

[4]States may impose small co-payments to discourage abusive overuse.

[5]Workers have the right to continue their employer-sponsored health insurance even after they quit or are fired. The problem is that most employers do not continue subsidizing the premiums, which means people are not likely to be able to afford to exercise this right.

PPACA PROVISIONS TO EXPAND COVERAGE

There are three significant provisions of the PPACA that serve to expand coverage to those who have been without it. First, beginning in 2014, employers of more than 50 full-time employees will be required to provide their employees with at least a minimal insurance plan or else pay a tax. Second, Medicaid will be expanded to cover everyone in families earning under 133 percent of the poverty line in those states that agree to pay a small portion of the added expense. Third, subsidies will be paid to those earning under 400 percent of the poverty line when they purchase health insurance through an approved exchange.

These provisions are not without controversy. The first provision forces employers that do not provide at least minimal health insurance to pay a fine if even one of their employees is given a subsidy to buy insurance. This provision has some economists worried that the PPACA lessens the incentive that firms have to employ new workers by raising the cost of that worker. The Medicaid expansion worries governors and legislatures regarding its impact on state budgets so much that (at this spring 2014 writing) fewer than 20 states have agreed to the expansion. Finally, because the PPACA was such a charged political issue for so long, fewer than 20 states have agreed to create the exchanges and it is unclear whether they will ever materialize.

same through time. On the other hand, health care tends to be changeable. The medical CPI has risen at or above the overall rate of inflation for several years. However, we cannot be sure how much of this increase is an increase in prices, how much is an increase in quality, and how much is the availability of new procedures or treatments.

To illustrate, let's discuss the treatment of acquired immunodeficiency syndrome (AIDS). In 1985 there was no standard treatment for AIDS. Morphine was sometimes given to ease pain—a terribly ineffective but "cheap" treatment compared to today. In 2001 the treatment became a "drug cocktail" of zidovudine (AZT) and a group of protease inhibitors. Newer drug cocktails cost more than $30,000 per patient per year, but they can sustain a good quality of life for several years. Which "treatment" costs more? You do not have to answer the question because you know that you are not pricing the same thing. The quality of the treatment has improved so greatly that to say that the price of the treatment has increased is simply wrong. The quality of the treatment has improved, and because there was no effective treatment to compare the current one to, the "price" has fallen from infinity.

Many of the complaints about the increase in the cost of health care over the past few years are misdirected. The cost of things that do not change in quality (syringes, bandages, etc.) has surely gone up. But, just as surely, we cannot measure the price of things whose quality is constantly changing. A night in a hospital, for instance, is not the same in 2011 as it was in 1985. Though some definitions are the same (semiprivate has meant and still means two beds in a room, for example), other aspects of the night's stay are different. Today television sets and other creature comforts and sophisticated medical equipment, including beds that monitor vital signs, are standard. Not long ago these were either optional or simply unavailable.

Another key problem with using a supply and demand model for health care services is that one of the assumptions that we made for such a model to work was perfect knowledge. One of the reasons we go to the doctor in the first place is that we do not know what is wrong with us. We go not only to stop the pain but also to find out why the pain exists. This is distinctly different from buying an apple. We know what an apple is, we know why we want it, and we know what it costs to get one. In health care we have to trust the seller (the doctor) to tell us what we need and how much it will cost.

Implications of Public Insurance

Though considerations such as these are important, we can still examine the effect of our financing system on the supply and demand model for health care services. As you can see in Figure 23.1, if there were no program to provide health care services to the poor, the nonpoor would get many services and the poor few. If D_{poor} is the demand for health care by the poor and $D_{nonpoor}$ is the demand for health care by the nonpoor, then $D_{poor\ 1\ nonpoor}$ is the market demand for health care services. This is arrived at by adding the two demand curves together horizontally. Specifically, at each price, the quantity demanded of the poor is added to the quantity demanded of the nonpoor. If the supply curve is as shown, then the price is P^* and the poor consume Q_{poor}, much less than the nonpoor $Q_{nonpoor}$.

FIGURE 23.1   Health care: who gets it without subsidies.

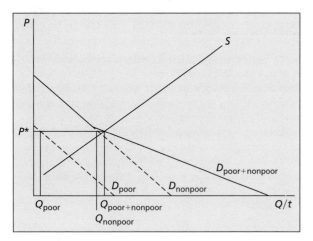

FIGURE 23.2   Health care: who gets it with subsidies.

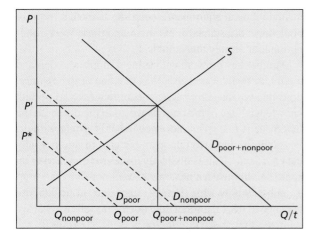

On the other hand, if the poor were to get the services at no cost, then the situation might be quite different. Figure 23.2 shows that in this case, the market demand is the amount that the poor would consume if it were free to them, Q_{poor}, plus the demand by the nonpoor. As you can see, the poor would consume much more, Q_{poor}, while the nonpoor would consume less. Prices would also be higher.

Efficiency Problems with Private Insurance

What private insurance does to the market for health care is as disruptive as public insurance. Recall the idea of co-payments: After the deductible is met, for every dollar of covered medical expense, a low percentage (usually 20 percent) is paid by the patient and the remainder is paid by the insurance company. How does that affect the demand for health care? For simplicity's sake, assume the deductible has either been met or is zero.

FIGURE 23.3   The effect of co-payments on the market for health care.

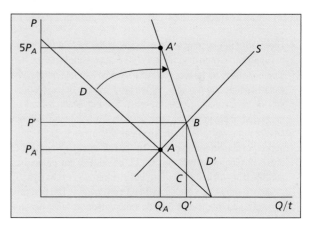

Figure 23.3 shows that the demand curve will rotate out to the right and that this will cause a greater consumption of health care services and higher prices. Let's look at why the curve rotates out to the right. Take the equilibrium point prior to any insurance; call that point A. A person is willing to pay P_A and consumes Q_A medical services prior to insurance. Suppose that person now has insurance with a 20 percent co-payment rate. If that is the case, that person would be willing to consume Q_A medical services even if the price were five times that of P_A. This is because the effective price to the insured person is 20 percent of $5P_A$, or just P_A. The reason it rotates out of the horizontal intercept of the demand curve is that if health care services were free, the effect of co-payments would not matter. Twenty percent of nothing would be nothing and five times of nothing would still be nothing.

Whenever there is a situation where someone other than the consumer is paying the bill, economists call this

third-party payer
An entity other than the consumer who pays part of the costs.

other entity a **third-party payer.** When this happens, the usual role of keeping costs down is taken out of the hands of the consumer.

Since our demand curve rotates out, we buy more health care services and pay more for them. The good news here is that this effect is lessened if the underlying demand curve D is itself inelastic. It can certainly be argued that the demand for health care services is relatively inelastic, and the evidence from an extensive study started in the late 1970s and published in 1987 suggests just that. This is because we would not have an unnecessary operation even if it got less expensive, and most people will have a necessary operation even if the price is high. This study suggests that patient sensitivity to price is greater for visits to doctors than for hospitalizations. Overall health elasticity estimates from this study indicate that a 10 percent increase in the out-of-pocket expenses of the patient is associated with a 1 percent to 3 percent reduction in health care utilization.

The increase in health care utilization also has an efficiency implication. Recall from the Chapter 3 discussion of consumer and producer surplus that the deadweight loss is the yardstick by which economists measure inefficiency. Here the triangle *ABC* is the amount of the inefficiency.

Another area of inefficiency with health care insurance in particular comes in the form of **moral hazard.**

moral hazard
Having insurance increases the demand for the insured good.

People who have insurance consume more health care. This is a problem with all forms of insurance, and the clearest example is in automobile insurance. If you drive more recklessly when you have insurance than when you do not, having insurance makes you more likely to need insurance. In the field of health care, if having insurance makes you more likely to get tested for certain diseases, or even worse, fail to exercise or eat right, then moral hazard is a problem.

A final area of inefficiency in the health insurance market is the greatest threat to its existence and that is

adverse selection
Those in most need of insurance are the most willing to pay for insurance and drive up the price of insurance with their illnesses to such a degree that those people who are not as sick leave the market altogether.

adverse selection. Adverse selection arises when, instead of a true cross-section of the population buying insurance, those in most need of insurance are the most willing to pay for insurance and drive up the price of insurance with their illnesses to such a degree that those people who are not as sick leave the market altogether.

To understand the problem, suppose there are three types of people who initially do not know their own health status and their own need for health insurance. Unbeknownst to them, they are the "healthy," "somewhat healthy," or "unhealthy." Suppose the healthiest category of people have no serious illnesses in the offing and face few risks other than accidents that are equally likely to occur throughout the population. Suppose the unhealthiest category of people face many risks associated with expensive treatments as well as those same injury risks. Now suppose there are two periods: now and later. If no one knows his or her health status "now" and everyone is risk averse, everyone will likely buy insurance "now." They will pay the costs

of that insurance (through premiums), which will equal the average cost of care plus the administrative costs plus the profit for the insurance company. In that sense, when no one knows anything, insurance works fine. Once they know their health status, they will be able to compare the premiums to their expected costs by going it alone. If the difference is dramatic, the healthiest group may drop out. Doing so will raise the average costs to everyone else left in the insurance pool. It may raise it so much that the somewhat healthy people drop their insurance. This has been labeled by some as the "insurance death spiral."

You can solve this particular problem of adverse selection in one of three ways: charging unhealthy people more than healthy people (which is what we do with car insurance in that bad drivers pay more), having a system in which everyone gets insurance through some means other than individual choice (which could be through their employer or through the government), or we can mandate that people buy health insurance. The first method is considered, by many, unethical because lack of coverage is frequently translated as lack of care and lack of care for the sick is considered immoral.

The second method, which is what most of those in group insurance live with, is the system that existed in the United States prior to health care reform in 2010. Prior to that time most Americans either got insurance through the government or through their employer, while some purchased it as individuals; and some of those in the individual market who were sick were denied coverage by insurers. The PPACA changed that. Insurance companies were required to cover them without considering their health status. Closing that option off for insurance companies, though, left the companies vulnerable to adverse selection.

The resolution to this problem and the final method of dealing with adverse selection is **mandation.** Mandation is the requirement that everyone buy insurance. By requiring the healthy to buy insurance (forcing them to

mandation
The requirement to purchase insurance.

pay a tax or fine if they do not), the problem of adverse selection disappears.

Major Changes to Insurance Resulting from PPACA

Several provisions of the bill change how the health insurance industry operates. Under laws existing prior to the enactment of PPACA, health insurers could cut off dependent children from coverage under their parents' health insurance the first year after their children reached

23 and were free to consider, charge more for, and deny coverage for any medical condition a prospective client had prior to purchasing insurance through the company.

They were free to set annual and lifetime limits on how much they would cover. They were free to set prior conditions by which they could rescind coverage, and they were free to raise the rates of those who became ill (and therefore expensive to the company). They were free to charge rates that were different for men and women. They were free from most government intervention when it came to premiums, profit, and the proportion of premiums taken up with administrative costs. Much of this ended or was scheduled to end with the passage of PPACA.

The law as it stands (or in some cases as it will soon stand) will require that health insurers allow dependent children to stay on their parents' health insurance through age 26, that the insurers accept everyone without regard to health status, charge the same to healthy and the unhealthy alike, and charge the same for men and women. They can no longer set lifetime limits, and after 2014, they can no longer set annual limits. They can no longer rescind coverage or raise rates on the sick.

To the untrained eye and ear, each of these provisions might be considered unambiguously good, but consider the fact that each one of them will come with a cost that will, in all likelihood, be passed on to the people who pay the premiums for health insurance, the people who work for companies who provide them with health insurance, and the people who buy goods and services from those companies. Take the most simple of these provisions, the extension of dependent coverage to children through age 26. This provision means that you (because the majority of those reading this book are college students under age 26) will be able to go to graduate school and/or have some time to find that first good job. However, your parents' employer will face extra costs associated with having you on their health insurance plan. How will they react? Depending on the elasticity of demand and supply for labor, the elasticity of demand for the good or service your parents' employer produces, and some other factors, that means your parents' paychecks will be smaller than they would otherwise be, your parents' employer may employ fewer workers than they might have and will have smaller profits than they might have had, the people who buy the goods or services your parents produce will have to pay more, or some combination of these. The cost of providing you with health insurance, or the cost of paying whatever health-related bills you face as a 24-, 25-, or 26-year-old will go from being

your problem (perhaps with your parents' help) to being someone else's problem. While that is good for you, it is not necessarily good for society.

All of these other provisions have a similar problem associated with them. Again the benefits to those not cut off, or not charged more, or not denied coverage will be greater. However, those costs and burdens will go somewhere. They will not disappear. Take another example. Women, on average, are more costly than men throughout the health care life cycle because they face cancer risks—specifically, ovarian, breast, and uterine cancer—that men either do not face or, in the case of breast cancer, with much less frequency. Just as in the auto insurance industry teenage boys pay more for car insurance than teenage girls because boys get in more serious accidents than do girls, women used to have to pay more for individual health insurance, and groups that were disproportionately women paid more than groups of the same size that were disproportionately men. What does that mean with regard to this provision? Men will pay more because women are paying less.

The aforementioned provisions affecting insurance that present the greatest challenge to the health insurance industry itself are the provisions that prevent insurance companies from denying coverage to the people based on pre-existing conditions. This, by itself, could (were it not accompanied with another provision requiring that everyone buy health insurance or have it provided to them) lead to the end of all private health insurance, through the aforementioned death spiral.

The resolution to the death spiral imagined by the PPACA is through a combination of provisions that expand coverage. Through a large expansion of Medicaid through state-run insurance exchanges, and through an employer requirement (all explained later in this chapter), coverage will likely be extended to three-quarters of those who are currently uninsured. Still, those provisions alone would likely not be enough to forestall the death spiral. It is mandation that does this. Mandation is the requirement that everyone buy insurance if insurance is not provided to them. Requiring the healthy to buy insurance (forcing them to pay a tax or fine if they do not) makes the problem of adverse selection disappear.

In the individual health insurance market, insurance companies will have significantly less freedom to charge differential prices to buyers. They will be allowed to charge older customers no more than three times what they charge younger ones (though younger ones typically cost one-fifth or less than what older ones cost), and only be able to charge 50 percent more to tobacco users.

They may set up broad geographic price differences and may charge more for larger families than smaller ones. This all is opposed to few, if any, federal limits that had been in place with regard to market segmentation. Remember that, under normal circumstances, insurers maximize profits by charging premiums based on actual experience.

There is one other, in the grand scheme of things, relatively minor provision change that is potentially important to young people; that is the provision that requires that administrative costs and profits make up not more than 15 percent of premiums (in large groups and 20 percent for small groups). It is this provision that affects those in the relatively low-wage restaurant and retail industries. Full-time employees are frequently offered the ability to buy mini-med policies that provide, for a low premium, some minimalist benefits. These policies tend to be very expensive to administer.

The Blood and Organ Problem

One problem associated with our current system is the scarcity of blood and organs. To an economist, the shortage of blood and organs is directly and unambiguously determined by the fact that it is illegal for people to sell these items for medical use. The ban on the sale of blood and organs for medical use is almost entirely justified on moral grounds. For instance, it is not illegal to sell your blood for use in cosmetics.

If a price can be forced to be zero, the quantity supplied will be reduced and the quantity demanded enhanced. This offers another moral dilemma. If a market were allowed, there would be people who would not be able to pay the price for a needed organ, and, as a result, they would die while someone else who could afford that organ would live. On the other side of that moral debate, though, is the fact that if there were a legal market, more organs would become available and more people would live.

Note that although both the supply and demand for organs are inelastic, neither is perfectly inelastic.[6] There are people who would choose not to pay an exorbitant price to live, and there are people who would be more likely to sign their donor cards if there were a high reward that they could bestow on their heirs by doing so.

The downside of such a market is similar to the downside of the market for tobacco. Poor information can cause people to make life-altering mistakes. For instance,

[6]If both were perfectly inelastic at different quantities, there would be no market-clearing price.

you can live on one kidney, and therefore you could sell the other if the price were right. However, you might underestimate the likelihood that you will ultimately need that other kidney. The sale of organs may be a poor idea, but selling blood may not. There is little economic reason to ban the sale of blood for medical purposes because, unlike organs, blood is self-replenishing.

Comparing the United States with the Rest of the World

Every industrialized nation on earth has a distinct health care system. The one thing that is common throughout the rest of the developed world, though, is that government is the health care provider, insurer, or insurer of last resort. There are distinct advantages to the way the rest of the world does this, but there are disadvantages as well. Having a **single-payer system,** where the government collects significantly high taxes to pay for everyone's health care, benefits those who could not afford health care any other way. It creates serious shortages as well.

single-payer system
The government collects (usually very high) taxes to pay for everyone's health care.

In Canada, England, and much of Europe, being a citizen of the country grants you unlimited rights to necessary health care that is either free or close to it. While the financial arrangements (shown in Table 23.2) in these countries differ, the citizenry need not worry about access to basic health care regardless of their ability to pay. This helps explain the very low occurrences of infant mortality and relatively long life spans in these countries, as seen in Table 23.3. The unemployed and the employed, the working and the retired, the young and the old, the rich and the poor are treated with a degree of equality that cannot be claimed in the United States. In addition, because the doctors are paid salaries by the government instead of fees for seeing patients, they do not have an incentive to order expensive tests and perform costly surgeries. Further, as government employees, they are usually protected from lawsuits. Thus universal access is accomplished at lower overall costs than in the United States.

This, however, comes at a cost. These countries have severe doctor shortages because, in an effort to keep costs down, physicians are paid much less than they are paid in the United States. One principal reason why you see many foreign-born physicians in the United States is that they can make a great deal more money here than in their own countries. Additionally, there is no monetary

TABLE 23.2 International health care finance schemes.

Source: OECD Health Data, www.oecd.org

Country	Public Expenditures as a Percent of Total, 2009–2011	Hospitals	Physicians	Function of Private Insurance
Australia	68.5	Mostly public	A	a
Canada	70.4	Mostly private	A, B	a
France	77.0	Mostly public	A	b
Germany	76.8	Mix of public and private	A	a
Japan	80.5	Mostly private	A, B	None
United Kingdom	83.2	Mostly public trusts	C	a
United States	48.2	Mostly private	A	c

A—mostly private fee for service.
B—government-imposed fee schedule.
C—public employees.
a—option to purchase private insurance for all expenses.
b—option to purchase private insurance for noncovered expenses.
c—all non-Medicare, non-Medicaid.

TABLE 23.3 International comparisons of health expenditures, infant mortality, and life expectancy.

Source: U.S. Census Bureau, www.census.gov/compendia/statab/cats/international_statistics/vital_statistics_health_elections_education.html; OECD Health Data, www.oecd.org

Country	Health Expenditures/ GDP, 2010	Infant Mortality Rate per 1,000 Births, 2010	Life Expectancy, 2010	Five-Year Survival Rates	
				Prostate Cancer	Breast Cancer
United States	17.6	6.1	78.7	98.6	88.7
United Kingdom	9.6	4.2	80.6	71.0	81.0
France	11.6	3.6	81.4	61.7	80.3
Germany	11.6	3.4	80.5	67.6	71.7
Japan	9.5	2.3	83.0		

incentive to become a doctor when you cannot get rich by being one. The effect of having doctors on salary also is seen when these doctors are reluctant to put in long hours. Physicians are among the hardest-working people in the United States. You can also see the effect of this public health provision in the five-year survival rates of breast and prostate cancers. The United States enjoys the highest survival rates among these countries. Another factor weighing in favor of the U.S. system is immediate access to procedures that require long waiting periods elsewhere.

In the United States a 50-year-old man with blocked arteries is hospitalized and operated on within hours of being admitted, whereas the waiting period for bypass surgery in Canada has been as high as six months. Though some waiting periods have shortened, this is in part due to the recognition by physicians that expensive procedures must be rationed. In the United States the elderly with kidney disease will be given dialysis as long as they are physically able to stand it (lengthening life by

a year or more). A similar English patient cannot schedule routine dialysis treatments under the British government-run system.

Another important area that would be lost if the United States were to go to a single-payer system would be innovation. Prescription drug, medical device, and medical procedure innovation has been highly concentrated in the United States, largely because the innovator makes money that cannot be made in the single-payer countries. Furthermore, the innovation that takes place abroad is likely motivated by profits that can be made in the United States. As a result, very few health care economists believe that turning the United States into a single-payer environment would be good for health care innovation.

Last, because doctors are typically immune from lawsuits in countries with single-payer systems, accountability for mistakes is left to professional standards boards. While these mechanisms can work, very often they end up being a system for physicians to protect their own.

Summary

You should now understand how the system of health care finance seriously alters the market for health care services. You also understand that in the United States 52 percent of the health care tab is picked up by the taxpayer, with the remainder being picked up either by patients directly or through their insurance companies. You understand why health care is not like most other goods that economists study but that we can look at it using the same supply and demand tools discussed earlier. You understand that both taxpayer-financed health care and private insurance–financed health care increase the overall price of health care. Last, you understand why a single-payer, taxpayer-financed health care system would have both advantages and disadvantages.

Key Terms

adverse selection, 263
co-payment, 259
deductible, 258
mandation, 263
maximum out of pocket, 259

Medicaid, 258
Medicare, 258
mini-med, 259
moral hazard, 263
primary care physician (PCP), 259

risk averse, 258
risk neutral, 258
single-payer system, 265
third-party payer, 262

Quiz Yourself

1. The primary motivation for the purchase of any insurance lies in the fact that most people are
   a. risk lovers.
   b. risk averse.
   c. risk neutral.
   d. risk tolerant.

2. The risk-averse person will buy health insurance
   a. only if the expected health costs equal the insurance premium.
   b. only if the expected health costs are greater than the insurance premium.
   c. even if the expected health costs are less than the insurance premium.
   d. under no circumstances.

3. The government, in the form of Medicare, Medicaid, and the Children's Health Insurance Program, pays for _____ of health care costs.
   a. less than 10 percent
   b. slightly less than half
   c. about 75 percent
   d. all

4. If you have a $2,000 covered health expense, a deductible of $500, and a 20 percent co-pay, then you pay _____ and the insurance company pays _____.
   a. $1,500, $500
   b. $1,000, $1,000
   c. $800, $1200
   d. $700, $800

5. Which of the following forms of private insurance is likely to have the lowest premiums and least doctor choice flexibility?
   a. Medicare.
   b. An HMO.
   c. A PPO.
   d. A fee-for-service plan.

6. Medical care inflation is likely to be easily overstated (if you look simply at the increase in the cost of a hospital stay) because that calculation ignores
   a. the original costs.
   b. the new costs.
   c. quality increases.
   d. quality decreases.

7. The problem of the "third-party payer" arises in health care in the form of
   a. doctors having to pay part of their own expenses.
   b. government and/or private insurance paying a significant part of the costs.
   c. patients having to pay a significant part of the costs.
   d. hospitals not being able to collect from many patients.

8. One significant feature of a "single-payer" system lacking in the U.S. system is
   a. government involvement in health care.
   b. coverage for the elderly.
   c. coverage for the poor.
   d. universal coverage.

Short Answer Questions

1. Why would eliminating the ability to deny coverage to those with pre-existing conditions require mandation to accompany it?

2. Why would risk-averse people be more likely to buy insurance?

3. For who would a mini-med health insurance policy be a good policy to have relative to the alternative and why?

4. Why is it more likely that health expenses will rise faster in the United States than in Canada or the United Kingdom?

5. How might you apply the notion of "moral hazard" to decisions you make about exercise?

Think about This

List the pros and cons associated with the U.S. system of financing health care relative to the U.K. system. Do the same relative to the Canadian system. Use your understanding of opportunity cost to think about why we can't have "the best of both worlds."

Talk about This

In the United States a terminally ill patient can decide to decline extraordinary medical treatment, but in all cases the patient, or the spouse, is the one who makes that decision (either with prior instructions or by making his or her wishes known to the health care provider). In the United Kingdom, the government can, and does, limit the availability of extraordinary medical treatment. Thus, though care is free (or nearly free) to the patient, it can be limited against their will. The U.K. government's contention is that health care resources are scarce and they would be wasted extending the life of a terminally ill patient by a few days. Which is worse, the aspect of the U.S. system where people are denied care when they are unable to pay, or the U.K. system where they are denied care because their treatment would not lead to a significant increase in the quality of life?

For More Insight See

Health Care Finance Association statistical tables—www.hcfa.gov

Phelps, Charles E., *Health Economics* (Reading, MA: Addison-Wesley, 2009).

www.census.gov/prod/2004pubs/04statab/health.pdf

International Comparisons of Types of Health Care Finance Systems—www.nao.org.uk/publications

Behind the Numbers

International comparisons of vital statistics and health care expenditures.

Statistical Abstract of the United States; comparative international statistics—www.census.gov/compendia/statab

Health care expenditures.

Centers for Medicare and Medicaid Services; historical tables—www.cms.gov/NationalHealth ExpendData

Health insurance coverage.

Coverage type—
www.census.gov/hhes/www/hlthins/hlthins.html

Lack of coverage.

Centers for Disease Control and Prevention—www.cdc.gov/nchs/nhis.htm

Medicare premiums.

Centers for Medicare and Medicaid Services—www.cms.hhs.gov

Government-Provided Health Insurance: Medicaid, Medicare, and the Child Health Insurance Program

Learning Objectives

After reading this chapter you should be able to:

LO1 Describe Medicaid as a program that covers medical expenses for many of this nation's poor.

LO2 Describe Medicare as a public insurance program for the elderly.

LO3 Distinguish Medicaid from Medicare and understand their relationship.

LO4 Describe the Child Health Insurance Program as one that serves the children of the working poor.

Chapter Outline

Medicaid: What, Who, and How Much

Why Medicaid Costs So Much

Medicare: Public Insurance and the Elderly

Medicare's Nuts and Bolts

The Medicare Trust Fund

Child Health Insurance Program

Summary

Since the early 1900s, the United States has been subsidizing medical care for citizens whose incomes are extremely low. The number of people who were covered by some form of federal medical care increased until 1967, when the Medicaid program came into full fruition. From that point on, millions of Americans have benefited from free medical care. Today, 39 million children and another 30 million adults have nearly all of their medical expenses paid for by Medicaid and its companion program, State Child Health Insurance Programs.

In this chapter we describe the Medicaid program in full, and we provide information about the people who are eligible for its benefits and what coverage they receive. We also discuss the groups that draw most heavily on Medicaid benefits. We describe the relationship between the federal government and the states in funding and administering the Medicaid program. We outline how doctors and hospitals are reimbursed when they work with patients whose costs are paid through Medicaid. We move on to use our supply and demand model to explain why Medicaid costs so much, and we focus attention on Medicaid's treatment of two very different populations: the very old and the very young. Then we consider provisions in Medicaid that are intended to keep costs down.

Medicare and Social Security are the centerpieces of the United States' policy toward its elderly. Social Security ensures an income for the retired, and Medicare guarantees heavily subsidized health insurance for everyone over 65, retired or not. Social Security began in the New Deal 1930s; Medicare in the second great wave of social programs during the Johnson administration's Great Society of the 1960s. In its first full year in operation, 1967, the cost of its benefits totaled $2.7 billion; by 2011 it cost $554 billion.

Medicare comprises two programs: Medicare Part A, a mandatory program that covers expenses derived from hospital stays; and Medicare Part B, a voluntary program that covers doctor visits. This section begins by laying out why a government health insurance program for the elderly makes economic sense, and reviews the problems that such health insurance programs inevitably face. After discussing how each part of Medicare works, we focus on ways that each part has attempted to control costs. We then look at the Medicare Trust Fund and its projected problems in staying solvent, and we suggest ways Medicare can stave off bankruptcy. As part of that discussion, we talk about the relationship between Medicaid and Medicare, the program for Americans 65 or older.

Finally we take up the relatively new Child Health Insurance Program and its function of providing health insurance to the children of working families where the parents have no employer-provided health insurance.

Medicaid: What, Who, and How Much

Medicaid was established in 1964 to consolidate and expand existing programs that had been charged with providing health care to those who could not otherwise afford it. In 2011 the program cost the federal and state governments $408 billion. We begin our discussion of the Medicaid system by describing who is eligible, what is covered, who is enrolled, which groups cost the most, what relationship the federal government has to the states, and how doctors and hospitals are reimbursed.

People who are eligible for Medicaid must meet one of many criteria. In general, anyone who is in a family that is eligible for cash assistance under Temporary Assistance to Needy Families (TANF) or Supplemental Security Income (SSI) is automatically eligible for Medicaid. Eligibility standards were altered by the Patient Protection and Affordable Care Act (PPAPA) such that in 2014 many more adults were to have been covered by Medicaid. Prior to that act's passage, any children under 19 whose parents' income was less than 133 percent of the appropriate poverty line for their family size or pregnant women and children under a year old whose family income was less than 185 percent of that poverty line were also eligible, as were relatively few others who were affected by a variety

of other rules. Under the rules prior to 2014, adults who did not have children under the age of 19 could have very little income and not be covered by Medicaid because their wealth made them ineligible for TANF or SSI.

The PPACA, as originally passed, required states to expand Medicaid eligibility to include anyone in the household if the household income was less than 133 percent of the poverty line unless the states were willing to forgo all federal money for Medicaid. The Supreme Court decision that validated many parts of the act invalidated this provision. This meant that states could decide whether or not to participate. This also meant that although Medicaid enrolled more than 61 million, and SCHIP enrolled another 7.9 million, only half of those whose incomes were below 150 percent of the poverty line received its benefits. Approximately half of states had formally declined the Medicaid expansion or were leaning that way in 2013, despite the provision that the federal government would pick up the vast majority of the extra costs. Whether this was rationally or politically motivated, the impact on Medicaid eligibility remained cloudy through 2013.

Medicaid pays for nearly everything that is considered necessary from a medical standpoint, and it pays for some things that can be questioned. Doctor visits, emergency room visits, surgery, outpatient procedures, medicines, birth control pills, permanent and semipermanent birth control procedures and devices, eye care, long-term care—you name it, Medicaid probably pays for it. Literally, the only things that are not covered are most abortions, cosmetic surgeries, and drugs for weight loss and hair growth. Abortions are paid for by Medicaid in only a few states, and in those states the state must pay the whole fee. Whenever a pregnancy is the result of rape or incest, or threatens the life of the mother, Medicaid pays as it would for any other procedure.

Far more women and young people are served by Medicaid than their proportion in the general population. Whereas 51 percent of the population is female, nearly 59 percent of the Medicaid population is. Only 25 percent of the population is under 18, yet 50 percent of the Medicaid population is under 18. If you look simply at the adults on Medicaid, 70 percent are female. Additionally, though the population of Medicaid recipients is disproportionately young, we will show that the dollars spent are disproportionately allocated to care for the elderly.

In racial makeup, Medicaid recipients mirror the population of those who live in poverty nearly perfectly: 37 percent white, 21 percent black, and 19 percent Hispanic.

Medicaid is a cooperative effort of federal and state governments. The federal government mandates that the states enroll all people who are eligible, and it gives them guidelines to use if they wish to enroll others. States have the option of covering or denying coverage of certain specified expenses (like the previously mentioned abortions), as they wish.

The federal mandates are partially covered by federal matching money, and states are reimbursed according to their relative GDPs. Poorer states are given greater reimbursement rates, and richer states are given smaller ones. Fourteen states get the minimum 50 percent matching percentage from the federal government, while 6 other states and the District of Columbia get at least a 70 percent match. To motivate state participation in Medicaid's eligibility standards, the Patient Protection and Affordable Care Act temporarily raised these rates 7.6 to 15 percentage points to assist states' transition. The differential rates make Medicaid less of a burden for poorer states to fund.

Whether or not they participate in the expanded Medicaid provisions, some states make it easier to get on Medicaid than others. States have different income and wealth standards for TANF, and people who are eligible for Medicaid in New York and Wisconsin, for example, would not be eligible in states like Texas and Arkansas. This difference is effective only for adults, since children under one year of age are eligible, regardless of the state they live in, under a federal standard that makes them eligible if their family's income is less than 185 percent of the poverty line. All other children are similarly eligible as long as their family income is less than 133 percent of the poverty line.

When they treat patients whose bills are paid by Medicaid, doctors and hospitals are reimbursed at widely varying rates. States pay different amounts for the same procedures. These variations come about because Medicaid payments start at the state level with the federal government matching the state's payments. States must set reimbursement rates high enough that there are enough physicians and hospitals in all areas to treat Medicaid patients adequately. When many physicians are in competition with one another, rates can be lower; when there are few, rates must be higher.

For doctors and hospitals, Medicaid is an all-or-nothing proposition. When doctors and hospitals agree to take Medicaid patients, they agree to accept the state reimbursement rate as payment in full. They also agree to take any and all Medicaid patients who show up for treatment. They cannot limit their practice to a certain percentage, and they cannot accept patients with one disease and not another. Finding these restrictions to be unreasonable and reimbursement rates too low, many private hospitals and prestigious doctors do not take Medicaid patients.

Why Medicaid Costs So Much

Medicaid is an expensive program. To examine why it costs as much as it does, it will be helpful to put it into our supply and demand context. In 2011, the federal and state governments spent $420 billion to provide health care for 69 million Americans of Medicaid and Medicaid's companion program, State Child Health Insurance Programs (SHCIPs). Netting out the SCHIPs enrollment and costs, that amount translates to just under $7,000 per recipient. People not on Medicaid spend about the same as that. As a matter of fact, until quite recently those on Medicaid accounted for substantially greater per capita expenditures than those not on Medicaid. Why is it that the expenses of people who pay for their own health care are almost identical to the expenses of people whose health care is paid through Medicaid?

Let's turn to our supply and demand model for an explanation. As it is with any other good, the demand for health care is downward sloping. This is because when the price is high, people forgo care for ailments that are not all that troubling. Although price is always a concern, there are ailments that people will have treated pretty much regardless of cost. Keeping our upward-sloping supply curve makes sense because it takes more money to get doctors and hospitals to provide the greater quantities of care we desire and the higher quality of care that we also desire.

Figure 24.1 differs from every other supply and demand diagram you have seen, though, in that we have

FIGURE 24.1   The supply and demand for health care without Medicaid.

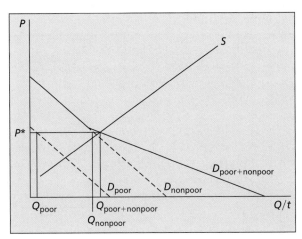

separated the demand by people in poverty from the demand by the people whose incomes are above the poverty line. The demand curve $D_{nonpoor}$ for the nonpoor is further to the right than the demand curve D_{poor} for the poor. To get the market demand curve $D_{poor + nonpoor}$, we must add the quantities of care that both the nonpoor and poor want at each price. At some prices the poor cannot afford any health care, and they therefore do not demand any health care. As prices fall, the poor begin to demand health care, and the nonpoor begin to demand more health care. To find where the market demand curve cuts the horizontal axis, you add the quantity of health care that each would want if it were provided free of charge. This horizontal adding of demand curves gives us the market demand curve.

Where the market demand curve $D_{poor + nonpoor}$ crosses the market supply curve S, we get the equilibrium price $P*$ and quantity $Q_{poor + nonpoor}$. When we take that price over to the nonpoor person's demand curve, we can read off the quantity of health care the nonpoor person will get as $Q_{nonpoor}$. Taking it further, to the poor person's demand curve, we can read off what the poor person wants as Q_{poor}. If the health care system is such that the poor cannot get access to care at affordable prices, there will be a disparity between the health care received by the nonpoor and that received by the poor that some people will consider to be unacceptable.

If the poor are provided health care free of charge, as they are with Medicaid, a different problem arises. The market demand curve does not stay as it was in Figure 24.1 but moves to its position in Figure 24.2. This new demand curve is made up by adding the quantity Q_{poor} of care poor people will want if it is free

FIGURE 24.2 The supply and demand for health care with Medicaid.

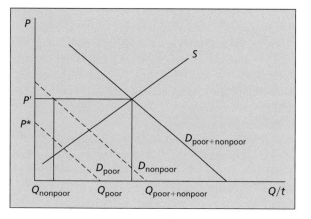

to the demand curve $D_{nonpoor}$ for the nonpoor. At the intersection of market supply and market demand, the price rises to P', which is substantially above its old price at $P*$. It also results in greater access for the poor and less access for the nonpoor. Figure 24.2 exaggerates this effect, but in the real world Medicaid recipients consume slightly more health care than those who have private insurance.

Why Spending Is Greater on the Elderly

In terms of expenses, Medicaid dollars are spent disproportionately on the elderly. This stands to reason in that older people need care that tends to be more expensive, and they need it more often than do those who are younger. The average Medicaid recipient utilized more than $8,000 in medical care in 2011. In 2009, the average child who was covered by Medicaid cost the government only $2,848, while the average covered person over 65 cost $15,678. Thus, though children make up slightly less than half of Medicaid's population, they account for only 20 percent of the bills, and although those over 65 (and not disabled) make up less than 10 percent of its population, they account for 22 percent of the bills. This is in addition to the $554 billion that they account for in Medicare bills.

As mentioned previously, the central reason for Medicaid's spending more on the elderly than it does on the young is that older people tend to get illnesses that cost more than those of younger people. However, there is a reason that comes in a close second: nursing home care. Nursing home care is not part of either Medicare Part A or Part B. People who are elderly must therefore pay for this care themselves, unless, of course, they cannot. When elderly people's incomes are low enough that they qualify for assistance, Medicaid will pick up the tab for nursing home care. This can cost anywhere between $30,000 and $70,000 a year, constituting a substantial outlay for Medicaid. In the final analysis, Medicaid spends 35 percent of its total budget on long-term care, of which about three-quarters is on care for the aged.

The problem that this generates for elderly Americans is that they have to qualify for Medicaid before Medicaid will start paying. For widows and widowers this is not that difficult; they simply pay all their medical and nursing home expenses until their money is gone. Then Medicaid starts paying. Oftentimes, adult children with power of attorney try to hasten the point at which Medicaid pays their parents' medical expenses by draining the wealth of their parents by making gifts of it to themselves and their own children. It is legal to do this but only up to a point. Any money that is given to children and grandchildren in the name of the elderly relatives in the two-year period leading up to their enrollment in Medicaid is treated as a semifraudulent way of avoiding paying for nursing home care. The government monitors this and takes back any money that was given away within that period.

Giving away an elderly person's assets does not solve the nursing home problem entirely, in any case, because many times an elderly married couple has one partner who needs care and another who does not. This is especially true when an otherwise healthy person gets Alzheimer's disease. Medicaid used to require that the entire household's wealth be spent down before it would pay anything to a nursing home. This left many healthy spouses destitute because of the need to finance health care for their partner. At the time, the only alternative for the couple was to file for divorce the minute one of them was placed in a nursing home. That way, the assets were divided in half so that only half would be spent down, and the other half would be available for the healthy spouse. The needless emotional trauma of divorcing a long-time spouse is now avoided because the law now allows the assets of the couple's household to be divided equally between what will be spent down and what will be left untouched when one member of the married couple is admitted to a nursing home.

Cost-Saving Measures in Medicaid

During the early 1990s Medicaid costs were rising by more than 10 percent a year. This trend, coupled with other welfare concerns, motivated many of the welfare reform measures of the middle part of that decade. During that time states began to shift their Medicaid systems from individual doctors reimbursed for expenses to health maintenance organizations (HMOs). From 1990 to 2004, doctors in HMOs went from treating fewer than 5 percent of Medicaid patients to treating 60 percent of them.

When HMOs are in place, people are denied coverage unless it is authorized by the doctors who have been designated as their primary care physicians. Under HMOs, primary care physicians are charged with providing basic care, and they are the only people who can refer patients to specialists. The use of HMOs has stemmed the unfortunate practice of Medicaid patients' use of emergency room treatments for basic care. Nonemergency Medicaid patients are now counseled that if they show up at an emergency room for treatment of nonserious matters, they may be turned away. They are also counseled about the benefits of having a physician who follows their particular health needs. In this way HMOs are saving the state and federal governments money and, at the same time, are helping to improve the health of the people they are serving.

One other way in which states began cutting their Medicaid budgets in 2011 was to drop many optional coverages. Specifically, states that covered eyeglasses began to consider dropping such coverage for Medicaid recipients.

Medicare: Public Insurance and the Elderly

Why Private Insurance May Not Work

There are two main arguments for government provision of health insurance for the elderly: equity and efficiency. While it was appropriate in earlier times to argue that it was only fair to provide for the elderly in that the elderly were poorer than younger people, such arguments are less appropriate today. Today's elderly are among the least likely of our citizens to be in poverty, due in some measure to these programs. What remains are arguments that the market cannot provide health insurance efficiently to people who are not in groups.

The problem with health insurance, in general, is that people who really need it, those who are sick, are more than willing to pay very high prices for it; and those who are healthy are only willing to pay low prices. Most people have in mind two kinds of health expenses when they are thinking about buying insurance, the expenses they are rather sure they will incur and expenses of which they are not as certain. They will buy insurance readily if the expenses they expect are greater than the premiums they have to pay. People will pay for insurance that covers them in areas they are not certain they will need, but if premiums are too high, only the sickest will want to buy insurance. If this group were to become the only one that buys insurance, the expenses to the insurance company would be greater than the premiums received and premiums would have to rise. This would make the problem worse, as only the sickest of the sick would buy the insurance. This problem is referred to by economists as adverse selection.

This vicious cycle would go on and on until there was no insurance at all. Fortunately, this is not much of a problem in the United States because most private health insurance is group insurance that employers buy for their employees. In each group there are undoubtedly some people who are sick, some who are healthy, and many who are somewhere in between. The healthy subsidize the sick. Because being part of a group affords such important benefits both to the insurance companies and to members of the group, people who buy health insurance as individuals always run into problems not encountered by people who buy into group health insurance.

This would not be a problem if the elderly were still with their employers. They are not; they are retired, and many employers do not offer membership in company health groups to retirees. With the efficacy of offering health plans to people in groups, and with millions of individual retirees needing health insurance, it has made sense for the government to offer such insurance, and it does so through Medicare.

What remains debatable about Medicare is who pays for it—its beneficiaries (as with normal health insurance), or all taxpayers, or a combination of these groups. At the outset it was intended that the cost split would be about 50–50, proportions that offered the elderly a substantial subsidy. Today the subsidy is such that about three-quarters of the total expenses are paid out of tax dollars and only about a quarter by its beneficiaries.

Why Medicare's Costs Are High

All government health insurance programs suffer from problems of cost control, problems that are compounded in an era of rapid advances in medical technology that vastly improve health care but increase costs as well.

Anytime the consumption of a good is subsidized via insurance, several basic problems ensue. The first problem is that you risk increasing its consumption to an inefficient level. The second problem, referred to by economists as the third-party payer problem, is that by insuring consumers and thereby insulating them from costs, neither consumers nor producers have incentives for holding down costs. These and other insurance problems were explained in detail in Chapter 23 on health care.

As with all other government health insurance programs, then, the costs of Medicare have escalated dramatically. Figure 24.3 shows the increase in the costs of Medicare since its inception in 1967.

For most programs, spending can rise only because prices rise or beneficiaries become more numerous. Medicare spending has risen for these reasons and one other: increases in numbers of available medical services. Medicare beneficiaries are not limited to the medical procedures that existed in 1967. They can avail themselves of the best that medical science has to offer in the 2000s. This means that some patients who would have died 20 years ago, and who therefore would no longer be drawing on Medicare's resources, are now given medicines and procedures that are allowing them to live much longer.

It would be unconscionable to deny medical treatment to Medicare patients, even if it would be expensive, to improve their life or their life span. Moreover, it would be unrealistic to assume that they would deny themselves expensive treatments in the name of cost savings. Thus,

FIGURE 24.3   Medicare spending in billions of 2005 dollars.

Source: Refer to Table 8.6: www.whitehouse.gov/omb/budget/Historicals

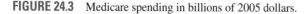

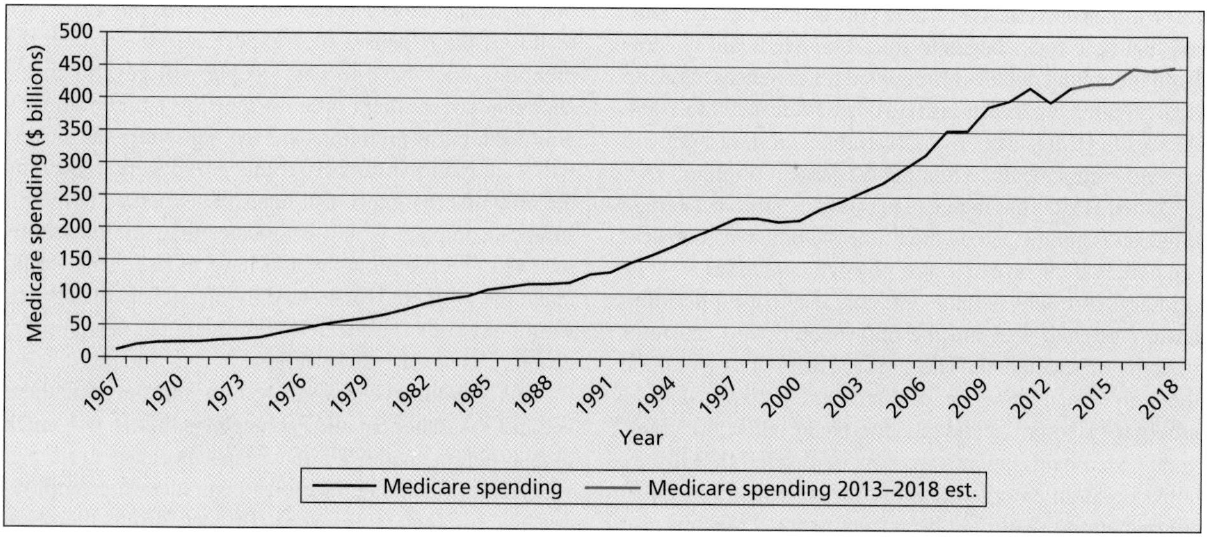

as treatments for health problems continue to become more effective and life expectancies increase, we will see a continued escalation of Medicare spending. As you will see in our section on the Medicare Trust Fund, it is this quickly increasing expense that has put Medicare on a course that is likely to lead it to bankruptcy.

One of the ways to deal with this kind of problem is to transfer the incentive to save money from the consumer to the producer. While it is usually consumers who want to limit the amount of money they pay, with insurance this incentive is either drastically reduced or even eliminated. As discussed above, if no one has an incentive to keep expenses down, no one will keep expenses down. It is possible, though, to make producers the cost-conscious parties by paying them prospectively rather than retrospectively.

Retrospective payment is what people are used to when they buy services. When a person has a car repaired, a garage worker finds the problem, asks whether the customer wants it fixed, tells what it will cost, and fixes it. At that point the retrospective payment is made. Under normal circumstances, this is not a problem because the customer still has the incentive to keep costs down. Problems arise when retrospective payments are used with insurance. When you have an accident that is someone else's fault, it is the other person's insurance that is paying the bill. Here you want everything fixed perfectly, with original parts, and the repair shop is only too happy to oblige because the mechanic can rack up the charges. If you had to pay for the repair, you would be more likely to be satisfied with "good enough" and to accept substitute parts. That is why either you are required to get two or three estimates before the work starts, or the single estimate and the repairs must be preapproved by an insurance adjuster. Both multiple estimates and insurance adjusters' oversight serve to keep repair shops competing with one another and prevent or lessen overbilling.

In health care it is unusual for an insurance company to have you go to several doctors to get estimates, though some may require second opinions. This is why some insurance companies and Medicare have gone to a system of prospective payments. Prospective payments are made prior to the service being performed. The hospital gets paid up front to treat its patients, and it then has an incentive to keep costs below what it has been paid. In the private arena, health maintenance organizations (HMOs) are designed to take advantage of such payments. Gatekeeper doctors, who are usually family practice physicians, pediatricians, or obstetrician/gynecologists, are paid specified sums per patient under their care, and they are paid

the sums whether the patients require a great deal of care or no care at all. Medicare HMOs work this way as well, and, as we will see, so does Medicare Part A.

Medicare's Nuts and Bolts

As we discussed before, Medicare is divided into two categories. Medicare Part A is mandatory for people over age 65, and it covers hospital care. Medicare Part B is voluntary, and it covers doctor visits. No part of Medicare covers common out-of-the-hospital prescription drugs or long-term nursing home care.

Provider Types

The first choice a Medicare recipient has to make is whether to choose traditional Medicare or a Medicare HMO. Medicare HMOs are approved by the government, and doctors who participate in them are paid per patient under their charge. The government pays less per HMO patient than per non-HMO patient on average, probably because healthy elderly people are more likely to enroll in an HMO. The cost controls that HMOs offer are usually enough that HMO premiums are significantly lower than normal Medicare premiums. People who opt for traditional Medicare are automatically enrolled in Part A; they may choose to enroll in Part B.

Part A

For people who work 10 years before reaching 65, Medicare Part A has no premium. For everyone else, the premium charged for Medicare Part A differs, depending on how long they worked. In 2013 the deductible was a relatively high $1,184 for the first day in the hospital. The costs for the next 60 days were paid by Medicare. After 60 days in the hospital, patients paid $296 per day, Medicare paid the rest, and after 90 days patients paid $592 per day. From day 91 on, patients have a 60-day reserve of days upon which to draw. When that reserve is gone, patients must pay the rest themselves.

From the hospital's position, Medicare is paying amounts that it has settled on for specific diagnoses. These payments, and they are prospective payments, are determined by where the patients' ailments put them on a list of more than 500 diagnosis-related groups (DRGs). All Medicare patients who enter the hospital are placed in a DRG, and rather than paying for specific expenses that are incurred, Medicare pays the hospital a predetermined amount that is considered appropriate for that DRG. This motivates the hospital to keep costs down.

Medicare had paid for every bandage, meal, and service until the mid-1980s, when it found that hospitals were racking up costs of questionable medical value just to increase their profit margins. Under fixed payments for DRGs, Medicare has kept much better control of cost increases. This policy has also led to a significant shortening of average hospital stays for specific problems. The current system also provides an incentive for hospitals to discharge patients as soon as possible.

This system for reimbursement is not without its critics. Specifically, President Obama derogatorily labels this prospective payment system as paying hospitals based on what the patients have when they walk in the door not for what the hospitals do to make the patients better, or even by what services they perform. This criticism is not new, but the balance that was struck when the DRG-based prospective reimbursement was instituted was that paying hospitals on performance (how much patients improve from when they were admitted) will cause hospitals to specialize in low-mortality, low-risk treatments, and that paying hospitals based on the services they provide will motivate hospitals to over-treat patients, thereby running up the costs. Though not without its critics, the current system is favored by most health economists as being one that keeps costs down, and with Medicare costs rising rapidly in the near future due to the aging of the baby boom generation, this is of primary concern.

Part B

Medicare Part B, the voluntary insurance program that pays for visits to doctors, has a monthly premium and an annual deductible. In 2013, the premium depended on your income. For those with incomes under $85,000 ($170,000 for married couples filing joint tax returns), the premium was $104.90 and the deductible was $147. Because neither the premium nor the deductible has increased at the rate of medical inflation, this part of the program is now being subsidized at a rate approaching 75 percent. What this means is that for every dollar a patient pays, Medicare Part B pays $3 out of tax revenues. Accordingly, there is virtually no reason for an elderly person not to enroll in Part B. For those who cannot afford the premium, Medicaid, the parallel program that provides health insurance for the poor, typically steps in. For everyone else, that $104.90 premium is a small enough amount that nearly 100 percent of the non-Medicaid eligible elderly are enrolled.

From a doctor's perspective, Medicare Part B pays a regional standard for each treatment. Unlike Part A,

Part B is billed expense by expense with retrospective payment. Medicaid pays a fixed amount for each service, but each service is billed individually rather than being grouped in a DRG.

The reason that prospective payments do not work for non-HMO Medicare Part B is that, with a huge range of possible ailments, there are many potential doctors a patient may want to see. In a Medicare HMO, a gatekeeper is in charge of referrals to specialists, but non-HMO patients can go at any time to the doctors of their choice. It would be impossible to predict such choices in advance, and since no single doctor, HMO, or hospital is in total charge of their care under Part B, prospective payments cannot be made to work.

Prescription Drug Coverage (Part D)

As part of the 2003 reauthorization of Medicare, the costs of prescription drugs are now covered. Prior to this change, health care economists were of two minds. First, they saw a distortion of the market when surgery was covered but medicines were not. Second, they noted Medicare's precarious financial state and worried that the additional benefit would make it that much worse.

As expensive as most drugs are, drug-based treatments are less expensive than their surgical alternatives. Because Medicare did not cover prescription drugs and it did cover surgery, patients may have elected surgery even though it may have been more expensive.

On the other side of the debate were the concerns over the cost of any prescription drug program. Initial estimates in the 2003 Medicare reauthorization placed the cost of such a program at $400 billion over 10 years. Those estimates were quickly revised. Currently the program is anticipated to cost at least $1 trillion over 10 years. What must be understood about any such estimates is that they are highly sensitive to assumptions about price elasticity for drugs. If the estimator uses data on the number of prescriptions filled and multiplies that number by the cost per prescription covered by the government (assuming perfectly inelastic demand), this would seriously underestimate costs. There are people who will benefit from prescriptions who did not go to the doctor because they knew they would get a prescription slip they could not afford to fill. Additionally, there were elderly who used to get multiple prescriptions and fill only a fraction of them because they could not afford to fill them all. Taking this into account, cost estimates are likely to be exceeded and higher deficits will ensue.

The 2003 reauthorization also introduced means testing to Medicare. The Republican-authored bill made premiums and coverage dependent on income and required most seniors to pay as much as $3,600 out of pocket. Medicare Part D is not really a national plan but was intended to foster many private alternatives with substantial government subsidies. Premiums, deductibles, and co-pays are features of each plan and are highly localized, and as a result much more confusing to beneficiaries than Medicare Part A or B. Democrats, who had sought a government-run program akin to the other parts of Medicare, generally opposed the plan. Republican defenders sought to introduce private market incentives to keep costs under control. Neither seems to have the upper hand on this issue as the system was initially very confusing, but the most recent estimates suggest that it will cost the government 30 percent less than it was originally projected to cost. A particularly troubling part of the original law was the existence of a "donut hole" where coverage began at one level of individual spending, then stopped until another higher level of spending was arrived at, and then began again. The donut hole is slated to be reduced under the Patient Protection and Affordable Care Act.

Cost Control Provisions in Medicare

Medicare has been attempting to keep costs under control since its inception, but, unfortunately, it has enjoyed little success. Ultimately the reasons for this lack of success boil down to two:

1. Medical care is increasingly sophisticated, with continually improving success rates, and it is therefore more costly.
2. There is no economic incentive for either patient or doctor to control costs.

While the aforementioned DRGs have helped control costs in Part A, and Medicare HMOs have helped control costs in Part B, neither has been foolproof. The DRGs, however, have succeeded in doing a couple of important things with regard to costs. First, basing the payments on DRGs has given hospitals the incentive to take many procedures that used to require one night in the hospital and turn them into outpatient procedures. Second, hospitals have put pressure on doctors and patients to shorten the average length of stay of many multiday procedures.

Given that DRGs pay a fixed amount for a procedure, hospitals have the incentive to cut costs. Since one of a hospital's greatest costs is keeping someone in a bed

overnight, converting a procedure that formerly involved a hospital stay to one that is done on an outpatient basis helps to raise profits. Heart bypass surgery is not likely to be an outpatient procedure anytime soon, but many other procedures are candidates. While many people are concerned about the health consequences of turning out patients who would have stayed a night, there has been little medical evidence that sending people home right away has had adverse effects.

A second area where costs have come down is the shortening of the length of stay for many multiday procedures. Surgeries that used to require a three- or four-day stay in the hospital to recuperate now require only two or three. In part this is because surgeons are better at limiting the trauma to the body from surgery, and in part it is because postsurgical rehabilitation has improved.[1]

The Medicare Trust Fund

One of the greatest concerns today is the fiscal health of the Medicare program that provides for our elderly's physical health. The Medicare Trust Fund enjoyed assets of $325 billion in 2011. This trust fund was set up to handle the anticipated medical expenses of the baby boom generation. Like the Social Security Trust Fund, it deliberately collected more in taxes than was necessary in order to build savings for the period between 2015 and 2035, when it was anticipated that the high numbers of the baby boom generation were likely to strain the system. Like the Social Security Trust Fund, the Medicare Trust Fund is invested only in U.S. government debt. In 1997, however, the trustees of the Medicare Trust Fund issued an alarming report. They estimated that long before the serious crisis hit, the trust fund would be bankrupt. While later trustees' reports have been somewhat more optimistic about the fiscal health of the program, eventual bankruptcy remains its conclusion. In fact, in 2008 the balance of the trust fund began to shrink for the first time in its history.

The annual reports of the trustees have been based on three different projections of the future: one very optimistic, the second very pessimistic, and the third on

[1] While the data on length of stay have not shown a decline, this is misleading because of the aforementioned outpatient substitution. Since the length-of-stay data are based on the number of days a patient stays in a hospital, the procedures that are now outpatient do not count at all. If length of stay for the other procedures had remained the same as it was before the outpatient substitution, then the overall average would have risen substantially since whenever you remove short stays and leave only the longer stays, the average rises. Since the overall average has remained constant, we know the length of stay for longer-stay procedures has fallen.

FIGURE 24.4 The Medicare Trust Fund under alternative assumptions.

Source: Medicare Trustees Report.

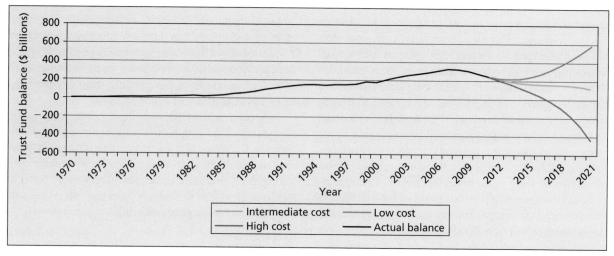

what the trustees judged to be the most realistic assumptions. Assumptions have been made about two economic variables and two demographic variables. The economic considerations have been the growth in inflation-adjusted wages and the real interest rate. The demographic variables have been the fertility rate and life expectancy. The higher the projected growth rate in wages, the more projected tax revenues would be; the higher the projected real interest rate, the better return on the trust fund would be; and because it is held that greater numbers of children will produce more tax revenue, the higher the projected fertility rate, the greater the projected tax revenues. Last, longer projected life expectancy would be anticipated to create greater Medicare expenses.

Figure 24.4 shows the actual balance of the Medicare Trust Fund from 1970 to 2011 and the projected balance of the trust fund until 2021 under the alternative assumptions just outlined. The estimates of low costs are based on the following assumptions: Real wages will grow quickly, at a rate of 1.6 percent; real interest rates will be a high rate of 3.7 percent; and fertility will be high, at 2.2 children per woman. The figures that reflect the estimate of high costs are just the opposite: Real wages will grow at 0.6 percent; real interest rates will be 2.2 percent; and fertility will be 1.7 children per woman. The intermediate cost projections are that real wages will rise at 1.1 percent; real interest rates will be at 3.0 percent; and the average woman will have 1.95 children.

If the assumptions leading to high costs are correct, Medicare is genuinely on the verge of bankruptcy. If the costs turn out to be low, the year of bankruptcy is beyond

the immediate projections of the report, but it still happens in the middle of the 21st century. The 1997 report used the intermediate assumptions and projected bankruptcy in 2008. The 1999 update of the report projected that the system would be bankrupt in 2015. The 2000 through 2008 versions have produced a relatively stable projection for around the 2020s.

The 2009 report was significantly less optimistic, while the 2010 report returned to projections of difficulties in the 2020s. These estimates have become somewhat political in that they were used to justify the need for the Patient Protection and Affordable Care Act, and assumptions were made in them that most political observers understood would never actually take place. Specifically, the rate at which Medicare reimburses hospitals and doctors was, by previous statute supposed to decline 20 percent as a result of cost estimates exceeding previously established benchmarks. Every year since the benchmarks were surpassed, Congress has acted to waive those rate reductions. As unrealistic as it is, the trustees are required to assume that Congress will not change the law, which means that they are supposed to assume that the last time Congress waived the rate reductions will be the last time they ever do.

To forestall the projected bankruptcy, it seems reasonable to consider simply raising taxes along the way in a pay-as-you-go format. This would presuppose that nothing is done to alter the current program. If we go to a pay-as-you-go system where taxes have to increase each year to meet the health care needs of the elderly, tax rates may rise substantially.

Under current law, the payroll tax that funds Part A of Medicare is 2.9 percent. That is, you and your employer each contribute 1.45 percent of everything you make on the job. (The self-employed contribute the full 2.9 percent.) Under the most likely scenario, the rate would more than double to 3.3 percent each.

If raising taxes to the necessary levels is unacceptable, other solutions may be explored. The age at which people become eligible could be raised, premiums and deductibles could be raised to their inflation-adjusted 1970 level or beyond, all beneficiaries could be required to have gatekeeper physicians (as in HMOs), and it could be mandated that at certain income or wealth levels the elderly would get reduced subsidies. Many people are dissatisfied with these alternatives, and none meet with the approval of the main lobbying organization for the elderly, the American Association of Retired Persons.

The Relationship between Medicaid and Medicare

Besides beginning with the same act of Congress and besides sharing the first six letters of their eight-letter titles, Medicare and Medicaid share other features. The most significant is a commingling of tasks when people are both old and poor. Medicare was set up to deal with only the aged and Medicaid was set up to deal with only the poor. When someone is both old and poor, both programs come into play.

When a person is of an age to be eligible for Medicare and is also poor and qualifies on that ground for Medicaid, the first to pay is Medicare. Medicaid is the payer of last resort. Since Medicare has two parts and since Medicaid's costs are shared by both the federal and state governments, the story gets even more complicated.

All elderly are required to participate in Medicare Part A, which covers hospital expenses, and they can elect to participate in Medicare Part B, coverage for doctors' visits. When people are poor as well and qualify for Medicaid, the Medicare premiums and deductibles for Part A are paid by Medicaid and the remainder are paid by Medicare. For Part B, the state can then elect to pay the Medicare Part B premiums and deductibles and have Medicare Part B pick up the bulk of the expenses. In any event, when elderly people are eligible for Medicaid, there is significant overlap between Medicare and Medicaid.

Child Health Insurance Program

In 1997 the Child Health Insurance Program was created to help the children of the working poor. It allowed states either to expand Medicaid coverage to those making less than 200 percent of the poverty line or to create a separate program to serve that population. The states have chosen a variety of strategies to implement their programs. In general, though, when a child's low-income parents have no insurance through their employer, they can purchase highly subsidized health insurance. The premiums are held below $20 per family per month, a tiny fraction of what they would be for private insurance. Similarly, the deductibles and co-payments are low as well. An interesting feature is that well-baby visits and immunizations are required to be free for children in the program.

The program is structured very much like Medicaid in that there is a matching rate for states depending on their per capita income and minimum coverage expectations to ensure that all covered children are given adequate care regardless of where they live. The matching rates are closely tied to the regular Medicaid matching rates but are, on average, 12 percentage points higher. The program now serves more than 7.9 million children at a cost of more than $11 billion per year.

Summary

At this point you understand that Medicaid is a program that covers medical expenses for a subset of this nation's poor. You understand that eligibility for Medicaid benefits is tied to family income and the age of dependent children, and, as a result, there are many people who are in poverty and not covered by the program. You understand that the beneficiaries are disproportionately women but that in other demographic dimensions they mirror those who are in poverty. You understand how much the program costs, and you know why those costs are high relative to the costs of those who are covered by private insurance. You know that a disproportionate amount of money is spent on the elderly, and you are able to articulate why that is the case. You understand the relationship between Medicaid and the companion program for the elderly, Medicare. Last, you are aware of the cost-saving measures that have been put in place for Medicaid.

Quiz Yourself

1. In 2011, a five-year-old child from a family making more than 133 percent but less than 200 percent of the poverty line is
   a. ineligible for any health care assistance.
   b. eligible for Medicare's prescription drug plan only.
   c. eligible for all of Medicare.
   d. eligible for Medicaid.

2. When a 65-year-old goes to the hospital, the part of Medicare that pays for the hospital bill is
   a. Part A.
   b. Part B.
   c. Part C.
   d. Part D.

3. When a program like Medicaid is introduced, the market demand curve for health care will
   a. increase and flatten.
   b. increase and become more steep.
   c. decrease and flatten.
   d. decrease and become more steep.

4. Medicaid spending per recipient is
   a. twice that of the average citizen's use of health care.
   b. somewhat less than the average citizen's use of health care.
   c. somewhat greater than the average citizen's use of health care.
   d. half that of the average citizen's use of health care.

5. The DRG system controls Medicare expenses by
   a. preventing doctors from using particular procedures.
   b. paying hospitals after they submit bills.
   c. paying hospitals on the basis of a disease or injury rather than expenses.
   d. paying the patient who then pays the hospital.

6. The Medicare Trust Fund is necessary because
   a. current expenses are greater than current revenues.
   b. current expenses are less than current revenues.
   c. future expenses will be greater than future revenues.
   d. future expenses will be less than future revenues.

7. Medicare's prescription drug coverage will likely
   a. cost substantially more than it was estimated to cost in 2003.
   b. cost substantially less than it was estimated to cost in 2003.
   c. cost slightly less than it was estimated to cost in 2003.
   d. cost about what it was estimated to cost in 2003.

Short Answer Questions

1. How might the elasticity of demand for a health care service be used to estimate the demand created for a health care service when there is a new program for government coverage?

2. Why is the Medicare Trust Fund estimated date of fund exhaustion so dependent on the assumption made with regard to economic growth, interest rates, and political changes?

3. What are the benefits and costs associated with reimbursing hospitals based on their actual services performed rather than based on the problems the patients have when they come to the hospital?

Think about This

One of the suggestions for providing the working poor with health insurance has been to require employers to provide health insurance benefits for all workers by having employers "buy them into Medicaid." Requiring this would raise the cost to employers of hiring new workers. Under what circumstances would this be good for workers? Under what circumstances would it not be good?

Talk about This

When public provision of health care is discussed in most political arenas, providing more coverage (e.g., prescriptions and long-term care) for the elderly typically garners more attention than expanding coverage to the working poor. Why is that? Is this the right priority in your mind?

For More Insight See

Garrett, Major, "Medicare: Healthier for Now," *U.S. News & World Report,* April 12, 1999, p. 29.

Lee, Ronald, and Jonathan Skinner, "Will Aging Baby Boomers Bust the Federal Budget?" *Journal of Economic Perspectives* 13 (Winter 1999), pp. 117–140.

Miller, Matthew, "Premium Idea," *The New Republic,* April 12, 1999, pp. 24–27.

Newhouse, Joseph, "Policy Watch: Medicare," *Journal of Economic Perspectives* 10 (Summer 1996), pp. 159–168.

Phelps, Charles, *Health Economics* (Reading, MA: Addison-Wesley, 1997), esp. Chapter 13.

"Survey: Health Care," *The Economist,* July 6, 1991.

2000 Annual Report of the Board of Trustees of the Federal Hospital Insurance Trust Fund.

Behind the Numbers

Historical data.

Federal Medicare spending.

Budget of the United States Government; historical tables—

www.whitehouse.gov/omb/budget/Historicals

Matching rates to the states—

http://aspe.hhs.gov/health/fmap11.pdf

Historical and projected Medicare Trust Fund assets, 1970–2019.

Centers for Medicare and Medicaid Services; Trustees Report—

www.cms.gov/Research-Statistics-Data-and-Systems/Statistics-Trends-and-Reports/Reports TrustFunds/downloads/tr2012.pdf

Medicaid spending and population characteristics, Medicaid and Medicare recipients, eligibility, and costs; Centers for Medicare and Medicaid Services—

www.cms.hhs.gov

www.cms.gov/ActuarialStudies/downloads/Medicaid Report2010.pdf

www.cms.gov/MedicaidDataSourcesGenInfo

Health, United States, 2010, with chartbook on trends in the health of Americans, National Center for Health Statistics—www.cdc.gov/nchs/data/hus/hus10.pdf

The Economics of Prescription Drugs

Learning Objectives

After reading this chapter you should be able to:

LO1 Apply the concepts of monopoly as well as consumer and producer surplus to the economics of prescription drugs.

LO2 Summarize why most health economists view prescription drugs as relatively inexpensive, even while most noneconomists view them as very expensive.

LO3 Explain why it is that most health economists do not favor price controls on prescription drugs.

LO4 Identify the consequences of an approval process that is too stringent or too lax.

Chapter Outline

Profiteers or Benevolent Scientists?

Monopoly Power Applied to Drugs

Important Questions

Summary

When people go to the doctor because they are sick or injured, they want the doctor to make them better. For certain injuries they may expect active treatments, like surgery. It is just part of the human psychological makeup to want to know that "everything is being done" to restore the patient's health. The same holds for the treatment of illnesses. Nothing is more frustrating to patients than to be told they have a "virus," because they accurately translate that to mean "go home and go to bed because there is nothing we can do for you." On the other hand, if patients go home having filled a prescription for a drug, they feel better simply because they think that taking medicine will make them well. In part they think this because the prescription drug industry has been so successful in treating everything from infections to impotence. When we have a virus and there is no prescription forthcoming, we lose hope for a quick end to our illness. In this sense we go to the doctor hoping for prescriptions because it is usually a drug the doctor prescribes, rather than something the doctor actually does, that makes us better.

It seems all the more strange to economists, then, that prescription drugs get as much criticism as they do when it comes to expense. The amount of money spent on prescription drugs is actually trivial relative to all health spending. In 2011, for example, all U.S. health spending amounted to more than $2.7 trillion dollars, and 10 percent of that was spent on prescription drugs.

This chapter has several purposes. We look at the degree to which prescription drug manufacturers are profiteers or good Samaritans. We use our monopoly model to discern why drugs are so costly, and we examine some of the new drugs and discuss whether they are expensive necessities or relatively inexpensive godsends. In doing this we will see the fundamental reasons why prescription drug companies are likely to remain unpopular even as they continue to provide important medicines. Last, we look at how other countries control prescription drug prices, and we offer a perspective on whether the United States should follow suit.

Profiteers or Benevolent Scientists?

Among the more interesting advertisements of the 1990s were the pharmaceutical industry's feel-good television spots that focused on a variety of hardworking scientists endeavoring to conquer a disease. These ads differed somewhat from the ads that commonly try to get us to go to the doctor to ask about problems like hair loss, seasonal allergies, or other afflictions. Just as McDonald's wants to sell burgers, so also the pharmaceutical ads are trying to sell us a particular drug. The feel-good ads are there, not to have us buy any particular product, but to persuade us to feel better about the industry in general.

Usually, the earlier ads discussed an emotional attachment the scientists had with curing the disease they were working on. A friend, spouse, relative, or parent had the disease and this, we were supposed to believe, motivated the scientist to spend long nights crouched over a microscope in search of a cure. With no attempt to criticize the scientists' sincerity, however, we know deep down that whether or not something altruistic motivates the scientist, what motivates the drug company is profit.

As with any invention, the fundamental economic problem is how to reward the inventor. Unless the inventor is given exclusive rights to his or her idea once the item has been invented, copycats can steal it. Knowing this, inventors will have little economic incentive to innovate. This is why we have laws that govern copyrights and **patents**. Within existing laws, a patent-holding inventor is the only person who can sell the invention for as long as the patent exists.

Monopoly power is particularly important in the so-called **orphan drug** industry, an industry that deals with diseases that afflict few people. Therapies that benefit small numbers of patients cannot hope to generate sufficient profits during normal patent lives for companies to justify research. For this reason drugs that are labeled orphan drugs are granted very long patent lives so that profits, though small, can be expected to last long into the future. Without this aspect of the patent law, research on such diseases would never be instituted by scientists working in the private sector.

In economic terms what this monopoly power does is give the inventor total control. As you recall from Chapter 5, monopoly means that there is one seller. It means, in turn, that there are no other companies producing the particular drug. When the drug is one-of-a-kind, as AZT was in the early 1990s, and it is the only hope a patient has, its monopoly power is dramatic. It is all the more dramatic when the disease it treats is fatal. Since most drugs cost very little to produce but may, as in the case of AIDS drugs, cost billions to discover and test, we are conflicted about high prices. We know that companies need to be rewarded for their investments, but we also find it troublesome that money has the power to determine whether a person gets a drug and lives or does not get a drug and dies.

On the other hand, when the drug is one of many, and it treats a non-life-threatening condition, as do the antiheartburn medications Nexium and Zantac, we are not at all conflicted. The problem is not life and death, and the power the companies have to charge high prices is limited only by competition and consumers' willingness to suffer through ailments that are merely annoying.

Whether we view drug companies as profiteers or benevolent scientists rests on whether they, in the end, do good and whether they charge what are perceived to be fair prices. Drug companies make a great deal of money, but they incur a great deal of risk. Much economic research has gone into studying whether their profits are out of line in comparison with those of similar industries. Although that research has not settled on a definitive answer, it does suggest that the rate of return to stockholders in the pharmaceutical industry is either at or slightly above that of similar industries. What is clear is that prescription drugs have both improved the quality of life for millions and made companies billions in profit.

Monopoly Power Applied to Drugs

As stated previously, the key economic attribute of the prescription drug industry is monopoly. While patents do run out and competition takes place in the form of generic drugs, monopoly reigns for several years at least. Figure 25.1 is the same graph that we saw in Chapter 5 for a monopolist's decision on price and production. As you know, a monopolist is the only seller of a good. This means that the demand curve that a monopolistic firm faces for its goods is the entire market demand curve. For such a firm, this has good and bad aspects. In contrast to perfect competition, the seller does not have to worry about other firms. On the downside, if the firm wants to

patent
A right granted by government to an inventor to be the exclusive seller of that invention for a limited period of time.

orphan drug
A drug that treats someone with a disease that afflicts few people.

FIGURE 25.1 The prescription drug monopolist.

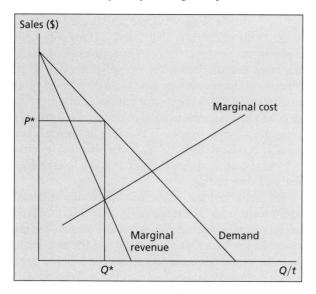

FIGURE 25.2 Comparing monopoly and perfect competition in prescription drugs.

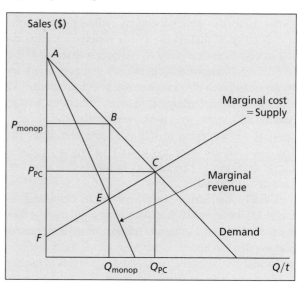

sell more goods, it not only has to lower the price to the people who will buy the extra goods; it has to lower the price to everyone else as well. This includes the people who would have purchased their goods at high prices, so the money gained from increasing sales is partially offset by the money that is lost from having to lower prices. The good news for the firm is that raising the price does not cause all customers to leave, as it does under perfect competition.

Figure 25.1 depicts a drug company that is the sole provider of a certain drug. It indicates that the marginal revenue curve, the curve that represents the additional revenue to the firm associated with the sale of one more unit of the good, is downward sloping rather than flat, as it would be under perfect competition.

Using the tools of consumer and producer surplus, we can show that with the price equal to P^* and the quantity equal to Q^*, relative to the societal optimum, the price is too high and the quantity too low. This can be seen by looking at Figure 25.2 and the assumptions that go along with it. For a moment suppose that the proper comparison to make with regard to the monopolistic production of prescription drugs is perfect competition.[1] As you saw in Chapter 5, the marginal cost curve for a perfect competitor—out of the minimum of average

[1]Because of the large innovation costs, this is a poor assumption for the industry at all stages of production but a reasonable one after the drug has been invented and approved.

variable cost—was the supply curve. If you adapt that notion here, the marginal cost curve for this monopolist in Figure 25.1 is also what the supply curve would be if the market were under perfect competition.

In Figure 25.2, monopoly is compared with perfect competition. The perfectly competitive market would produce Q_{PC} at a price of P_{PC}, because this is where supply crosses demand. The monopolistic producer charges much more, P_{monop}, and produces less, Q_{monop}, because this is where marginal cost equals marginal revenue. Our consumer and producer surplus analysis, then, allows us to show that companies profit not only at the expense of sick people, but also at the expense of society as a whole.

Figure 25.2 indicates that the consumer surplus (the area under the demand curve but above the price line) at the perfectly competitive price–quantity combination is $P_{PC}AC$, and the producer surplus (the area above the supply curve but under the price line) is $FP_{PC}C$. Under monopoly, the consumer surplus shrinks to $P_{monop}AB$, and the producer surplus rises to $FP_{monop}BE$. This means that producers are better off but not by as much as consumers are worse off.

deadweight loss
The loss in social welfare associated with production being too little or too great.

Stated differently, the **deadweight loss,** or loss to society of producing at the wrong price–quantity combination, can be shown as the difference between the sum of consumer and producer surplus between the perfect competition and monopoly situations. That area is depicted as *EBC* in Figure 25.2.

Important Questions

Expensive Necessities or Relatively Inexpensive Godsends?

In addition to the fact that we can show prices to be "high" in a theoretical sense, the data show they are also high in real life. In the United States in particular, drugs are often priced at 10 times their marginal production costs. In addition, drug prices are increasing far more rapidly than the overall inflation rate. As a matter of fact, from 1986 to 2013 drug prices went up more than 253 percent at a time when overall inflation increased general prices 111 percent. While some difference could have been expected, this difference is remarkable given that nonprescription drugs saw only a 61 percent price increase over the same period.

The reasons for increased prescription drug prices are many and varied, but they boil down to a few important issues: development costs, regulation, and litigation. There is also a problem with the mismeasurement of inflation in drug prices.

Development of new drugs costs a great deal of money, and drug companies need to recoup costs before they can make a profit. Since the "easy" diseases already have cures or treatments, we are left with some very difficult diseases to research. The training required to even understand how to start researching drug therapies takes several years after a researcher has earned a doctorate or a medical degree. People who get that kind of education for that long a period of time are going to command very high salaries once they start working. In addition to high labor costs, the equipment needed for this kind of work is specialized and expensive.

The capital and labor costs of drug research are extended even further by the years required to take a drug from successful trials to government approval. Typically, new drugs are first tested on small animals. They are then tested on primates. These tests are followed by small-scale human trials, designed primarily to gauge safety. Finally, a large-scale human trial requires that the drug be shown to work effectively while not causing unacceptable side effects. This lengthy process is expensive and it significantly extends the time before the company's revenue stream starts.

The concept of present value can shed light on how this contributes to the high costs of drugs. Let's use a numerical example to illustrate these issues. Assume a drug company sees that 1 million patients with a particular ailment are willing and able to pay for a treatment.

Suppose it costs $10 million a year for 10 years to invent a drug. Suppose it then takes another $10 million a year for another five years to test it and get it through the approval process. The law on how long a drug company has monopoly power over a drug is somewhat complicated, but we will assume that the company has that power for 10 years; after that, perfect competition takes hold and all economic profits disappear.[2] Add to this scenario the fact that few drugs make it from the scientist's lab to the pharmacy. Drug companies claim that the number of unsuccessful attempts is very high and that this is an additional reason for high costs.

Let's examine a hypothetical situation drug companies might face. Assume for every five drugs that reach the testing phase another five do not make it that far. Further, suppose that only one of every five that is tested is shown to be safe and effective. Thus for every 11 that incur invention costs, there are five that also incur testing costs. Only one produces revenue. Suppose at the very beginning of this process the manufacturer does not know which of these 11 plausible ideas will pay off, but it does know that one of them will. Also suppose that the manufacturer has a good idea that marginal production costs will amount to $10 per patient per year. Given all that, at a 10 percent real rate of return, the anticipated profit to the manufacturer from this one drug would have to be $520 million per year for the drug company to make back its initial investment. Thus, even if you ignore all of the markups that wholesalers and retailers charge from the manufacturer to the patient, the price per patient per year for our hypothetical example will have to be $530 dollars ($520 million dollars in profit/1 million patients +$10 in production costs).

In addition to all the preceding considerations, drug prices are made higher by our society's propensity for suing pharmaceutical companies. Americans sue each other more than any other group of people. Pharmaceutical firms have deep pockets. They produce products that do not work all the time and that sometimes do more harm than good. In the last 15 years, Vioxx and other Cox-2 inhibitors were approved and later had their safety called into question because they were shown to cause heart problems. Subsequent multimillion-dollar lawsuits were filed against their makers and, if upheld, they will completely wipe out the profit from the sale of these

---

[2]Manufacturers typically will make some economic profits on drugs after the expiration of the patent because of brand loyalty among physicians and patients. Drug company representatives encourage that loyalty with gifts. Sometimes these gifts are as innocuous as drug company pens while at other times they are expensive company-sponsored vacations.

drugs. With the fear of such judgments in mind, pharmaceutical firms will increase their prices so they have enough money on hand to account for such judgments and to have profit left over. In countries where lawsuits and judgments are limited, the prices of drugs tend to be commensurately lower.

Another phenomenon we must account for in analyzing the prices of drugs is that drug price indexes suffer from all of the problems that other price indexes suffer from. The consumer price index's lapses, discussed briefly in Chapter 6, are especially problematic with drugs. For an illustration of this, you need look no further than birth control pills. The pills your grandmother took in the early 1960s are nothing like those that are available now. The side effects of the early pills were much more severe than they are today. Part of the increase in the current price of birth control pills can be attributed to the improvement of quality rather than to the effects of inflation.

Taking all of the preceding into account, we are left with the fact that either drug prices are high or they seem to be high. The problem of the high expenses of drug therapies is shown very clearly in the cost of AIDS treatment. The drugs necessary to keep AIDS under control cost more than $12,000 a year. The "drug cocktail," a combination of AZT and protease inhibitors, can render AIDS a manageable disease in many. Instead of simply sedating patients as they die painfully, the only therapy in the middle 1980s, doctors can now offer many AIDS patients hope that they can manage the disease in a manner that is similar to the way patients with high blood pressure deal with their disease. That is to say, although the disease may eventually still kill them, the length and quality of their lives will be greatly enhanced. This is quite literally a life-saving cocktail of drugs, but it is one that forces many people into debt or requires that they quit work in order to qualify for Medicaid's health coverage. While bankruptcy is better than death, we can safely say that for AIDS patients this is an expensive necessity.

To counter some of the preceding negative characteristics, it must be said that the prescription drug industry can also lay claim to lowering health costs in some areas and to improving lives in nearly all areas. Drugs treat some diseases that either used to require surgery or, worse, that simply went untreated. There are drugs, also, that improve the quality of life and do so in a number of important areas. Some nonemergency heart conditions can now be treated with drug therapies rather than $30,000–$50,000 bypass or $10,000–$20,000 catheterization surgeries. Although the drugs are expensive and cannot be used when a patient is suffering from near-complete arterial blockages, they can slowly open up the arteries, and they have been shown to have a success rate that is comparable to more invasive alternatives.

In other areas new drugs have simply improved life. From ailments as irritating as seasonal allergies to those as trivial as heartburn, to those as debilitating as asthma, new drugs have made the lives of people of all ages much better. While seasonal allergies and heartburn are never life-threatening, people's lives are changed when they are successfully treated.

Before the invention of nonsedating antihistamines such as Seldane[3] and Claritin, allergy sufferers like me were hard pressed to accomplish much out of doors in the spring and fall. These medications let allergy sufferers play golf, mow the lawn, and do many other enjoyable and productive things that used to only induce fits of sneezing. Claritin was also shown to be safe enough that the FDA allowed the drug to go "over the counter" (meaning no prescription is required) in 2003. Before antiheartburn medications such as Nexium,[4] spicy, high-acid, or rich dishes were simply off-limits for many middle-aged people. While it may seem trivial to the young, being unable to eat favorite foods affects people's quality of life. Being able to eat pizza, Cajun wings, or a piquant sauce does not rank high in the sphere of important medical issues, but being able to indulge once in a while does make life a little more enjoyable.

These latter cases are also not life-threatening, but they do represent serious quality-of-life issues. The drugs that treat these ailments may not be critical to life but they represent significant advances for people. Some would classify them as luxuries, but compared to not having the treatments available, others consider them to be inexpensive.

Why then do prescription drugs get such a bad rap? It is the reality that drug prices have increased significantly faster than inflation along with perceptions that economists claim are not well founded. Our perceptions tell us that the costs of prescription drugs are much higher than the actual 10 percent of medical spending for which they are responsible. For every dollar of expense incurred in hospital or doctor visits, less than 25 cents is paid by the patient in out-of-pocket expenses. On the other hand, more than 50 cents on the dollar is picked up by the patient for prescription drugs. This leaves the patient more

---

[3]This drug was pulled from the market because it was shown to interact in potentially fatal ways with heart medications.

[4]In extreme cases this drug has reduced the risk of esophageal cancer.

RESTLESS LEGS SYNDROME?

In 2006, a major pharmaceutical manufacturer, GlaxoSmithKline (yes, it is all one word) began producing and marketing Requip. The first thing it had to do was market the disease that Requip treated. So instead of describing the drug's ability to solve an obvious medical problem, like high blood pressure or heart disease, it had to tell people about "restless legs syndrome." This is what they say about this particular malady on their website (www.requip.com).

> Are your legs keeping you up at night?® Do you dread long business meetings, going to the movies, or traveling on an airplane because you know your restless legs won't let you sit still? You just know you'll have to get up to relieve the discomfort in your restless legs—disturbing your work colleagues, other moviegoers, and fellow passengers.

The drug has made millions for the company because they have effectively convinced people who can't stand to sit in confined areas that they have a curable ailment. They have also succeeded in marketing their product to people who can't get to sleep or stay asleep because they feel a compulsion to move. The cynical among us might suspect that this is an example of marketing a drug to a population who has money. Who has trouble on long flights? Who sits in long meetings? Who can't get to sleep or stay asleep? Middle-aged businesspeople with money and prescription drug coverage, that's who. Economically speaking, the purpose of advertising is to move the demand curve to the right. In this case, GlaxoSmithKline may have created it for themselves.

aware of and sensitive to increases in drug costs than increases in the costs of hospitals and doctors.

Price Controls: Are They the Answer?

Another of the facts that must be faced with regard to drug prices is that they are higher in the United States than anywhere else in the world. That is because in most other countries drug prices are regulated. Whether the drug prices themselves are controlled or the profits from their sales are controlled, people in other countries pay much less for drugs than we do. Go to El Paso, Texas, and price a drug, and you will find it at half price or less across the border in Mexico. You find the same thing in Detroit relative to Windsor, Canada. The drug is not safer in El Paso or Detroit; it is only more expensive. As a matter of fact, it is often in exactly the same package. Prices are lower in other parts of the world and one of the reasons is certainly price controls.

Would we be better off if the government controlled the price of drugs? Probably not. The world's drug inventors eye the profit that they get in the United States when they pour billions into their scientists and laboratories. If they could not make a profit in the United States, there would be no place to make one and they would not put the money into innovation. To mix metaphors, the United States is the drug industry's cash cow; by controlling prices, we would be killing the golden goose just as she is producing some very important life-improving and life-saving eggs.

The law with respect to prescription drugs is in flux. It has been against the law for companies to buy prescription drugs in a foreign country and resell them in the United States. Otherwise, a drug company could sell its products to a Canadian company at a low price determined by Canadian law. That Canadian company would then resell them to a U.S. retailer, thereby avoiding the high price in the United States. This would have the same effect as allowing Canada to control U.S. prices. This law has been under review for some time and with the election of President Obama is likely to be changed in favor of allowing reimportation.

FDA Approval: Too Stringent or Too Lax?

The approval for, and the regulation of, prescription drugs is performed by the Food and Drug Administration (FDA). In the early 1990s the FDA was under scrutiny for not allowing drugs to come to market quickly enough. The issue then was magnified by the excruciatingly slow process of getting AIDS drugs approved. As described earlier, the FDA's process is a multistage one where a drug is tested first for its safety and then for its effectiveness. A drug can be marketed only if both meet a high scientific standard.

While this sounds very good, the problem is that people will die of afflictions for which there are already existing drug therapies. For example, in the early 1990s the AIDS-combating protease inhibitors had been shown to be safe but scientists had not yet had the time to show their effectiveness. Reasoning that unforeseen drug interactions were the least of their worries, dying AIDS patients wanted the drugs immediately. The problem of overly stringent FDA regulation is that people die when they could be saved with a less stringent process.

During the middle 1990s the FDA began to experiment with a fast-track approval process. Here, drugs that are shown to be safe get an expedited review for effectiveness. The problem is that the initial safety review is conducted using a relatively small sample of people, while the effectiveness review is conducted using a much larger one. Adverse drug interactions and relatively rare and unforeseen safety issues come to light during this effectiveness testing. Expediting the effectiveness testing causes some safety issues to be missed, and as a result the FDA sometimes has to subsequently pull drugs off the shelves. This was Fen-Phen's fate and it may end up being the fate of all Cox-2 inhibitors.

This is a prime example of how the marginal analysis of economics can be used to aid in decision making. The marginal benefit of increasing FDA stringency is the decrease in the health problems accruing to those who take approved drugs that later are found to be unsafe. The marginal cost of increasing FDA stringency is the forgone increase in the health of people who could have been treated but were not. The optimal degree of FDA stringency is where the marginal cost equals the marginal benefit.

Whether a particular drug goes over the counter is also a matter for FDA approval. When a new drug shows that it is sufficiently safe that it can be used by consumers with little or no consultation with a doctor, the FDA will approve it for use over the counter. When that occurs, the price of the drugs falls precipitously because it can be more easily mass-marketed. Whether that translates into consumers saving money is another story. It is ironic that when Claritin went over the counter in 2003, consumers without prescription drug coverage on their health insurance saw the price fall from more than $100 per month to around $35 per month, while those with insurance saw the cost to them rise because no insurance companies cover over-the-counter drugs. Former Claritin users with insurance were then motivated to seek more expensive prescription solutions such as Allegra. Insurance companies have since responded to this trend by requiring over-the-counter options to be tried before prescription options are tried.

Summary

You are now able to apply the concept of monopoly as well as consumer and producer surplus to the analysis of the costs of prescription drugs. You are able to apply those concepts to see the reasons most health economists view prescription drugs as relatively inexpensive even while most noneconomists view them as very expensive. You also understand why it is that most health economists do not favor price controls on prescription drugs. Last, you understand how economists see the issue of FDA approval and the appropriate degree of stringency.

Key Terms

deadweight loss, 284   orphan drug, 283   patent, 283

Quiz Yourself

1. The prescription drug industry is characterized by products that have
   a. low fixed costs and low marginal costs.
   b. low fixed costs and high marginal costs.
   c. high fixed costs and low marginal costs.
   d. high fixed costs and high marginal costs.

2. A patent is necessary to motivate innovation in areas where the innovation is
   a. costly to figure out and easily copied.
   b. cheap to figure out and difficult to copy.
   c. costly to figure out and difficult to copy.
   d. cheap to figure out and cheap to copy.

3. The reason orphan drug laws were created was that the motivation to invent drugs for these diseases was
   a. much greater than normal because prices could be high.
   b. much less than normal because prices would be too low.
   c. much less than normal because firms anticipated few sales.
   d. much greater than normal because firms anticipated high sales.

4. The market form for a new drug in an area where there are no competitors is
   a. perfect competition.
   b. monopolistc competition.
   c. oligopoly.
   d. monopoly.

5. The market form for a new drug in an area that has one other drug is
   a. perfect competition.
   b. monopolistc competition.
   c. oligopoly.
   d. monopoly.

6. The approval process for new drugs, if governed by economic thinking, should set stringency standards so that the _____ equals the _____.
   a. total cost; total benefit
   b. average cost; average benefit
   c. marginal cost; marginal benefit
   d. cost of production; revenue from sales

7. When an existing prescription drug goes over the counter
   a. everyone wins.
   b. drug companies win but consumers lose.
   c. drug companies lose but consumers win.
   d. drug companies likely win because of the increase in sales, and consumers may win depending on whether prescriptions are covered by insurance.

Short Answer Questions

1. What reasons are there for not limiting the price, or at least the increase in the price, of prescription drugs that have already been invented?

2. What are the reasons why, even if it is in the best interests of every other country to limit prescription drug prices, it might not be in the best interests of the United States to limit those prices?

3. Why might legalizing drug re-importation be equivalent to limiting drug prices?

4. What is lost in terms of societal welfare if, in the cause of safety, a drug or medical device has its approval delayed by a year or two?

Think about This

Vioxx and other Cox-2 inhibitors were invented because the existing pain medications (when taken for persistent pain) did damage to the lining of the stomach. After years of clinical trials, they were determined to be safe. It was only after use by millions of people that we became aware of the fact that they affected the heart. Under what conditions should their makers be legally liable for these side effects?

Talk about This

When a disease has no cure, people with the disease have no options. Suppose a prescription drug is invented but is so expensive that some patients cannot afford it. Are we better off with a drug being available, but only to those with insurance? What are the social consequences of this?

For More Insight See

Scherer, F. M., "Pricing, Profits, and Technological Progress in the Pharmaceutical Industry," *Journal of Economic Perspectives* 7, no. 3 (Summer 1993), pp. 97–115.

Behind the Numbers

Health, United States—www.cdc.gov/nchs
Overall and prescription drug prices—www.bls.gov/cpi/home.htm

CHAPTER TWENTY-SIX

So You Want to Be a Lawyer: Economics and the Law

Learning Objectives

After reading this chapter you should be able to:

LO1 Describe private property, intellectual property, and contracts and relate their importance in enabling economic growth.

LO2 Explain why a system of bankruptcy laws is necessary to a thriving economy and show why those laws must be carefully crafted.

LO3 Describe the role of civil litigation in a society and discuss how economists participate in that arena.

Chapter Outline

The Government's Role in Protecting Property and Enforcing Contracts

Private Property

Bankruptcy

Civil Liability

Summary

This chapter outlines the importance of government and a legal environment in promoting economic activity. It starts by describing why a system of laws is a prerequisite to a healthy economy and then lays out the legal framework for private property, intellectual property, contracts, and bankruptcy. It ends by describing a liability and tort system that can either aid or detract from economic efficiency depending on how it is applied.

The Government's Role in Protecting Property and Enforcing Contracts

As Chapter 3 laid out, there are times when markets fail and governments are needed to step in to correct those failures. That was not meant to leave the impression that without those "failure" conditions, the economy would function well with no government. Clearly, government is necessary to protect us from physical harm. We need

armies and police forces to keep others from hurting us. Those services are provided by government in response to a clear market failure. This chapter focuses on the legal framework under which our economy operates.

Private Property

Suppose you have a quiz on this chapter in the next hour and you are reading this book so you can study. Now also suppose that you are smart and could get a decent grade on that quiz without reading carefully and the friend sitting next to you does not have a book and is not as smart as you are. He could claim to "need" it more than you and that the gain to him of reading it is greater than the loss to you of not reading it. All that may be true, but the book is your **private property** to

private property
Land and other physical items that are owned by individuals or a group of individuals.

do with what you wish. You sacrificed $110 to buy it. It is yours. If your friend took it from you, you could have him brought up on charges of theft. Here government plays the role of protecting and respecting the importance of private property.

Why does protecting private property foster economic growth? First, it motivates you to work hard. If you work hard and produce goods and services for others, they will pay you. If you make a lot of money from working hard, you can buy stuff. You cannot count on getting to enjoy the benefits of that hard work if your earnings, or the stuff you buy with those earnings, can be taken by others without consequence. Second, government's protection of private property motivates you to save. If you save your earnings rather than immediately consuming them, you are providing the financial capital for others to buy productive machinery that they would otherwise not be able to buy. You get the reward of interest and they have the opportunity to increase their business's profit. If fear of theft caused you to consume everything you earned right away, you would not save. You would be worse off because of the forgone interest and the borrower would be worse off because of the forgone profit.

Intellectual Property

intellectual property
Written and recorded works, ideas, formulas, and other creative intangible property that are owned by individuals or a group of individuals.

copyright
A right granted by government to a creator of a written or recorded work to be the exclusive seller of that work for a limited period of time.

patent
A right granted by government to an inventor to be the exclusive seller of that invention for a limited period of time.

trademark
A right granted by government to a business to be the exclusive user of a phrase, logo, or name of such a business.

Usually, private property is the product of your hard work. Once in a while that hard work is a result of your brain power, your imagination, your creativity, or your insight. This **intellectual property** is also protected from those tempted to steal it. This book is protected by a **copyright**. So is 50 Cent's *(pronounced fiddy cent)* music . . . if that's what you call it. Similarly the recipe to the vaccine protecting you from HPV and its cancerous consequences is patented. For the life of the **patent**, only the inventing company can produce it. Finally, if you created a brand name for a blockbuster product, like BlockBuster did for renting videos and games, that name could not be used without your consent. The instrument that protects your intellectual property is called a **trademark**.

Contracts

In more advanced economies contracts are necessary to lay out the promises made by two or more parties. This typically occurs because the exchange between parties is not at the same time. When I buy a Snickers bar at a gas station, I do not need to sign a contract because I have paid for the Snickers bar when I received it. I need a **contract** with my publisher because I wrote this book several months before you bought it. I was paid my portion of the amount you paid for it about six to nine months after you bought it. Without a contract, the publisher could simply keep the money, or perhaps hold onto it for years rather than months. My contract protects me from my publisher should it decide to be dishonest. That contract also protects my publisher from my laziness. When I wrote the first edition, they paid me money in advance on the condition that I would deliver on my promise of a book they could sell.

contract
Written agreement by which each party is bound to provide other parties with goods, services, or financial consideration in exchange for other goods, services, or financial considerations.

Contracts protect both parties and make their promises binding by something other than their good word. If I thought there was a chance that I would not be paid, I would not have taken the many months to have written it and the publisher would not have made money on it. If the publisher could not hold me to our agreement that I would deliver a book, they would not have paid me in advance. From our Chapter 3 concepts of producer and consumer surplus, society is better off when the book is produced. I make royalties, my publisher makes a profit, and a student learns about why contracts are necessary. Everyone is better off because of the existence of contracts.

Enforcing Various Property Rights and Contracts

Just because we have a law that says you cannot do something does not mean that it is not done. Someone has to enforce the law. If someone steals your money, you call the police. Assuming that person is caught and convicted, the punishment is jail time. If someone copies your song, book, drug, or marketing trademark, or violates his or her part in a contract, you have to appeal to a different part of government: the civil court system. That means you have to hire a lawyer and get a court date for a judge and jury to settle who is in the right and who has to pay whom. If they agree with your claim, the intellectual property thief or contract violator is punished by being ordered to stop the violation and to pay you the money you are owed.

So even when markets are perfectly competitive, contracts and property rights are imperative to an economy's success, and government, whether it be the police or the courts, is needed to enforce those rights. Countries without stable and effective governments are typically not successful in fostering healthy economies. During the 1990s, Somalia's economy collapsed because of lawlessness. No one could count on agreements being upheld, and no one had the incentive to create goods for the market because they were easily stolen. During more recent times, lawlessness in Iraq not only prevented the U.S. military from leaving as quickly as the American people had hoped, but also prevented Iraq's economy from recovering.

Negative Consequences of Private Property Rights

Though a system of private property rights clearly motivates people to work hard and be creative, it also creates other ethical and economic issues. If you have discussed the issue chapters on prescription drugs or the cost of college textbooks, you have become acquainted with some of these issues. Ethically, how do we accept a level of global wealth inequality that arises from our system of private property? Is it ethical to possess the means by which to manage the AIDs problem and not allow the poor countries in Africa to produce the medications to do so? Is it ethical to charge $125 for a textbook that costs $15 to produce? Is it economically efficient to have monopoly production, with the resulting deadweight loss, in these goods? Economists generally agree that the system of private property motivates these goods to be produced in the first place and that removing the property rights protections would seriously reduce the incentive to produce them. The ethical conundrum and the monopoly-induced inefficiency are the price we pay for creating those incentives.

Bankruptcy

Sometimes people and firms are unable to meet their financial obligations. Either because they have come on hard economic times, have had health issues that turned into financial troubles, or simply spent more than they had, sometimes people cannot repay the money they owe. **Bankruptcy** allows people to start fresh with

bankruptcy
The legal state that allows debtors to be protected from the actions of their creditors.

their debts. The bankruptcy laws have built-in options. Some people want to keep homes and cars by agreeing to continue to pay mortgage and car payments. Some people want to get out of debt altogether.

A perfectly reasonable question to ask at this point is why, if we need government to enforce contracts, would it make sense to allow people to not repay their debts? For the answer we have to appeal to our Chapter 1 notion of incentives. Suppose you are in great debt and whatever you earn would go to paying on that debt. You would have no incentive to work if you knew there was no way out. Providing a system of bankruptcy that allows people a way out also reenergizes their incentives to work hard. Of course, when abused, a system of bankruptcy allows people to consume without ever intending to pay for it. In 2005, Congress recognized this concern when it reformed the bankruptcy laws to put tighter controls on who could declare bankruptcy and for what purposes.

Since this is a college textbook and you likely are a college student, it is also important for you to know that part of the way society pays for the subsidized interest rates on student loans is to make it so that you cannot escape them if you declare bankruptcy. They will follow you forever.

Civil Liability

Sometimes the harm one person does to another is not from taking something from them but from accidentally, negligently, or purposefully injuring them. Suppose you are driving along and crash into me in your car, and I die. My wife and children are clearly harmed. How much they have been harmed depends on what their lives are like without me compared to the way life was with me. Using this fairly straightforward principle and the notion of liability, we can determine how much my family should get from you and your insurance company.

Before we get into how much harm you have done, let's think about how the accident came about. If you were driving the speed limit, had adequately maintained your car, were not impaired by alcohol, and were not talking on your cell phone, but instead were blinded by the sun when you came around a corner we can argue that this was an accident. In most states your liability here is limited because, though you were at fault, it was an accident. Most states protect the perpetrator of true accidents with limits on their liability. If you were drinking, or had neglected your brakes, or were chatting on your cell phone, it can overcome this shield of liability and you have now become negligent and your liability is unlimited. Similarly, if you killed me on purpose because this book had bored you to tears one too many times, you would not only face civil liability, but criminal liability as well.

How much my wife has been harmed, though, is independent of the degree of your liability. So now let's assume that you were drunk and your employer knew it when he sent you out on a delivery. There is no limit on your liability or your employer's. We can now look at your legal exposure by dividing it into monetary losses and nonmonetary losses. This division is similar to the accounting cost versus economic cost division from Chapter 4.

Let's start with the monetary losses that are relatively easy to quantify. Suppose I make $75,000 per year as a professor at my university and I get pension, health, and other benefits totaling another $25,000 per year. You could find the present value of $100,000 per year for the rest of my working life and, depending on the interest rate chosen and the length of time I am likely to work, get a pretty good starting point for how much monetary damage you have done to my family. The present value of $100,000 per year for 25 years discounting at 5 percent is a little more than $1.4 million.

The problem is that you have not taken into account any pay increases I might get. You have not figured in how much this book will earn in royalties that will now be paid to a substitute author. You have not taken into account the fact that I might have died from something else. You have assumed that I will not be fired or will not just up and quit well before retirement age. You will have assumed I will retire at the "average" time. You have assumed an interest rate that is based on an assumed inflation rate. Economists make assumptions about these types of variables when testifying in trials, and all go into creating an expected present value of losses. Let's pretend for a moment that your estimates on these variables are accurate and you can modify your simple present value calculation appropriately. Having done so, you are still missing the nonmonetary losses.

If you go back and review the reasons real GDP is not synonymous with social welfare from Chapter 6, you will remember that real GDP only accounts for transactions that take place in markets. My choice to sell my labor to my university is a market decision, and both my salary and my benefits count. What does not count there, and has not counted so far, is my work around the house. Every day I get up with my children to make them breakfast and pack them each a lunch. I am a good husband

and father in that I do my share of the cooking, cleaning, and shopping. I mow the lawn, split firewood, stoke the fire in the fireplace, help my children with homework, help them sort through boyfriend/girlfriend issues, and appropriately discipline them for their errant Internet usage and excessive text messaging. What's the loss associated with all that? What about the loss to my family's psychological well-being? These implicit losses are real but difficult to quantify.

Let's suppose, for now, that the jury takes all of this into account and generates a solid, defensible verdict and jury award. Is it good for the economy? Many would argue that it is because this type of jury award forces people to understand and account for the actions they take that risk harming other people. If you recall from Chapter 3, markets fail when a person makes an economic decision without thinking about the harm done to an innocent third party. Having people think about all the economic consequences of their actions helps ensure that those actions are the correct ones. So if juries get their awards right, this serves to cause individuals and businesses to consider all the costs they impose on a society.

The problem is that juries sometimes wildly inflate the less easy-to-quantify losses. Though I am a good father, I am not worth $100 million even if the jury wants to make a statement against drunk driving or driving while cellphone talking. When firms are concerned that even when they make good-faith mistakes, they will jeopardize their very existence, they will be overly cautious. A good example of this concern is the arena of prescription drugs.

When drugs go through the FDA approval process, they are tested for both their effectiveness in treating the specific ailment for which they are prescribed as well as their safety. Assuming they are approved, they are marketed. The advertisements are often humorous without intending to be. The pitch person talks very calmly about the drug and its uses and then someone else talks very fast about possible side effects. Part of the rationale behind the fast-talking discussion of side effects is to limit the liability of the drug maker.

Consider Vioxx. It was the first in a line of painkillers designed for arthritic patients who cannot take aspirin or Tylenol because these cheap over-the-counter medications damage the lining of the stomach. After Vioxx and several other similar Cox-2 inhibitors passed the approval process, a link between heart problems and these drugs was discovered. The companies that invented and marketed them did not immediately pull the drugs at the moment the first questions were raised, but rather waited until the links were confirmed. When those ill effects were confirmed, it was off to the races with civil liability lawsuits because they waited.

Why would individuals hire attorneys when they might lose? The answer is because they don't have to worry about losing. **Contingency attorneys** are lawyers who agree to take a case on the stipulation that if their client loses, the client owes nothing. If they win, the lawyer typically gets one-third of the judgment or settlement. Contingency attorneys take cases knowing that they may only win a few of them, but as long as the payoff to the wins is very high, as it often is, they can still make a handsome living.

contingency attorney
A lawyer who agrees to take a percentage of any judgment or settlement. The attorney is paid only if the client wins the case.

class action lawsuits
Suits where similarly harmed people are joined together into one party so as to sue one or more defendants.

In other cases, where the losses to individuals are very low but where there are many similarly situated victims, attorneys create class actions. **Class actions lawsuits** are suits where the concerns of many wronged parties are grouped into one "class." A good example here is my 2002 Honda Odyssey. For whatever reason, it is alleged that the odometer on that model overestimated the true distance traveled by 5 percent. The losses to individuals are likely to be small, but the losses to the estimated

6 million Honda owners are not small in total. Because Honda settled the suit, they agreed to pay for any repairs that they would have paid for had the odometer reading been accurate. So if I had a 36,000 mile warranty and my engine blew at 37,000 miles, they would agree to fix it for free. Under the settlement, if I had already had the repair done, I could submit receipts to get my money back. Those who leased their minivans could recover a portion of their mileage overage charges. What also happened in this case, and what happens in many class action lawsuits, is that the lawyers get paid, usually rather handsomely. In the Honda case, the lawyers netted close to $10 million.

Whether this is good for the economy generally depends on whether the losses recovered by the wronged parties are significant, whether firms are more careful to account for these types of errors, and whether the firms overcompensate for the fear of losses by not producing useful goods that might generate such suits. The question of whether class action suits are, on the whole, useful devices to protect people and compel businesses to ensure their products are working properly or whether the lawsuits and the threat of lawsuits are a drain on the economy also separates the political parties. Contingency attorneys overwhelmingly favor Democrats while business interests seeking a limit on their liability overwhelmingly favor Republicans.

Summary

In this chapter we have explored the role of government and the law with respect to property, intellectual property, contracts, bankruptcy, and civil liability. We have seen that their enforcement adds to economic efficiency but comes at a cost. We have also seen that bankruptcy and civil litigation can be used as tools to enhance economic efficiency but can also be a drag on the economy.

Key Terms

bankruptcy, 292
class action lawsuit, 294
contingency attorney, 294

contract, 291
copyright, 291
intellectual property, 291

patent, 291
private property, 290
trademark, 291

Quiz Yourself

1. For a market economy to function, economists insist that government must protect
   a. private property.
   b. rights to free speech.
   c. freedom of assembly.
   d. free access to health care.

2. The type of private property that is protected by a copyright or patent is
   a. land.
   b. financial capital.
   c. intellectual property.
   d. personal property.

3. A monopolistic competitor's brand identity is protected by a
   a. trademark.
   b. patent.
   c. copyright.
   d. bond.

4. Economists insist that bankruptcy laws are always harmful to a well-functioning economy.
   a. True.
   b. False.

5. When one party harms another and the harmed party hires a lawyer who will collect only if the harmed party wins the suit, that party has hired a
   a. personal injury attorney.
   b. contingency attorney.
   c. corporate lawyer.
   d. disbarred attorney.

6. If an attorney wishes to combine the small claims of many people into one lawsuit against a defendant, he or she is engaging in a
   a. summary judgment.
   b. frivolous tort.
   c. pointed claim.
   d. class action lawsuit.

Short Answer Questions

1. Mortgages are a form of contract. Why might it not be in the best interests of the borrower, the lender, or the house buyer that such a contract be enforced if the value of the house is much less than the outstanding balance on the mortgage?

2. What are the potential costs and benefits associated with allowing for intellectual property rights? Do they always motivate innovation? Could they inhibit innovation? How?

3. What are the benefits of having a system that allows for bankruptcy? What are the costs?

4. In 2011 the Supreme Court heard a case in which lawyers were attempting to certify that all women who worked for Walmart were a single class. What would make you skeptical of such a large "class," and why would having a large class such as this make it more likely that the plaintiffs would get some settlement in their favor?

Think about This

When an economy creates intellectual property rights, it must enforce those rights. This is somewhat easy to do within a country but very difficult to do when the violator is outside the country. In China copyright infringement runs rampant, and DVDs and CDs are copied and sold by street vendors for much less than these movies and albums sell for in the United States. The United States made this an important part of trade negotiations and emphasized it more than it emphasized adherence to international labor standards. Which issue is more important to you and why?

Talk about This

The Republican and Democratic parties differ greatly on their view of personal injury and class action lawsuits. Republicans argue that these suits place a significant drain on the economy and reduce the motivation for innovation, especially in the medical arena. Democrats counter that consumers must have recourse when they are hurt or their interests are damaged by corporations. Suppose, at some level, they are both right. Where would you balance the interests of everyone in a growing but safe economy?

CHAPTER TWENTY-SEVEN

The Economics of Crime

Learning Objectives

After reading this chapter you should be able to:

LO1 Describe how economics can contribute to the debate over crime and crime control.

LO2 Describe who generally commits crime and why.

LO3 Conclude that economists who study crime often assume that criminals are rational.

LO4 Analyze the cost of crime to society and whether we are currently spending the right amount, focusing on the right criminals, emphasizing the right crimes, and enforcing the right sentences.

LO5 Apply the principles of incentives, marginal cost, and marginal benefit to crime control.

Chapter Outline

Who Commits Crimes and Why
The Rational Criminal Model
The Costs of Crime
Optimal Spending on Crime Control
Summary

Crime is a problem that does not naturally spring to mind as one for which economists would have much of value to contribute. Other than early work on crime by Nobel Prize–winning economist Gary Becker, we have not used much of our research time and money on this subject. Still, there are areas where economic analysis is uniquely suited to deal with the problems of crime. For instance, a potential criminal makes a decision to commit a crime based on the income potential of legal work, the booty to be gained from the crime, and the chance and consequence of getting caught. Couched in different words, this is not all that different from an investment decision in which small gains in safe assets are compared to large gains in risky assets. When looked at this way, economics and criminology have some important links.

The first thing we do in exploring the economics of crime is to look at who commits crime. We then see what a theoretical "investment-like" decision would tell us about who we should expect will commit crimes. Next, we use cost–benefit analysis to discuss how the

noncriminal public should devote resources in the areas of crime prevention, detection, apprehension, and punishment. Last, we use economics to study whether the goals of life imprisonment and the death penalty have the desired effects of deterring or preventing future crime.

Who Commits Crimes and Why

Most crime is committed by young men who are socially and economically disadvantaged. The victims of their crimes are disproportionately from the same group. Young black men, for example, overwhelmingly commit crimes against other young black men. Moreover, when we examine the disadvantages attributed to racism and compound them with the economic disadvantage of poor job opportunities, the problem seems to magnify. For instance, in the latest data where we have the race of both the perpetrator and victims, white people are killed by other whites in about the number that would be predicted by the overall population (86 of 100), whereas 94 of every 100 murdered blacks are killed by other blacks. In this case the number predicted by the distribution of the population as a whole would be 12 out of 100, rather than 94 out of 100.

Crime statistics generally come to us from two sources: police reports and surveys of crime victims. Those who view the police to be racially biased may argue that statistics that come from police reports are racially biased, but it is hard to believe that crime victims would have an interest in biasing their reports. Falsely reporting an attacker to the police would diminish the likelihood that the perpetrator would be caught, and doing so in a survey would not serve any useful purpose. No matter whether you measure crime by looking at arrest reports sent to the FBI or by looking at victimization surveys, the data indicate conclusively that minorities commit far more crimes than their 28 percent proportion of the populace. The question is not whether poor blacks, Hispanics, and other needy members of minority communities commit more crimes, but why.

The Rational Criminal Model

In the late 1960s, Gary Becker came up with a model of criminal behavior that explained crime in terms of a simple investment decision. According to Becker, the decision to commit a crime is one of risk versus return. The low-return investment, work at a legal job, has a low return, but the worker carries no risk of being arrested. On the other hand, the high-return investment, stealing or selling illegal goods, has a high return, but it puts the thief or drug dealer at risk of being caught and punished. In this context, a criminal is no different from an investment banker who is deciding whether to invest in tried-and-true U.S. Treasury bonds or a risky initial public offering of an Internet stock. Just as investors have a portfolio that contains a mix of risky and safe assets, you would expect to see that most criminals would have legitimate jobs as well. This is, in fact, the case.

We should take some time to explain what economists mean when they use the word "rational." To an economist, if people know what it is they want, know the constraints they face, know the costs of getting what they want, and choose to proceed with getting it, then they are rational. This does not mean that these rational people will do what society thinks is best for them. It means only that their actions are consistent with their goals, constraints, and costs. By this standard all but the insane are rational.

Crime Falls When Legal Income Rises

If a person has the potential for earning a higher income through legal means than illegal ones, then the person would be just plain stupid to pick the risky and lower-earning alternative of a life of crime. If you have the skills to be a doctor or lawyer and have a six-figure salary, the alternative of clearing $50,000 while selling cocaine is not all that attractive. Thus the rational criminal theory correctly predicts that people with high legal incomes are not likely to be prevalent in the criminal and prison population.

This conclusion may seem trivially easy to come to, but what is not trivial is how a person with a set of intermediate skills, earning $10 an hour, or about $20,000 a year, would treat the issue. To be at that level of income in today's society, most people have completed high school. It is therefore significant that less than half of those in the prison population graduated from high school, and 33 percent were not working at a legal job just prior to being arrested. Weighing a $20,000 a year job against a high-risk, high-income criminal life is hard, and the decision could go either way.

A full-time minimum-wage worker, earning approximately $14,500 (in 2013), would see the opportunity of earning a high criminal income as a significantly greater temptation than would a person making much more. We would expect that greater economic alternatives in the legal realm would translate into less crime, and fewer opportunities would lead to more crime. Why, then, did crime escalate during the sustained economic growth in the middle to late 1980s and fall during the sustained growth of the middle to late 1990s? The answer lies in the placing of economic opportunities.

If our rational criminal theory is accurate, raising a middle-, upper-middle-, or high-income person's economic prospects should have little to no effect on crime. Even without a growth in income, such a person would have virtually no incentive to turn to crime. An increase in income would simply lessen a trivially small temptation and would have no appreciable impact on crime. On the other hand, if the economic prospects changed at the low end of the economic scale, the effect on crime would likely be substantial.

In the decade and a half from the mid-1970s to the early 1990s, income inequality rose. Average income rose because the upper half of the income scale did very well, while people with little education and few job skills saw their real spending power remain stagnant or fall.[1]

---

[1] Of course, the material in Chapter 6 lays out the case that because the CPI overstates the effects of inflation, real incomes for the poor did not fall but rose slightly.

What you would expect to see from our rational criminal model did, in fact, happen. Crime increased substantially through the period, and it did so more in the lower-income groups than in the higher-income groups.

After the recession of 1990–1991, however, when crime was at a near-term high, the economic prospects of low-skill workers began to increase. The minimum wage was raised from $3.35 to $5.15 during the period, and both the overall unemployment rate and the unemployment rate for minorities and for low-skill workers fell. At the same time, either because of coincidence or because the model is right, crime fell, and it fell quickly.

The rational criminal model has a more difficult time explaining the general increase in crime during the 1960s, when incomes rose both in general and within the poor communities. This highlights an important thing to keep in mind when it comes to using economics to explain complex social phenomena. Sometimes a change in social norms, an area better left to sociologists, or a change in moral values, an area better left to the clergy, is at the heart of these social phenomena. Economics is then less capable of explaining them.

Crime Falls When the Likelihood and Consequences of Getting Caught Rise

The other variable that can change things in this rational criminal model is the probability and consequences of getting caught. We know that crime pays when you do not get caught. We also know that choosing to become a criminal becomes less attractive when the chances of getting away with crime diminish and when the potential punishment becomes more severe. It is usually true that if you knew you would get caught, you would choose a legal occupation. Sometimes, however, this is not true. For women who possess low levels of education and few marketable skills, for example, the occupation of prostitute entails getting caught regularly and going to jail for a few days as a part of the cost of doing business. The important thing here is that even given the lost time in jail, for such women, prostitution pays better than legal work.

To deter potential criminals from committing crimes, there are two things that we can do. We can make the chances of meeting punishment greater, and we can make the punishment more severe. In its simplest terms, the first implies that by having more police, judges, and jails we can increase the likelihood that criminals will be caught, be convicted quickly, and go to jail. The second suggests that we make the sentences longer or the fines greater.

Though these may seem like two aspects of the same approach, in part because we are talking about increasing spending on the same kinds of people, they are really distinct in their intent. The first is intended to make criminals less confident that they will get away with their activities. Depending on where in the judicial system the money is spent, this can provide additional funding for cops on the street, making detection and apprehension more likely, or it can provide funds for greater numbers of effective prosecutors, who may garner greater numbers of postarrest guilty verdicts. This differs from spending more money on prisons and allowing judges to sentence convicted criminals to longer terms.

Problems with the Rationality Assumption

Criminologists and sociologists have a hard time granting the assumption that the decision to become a criminal is a rational economic decision made by people capable of evaluating complex choices. In support of their view, you only have to look at the percentage of crime that is seemingly senseless. School shootings are not explainable using economic methods. One of the main criticisms of economic models is that they assume too much intellectual capacity on the part of humans. For instance, it might be argued that if criminals could evaluate the options as rationally as economists claim they can, they probably would be smart enough not to have to turn to crime. In any event, economists use the idea of the "rational criminal" when looking at criminality; and, as was seen above, the rational criminal model is often consistent with what we know about crime.

The Costs of Crime

In the latest year for which there is comprehensive national data, 2009, we spent a total of $258 billion on the police, the judiciary, and prisons. Every year 12.4 million persons are arrested and some 668,800 of that number get jail time. Currently there are more than 2.4 million Americans in state or federal jails and prisons. This is all done in response to the 1.2 million violent and 9.1 million property crimes that are reported each year. When we see these numbers, we wonder whether the money we spend is worth it, and whether the distribution of spending on police, justice, and prisons is a good one.

If we put any faith in the model we have been discussing, we are convinced that by spending money in this arena, we can change the probability of a criminal's being punished and the extent of the punishment.

Of course, we could also talk about spending the money to raise the legal income potential of people. Some people argue, for example, that we should take money that is earmarked for building new prisons and put it into education and social programs like Head Start and employment training programs that might help people to get out of poverty legally. Others point to data that indicate that these programs do not work and suggest that building prisons is the best of a set of bad alternatives.

On the central questions of whether we are spending the right amount of money on crime control and whether we are spending on the right mix of control mechanisms, we need to examine how much crime there is and how much it costs us. Using a variety of criminological surveys, we know that, of the 12.4 million crimes reported annually, more than twice that number are actually committed. Though most murders get reported, robberies, rapes, and other crimes tend not to be universally reported. Some of this may be attributed to the rationality of crime victims. If the chances of catching the perpetrator of a crime are low and the psychological and monetary costs of testifying are high, then it is quite likely that some victims will not report crimes committed against them.

How Much Does an Average Crime Cost?

When a crime is committed there are several different kinds of costs to consider. If we could put a dollar value on the average crime, we could, at least theoretically, come to an estimate of the cost of crime in general. The first and most obvious cost of crime is the value of items taken or stolen. This is fairly easily measured but it is not always very important, especially if the crime is a form of assault rather than a form of theft. Even when the crime is a simple theft, if the stolen item is replaced with insurance, the cost of the crime to the victim doesn't account for the loss to society of the theft. Insurance rates, for instance, will rise when thefts are prevalent as will extraneous theft-prevention activities that add little to actual economic well-being.

As difficult as it is to estimate tangible costs of crime, it is much harder to estimate the costs of crimes like murder, rape, and assault, because so much of those costs are intangible. There are some aspects of the loss that are easier to estimate than others. For example, an assault victim who cannot work for a few days has a loss that is at least quantifiable. On the other hand, a sexual assault victim's loss in terms of quality of life is not so easily quantified. Moreover, there is no way of knowing whether having been a victim of a crime causes people to be less ambitious or productive than they would have been otherwise.

The monetary value of psychological trauma that comes with victimization is also difficult to estimate.

There are two general methods that are used to estimate these intangible losses. The first looks at how much money individuals pay to avoid crimes by looking at the relative price of homes in high- and low-crime neighborhoods. This allows economists to create a "willingness-to-pay" measure. If people have to pay $100,000 extra to reduce their likelihood of victimization by half, then crime "costs" $200,000. This method can be used to estimate the value of a human life. If someone is willing to pay $100 to reduce their likelihood of death from one in 5,000 to one in 10,000, then they are implicitly saying their life is worth $100/.0002 = $500,000.

Another method uses jury awards in wrongful death and personal injury cases to establish loss estimates. In this method, the average jury award to the widow of a drunken driving victim is used as a proxy for the value of the life lost. The average jury award to a nonfatal accident might stand in for the intangible loss from a nonfatal assault.

If we simply ignore all of the estimated costs of pain and suffering and lives lost, then the cost of the average crime has been estimated at a little more than $1,000. Adding the pain and suffering and other intangible costs, some economists have estimated the costs at up to $10,000 per average crime.

How Much Crime Does an Average Criminal Commit?

We can use these figures to estimate the cost of letting criminals go free and compare that to the cost of keeping them in jail. If we know how many crimes the average criminal commits, we can multiply the average cost per crime by the average number of crimes committed in a year to come up with the costs imposed on society by the early release of a still violent criminal. Looking at it another way, we can compute the average cost of not catching and imprisoning a criminal.

Even when we interpret sophisticated criminological surveys, we find that the average number of crimes committed by the average criminal ranges all the way from 180 down to 10. Most economists are comfortable with estimates in the range of 10 to 20 crimes. If we assume for a moment that crime would stay the same if we eliminated all expenditures on law enforcement, the average savings from keeping average criminals off the street would range from 10 crimes per criminal times $500 per crime, or $5,000, to 20 crimes per criminal times $10,000 per crime, or $200,000.

THINGS THAT MATTER IN CRIME

An interesting investigation of this issue was conducted by economist Steven Levitt. What he found was that "community policing," whereby police are in constant communication with the communities and subcommunities that they patrol, was less effective than simply increasing their numbers. What this implies is that visibility deters crime more than anything the police actually do.

Similarly, he found that stiffening the sentence for crime had little deterrent effect, but having more criminals locked up longer decreased crime. The reason for this is deceptively obvious. He argues that the patterns of drug dealers, for instance, fly in the face of the rational criminal model. These criminals are less apt to react to increases in potential punishment when they have already chosen an occupation where death at the hands of competitors is an occupational hazard. What he found was that longer and more certain sentences worked because they prevented the convicted criminal from offending again any time soon.

In terms of economics and crime, what Levitt found was that the significant decrease in crime in the 1990s was less associated with the growing economy of the time than it was of a higher degree of "wantedness" of the children born 15 to 20 years before. In one of those conclusions that only an economist could come up with (see the discussion of how smokers help Social Security in Chapter 21), Levitt argues that the legalization of abortion in the 1970s increased the proportion of children born into homes where they were wanted. The argument, which some economists have taken issue with, is that children born into homes in which they are not wanted will grow up to commit more crime than children born into homes in which they are wanted.

Another completely separate but similarly time-separated explanation was introduced into the crime and economics literature by Jessica Reyes. Her explanation centers not on the opening up of abortion rights during the 1970s, but on the crackdown on lead in paint and in gasoline that occurred during that decade. What she found was that if you overlay a graph of the time series of the levels of atmospheric lead from 1950 to 1980 on top of the time series of violent crime from 1970 to 2002, you get a near-perfect match. The rise in crime that occurred during the 1970s through the 1990s was matched by the increase in atmospheric lead (using her approximations and estimations that were derived from lead content in gasoline and aggregate miles driven); the decrease in violent crime that was evident in the United States beginning in the middle 1990s was matched with the decreasing lead levels that resulted from a banning of leaded gasoline (and then, 10 years later, lead additives). Before you say "eureka," remember the caution from the first chapter. Even when two variables are related, that doesn't mean that one caused the other unless you can create the causal link. In this case, her proposed and plausible causal link is that lead in the air is ingested into the lungs of children and fundamentally alters their brain. This last aspect of her case is completely in line with medical evidence on the effects of lead. She then cites the medical evidence that it is how the brain is affected by lead that leads to violent crime. Specifically, lead alters the portions of the brain that allow for concentration and other portions that allow us to inhibit compulsive behavior. When both are damaged, we are less able to focus on productive work and are more likely to act on our (perhaps violent) impulses.

Which of these explanations is accurate? Perhaps both.

Optimal Spending on Crime Control

What Is the Optimal Amount to Spend?

The average cost of holding a criminal in jail is $51,250 per year. Assuming that crime rates would rise if we eliminated all expenditures on law enforcement—either by the average criminal's committing more crimes or because otherwise law-abiding citizens turned to crime—it is quite clear that the money we spend on prisons is worth it. Even though more than 1.6 million people are in state or federal prisons at a cost of approximately $82 billion a year, this may be a good expenditure.

The question of whether we spend the optimal amount on keeping people in prisons, however, remains to be answered. At this time, there are far more than double the number of felons on the street than in prison. These are people who have served their sentences, been released on parole, or were never imprisoned in the first place. If they are committing crimes at a rate similar to the 15 to 20 crimes a year that incarcerated criminals were committing, then we have too few people in prison.

Of key concern to economists is not necessarily whether the total amount spent on crime control exceeds the total amount saved from preventing crime, but whether we are spending the correct amount. At its heart, the problem is exactly the same as the profit-maximizing problem for a business firm. The mere fact that a firm's revenues exceed its costs does not mean that profit is as high as it could be. That means we are less interested in the costs and benefits of capturing, trying, and incarcerating the "average" criminal than we are in incarcerating the "marginal" criminal.

Think of it this way. Suppose we catch a prolific thief who costs society $100,000 a year, and it costs $51,250 a year to lock him up. Now suppose we catch a part-time thief who costs society only $10,000 a year, and it still costs $51,250 a year to lock him up. The intermediate or average thief costs society $55,000 each year, and we spend $51,250 per year keeping him locked up. This does not mean we should not have locked up the part-time thief. The marginal benefit to society of locking him up was less than the marginal cost.

Applying this information to the problem of optimal crime control means that we would need to look at who the people are who get arrested and put away when we increase spending on criminal justice. The practical problem is much harder to figure out than it is for a firm. In business we can see how much extra material and labor costs go into producing another unit of output and judge whether that is greater than the price, but we cannot easily determine which extra criminals are caught as a result of our spending more on police. Are these criminals more or less prolific than the average criminal caught before the spending increase? For this reason, much of the research on crime assumes that the "marginal" criminal is just like the "average" criminal.

Is the Money Spent in the Right Way?

Whether we spend the right amount of money is interesting but equally interesting is whether we spend the money in the right way. Again, marginal analysis is of use. If we spend $258 billon on the system, the allocation between police, justice, and incarceration should depend on how effective the marginal dollar is in combating crime in each category. If the optimal distribution is accomplished, the marginal benefit of a dollar should be equal in the three areas.

Are the Right People in Jail?

Of course there is the related issue of whether the right people are in jail. Of the 1.6 million people who are in prisons and 750,000 in local jails, just under half are there for violent crimes. The remainder are there for nonviolent crimes such as burglary, drug possession, and drug distribution. If these prison spaces are being used for drug offenders rather than violent criminals or thieves, perhaps the wrong people are in jail. If we release violent criminals in order to make room in prisons for drug users, we will have to either build more prisons or let the drug users go.

In recognition of this choice, state and local governments decided to go on a prison-building spree. In Texas, for example, prison capacity during the 1980s and 1990s was nearly doubling every four years. This phenomenon was certainly not confined to any one state, as state after state went to "truth in sentencing" laws that required criminals to serve at least 85 percent of their sentence. In Florida and Texas, felons had been serving less than a third of their sentences, a disparity these states and others found unacceptable.

What Laws Should We Rigorously Enforce?

In a formal way, economists look at crime control measures from a cost–benefit point of view. In Figure 27.1 the vertical axis represents the amount of marginal benefit and marginal cost associated with catching, adjudicating, and imprisoning an additional criminal. We will make three assumptions:

1. The marginal benefits are decreasing for each additional criminal.
2. We will deal with serious crimes first and petty crimes last.
3. The dollar benefits of preventing these crimes will fall.

FIGURE 27.1   Marginal cost and marginal benefit analysis and crime.

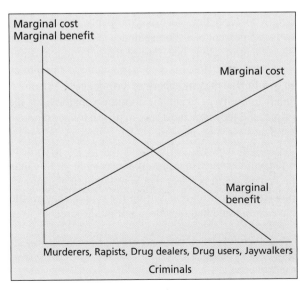

Furthermore, we will assume that the marginal cost of dealing with criminals increases because the petty criminals violating trivial laws are assumed to be more expensive to catch and convict than are criminals whose crimes are more serious. This assumption is predicated on the idea that we would have to have very many and, most important, less competent police[2] to catch such violators.

Figure 27.1 indicates that it makes sense to spend the money to catch, prosecute, and imprison all murderers, rapists, and high-end drug dealers. It also indicates that it makes no sense to do the same for jaywalkers, drug users, and low-end drug dealers. Though this picture is simplistic in its assumptions, you can see, roughly, how an economist reasons on the issue of crime control. Spend the money on the really bad guys and do not spend it on the not-so-bad guys.

That leaves one last issue to deal with in determining how we spend our law enforcement dollars: How do we divide the money among the various sectors? States, for example, have spent a growing part of their budgets to deal with crime and in doing so have changed the percentage that they allocate to the different sectors. The increase in resources has gone mainly to prisons and police, with a smaller percentage of money allocated to adjudication. Competent police are more effective in deterring criminals and apprehending criminals who have not yet been deterred. It also means that people sentenced stay in jail longer. The downside of this is that more cases are plea-bargained than ever before.

Since the increases in spending have not funded all sectors of the system evenly, criminals are more likely to be caught, plea to a crime that is less severe than the one they actually committed, and go to jail. The length of term they face has probably increased because 85 percent of a short sentence is often longer than 33 percent of a long one. Part of the reduction in crime since the early 1990s is also attributable to this policy of sending greater numbers of criminals to prison. A small minority of criminals commit a majority of the crime, and they now must stay in prison longer. Though estimates vary, an increase of 10 percent in the prison population has been shown to result in a 4 percent to 6 percent decrease in crime. Whereas some of this may be deterrence, it is likely that simply holding criminals prevents them from committing the crimes they would have committed had they been left on the streets.

[2]We assume they are likely to be less competent because cities hire the more competent of their applicant pool first, and these are all gone when it comes time to hire more.

What Is the Optimal Sentence?

One of the major debates of our time is whether criminals convicted of murder and other of the most heinous crimes should be put to death or be locked up with no opportunity for parole. While many religious leaders and lay persons alike approach this as a moral issue, economists again tend to look at it from the standpoint of the costs and benefits. If you sentence men and women to death, the sentences are carried out only after a long and drawn-out appeal process. Even then, many death row inmates die on their prison cots rather than face injection, asphyxiation, or electrocution. In economic terms we have to decide whether spending a lot of money over a 10-year period is worth the savings in imprisonment expenses. Life sentences, which are routinely given in murder cases, also have cost issues to face. If a 75-year-old is released from prison, is he or she likely to again become a menace to society?

To examine whether the death penalty saves money or costs money we need to recall the Chapter 7 concept of present value. Suppose it would take $1 million invested now to make the payments to house, adjudicate appeals, and put to death a condemned inmate. Suppose it would cost less than $1 million invested now to simply house the inmate from the time he or she is sentenced to the time that inmate would have died if given a life sentence. In such a circumstance the death penalty costs money. Otherwise it saves money. This of course assumes that the death penalty is not a deterrent. It may also be that it costs $1 million in present value to execute a person and $900,000 to imprison the same person for life, but we get $100,000 or more worth of satisfaction knowing that the worst of the bad guys got his or her due.

The cost–benefit trade-off is important also in establishing sentence length. Since nearly no crime is committed by 80-year-olds, does it make sense to sentence people to life in prison? Why not let them out when the chances of their committing a crime have gone away? It is not hard to figure that, as time goes on, a person violent enough to kill at age 18 is not as likely to commit murder at 50 and is even less likely to at 70. This point may not be worth considering since the life expectancy in prison is such that few inmates sentenced to life live long enough to outlive their own violent tendencies. Prison life is hard, and the food and medical care are not geared to keeping people healthy in their "golden years." Ironically, this makes the death penalty even less economically sensible since the "lifer's" life is not going to be that long.

Summary

You should now understand how economics, and in particular the use of marginal benefit–marginal cost analysis, can contribute to the debate over crime and crime control. Besides knowing who it is that generally commits crime and why, you have seen that economists often model criminals as rational human actors who are influenced by the risks and rewards of their decisions. You have seen how much crime costs society and how much we spend to control it. You have seen how an economist looks at issues of crime control to answer questions about whether we are spending the right amount on the right criminals and the right crimes and enforcing the right sentences.

Quiz Yourself

1. If judges had to be trained as economists before taking their position, they might use _____ analysis when deciding on the right sentence.
   a. marginal
   b. punitive
   c. religious
   d. average

2. The optimal level of police protection would compare the _____ with the _____.
   a. marginal cost of hiring an additional officer; marginal benefit of crime reduction
   b. average cost of all officers; average benefit per officer of crime reduction
   c. total cost of all officers; average benefit of crime reduction
   d. length of the average sentence; history of sentences, per crime

3. Economist Steven Levitt has drawn an unexpected connection between crime and
   a. obesity.
   b. the political party in office.
   c. abortion rights.
   d. global warming.

4. The average cost per crime has been estimated at between
   a. $500 and $2,500.
   b. $1,000 and $10,000.
   c. $10,000 and $100,000.
   d. $100,000 and $1,000,000.

5. To an economist, the correct distribution of money among police, the justice system, and prisons is one that
   a. sets an equal amount to each.
   b. sets the amount each gets equal to its average benefit.
   c. sets the amount each gets so that none is wasted.
   d. sets the amount each gets so that no other element could get better use (in terms of crime reduction) of the marginal dollar.

6. The rational crime model explains crimes of
   a. passion.
   b. stupidity.
   c. profit.
   d. love.

7. The rational criminal model draws a parallel to the thought processes of
   a. investors.
   b. educators.
   c. law enforcement officers.
   d. politicians.

Short Answer Questions

1. How would you use marginal benefit and marginal cost analysis to determine the correct sentence length for a particular crime?

2. How could you use marginal benefit and marginal cost analysis to determine whether money would be better spent keeping prisoners incarcerated or on employing more police?

3. Why is it important to use marginal analysis in examining crime policies rather than "average" (cost and benefit) analysis?

4. What other policy changes could you make now that would have a similarly delayed impact on crime several years from now?

Think about This

The rational criminal model is often invoked to explain the behavior of drug dealers and their pushers. Economist Steven Levitt disputes this by suggesting that drug dealers engage in behaviors that are just as irrational as those who play the lottery. Is drug dealing rational?

Talk about This

Under what circumstances would you engage in a criminal activity? Would your actions be rational?

For More Insight See

Journal of Economic Perspectives 10, no. 1 (Winter 1996). See articles by John J. DiIulio; and Richard B. Freeman and Isaac Ehrlich, pp. 3–8.

Cohen, Mark, *The Costs of Crime and Justice* (New York: Routledge, 2005).

Levitt, Steven D., "Understanding Why Crime Fell in the 1990s: Four Factors That Explain the Decline and Six That Do Not," *Journal of Economic Perspectives* 18, no. 1 (Winter 2004).

Reyes, Jessica Wolpaw, "Environmental Policy as Social Policy? The Impact of Childhood Lead Exposure on Crime," *The B.E. Journal of Economic Analysis & Policy* 7, no. 1 (2007), Contributions, Article 51.

Behind the Numbers

Federal justice system statistics on crime, federal justice system expenditures; number of arrests and inmates, Bureau of Justice Statistics; characteristics of victims, criminals, and types of crime committed, U.S. Department of Justice; Bureau of Justice Statistics; crime and victim statistics—www.bjs.gov

Crime in the United States, Federal Bureau of Investigation—www.fbi.gov/about-us/cjis/ucr/crime-in-the-u.s

CHAPTER TWENTY-EIGHT

The Economics of Race and Sex Discrimination

Learning Objectives

After reading this chapter you should be able to:

LO1   Describe how economists measure the income disparity between the races and sexes.

LO2   Define what discrimination is, how it is measured, and how it is detected.

LO3   Model discrimination in the labor market and summarize the evidence for its existence in the markets for real estate, automobiles, and lending.

LO4   Describe what affirmative action is; how, why, and when it came about; and what forms of it exist today in the United States.

Chapter Outline

The Economic Status of Women and Minorities

Definitions and Detection of Discrimination

Discrimination in Labor, Consumption, and Lending

Affirmative Action

Summary

African Americans and women have been subjected to discrimination throughout history. That discrimination exists is not a surprise, but its precise detection and measurement are not as simple as they may seem. Some of the differences in income and wealth are diminishing over time but nontrivial gaps remain. This chapter explores the economic status of women and minorities, discusses the varieties of discrimination economists recognize, and moves to explain them. In so doing, the chapter discusses the means of detecting discrimination and seeks to model its impact on wages. The chapter moves on to explain why, absent legally sanctioned discrimination, some economists thought wage gaps would close quickly and why other economists correctly predicted that those gaps would remain, even in the presence of laws forbidding discriminatory practices. Finally, the chapter ends with a discussion of affirmative action, its economic justification and machinations.

The Economic Status of Women and Minorities

Women

Women are becoming an ever-growing part of the U.S. economy. Economists call the percentage of people in a particular category who are over 16 and working the **labor-force participation rate.** The rate for women has been rising steadily for decades, from 38 percent in the early 1960s to 57 percent today. While the rate for men is higher than that for women, 70 percent, it has been steadily decreasing. Demographers, the people who study population trends, adjust the labor-force participation rate to reflect the fact that as the U.S. population ages, more people

labor-force participation rate
The percentage of the population of a group that is employed or seeking employment.

are in age groups likely to be retired from work. For this reason, they suggest that the real importance of women in the workplace is even greater than the raw participation rate suggests.

What is also important from an economic perspective is that though men and women are approaching equality in income and wealth, men still have 56 percent more income than women, make 24 percent more in wages for full-time employment, and are less likely to be in poverty. Though more couples file for bankruptcy than single men or single women, the incidence of single women filing for bankruptcy has increased substantially, while the incidence of couples or men filing alone has remained steady. Finally, single men have 46 percent more wealth than single women. The differences are summarized in Table 28.1.

This is not to suggest that the economic status of women is not improving. Figure 28.1 shows that the ratio of women's to men's weekly wages for full-time employment and the similar ratio for money income from all sources continue to increase. Still, as Table 28.2 suggests, even when you look at identical professions, women currently make less than men.

Minorities

There are two clear trends in the data on economic and social conditions affecting the races. Inequality within the

TABLE 28.1   Economic differences between men and women.

Sources: www.census.gov/hhes/www/income
www.bls.gov/cps/cpsaat39.pdf
www.census.gov/hhes/www/poverty
www.census.gov/hhes/www/wealth
www.financiallit.org/PDF/2010_Demographics_Report.pdf

	Men	**Women**
Income from all sources	$ 32,986	$ 21,102
Median weekly wages for full-time employment	$ 854	$ 691
Mean net worth (singles)	$136,607	$93,732
Poverty rate	13.6%	16.3%
Percentage of single-filing bankruptcies	48%	52%

TABLE 28.2   Median full-time wage earnings: selected occupations.

Source: www.bls.gov/cps/cpsaat39.pdf

Occupation	Women's Earnings as a Percentage of Men's
Physicians	68
Lawyers	80
Managers/Executives	73
Teachers (elementary)	82

FIGURE 28.1   Ratio of women's income to men's.

Sources: United States Census Bureau, www.census.gov

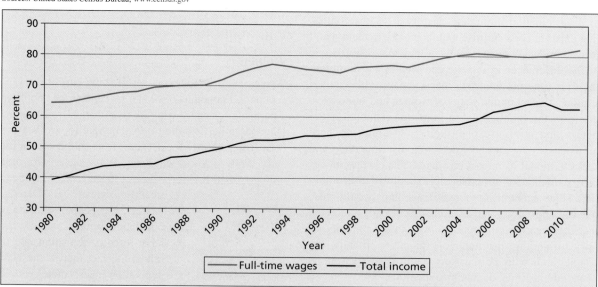

races is clearly documented, and the degree of inequality is lessening. The clearest sign of this phenomenon of shrinking-but-not-yet-zero inequality can be seen in the data on median family income for white and black families. Figure 28.2 shows us that since 1967 median family income has risen from $8,234 to $64,081 for white families and from $4,875 to $40,472 for black families.

Figure 28.3 indicates that while the gap in income between black people and white people is widening in absolute terms, the ratio of white median family income to black median family income is narrowing. This means that while white families still enjoy the benefits of more income, the income of black families is increasing at a faster rate than that of white families. The ratio of white family income to black family income remains significantly less than 1.0 (its value if perfect equality existed),

but it has grown from .52 in 1950 to .632 in 2011. It is worth noting that the 2007–2009 recession was harder in economic terms on African American families than it was on white families.

Other economic measures provide us with additional data on the inequalities that exist between African Americans and whites. For instance, in 2010, for salaried and full-time hourly workers, median weekly earnings are $792 for white workers and $621 for black workers. In this arena, the ratio of .78 shows we are closer to equality, but this ratio has remained constant for nearly 20 years, and in fact declined following the recession of 2007–2009.

Although there remain many signs of astonishing economic inequality, there are also signs of significant progress. Nevertheless, only 24 percent of African

FIGURE 28.2 Median family income.

Source: United States Census Bureau, www.census.gov/hhes/www/income

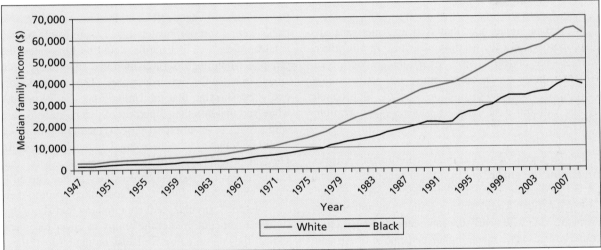

FIGURE 28.3 Ratio of black to white family income.

Source: United States Census Bureau, www.census.gov/hhes/www/income

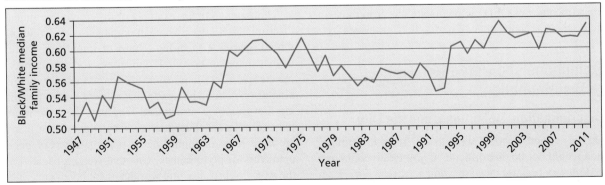

Americans are in the top 40 percent of income earners, whereas 57 percent are in the bottom 40 percent; moreover, unemployment rates across age categories are several percentage points higher for blacks than whites. A particularly troubling aspect of the 2007–2009 recession was that while unemployment was rising across the board, it was affecting African Americans disproportionately. In particular, black teenage unemployment rose to 49.2 percent in September of 2010. That level was more than twice white teenage unemployment. Encouragingly, the growth in the number of businesses owned by members of minority groups has been astounding. Between 1987 and 1996 the number of such firms grew by 46 percent and their receipts by 63 percent.

We cannot escape the fact that black children are more than twice as likely as white children to be in a female-headed household. Because family structure is a key determinant of economic well-being, this social problem of single-parent (overwhelmingly female) households is a major cause of the economic disparity that African Americans face.

It must be noted, too, that African Americans are disproportionately the victims of crime. In any given year, 2.4 out of 100 African Americans are victims of violent crime, whereas only 2 out of 100 whites are so victimized. The racial distinction is greatly highlighted by the difference in rates of robbery victimization. Blacks are three times more likely to be victims of robbery than whites.

In the arena of educational achievement, African Americans are graduating from high school at a much faster rate than they were in 1960. Unfortunately, the rate at which African Americans are graduating from college is not growing with nearly the same rapidity. In part, this could be because a much higher percentage of African Americans get their high school diploma with a general equivalence degree (GED) than whites. Many colleges, moreover, are less enthusiastic about GEDs than actual high school diplomas. Further, white or black, the average incomes of GED recipients are closer to those of high school dropouts than of high school graduates.

Definitions and Detection of Discrimination

Discrimination, Definitions, and the Law

On the surface, it would seem that defining discrimination would not be that difficult. If you treat people in a certain way because they are women, African American,

or Hispanic, you are discriminating. To make matters more complicated, however, there are two types of discrimination rather than just one. If you treat two otherwise equal people differently and do so on the basis of their sex or race, then this is called **disparate treatment discrimination**. If, on the other hand, you do something that is not necessarily discriminatory on its face but that impacts some groups more negatively than others, you are engaging in what is called **adverse impact discrimination**.

disparate treatment discrimination
Treating two otherwise equal people differently on the basis of race.

adverse impact discrimination
Doing something that is not necessarily discriminatory on its face but that impacts some groups more negatively than others.

While both forms of discrimination are usually illegal, adverse impact discrimination can be acceptable as long as the persons or companies doing the discriminating can show that what they are doing makes sense for their needs. For instance, if whites sued the National Football League (NFL) on the basis that defensive backs were disproportionately black, there would be two legal hurdles. The first hurdle would be for whites, the group at whom the discrimination had supposedly been aimed, to show the "adverse impact." They could do this easily, by showing that the United States is 70 percent white and that less than 3 percent of defensive backs are white. With adverse impact proved, the burden of proof would be transferred to the accused, in this case the NFL. The NFL would have to show a "business necessity" that led the teams to make the choices they made. The NFL would win in court if the teams could then point to their tests of speed, strength, and conditioning and show that (1) these tests did predict the ability to cover receivers, and (2) they chose defensive backs on the basis of these tests. Thus, while differential treatment discrimination is always illegal, adverse impact discrimination is illegal only when it cannot be defended on the grounds that it stems from a business necessity.

The more common example of differential treatment discrimination arises when an employer uses a rule-of-thumb approach to hiring. Rules of thumb are useful in that they can be simple guidelines for people making complex decisions. Some economists who study this kind of discrimination assert that rules of thumb for hiring are generally perpetuated long past the time when they are relevant. Furthermore, they suggest that many of those rules of thumb never really were very good predictors of performance. One that was propagated in the world of broadcasting was that men, being generally

SOCIOLOGY OR ECONOMICS: WHY WOMEN EARN LESS THAN MEN

A multitude of studies compare women's pay to men's. Many economists do the comparison by controlling for education, full- or part-time status, experience, job requirements, and a host of other factors to determine whether men and women earn the same money for the same work. Sociologists and nearly all feminists view this as fallacious because they see these as symptoms of continued mistreatment of women, rather than economic phenomena that should be statistically controlled. The issues are:

- All income versus earned income: As shown in Table 28.1, if you focus on the broad issue of relative incomes, women earn only 64 percent of what men do, but if you focus more narrowly on the differences between what women and men earn when they both work full time, the ratio is narrower: Women earn 81 percent of what men do.

- Experience with the same employer: Men have been with their current employer for a median 4.7 years; the comparable figure for females is 4.6 years. It is notable that this gap has nearly been eliminated in recent years.

- Different professions: Only 31 percent of lawyers, 34 percent of doctors, and 14 percent of engineers are women. On the

other hand, women account for 95 percent of secretaries, 89 percent of nurses, 81 percent of elementary school teachers, 93 percent of day-care workers, and 81 percent of social workers.

- Pregnancy and child rearing: While it is illegal to discriminate based on pregnancy, any opportunity that a woman loses and a man gains can result in young professional fathers being promoted more quickly than young professional mothers. Since only women can give birth and 98 percent of stay-at-home parents are women, women lose opportunities.

- Flexible employment: For reasons that are primarily sociological, women rather than men pick flexible employment so that they can deal with their family's needs. Flexible jobs also happen to be lower paying.

Are these legitimate economic consequences of choices that people make freely and knowingly or are they manifestations of discrimination itself? That is a debate for you to have with your fellow students and your professors of economics and sociology.

---

more interested in sports, would make better sports broadcasters. Although it may be true that men watch more sports, that does not say anything about whether a particular man or a particular woman would be better for a particular job. Furthermore, many rules of thumb, like the notion that men are better drivers, never were good predictors of performance on the job.

Even when there is a concretely accurate rule of thumb, discrimination is illegal. This form of discrimination is the economic equivalent of racial profiling, which we hear about with regard to police tactics. In economics,

rational or statistical discrimination
Unequal treatment of classes of people that is based on sound statistical evidence and is consistent with profit maximization.

such discrimination is labeled by some as **rational or statistical discrimination** because it is based on sound statistical evidence. It is referred to as "rational" only because it is consistent with the recognized goal of firms of maximizing profit. For instance, it is a

fact of life in the United States that when a bank consults with the best statisticians and economists, it finds that African Americans are 2 percent more likely to default on a home loan. This is true even when the study holds income, occupation, and a host of other important variables

constant. If lenders use this information to charge blacks a higher interest rate for mortgages, or if they use this information to set a higher standard for blacks to qualify for a loan, they are guilty of "statistical" discrimination.[1] Regardless of whether it makes economic sense, it is illegal to use race in any part of the lending decision.

Detecting and Measuring Discrimination

Detecting and measuring the extent of discrimination in an authoritative way are not always easy. If a Hispanic female high school dropout and an affluent white male college professor each went into a bank to ask for a loan, and the high school dropout was denied the loan and the professor got one, we would not automatically assume we were looking at a case of gender or race discrimination. We would have to separate out the reasons why one person got the loan and the other did not.

There are two ways that economists try to do this. First, they use the statistical technique called "regression" to look for systematic patterns in the data. Once

[1]Another interpretation of this finding is that it is actually whites who are being discriminated against since, all else being equal, they are defaulting less frequently than blacks. This implies that they are being turned down too often.

they figure the appropriate values using a statistical computer program, regression analysis tells them the impact of one variable on another holding the effects of other variables constant. It allows them to say, with degrees of certainty, that a variable like race or sex has a specific impact on another variable, like whether or not a loan was approved, even when they hold other variables like income constant. When many different people, from many different backgrounds, with different incomes and debt histories seek loans from many different banks, the regression technique can, when correctly applied, determine whether being African American or female makes an applicant less likely to get a loan.

The second technique involves creating fake identities for people who are exactly alike except for their race or sex. These "auditors" approach a situation one after the other to see if they are treated differently. Since everything other than race is held constant, any differences in the way the auditors are treated must be related to race. A fascinating example of this work was conducted by economists Bertrand and Mullainathan. They showed that on purely fictitious and functionally identical resumes, applicants with names like "Emily" and "Greg" were statistically, substantially, and depressingly more likely to be called for an interview than applicants with names like "Lakisha" and "Jamal."

These two techniques have their critics. This may, at least in part, be because of the somewhat different conclusions the techniques have led economists to make. Generally, regression techniques expose a smaller race bias problem across the board than is exposed by audit techniques. Typically, those who advocate regression measurement rather than using auditors say that the fictitious auditors themselves may create part of the disparity by the way they act. They also say that the exactness of the match is less than reliable. On the other hand, the advocates of auditing suggest that variables included in regressions, like intelligence scores, are themselves biased or indicative of other past discriminatory practices and therefore always understate the true problem.

Discrimination in Labor, Consumption, and Lending

Keeping these basics in mind, we turn now to three areas of the economy in which professional economists have studied discrimination in some depth. These areas are the labor market, where people sell their labor to firms; the goods market, where people buy things; and the lending market, where people borrow money.

Labor Market Discrimination

We can start exploring the effect of discrimination in the labor market by assuming a world, like the 1960s, where it is legal and openly practiced. In Figure 28.4, suppose there are two kinds of jobs: jobs that only whites are allowed to do and jobs that whites are allowed to do but blacks must do if they want jobs.[2] In a world where there is no discrimination, the nondiscriminatory supply curve S_{ND} crosses the demand curve at a wage W_{ND} that is equal for blacks and whites. In the world where such discrimination is legal and binding, the supply of workers available to perform tasks limited to whites only (left panel) is less, S_D, and therefore the wage that must be paid to whites is greater. Because blacks must perform the other tasks, the supply of workers available in that market (right panel) is greater and therefore the wage is lower.

Thus with discrimination that is legal, whites make more than blacks. The question is: If discrimination is held to be illegal, is that sufficient to eliminate the wage differential? Beginning with the work of economist Gary Becker, the profession showed theoretically that without a legal basis, discrimination and wage differentials would go away. In the 1960s the economics profession was confident that profit-oriented but open-minded business owners would want to make as much money as possible and would therefore ignore skin color. If employers employed people to do what used to be considered "a white man's job" and were right in assuming that the only reason blacks had been previously prevented from doing the job before was racism, then the African Americans would be able to do the job just as well as whites. That, in and of itself, however, would not motivate

FIGURE 28.4 The effect of racism on white and black wages.

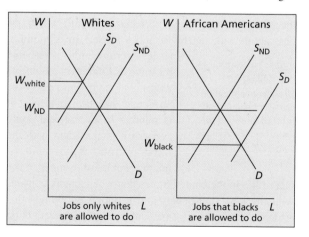

profit-oriented business owners to hire blacks. What would motivate them would be that they could offer blacks a little bit more than their other jobs paid but less than they were currently paying whites. In Figure 28.4 this would be between W_{black} and W_{white}.

If profit-oriented managers were to hire African Americans at just above the W_{black} wage that is depicted in the right panel of Figure 28.4, they could get all the labor they need at much lower cost than they would have had to pay white workers, W_{white}. Thus the business manager's desire to make money can serve to narrow the wage gap, at least a little.

As other managers see the advantage of hiring lower-paid, equally skilled African American labor, the wages among African Americans would continue to rise as firms seeking cheaper labor attempt to outbid each other. Thus a traditional economist argues that in time nothing more than removing legal impediments is required to achieve equality. The idea that greed prevails over bigotry remains steadfast in the minds of many economists.

Considering that wages are not equal 35 years after the civil rights movement's heyday, however, there must be obstacles that simple economic incentives have not been able to overcome in equalizing wages. The first thing to consider with regard to whether economic profit incentives will overcome racism is that people will pay extra, when they want to, to satisfy their bigoted nature. Managers will pay a little extra not to have to work with "them," regardless of whether "them" is women, blacks, gays, whites, or anyone else. Presumably bigots are willing to pay to support their bigotry.

Another problem is that some people will patronize only businesses where not any of "them" are around. Even if you are an open-minded, profit-oriented manager, if you see that your business decreases whenever you hire more African Americans, you may decide to hire only whites, and you will pay more to attract them. You may do this even though you know it is illegal and morally wrong. It is a fact of life that if you are a manager and your livelihood depends on satisfying your customers, you may do things you would not otherwise do.

It is for these reasons that, even though the wage gap between whites and blacks has shrunk, it has not disappeared. Regression analysis shows that it remains at between 12 percent and 15 percent.[3] Remember that the

regression results hold constant things that are supposed to determine pay such as education and occupation. Because African Americans have attained a lower average level of education and because they are less prevalent in high-income occupations, you would expect that they would be paid less. What this also means is that the actual difference in pay is much greater than the 12 percent to 15 percent that these regression studies indicate. In an apparent contradiction, studies limited to well-educated professionals show that being a black woman actually pays a premium. This is interesting but it lacks practical significance since most African American women are not well-educated professionals.

Consumption Market and Lending Market Discrimination

While it is easy to imagine discrimination in the labor market, where people either are denied positions or are hired for lower pay, it is harder to imagine in the market for goods. You never see a Walmart charge a white man $65 for a car battery and then charge a Hispanic woman $75. There are areas in the goods market, however, and especially in the services market, where the races can be and are treated differently.

At first it would seem rather silly for a business to discriminate and turn away profitable sales. What you have to consider, though, is that audits performed by various economists and government investigators have shown that discrimination is in fact quite prevalent in real estate sales, rentals, and car sales.

In real estate, audits show that real estate agents of both races tend to show white clients more houses. Moreover, they show white families houses in all-white neighborhoods while diverting black families to houses in black or integrated neighborhoods. The same results were evident when auditors looked for rentals. Why would real estate agents do this? Why, in particular, would black real estate agents do this? There appear to be a couple of explanations.

The first possibility is that agents are simply trying to make the clients happy, and they think they are doing this—and may in fact be doing this—by showing housing in areas where they think the clients want to live. Salespeople make judgments all the time about what will make their clients happy, and they do so with very little to go on. The economists who uncovered this form of discrimination attribute this behavior to racism and call it discrimination. If a significant segment of African Americans really do want to live in already-integrated neighborhoods rather than move into another

[3]Some economists have found that when they include standardized tests of intelligence, this remaining difference disappears. These tests and their use in this context are hotly debated by economists. The economists who employ the results of the tests believe the tests are truly tests of intelligence, whereas others contend that the tests are racially biased and therefore of no value.

neighborhood to become the only minority family in the area, the economists are incorrect when they label this behavior as discrimination.

The second possibility is that both the black and white agents have regular clients in the neighborhoods that contain the apartments or houses that are available, and they do not want to anger their regular clients by upsetting the racial "balance" in the neighborhood. The audits do not include interviews of the agents, so the data do not show whether either of these scenarios accounts for the discriminatory practices that exist when realtors are showing properties to their clients. If you live in a neighborhood originally developed before 1975, you might be shocked to find the covenants for your property probably include a line like the one I found in mine:

> No person of any race other than Caucasian shall own, use or occupy any lot or building in this subdivision, except that this covenant shall not prevent domestic servants or employees of a different race domiciled with an owner tenant.

Another area where economists have found race and sex discrimination in the market for goods is in automobile sales. Auditors found that even when they used the same bargaining strategy, made it clear they would be paying cash, and were talking about the same car, dealers charged blacks and women more. The usual method of the audit had blacks and whites, men and women going into the same dealership within a short period of time and asking a salesperson to tell them the asking price for a specific car. In each case the auditors would then offer a price they had previously decided to offer and then they would use a "split the difference" bargaining technique until the salesperson and they arrived at a final price. What happened was that the initial offer made by both black and white car dealers was lower for whites than it was for blacks. The dealers also agreed to sell cars to whites for lower prices than those for blacks. The economists who performed these audits concluded that, on the average, black women pay $1,000 more, black men pay $800 more, and white women pay $400 more for a car than do white men.

Why would dealers do this? Though the bias was less evident when the dealers themselves were women or minorities, they still discriminated against blacks and women. It seems as if either the dealers did not want the sales or dealers have preconceived notions of sales resistance and bargaining strategies. It may be they believe they can outmaneuver African American and female customers.

Another area where economists have investigated and found serious race discrimination is the area of mortgage lending. Because it is rare that banks offer anything but a single interest rate, the question is whether blacks are more likely to be turned down for loans than are whites. Again, audits found that given nearly identical economic characteristics, blacks were somewhat more likely than whites to be turned down for a loan. It seems likely here that, short of bigotry, banks, which use both objective standards and subjective standards in making their decisions, have discriminatory prejudice in their subjective standards. As we said before, it has been shown that blacks and whites of equal economic standing have different default rates on mortgage loans. It may be that the loan officer who denies a mortgage to a black couple that would have been approved for a white couple is doing so in a "rational" sense. Nevertheless, this discrimination remains a violation of law, and banks are currently being monitored and penalized for such practices.

Some economists claim to have noted sex discrimination in retirement annuities. Whether it is actually discrimination, men have better choices than women because women live longer than men by more than half a decade. Insurance companies that offer annuities have to charge women more than men, offer fewer benefits to women than men, or split the difference in some other way so that women end up paying somewhat more and being paid somewhat less. Making it illegal to charge women more than men for such annuities would not change these facts. It would merely force companies to indulge in what would amount to a redistribution of wealth from men to women.

Affirmative Action

The Economics of Affirmative Action

As you saw in the preceding discussion, there are conditions under which discriminatory behavior can continue long after it is declared illegal. Either because employers may be bigoted or because employers may have customers who are bigoted, discrimination in employment exists even in a perfectly competitive market. This means that the perfectly competitive market may fail to arrive at the socially optimal level of employment for minorities. Minorities will be underemployed and underpaid, and whites and men will be overpaid for the work they are doing and get jobs for which they are not as qualified.

Anytime a market fails to achieve a situation where consumer and producer surplus combined are maximized, economists are interested in actions that can correct that market's failure. Though corrective policies for failed markets have costs, they are seen by economists as necessary investments that will ultimately pay dividends. In this context the corrective policies are called **affirmative action**. Affirmative action is any policy that is taken to speed up the process of achieving equality.

affirmative action
Any policy that is taken to speed up the process of achieving equality.

The costs of affirmative action policies range from the costs of more thorough searches for employees to the cost of monitoring fair hiring practices with a fully staffed human resources office. These costs can be seen in the same context as any costs associated with correcting a failed market. For example, though it costs industry money to clean up pollution, expenditures to do so by industry, which are mandated by the government, make us better off in the aggregate than we would be without them. When affirmative action is utilized to correct an inequality that is seen as permanent, affirmative action supporters view it very much like scrubbers on coal-fired plants: It is money spent to fix a market failure. If affirmative action exists to speed up a transition from inequality to equality that would have happened eventually anyway, these are seen as costs that diminish the market failure by shortening the time it exists.

On the other hand, if the market differences between minorities and whites and between men and women only reflect the differences in the skills of the groups, then the market is not failing. If this is the case, then any attempt at affirmative action imposes a cost on, rather than a benefit to, the economy. In such a case, the costs of affirmative action should be viewed as buying "fairness" rather than fixing a market failure.

What Is Affirmative Action?

Even if traditional economic models correctly predicted that pay gaps between men and women and between whites and minorities would eventually be eliminated without needing such influences as affirmative action, there is the problem of time. Affirmative action came about because proponents wanted to achieve equality more quickly. To the degree that equality is not arriving fast enough through economic incentives, advocates have asserted that further affirmative action be taken to speed up the process.

Gradations of Affirmative Action

Affirmative action's many forms range from the inconsequential to the highly consequential. For instance, many citizens hold as conventional wisdom that affirmative action consists of quotas that mandate the number of people who must be hired, promoted, or admitted. As a matter of fact, explicit quotas are rare and, unless they have been ordered through a court decision, they are illegal. On the other hand, many other policies can be engaged in that stop far short of quotas.

One form of affirmative action is simply to make sure that all potentially qualified employees know about a particular job. So, for instance, if you were hiring production workers in a southwestern city, affirmative action could consist of your advertising in both the English- and Spanish-language newspapers. If you were hiring in a city that had a radio station whose audience was primarily African American, under this form of affirmative action you would advertise there alongside radio stations where audiences were predominantly white. This form of affirmative action requires that employers cast the net wide when looking for new hires. It places very little burden on employers and it gives no one any sort of unfair advantage. The only people who might be perceived as disadvantaged would be those who previously had an unfair advantage. These might be those who were less qualified but got jobs because minorities were not aware particular jobs were available.

Another form of affirmative action has held that if two applicants are judged to have equal qualifications for a position, then the one who is a member of a minority should automatically be hired. Just as in baseball where "tie goes to the runner," this form of affirmative action suggests that "tie goes to the minority." The advantage to the minority group members here is that once they have shown they are equally qualified, their chance of being hired goes from 50–50 to 100 percent, and the disadvantage to the member of the majority is that the chance of being hired goes from 50–50 to 0 percent.

A third, higher level of affirmative action is one in which an employer sets a level of qualification that is appropriate for a job, hires all minorities who meet the standard, and then fills out the remaining slots with nonminorities. When universities make decisions about whom to admit, and they use criteria to further affirmative action, they often conduct them in the following way: A school will decide that an SAT of 1,000 is sufficient to make graduation likely and admit all minorities who meet that standard. The remainder of the student body is then generated from the best of the rest, a pool of students whose SATs may well be above 1,000.

A fourth version of affirmative action, just short of a quota, is establishing a guideline that employers should

MYTHS OF AFFIRMATIVE ACTION

Economists Roland Fryer and Glenn Loury studied affirmative action policies and concluded that the mythology of the practice sometimes overwhelms the reality.

Myth 1: Affirmative Action Can Involve Goals and Timetables While Avoiding Quotas

They argue that because those looking for discrimination cannot see into the heart of the potential accused, the hiring, loaning, or admitting entity will likely create an "implicit quota" to achieve its goal.

Myth 2: Color-Blind Policies Offer an Efficient Substitute for Color-Sighted Affirmative Action

They point to reactions in California, Florida, and Texas when affirmative action policies were banned in college admissions. They argue that the attempt to use income or high school location as a proxy was ineffective and that getting the best, most diverse class of students is hampered by using proxies for race rather than race itself.

Myth 3: Affirmative Action Undercuts the Incentive to Invest in Yourself

They argue that though whites may not see as much payoff to educational investments, African Americans will see a greater payoff to education. Which effect is greater, they argue, is an unsettled empirical question.

Myth 4: Equal Opportunity Is Enough to Ensure Racial Equality

They argue that because social networks ("who you know") matter a great deal in hiring practices, previous advantages are likely to maintain themselves for a very long time.

Myth 5: The Earlier in, the Better

They argue that this is an empirical question where the data have not yet shown that earlier investments in more equal education will assist later outcomes in graduation rates.

Myth 6: Many Nonminority Citizens Are Directly Affected by Affirmative Action

They argue that far more whites and men believe they are passed over because of affirmative action policies than actually are.

Myth 7: Affirmative Action Always Helps Its Beneficiaries

They argue that affirmative action has reduced the graduation and bar passage rates of African American law school students because they are admitted to schools where they are less likely to flourish.

try to meet. The idea behind this is to ensure that employers can be somewhat flexible while also ensuring that the proportion of minorities not be allowed to drop too low. In military promotions, for example, if the racial, ethnic, and gender proportions of those promoted are not roughly equal to the racial, ethnic, and gender proportions of those eligible for promotion, the promotions board must file a report justifying the discrepancy. That means that though there is no specific number that must be promoted, any deviation from the guideline is suspect.

The final version of strictness associated with affirmative action is quotas. Surprisingly, the quotas that most people think of when they think of affirmative action are actually against the law as a general practice. Quotas are legal only when court-mandated, either through a verdict or a consent decree. Sufficient grounds must exist to show that a particular employer or university has been guilty of discrimination in the past to make quotas legal. What troubles some economists is the degree to which businesses engage in quota-like hiring practices designed to protect themselves from legal troubles.

Summary

You now understand the economic implications of discrimination. You know how economists measure the impact of discrimination, detect its existence, and explain its importance. You know how labor market discrimination can be modeled, which implies that discriminatory pay gaps should close over time, but the reality is that the rate of closure is slow. You know what affirmative action is in its various forms.

Key Terms

adverse impact
   discrimination, 308
affirmative action, 313

disparate treatment
   discrimination, 308
labor-force participation rate, 305

rational or statistical
   discrimination, 309

Quiz Yourself

1. How academics look at the evidence on how much women make relative to men is an issue that very much depends on
   a. which year you look at.
   b. which state you look at.
   c. whether you take some variables as "choices" or as "further evidence of discrimination."
   d. which court you are in.

2. The earnings of African Americans relative to whites has
   a. increased from 40 percent in the 1920s to 90 percent today.
   b. increased from 50 percent in the 1950s to around 60 percent in the 1970s, remaining in that area since.
   c. remained constant since the 1950s.
   d. decreased steadily since the 1960s.

3. The method of detecting sex discrimination most likely to minimize it would be to use
   a. simple differences in income between men and women.
   b. simple differences in full-time wages for men and women.
   c. regression techniques.
   d. auditing techniques.

4. The method of detecting sex discrimination most likely to maximize it would be to use
   a. simple differences in income between men and women.
   b. simple differences in full-time wages for men and women.
   c. regression techniques.
   d. auditing techniques.

5. If a woman does not get an interview for a job requiring heavy lifting because the manager has noted that the average woman can lift less than the average man, this is
   a. a legal example of statistical discrimination.
   b. an illegal example of statistical discrimination.
   c. a legal example of adverse impact discrimination.
   d. an illegal example of adverse impact discrimination.

6. Those who believe that wages paid to minorities will rise without government intervention believe that bosses are primarily motivated by
   a. profit.
   b. religion.
   c. doing right.
   d. helping the downtrodden.

7. Affirmative action
   a. can take many forms.
   b. is almost always a racial quota.
   c. applies only to women.
   d. has typically been declared unconstitutional.

Short Answer Questions

1. Describe the process by which greed, absent sexism or bigotry on the part of business owners, can lead to the reduction in wage gaps between men and women and between whites and nonwhites.

2. What are the reasons that income gaps between men and women and whites and nonwhites may persist even in the absence of sexism or racism by business owners.

3. Suppose an establishment has absolutely no overt history of employment discrimination but has a goal of reducing race or gender gaps in its employment. What are the legal means by which it may reduce that gap?

Think about This

Think about your chosen major, your favorite restaurant, the place you live. Are they predominantly male, female, black, or white? Would you feel comfortable going outside the social norms in your choices? Are those social norms limiting?

Talk about This

Who is going to raise your children? Who is going to sacrifice a career for their care, an illness, their after-school activities, etc.?

For More Insight See

Bertrand, Marianne, and Sendhil Mullainathan, "Are Emily and Greg More Employable Than Lakisha and Jamal? A Field Experiement on Labor Market Discrimination," *America Economic Review* 94, no. 4 (September 2004).

Blau, Francine, Marianne Ferber, and Anne Winkler, *The Economics of Women, Men and Work,* 3rd ed. (Upper Saddle River, NJ: Prentice Hall, 1998).

Curry, George E., ed., *The Affirmative Action Debate* (Reading, MA: Addison-Wesley, 1996).

Feiner, Susan F., *Race and Gender in the American Economy* (Englewood Cliffs, NJ: Prentice Hall, 1994).

Fryer, Roland, and Glenn Loury, "Affirmative Action and Its Mythology," *Journal of Economic Perspectives* 19, no. 3 (2005).

Journal of Economic Perspectives 12, no. 2 (Spring 1998). See articles by John Yinger; William A. Darity, Jr., and Patrick L. Mason; Helen F. Ladd; and Kenneth J. Arrow, James J. Heckman, and Glenn C. Loury, pp. 23–126.

Sowell, Thomas, *Race and Economics* (New York: David McKay, 1975).

Waldfogel, Jane, "Understanding the 'Family Gap' in Pay for Women with Children," *Journal of Economic Perspectives* 12, no. 1 (Winter 1998), pp. 137–156.

Behind the Numbers

Income and wealth.

Median family income; Income by Race and Gender.
U.S. Census Bureau; historical income tables— www.census.gov/hhes/www/income

Wealth.
U.S. Census Bureau; historical income tables— www.census.gov/hhes/wealth

Median earnings and ratio of men's to women's income.
Bureau of Labor Statistics—www.bls.gov/cps/cpsaat39.pdf

CHAPTER TWENTY-NINE

Income and Wealth Inequality: What's Fair?

Learning Objectives

After reading this chapter you should be able to:

LO1 Understand how income inequality is measured.

LO2 Understand how wealth inequality is measured.

LO3 Explain why income and wealth inequality exists in the United States.

LO4 Enumerate and explain the costs and benefits of income inequality.

LO5 Explain income mobility and note its extent in the United States.

LO6 Explain intergenerational income mobility and compare its degree across the developed world.

Chapter Outline

Introduction

Measurement of Inequality

Causes of Household Income and Wealth Inequality

Costs and Benefits of Income Inequality

Summary

Introduction

In 2011, the *Occupy Wall Street* movement made headlines regarding the concentration of income and wealth in the hands of the top 1 percent by claiming to represent the other 99 percent. As a result, there was quite a stir in the popular culture as well as in the economics literature about income and wealth inequality generally and the increase in the percentage of income held by the top 1 percent specifically. Income inequality has many measures, causes, and consequences. This chapter will begin by showing narrow and broad measures of income and wealth inequality and how those measures have changed through the years. The chapter will move forward to discuss the causes and effects of that inequality and conclude by discussing why some inequality is necessary to reward productivity and success while excessive inequality has potentially troublesome social and economic consequences.

Measurement of Inequality

Income Inequality

The popular press measure of inequality looks at the percentage of total income going to the top 1 percent of earners. The data available for this type of analysis are garnered from an IRS publication (*Statistics of Income: Individual Income Tax*). The data only become available three years after the fact. As can be seen in Figure 29.1, the same year the inequality issue gained widespread attention in the United States coincided with the worst of the financial-crisis-precipitated recession. This happened for two reasons: First, conventional wisdom placed the blame for the recession on wealthy financial interests; and second, the IRS report for 2007 became available in mid-2010 and showed that the "top 1 percent" share of income had risen to 22.49 percent. Those decrying this level of income inequality noted that in 1978 that same

FIGURE 29.1   Conventionally Measured Income Inequality.

Source: The Internal Revenue Service, www.irs.gov

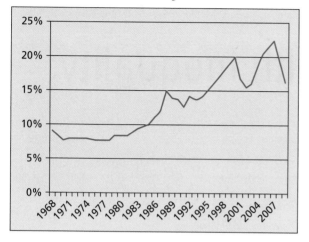

FIGURE 29.2   Conventionally Measured Income Inequality.

Source: The Internal Revenue Service, www.irs.gov

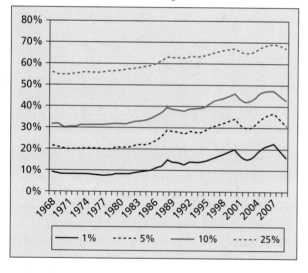

measure showed the "top 1 percent" share stood at only 7.55 percent. For that period and using that measure, the share of the top 1 percent of income earners had tripled.

Clearly, as can be seen in both Figure 29.1 and Figure 29.2, and using the share of income from more broadly defined groups, as more data became available, they showed that the increase from 2001 to 2007 was largely transitory. It peaked at the time of the tech boom in the 1990s and peaked again just prior to the financial crisis. The biggest increase in systemic inequality had

FIGURE 29.3   Ratio of Returns to Population.

Source: The Internal Revenue Service, www.irs.gov

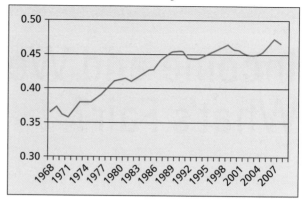

actually occurred during the 1980s and 1990s. The period of the 2000s was marked by highly variable income inequality measures.

As compelling as this may appear, there are problems using only this measure of income inequality. The first of these relates to the rapid increase in the proportion of Americans filing tax returns, while the second relates to the special tax treatment of capital gains.

Regarding tax filings, Figure 29.3 shows that from 1971 to 1998, there was such a rapid increase in the number of income tax returns filed that the proportion of the population completing income tax returns rose from 36 percent to 47 percent. There are three basic reasons this occurred: (1) More people were filing as "single head of household" because more people who were not married or were divorced had children; (2) more young people (under 24) were working at part-time jobs during this period than had been in previous generations; and (3) the new Child Tax Credit combined with the refundable[1] and greatly expanded EITC was creating a motivation for low-earning households to file tax returns when they were not legally required to (because they could garner a tax refund in an amount vastly exceeding their tax withholding). When filings increase faster than the population increases, and when nearly all of those extra

---

[1] A refundable tax credit is one whereby a household can receive more from the federal government in the form of a return than is owed in tax or withheld. The Earned Income Tax Credit (which was greatly expanded in both the Reagan and Clinton administrations) and the Child Tax Credit (which was created in the Clinton administration and doubled in size during the G. W. Bush administration) are both refundable. Portions of the tax credits to support a college education are also refundable.

FIGURE 29.4   1 Percent Adjusted for the Increase in All Returns.

Source: The Internal Revenue Service, www.irs.gov and author calculations.

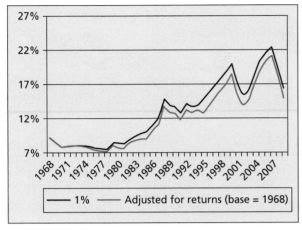

FIGURE 29.5   Maximum Capital Gain Tax Rate.

Source: The Internal Revenue Service, www.irs.gov

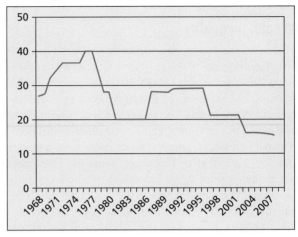

filings are in the lower 99 percent, that expands the 1 percent group to cover more people than it otherwise would. For instance, in 2007, 32 million more filings were received than there would have been had only 36 percent of the population filed. With 32 million more filings, there were 322,000 more in the 1 percent. Essentially, the conventional measure scooped some of the 2 percent into the 1 percent. Correcting for that effect results in a 1.4 percent decrease in the top 1 percent's systemic share. This is displayed in Figure 29.4.

Regarding the impact that changes to the tax treatment of capital gains have had on the measure of inequality, there is potentially a much larger effect. For the benefit of those not steeped in finance or tax issues, capital gains are those gains garnered from selling an asset for more than was paid for it. In the United States, capital gains are only taxed on "realization" rather than "accrual." This means that taxes are only owed on the gain if the gain is "realized" in the form of a sale. Further, capital gains are forgiven at death, which means that if there is an accrued gain and a person sells, he or she realizes the gain and owes the tax. If the person dies prior to the realization, the gain is tax free (except for inheritance taxes) and the heirs can immediately sell that asset (with its gains) tax free. It is only if the heirs hold the asset that any gains are taxed, but even then the "stepped-up basis" means that its value on the day the person died becomes its effective purchase price. There are good economic reasons for this treatment that are beyond the scope of this chapter, but the upshot is this: Capital gains

realizations, and therefore payments of capital gains taxes, are almost entirely voluntary and easily avoided. Higher rates of tax encourage tax avoidance through nonrealization and lower rates of tax encourage realization. Figure 29.5 shows that the rate that high-income earners pay on those capital gains has changed over the years. That rate reached a peak in the late 1970s at nearly 40 percent and from 2003 to 2012 was at its all-time low level of 15 percent. This impacts the measure of income inequality markedly in that, were capital gains tax rates as high in 2007 as they were in the late 1970s, far fewer gains would have been realized, and therefore far fewer gains reported to the IRS. The accrued income would have existed, but the measured income would not have. If tax rates on capital gains had remained the same, presumably the rate of realization would have remained the same. Because a higher percentage of capital gains probably went unrealized during the 1970s, incomes of the top 1 percent were likely understated. Looked at differently, if tax rates had remained at their mid-1970s peak, fewer realizations would have occurred and less income would have been reported by the top 1 percent. Either way, a decrease in the capital gains tax rate would be reflected in an increase in the observed measure of the share of income of the top 1 percent though inequality may not have changed at all. A simple analysis of the impact of a 20 percentage point drop in the maximum capital gains tax rate suggests that 8 percentage points of the increase in the share of the 1 percent can be attributed to the drop in the capital gains tax rate. Accounting for the tax-returns effect and the capital gains effect, the top 1 percent's share would have increased from 7.55 percent to 13.09 percent rather than to 22.49 percent.

Wealth Inequality

A parallel issue to income inequality is wealth inequality. Here there are fewer measurement concerns as there is no direct tax in the United States on wealth (except perhaps inheritance taxes that only occur at death). As a result, there is no issue associated with who is filing and who isn't or capital gains accruals or realizations. The data on wealth concentrations come from a unique dataset: the *Survey of Consumer Finances*. These data are garnered from 4,500 individuals who are carefully selected to accurately represent the U.S. population's demographics (age, gender, household type, etc.) but also to achieve an appropriate representation of households according to economic characteristics (homeowners vs. renters, high-income vs. low-income individuals, as well as those with defined benefit pensions vs. those with defined contribution pensions). Part of the survey's usefulness is that there is what in the statistics world is called "oversampling" of high-income and high-wealth households to get a more accurate representation of households in those categories. Those "oversampled" households are then weighted downward to make sure they do not bias the results of the survey. Conducted on behalf of the Federal Reserve by the University of Chicago, it is widely considered the gold standard of economic surveys.

Its results show that wealth inequality is similarly high and is higher than it once was. The share of the top 10 percent, which was 67 percent in 1989, grew to 74.5 percent by 2010. Figure 29.6 shows that the share of the top 1 percent grew markedly (from 30 percent to 34 percent) with the rise in the stock market during the 1990s and has been relatively stable. The relatively (but not extraordinarily) rich (i.e., the 9 percent in the top 10 percent but not in the top 1 percent) faired very well during the period after 1995. Figure 29.7 shows that the upper-middle class and the bottom half have seen their relative wealth shares fall. While the bottom half's share drop from 2007 to 2010 (from 2.5 percent to 1.1 percent) is likely the result of the bursting of the housing bubble in 2008 through 2010, both household types have seen systematic declines in their wealth shares since 1989.

Another measure of wealth inequality is the ratio of mean wealth to median wealth. Mean (the simple average of) wealth differs from the median (the mid-point of) wealth because rich people are very rich, and modest percentage changes in their wealth are still very large

FIGURE 29.6 Share of Wealth Top 10%.

Source: *Survey of Consumer Finances.*

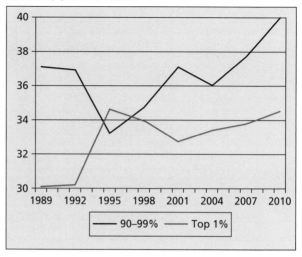

FIGURE 29.7 Share of Wealth: Bottom 90%.

Source: *Survey of Consumer Finances.*

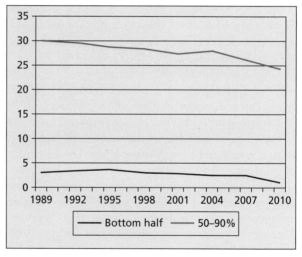

and as such will change the mean significantly even if they have no effect on the median person's wealth. Figure 29.8 shows that during the 1989 to 2007 period, wealth (in inflation-adjusted dollars) rose 60 percent for the median household, but the mean rose 86 percent; that is, the rich got richer faster than did others. Again, most of that effect was a result of the increase in the stock market from 1989 to 2000. The gains from 2001 to 2007 were more the result of the housing bubble, and because

FIGURE 29.8 Median and Mean Wealth and Their Ratio (2010 Dollars)

Source: *Survey of Consumer Finances.*

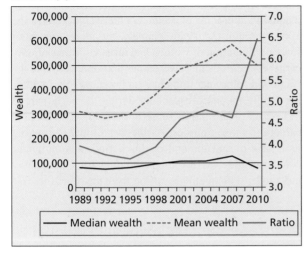

the average household benefited more (in net wealth terms) from the increase in housing-related wealth than did the rich (who have far less of the wealth tied up in their homes), the relative increase in median and mean wealth for that period was approximately equal. When the housing bubble collapsed, however, the median household's wealth fell 40 percent, all the way back to its 1989 inflation-adjusted level, while the mean value dropped only 15 percent. This caused the mean to median ratio, which had been rising steadily from 1995 to 2004, to spike to a level of 6.5. This means that the high end is so high that mean wealth is 6.5 times higher than the median household's wealth.

Causes of Household Income and Wealth Inequality

The reasons for the increase in household and wealth inequality are not particularly contentious. Some economists and sociologists, however, might debate whether these increases were avoidable, how the increases might have been avoided, and even whether combatting the increases would be wise. Let's begin with the causes, as they have been enumerated.

First, there is the decline of the American manufacturing sector generally and the decline of union-represented manufacturing employees specifically. Union-represented manufacturing employment, in autos, steel, and consumer

durables (televisions, household appliances, etc.) has largely collapsed in the last 40 years. The jobs created by these sectors (and now lost) were well-paying positions requiring relatively little education. These jobs were, to the hard-working, a ticket to a middle-class lifestyle.

So why did this happen? Robotic production and international competition for the goods produced by these industries are largely to blame for the elimination of these manufacturing jobs. Specifically, fewer and fewer jobs are being performed by physically challenging labor, and more and more jobs are being performed by intellectually challenging labor. As a result, the premium paid to the brightest and most well educated continues to grow, and the relative wage of those performing manual labor has diminished. A worker today can be responsible for the output, while supervising the actions of computer and robotically driven manufacturing that once required several workers to perform physically demanding tasks.

International competition for goods-producing industries has made it extraordinarily difficult for domestic manufacturers to compete if and when they have high wages and generous benefit packages. Domestic steel and auto production declined in the 1970s and 1980s, and while their decline continued through to today, the 1990s and 2000s saw a significant decline in the production of consumer electronics, appliances, and household products. Many economists consider this aspect as having been inevitable. In the immediate aftermath of World War II, there was no major economy, other than the American one, with its economy and infrastructure more or less intact. For that reason, American manufacturing had significant market power relative to the rest of the world. If someone wanted steel, for the better part of the 1950s and into the 1960s, he or she had to buy it from the United States. The same was largely true of automobiles through the 1970s and for consumer electronics and durables through the 1980s. With that market power, companies in the United States could pass on their higher wage costs to the world's consumers. American unions could therefore bargain for higher wages and, because there was no international competition in these areas, the manufacturers were motivated to back down and pay those wages and offer better benefits. Again, because they could pass on the increased costs, they were not only not compelled to keep costs under control, but rather it was more in their interests to avoid sales-reducing strikes. As time progressed and the economies of first, Germany and Japan, then Korea and China, and perhaps soon, India and Africa were able to undercut high American prices with the one advantage they had: lower wages. Short of walling off the U.S. economy, there was nothing the United States could have done to stop this pressure. As a result, downward pressure on American wages, under the story accepted by many, was an inevitable outcome of the late twentieth century.

All of this speaks to why incomes (and wealth) of those at the bottom would remain stagnant or decline, but what would explain why those at the top did so well? For this we have to turn to the aspects of global changes that benefited those at the top. The first of these changes involves the movement of global capital, while the second involves changes in the consumption-saving patterns of those not at the top.

In the aftermath of World War II and through the 1980s, the vast majority of financial capital used to grow businesses was locally generated. That is, Americans lent their money to other Americans to build businesses, finance homes, and so forth. Today, a bond used to finance a company or a mortgage taken out to buy a home could very easily have its origins in Saudi Arabia or China. The foreign entity saves the money from profits earned in their global enterprises, converts that money to dollars, and invests it in U.S. markets. Capital markets have become much more profitable to those engaged in them and those engaged in them are, almost always, very wealthy people.

Furthermore, American saving rates have fallen precipitously since the 1960s. A home that used to require a 20 percent down payment can now be had for 10 percent (or less) down. A car that used to be purchased for cash is now far more likely to be financed with a loan or leased with terms often so generous as to allow the consumer to simply sign his or her name and drive away with a new car. What that means is that the savers, who used to come from all walks of life, are now far more likely to come from the higher end of the income scale.

To some degree, public policy since the 1980s has been more favorable to those at the high end of the income and wealth distribution than it was in years prior. Inheritance tax rates have fallen throughout the United States relative to where they were in the 1970s. Nationally, in inflation-adjusted terms, inheritance taxes are collected on fewer households than used to be subject to them and at lower rates. This is true at the federal and state levels. If there are two ways of being rich—inheriting your wealth or earning your wealth—policy changes are making the former easier.

The other significant tax policy change prior to the 1980s is the treatment of investment-based income. Capital gains tax rates as well as tax rates on carried interest (a form of income associated with an investment or hedge fund manager's exceeding a specified return

goal), which had been treated as ordinary income in the late 1980s and early 1990s, are now taxed at a lower rate than other earned income.

Finally, with all of this happening to increase income inequality, there had existed a counterweight to it in the 1960s through the 1980s: namely, the increasing labor force participation of women had turned millions of one-earner households into two-earner households so that the wage-and-salary earning class had seen rapidly increasing family incomes, especially during the early part of this period, from the increase in the number of income earners in those families. As the trend finished running its course during the end of this period, this particular counterweight was no longer holding back the movement toward inequality resulting from the other forces.

Costs and Benefits of Income Inequality

Market economies rely on the principle that individuals earn an income that is positively related to the value of what they provide to that society where that value is measured by what others are willing to pay. If it is not positively related, some (perhaps many) individuals will stop doing what they are doing and do something else more lucrative or less demanding. If physicians and other professionals that require higher levels of education do not earn more than ordinary laborers, then only those who wish to stay in school for long periods of time to engage in their desired profession will do so. If that happens, there will be too few people trained to be physicians, engineers, scientists, and managers. Income inequality provides a motivation for both those who wish to be at the high end of the income distribution to work to achieve it and those who wish to avoid being at the low end of the income distribution to work to avoid that result as well.

To see this in your own life, imagine that the profession you wish to embark upon paid only the minimum wage. Would you continue pursuing a degree in order to engage in that profession? Some of you might, but most of you would change your degree program to do something more lucrative—if for no other reason than to pay off your student loans or make the time in college worth the expense.

Significant income inequality has a social downside as well, especially when the level of inequality is viewed by those in the middle and at the bottom of the distribution as unjustified by the aforementioned social benefits associated with meeting market needs. When the poor believe that their poverty is a result of choices they made or as a result of things they did or failed to do, income inequality does not challenge the social order. On the other

TABLE 29.1 Income mobility from 1987 to 1996 and from 1996 to 2005.

Source: United States Department of the Treasury www.treasury.gov/resource-center/tax-policy/Documents/incomemobilitystudy03-08revise.pdf

		Lowest	Second	Middle	Fourth	Highest	Total	Top 1%
Lowest	1987–1996	38.9	28.3	14.9	10.6	7.3	100	0.3
	1996–2005	37.8	27.1	16.1	11.8	7.2	100	0.3
Second	1987–1996	14.2	33.8	26.4	16.4	9.3	100	0.2
	1996–2005	15.8	30.1	28	17.2	9	100	0.2
Middle	1987–1996	6.1	17.4	33.9	28.4	14.2	100	0.3
	1996–2005	5.9	14	32.6	31.1	16.3	100	0.3
Fourth	1987–1996	3	7.5	19.4	40.1	30	100	0.5
	1996–2005	3.1	5.7	15.5	41.9	33.8	100	0.3
Highest	1987–1996	1.8	2.5	7.3	20.6	67.8	100	5.4
	1996–2005	2	2	5.7	17.2	73.2	100	4.8
Top 1%	1987–1996	2.1	0.9	2.5	4.7	89.9	100	46
	1996–2005	2.7	1	1.5	4.5	90.3	100	44.7
All Income	1987–1996	11.3	16.5	20.1	24.1	28	100	1.5
	1996–2005	11.7	14.7	19.1	24.4	30	100	1.3

hand, when those in the middle or at the bottom of the distribution believe that the system is rigged in favor of the rich remaining rich, social disorder can be the result. Social disorder can threaten the system that allows for income inequality in the first place and, as a result, it is frequently in the interests of those at the top of the distribution to ensure that those in the middle and at the bottom believe that the inequality is justified.

A positive view of income inequality by those in the middle and at the bottom can be achieved as long as there is the widespread belief that there exists upward income and wealth mobility in society. It is therefore important for those at the top of the income distribution to create the reality of opportunity or at least maintain a widespread belief in a myth of opportunity. Table 29.1 shows the degree of income mobility from 1987 to 1998 and from 1996 to 2005. What it shows is that 38.9 percent of those in the lowest quintile in 1987 were also in the lowest quintile in 1996. What it also shows is that 17.9 percent of those in the lowest quintile in 1987 were in one of the two highest quintiles in 1996. From 1996 to 2005 these figures were largely the same, given that 37.8 percent of the poor in 1996 were also poor in 2005 and that 19 percent of the poor in 1996 were in one of the top two quintiles in 2005. At the other end, it shows that 55.3 percent (100% − 44.7%) of those in the 1 percent in 1996 weren't in the top 1 percent in 2005.

Another way of looking at income mobility is the degree to which the income quintile of parents and the income quintile of their children are related; that is,

TABLE 29.2 Cross-country intergenerational income elasticities.

Source: Miles Corak, "Do Poor Children Become Poor Adults? Lessons from a Cross-Country Comparison of Generational Earnings Mobility," http://ftp.iza.org/dp1993.pdf

Country	Elasticity
Denmark	0.15
Norway	0.17
Finland	0.18
Canada	0.19
Sweden	0.27
Germany	0.32
France	0.41
United States	0.47
United Kingdom	0.50

whether or not you inherit your parents' wealth, you often inherit your parents' values, work ethic, and social standing and that translates into higher income.[2] This intergenerational income relationship has been estimated by economists for a variety of countries using a variety of methodologies. Canadian economist Miles Corak summarized the results that are displayed in Table 29.2. Higher numbers suggest a stronger relationship between parental and child income. This analysis shows that the U.S. claim to be "the land of opportunity" isn't backed up by the data, at least not recently.

[2]For instance, my fraternal grandfather earned a law degree; my father, brother, and sister (as well as I) earned PhDs; and my daughter is in a PhD program. That is highly unlikely to be random.

Summary

The United States has significant income and wealth inequality. Part of the increase in income inequality is explained by measurement issues. The systemic increase in income inequality is explainable demographic factors and factors relating to tax policy. Inequality has benefits in that a higher income is a market reward for higher productivity while it has costs related to social discord. Social discord is a more likely outcome when income mobility is low or decreasing, and in the present-day United States, both are the case.

Quiz Yourself

1. Income inequality, when measured as the percentage of total income going to the top 1 percent, increased most rapidly during the
   a. 1950s.
   b. 1960s.
   c. 1980s and 1990s.
   d. 2000s.

2. Income inequality as conventionally measured is _____ when you ignore the fact that a higher percentage of the population is filing tax forms.
   a. overstated
   b. understated
   c. properly stated

3. Income inequality as conventionally measured is _____ when you ignore the decreases in the capital gains tax rate.
   a. overstated
   b. understated
   c. properly stated

4. Wealth inequality is _____ related to the ratio of mean to median wealth.
   a. positively
   b. negatively
   c. not

5. Which of the following had the effect of decreasing income inequality?
   a. The increase in the female labor force participation rate.
   b. The increase in globalization of capital.
   c. The increase in globalization of trade in steel, autos, and consumer durables.
   d. The increase in robotic production.

6. Which of the following had the effect of increasing income inequality?
   a. The increase in the female labor force participation rate.
   b. The decrease in globalization of capital.
   c. The increase in globalization of trade in steel, autos, and consumer durables.
   d. The decrease in robotic production.

7. The benefits of income inequality are
   a. always greater than the costs.
   b. always less than the costs.
   c. associated with rewarding hard work and work that society values.
   d. associated with the social discord that it creates.

8. Social discord resulting from income inequality can be lessened if there is (are)
   a. high levels of intergenerational income mobility.
   b. high levels of income mobility of individuals.
   c. belief that the economic system is rigged in favor of the rich.
   d. a and b

9. The notion that the United States is the "land of opportunity" where who your parents are and how much they earn is unrelated to your income is (relative to other industrial powers)
   a. clearly shown in the data to be accurate.
   b. clearly shown in the data to be inaccurate.
   c. not supported but there aren't data to support the conclusion that it isn't true either.

Talk about This

Suppose you were rich. How would you structure your tax and welfare systems to make sure you could stay rich? Would you try to rig the system in your favor or could that be self-defeating?

Fact 1: Americans tolerate a level of income inequality that is higher than it is in much of the rest of the world.

Fact 2: Our "liberal" political party, the Democrats, are frequently more conservative than the members of European conservative political parties.

Question: Which is the cause and which is the effect?

Think about This

Are the poor adults with whom you are familiar poor because of things they did (got pregnant at an early age, committed a crime that prevented them from a getting a good job), things they failed to do (finish their education, work hard), things that happened to them (they were the victim of an accident, or were left with children to attend to), or is the system rigged against poor people?

What policy would you suggest to a national leader to increase income mobility?

Behind the Numbers

Income—www.irs.gov/uac/SOI-Tax-Stats-Individual-Income-Tax-Returns

Wealth—www.census.gov/people/wealth/data/dtables html; www.census.gov/people/wealth

Income mobility—www.federalreserve.gov/pubs/feds/2009/200913/200913pap.pdf

International statistics on intergenerational income mobility.

Corak, Miles, "Do Poor Children Become Poor Adults? Lessons from a Cross-Country Comparison of Generational Earnings Mobility," ftp.iza.org/dp1993.pdf.

CHAPTER THIRTY

Farm Policy

Learning Objectives

After reading this chapter you should be able to:

LO1 Conclude that economists generally are not in favor of price supports in agriculture.

LO2 Conclude that price variation is the leading economic justification for farm price supports, while also concluding that this is insufficient justification for most economists.

LO3 Apply supply and demand and consumer and producer surplus analysis to demonstrate economists' reasoning in opposing farm price supports.

LO4 Describe and illustrate the mechanisms that are typically used to enforce price supports and know some of their history.

Chapter Outline

Farm Prices Since 1950

Price Variation as a Justification for Government Intervention

Consumer and Producer Surplus Analysis of Price Floors

Price Support Mechanisms and Their History

Is There a Bubble on the Farm?

Kick It Up a Notch

Summary

Farm policy in the United States has been schizophrenic. Sometimes farmers are depicted as strong, independent men and women who simply need the government to stay out of their way. At other times they are depicted as desperate victims in need of help. In political speeches, family farms are spoken of with the same reverence as motherhood and apple pie, and to hear politicians talk, you would think farmers were demigods.

It is ironic, then, that without almost continuous government grants and low-interest loans, many farmers would have declared bankruptcy long ago. Help for farmers has come from government in many forms. The government has bought and stored excess production, bought and given away excess production, bought livestock to prevent oversupply, and paid farmers not to farm.

We look here at the history of farm prices since 1950, and we draw on that history to discuss why government has intervened and will probably continue to feel motivated to intervene in agriculture. We use our basic supply and demand model and our consumer and producer surplus knowledge to discuss the impact of farm price supports. In that discussion, as we said, we review the history of farm price supports and the various ways that farmers have received assistance.

Farm Prices Since 1950

A look at Figure 30.1 quickly tells you that farm prices are anything but stable. While beef, hogs, milk, corn, and soybeans are sold in different units, by displaying prices relative to where they were in 1982, we can show all of them on one graph. A number higher than 100 indicates a price in a selected year for that commodity that exceeds its 1982 level. A number below 100 indicates the opposite.

Whereas the prices of all the products shown in Figure 30.1 were higher in 2013 than they were in 1950, it was not that long ago that several were lower than they were in 1982. Since, according to the CPI, overall

FIGURE 30.1 Farm prices relative to their 1982 levels.

Source: Bureau of Labor Statistics, www.bls.gov/ppi

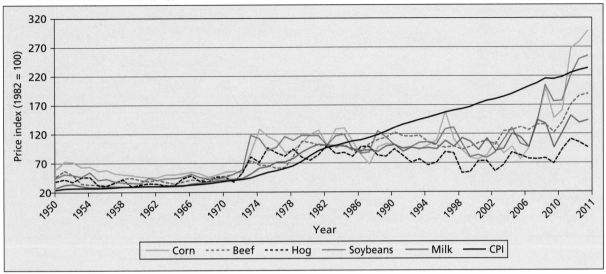

inflation was 130 percent from 1982 to 2013, farmers who produced the same crops in the same amounts and with the same costs would have experienced a 56 percent (100/230) loss in real income if they were only able to get the same price they received in 1982. Hog prices in particular took a beating between 1998 and 2000, yielding at times less than 45 percent of their 1982 levels. Any farmers who had not gotten more productive by this time would have seen a standard of living only 33 percent of their 1982 level. Until quite recently, prices for most farm commodities have risen far more slowly than overall consumer prices. Since 2007, farm prices have seen a significant increase, and two of them, corn and soybeans, saw such a spike between 2010 and 2013 that their overall increase since 1982 exceeded that of the CPI.

If you look carefully at Figure 30.1, you will see that there was a sharp jump in all of these commodity prices in the early 1970s and again in 2008, and then again between 2010 and 2013. Corn, soybean, and hog prices doubled in the four years from 1972 to 1975. Before 1975, corn, soybean, and milk prices had been the most stable, but since 1976, corn has joined beef as a commodity whose price is not stable.[1] In 2007 and 2008 most farm commodities doubled or even tripled in price. By far the greatest increase was seen in corn and soybeans. Going back to Chapter 2, you will remember that when one good is an input into another, an increase in

[1] We are defining stability here as the ratio of the standard deviation of real prices to their mean.

that input price will drive the price of the output to rise. Corn and soybean meal are frequently used as animal feed, thus the relationship between corn, soybeans, and beef and hog prices. Also in Chapter 2 and the notion of "alternative outputs," recall that when two can be easily produced from the same inputs, the two prices will almost always mirror one another. If you have ever traveled from Ohio through Indiana, Illinois, Iowa, or Missouri, the farms along the highway are almost always planted in corn and soybeans. An increase in the demand for one will cause a decrease in the supply of the other. Farmers will plant whatever makes them the most profit, and as a result the prices will move in tandem. What occurred in 2007 and 2008 was a spike in the demand for corn owing to its potential use in corn-based ethanol.

Corn and Gasoline

Let's examine that corn–gasoline relationship in greater detail. What had once been a nonexistent relationship began to emerge in 2004 as subsidies and mandates for alternative fuels for cars and trucks became part of the U.S. energy landscape. Corn-based ethanol was a major part of President Bush's energy strategy and will likely play an important role in President Obama's energy strategy. Flex-fuel vehicles are an increasing portion of the rolling stock on American roads and as a result the overall demand for corn has risen. In addition, ethanol is now an increasing portion of the total fuel demand, so much so that 40 percent of the corn grown is now used for that

FIGURE 30.2   Relative prices of gas and corn.

Source: Bureau of Labor Statistics, www.bls.gov/ppi

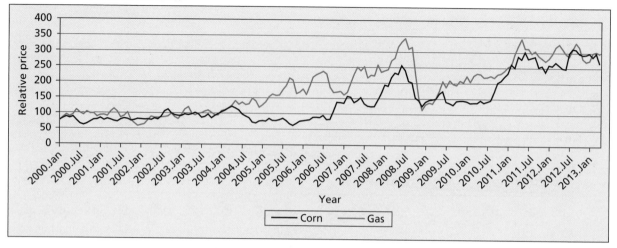

purpose. As can be seen in Figure 30.2, prior to 2004 there was almost no relationship between the two prices, but between late 2004 and early 2009 the price per bushel of corn more than tripled in reaction to the tripling of gasoline prices. Going back to our Chapter 2 discussion of demand and supply determinants, ethanol is a substitute for gasoline and corn is an input to ethanol. A steadily high gasoline price would be expected to, and in fact did, lead to an increase in corn demand and corn prices.

Had gasoline prices remained at their summer 2008 highs, corn probably would have as well. When the demand for gasoline fell dramatically with the declining economy, the price of corn fell dramatically as well. By the end of 2008 the price of corn was about half of its mid-2008 high. The prices once again mirrored each other in the rise through late 2010 and into 2013.

Price Variation as a Justification for Government Intervention

Economists agree on few things, but one area where there is wide agreement is on the inadvisability of government intervention in agriculture. As a result, appeals for intervention tend to be based on sentiment rather than analysis. Although such sentimental appeals have not persuaded many economists, they have swayed politicians. The family farm is so revered in America, even by people who have never lived on or even near one, that economists have had little success forestalling farm

bailouts. That said, there are reasons for government intervention in agriculture that a few academic economists, particularly agricultural economists, accept.

The Case for Price Supports

The most compelling of the reasons for government intervention in this market is that price variability makes farming a necessarily economically risky occupation. Supporters think that farmers whose farms are small need some government action to survive the aforementioned variability. The government's assistance in this might take the form of buying and storing excess crops when prices are too low and selling them out of inventory when prices rebound. This would do nothing to change the long-term price of crops, but it would stabilize prices. When the government does this for farmers, it acts as it does when it controls the value of its own currency.

There are two sources of price instability for any good: supply uncertainty and demand uncertainty. Sources of supply uncertainty are obvious: the weather and other natural phenomena like diseases and insect damage. The source of demand variability is mostly the unpredictability of international markets and whether there is demand for American crops by other countries.

The weather and other aspects of nature determine whether crops will do well, and there is not a great deal farmers can control once the planting is done. They can plant different varieties of corn and soybeans based on the lateness of the planting season, but once the seeds are sown, most of the economic decisions are made. Grain farmers, for example, are powerless to do anything if market conditions change after planting. At harvest time they will reap what they sowed—no more, no less.

On the demand side, variability comes from the quantities of goods foreigners will buy. In part this is supply-side variability in other nations. For instance, if the weather is bad in the other major exporting countries of Argentina, Australia, Canada, and Russia, then demand will be high in the importing countries for American grain. The United States is the largest source in grain production, but prices in the United States are usually somewhat higher than in other countries. For this reason, food importers buy all they can from these other countries; then they buy the rest of what they need from the United States. If the weather in these other exporting countries is bad, then importing countries will need great quantities of U.S. grain. If their weather is good, importing countries will not need much U.S. grain. With the weather and other forces of nature as variable as they are, there are few goods whose prices fluctuate as much as basic farm prices.

The Case against Price Supports

Though price variability is the most compelling reason for government interference in agriculture, it is not a persuasive reason for many economists. Option markets for agricultural goods exist and offer many opportunities to ensure that prices at harvest time are known in advance. Such markets serve as insurance to farmers on prices.

To see how using an option market might work, suppose you planted your crop in May and expected it to yield 10,000 bushels. At planting time in May you can buy an option to sell 10,000 bushels at harvest time for a specific price. If the price at harvest time is lower than the price specified in the option, you can exercise the option and sell your harvest at the higher contract price. If the price is higher, you do not need the option. This is comparable to buying automobile insurance. You will use it if you have an accident; you will not if you avoid a wreck.

If you fear your crop might fail, you can protect yourself by buying crop insurance. Crop insurance will pay off if crops fail. With these two forms of insurance (options and crop insurance), farmers can deal with the aspects of farming over which they have no control without government help. If farmers do not buy options

or crop insurance, it is because they cost money. Even when things go well, profit margins on farms are low enough that some farmers believe they cannot afford insurance.

Consumer and Producer Surplus Analysis of Price Floors

One Floor in One Market

All of the many forms of support that government can give to farmers can be modeled with our supply and demand model, and we can discuss their implications using the consumer and producer surplus language that was introduced in Chapter 3. This section quickly reviews that language and uses Figure 30.3 to look at the impact of farm price supports on the economy.

Chapter 3 told us that consumer surplus is the difference between how much consumers value a good and the price they have to pay for it. It also told us that producer surplus is the difference between the amount producers get from consumers and the variable cost of production. The demand curve represents what consumers are willing to pay for a good, and we interpret that as how much they value the good. In Chapter 5, we saw that the supply curve in a perfectly competitive market is made up of the marginal cost curves of the many entities that comprise

FIGURE 30.3 Price floors in a supply and demand model.

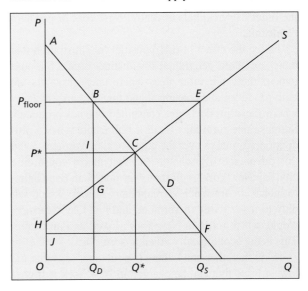

the market. The area under the supply curve thus represents the variable costs of production.

At equilibrium, $P^* - Q^*$, consumers have a consumer surplus of P^*AC. Similarly, the producer makes out well, too. The firms net a producer surplus of HP^*C. The combined surpluses make up the value to society of the exchange, a value represented as HAC.

If the government sets a **price floor** of P_{floor}, it will have to enforce it somehow. While we will not talk until the next section about how government might enforce the floor, assume for the moment that it is possible. Since consumers will want only Q_D, this is all that will be sold to consumers. The consumer surplus will shrink (to $P_{floor}AB$) while firms' producer surplus will grow (to $HP_{floor}BG$), but the combined surpluses are less than without the floor by GBC. Economists label this deadweight loss. To see why this is the case, turn to "Kick It Up a Notch" at the end of the chapter.

price floor
Price below which a commodity may not sell.

Variable Floors in Multiple Markets

Support for farmers and their price supports dates back to the Great Depression, when dairy farmers could not sell their products, and they convinced the government to set minimum prices. The so-called Eau Claire Rule came about at this time. Put in place so that farmers outside Wisconsin could survive and remain in business, the Eau Claire Rule sets the minimum price for milk as a function of a farm's proximity to this small Wisconsin city. To this day, a dairy farmer in central Wisconsin gets a substantially lower subsidy than a similar farmer in the other dairy capitals of central New York or northern California.

To see the effect of this, consider for illustration that there are three geographically distinct areas. Suppose two of these are rural areas where dairy products are both produced and consumed and the third area is a city where these products are consumed but not produced. Suppose one rural area—call it Eau Claire—has a production advantage over the other—call it Vermont—and this advantage overwhelms the fact that a consuming city, say New York, is closer to Vermont than Eau Claire. In such a circumstance Vermont dairy farmers would sell only to those living in Vermont, and Eau Claire farmers would sell to those in New York as well as Eau Claire. This is the economically efficient scenario.

If, on the other hand, there is a rule that says that the lowest price that can be charged in New York is higher than the market equilibrium, it might be high enough that Vermont rather than Eau Claire produces the dairy for New York. Thus not only do New Yorkers have to buy milk at high prices, but the fact that they do tends to reward less efficient means of production. This is, unfortunately, precisely what the Eau Claire Rule does in the United States.

What Would Happen without Price Supports?

If there were no price supports, how low could prices go? The first thing to understand is that like everyone else, farmers have options other than farming. If prices go low enough, they will sell out and work somewhere else. In this sense farmers are like any other small businesspersons who must decide when they have had enough. While being your own boss has clear advantages, they must also be weighed against risks and the frayed nerves associated with being in charge.

For most farmers, the lack of a boss outweighs the frayed nerves. Even with lower income, they would rather continue farming than work for someone else. On the other hand, there is a price for which the rate of return to farming is just too low. When that point is reached, farmers auction off their assets, pay their debts, and move on. As a result, prices cannot fall below the level where farmers are better off not farming. If they did, the farmers would leave the market, thereby reducing the number of sellers, and that would put upward pressure on the price.

Price Support Mechanisms and Their History

Price Support Mechanisms

As we noted in the previous section, there are many ways of enforcing a price support. The reason an enforcement mechanism is required in agriculture and not in other price floor situations is that production happens and most costs are incurred well before sales are made or even arranged. For instance, the minimum wage is a form of price floor. The buyer of labor, the boss, cannot pay the seller of labor, the worker, any less than the minimum wage, just as the buyer of the agricultural product cannot pay the farmer any less than the price floor. The supply and demand analysis in the minimum wage shows that more people want to work than there are jobs available. This is not as much of a problem in normal working situations as it is in farming because, unlike farming, the workers are not working and then looking to see if the boss will pay them. They are hired and then they do the work. Farmers, on the other hand, grow and harvest their crops before they have a known buyer. Raising the price that farmers get to P_{floor} will not do farmers any good if many of them end up having truckloads of grain to sell and no one willing to buy them. They will have incurred all of the costs of working, but they will not derive any revenue from their work.

For this reason, the government has to enforce the price floor in a manner that makes sure either that only Q_D is produced or that Q_S is wanted. There are several ways that this can be done. The government can limit what farmers produce by allocating rights to sell among farmers. With rights to sell, farmers can sell only what their rights allow. The government can pay farmers to participate by allowing anyone to sell at P^* while allowing only those who agreed to limit production to sell at P_{floor}. The government can then buy all that farmers want to produce. At its discretion it can then give the good away to foreign or domestic recipients that could not afford to buy it at P_{floor} or the government can buy and store all that farmers want to produce at P_{floor}.

The government's least expensive option to keep prices high, however, is to limit the amount that a farmer can produce. It can do this by allowing only licensed farmers to produce specific quantities. Peanuts and chewing grade tobacco are two crops that are produced under licensing. You cannot grow and sell these products unless you have a license. If you examine Figure 30.3 again, you will see that by limiting the number of farmers and the amount of acreage that can be devoted to this production, the P_{floor} price can be maintained and farmers will produce only Q_D.

The government's next least expensive option is to pay farmers not to produce as much as they might otherwise choose to. In the past the government paid farmers not to plant in certain fields, and it even paid them not to farm altogether. Moreover, to affect the price of milk, the government bought dairy herds and sent them off to slaughter. The government, of course, keeps production down when it pays farmers not to produce. The effectiveness of this method is lessened, however, by increases in productivity and by new people becoming farmers. In the case of milk, farmers who had their herds bought were not allowed to get back into dairy farming for several years, even if they wanted to, but that did not prevent others from becoming farmers. It did not prevent

remaining farmers from increasing their herds, and it did not prevent others from increasing the productivity of their cows, using artificial hormones. Grain farmers also experienced this form of price support. Many were paid to have idle fields, fields that could be used for hay but not for cash grains like wheat, soybeans, or corn. In general, the government subsidies have had the effect of persuading significant numbers of farmers either to do something else or to limit production.

An expensive option for the government has been to let farmers grow all they want and either pay them the difference between the market price and the price floor or simply buy up whatever was not purchased by consumers. Figure 30.3 shows that it is very expensive for the government to choose either of these options. If it chooses the former, it will have to pay farmers the difference between P_{floor} and the price that Q_S will sell for on the open market, shown in Figure 30.3 as J, for all Q_S. This totals $JP_{floor}EF$. If the government chooses the latter option, it will have to buy the difference between Q_S and Q_D for the P_{floor} price. That totals Q_DBEQ_S.

If it buys up what is left by consumers, the government still has to figure out what to do with the excess. There are three options here: Let it spoil, give it away, or store it. The first does not cost anything more than trucking the surplus to a place where it can be dumped. Giving the excess away sounds more appealing, but if you give people something that they would have ordinarily paid for, you still are not solving the agriculture price problem. You are reducing demand even further by the amount you are giving away. You can only give the good to people who are so poor they would have gone without, and you are most likely to find such people in the developing world. It may sound somewhat cynical, but the government of the United States is a leading contributor of foodstuffs to victims of starvation and natural disaster in the developing world in part because the United States has an excess that it needs to dispose of.

Even though the most expensive option for the government is to store the excess, it has, at various times, stored milk and grains. Milk has been stored either as a powder or in the form of block American cheese. While both can be stored at near room temperature, a cool, dry environment is more conducive to long-term storage. Abandoned salt mines have served that purpose well.

Storing grain is somewhat easier. It does not require any processing, the way milk does, but it is still subject to rotting if it gets wet. However it is stored, storing food is very expensive.

History of Price Supports

At various times the United States has employed every imaginable way of supporting agriculture prices. At one time it could have idled all grain farms in the United States for a year and still had enough in storage to process into food and to feed livestock. In the middle of the 1982 recession, there was enough excess dairy in storage that the government gave every poor person who showed up for it several pounds of cheese and several boxes of powdered milk. In the middle 1980s, thousands of dairy farmers around the country went into early retirement when the government paid top dollar to buy up their herds.

As we said before, the support for agricultural price supports grew out of the depression of the 1930s. Agricultural prices fell so far so fast that farm bankruptcies skyrocketed. Politicians reacted by putting price floors on a number of agricultural products, most notably dairy. In the middle 1980s, the Reagan administration tried to lessen the cost of agriculture subsidies by limiting supply, rather than serving as a buyer of last resort. First it sold off and gave away much of the government's excess stocks of grain and dairy products. Then it offered farmers payments not to farm. The ultimate act in this regard was the middle 1980s policy to thin dairy herds. This led to nearly a 10 percent reduction in farmland under active cultivation since 1988. While we proceed down a path of restricting output rather than buying up excess, many thousands of farmers still are paid many billions of dollars not to farm many millions of acres.

The 1996 Freedom to Farm Act began yet another long phase of practices leading away from agricultural price supports. By 2002 the United States was supposed to exist without supports for milk or grain, but alas, support continued with the federal government spending $19 billion in 2009. Cuts to the program and the increase in the price of corn are projected to bring this down to $12 billion in 2015. Farming is still considered as sacrosanct as motherhood and apple pie, so if mom or the pie gets in trouble, politicians will always be strongly tempted to help them out.

Is There a Bubble on the Farm?

The housing bubble of the 2000s was the result of a more than doubling of home prices between 2000 and 2006. When it burst, many people looked around and

FIGURE 30.4 Agricultural land values.

Source: USDA Agricultural Research Services.

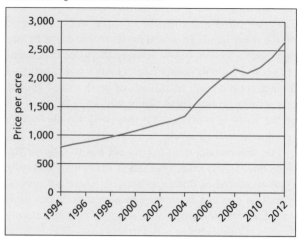

wondered why few had recognized the danger. Beginning in 2011, agricultural economists were expressing concern that a bubble was forming in agricultural land values. Figure 30.4 shows why. As corn and soybean prices rose, agricultural land values rose along with them. The obvious reason for this is that the value of the land is directly related to the profit that can be made by growing crops on that land. Higher crop prices lead to higher farm profits, which leads to increased demand for farmland, which leads to higher farmland prices.

That chain of events is factual and reasonable. The real or imagined bubble problem comes when either of the following is true: the prices for the crops are artificially high or the interest rates on the farm loans are artificially low. It is difficult to argue from Figure 30.1 that crop prices are artificially high as only corn and soybean prices are above their inflation-adjusted levels from the 1980s. It is easy to argue, using Figure 10.5, that interest rates from 2003 to 2006 and from 2009 to 2013 were artificially low. With Federal Reserve policy pushing interest rates low during these periods, one outcome has been inflated farmland prices. When the quantitative easing policy ends, it is likely that the run-up in farm prices will also end. Whether that results in a collapse in farmland prices (akin to the early 1980s collapse that resulted in hundreds of thousands of farm foreclosures), only time will tell.

Kick It Up
a Notch

Referring back to Figure 30.3, at equilibrium, $P^* - Q^*$, consumers pay the producers OP^*CQ^*, but they value what they get at $OACQ^*$. This means they have a consumer surplus of P^*AC. Similarly, the producer makes out well, too. The producer receives the OP^*CQ^* in revenue and the variable costs are only $OHCQ^*$. This nets the producer surplus of HP^*C. The combined surpluses make up the value to society of the exchange, a value represented as HAC.

If the government sets a price floor of P_{floor} consumers will want only Q_D. They will pay the $OP_{floor}BQ_D$ to producers. Consumers will value this at $OABQ_D$ and will net a consumer surplus of $P_{floor}AB$. It will cost producers $OHGQ_D$, so their producer surplus will be $HP_{floor}BG$. The combined surpluses are $HABG$. The deadweight loss is the difference between the combined surpluses with and without the floor, GBC.

Summary

Now that you have plowed your way through this chapter, you understand why economists generally are not in favor of price supports in agriculture. You understand that though price variation is real, there are mechanisms that farmers can use to compensate for that without government intervention. You are now able to employ consumer and producer surplus analysis to demonstrate the inefficiency caused by price floors. Last, you understand how price floors work in practice, and you have an appreciation for their history.

Key Term

price floor, 330

Quiz Yourself

1. The economic rationale for farm price supports is generally
   a. weak, but relies on price variability.
   b. weak, but relies on the unavailability of crop insurance.
   c. strong, and relies on the fact that prices are too high.
   d. strong, and relies on the importance of Iowa in presidential elections.

2. Price supports in the United States have
   a. always relied on the government paying farmers to set aside land.
   b. always relied on the government buying excess crops.
   c. always relied on forbidding production above certain levels.
   d. utilized a wide variety of means to raise prices and reduce output.

3. Farm price supports are typically for
   a. basic commodities like raw milk and grain.
   b. fruits and vegetables.
   c. refined products like flour.
   d. manufactured products like breakfast cereals.

4. A price support mechanism
   a. can only regulate supply.
   b. can only regulate demand.
   c. must involve government purchases.
   d. can involve government manipulation of the supply or demand of the good.

5. In Figure 30.2, maintaining P_{floor} as the target minimum price (rather than equilibrium) would
   a. raise consumer surplus more than it would decrease producer surplus.
   b. raise producer surplus more than it would decrease consumer surplus.

c. involve creating deadweight loss.

d. enhance the welfare of consumers and producers.

6. Looking at Figure 30.3, maintaining P_{floor} as the target minimum price (rather than equilibrium) by having the government purchase how much of the product farmers wished to produce would cost the government _____ dollars.

a. $OP*CQ*$

b. Q_DBEQ_S

c. $OP_{floor}BQ_D$

d. BCG dollars

Short Answer Questions

1. Given what you know about the relationship between corn and beef and corn and soybeans and corn and gasoline, an increase in the price of corn (due to a new insect that eats the roots out of corn) would have what impact on soybeans, beef, and gasoline?

2. If the price floor for corn is $3 per bushel and it is raised to $4 per bushel, what is the impact of that policy if the market price of corn is $6.50 per bushel?

3. During the 1980s many considered urban sprawl to be a serious problem for farm land. What would the mechanism be for "farm sprawl" reversing that?

Think about This

How much does it matter from the perspective of market form (monopoly, oligopoly, perfect competition) if there are 100, 1,000 or 1,000,000 farms producing raw grain?

Talk about This

Farm price supports are intended to help "the family farmer" but in reality often help multimillion-dollar farms. When Congress limited the size of the check that any particular farm could receive, farmers divided their farms into separate entities with different family members owning different farms so that they could continue to collect money. The "family farmer," defined as a simple farm with one house and the occupants of that house working the land, no longer produces a significant portion of the raw grain, cattle, or milk in the United States. Is the family farm more of a social myth than an actual entity?

For More Insight See

Gardner, Bruce L., "Changing Economic Perspectives on the Farm Problem," *Journal of Economic Literature* 30, no. 1 (March 1992), pp. 62–101.

Behind the Numbers

Farm product prices.

Bureau of Labor Statistics; Producer price index—www.bls.gov/ppi

CHAPTER THIRTY-ONE

Minimum Wage

Learning Objectives

After reading this chapter you should be able to:

LO1 Apply supply and demand to a labor market.

LO2 Define and describe the purpose of a minimum wage.

LO3 Conclude that the minimum wage must be higher than the equilibrium wage in order to be relevant.

LO4 Apply consumer and producer surplus to identify real-world winners and losers of a minimum wage increase.

LO5 Apply the concept of elasticity to the question of whether a minimum wage increase would increase unemployment.

LO6 Describe the earned income tax credit as an alternative to a minimum wage.

Chapter Outline

Traditional Economic Analysis of a Minimum Wage

Rebuttals to the Traditional Analysis

Where Are Economists Now?

Kick It Up a Notch

Summary

The **minimum wage** is the lowest wage that may legally be paid for an hour's work, subject to government restrictions. In 1938 the first minimum wage was set at 25 cents

minimum wage
The lowest wage that may legally be paid for an hour's work.

living wage
A wage sufficient to keep a family out of poverty.

per hour, and the amount has been increased periodically over the years. As of June 2013, the minimum wage was $7.25.

The minimum wage has traditionally been justified as a mechanism to ensure a **living wage**, that is, a wage sufficient to keep a family out of poverty.

As you can see in Figure 31.1, the minimum wage was always sufficient to keep an individual above the poverty line. It has been less successful for families. Since 1985 the minimum wage has been insufficient to maintain a one-earner, minimum-wage family (constituting more than an individual) above the poverty line. For instance, to accomplish the feat of keeping a family of four above the poverty line, the minimum wage for

a single full-time earner would have to be nearly $11 an hour.

Figure 31.2 indicates that although the minimum wage itself has been increased several times over the last 60 years, its real value, that is, the value adjusted for inflation in 1999 dollars, rose for the first 30 years of its existence and has steadily fallen since. Since 1950, the lowest it has been in inflation-adjusted dollars was its early 2007 level. It reached its highest inflation-adjusted level in 1968 at $7.65 per hour.[1] With solid majorities gained in the 2006 mid-term elections, Democrats pushed through a significant increase in the minimum wage. What had been $5.15 an hour in 2007 became $7.25 per hour in 2009. Even with that significant increase, in terms of its inflation-adjusted level, the minimum wage in 2009 was at its long-term historical average. With Republicans

---

[1]The poverty line used here is the official poverty line, with which there are many problems. Review Chapter 35, "Poverty and Welfare," to understand this issue.

FIGURE 31.1   The ratio of the earnings of a full-time minimum-wage worker to the poverty line for various family sizes.

Sources: U.S. Census Bureau, www.census.gov/hhes/www/poverty/data/threshld; United States Department of Labor, www.dol.gov/dol/topic/wages/minimumwage.htm

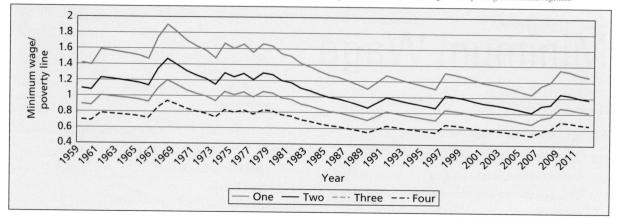

FIGURE 31.2   The nominal and real minimum wage, 1938–2013, in 1999 dollars.

Source: United States Department of Labor, www.dol.gov/dol/topic/wages/minimumwage.htm

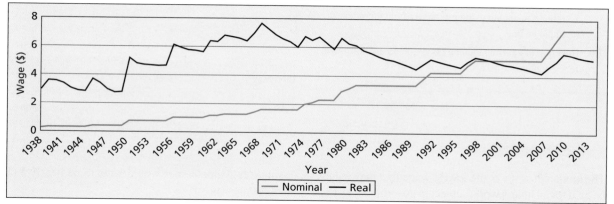

retaking the House of Representatives in 2010, there has been no increase since the last step increase in 2009.

Over time, economists have tended to argue against the minimum wage. In this chapter we explain those arguments along with the reasons why, until recently, most economists thought raising the minimum wage was wrong-headed. We also look at the arguments that suggest it may have been economists who were wrongheaded.

Traditional Economic Analysis of a Minimum Wage

Labor Markets and Consumer and Producer Surplus

Most economists have had few good things to say about the idea of establishing a minimum wage, and they have based that opinion on a traditional supply and demand analysis of the issue. Figure 31.3 represents a market for low-skill minimum-wage labor. The good being sold in this market is labor, and the price at which it is sold is the wage. The supply is made up of workers who will want to work more at higher pay, implying an upward-sloping supply curve; demand is made up of bosses seeking to hire that labor. The employers are assumed to want fewer laborers at higher wages, implying a downward-sloping demand curve. Without a law that sets its actual dollar amount, the wage would be set in this market at the point where the supply and demand curves meet. At this point there would be no shortage and no surplus. The wage would be W^* and there would be L^* work. Being a market clearing equilibrium, this is a wage at which no one who wants a job at that wage is without one, and no employers who want workers at that wage are unable to get them.

STATES AND CITIES INCREASE THE MINIMUM WAGE ON THEIR OWN

Because the federal minimum wage remained constant for nearly a decade, states and cities began to take the initiative to impose a higher minimum wage within their jurisdictions. As of May 2013, 19 states and several cities have minimum-wage laws that are higher than the federally mandated minimum wage. Moreover, in an effort to prevent the inflationary erosion of their state minimum wage, 11 states index their minimum wage to some measure of inflation.

FIGURE 31.3 Labor market.

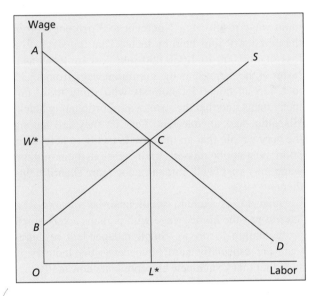

In this situation workers would be paid a total of OW^*CL^* dollars. When we addressed the notion of consumer and producer surplus in Chapter 3, we stated that the consumer surplus is the area under the demand curve but above the price line, while the producer surplus is the area under the price line and above the supply curve. Of course, in this case the price is the wage.

The key difference here is that businesses are getting the consumer surplus W^*AC, because it is they who are buying the good, that is, hiring the labor. We interpret consumer surplus here as the money that businesses make from the work of their employees that exceeds the amount they have to pay workers.

The producer surplus BW^*C is also different in that it is what workers get, since it is they who are doing the selling. The interpretation here is that it represents the amount of money that workers get in excess of what they would have worked for. So, just as in any other market,

the consumer gets something and the producer gets something.

A Relevant versus an Irrelevant Minimum Wage

If a minimum wage is set below W^*, would businesses pay the minimum wage rather than the higher W^*? Surprisingly, the answer is no, they would not: To get workers in the numbers that are most profitable to the business, employers have to pay the higher W^*. They would rather pay more than the minimum because, even though their labor costs then rise at a higher rate, the output of the extra workers will generate enough additional revenue to pay workers and to produce an increased profit as well. In addition, it is in their best interests to pay W^*, because otherwise their competitors will outbid them for labor. Thus any minimum wage set below W^* is irrelevant, because firms make more profit offering W^* rather than a lesser amount.

If you are not yet convinced that setting a minimum wage may be irrelevant, consider what would happen if your professors told you that you would fail if you showed up in class naked. Unless you had planned to do this anyway, an unlikely event since you would be kicked out of school, the rule would not affect your behavior in the least. Any rule that tells you that you cannot do something that you had no intention of doing anyway is not much of a rule. It does not alter your behavior, and it is therefore irrelevant. For the minimum wage to be relevant, it has to be an amount that is set above the equilibrium wage.

What Is Wrong with a Minimum Wage?

As seen in Figure 31.4, a minimum wage that has been set above the equilibrium wage has several effects. First, it raises the wage from W^* to W_{min}. Second, it reduces the amount of labor sold from L^* to L_{min}. Third, as long as the money gained from raising the wage to workers

FIGURE 31.4   Minimum wage.

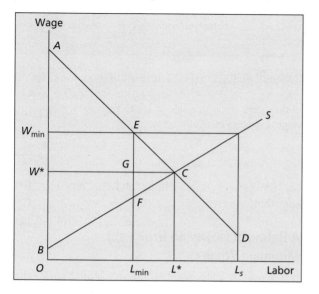

area *FEC*. To see this precisely, go to "Kick It Up A Notch" located at the end of the chapter.

Real-World Implications of the Minimum Wage

Though rather elegant as a mechanism to analyze the impacts of a minimum wage, consumer and producer surplus analysis does not put it in terms easy for the average person to see. The winners are the more than 4 million people who work for the minimum wage and get a pay increase because they keep their jobs.

The losers are the people who lose their jobs. Research on the subject has led economists to use the rule of thumb that a 10 percent increase in the minimum wage results in a 1 percent to 3 percent drop in the number of jobs held by teens. That translates to a loss of 360,000 to 1,050,000 jobs lost by teens as a result of the increase in the minimum wage from $5.15 to $7.25 an hour.[2] Economists who study those unlucky teens find that they are disproportionately black, Hispanic, and uneducated. That is, they are among the very people that an increase is trying to help. This point must not be missed. An increase in the minimum wage may very well hurt the poor more than it helps them.

Other losers include small business owners who have to pay the higher wage with perhaps a very small profit margin to do so. Small independent restaurateurs are especially hard hit because the industry is such that many such new entrepreneurs constantly teeter on the edge of bankruptcy and can afford to pay only minimum wage. That means that an increase in the minimum wage may destroy not only the jobs these entrepreneurs are creating, but also the entrepreneurs themselves.

Finally, the losers include anyone who buys goods or services produced by minimum-wage workers, because part of the increase is passed on to them in the form of higher prices.

Alternatives to the Minimum Wage

It is for all of these reasons and more that until recently most economists could not endorse increases in the minimum wage. Those who took the position that the minimum wage was an inappropriate cure for

is greater than the money lost as a result of having fewer people working, workers in general have more money than they had before. From your earlier study of the concept of elasticity, you will recognize the condition for this is that the demand for labor has to be inelastic. Finally, the imposition of a minimum wage will raise the unemployment rate for workers in this market. This will happen because either more workers will want to work or existing workers will want to work more hours. With a minimum wage set above the equilibrium wage, workers want to provide L_s labor, whereas they used to want to work only L^*. Further complicating this is that employers now want to hire labor only up to L_{min} rather than the L^* they had wanted previously.

In the end, the consumer surplus shrinks to $W_{min}AE$ and producer surplus grows. The sum of the consumer and producer surpluses is less than it was without the minimum wage, by the triangle *FEC*.

What this all leads to is that under this economic analysis of the minimum wage, there are winners and losers. The winners are those workers who get a wage increase and who are still able to continue working as much as they want. The losers are men and women who used to be working and who are now unemployed ($L^* - L_{min}$). The important part of this analysis is that what is gained by workers is less than what employers lose. We are thus confronted with what economists label deadweight loss, the net loss to society by the

[2]This assumes that at $5.15, the minimum wage was above equilibrium. The evidence is that the equilibrium wage was higher than $5.15 for much of 2004 and beyond, making $5.15 an irrelevant minimum wage.

the problems of poorly paid workers highlighted the fact that most workers who made the minimum wage were under 24. Nearly a third of these were under 19 and therefore very unlikely to be supporting a family. Combine this with the fact that many of those who earn the minimum wage and are over age 24 are spouses who work only to supplement the income of the family's primary income producer and are nowhere near poverty.

In the eyes of many economists a better alternative is the Earned Income Tax Credit (EITC). Low-income working families with children are eligible for up to $4,824 that arrives in the form of a tax refund. The benefits of the EITC are concentrated on the people who actually need the money to feed their families. More than 70 percent of the money goes to households that are or would otherwise be in poverty. This contrasts dramatically with the minimum wage, where upward of 70 percent of the benefits accrue to households not in poverty.

The EITC, while born in the 1970s, saw great increases starting during the administration of President Ronald Reagan. It was during this administration that the minimum wage saw a long period of real decline in its value. It was President Reagan's view that the minimum wage was a poor mechanism to help the poor and that the EITC could help working poor families without hurting businesses. While President Clinton's first budget increased taxes for many, it also greatly increased the EITC. Moreover, though he pushed through an increase in the minimum wage as well, the increased level of the EITC has had a greater effect on the working poor.

Rebuttals to the Traditional Analysis

In contrast to the preceding section, important points of rebuttal to the traditional analysis have gained respectability in recent years among economists. They center on three main lines of argument. Macroeconomic analysis suggests, first, that the effect of a decrease in income by owners of businesses is somewhat offset by the effect of an increase in income by the lower-income people. Low-income people spend more and high-income people save more. A second line of argument is that the good in question, labor, is not as definable as most other goods and that with better pay, workers can be induced to work harder. If they do so, the increase in the wage becomes less of a burden on employers. The remaining

argument is that the elasticity of demand for labor may be so low that the traditional analysis needs to reflect this fact. If it does, the negative aspects of the minimum wage will be small.

The Macroeconomics Argument

The first argument in rebuttal to the traditional analysis relies on an aspect of macroeconomics that suggests that if you track all of the times a particular amount of money is spent, you can figure up the total impact of new spending. Or, as is appropriate in this case, you can examine the net effect of monies being spent by different people. If, for instance, business owners save most of their profit rather than spend or invest it, then something less than the entire profit of the business works its way through the economy in the form of additional spending. On the other hand, if the business owners have to relinquish more of that profit to workers because of the imposition of a higher minimum wage, then almost all of that money will be spent. Men and women who are paid the minimum wage save very little, and they spend nearly all of their additional income. Because money is spent rather than saved, total consumption in the economy rises. From a macroeconomic standpoint, any negative effects of a minimum-wage increase range from being offset, to being nonexistent, to being positive.

Suppose, for example, that the result of an increase in the minimum wage is to increase the incomes for workers by $75 while creating a $100 loss in profit to businesses. Remember that it is not simply a direct transfer; workers' gains are offset by losses to business that are greater. The $25 difference, the deadweight loss, is the amount of damage to an overall measure of economic activity like the gross domestic product. This gap can be made up if the effect of low-skill workers' spending it is greater than the effect of bosses spending it. If low-skill workers spend all of their increased income, and bosses spend or invest only 80 percent of theirs, the net effect of raising the minimum wage is that the GDP shrinks by $5 rather than $25. This is because 80 percent of $100 is only $5 more than 100 percent of $75. This is, of course, predicated on the assumption that a higher minimum wage has the net effect of increasing the income of minimum-wage workers.

The Work Effort Argument

The second argument is probably correct in assuming that people adjust the effort they put in at work depending on how happy they are with their employer. This means that the graphs in Figures 31.3 and 31.4 are not as stable as we previously thought them to be. The good "labor" is not as fixed in its meaning as are most other goods for which we use this supply and demand model. People can work hard or slack off, and there is not a great deal that an employer can do to force slackers to work harder. If higher pay translates into workers who are happier and who do more work per hour, it may be the case that some if not all of the impact of forcing wages to rise will be mitigated. In this way the minimum-wage increase may pay for itself. On the other hand, if it did pay for itself, we would have to assume that employers were either ignorant of this fact or not maximizers of profit. Neither of these assumptions sits well with most economists. It is more plausible that such an increase merely lessens the negative impact.

The Elasticity Argument

The last argument used to rebut traditional analysis simply tweaks the traditional analysis a little to suggest that the negative impact of an increase in the minimum wage is very small. Any increase can thus be interpreted as simply a transfer of money from business owners to workers. Comparing Figure 31.5 to Figure 31.4, you will find that the only real difference is that the demand curve is steeper, that is, more inelastic, in Figure 31.5. The net amount that workers gain is very great, and the resulting unemployment of those who had jobs before, $L^* - L_{min}$, is very low. As we said when we discussed elasticity in Chapter 3,

there are two things that will influence elasticity: the number of close substitutes and time to invent them.

Given that in the short run there are very few substitutes for having workers on the job, this rebuttal seems, of the three mentioned, the most persuasive to traditional economists. Most economists still believe that the existence of a minimum wage will reduce employment in the long run. They maintain that the only reason the gain to workers is great and the net loss to society is small is that this is an analysis that works only in the short run.

They argue that in the long run business owners will search until they find substitutes for labor such as easier-to-use machines and self-serve devices. If you look at the fast-food industry and the equipment that it uses, you will find that the companies involved are always looking for new ways to reduce the need for employees, and they have had great success in their endeavors. Putting the drink machines in the lobby and using chain ovens or broilers that cook the food for exactly the correct amount of time without needing employee monitoring are just a couple of examples of how employers of minimum-wage workers have substituted capital for labor.

Where Are Economists Now?

If the more recent nontraditional analysis is correct, it is probably because in the short run there is not much deadweight loss to be made up. The combined impact of the macroeconomic effect and the harder worker effect is therefore enough to completely eliminate the problem. The data on whether recent minimum-wage increases have had a net negative impact on unemployment for the 1990 and 1996 increases are mixed. Two influential economists, David Card and Andrew Krueger, published a study of the minimum wage utilizing data on fast-food employment. They surveyed establishments in two neighboring states in a period where one increased its minimum wage and another did not. They found that the increase did not negatively impact, and perhaps positively impacted, employment in the state that raised its minimum wage.

Since this study ran against the conventional wisdom of labor economists, many were quick to try to duplicate their results. The attempts to replicate the work of Card and Krueger turned up serious data and methodology problems with their work. As a result of the newer work casting doubt on the Card and Krueger conclusion, most labor economists have not moved much from their earlier assessment. In particular, many still use the teen

FIGURE 31.5 The minimum wage in the short run.

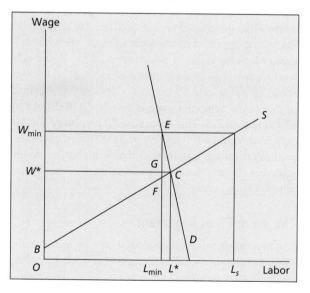

employment rule of thumb mentioned earlier but concede that a 10 percent increase in the minimum wage translates to a 1 percent or 2 percent decrease in teen

employment. In any event, economists have expended considerable time rethinking an issue that they thought they had put to bed a long time ago.

Kick It Up
a Notch

Referring back to Figure 31.4, we can firmly establish the winners and losers and more rigorously defend the claim that the gain to workers from a minimum wage is less than the loss to firms and unemployed workers. Remember that the benefit to workers from an increase in the minimum wage is the increase in their producer surplus. Without a minimum wage the producer surplus is $BW*C$, while with the minimum wage it is $BW_{min}EF$. The

consumer surplus is the benefit to firms hiring the labor. They go from having a consumer surplus of $W*AC$ without the minimum wage to a consumer surplus of $W_{min}AE$ with it. The gain to workers is $W*W_{min}EG - GFC$, while the loss to firms is $W*WminEG + GEC$. The net effect is the gain to workers minus the loss to firms, which is $-FEC$. Because the net effect is negative, this is a loss, one that economists call the deadweight loss.

Summary

After this exploration of the minimum wage, you understand why it exists in the first place and what its implications are for our supply and demand model for labor. You know how to use our consumer and producer surplus techniques to identify the winners and losers of any minimum wage increase and then apply real-world observations. You understand the diversity of opinion among economists on the subject, and you know the Earned Income Tax Credit is an alternative to it.

Key Terms

living wage, 335   minimum wage, 335

Quiz Yourself

1. Between 1998 and 2007 the real minimum wage
   a. rose rapidly.
   b. rose slowly.
   c. remained constant.
   d. fell rapidly.

2. In order for the minimum wage to reach its 1968 high in real terms (1999 dollars), it would have to rise to approximately _____ per hour.
   a. $8
   b. $9
   c. $10
   d. $11

3. The last time the minimum wage alone was sufficient to keep a family of three above the poverty line was
   a. 1979.
   b. 1985.
   c. 1990.
   d. 1998.

4. The argument that the minimum wage is worse than the earned income tax credit is based on the idea that
   a. the people who earn the minimum wage are really poor.
   b. the minimum wage applies to all workers, not just the working poor.
   c. the earned income tax credit goes to all workers.
   d. the minimum wage applies only to those younger than 25.

5. The argument that the minimum wage does not significantly increase unemployment is based on
   a. producer surplus.
   b. consumer surplus.
   c. elasticity.
   d. aggregate demand.

6. The argument that the minimum wage hurts society more than it helps is based on _____ analysis.
    a. consumer and producer surplus
    b. production possibilities
    c. aggregate supply–aggregate demand
    d. marginal

7. The argument that employers would actually not lose money if the minimum wage were raised is based on
    a. the idea that workers would spend the extra money buying goods from their employer.
    b. the idea that workers would work overtime without having to be paid.
    c. the idea that workers would be more productive if they felt they were adequately compensated.
    d. the elasticity of demand for labor.

Short Answer Questions

1. Who is most likely to benefit from an increase in the minimum wage?

2. Who is most likely to lose from an increase in the minimum wage? Who of those might have thought an increase was in their best interests?

3. Suppose you knew that there was going to be 20 percent inflation between now and five years from now, and suppose you knew that the minimum wage was only enough to get a family of three to 80 percent of the poverty line. How much would you have to raise the minimum wage over that period in order to make the minimum wage earn enough to be at that poverty line?

Think about This

Several states have set the minimum wage in their states higher than the federal minimum wage. If doing so places them at a competitive disadvantage for new business this might be counterproductive. On the other hand, the minimum wage is typically relevant only in low-paid service jobs. Who makes the minimum wage in your community? Would your community be better off with a higher minimum wage?

Talk about This

One of the principal opponents to minimum wage increases is the umbrella organization for small business. Many states with higher minimum wages than the federal level exempt businesses with few employees. Should small businesses be exempt from minimum wage laws?

For More Insight See

Brown, Charles, "Minimum Wages Laws: Are They Overrated?" *Journal of Economic Perspectives* 2, no. 3 (Summer 1988), pp. 133–146.

Brown, Charles, Curtis Gilroy, and Andrew Kohen, "The Effect of the Minimum Wage on Employment and Unemployment," *Journal of Economic Literature* 20, no. 2 (June 1982), pp. 487–528.

Card, David, and Alan Krueger, *Myth and Measurement: The New Economics of the Minimum Wage* (Princeton, NJ: Princeton University Press, 1995).

Behind the Numbers

Historical data.
Minimum wage.
    U.S. Department of Labor; Employment Standards Administration—www.dol.gov/dol/topic/wages/minimumwage.htm
Poverty line.
    U.S. Census Bureau; historical poverty tables—www.census.gov/hhes/www/poverty/data/threshld/
EITC eligibility and amount.
    Internal Revenue Service—www.irs.gov
Adams, Scott, and David Neumark, "A Decade of Living Wages: What Have We Learned?" Public Policy Institute of California—www.ppic.org/main/publication.asp?i=620

CHAPTER THIRTY-TWO

Ticket Brokers and Ticket Scalping

Learning Objectives

After reading this chapter you should be able to:

LO1 Define ticket scalping and describe why it exists.

LO2 Conclude that the market form appropriate to analyze ticket sales to an event is the monopoly model.

LO3 Contrast the marginal cost curve presented in Chapter 4 with the one appropriate for ticket sales.

LO4 Enumerate the reasons why promoters may rationally charge less for an event than they could, and conclude that the result of this is a shortage of tickets.

LO5 Describe why the conditions of a shortage typically create a scalping market, where people buy tickets below, at, or above their face value and sell them for a profit.

LO6 Conclude that economists generally value the scalping market, see very little reason to make laws regulating it, and see very little functional distinction between the legal and illegal forms of scalping that exist across the country.

Chapter Outline

Defining Brokering and Scalping

An Economic Model of Ticket Sales

Why Promoters Charge Less Than They Could

An Economic Model of Scalping

Legitimate Scalpers

Summary

If you want to see a concert, a game, a race, or any other event that is sold out, you probably know that you can always get a ticket—for a price. Some tickets command prices that are many times their face value. In the 1990s scalpers were getting more than $1,000 for a ticket to see Michael Jordan's last game as a Chicago Bull and Mark McGwire's attempt to break the single-season home run record. Some events are once in a lifetime, whereas other reoccurring events like the Super Bowl and the World Series are events that are important enough to some people that they are willing to pay more than face value for a ticket.

While in many cities it is illegal to sell a ticket for more than face value, in every major city there is a way of getting such tickets when they are the only ones available. Economists are almost always against laws that prevent people from selling things they possess. They reason that if one person would rather have $500 than a ticket to a game and another person would rather have a ticket to a game than $500, then both are better off with the trade than without it.

This chapter defines ticket scalping and offers an economic explanation for it. We begin that explanation by using our monopoly pricing model from Chapter 5 to understand the promoter's ticket-pricing scheme.

We show that for scalping to exist, promoters have to be underpricing their tickets, and we consider why they do this. We use our supply and demand model and our consumer and producer surplus language to see how scalping helps consumers and scalpers alike. We talk about the mechanism by which scalpers become "legit" by calling themselves "brokers" or by offering packages that combine the tickets with other amenities.

Defining Brokering and Scalping

Brokering tickets is the act of buying a ticket and selling it at a price higher than its face value when such a trans-action is legal. **Scalping** tickets is the act of buying a ticket and selling it at a price higher than its face value when such a transac-tion is illegal. Thus, the practice is scalping only when it is done illegally. Regardless of semantic differences, for many fans and performers, scalpers and brokers are the worst form of predator; they obtain large blocks of tickets before other people get them and then they sell the tickets at prices that net them a profit. They do not produce any-thing. Those who engage in this trade view themselves as simply providing a service from which they make a living. To others, they are simply leeching off the talents of others.

brokering
The act of buying a ticket and legally selling it at a price higher than its face value.

scalping
The act of buying a ticket and illegally selling it at a price higher than its face value.

For economists, scalpers perform a function that "fixes" pricing that promoters get wrong. As we will see, scalping can exist profitably only when enough fans are willing to pay more for tickets than the face value of the ticket and there are more buyers willing to pay face value than there are seats.

This does not necessarily mean the performance is a sellout. If some seats are really good and others are re-ally terrible, then the good ones, at courtside, say, might be scalped while those in "nosebleed territory" might re-main unsold. What is true is that there cannot be unsold seats right next to seats for which scalpers wish to charge more than face value. When traditional ticket outlets that sell for face value have open, decent seats, these will be sold out before scalpers can sell any.

An Economic Model of Ticket Sales

The question we can pose at this point is, "Why would a promoter charge less for a ticket than it is worth?" To answer the question we need to look at what determines

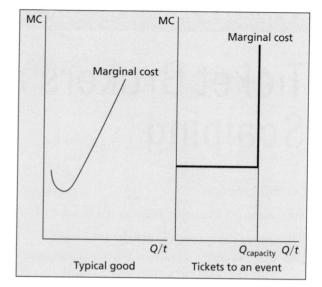

FIGURE 32.1   Marginal cost.

the price a promoter should charge. To model that, we need to go back to Chapter 5 to see which model of the market is more appropriate for ticket sales, perfect com-petition or monopoly. Because there is ultimately only one seller of the tickets, the promoter, our monopoly model is clearly more appropriate to this than the perfect competition model, in which there are many sellers.

Marginal Cost

To complicate things somewhat more, remember the shape of the marginal cost curve that was introduced in Chapter 4. It is a check-shaped curve, as seen in the left panel of Figure 32.1. For ticket sales to a sporting event or a concert, the marginal cost looks a little different. The right-hand side of Figure 32.1 shows that up to the capacity of the stadium, the marginal cost is probably more likely to be a constant. The costs of printing and selling the tickets and the costs of cleaning up after each additional fan remain relatively constant. These extra costs are likely to be the same for the thousandth fan as the hundred-thousandth fan. At capacity, however, the extra cost of selling to another person grows astronomi-cally, as new construction would have to take place to add more seats.

The Promoter as Monopolist

When promoters are attempting to maximize profits and are trying to figure out what price to charge for events, they have to gauge what the demand will be for the event. Once they

FIGURE 32.2   The profit-maximizing promoter's choice of price and ticket sales.

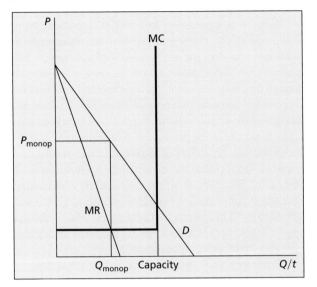

FIGURE 32.3   The perfect arena.

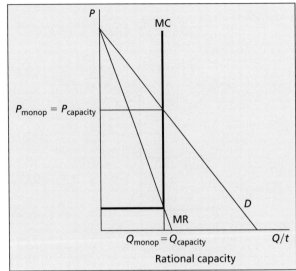

have done that, they can look at this problem as any other monopolist would. Recall that we have always assumed that firms are profit maximizers. Though revenue would be maximized where marginal revenue cuts the horizontal axis, this is not where the profit-maximizing promoters operate. As is depicted in Figure 32.2, they project the number of sales and set the price so that marginal revenue equals marginal cost. This means that they would sell Q_{monop} tickets for P_{monop} each.

An interesting aspect of this is that it may make sense for promoters to see that the arena is only partially filled. Promoters hold back tickets when they would have to lower the price too far in order to sell out the facility. You should not be surprised by this conclusion, especially if you are at a school that does not have a popular athletic program. Consider a school whose men's basketball team draws between 4,000 and 6,000 fans a game, while the women's team draws fewer than 1,000 a game. If the athletic department were to price tickets to sell out the arena, tickets would be nearly free for the men's games and the department would have to pay people to see the women. That is not a slam at the women; it is just a fact of life at a school without a national sports reputation. Clearly, it makes sense for this university to charge more for the men's games and to charge something for the women. The university makes the most money possible that way, even with only one sellout per decade.

The Perfect Arena

To a promoter, the size of the facility is significant. In a promoter's eyes, the perfect facility would be represented as seen in Figure 32.3, where the capacity is exactly the number of seats that the promoter wants to sell anyway. That is, the facility with perfect capacity is the one where marginal cost intersects marginal revenue at the quantity that is exactly the capacity of the facility. Of course, promoters cannot always find the perfect facility. Most medium and small cities have only one or two places to hold an event like a concert, and even in other places, the perfect arena or concert hall may not be available.

In a big city with many venues of many different sizes, a promoter should seek the facility whose size ensures that the marginal cost will cross marginal revenue at exactly the capacity. On the assumption that facilities that are unnecessarily large cost the promoter more to rent, booking this "perfect" facility maximizes profit.

In each case mentioned so far, there is no market for scalpers because the face value of the ticket is the price at which it is sold. Scalping makes sense only if the market price of the ticket is greater than the face value. The only way for that to happen is if the promoter charges less than the profit-maximizing amount. This is seen in Figure 32.4, where the ticket is priced at or below the price that would sell out the facility rather than the price that would maximize profits for the promoter.

FIGURE 32.4   Capacity versus profit-maximizing prices.

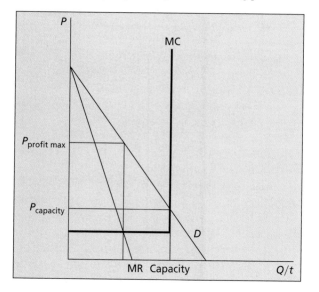

Why Promoters Charge Less Than They Could

Why might promoters sell out a facility rather than maximize profits? First, they may not have good information on the price they ought to charge. This uncertainty might motivate them to err on the safe side and charge a lower price. Second, there may be some "excitement" factor to a full stadium that appeals to the performers and that is worth the loss of profit. Third, the performers may want a reputation of charging a "fair price" for their events and be willing to forgo maximum profit in order to further that reputation. Fourth, the performers may want some mechanism other than price to separate the "real fans" from those who go to events simply because they have money. Fifth, ancillary sales of shirts and other memorabilia are important sources of revenue for performers and promoters alike. Since it may be that the revenue gained by these sales exceeds that lost by having low ticket prices, low ticket prices may lead to increasing audience size and may therefore maximize profit after all. Last, it may be in the long-run best interest of the performers to charge a low price for tickets so that the largest possible audience can provide word-of-mouth advertising for them and generate interest for their talent.

Sometimes promoters do not have an exact idea of what price to charge for an event. More often than not, promoters of a new act must guess what the market will bear for the ticket. If they guess too low, scalping may ensue. In addition, promoters may want to play it safe

and not run the risk of pricing too high, thereby purposefully pricing less than even their best guess. This might also result in scalping.

There is an excitement to being at a sold-out event in a large arena. The sound and feel are different for a sold-out event than for one in a half-full auditorium. The performer enjoys it more and the fans enjoy it more. Although this may not seem like an important function for a promoter, consider that promoters are hired by athletes or performers to promote the event as effectively as possible. It may be in the promoters' best interests to cater to the performer, regardless of what maximizes profit.

Some performers try to establish a closeness with their fans. Some try to signal their empathy by making sure ticket prices are low enough that "ordinary" fans can afford to go. This means that performers and promoters are willing to accept less money for the good feeling that charging "fair" prices gives them.

Performers may appreciate fans who are willing to camp out for tickets more than those simply willing to pay a lot of money. You have to be much more excited about a band to camp out than to simply buy tickets. The people who are willing to camp out to get front-row seats are far more likely to convey enthusiasm for performers than those with deep pockets.

When you go to a concert, you often spend as much on shirts and other promotional items as you did on the ticket. If promoters keep you out by charging a price that is too high, they forgo that important other revenue as well. In the big picture, low ticket prices may be profit maximizing after all.

Promoters of new bands may decide that it is in their long-run interest to keep ticket prices low so that the band is seen by as many people as possible. By setting low ticket prices early in a performer's career, they may be more likely to turn a one-hit wonder into a star.

For any one of the reasons just outlined, promoters may choose to sell their tickets at prices below their monopoly market value and perhaps even below the price that would guarantee a sellout. In any event, a price below what they see as the free market value will cause scalpers to buy tickets at the lower price in order to sell them at a higher price.

An Economic Model of Scalping

A market characterized by ticket scalping is going to have a typical demand curve. It will reflect the demand by those who do not get tickets by normal means. For many events, such as any home game played by the Green Bay Packers, tickets only go to those who subscribe or have had tickets for many, many years. This "right of first refusal" on tickets is so valuable that married couples' divorce agreements have been held up over this right. If you want to go to a single Packers game, you have to resort to the scalpers market.

The demand curve for these tickets is downward sloping just as it is for any other good. If the event is a "must see," then you expect a demand curve further to the right or perhaps more inelastic, or steeper, because tickets for a "once-in-a-lifetime event" have fewer substitutes than tickets for events that will be repeated. The elasticity of demand will be expected to be less.

The supply curve for this market is upward sloping (and not vertical), not because the number of tickets is not limited but because in order to get tickets away from those who have them, you have to give up more and more to persuade more and more rabid fans to give up their tickets. Figure 32.5 reflects the market for scalped tickets.

If the price is required to stay at the face value of the ticket, then there will be fewer tickets than potential buyers. To an economist this is the very definition of a shortage. Note that the supply curve may start below $P_{\text{face value}}$ or above it. In Figure 32.5 it starts below. To understand why, consider that there are people who have tickets for an event who are willing to sell them for less than they paid because they do not want to go to the event. Why would you buy a ticket for an event you did not want to go to? Suppose you had season tickets to the Los Angeles

Lakers and a ticket to the California 500 NASCAR race. Suppose the L.A. Clippers were playing the Lakers on the day of the race. You paid face value for the ticket, and you are willing to take almost anything for that game's ticket because you have decided to go to the race.

If scalping is illegal, only $Q_{\text{face value}}$, the tickets that people are willing to unload for the face value, will be sold. If those are the only tickets that are sold, then the people who are willing to pay more than face value will not find any to buy. Some people will go to the game when they would rather have received P_{market} and stayed home. Others will stay home, when they would rather have paid P_{market} and gone to the game.

Without scalping, there is a shortage and a loss of societal benefit. That loss, measured by the loss in consumer and producer surplus, can also be seen in Figure 30.5. The loss of welfare to people who want to see the game at the scalper's price is *EFB*, while the loss to people who would like to have sold their tickets is *GEB*. The total loss to society when scalping is forbidden is *GFB*.

In this circumstance, is the permission to scalp tickets creating a problem or solving one? Economists posit that scalpers are solving the shortage by taking tickets from those who have them and who value them least and transferring them to those who do not have them and who value them most. For this the scalper takes a cut. Performers take a dim view of this. They view it as a practice in which people profit from something they had no hand at all in creating.

FIGURE 32.5 A scalper's market.

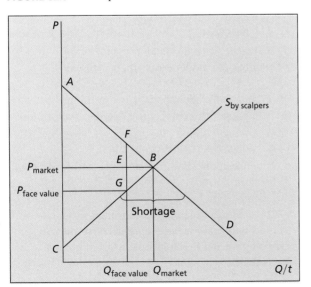

Legitimate Scalpers

In some states, all forms of scalping are legal; in others, none are. In a growing number of states scalping remains illegal, but "brokers" are allowed to sell tickets for more than they pay for them. The only difference between a scalper and a broker is that the scalper walks around an event's perimeter trying to sell tickets, while the broker does it from a desk and a phone. The scalper demands cash; the broker takes credit cards.

Another way that scalpers have become legitimate is by pairing their services with that of a travel agent. It is legal in nearly every state for travel agents to create packages with hotel rooms, cab rides, and the like, and then offer these along with the tickets. Suppose you want a ticket to the latest "fight of the century." If it is in a no-scalping state and you cannot get tickets the normal way, you can still get the ticket because travel agents now can combine a $100 ticket with a $100 hotel room and a $10 dollar cab ride and call it a $500 "excursion." (Do the math!) This is legal nearly everywhere, even when "scalping" is not. It is also what an economist would call a distinction without a difference.

It must be reinforced, therefore, that economists generally disapprove of antiscalping regulations. Whether as legal brokers or illegal scalpers, the sellers are providing services. They are not only fixing the market shortage left over by the promoter, they are also providing convenience. The hours of ticket offices at major arenas are not always amenable to customer desires. Lines at the ticket booth or at "will call" windows are often very long the day of the event. Because scalpers and brokers provide us with a convenience and harm no one in the process, there is little economic reason to ban their activities.

Summary

You now understand what ticket scalping is and why it exists. You understand that the market for tickets falls within the monopoly model and that the marginal cost curve presented in Chapter 4 is not appropriate for ticket sales. You understand why promoters may rationally charge less for an event than they could and that the result of this is a shortage of tickets. You understand that under the conditions of a shortage there is typically a place for a scalping market in which people buy tickets below, at, or above their face value and sell them for a profit. Last, you understand that economists generally value such services, see little reason to make laws regulating them, and see little functional distinction between the legal and illegal forms of brokering or scalping that exist across the country.

Key Terms

brokering, 344   scalping, 344

Quiz Yourself

1. Ticket scalping is a symptom of
   a. stupid promoters.
   b. market prices being greater than the face value of the ticket.
   c. market prices being less than the face value of the ticket.
   d. stupid consumers.
2. Economists _____ the activities of ticket brokers and scalpers.
   a. draw no distinction between
   b. separately model
   c. draw a stark contrast between
   d. ignore
3. The optimal venue for an event is one where
   a. the number of seats exceeds the number where marginal cost equals marginal revenue.
   b. the number of seats is less than the number where marginal cost equals marginal revenue.
   c. the number of seats is exactly the number where marginal cost equals marginal revenue.
   d. marginal revenue exceeds marginal cost for all seats.
4. The distinct feature of the marginal cost curve in the analysis of venues is that it is
   a. a vertical line.
   b. a horizontal line.
   c. a check-shaped curve.
   d. a backward L.
5. The model for a promoter is _____ whereas the model for scalpers is that of _____ _____.
   a. monopoly; monopolistic competition
   b. monopolistic competition; perfect competition
   c. monopoly; oligopoly
   d. monopoly; perfect competition
6. If antiscalping laws are perfectly enforced, it will result in
   a. deadweight loss.
   b. a significant increase in consumer surplus.
   c. a significant increase in producer surplus.
   d. a significant loss to people who are going to the event.

Short Answer Questions

1. What is the difference between StubHub! and a ticket scalper walking in front of a stadium?

2. Explain why it is not a contradiction for a ticket scalper to carry a sign that says "Need Tickets" on one side when it says "Have Tickets" on the other side (indicating he is both buying and selling tickets)?

3. Suppose you have a ticket to an event that is on a very important day to your spouse and you know it will cost you if you go to the event. How is the scalper good for you?

4. Suppose you need a ticket to a sold-out event for which your spouse had asked you to buy tickets a long time ago (and you forgot). Would you be made better off with or without antiscalping laws when those laws are closely enforced?

Think about This

There are laws in many states and communities against scalping. Many promoters will let people buy only a limited number of tickets for fear that the buyer will simply resell them later. Why would a promoter care who buys the tickets? If you became a performer, would you care?

Talk about This

Some scalpers will pay college students who have camped out for a concert to buy extra tickets for them so that they can later resell them. Because this is against the law in some places, there is some risk for the scalper in that the student could simply resell the tickets themselves. If you were standing in line for tickets, what would you do?

For More Insight See

Happel, Stephen, and Marianne Jennings, "The Folly of Anti-Scalping Laws," *The Cato Journal* 15, no. 1 (Spring/Summer 1995), pp. 65–76.

CHAPTER THIRTY-THREE

The Economics of K–12 Education

Learning Objectives

After reading this chapter you should be able to:

LO1   Analyze education as an investment and as one that not only pays dividends to the person getting the education, but also positively affects society at large.

LO2   Summarize the debate over whether spending more on education will yield more significant returns.

LO3   Summarize the economics behind the school reform issues.

LO4   Describe why many economists argue that the current structure of education prevents more money from doing any good.

Chapter Outline

Investments in Human Capital

Should We Spend More?

School Reform Issues

Summary

From a strictly economic perspective, the amount of time and money we spend on educating ourselves and our fellow citizens is amazing. Required to stay in school until we are at least 16, and in some cases until we are 18, we are strongly encouraged to graduate from high school and, when we do, we are offered substantial subsidies to get some form of higher education. Some of us even press on to earn graduate degrees. In the end, it is easily possible that we have spent the first third of our lives acquiring an education. Our parents and our government have encouraged us to invest in ourselves even while contributing nothing of substance to society during that time. Since most people retire before they die, the typical postgraduate educated person has fewer than 40 years to earn enough to pay back, figuratively, what he or she invested in formal education.

In general, parents and grandparents are staunch supporters of schools, at least financially. People without children in school have other reasons for supporting them. In this chapter we explore some of the reasons people give for supporting education. We try to determine whether society is getting its money's worth for elementary and secondary education.

In considering the elementary and secondary level, we look at how much money is spent on education and attempt to determine whether taxpayers are getting what they pay for. To that end we plot measures of cost, and we look at the ratio of the numbers of students to teachers. Next we examine measures of success such as students' performances on standardized tests and the numbers of degrees that are granted.

Investments in Human Capital

In Chapters 4 and 5 we spoke of capital as though the concept were confined to machines. In this chapter we

human capital
The ability of a person to create goods and services.

turn to another form of capital, **human capital**. This refers to the ability of a person to create goods and services. Education and training play an important role in developing human capital.

Present Value Analysis

In Chapter 7's discussion of present value and investments, we learned it is possible to invest too little or too

net present value
The difference between the present value of benefits and the present value of costs.

much in anything, including human capital. Determining the right amount depends on the value of the **net present value**, the difference between the present value of benefits and the present value of costs.

The investment we make in the education of our own children we do out of love for them, but it also makes sense from an economic point of view. If there were no "free"[1] public schools, we would look first at the present value of costs of educating a child from kindergarten through high school. We would then subtract that from the present value of the child's increased earning potential because of that education. If at that point we found that the net was positive, then we would conclude that, for the parent, the investment would be a wise one.

Again, from the view of the parent, an even more refined look at this analysis would subtract out those costs that would occur anyway. Consider the modern family with two working parents or a single parent. If there were no public school, they would have day-care expenses whether or not the child were educated. That means, at the margin, a cost of educating the child is the difference between the tuition to the school and the day-care costs. This reduces the relevant costs, and it makes education an even better investment.

---

[1] "Free" is in quotes for two reasons. First, some states require a textbook rental fee that, in Indiana at least, is between $100 and $200 per student per year. This fee is waived for students qualifying for the Federal School Lunch program. Second, the taxpayer pays for this public education. Thus "free" should be read as "free to the parents except for any fees that might be involved."

External Benefits

Of course, K–12 education is public and it has been for so long that we may not even think of asking why. There are societal as well as economic reasons for having free public education. Societally, benefits accrue to us all from having children become educated, whether or not they are our own children. Economically, benefits accrue to us because people who are educated are less likely to be on welfare or commit crimes against us and are more likely to be productive citizens who pay more in taxes than they cost in government benefits. An additional benefit that we derive from public school education is that having children of all races, ethnic groups, religions,

external benefits
Benefits that accrue to someone other than the consumer or producer of the good or service.

and income classes in the same schools may foster social stability. Thus, the **external benefits** of K–12 education justify having a considerable subsidy to that education.

We can use our supply and demand diagram to illustrate the inefficiency of just having unsubsidized private education. Consider Figure 33.1 and what it suggests the price of education should be to the parents of the children to be educated. The price is the annual tuition, and the quantity is the number of kids educated in a year. At low tuition rates, more will invest in education, and when it is free, everyone will take advantage of it. The resulting demand curve is downward sloping, but if tuition is low, schools will be willing to educate fewer students.

FIGURE 33.1   External benefits of K–12 education.

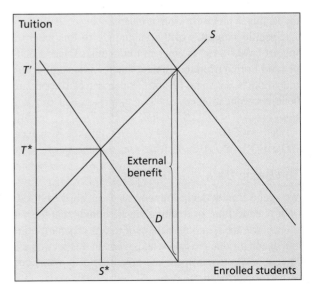

FIGURE 33.2   Spending per pupil in 2012 dollars.

Sources: *Digest of Education Statistics*, http://nces.ed.gov/programs/digest

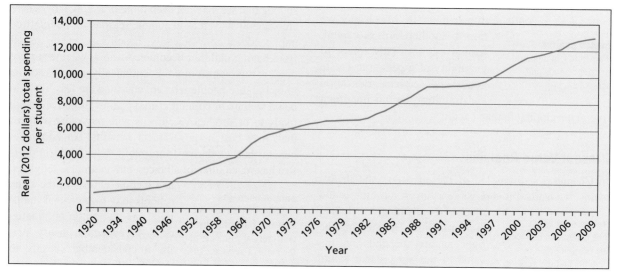

The equilibrium tuition $T*$ and the equilibrium number of enrolled students $S*$ are what the unsubsidized market would yield. If there is an external benefit of the size shown, then the optimal number of students is much greater than the market amount. In this case the optimal number of students is everyone and the optimal price is zero. This means that taxpayers will have to pay the T' per student. From a theoretical point of view, this does not necessarily mean that the school must be government-owned and operated. In the United States, except for some experiments in Milwaukee and other cities, this is precisely what it means.

Specific estimates of the magnitude of this external impact have started to emerge. Economists Lance Lochner and Enrico Moretti estimate that the impact of crime reduction is between 12 and 26 percent of the private benefit to education.

Should We Spend More?

The Basic Data

We spend a great deal of money on elementary and secondary education. In so doing we are hoping that the tax money we are spending nets us a return of smart, educated, and productive future taxpayers. In this section we look at how much is spent and how it is spent, measures of performance, and reasons why our dollars apparently

are not buying us what they used to. We also explore the alternatives to public elementary and secondary schools and ask whether the near monopoly that is our current public school system is serving our interests adequately.

As of 2012 the United States was spending more than $660 billion to educate 55 million elementary and secondary students. In exploring whether this amount of money is justified, we can look at how inflation-adjusted spending per pupil has been tracked over time and compare the amounts that have been spent with outcomes such as test scores and graduation rates. It is important that we look at things in this way because as the number of students rises, the number of classrooms needed rises too. This not only raises construction and maintenance costs; it also increases the number of teachers that are needed. Thus, whether or not spending increases, it is spending per pupil that matters. In addition, because inflation makes a 1960 dollar more valuable than a 2006 dollar, we need to adjust the spending figures for inflation. Though a flawed measure, the CPI is what we typically use to perform that adjustment.[2]

From Figure 33.2 you can see that even when it is adjusted for inflation, spending per student increased dramatically over the last 50 years. Although it leveled off in the 1990s, there is, nonetheless, a marked increase from $3,408 (2012 dollars) per student in 1960 to $12,957 in

[2]See Chapter 6 for a brief review of this.

FIGURE 33.3   Student-to-teacher ratios.

Sources: *Digest of Education Statistics*, http://nces.ed.gov/programs/digest

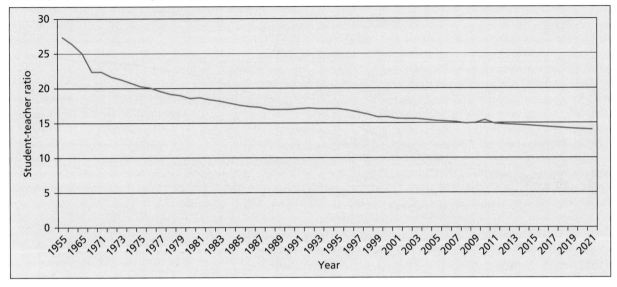

FIGURE 33.4   SATs for college-bound students.

Sources: *Digest of Education Statistics*, http://nces.ed.gov/programs/digest

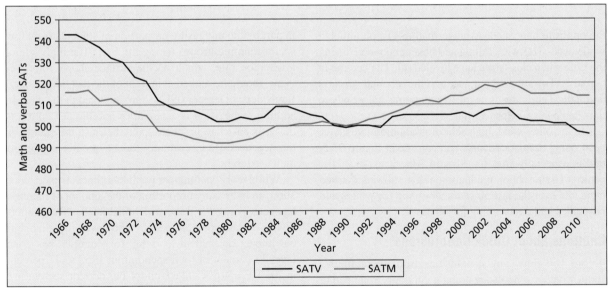

2010. While that spending went for many other things as well, it served to decrease average class size dramatically. As can be seen in Figure 33.3, in 1960 there were more than 26 students per class; there are currently less than 15. If the demands on what needs to be taught have remained constant, such a significant reduction in the number of students in a class would be expected to have a similarly significant impact on the success of students. By some measures it has, and by others, it has not.

Figure 33.4 indicates that students' scores on the SATs over the same period did not respond in proportion to the reductions in class sizes, and there is no clear evidence that reducing class size led to an improvement in SAT scores for college-bound students. If anything,

FIGURE 33.5 High school graduation rates.

Source: United States Census Bureau, www.census.gov/hhes/socdemo/education/data/cps/index.html

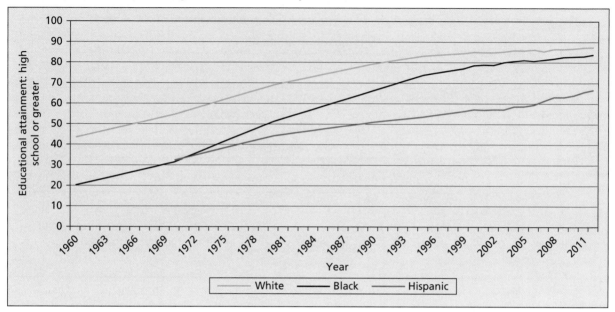

the opposite happened. Average math SATs plummeted while class sizes were falling and have rebounded during the time when class sizes have leveled off. The decline in verbal SATs bottomed out later and the rebound was less dramatic. These scores are nearly 40 points below where they had been 50 years earlier.[3]

On the other hand, high school graduation rates have been rising dramatically. As you can see in Figure 33.5, this is especially true for African Americans and Hispanics. High school graduation rates showed marked increases over the last 50 years, doubling for whites and Hispanics and quadrupling for blacks.

Cautions about Quick Conclusions

Before you draw any conclusions from these figures about whether schools are doing a good job, you need to consider some mitigating issues. The data, which on the surface indicate that there has been more than a doubling of real spending per pupil, are easily misinterpreted because much of the increase has gone for noninstructional purposes and special education. Though it is depressing on the surface, the low SAT scores can be accounted for

in part by the increasing proportion of students from low socioeconomic groups taking the SAT. The high school graduation rate, which on the surface shows improvement, should be looked at in light of the fact that General Equivalency Degrees (GEDs) are included in the data. In addition, whether it is accurate or not, the perception is that it is easier to graduate today because the standards that teachers use to evaluate students are not as high as they used to be.

While real spending per pupil has almost tripled since 1960, an increasing proportion of the amount of increase has been going for noninstructional needs. The proportion of dollars spent on people who have only a tangential impact on student learning, for example, has gone from 32 percent of total spending in 1960 to 47 percent in 2010. Employees like janitors, bus drivers, secretaries, and administrators do not teach children, and therefore we should not count the money spent on them as though it has an impact on learning. The proportion of the total staff in the classroom has fallen from 70 percent in 1960 to a little less than half in 2010. If the proportion of total spending on noninstructional employees had remained constant, then the overall rate of increase could be telling us something about whether we have been getting what we paid for. It has not remained constant so we cannot. It

[3]The 3-test version of the SAT may have had an impact as the scores dropped markedly for the year in which it was adopted.

is still the case, however, that real instructional spending per pupil has doubled.

Some of the real instructional spending per pupil that has doubled since 1960 has been devoted to legally mandated special education instruction. In 2011, 13.0 percent of the student population was labeled with disabilities and thus eligible for help that was subsidized through various state and federal programs. Most students who have been labeled as having physical disabilities do not require many extra resources, but some require quite expensive services. Although the Americans with Disabilities Act requires that the school provide all necessary assistance to such children while they are in school, the money that it costs to do so should not be called a spending increase for purposes of deciding whether annual costs per pupil are too high. Such spending does not directly benefit students without disabilities, and it therefore should be netted out of the analysis. Doing so reduces the per-pupil spending by around $700.

If we include the spending that funds special education programs in our analysis, the figures on class sizes are understated. Because the figures are derived by simply dividing the number of students by the number of teachers, and because many of the additional teachers focus on only a few special education children, the correct number for analysis should be the number of non–special education students divided by the number of non–special education teachers. When we do that computation we see that classes are not as small on the average as we thought. The student-to-teacher ratio has not fallen to 15 but only to 19.

In the past 50 years real total spending per pupil has increased, real total instructional spending per pupil has increased, and real total instructional spending has increased for students without eligible handicapping conditions. The SAT and other test scores are lower today than they were 45 years ago. While we would not expect increased spending on bus drivers or students with severe academic problems to increase SAT scores, we have every reason to expect a real increase in spending on instruction of students without disabilities to increase test scores. Because spending has increased and the test scores have decreased, it seems logical to conclude that we are not getting what we pay for in education spending. That conclusion may not be warranted, though, because the number of students taking the tests has increased and the number going to college has increased. If we look at the entire range of students, moreover, we will see that greater numbers of those who earn lower scores are represented than used to be the case. For instance, if a high school senior class of 10 has 5 going to college and they averaged a combined score of 1,000, is that better than a class of 10 where the first 5 average a 1,000 and the sixth, a less-qualified student, gets an 800? Since more people are taking the SAT now than in 1960, and since the quality of the students who would not have taken it then but take it now is lower than the quality of students who would have taken it anyway, we should expect average SAT scores to decrease. Even a level SAT average would indicate that today's schools are doing a better job.

Test scores have fallen as spending has increased, and we have speculated about why increased spending has not resulted in higher test scores. Let's look now at graduation rates. Though graduation rates have risen substantially over the decades, there is an open question as to whether this can necessarily be viewed as an improvement. For one thing, more people earn a GED diploma today than at any other time in our history. Some of them have dropped out of school for various reasons. Others are prisoners who have learned that completing a GED shaves time off their sentence. It is admirable that they do this, regardless of who they are, but even though the "E" stands for equivalence, few employers consider it to be the equal of a high school diploma. The best evidence for this assertion is that the income of GED holders is far closer to the income of high school dropouts than it is to high school graduates who have not gone to college. We need to consider this when we make positive statements about the marked increase in graduation rates for blacks. Because blacks hold a vastly disproportionate number of the GEDs, we have to be careful to interpret the increases in graduation rates.

Additionally, there is the common perception that high schools engage in what is referred to as "social promotion," that is, the granting of diplomas for survival rather than for achievement, a trend that critics say has increased in recent years. States have begun implementing exit exams for students to combat this perception, but the data are not yet in on whether graduation rates will fall as a result. If they do, the evidence will show that standards have indeed been lowered and that social promotion, rather than anything to be proud of, is responsible for increased graduation rates.

Literature on Whether More Money Will Improve Educational Outcomes

There is a vast literature written by economists on whether increases in spending can be counted on to increase educational outcomes. The premise that "you get what you pay for" and that more money will make things better can be traced to the production function that we outlined in Chapter 4. Recall that this function maps the relationship between inputs and the resulting outputs. We used workers as the example for that chapter. We showed that more inputs translated into more outputs until the point where the limited capital stock or the structure of the business prevented the new workers from having a positive impact on output.

Applying that idea to education, let's assume that the input is teachers and the output is some agreed-on measure of education outcomes. Each of these assumptions requires some clarification. First, whether it is best to hire more teachers (a higher quantity) to reduce class size or whether it is best to pay teachers more to get better ones (a higher quality) or both is certainly an open question. For the purposes of our graph, we will simply assume quality and quantity are interchangeable concepts. Second, while standardized test scores do not necessarily qualify as an agreed-on measure of outcome, for simplicity of explanation we will assume that they do. Given all that, Figure 33.6 shows the relationship between teachers and test scores.

Eric Hanushek, a leading economist on the issue of education, summarized 377 studies where one or more measures of input like student-to-teacher ratio (the quantity of teachers), teacher education, and teacher experience (the quality of teachers) were used to explain test scores. He reported that most of these studies found no relationship between test scores and these inputs and that nearly as many found a negative one as a positive

FIGURE 33.6   Educational production function.

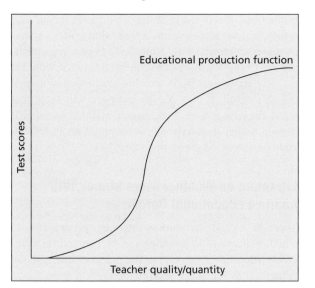

one. This stunning conclusion, however—that money does not matter and that spending more is a waste of taxpayer resources—is in some dispute by other economists. These economists contend that test scores are less important than the earnings of the graduates. They state that over the last century graduates of schools in states that spent more had more earning power than those who graduated in states that spent less. All economists who study the issue have found, moreover, that educational outcomes are determined mostly by factors that are largely beyond the control of schools, such as family income and family structure.

These results are not as contradictory as they might seem. Figure 33.6 indicates that it might very well be that the structure of public schools has been such that more money had a significant impact in the 1940s through the 1960s because we were spending so little and were on the steep, upward-sloping part of the curve. The argument that Hanushek and others make is that it appears that we are now "on the flat of the curve," meaning that we have done all we can do with more teachers. Now we need to look at something else.

School Reform Issues

If we are in fact on the flat part of the educational production function and more money will not help until the structure is changed, it is reasonable to ask what the structure is and why it is limiting. There are two separate issues with regard to the structure that we explore in this section. The first is that the public education system operates as a monopoly and as such tends not to be responsive to the desires of individual students and parents. The second is that teachers' salaries are usually not dependent on their performance. The debate about whether private schools and vouchers to pay for them might help to improve formal education makes up the remainder of this section.

The Public School Monopoly

In Chapter 5 we saw that in industries dominated by monopolies, prices are higher and output is less than it would be under perfect competition. Public schools operate in most communities as a monopoly. Though there are private schools and home schooling, these are not real options to most parents. Even more interesting is that this monopoly charges you, in the form of state and local taxes, whether or not you use the schools. It would be as if your electric company could continue sending you a bill even after you decided to buy your own electric generator.

There are reasons for this. If you believe that the external benefits of K–12 education are so great that they justify being subsidized, then parents who choose to send their children to private schools should have to continue paying school-related taxes because they are getting those external benefits.

Ultimately, the problem that seems to come to the fore with a monopoly is that it becomes unresponsive to the needs and desires of its customers. In the case of public schools, there is no compelling monetary incentive for the school to help a child with a particular need or to foster excellence in another child. Consider the following problem that exists at the beginning of every school year in nearly every school in the country. Every school has teachers of varying quality and many parents know who the better ones are. Parents want the teachers they consider to be better, and the principal must disappoint some of these parents. Under competition, a disappointed parent could threaten to move to another school. Under competition, the principal would have at least a budgetary incentive to make bad teachers better. Under the current system in most school districts, the parents are simply told, "That's the way it is."

Merit Pay and Tenure

One of the areas that distinguishes teachers from other professionals is the lack of economic performance incentives and the presence of lifetime job security. One recent study has found that individual teacher quality does matter. Economist Jonah Rockoff, in particular, found that he could isolate the impact of individual teachers and found that he could identify the better ones statistically by carefully matching student achievement to their past teachers. The reason is that most teachers in the United States are represented by a union that is an independent union, an affiliate of the National Education Association, or the American Federation of Teachers. Unions in general, and teachers' unions in particular, prefer that pay be based solely on education and seniority.

This means that a poor teacher with more experience earns more than a good teacher with fewer years in the classroom. This is a problem because energetic teachers can become discouraged by the lack of monetary recognition for their efforts. Any time pay is based strictly on who you are rather than what you do, there is an incentive to do as little as possible.

The other serious obstacle to rewarding good teachers and getting rid of bad ones is teacher tenure. Much like the institution of tenure in colleges and universities, K–12 educators are often granted tenure after they have successfully met certain criteria and taught for a set number of years. This means that, short of some abusive behavior, they cannot be fired. This further adds to the lack of performance incentives in older teachers.

Many teachers and their union representatives argue several points in defense of this system. First, they argue that as professionals they are above economic considerations and teach to the best of their ability all the time. Second, they argue that granting a principal the power to fire senior teachers and hand out merit pay would foster cronyism. Only those who did the principal's bidding would keep their jobs or get large pay increases. Last, they argue that pay in general is low relative to other professionals and that any additional money should raise all teachers' pay to a higher level.

An additional obstacle facing the current educational system is the degree to which talented women have fled teaching jobs. Economists Caroline Hoxby and Andrew Leigh have identified a frightening degree of movement of brighter women away from teaching and an even more frightening shift of less bright women toward teaching. This, combined with the fact that very few men, bright or otherwise, choose teaching as a profession, means that salaries will have to rise in order to reattract bright men and women to the profession of teaching. Teachers' salaries, although they have risen with inflation, have fallen relative to the salaries of equally credentialed occupations. These economists argue that economics has overcome the sociological tendency of women to be attracted to teaching as a profession and only more pay will reverse this trend.

Private versus Public Education

In the presence of failed or failing public schools, many have come to ask whether private schools should be allowed to receive public funds. In general, students from private schools perform dramatically better and have far fewer discipline problems than students in public schools. This happens even though most private schools exist with funding that is far less than that of public schools.

When private schools outperform public schools, it can be attributed to a variety of factors. Because the parents pay tuition to private schools out of their own pockets, we can surmise that the students come from homes where education matters, they are wealthier on average than their counterparts in public schools, and it is unlikely they possess academic or physical disabilities.

The question is whether, after separating out these factors, private schools do outperform. The answer is an equivocal "yes." If you look at public school students who fit a profile similar to private school students, private schools do a little more with a little less. The difference is not as dramatic as it is without this filter, but it still exists. The primary reason is that parent involvement is higher and administrative costs are lower in private schools.

There is a concern, however, as it relates to private schools and that is that the schools would be motivated to admit the easiest to educate. By-and-large, students with higher test scores, students from two-parent households, and students without significant physical or psychological challenges are easier to teach than other students.

cherry picking
The act of admitting only students who are easy to educate, leaving the harder and more expensive ones for public schools.

Cherry picking, the act of choosing students easy to educate, would leave the hardest and most expensive students in the public schools.

School Vouchers

The question raised by the preceding analysis is whether parents should be allowed to take their children out of a public school and have them placed in another public school or a private school that is then given the taxpayer money that would have gone to educate the child in the first public school. This would amount to about $2,500 per year for an "able" student. With cost savings and a general dislike of teachers' unions in mind, this option is popular among Republicans. Democrats, strict believers in the "public" part of public education, generally oppose attempts at privatization.

There are, however, ongoing experiments with school vouchers. The school system in Milwaukee, Wisconsin, for example, has been operating a school choice program since 1990. In this system low-income parents can obtain vouchers to send their children to secular (i.e., nonreligious) private schools. The degree of parental disgust with public schools can be seen in the fact that there was space for only a third of those who applied for the vouchers.[4]

The results of this experiment and others like it are mixed. Until recently, only a research team at the University of Wisconsin had access to the data and they concluded that, compared to all other Milwaukee public school students, children did no better. Research that ensued after the data were released to the general academic community suggests that those in the program for three or more years did better (3 to 5 percentile points

on reading and 5 to 12 on math) than those who applied but could not get in.

The debate continues on the wisdom of school vouchers from a variety of perspectives, political, ethical, and economic. Research conducted separately by Helen Ladd and Derek Neal suggests that vouchers and charter schools have not performed so well, or so badly as to settle the issue from the perspective of effectiveness. Part of the problem in such analysis is that parents who show an interest in getting their children out of failing public schools are likely to nurture their children in either setting. If those who succeed in getting their children out of the failing schools and into charter schools are highly motivated parents, then any success in the charter schools is likely to be overstated with simple analysis. These researchers found that controlling for that bias, the impact of charter schools is modest at best.

Collective Bargaining

An issue that developed in the aftermath of the 2010 mid-term elections was the degree to which the collective bargaining rights of teachers had led to, or even contributed to, a perceived decline in education outcomes in public elementary and secondary education. States with Republican governors that also elected solid Republican majorities, specifically Indiana and Wisconsin, saw moves to limit the collective bargaining rights of their teachers (as well as other public employees). The moves were, at least in part, motivated by the desire to reign in non-salary-related costs.

If you read Chapter 16 and its discussion of the public employee pension crisis that is about to hit many states, you understand that it is not current teachers' salaries that are considered the problem, but instead it is their pensions. These pensions are frequently defined benefit pensions with a "rule of 85" clause that allows any teacher in a state to retire with full benefits (typically 75 percent of their salary) when their age plus their years of service equals 85.

The aforementioned legislatures went after the collective bargaining rights of the public employees (specifically the teachers in Wisconsin) because it was collective bargaining that led to these types of pension arrangements, which, because they allowed teachers to retire at full benefits at age 55, were considered (by the Republicans) to be more generous than the state could afford.

Associated with that same collective bargaining issue was the realization that state education budgets across the country were going to be cut, and it was through

---

[4]State law mandated that in such a circumstance the awarding of vouchers would be determined at random.

collective bargaining that teachers unions had negotiated "last in, first out" clauses for layoffs. Those in favor of significant educational reform felt that these provisions would inappropriately require that excellent young teachers be let go while poor (yet experienced) teachers remained. Those opposed to the stripping of collective bargaining rights for teachers objected to what they described as the vilification of experienced teachers.

Summary

You now understand that education is an investment in human capital and that this investment not only increases the earnings of the person being educated but has positive externalities as well. You also understand that spending more money will not necessarily yield even more returns. Moreover, you are well aware of the debate centering on whether, with the current education structure, we are on the "flat" of the education production function. You now understand the economics behind the school reform issues.

Key Terms

cherry picking, 358

external benefits, 351

human capital, 351

net present value, 351

Quiz Yourself

1. The evidence on the impact of spending on K–12 education outcomes suggests that, ceteris paribus,
   a. the more a school district spends, the better it does.
   b. the more a school district spends, the worse it does.
   c. the more a school district spends on expensive buildings, the better it does.
   d. the amount of money a school district spends has no consistent positive or negative impact on outcome.

2. The fact that education benefits not just the person being educated but society as a whole suggests that there is a
   a. positive externality.
   b. negative externality.
   c. congestion.
   d. monopoly.

3. The argument that spending more money on teachers has little impact on educational outcomes in K–12 is
   a. inconsistent with any economic model.
   b. consistent with the upward-sloping nature of a production function.
   c. consistent with the downward-sloping nature of a demand curve.
   d. consistent with the flat part of the production possibilities frontier.

4. The institution of teacher tenure is meant to
   a. ensure job security for teachers with 10 years of experience.
   b. ensure that teachers do not get fired for political reasons.
   c. allow teachers to engage in any behavior they wish.
   d. allow the easy firing of incompetent teachers.

5. The evidence on charter schools is that they
   a. have had no impact in any locations they have been tried.
   b. have had an enormously positive impact on education generally.
   c. have had a negative impact on students.
   d. have had some impact in some locations, but there is no generally obvious positive impact.

6. If all K–12 schools were privately owned with a constant subsidy paid by the government to the school for each student enrolled, what would be one potential and likely negative consequence?
   a. Cherry picking.
   b. Collective bargaining.
   c. Tenure.
   d. Vouchers.

7. In most school districts, all other characteristics held constant, an excellent teacher earns _____ a poor teacher.
   a. the same as
   b. more than
   c. less than

Short Answer Questions

1. Explain how the data in Figures 33.2 through 33.5 (increasing real spending per pupil, decreasing class sizes, decreasing SATs, and increasing graduation rates) can be occurring at the same time.

2. Use the production function "flat of the curve" explanation to describe why more money spent on education may not have a significant impact.

3. Provide an explanation for why it is possible that average SATs that are declining might be consistent with the assertion that more people are prepared for college than ever before.

4. Suppose you were to find yourself between an advocate for education who claimed that you have to pay teachers more in order to get more qualified teachers and an advocate for education reform who claimed that paying the same teachers more money won't help. Explain why they both might be correct.

Think about This

As bad as the gender discrimination of the 1950s and 1960s was to the career aspirations of smart women, there was a silver lining to the dark cloud: School systems could hire very smart, very capable, and very motivated women to be elementary school teachers and do so for relatively modest salaries. Suppose you were a school board member in the 1980s and noticed the decline in abilities of the new graduates. What would you have done to reattract great women to the teaching profession?

Talk about This

Should teachers' salaries be tied to their performance? How would you measure their performance? Should the performance-evaluation mechanisms be strictly based on quantitative factors (e.g., test scores) or should they reflect the subjective judgments of administrators?

For More Insight See

Greene, P., Paul E. Peterson, Jiangtao Du, Leesa Boeger, and Curtis L. Frazier, *The Effectiveness of School Choice in Milwaukee: A Secondary Analysis of Data from the Program's Evaluation.*

Lochner, Lance, and E. Moretti, "The Effect of Education on Crime: Evidence from Prison Inmates, Arrests, and Self-Reports," *American Economic Review* 94, no. 2.

Hoxby, Caroline M., and Andrew Leigh, "Pulled Away or Pushed Out? Explaining the Decline in Teacher Aptitude in the United States," *American Economic Review* 94, no. 2.

Journal of Economic Perspectives 10, no. 4. (Fall 1996). See articles by Francine D. Blau; Eric Hanushek; David Card and Alan B. Krueger; and Caroline Minter Hoxby, pp. 3–72.

Journal of Economic Perspectives 16, no. 4 (Fall 2002). See articles by Helen Ladd and Derek Neal, pp. 3–44.

Rockoff, Jonah E., "The Impact of Individual Teachers on Student Achievement: Evidence from Panel Data," *American Economic Review* 94, no. 2.

Behind the Numbers

National Center for Education Statistics; *Digest of Education Statistics*—http://nces.ed.gov/programs/digest

College and University Education: Why Is It So Expensive?

Learning Objectives

After reading this chapter you should be able to:

LO1   Understand why a college education is so expensive and why those costs have been rising faster than inflation.

LO2   Explain the role of textbooks in those rising costs.

LO3   Apply the principle of present value so as to see why borrowing money to pay for a college education is a wise, if potentially risky, investment in future income potential.

LO4   Understand that the United States has a greater percentage of citizens with a college degree than other developed countries, though that advantage is rapidly evaporating.

Chapter Outline

Introduction

Why Are the Costs So High?

Why Are College Costs Rising So Fast?

Why Have Textbook Costs Risen So Rapidly?

What a College Degree Is Worth

How Do People Pay for College?

Summary

Introduction

In the preceding chapter, we raised questions about the costs and effectiveness of education through grade 12. Here we explore whether students in colleges and universities are receiving good value for their money. In 2010, a little more than $471 billion was spent educating 21 million college students, which works out to $22,429 per student, per year. Obviously it costs substantially more for higher education than it does for students in elementary or secondary schools. Moreover, tuition, room, and board have increased 629 percent over the last 31 years—a period when overall prices increased only 131 percent. Figure 34.1 shows that both college tuition and college textbook prices have increased much more rapidly than has inflation.

To find out why this is so, we examine some of the economic issues for higher education. We include a discussion of why it costs more and whether those costs are worth it to the college student consumer. We proceed to discuss how higher education is financed in the United States and finish with a discussion of one of the most significant expenses in college textbooks.

Why Are the Costs So High?

The reasons why college costs more than high school per student are both obvious and hidden. First, the obvious: On the average, college professors earn salaries that are almost twice those of elementary and secondary teachers.

FIGURE 34.1 College costs relative to CPI.

Source: Bureau of Labor Statistics, www.bls.gov/cpi/home.htm

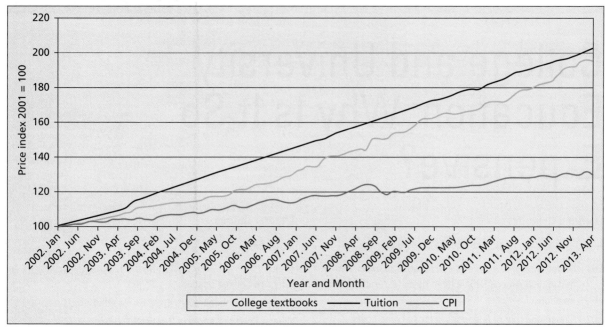

Colleges have libraries that dwarf what we might see in a high school, and librarians have no choice but to subscribe to wildly expensive journals, including many in the sciences that have five-figure subscription prices. If you have not already noticed, college professors teach far less than high school teachers do. A professor at a research-oriented university may teach only 3 to 6 hours a week, while a professor in a teaching-oriented community college may average 12 to 15 hours a week. High school teachers are in the classroom from around 8 a.m. to around 3 p.m., with some time off for lunch and preparation. They may teach five- or six-hour-long classes, five days a week. In net, a high school teacher is in class more in a single day than some professors are in a week.

Exploring reasons for the disparities between K–12 and college teachers gets us into some less obvious reasons why per-pupil college costs are so high. Educators at all levels must maintain a high level of expertise in their field. At the college level, it is accepted that professors need time for reading and studying. Professors who teach at the higher end of a discipline need particularly great amounts of time for scholarly study. Many professors are also judged by the degree to which they advance knowledge in their academic discipline. This research commands most of a professor's time at most universities, whether or not they are regarded as prestigious. A sad fact of life in modern college education is that for a professor to advance within an institution, or to advance from a less prestigious school to a more prestigious school, research and other scholarly activity are more important than teaching.

That research is expensive. Research for an English professor requires a well-stocked library and a state-of-the-art computer. This is cheap compared to what it costs to set up a biologist to do advanced research. Not only do biologists require the well-stocked library; they require a fully stocked laboratory with equipment that can separate out DNA and that can magnify samples so that individual cells can be seen. The cost of some of this equipment is so high that if you used the money to equip high schools, you could equip all the high school labs of a medium-sized city for what it costs to fund the laboratory of a single professor at Harvard, MIT, or Stanford. On the other hand, research brings in a considerable amount of money to universities. At nearly $50 billion in 2011, the revenue associated with grants and contracts contributes almost as much money to higher education revenue as tuition does ($60 billion).

A final reason why college is so expensive relates to the subsidies. As shown in the previous chapter about

FIGURE 34.2 External benefits of a college education.

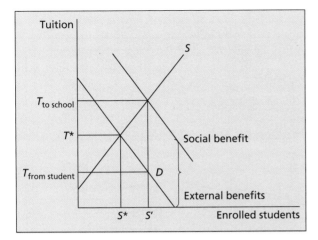

K–12 education, a college education provides private benefits to its students as well as external benefits to the public at large. The private benefits include the higher incomes college graduates earn as well as the fun college students have in and especially out of the classroom. The external benefits include the fact that the college educated pay far more in taxes over a lifetime than do those without such an education as well as the increased knowledge they bring to their voting and leadership activities. Thus, though perhaps not as significant as the external benefits of K–12 education, they are still high enough to justify having a considerable subsidy to that education.

Just as we used our supply and demand diagram in the previous chapter to illustrate the inefficiency of just having unsubsidized private K–12 education, we can apply the same models and principles here. Consider Figure 34.2 and what it suggests about the price of a college education. The price is the annual tuition and the quantity is the number of college students educated in a year. At low tuition rates, more will invest in a college education, so the resulting demand curve is downward sloping. However, if tuition is low, colleges and universities will be willing to educate fewer students.

The equilibrium tuition T* and the equilibrium number of enrolled students S* are what the unsubsidized market would yield. If there is an external benefit of the size shown, then the optimal number of students is much greater than the market amount. Unlike the K–12 case, the optimal number of students is likely not everyone and the optimal price is likely not zero. It does mean that students should not have to pay all of the costs and that taxpayers will have to pay a subsidy. Students should

pay $T_{\text{from student}}$, and taxpayers should pick up the rest so that the school gets the amount they need, $T_{\text{to school}}$, to teach S' students. Notice, though, what happens to the cost per student (not just to the student). It rises from the T* to $T_{\text{to school}}$. Subsidizing something contributes to its higher costs.

Why Are College Costs Rising So Fast?

As can be seen from Figure 34.3, though tuition has been rising fast, the rise in the revenues to universities has more to do with their other enterprises than it does with tuition. Total revenues to public universities increased by $200 billion over the period 1995 to 2011. Tuition increases only accounted for $37 billion of that increase. The staples of a public university's budget— especially a public university that is not the flagship of the state—are its tuition, its state (and to a lesser degree federal and local) appropriation, and its housing-based auxiliaries (shown in the figure as "aux-non-hospital").

There is little doubt, however, that the mix in revenues has changed dramatically throughout the years, even ignoring the largest part of the increase: that is, the increase in gift, investment, grant and contract, and affiliated hospital derived income.[1] Zeroing out those elements, the relative sizes of the wedges of the pie have changed markedly. Specifically, from 2007 to 2011, total federal, state, and local appropriations to public universities fell from nearly $80 billion to less than $75 billion. At that same time tuition revenue increased by 25 percent. Figure 34.4 shows that the share of revenues attributable to appropriations fell from 57 percent in 1995 to 47 percent in 2010, with almost the entirety of that difference being absorbed within tuition. Essentially, public universities are justifying their rapid increases in tuition on the relative decline in state appropriations.

Another reason for the increase in the cost of higher education is the degree to which student expectations of their environment have changed. The contrast between post–World War II student housing and modern student housing is remarkable. The floor of 40 two-to-a-room 10 × 15-foot prison cells with a common shower and bathroom facility has been replaced by suite-style housing with private or semiprivate showers and bathrooms.

---

[1]Some larger state universities operate hospitals as part of their medical schools, and the revenue from those hospitals significantly distorts the relative size of the revenue sources.

FIGURE 34.3 Revenue to public degree-granting universities.

Source: National Center for Education Statistics, http://nces.ed.gov/programs/digest
*2001–2002 and 2002–2003 interpolated from available data.

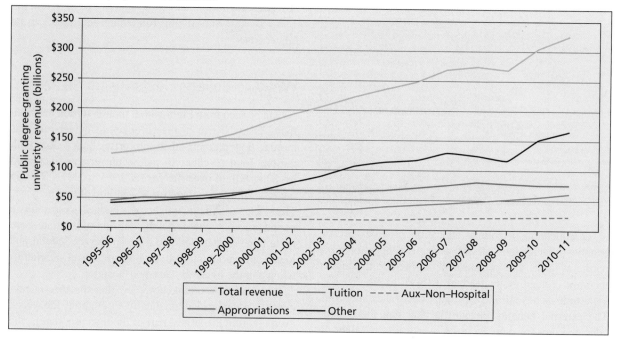

FIGURE 34.4 Share of university revenue: Appropriations, tuition, and non-hospital auxiliaries.

Source: National Center for Education Statistics, http://nces.ed.gov/programs/digest

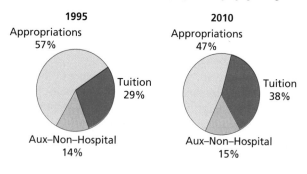

Building those newer facilities has led to a tenfold increase in debt for public universities in 10 years. Those costs have been passed on to students. Further, while not always directly demanding modern exercise facilities, students have chosen to enroll on campuses that have built them. The costs of constructing and equipping these recreation centers have been passed on to students either in the form of dedicated fees or in the form of higher tuition. Universities have built them largely for enrollment reasons. As public universities have come to increasingly depend on tuition revenue, they have become increasingly sensitive to student desires.

Why Have Textbook Costs Risen So Rapidly?

The market for college textbooks is a good example of a great many economic concepts: fixed and variable costs, the impact of patents and copyrights on the market for a good, the fuzziness of the line between oligopoly and monopolistic competition, and the degree to which increased technology increases supply. Before we get too deep into the analysis, you should understand how a textbook comes to market.

Either solicited or unsolicited, a faculty member will write a chapter or two to show a publisher why this new book would be better than those that exist. Very few of these prospective books make it past this step. Those sample chapters that meet with the publisher's expectations are sent out to faculty who, when the book is published, might consider using the book for their course. They are compensated for their feedback and, if the publisher senses from that feedback that the book will be successful, a contract is drawn up that specifies how the

FIGURE 34.5 Where the money goes.

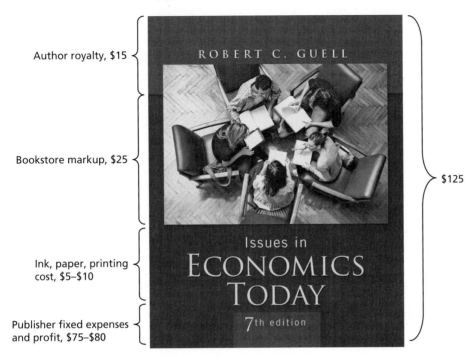

Author royalty, $15

Bookstore markup, $25

Ink, paper, printing
cost, $5–$10

Publisher fixed expenses
and profit, $75–$80

$125

author is to be paid. Typically the author will get a percentage of the sales (in the neighborhood of 15 percent)

advance
The amount of money paid to authors prior to a book's publication. This is typically counted against future royalties.

royalties
The amount of money paid to authors. Typically paid on a percentage basis.

to bookstores (based on the wholesale price, net of returns). An **advance** is usually offered to the author against future **royalties**. The book takes at least a year to write, revise, edit, and publish. Often, a first edition takes

much longer than subsequent editions because it is typically reviewed by a different collection of faculty around the country.

Once available for sale, the book is mailed, free of charge, to faculty all around the country that teach a course in which the book might be used. This could be thousands of books, as is the case when there is a roll-out of a principles of economics book (that which is appropriate for business and economics majors) or a few hundred (when the book has a more limited audience). Faculty place their orders with their respective bookstores and the bookstores order them in the month leading up to the beginning of the semester.

To see where the money goes on the sale of a new book, consider the one you are reading. As shown in Figure 34.5, the previous edition of this book sold for $125 as a new book in my university's bookstore. The book was sold to the bookstore for $100 so its expenses and profit come out of the store's $25 markup. I get 15 percent of the amount that the publisher gets, or $15. The publisher keeps between $75 and $80. The publisher's costs include very high fixed costs for such things as supplements (recent textbooks have all needed to have expensively produced testbanks, instructor's manuals, website materials, study guides, PowerPoints, etc.) as well as costs associated with editorial staff and marketing. The variable costs also include the cost of the paper, ink, and printing of the book itself. In all, the marginal production cost of a textbook is less than $10, sometimes as little as $5. When all is said and done, the $75 to $80 margin that the publisher makes must cover all the fixed costs of production.

Here it gets tricky because the publisher, and by extension the author, makes money only when a new book is sold. You do not have to be in college very long to know that you can buy used textbooks for much less than new ones and that you can sell your books back to the bookstore at the end of the semester. Typically a book that sells new for $125 will sell used for $100. The bookstore will have purchased that used book from a previous student at the same university for around $62.50.[2] The bookstore then stocks both new books and used books and makes a profit on either. There is some risk for the bookstore in overstocking a new book, since they have to pay a restocking fee to return new books to the publisher, but there is enormous risk in overstocking used books.

The bottom line for publishers is that they are in business to make money, and new sales increase profits and used book sales eat into profits. The break-even point on a book such as this one is around 5,000 units. The next 5,000 units can easily generate nearly a half million in profits for the publisher. This is why books are on relatively short production cycles. Calculus books, though the content hasn't changed since Newton figured it out, are revised regularly because publishers and authors make money only when the new edition sells for the first time.

A second significant cause behind the expense of textbooks is the market form. The book you are reading is the intellectual property of its owner. I gave that intellectual property to the publisher in exchange for the royalties they pay me for sales on the book. What the copyright does is to give McGraw-Hill Education the exclusive right to sell this material. It also prohibits you from walking down to FedEx-Kinko's and running off copies for your friends. Copyrights are necessary to bring intellectual property to market because without them producers of the books, songs, and inventions would have no financial motivation to produce them.

In some disciplines there is one standard textbook that everyone uses, while in others there are multiple texts that look very much the same. Though there are hundreds of textbooks on the market, most are not good substitutes for another. It does little good to bring your economics text to your poetry class. In the end, your professor probably had a relatively small number of books from which to choose. If you are using this book while taking a general education economics course for non-majors, your professor had to decide whether to cram a bunch of theory in or do an issues approach. Having chosen this book, your professor chose the issues approach. There are four books that really work in this niche. McGraw-Hill has a monopoly on this book but it

is a competitor in this niche. The market form best suited to this area is monopolistic competition.

The market for principles of economics texts is much greater and there are many more choices. There are four really big sellers and several scattered players. This is also an example of monopolistic competition. The differences between books is quite slight (mostly in presentation and emphasis), but the publishers still retain their monopoly rights. For an example of an area in which there are fewer sellers, consider the market for graduate-level textbooks in mathematical economics. For all intents and purposes, there are two. One is older than dirt and the other one is a few years old. This is an example of oligopoly. Some areas of economics are so narrow, with such a small market, that there is only one book.

A third reason why textbooks have increased rapidly in price is that, like prescription drugs, in most cases the consumer doesn't get to pick a cheaper alternative. Textbooks are chosen for you by faculty members who are often completely oblivious to the price that will be charged for the book because they get the book mailed to them free. When students go to the bookstore and get their books, they cannot choose which book to buy (beyond their choice of used versus new, buy versus rent, or print versus e-book). They have to decide to obtain the book or not. Thus the price of the book is irrelevant in the adoption decision. Under good circumstances, the adoption decision is typically made after a professor has looked at the choices in the area and selected the one that goes best with the course and the way the professor teaches. In the end, faculty often pick books that have the supplements they are looking for, have illustrations that simplify the subject, and that are pleasing to the eye. All of these add to the price of the book but the price often does not enter into the decision to adopt the book. The student is then made to choose between buying the book or not.

What a College Degree Is Worth

Now that we have seen a few reasons why college costs so much, we can ask whether it is worth the expense. To explore this question, we need again to understand and to use the concept of present value. If the interest-adjusted amount of money you spend on your education, the present value of the costs, is less than the interest-adjusted amount of the extra money you earn as a result of your education, the present value of the benefits, then your college education is worth the money you pay for it.

---

[2]There are several reasons why a student might get less than the full buy-back price. Some include the existence of key codes for online content or custom content, or the fact that the book came in loose-leaf form.

AVOIDING HIGH TEXTBOOK PRICES

In recent years, there have been three significant changes to the textbook market that have jolted textbook companies. The first of these is the advent of a relatively old niche market for textbook rentals. Chegg and other Internet companies have revived this relatively small market in a significant way. These companies typically charge approximately half the retail price of the book but compel you to return the book to avoid being charged for the other half. To accomplish this, they will typically take a customer's credit card information for the sale and, if the book is not returned, charge it again. This amounts to the same issue as buying new books and selling them back, but the student doesn't take the risk that the book will be out of edition (and therefore worth much less).

Additionally, companies are beginning to see their e-book alternatives grow in popularity, in part thanks to the iPad. While some text-only books work well with e-readers such as Amazon's Kindle, graph and mathematics laden books with color are ill suited to the Kindle platform but are well suited to the iPad and PC platform. Again this is like renting a book but the book does not have to be returned; it simply becomes inaccessible after a semester (or year, depending on the seller's policies.)

Finally, an increasing number of faculty who have seen their students struggle with being able to afford their textbooks have chosen a path that is both interesting as an economist and troublesome as an author. It had been the case that when a new edition of a textbook came out, nearly every faculty member would adopt that new edition and the old editions would be of almost no value in the market. For instance, when the fifth edition of this book became available in the spring of 2010, it sold in bookstores for $125 and rented on Chegg for half that. At the same time, the fourth edition, which had sold in bookstores for $120 the semester before, was selling for less than $10 on the Internet's many used book outlets.

What seems to be occurring now is that some faculty order the old edition for everyone in their class so everyone in the class is in the same position. The faculty member has stayed with the author's book but there are no profits for the publisher or royalties for the author. The long-run impact of this strategy will, however, result in decreasing its viability as a strategy. As more faculty fail to "roll" to the new edition, the price of old editions will rise on the Internet as their easy availability shrinks. In addition, traditional bookstores will have an increasing difficulty finding and stocking the old editions in sufficient quantity to meet the demand. This new faculty strategy is both interesting and probably unsustainable.

Assume for a moment that your four years of college cost you $10,000 a year in out-of-pocket expenses and you give up another $12,000 a year in what you would have earned had you worked full time. The total cost of your education is then $22,000 a year, or a total of about $88,000. Since the expenses incurred in the second, third, and fourth years are in the future, you must discount them by the appropriate interest rate. Now assume that instead of making $12,000 a year without a degree, you will earn the degree and then make $30,000 a year. The benefit from going to college is the extra $18,000 you earn a year. We use $18,000 because this is roughly the difference in median income of households headed by people who have college degrees over that same figure for households headed by people with only a high school education. We must again discount these benefits, as they will happen in the future. If we assume that all of these dollar figures are inflation-adjusted and the real interest rate is 3 percent, then the present value of the costs is roughly $82,000 and the present value of 40 years of $18,000 extra a year is roughly $415,000. The net present value of a college degree is $333,000, making it so that dropping out of college is likely the most expensive noncriminal mistake you could ever make. Conversely, doing well in college may be the most lucrative thing you ever do.

How Do People Pay for College?

Many college students recognize the benefits of education but cannot see themselves paying for them. While we have just shown that it makes sense to complete college even if you have to borrow all of the money to do it, you know that merely racking up student loans does not mean you get a degree. This means that there is some risk involved. You have to weigh the risk of having the only thing you take away from college be debt against the benefit that you get the $333,000 in net present value. In addition, though it seems as if a college degree costs you a lot of money, consider the fact that at a public university you are getting a subsidy of nearly $1.50 for every $1 you spend. The subsidy of $1

FIGURE 34.6   College graduates as a percentage of the 24 and older population.

Source: United States Census Bureau, www.census.gov/hhes/socdemo/education/data/cps/index.html

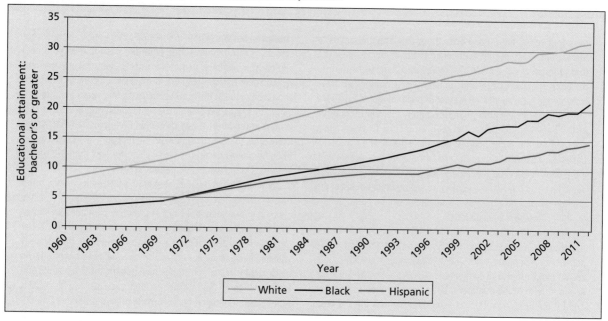

for every $1 at a private university is less, but it is still substantial. Subsidies to universities are computed from the value of interest-reduced loans and gifts to the universities. Whether you are a student at a public or private university, you are paying great sums of money, sums that would be even greater were it not for subsidies from national, state, and private sources.

One of the interesting changes over the last three decades has been the change in the way students pay for their portion of the costs of a higher education. In the 1940s, World War II veterans received the GI Bill, which allowed many former soldiers to go to college. Not only was their tuition paid, but they were also granted a stipend upon which to live. In the 1960s and 1970s, the federal government instituted programs such as the Pell Grant, which provided a similar benefit to children of poor families. In the 1980s, President Reagan shifted the focus to making student loans available at subsidized rates. In the 1990s, President Clinton reformulated the loan process by increasing federal government involvement and sponsored educational income tax deductions and credits. As a rarely discussed part of the Patient Protection and Affordable Care Act, President Obama's legislation reformed the student loan program to by-pass banks. The loans, instead, will be administered out of

the U.S. Department of Education. Taken together, these transformations have allowed more students to access some form of aid, but the aid is now more likely to come in the form of a subsidized loan.

Nationally, between 1992 and 2008, the percentage of students on some form of aid increased from 59 percent to 79.5 percent, and the percentage borrowing to pay for college increased from 31 percent to 53 percent, while the percentage receiving federally funded education grants has slowly increased to 33 percent.

Figure 34.6 shows that if we measure the success of higher education by looking at degrees granted, there is success. On the other hand, the United States is rapidly being caught (and surpassed) by other developed countries in the percentage of adults with a college education. The United States led OCED countries in 2008 with nearly a third of the adult population 25 to 64 having a college education. However, the U.S. rate for young adults (24–35) placed sixteenth on the list. The United States is not becoming less educated. It is that others are catching up. The college attainment rate for Americans has remained steady through the years, while the rate for other countries has increased rapidly. This could ultimately threaten the comparative advantage the United States had held in this particular area.

Summary

You now understand why a college education is an expensive thing to provide and why those costs have been rising faster than inflation over the years. You understand that a part of that rapidly rising set of costs is associated with the cost of textbooks. You understand that the principle of present value is useful in seeing why borrowing money to pay for a college education is a wise, if potentially risky, investment in future income potential and that the source of funds for students has increasingly moved from grants to loans. Finally, you understand that though higher educational attainment is higher in the United States than it is elsewhere, that advantage is evaporating as other countries' citizens are rapidly increasing their levels of educational attainment.

Key Terms

advance, 365

royalties, 365

Quiz Yourself

1. Which of the following has increased fastest?
   a. Overall prices.
   b. College textbook prices.
   c. College tuition.

2. What are the key reasons why college costs are higher than high school costs?
   a. The expenses of research.
   b. College faculty salaries are higher than K–12 faculty salaries.
   c. Subsidies to education cause increased demand for it.
   d. All of these.

3. The textbook production industry has a great deal in common with the pharmaceutical industry in that there are _____ fixed costs and _____ marginal costs.
   a. high; high
   b. high; low
   c. low; high
   d. low; low

4. Authors are typically paid for their work
   a. based on a percentage of the sales at college bookstores.
   b. based on a percentage of the sales from publishers to bookstores.
   c. a fixed amount regardless of sales.
   d. on a per-page basis.

5. The economic tool that proves the value of an expensive college education is
   a. production possibilities.
   b. the yield curve.
   c. supply and demand.
   d. present value.

6. The cost of educating a college student
   a. is less than the cost of educating a high school student because college classes are generally large.
   b. is equal to the cost of educating a high school student because, although college teachers make more money, their classes are generally larger.
   c. is less than it used to be.
   d. is much greater than the cost of educating a high school student because college professors make more money and teach fewer hours per week.

Think about This

Your education, from kindergarten through college, benefited you and it benefited society. The proportion of a typical college education paid by the student has risen in recent years. How much of your college education do you pay? (Consider the state appropriation to your school if it is public, the federal and state financial aid that you get, and the value of the guarantee on any of your student loans). Is this the right division of the burden?

Talk about This

How did cost figure into your choice of school? Did you have lots of options? If you could have gotten a "full ride," where would you have gone?

Behind the Numbers

Revenues, expenses, enrollments, sources of financing.
Digest of Education Statistics—http://nces.ed.gov/programs/digest

Costs relative to other goods—
www.bls.gov/cpi/home.htm

International comparisons—
www.cgsnet.org/data-sources-international-comparisons-educational-attainment

Educational achievement—www.census.gov/hhes/socdemo/education/data/cps/index.html

CHAPTER THIRTY-FIVE

Poverty and Welfare

Learning Objectives

After reading this chapter you should be able to:

LO1 Describe how poverty is measured, summarize the demographics of poverty in the United States, and show how the percentage of the population that is poor has changed through the last 40 years.

LO2 Enumerate the significant problems associated with the federal government's official poverty rate.

LO3 List and describe the myriad programs that exist for the poor.

LO4 Explain why the government prefers programs that grant the recipient goods and services rather than money.

LO5 List the incentives and disincentives of welfare.

LO6 Summarize the welfare reform issues that we currently face.

Chapter Outline

Measuring Poverty

Programs for the Poor

Incentives, Disincentives, Myths, and Truths

Welfare Reform

Summary

Welfare and the reforming of welfare have been political issues from the time when the first "relief" bills were passed by Congress in the 1930s. In more recent times, President Bill Clinton vowed to "end welfare as we know it," and in 1996 a compromise was reached between his administration and the Republican majority in Congress. Shortly thereafter the welfare rolls were significantly cut and welfare programs in general were significantly changed. Even so, there are myriad programs that provide assistance to people in need, and we review them in this chapter. Some of these programs, such as TANF, and WIC, read like an alphabet soup; others have catchy names, like Head Start and Medicaid; still others have more straightforward names, like Food Stamps and the School Lunch and Breakfast program. Each program is designed to help poor people in specific ways. Some

disburse cash; others provide goods or services at little or no cost.

After defining what constitutes a state of "poverty," we describe the people who meet the criteria. We present and discuss some of the modern history of poverty, and we discuss why the measure of poverty we outlined might not be adequate to the task of ascertaining who needs assistance and who does not. We then describe the programs that are available to the poor. We divide the programs into those that provide cash and those that provide goods and services. We discuss why we make such a division. Last, we discuss, in general terms, the incentives and disincentives endemic to welfare programs, and we show why it is so difficult to solve the problems of those who live in poverty.

Measuring Poverty

What does being "poor" really mean? Are you poor only if you are on the verge of starvation? This absolutist position would suggest that poverty in the United States is almost entirely gone. As we will see later in our discussion, one of the most significant health problems of America's poor is that they are obese rather than starving. On the other hand, there is the position that poverty is a relative concept. We note that someone who has the living standard of a median-income Somalian is in poverty in the United States but not in Somalia, and an American today with an average income has a living standard that 100 years from now will likely be considered unacceptably poor. To see this point, note that the poor of today live in larger homes than all but the very richest Americans did in 1900.

The Poverty Line

Surveys have established reasonably well that low-income families of four spend roughly a third of their income on food. Defining the **poverty line** as that level of annual income sufficient to provide a family with a minimally adequate standard of living, we created the first poverty line by multiplying the cost of a

poverty line
That level of income sufficient to provide a family with a minimally adequate standard of living.

minimally sufficient diet by 3, the reciprocal of one-third. In successive years, the amount has been raised by the amount of increase in the consumer price index. For other family sizes, a similar process takes place where the reciprocal of the fraction of income spent on food by low-income people of that family size is multiplied by the cost of the minimally sufficient diet. In 2012, these numbers were $11,484 for one person, $14,657 for two people, $17,916 for three people, and $23,021 for four people. The **poverty rate** is the percentage of people in households whose incomes are under the poverty line. In 2011, the poverty rate in the United States stood at 15.0 percent.

Another important measure of poverty is the **poverty gap**, a representation of the total amount of money that would have to be transferred to households below the poverty line in order for them to get out of poverty. The poverty gap in the United States was $91 billion as of 2011.

poverty rate
The percentage of people in households whose incomes are under the poverty line.

poverty gap
The total amount of money that would have to be transferred to households below the poverty line for them to get out of poverty.

Who's Poor?

Table 35.1 displays indicators of who is poor and compares that to their general portion of the population. Many

TABLE 35.1   Who's poor.

Source: U.S. Census Bureau: Current Population Survey, www.census.gov/hhes/www/poverty/data/index.html

Demographic	General Population (in millions)	Percentage of the General Population	Percentage of Those in Poverty	Poverty Rate (%)
White, non-Hispanic	195.0	63.2%	41.6	9.8
Hispanic	52.3	17.0	28.6	25.3
Black, non-Hispanic	39.6	12.8	23.6	27.6
Other race	21.6	7.0	6.3	13.4
Male	150.9	48.9	44.4	13.6
Female	157.6	51.1	55.6	16.3
Under 18	73.7	23.9	34.8	21.9
18–24	30.1	9.8	13.4	20.6
25–64	163.1	52.9	43.7	9.8
65 and over	41.5	13.5	7.8	8.7
Female-headed household, no husband present	48.1	15.6	35.7	34.2
High school dropout*	43.5	14.1	23.8	25.4
High school graduate (no college)*	70.6	22.9	22.7	14.9
College (without a degree)*	67.3	21.8	16.0	11.1
Bachelor's degree or greater*	66.2	21.5	7.4	5.1

There are different thresholds for different compositions of each group. These figures are for a single adult under 65, two adults, two adults and one child, and two adults and two children, respectively.

people think that most poor people are African American. While many academics are quick to dispel that myth, they often perpetuate another with a counterassertion that most poor people are white. Neither is true if you separate European Americans from Hispanic Americans. Table 35.1 shows disproportionate numbers of blacks and Hispanics are in poverty and that they, together with American Indians, Asians, and Pacific Islanders, comprise a majority of the Americans living below the poverty line. It is obvious that there is a significant degree of racial and ethnic distinction in U.S. rates of poverty.

The data indicate that women are more likely to be in poverty than men; and, if we define "families" as not including single adults, then of families in poverty, half are in female-headed households while half are families of married couples. Given that female-headed households with children make up only 15.6 percent of the general population, poverty is clearly a women's issue.

It is also true that children under 18 make up 34.8 percent of those who are poor, though they comprise only 23.9 percent of the general population. This is a poverty rate among children of 21.9 percent. Whether this indicates that the poor have more children or that raising children can itself lead families into poverty can be debated. Clearly, the picture of poverty is this: Minorities, women, and children are poor in numbers vastly out of proportion to their numbers in the general population.

Another key indicator of poverty is education or, more properly, the lack of it. Those with a bachelor's degree experience poverty at one-sixth the rate of high school dropouts. Simply completing high school cuts the chance of being in poverty by about half, and simply attending college reduces the chance of being in poverty from 14.9 percent to 11.1 percent. Completing college reduces the rate even further. Only 1 in 20 households headed by a college graduate is in poverty.

Poverty through History

Figure 35.1 indicates that although the number of people in poverty is roughly the same as it was in 1959, the poverty rate has fallen dramatically. As we will discuss later, the poverty rate shown fails to account for the many government benefits. This means that the reduction in the poverty rate since 1959 can be attributed to an economic strengthening for those whose incomes are at the bottom of the economic scale.

In considering the decline in the general trend in poverty, be aware of the following caveats. The poverty rate has remained largely unchanged since the middle 1960s when the "war on poverty" actually began. From that time to the present it has neither fallen below 11 percent nor, until the Great Recession, gone above 15 percent. The systemic reduction, as a matter of fact, occurred between 1959 and 1969, before the enactment of many of the antipoverty programs. Noting that the shaded bars in Figure 35.1 indicate recessions, we can see that the poverty rate has increased during recessions and lessened during periods of growth. Democratic presidents

FIGURE 35.1 Poverty since 1959.

Source: U.S. Census Bureau, www.census.gov/hhes/www/poverty.html

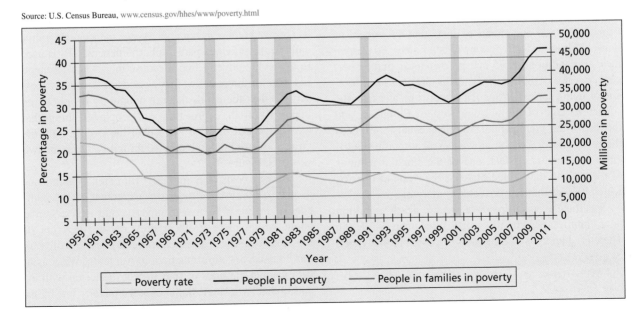

Kennedy and Johnson get much of the credit for the pre-1969 reduction in the poverty rate. However, this was a result more of a strong economy's providing excellent economic opportunities than anything these administrations did for the poor. The bulk of the pre-1969 decline took place prior to 1965 when these programs first began to become law. Since 1969 Democrats and Republicans have nearly identical records with respect to poverty. Generally speaking, the poverty rate is a reflection of the health of the overall economy.

Problems with Our Measure of Poverty

There is a host of reasons why using three times the cost of a minimally sufficient diet as a measure of poverty is inadequate to the task of measuring who is poor. First, it does not distinguish among families that are intact with one income earner and families that either are not intact or for other reasons have day-care costs. Since nearly 36 percent of families living in poverty are headed by single women with children under 18, this is potentially a significant problem. Since the one-third fraction that was used in the original poverty measure came from a survey conducted when there were fewer such female-headed households, the poverty line could be understated by all or part of the cost of day care. Since day-care costs can be between $4,500 and $14,000 per year per child under 12, this is a substantial area of mismeasurement.

Although this indicates that poverty is understated, there are problems with the measure that indicate that poverty may be overstated. Robert Rector of the conservative Heritage Foundation repeatedly updates statistics that purport to show that poverty is not a problem in the United States.[1] He uses government surveys and published statistical documents to show that 43 percent of households considered poor own their homes, 80 percent have air conditioning, 75 percent own a car, and 31 percent own two or more cars. He notes that the square footage of living space of America's poor is greater than the square footage of the average western European, and the diet of the average poor American equals or exceeds the recommended daily allowances of important nutrients. As a matter of fact, one of the singular features of the poor in the United States is their rate of obesity, which implies that few are actually starving.

Specifically on the point of wealth, nearly a million poor families own homes worth more than $150,000. There are hundreds of thousands of people in the United States who have little income but who are worth hundreds of thousands of dollars. Some are even millionaires. Admittedly, it is a small number of people like this who are rich, but called poor. However, it is important to note that the poverty line measures only people's income relative to a fixed standard that ignores measures of wealth.

Another shortcoming of the formula that is used to determine the poverty line is that it only includes income that is in cash. Thus programs that the poor take advantage of that are not cash-driven are incorrectly and absurdly omitted as if they have no value. For instance, the $200 in food stamps that a family might get a month is not counted and, if they found a subsidized rental apartment and free medical care, these also would not be counted. Depending on the study you believe, this failure to include income that is in forms other than cash overstates poverty by between two and four percentage points.

As we saw in Chapter 6, the consumer price index that is used to update the poverty line each year has many shortcomings. Best estimates are that it has overstated the cost of living by at least a full percentage point a year. Since the increase in the poverty line is generated using this flawed measure, it is likely that the poverty line has long been overstated relative to its real value in the 1960s. Figure 35.2 indicates that although the lower line, the adjusted version, tracks the upper line throughout the 1960s, the spread is significant enough that if you take the 1959 poverty line as the base on which to build the adjusted poverty line, you see that instead of being $23,021 in 2012 it should have been $13,531.

Besides the possible overstating of poverty that we have seen up to this point, there are additional problems with this measure that result in mislabeling some people as poor and others as not poor. As we mentioned specifically in the previous paragraph, the general CPI is used to adjust the poverty line. Because the CPI is a general indicator of the prices of many goods, it does not necessarily reflect the goods that are bought by people living in poverty. To the degree that poor people buy things that have increased in price more than the overall CPI, the "true" poverty line probably would fall between the two shown in Figure 35.2.

The way costs of living vary from area to area leads to yet another source of mismeasurement of the numbers of people who live in poverty, and it is a source about which there is uncertainty of the direction of the bias. Because it is much more expensive to live in San Francisco, California, than in Appleton, Wisconsin, for example, families of four in San Francisco with incomes that are a single dollar over the poverty line figure

[1] A recent version is available at www.heritage.org/Research/Reports/2007/08/How-Poor-Are-Americas-Poor-Examining-the-Plague-of-Poverty-in-America.

FIGURE 35.2 Poverty line with and without CPI adjustment.

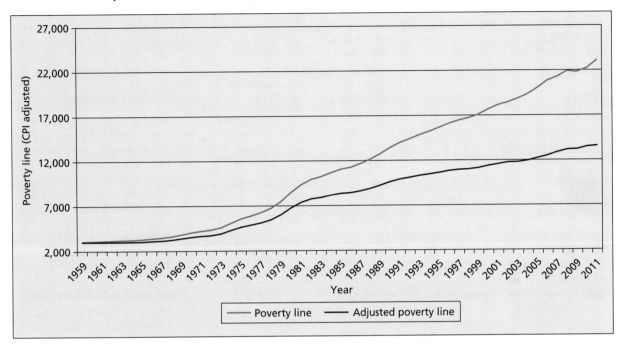

of $23,021 are significantly worse off than families of four in Appleton with incomes one dollar under the poverty line. In this way the poverty rate underestimates both urban poverty and poverty on the coasts. It overestimates the incidence of poverty in rural areas, small cities, in the South, and in the Midwest.

There is a final reason to doubt official poverty numbers, and that is a missing $2 trillion. In Chapter 6, when we talked about national income accounting, we briefly explained the sources of the numbers that make up the gross domestic product. It turns out that data used by the Census Bureau add up to substantially less, $2 trillion less, than the source numbers for personal income used in GDP calculations. While much of the missing $2 trillion is the in-kind transfers mentioned above, this certainly does not account for all of it. It is clearly true that most of that probably goes to the nonpoor. Some of it must also be in the hands of the poor, so there are clearly some who are labeled poor who are not.

Poverty in the United States versus Europe

As referred to in the opening, most countries have their own measures of poverty and they are not directly comparable. Timothy Smeeding, one of the foremost economists on the subject of poverty and income inequality, has attempted to create those comparable measures. He used the U.S. poverty line, adjusted it for different currency values, and looked at the percentage of people in various European countries who would fall below this line. Using this measure, he noted that U.S. poverty rates were higher than eight of the nine countries examined. When he focused strictly on income inequality, measured by the percentage of people living on incomes below 40 percent of a country's median disposable income, he found that the United States had the most unequal income of any of the countries compared.

Programs for the Poor

In Kind versus In Cash

The programs available to the poor are many and complicated. They are better understood as varying from state to state rather than being one consistent program across the country. Further, these programs are best understood as being divided between cash payments and provisions of goods and services in forms other than

in-kind subsidies
Provisions of goods and services in forms other than cash.

cash. Economists refer to the latter types as **in-kind subsidies**. Table 35.2 describes the different programs, the functions, and the populations they serve, as well as the restrictions placed on eligibility to receive them.

TABLE 35.2 Programs for the poor and their characteristics, FY2014.

Sources: Data compiled by the author.

Program	Function	Cash or In-Kind and Annual Federal + State Cost ($ billions)	Population Served	Eligibility Requirements
Temporary Assistance to Needy Families (TANF); formerly called AFDC	Cash income to the poor (the welfare check)	Cash, $25	Poor parents and their children under 18	Though this varies from state to state, the following generalizations can be made: Recipients (1) have to have children; (2) cannot have much wealth (usually less than $5,000 net), including house and car; (3) can remain on the program for 24 consecutive months only
Women, Infants and Children (WIC)	Food, formula, and diapers	In-kind, $7.1	Pregnant women and new mothers	Low wealth and income; cutoffs depend on the state
Food Stamps (now called SNAP)	Vouchers that can be spent only on food	In-kind, $74	All poor	Low wealth and income; cutoffs depend on the state; recipients can remain on the program for only 24 consecutive months
Medicaid		In-kind, $408	All poor	Low wealth and income; cutoffs depend on the state
Section 8 or Housing Authority Apartment	Reduced rent or low-cost housing	In-kind, $35	All poor	Low wealth and income; cutoffs depend on the state
Head Start	Day care; preschool	In-kind, $9	Poor with children under 5	First come, first served for anyone below 1.25 poverty line
School Lunch	Lunch and breakfast	In-kind, $18	Poor with school-age children	Anyone below 1.25 poverty line
Supplemental Security Income (SSI)	Cash assistance to "deserving poor"	Cash, $53	Disabled and widow-(er)s and orphans Poor with school-age children	Someone (a parent, guardian, or spouse) must be disabled or must have died
Earned Income Tax Credit (EITC)	Negative tax; boost low-pay workers	Cash, $56	Working poor	Based on family size; phases in at incomes up to $12,549, then phases out for incomes between $16,450 and $40,362; family of four maximum now, $5,666

Why Spend $685 Billion on a $91 Billion Problem?

Given the preceding information on the extent of poverty and the dollar costs of poverty programs, the following should strike you: If the poverty gap is $91 billion, why do the various levels of government spend more than six times that on poverty programs? The answer is two-fold: (1) There are people above the poverty line in need whom we choose to help; and (2) poverty programs must be terribly inefficient if it genuinely takes $685 billion to cure a $91 billion problem.

Table 35.2 shows that billions more are spent on goods and services than are spent in cash benefits. Including some minor programs not mentioned in Table 35.2, cash benefits total around $134 billion, whereas in-kind benefits total $551 billion. Clearly the government spends far more money on programs that give it control over recipients' behavior. For instance, we think the poor do not have enough to eat, adequate medical services, adequate housing, and so on. Instead of providing them with enough money to pay for these things, the government provides them with what it thinks they need.

If there is a family whose members enjoy good health, it is conceivable they would rather have more money spent on food and less on medical care. They cannot make that substitution. People who live in poverty are denied the ability to make basic decisions when they are given specific goods and services rather than money. In many studies of the poor, it is clear that they value cash more than the goods they are provided. Some food stamp recipients show exactly how little they value food stamps and WIC vouchers by selling them on the black market for 50 cents on the dollar. Why haven't programs been designed so that people in need receive cash and are then encouraged to make their own decisions on how to spend it?

There are several reasons, but three are obvious. First, through their elected officials, voters have made it clear they do not trust the judgment of the people who receive government benefits concerning what goods they buy. Many believe that if the poor could make good decisions, they would not be poor to begin with.

Second, people are more concerned with the welfare of needy children than with the welfare of adults. If you look at the programs with this in mind, you will see that nearly all of them require the presence of a child for an adult to be eligible. If we want to guarantee services for children, it makes more sense to give the adult access to such services rather than cash. This minimizes the likelihood that the money will be diverted by adults away from the targeted children.

Third, some welfare benefits seem designed more to provide those who tender them with a feeling of magnanimity than to benefit the poor. If it is our own happiness we are maximizing and if our happiness is enhanced by the knowledge that we provided the poor with enough to survive, it may be even more important to us that we ensure that the poor are consuming what we think is good for them rather than what they want.

Is $685 Billion Even a Lot Compared to Other Countries?

Though the United States spends $685 billion on its antipoverty programs, the Smeeding analysis puts this in perspective by noting that European antipoverty programs are far more aggressive. He notes that after accounting for taxes and various welfare programs, the system in the United States reduces poverty (defined by him as the percentage of people living below 50 percent of median household disposable income) by only 26 percent, whereas the average European country's programs reduce their poverty by more than 60 percent.

Incentives, Disincentives, Myths, and Truths

While no one has ever intended this to be the case, many of the programs designed to help the poor are blamed for ensuring that people who live in poverty and who receive benefits have no incentive to become self-sufficient. The existence of welfare is accused of giving people a reason not to work. It is blamed for encouraging young women both to get pregnant and to carry the pregnancy to term. Welfare is indicted for encouraging recipients to have more children so that their WIC will be extended and their food stamps and TANF payments increased. The structure of TANF's predecessor, Aid to Families with Dependent Children (AFDC), was blamed for breaking up poor families by giving them the incentive to have the father leave. Together, these problems created the concern that welfare was becoming a way of life and that people were getting used to it.

From a theoretical perspective, each of the preceding arguments has merit, but the evidence from economic studies is not one-sided. First, there are several counterclaims. Birth rates among teenagers climbed steadily from the 1960s through the early 1990s and leveled off when the states and then the federal government

WELFARE'S BEST URBAN LEGEND

The world of welfare is replete with urban legends. My favorite goes something like this: "I was standing in line at the grocery store one day behind a nicely dressed woman who was buying beer, steak, shrimp, and a whole bunch of stuff I couldn't afford. She had them put the steak and shrimp on her food stamp card and used her cash to buy the beer. She packed up her groceries and went to her brand new SUV." In teaching this subject for years, I have heard this story in countless renditions from students who were either customers or grocery employees. The story is almost always the same. While the story may be about fraud, it is also quite likely about their misinterpreting the actions of a foster parent.

Most states give foster families Medicaid cards and an allotment on a food stamp card to pay for the food and medical expenses of the children in their care. That some of these families are wealthy enough to afford nice meals and nice vehicles does not diminish our obligation to pay them for the service they are providing us by caring for orphaned, discarded, or abused children or those children whose parents are in prison.

instituted welfare reforms designed to curb benefits. The truth is that the real dollar value of benefits per recipient is lower today than it was in the late 1960s. Thus, if poor teenagers were really considering the value of welfare in making decisions about having children, teen pregnancy rates would have fallen from the mid-1970s on as the real value of the benefits fell. It is more likely that the culture and teen sex drives had more to do with teen pregnancies than the prospect of receiving welfare checks.

Second, although it was and still is true that the more children you have, the more benefits you get, there is no systematic evidence that people on welfare had more children because they were on welfare. If welfare mothers were concerned only for themselves and the benefits they could get, it would make sense that they would have children so they would be eligible for more benefits. What had to have been evident to them, however, is that the increase in benefits does not cover any more than the increased cost of raising an additional child. Unless we want to claim that the poor do not care about their children, there is little likelihood that rational women would get pregnant and do the work of raising an additional child in order to keep a few extra dollars a month. They could make more money with less effort if they cleaned houses on the side.

Third, it is true that families on welfare are far more likely to have absent fathers, but it is hard to say whether the father's leaving was caused by the need to be welfare-eligible or the family became welfare-eligible because the father left. In order to accept the argument that welfare caused a rash of absent fathers, you must hold the cynical belief that a well-meaning father would abandon his children so they could receive benefits. Although this might have been the case prior to 1996, today, after welfare reform, the abandonment would have to be complete.

A mother now has to name and state the last known location of absent fathers to get benefits. Clearly, whether the need to apply for welfare leads to the breakup of families that would have stayed together is debatable. The reason that some welfare programs are contingent on a parent's being absent stems from the conviction that if there are two able-bodied adults in a household, one of them should be working. Either the problem of absent fathers is a coincidence or it is the price society is paying for building welfare requirements around a view that families with both parents present should not be eligible for assistance unless one is disabled.

Fourth, under AFDC, that is, prior to the welfare reforms of 1996, welfare dependency had been growing at an alarming rate. Some 26 percent of recipients had been receiving benefits from the program for 10 years or more at the same time that the percentage of families that had been on welfare for very short periods of time was falling. In addition, daughters of recipients were tending to become recipients themselves. These circumstances and others like them led Congress and the president to agree to change welfare programs to incorporate limits on the length of time people could receive benefits and to require that recipients become gainfully employed.

Welfare Reform

Is There a Solution?

To be successful, a social safety net must meet three goals:

1. The program that is designed cannot be so expensive that the taxpaying public will not sustain it.

2. The program must have an incentive built in that makes beneficiaries want to leave it.

3. The program must provide enough of a level of basic necessities that recipients have a socially acceptable standard of living.

The problem facing policy analysts in the United States has always been that these goals cannot be satisfied simultaneously.

Any program must have a phaseout level of income. If the phaseout is too quick, meaning that for every dollar you earn you lose significant welfare benefits, the disincentive to work will be too profound. The AFDC program reduced benefits by nearly a dollar for every dollar the recipient earned. This nearly 100 percent take-back rate meant that without a salary at least twice the minimum wage in a job, a single parent with two small children requiring day care would be far better off on welfare than working.

If the phaseout is too slow, then too many people will be getting welfare benefits and not enough will be paying taxes. Though this is possible, it violates the first goal, that of having a program that does not cost too much money. On the other hand, the phaseout could be slow and of low cost to taxpayers. The problem would then be that there would not be enough money for recipients to survive on.

The implicit choice made by policy makers prior to the reforms of welfare that were instituted in 1996 was to give up on providing incentives to leave the program. The increase in long-term dependency on the program can, at least in part, be blamed on this decision. The near 100 percent take-back rate on AFDC left people with no earned income better off than people making $10,000 a year. The result was that only those recipients who could invest in an education could ultimately afford to leave the program.

Welfare as We Now Know It

In the 1996 reforms, the problem of welfare dependency was tackled by simply ordering people to leave welfare. The institution of time limits was an acknowledgment of the concern that dependency was wrong and that monetary incentives for relinquishing benefits were too expensive. Instead of being offered incentives to leave the program, people are now told how long their benefits will keep coming. States are given block grants of money (TANF) that they are supposed to use to aid their poor. Instead of having to give it away in cash benefits, as they did under AFDC, they can now spend it on job training, child care, or tax breaks for businesses that are willing to hire welfare recipients. States must set time limits of 24 months or less and they must establish work requirements for some programs. Supplemental Security Income rules for disability have changed such that some people who were once eligible for full benefits are now eligible for only partial benefits.

By 1999, welfare caseloads had fallen to their lowest point in three decades. Though it is difficult to tell how much of this was due to the robust economy of the 1990s, it is clear that the reforms that were instituted have had some effect. Economist Rebecca Blank summarized the growing research that has been conducted on this issue by noting that through the reforms of providing assistance to work, monetary incentives to work, and requirements to work, the current array of programs is raising incomes and increasing employment in ways previous programs did not.

Is Poverty Necessarily Bad?

There are many economists who object to the implied premise of this entire chapter: namely, that poverty is a bad thing. Without a carrot—wealth, and a stick—poverty, these economists believe that people would have little incentive to "work hard and play by the rules."[2] If accepted as valid, this philosophy would suggest that there is a trade-off between rates of economic growth and rates of economic inequality. There is evidence from the 1980s through today that countries with low rates of economic inequality had low rates of economic growth, but there is much disagreement about whether the former caused the latter.

[2]This phrase was often used by President Clinton as a political mantra.

Summary

You now understand how poverty is measured, who is poor in the United States, and how the percentage of the population that is poor has changed through the last 40 years. You are able to describe some of the significant problems presented by the official poverty rate. You understand the myriad programs that exist for the poor, note that most of the programs grant the recipients goods and services rather than money, and understand why it is that government does this. Last, you are aware of the incentives and disincentives in the welfare state, and you know the welfare reform issues that we currently face.

Key Terms

in-kind subsidies, 375   poverty line, 372   poverty rate, 372
poverty gap, 372

Quiz Yourself

1. Poverty is a _____ concept in that a person with that income in the United States may be considered in poverty, while a person with that same income in Somalia may be in the upper quarter of income earners.
   a. relative
   b. absolute
   c. irrelevant
   d. ficticious

2. In a simple 300 million person world of all four-person families, if the poverty line is $12,500 and half of the 10 million families (with 40 million poor people) earn $10,000 and the other half earn $7,500, then the poverty gap is
   a. $125 billion (= 10 million * $12,500).
   b. $250 billion (= 20 million * $12,500).
   c. $150 billion (= 20 million * $2,500 + 20 million * $5,000).
   d. $37.5 billion (= 5 million * $2,500 + 5 million * $5,000).

3. In a simple 300 million person world of all four-person families, if the poverty line is $12,500 and half of the 10 million families (with 40 million poor people) earn $10,000 and the other half earn $7,500, then the poverty rate is
   a. 3.33% (10 million/300 million).
   b. 13.33% (40 million/300 million).
   c. 16.66% (50 million/300 million).
   d. 96.33% ((300 million − 10 million)/300 million).

4. Using a poverty line of $12,500, under the current system of calculating the poverty rate, which of the following people is not considered in poverty and probably ought to be?
   a. A rural family whose sole income earner is from a minimum wage ($10,300).
   b. A rural family whose combined income is $15,000.
   c. A New York City family whose combined income is $13,000.
   d. A retired couple whose multimillion dollar estate yields them no income.

5. Using a poverty line of $12,500, under the current system of calculating the poverty rate, which of the following people is considered in poverty and probably ought not to be?
   a. A rural family whose sole income is from a minimum wage ($10,300).
   b. A rural family whose combined income is $15,000.
   c. A New York City family whose combined income is $13,000.
   d. A retired couple whose multimillion dollar estate yields them no income.

6. The distribution of aid to the poor between in-kind and in-cash is
   a. roughly equal.
   b. weighted heavily toward in-cash benefits.
   c. weighted slightly toward in-kind benefits.
   d. weighted heavily toward in-kind benefits.

7. The most obvious pattern in poverty rates is the degree to which they are higher during
   a. Democratic administrations.
   b. wars.
   c. odd years.
   d. recessions.

8. The evidence is that welfare reform in 1996 resulted in _____ welfare rolls.
   a. a substantial increase in
   b. a slight increase in
   c. a substantial decrease in
   d. no impact on

Short Answer Questions

1. Compare the data on who is in poverty to whatever stereotype you may have had prior to reading this chapter.

2. What do the data suggest with regard to poverty and the age profile of those in poverty relative to the age profile generally?

3. What measure of poverty would give you the lowest possible estimate of the amount of money you would need to solve the nation's poverty problem? Why would only spending that amount not likely be a good solution to the problem?

4. If you were to construct a poverty measure, what would you put into the calculations to deal with the issues listed in the chapter?

Think about This

The wealth of one person, Bill Gates, is about equal to the annual poverty gap in the United States in one year, $91 billion. The United States has a more significantly unequal division of income than any other industrialized country. What are the consequences of that unequal distribution?

Talk about This

What other "urban legends" exist about the poor and welfare? What research could be conducted to dispel these legends or prove them to be factual?

For More Insight See

Blank, Rebecca M., "Evaluating Welfare Reform in the United States," *Journal of Economic Literature* XL (December 2002).

Journal of Economic Perspectives 11, no. 2 (Spring 1997). See articles by Peter Gottschalk; George Johnson; Robert Topel; and Nicole Fortin and Thomas Lemieux, pp. 21–96.

Journal of Economic Perspectives 12, no. 1 (Winter 1998). See articles by Dale Jorgenson; and Robert Triest, pp. 79–114.

Smeeding, Timothy, "Poor People in Rich Nations: The United States in Comparative Perspective," *Journal of Economic Perspectives* 20, no. 1 (Winter 2006).

Wolff, Edward, "Recent Trends in the Size Distribution of Household Wealth," *Journal of Economic Perspectives* 12, no. 3 (Summer 1998).

Behind the Numbers

Detailed Poverty Tabulations from the Current Population Survey—www.census.gov

Historical Poverty Tables, Current Population Survey—www.census.gov/hhes/www/poverty

Federal Spending on Programs for the Poor, Detailed Functional Tables—www.whitehouse.gov/omb/budget

Statistics of those in poverty.

The Heritage Foundation; paper by Robert Rector—www.heritage.org/Research/Reports/2007/08/How-Poor-Are-Americas-Poor-Examining-the-Plague-of-Poverty-in-America

CHAPTER THIRTY-SIX

Social Security

Learning Objectives

After reading this chapter you should be able to:

LO1 Describe what Social Security is and its basic tax and benefit structure.

LO2 Detail the history of changes to the program since its inception.

LO3 Explain the economic rationale for having such a system.

LO4 Enumerate the effects of the program on work and savings.

LO5 Show how economists use present value analysis to aid in determining for whom the program works and for whom it does not.

LO6 Explain the origin and purpose behind the Social Security Trust Fund.

LO7 Summarize present estimates of the future financial health of the Social Security system and evaluate the options for ensuring its long-run solvency.

Chapter Outline

The Basics

Why Do We Need Social Security?

Social Security's Effect on the Economy

Whom Is the Program Good For?

Will the System Be There for Me?

Summary

When most people think about Social Security, they envision retirement checks for the elderly. Social Security has a much broader scope, including benefits for eligible widows and orphans in addition to medical and disability insurance. In this chapter we concentrate on retirement benefits.

We begin by reviewing the history of Social Security as a government pension program, and we include its tax, benefit, and structure. We then turn to why it is needed. We discuss the effects of Social Security on the economy in general and show that as a retirement program, it is better for retirees who are poor than for those who are rich and much better for those who retired before 1960 than after 1980. Last, we discuss why bankruptcy is likely without reform and what reform might look like.

The Basics

The Beginning

In 1935 the Social Security Act was passed and signed into law by President Franklin Roosevelt. The stock market crash of 1929 and the Great Depression of the 1930s had caused great upheavals in people's financial circumstances. Unemployment had reached a high of 25 percent. People who had been wealthy investors before the crash were lucky if they had a job that would allow them to at least live from paycheck to paycheck after the crash. Many banks closed when, as a result of the stock market crash, their investments were insufficient to pay their depositors. In this circumstance, even people who had saved diligently and invested prudently for their retirement found themselves without savings. Social Security guaranteed a safety net, come good times or bad, to generations who retired from the late 1930s on. At the time, it was not intended that Social Security be the only income on which a person lived. To nearly a third of recipients today it is just that.

Today, Social Security provides guaranteed retirement benefits averaging about $1,199 a month to 36 million American people over the age of 62. Social Security is a **pay-as-you-go pension** system where current workers' taxes are used to pay pensions to current retirees. This is unlike a traditional **fully funded pension** system where, for every benefit dollar it is required to pay in the future, there is an offsetting amount currently invested that is sufficient to pay off that dollar. It is the pay-as-you-go aspect that allowed money to go to the elderly right away (the first checks went out in 1936) but, as we will see, it is also this aspect that currently puts Social Security in the most jeopardy.

pay-as-you-go pension
A system where current workers' taxes are used to pay pensions to current retirees.

fully funded pension
A system that has an amount currently invested that is sufficient to pay every benefit dollar it is required to pay in the future.

Taxes

Social Security taxes (technically called FICA, or Federal Insurance Contribution Act taxes) are **payroll taxes**. That is, the amount workers pay is based on what workers earn from their work. This is different from an income tax in that interest, dividends, and other forms of unearned income are not subject to this tax. In addition, not all payroll is taxed; taxes are paid only up to a limited amount of income called the **maximum taxable earnings**. In 2013, this amount was $113,700 which means that workers did not have to pay the old-age portion of the Social Security tax for income they earned beyond that point. Both the employer and employee pay an equal amount of this tax so that if you have to pay $1,000 in tax, so does your employer. The self-employed pay both parts of the tax.

payroll taxes
Taxes owed on what workers earn from their work.

maximum taxable earnings
The maximum of taxable earnings subject to the payroll tax.

As part of a temporary stimulus agreement after the 2010 elections, the employee portion was reduced to 4.2 percent from 6.2 percent for the 2011 and 2012 tax years.

Benefits

On the benefit side, eligible retirees get benefit checks that are based on what they made during their working years. The **average index of monthly earnings (AIME)** is the monthly average of the 35 highest earnings years (capped by the maximum taxable earnings for each respective year) adjusted for wage inflation. The AIME is put into a formula that generates the **primary insurance amount (PIA).**[1] Single people are paid the PIA and married couples get 1.5 times the highest of their PIAs, or the sum of their individual PIAs, whichever is higher. For full benefits workers cannot begin to collect until they reach the **retirement age,** though they can collect partial benefits at age 62.

average index of monthly earnings (AIME)
The monthly average of the 35 highest earnings years adjusted for wage inflation.

primary insurance amount (PIA)
The amount single retirees receive in a monthly check if they retire at their retirement age.

retirement age
The age at which retirees get full benefits.

Although the payroll tax structure is such that everyone with income under the maximum taxable earnings pays the same rate of tax, the benefit structure is such that, in net, Social Security redistributes income to the lower end of the income scale. To see this, consider the following example. Assume, inflation-adjusted, a person makes $5,000 per month for 35 years, so that person's AIME is $5,000. Inflation-adjusted, the employee and the employer each pay $382.50 (7.65% $\times$ $5,000) per month in taxes. That person would get a monthly Social Security check of $2,026. If someone else were in a similar situation with one-fifth the income, that person and his or her employer would combine to pay one-fifth the tax but the benefit would be $779 per month. Thus, this employee pays one-fifth the tax but receives one-third the benefit. This means that the person at the lower end of the income scale has a benefit dollar–to–tax dollar ratio that is twice that of the upper-income person. This is by design, and, as such, the program serves to redistribute money down the income line.

Changes over Time

Since its inception Social Security has added benefits. Payments to widows and orphans, called survivor

---

[1] The formula for 2013 was 90 percent of the first $791 plus 32 percent of the next $3,977 plus 15 percent of the remainder up to a maximum benefit that is computed using the maximum taxable earnings for each of the work years. This formula is adjusted yearly for inflation. For more information, see www.socialsecurity.gov

TABLE 36.1 History of Social Security's components at selected points in time.

Year	Maximum Taxable Earnings ($)	Old-Age and Disability Tax Rate (% of payroll)	Medicare Tax Rate (%)	Total Tax Rate That Both Employers and Employees Pay (%)	Retirement Age*		
					Year of Birth	Age	Benefits†
1937	$ 3,000	1.000%	0%	1.000%	1937	65	OA, S
1950	3,600	1.500	0	1.500	1950	66	OA, S
1955	4,200	2.000	0	2.000	1955	66 + 2 months	OA, S
1960	4,800	2.250	0	2.250	1960	67	OA, S, DI
1965	4,800	3.625	0	3.625	1965	67	OA, S, DI
1970	7,800	4.200	0.600	4.800	1970	67	OA, S, DI, HI
1975	14,100	4.950	0.900	5.850	1975	67	OA, S, DI, HI
1980	25,900	5.080	1.050	6.130	1980	67	OA, S, DI, HI
1985	39,600	5.700	1.300	7.000	1985	67	OA, S, DI, HI
1990	51,300	6.200	1.450	7.650	1990	67	OA, S, DI, HI
1995	61,200	6.200	1.450	7.650	1995	67	OA, S, DI, HI
2000	76,200	6.200	1.450	7.650	2000	67	OA, S, DI, HI
2013	113,700	6.200	1.450	7.650	2011	67	OA, S, D, HI

*Until 1983 the retirement age was 65. In 1983 the law was changed to increase it depending on year of birth. 1938, => 65 + 2 months; 1939, => 65 + 4 months; 1940, => 65 + 6 months; 1941, => 65 + 8 months; 1942, => 65 + 10 months; 1943–1954, => 66; 1955, => 66 + 2 months; 1956, => 66 + 4 months; 1957, => 66 + 6 months; 1958, => 66 + 8 months; 1959, => 66 + 10 months; 1960 on, 67.

†OA = old age; S = survivor; DI = disability; HI = health insurance (Medicare).

benefits, have been part of Social Security from its inception. Disability insurance, for workers who are unable to work for long periods of time, was added in 1956, and basic, highly subsidized health coverage (called Medicare) was added in 1966.

Table 36.1 shows how the tax rate, the maximum taxable earnings, and the retirement age have changed since the program began. This table shows how Social Security's components have been changed to ensure its survivability. As you can see, tax rates have risen, in part to pay for the other benefits described previously, but also to guarantee that retirement benefits would be there for each generation. The tax rate has risen from 1 percent to 7.65 percent while the maximum amount subject to tax has risen from $3,000 to $113,700. The retirement age has also risen. People born before 1938 can retire with full benefits at 65; those born after 1960 must wait until they are 67. A somewhat complicated transition formula determines the retirement age of those born between 1939 and 1959. In short, in contrast to the view that Social Security has been a monolithic and unalterable program, there have been many changes that have both broadened its scope and ensured its survivability.

Why Do We Need Social Security?

If you have worked through other issue chapters in this book by now, you know that it has been mentioned before that economists believe that government intervention in private enterprise must be justified on at least one of the following three grounds:

1. The need to control **externalities** that is, effects created by an unregulated market on people other than the buyer or seller, such as pollution, secondhand smoke, and drunk driving.

2. Concern about significant moral or ethical problems associated with the good being sold, for example, drugs, prostitution, and pornography.

3. Sellers or buyers are incapable of making rational decisions, because people either cannot be counted on to do the smart thing or have inadequate information upon which to base a decision.

externalities
Effects created by an unregulated market on people other than the buyer or seller.

It is a combination of the first and third reasons that makes some form of compulsory-saving/

retirement-benefit program necessary in the eyes of economists.

Ideally, rational and wise people will be able to save money for their own retirements based on their own preferences for consuming now versus consuming later. They will realize that money spent now has an opportunity cost, namely, money that cannot be spent later. Investment markets allow people to save or borrow as they please. If all the assumptions about well-functioning markets are valid in the investment market, then there is no reason for government to force people to save. They will save the right amount for themselves.

In opposition to the rationale put forth by economists is the contention that people may not be able to save the right amount for themselves. This is an argument that has little appeal among economists. Many economists maintain that if the government were not taxing workers for this purpose, workers could be saving the money on their own, and saving or not saving would therefore be their choice.

On the other hand, two arguments against a completely free market approach have some appeal among economists. First, our humanity prevents us from letting others starve. If people do not save for themselves, someone else will be forced to bail them out. Their decision not to save affects others. These "others" could be children, relatives, friends, or government. Social Security prevents people from not saving the right amount, and it protects others from having to bail them out.

Second, our rationality stems from our ability to learn from our mistakes. In most situations, and especially in most markets, we learn from our mistakes. For instance, if the first time you go grocery shopping for yourself you buy nothing but marshmallows and Red Bull, you will quickly learn that you need vegetables and fruits in your diet. If you do not save enough for retirement, you cannot just decide to live the first 65 years of your life over again. Government often prevents us from this sort of mistake. There are few guarantees that we will always do the right thing ourselves. There are other examples of this: (1) You cannot borrow money before age 18 without a cosignature; (2) you cannot drop out of school before you are 16; and (3) you cannot drink until you are 21. Society fears that you might suffer irreparable bankruptcy, poverty, or alcoholism, respectively; and it wants government to ensure that you will not make mistakes that cannot be undone. For these reasons, the question among economists is not whether some form of government-run retirement is needed but what form that system takes and how to fund it so that it is financially stable.

Social Security's Effect on the Economy

Effect on Work

Before Social Security was implemented, 51 percent of men over age 65 worked. Today, that number is 22 percent. While there is much dispute on the degree to which Social Security itself caused this to happen (in fact, this number has risen in recent years), Social Security has clearly made it easier for people to retire. This has good as well as bad aspects. Though the retired may be happier being retired, the economy is deprived of their labor and the fruit of their labor. On the other hand, as more people retire, positions are opened up throughout the labor scale as everyone moves up to fill vacated positions. Paradoxically, this is a circumstance in which the economy is hurt even though everyone in it is happier. (If this seems odd, revisit Chapter 6 and the section "Real Gross Domestic Product and Why It Is Not Synonymous with Social Welfare.")

Effect on Saving

Most economists believe that if people had to save for their own retirement, they would save more than they do now. Though these economists disagree on the magnitude of this effect, they have concluded that the existence of Social Security reduces the amount of money that is saved in the economy. This is primarily due to the **asset substitution effect**. If the government is taxing you on your earnings now and promising a pension payment later, the government is, in effect, saving for you. If the government is saving for you, you will save less for yourself.

asset substitution effect
Government is saving for you; thus you will save less for yourself.

induced retirement effect
People need to save more if they are going to retire earlier than they would have without Social Security.

Two counteracting effects to this are the **induced retirement effect** and the bequest effect. As mentioned, people are clearly retiring earlier than they did in the past. If Social Security did not exist, and people had no hope of ever retiring, they might not save anything. On the other hand, since Social Security makes retirement a possibility, people may save so as to retire. The induced retirement effect thus increases national savings because people need to save more if they are going to retire earlier than they would have without Social Security.

Another impact of Social Security is that it may increase national savings if the elderly are putting aside

TABLE 36.2   Present value analysis of Social Security.

Income ($)	Present Value of Social Security Taxes at 8% ($)	Present Value of Social Security Benefits at 8% ($)	Net Present Value of Social Security at 8% ($)	Real Rate of Return (%)
$ 15,000	$ 25,780	$ 11,434	−$ 14,346	2.6
20,000	34,374	13,836	−20,538	2.3
25,000	42,968	16,239	−26,729	2.1
30,000	51,561	18,446	−33,115	1.9
35,000	60,154	19,572	−40,582	1.7
40,000	68,748	20,698	−48,050	1.5

more money for bequests, that is, money that will go to younger family members when their elders die. It may be that Social Security provides a stable enough income for the elderly that they choose to save enough to pass on a larger inheritance than they would have if there had been no such program. The **bequest effect** thus increases national savings because people save more so as to give larger gifts to their descendants than they would have without Social Security.

bequest effect
People save more to give larger gifts to their descendants, thus increasing national savings.

Economists dispute the net effect of Social Security on savings. Martin Feldstein, in particular, was the first to estimate the effect of Social Security on savings. In 1974 he concluded that there was a dramatic reduction in savings. This was disputed by other economists, led by Alicia Munnell in 1977 and Dean Leimer and Selig Lesnoy in 1982, all of whom estimated that the net effect was zero. Not to be silenced, in 1996 Feldstein published revised estimates for 1992, when personal savings were actually $248 billion, indicating that it would have been $646 billion without Social Security. The upshot is that there is little agreement except for a middle ground that appears to indicate a small net negative impact of Social Security on savings.

Whom Is the Program Good For?

With a spreadsheet, a few assumptions, and some specialized terminology, you can compute whether Social Security is a good deal for you. To do this you will need to draw on the present value discussion of Chapter 7. We can then compare the taxes we pay today with the benefits we anticipate getting 40 or 50 years from now.

There is much literature on the present value of Social Security. C. Eugene Steuerle and Jon Bakija provide

detailed present value estimates for different categories of people born in different generations. Though exact estimates vary by marital status, by earners, and by age, the results show unequivocally that the program was a net winner across the income scale for those retiring before 1980. However, because of the rapid increases in FICA taxes, this situation has steadily eroded, leaving only married couples, with only a single low-income earner, to benefit.

To get a flavor of what this kind of analysis entails, consider the following example. First, we need to make some basic assumptions. To estimate the present value of your Social Security taxes and benefits, we need to know your age, your marital status, the starting salary you can expect upon graduation, the rate at which your income will grow, an assumption of yearly inflation, your age at retirement, and, finally, your age at death. For Table 36.2 we will assume the following: You are 19; you will graduate at age 23; you will not get married; you will work until you are 67; you will die at 88; inflation will be 3 percent every year; your income will grow at 4 percent per year; and 8 percent is the appropriate interest rate. Though the old age and disability tax rate is 6.2 percent, the old age part is only 5.3 percent. This tax is on both the employer and employee, so we will assume that your old age Social Security contributions amount to 10.6 percent of your earnings (up to, of course, the maximum taxable earnings).[2]

Table 36.2 indicates that today's 19-year-olds would do better if their Social Security taxes were invested at 8 percent per year (inflation plus a 5 percent real rate of return) than they would do under Social Security. The first column shows the income assumed for the calculations, and the second indicates the present value, at 8 percent, of all taxes to be paid. The third column shows the present value, again at 8 percent, of all the benefits that

[2] We assume that employees bear the entire burden of the Social Security tax because empirical estimates of labor supply elasticity are nearly zero.

people will be entitled to from their retirements at age 67 until their deaths at 88. The last column indicates the appropriate real interest rate that equalizes the present value of taxes and benefits.

As can be seen from the first two columns, as people make more money, they also pay more taxes. Starting with people making minimum wage ($7.25/hour × 2,080 hours in a year) and ending with people starting their working life with a $40,000 salary, the present value of their taxes increases from $25,780 to $68,748.[3] Also apparent from the table is that the present value of benefits for high-income people is greater than that for low-income people. This is because the more you make and contribute to the system, the bigger your benefit checks are at retirement. Note here that although the high earner makes much more than three times what the lower earner makes, the benefit check the high earner gets is a little more than twice that of the lower earner.

The fact that the net present value is negative means that Social Security will not pay as well as a private investment making 8 percent. As can be seen from the fourth column, everyone in your generation will do better if your money is privately invested. For those of you who are going to be high earners, this loss is significant. The last column shows that, as an investment, Social Security is a better deal, in terms of the real rate of return, for a low earner than for a high earner.

Two conclusions can be drawn from Table 36.2: (1) For no members of the current generation of college students is Social Security likely to beat their private alternatives; (2) the more money people are likely to make over their lifetimes, the worse the discrepancy between private investments and Social Security is likely to be.

There are a couple of logical questions that could be asked at this point so I'll ask them for you: (1) You assumed a 5 percent real interest rate. What would happen if you assumed something like 3 percent? In this case, the net present values would be near zero for the low earner and –$41,693 for the high earner. (2) What if I live until I'm 100? Can I beat the system? The power of compounding interest dwarfs your ability to live long enough to make the system work for you. Even though a high earner would get benefits in excess

of $100,000 a year, at age 90 the present value of this is around $2,000 a year.

If your parents, grandparents, and great-grandparents had run these numbers when they were your age, the outcomes would have been markedly different. For those retiring in 1960, the real rate of return averaged 15 percent while those retiring in 1980 saw an average 7 percent real rate of return. The basic reason for the difference in real rates of return between you and previous generations is that the Social Security tax rates they paid were much lower than the rates you can expect to pay. Those retiring in the 1960s faced tax rates of less than 3 percent for much of their working lives. Those who retired in the 1980s saw tax rates rise from 1 percent to 5 percent while they worked. You will face Social Security tax rates (old age) of at least 5.3 percent for your working life.

In part, Social Security has been viewed as a successful program because, until recently, it has been a good deal for everyone. For people alive when Social Security was introduced, it was an example of the great things that government can do. For people born between 1935 and the mid-1950s, Social Security provides a guaranteed retirement income that is about equal to, for married average wage earners, what they would have gotten in the stock market.[4] For those born after the mid-1950s, the real rate of return on Social Security is likely to be dwarfed by private investment opportunities. For those who are single people, for married dual-income earners, or for higher income earners, the year of birth for a breakeven status was as long ago as 35 years earlier. For such people, Social Security has returned to them much less than private investments would have.

The whole question of who benefits from Social Security is often seen as a loaded one. Simply asking it sometimes causes people to think that you favor its elimination. So given that this section may have struck you as a sales pitch for its elimination, remember that Social Security is part of what economists call "social insurance." It is not intended to be a good investment. It is intended to provide a secure source of income during retirement. As you will see when we discuss the reform question, that is where the debate centers. Those who favor some form of privatization judge the program using a yardstick, like rate of return, that others reject.

[3] The reason that the increase in taxes paid is less than proportional to the increase in income is that people with starting salaries of $40,000 and 4 percent growth per year will hit the maximum taxable earnings before they retire. So, whereas the taxes that a poor worker will pay will go up 4 percent every year, the taxes a richer person will pay will go up only 3 percent a year once they have hit that limit.

[4] Because the system has a built-in transfer from high-income earners to low-income earners, though the average earner would break even, the low-income earner would get more than the present value of taxes. A high-income earner would get less.

Will the System Be There for Me?

Why Social Security Is in Trouble

There has always been a concern about whether Social Security could survive. Tax rates have always risen faster than benefits have been added because the retired population has grown faster than the working population. In 1982 a significant concern was raised that the pay-as-you-go system could not handle the demographic bulge of the post–World War II baby boom. In the years following World War II, until around 1960, some 2.5 percent of all women gave birth each year. The advent of the birth control pill, the increased availability of abortion, and the social unrest of the 1960s and 1970s significantly altered America's birth rate. By 1976 only 1.5 percent of women gave birth each year.

As a result, the baby-boom generation, 50 to 68 years old in 2014, represents 22 percent of the current population. A comparable group before them, those between 70 and 85, are now only 7 percent of the population. Because of this, the number of taxpaying workers per benefit-receiving retiree will continue to fall precipitously. In 1950, there were more than 16 workers paying taxes for every retiree who was collecting benefits. Today, the number is 2.9, and current projections say it will drop to 2.2 by 2030 and to 1.9 by 2085. Figure 36.1 presents an overview of this situation.

The Social Security Trust Fund

To combat the demographic problem the **Social Security Trust Fund** was established in 1982 to collect more taxes than were needed to pay current benefits. In later years there would thus be money enough to pay benefits to baby-boom retirees. In 2012, there was approximately $2.7 trillion in U.S. government debt in this fund. As you may recall from Chapter 10, "Monetary Policy," or Chapter 12, "Federal Deficits, Surpluses, and the National Debt," the federal government owes itself $6.4 trillion.

Social Security Trust Fund
A fund established in 1982 to hold government debt which will be sold as necessary when tax revenues are less than benefits.

Whether this actually constitutes a true trust fund is debatable. It is a collection of debt that will either be issued for the first time or reissued to the public when there is less in Social Security tax revenues than benefits to pay. One way of looking at this issue is that the trust fund is money that was collected using the Social Security tax, rather than the income tax. This was begun in the 1980s and early 1990s to reduce what would otherwise have been a much larger deficit. If you look at it this way, the national debt that grew to $17 trillion by 2013 actually only grew to just $12 trillion (and just $10 trillion if you count Federal Reserve holdings of the national debt). As a result, should surpluses come in, we would be reducing the true national

FIGURE 36.1   Workers per retiree history and projections.

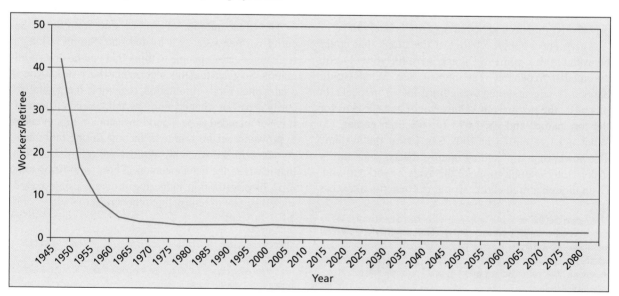

debt to allow ourselves the ability to borrow much more later. Either way it is essentially the same. Reissuing debt and borrowing money are functionally identical.

The Social Security trustees periodically issue reports that attempt to project how long this trust fund will suffice. They issue three different predictions based on three different sets of assumptions. The "optimistic" report is based on assumptions that economic growth will be higher than we have seen in the recent past, life spans will be shorter than current health trends are likely to yield, and interest rates will be lower than they are likely to be. The "pessimistic" report is based on assumptions of slow growth, long lives, and high interest rates.

The "intermediate" report is the most widely quoted, and it indicates that the Social Security system generally (except for 2010 through 2011 when revenues were down as a result of the recession) collects more in taxes than it pays in benefits and will likely do so through about 2025. Between 2025 and 2033 there will be less collected in taxes than paid in benefits, and the difference will come out of this fund. By 2033 the fund will run dry and the annual deficit could be as much as 23 percent of the benefits owed in 2033 and 26 percent of benefits owed in 2086. It is in 2033 that the system will have insufficient assets to pay off its obligations. This is what some would describe as bankruptcy, athough since the government could continue to pay the benefits with other revenues or borrowing, that term is not technically valid.

This intermediate view of whether Social Security will survive has to be balanced by the fact that much of it is based on assumptions that may or may not materialize. For instance, if the optimistic view holds, and the economy grows a single percentage point a year more than predicted, the problem is mostly solved. Changes, for example, in immigration policies that allow more workers to enter over the next 20 years, could help solve the remainder of the problem. Additionally, if inflation and interest rates are slightly less than predicted, Social Security bankruptcy is far from certain.

As a matter of fact, an increase in something as unrelated as the divorce rate would make the problem worse. Husbands and wives typically get less in benefits married than they do if they are divorced.

The long and the short of it is that economists cannot be sure that Social Security will be bankrupt. Significantly altering what many consider to be the nation's greatest social program on the basis of economic assumptions that may or may not come true strikes many as foolhardy. This is especially true, from the point of view of economist and Social Security expert Peter Diamond.

He notes that even if the trust fund is exhausted in 30, 40, or 50 years, the taxes paid will be sufficient to cover 75 percent of benefits. On the other hand, the possible solutions that we next describe also require several years to be effective if the goal is to make the program 100 percent solvent into the future.

Options for Fixing Social Security

The options for saving Social Security are plentiful, and they range from radical to timid. They all include a mixture of the following elements: raising payroll taxes, raising the retirement age further, cutting benefits to upper-income recipients, changing the target from indexing benefits using wage inflation to indexing using price inflation, investing the trust fund in corporate stocks and bonds, or carving out some of the payroll tax for privatized individual accounts.

Raising taxes is the option most preferred by those who like Social Security the way it is. This could be accomplished by raising the tax rate as well as raising or eliminating the maximum taxable earnings lid on what an individual has to pay. Estimates vary, but eliminating this provision so that the upper-income people would have to pay taxes on more than just the first of their earnings would solve about a third of the problem. Raising the overall payroll tax rate for the old age part from 5.3 percent to 6.3 percent would probably be sufficient to deal with the remainder.

Another alternative would be to raise the retirement age. Typically those who like this option argue that Social Security's original retirement age was pegged at life expectancy, which in 1935 was 65. If the retirement age is exactly life expectancy, then people who die at or before expectancy pay a lifetime of taxes and get no benefits. This ensures that there is enough money to pay for those who die after expectancy. Currently life expectancy is 78. For those who make it to 65, men can expect to live another 16 years, women 19 years. Though people are living much longer, the problem is that there is less Social Security retirement money to go around. Depending on how quickly we did it, raising the retirement age to 70 would also solve about a third of the problem. If the retirement age were not raised to age 70 until 2075, as some suggest, it would be of no help in resolving the problem scheduled to occur in 2033.

One of the great successes of Social Security is that it has brought the poverty rate among the elderly down greatly. On the other hand, many retirees have enjoyed financial success in their own right. Some have succeeded so well in this area that they are getting Social Security checks but have no need for them. The median net worth for a Social Security recipient is currently about twice that of a nonrecipient. One proposed solution to Social Security's problems is to subject its beneficiaries to a **means test**. Those with high incomes or great wealth would get less of their PIA than those who depend on the monthly check. Depending on how much a wealthy person's check is reduced, this could go a long way to staving off bankruptcy. Denying Social Security to anyone whose other income is greater than $50,000, for example, would eliminate the solvency issue altogether. Less radically, means testing could be introduced into the system by using a hybrid form of indexing espoused by economists Pozen, Schieber, and Shoven. They suggest indexing benefits for upper-income retirees using price inflation rather than wage inflation. Since the former is usually one percentage point lower than the latter, this would have the effect of slowly reducing the benefits paid to upper-income retirees. On the other hand, this could create problems. If benefits to the wealthy are reduced too much, this could seriously discourage savings among the upper- and upper-middle-income earners. Also, political support for the program might be seriously jeopardized, as it would resemble a welfare program more than a universal retirement program.

means test
Determination of the amount of one's government benefit on the basis of income or wealth.

Another way to save the system would be to invest the Social Security Trust Fund in corporate investments that yield higher rates of return. As mentioned above, the trust fund buys government debt and this debt "yields" between 2 percent and 3 percent. In this sense the government (the Treasury) owes the government (the trust fund) money and has to pay itself interest. Proponents of this solution contend that if the government invested the money in corporate stocks and bonds, the higher rates of return would generate enough to pay retirees' benefits.

There are problems with the approach. First, government would be in the business of picking stocks and might not do very well. Second, the process of picking government investments might be unduly politicized. Given politicians' penchant for succumbing to special interests, it is not beyond the realm of possibilities that such investment would not be in the general interest. Third, though corporate securities do better in the long run than government bonds, they are also riskier.

The last option suggests that individuals be allowed to invest part of their taxes themselves. In the 2000 presidential election, candidate George W. Bush made this a cornerstone of his solution to the Social Security crisis. The precipitous declines in global stock markets that began in 2000 and did not abate until 2003 seriously undercut the political support such an option was beginning to build, but with his reelection in 2004, President Bush again pushed this option front and center. What he suggested was a system by which younger workers would have a portion of their taxes placed in an account under their control. Opponents of the president's plan focused on the fact that the guaranteed Social Security benefit would be significantly reduced while supporters countered that the proceeds of the accounts, if investments returned their normal historical rates, would more than make up the difference.

In late summer 2005, Hurricanes Katrina and Rita took over the headlines and the subsequent political damage to President Bush ended his ability to sell a major change to Social Security.

During his 2008 presidential campaign, Barack Obama rejected all forms of privatization and instead suggested that the 6.2 percent old-age portion of the Social Security tax be reimposed on incomes over $250,000. He did not specify whether the employer portion would also be reimposed or whether the $250,000 line would be based on the household's income or the specific person's income. Without other elements, this would push back the date when Social Security could not meet its full retirement obligations, but it would not fully eliminate the impending funding problem. Sadly, neither the president nor Governor Romney offered any serious proposals to address the issue during the 2012 campaign.

Summary

You now understand what Social Security is. You know its basic tax and benefit structure as well as the changes that have been made to the program since its inception. You understand the economic rationale for having the system to begin with, and you know the effects of the program on work and savings. You understand how economists use present value analysis to aid in determining for whom the program works and for whom it does not. You understand that, under present estimates, the system will be bankrupt by 2033, what the Social Security Trust Fund is, and what the options are for fixing the system so that it will not only be there for you but be good for you as well.

Key Terms

asset substitution effect, 385

average index of monthly earnings (AIME), 383

bequest effect, 386

externalities, 384

fully funded pension, 383

induced retirement effect, 385

maximum taxable earnings, 383

means test, 390

pay-as-you-go pension, 383

payroll taxes, 383

primary insurance amount (PIA), 383

retirement age, 383

Social Security Trust Fund, 388

Quiz Yourself

1. Social Security's revenue emanates from taxes on
   a. all income.
   b. payrolls.
   c. capital.
   d. estates.

2. One of the reasons a government-run annuity system such as Social Security may be better for society than simply relying on private savings is that
   a. no one would save for themselves.
   b. people, being overly risk averse, will save too much.
   c. people, being risk neutral, will save too much.
   d. people, having imperfect foresight, will save too little.

3. The average index of monthly earnings is indexed
   a. for wage inflation.
   b. for consumer price inflation.
   c. for producer price inflation.
   d. via a combination of wage and price inflation.

4. Since its inception, the portion of earnings that has been subject to the Social Security tax has
   a. remained roughly intact.
   b. increased substantially.
   c. decreased slightly.
   d. decreased substantially.

5. In 2013, a worker who earned $125,000 would have _____ in Social Security taxes taken out of his or her pay and _____ would also be paid by the employer.
   a. $17,396; $17,396 (both equal to $113,700*.153)
   b. $8,860.45; $8,860.45 (both equal to $113,700*.0765+.0145*$11,300)
   c. $8,470.65; $8,470.65 (both equal to $113,700*.0765)
   d. $9,562.50; $9,562.50 (both equal to $125,000*.0765)

6. The asset substitution effect implies that Social Security will _____ from where it would have been without it.
   a. increase savings
   b. increase work
   c. decrease work
   d. decrease savings

7. The question of whether Social Security increases or decreases savings depends mostly on whether the _____ effect outweighs the _____ effect or vice versa.
   a. bequest; asset substitution
   b. bequest; induced retirement
   c. asset substitution; induced retirement
   d. interest; asset substitution

8. When compared to people of your grandparents' generation, you can expect the net present value of Social Security to be
   a. much better.
   b. about the same.
   c. slightly worse.
   d. much worse.

Short Answer Questions

1. Why would comparing the benefit and tax structure of Social Security to what might be achieved in a private investment alternative be valid, and why might it not be valid?

2. How would a change in immigration policy affect the projected solvency of the Social Security system?

3. How much would an individual receive in benefits if she had a constant (wage-inflation adjusted) monthly income of $6,000, and how would that compare to someone who had an income one-third that size?

4. What economic concept do you use to compare benefits received in the distant future with taxes paid in the past, currently, and in the near future?

Think about This

How much risk is appropriate for a government-run annuity system? Is there an appropriate risk-return calculation to be made? Is Social Security risk free? What about political risk?

Talk about This

Defenders of the status quo in Social Security note the extremely low administrative costs of the system relative to those associated with private investment houses. Critics of the status quo note that the real rate of return to future recipients is so much less than the long-term historical average of stocks that paying the extra administrative costs would be worth it. Who's right? Given the methods of saving Social Security described in this chapter, which combination would you employ to save it?

For More Insight See

Aaron, Henry, "The Myths of Social Security Crisis: Behind the Privatization Push," *NTA Forum* 26 (Summer 1996).

Clark, Robert, "Social Security Financing: Facts, Fantasies, Foibles, and Follies," *American Economic Review* 94, no. 2.

Cogan, John F., and Olivia S. Mitchell, "Perspectives from the President's Commission on Social Security Reform," *Journal of Economic Perspectives* 17, no. 2.

Diamond, Peter, "Social Security," *American Economic Review* 94, no. 1.

Feldstein, Martin, "Social Security and Saving: New Time Series Evidence," *National Tax Journal* 49, no. 2 (June 1996), pp. 151–163.

Hyman, David, *Public Finance: A Contemporary Application of Theory to Policy,* 7th ed. (Fort Worth, TX: Harcourt College Publishers, 2001).

Journal of Economic Perspectives 10, no. 3 (Summer 1996). See articles by Edward M. Gramlich; and Peter A. Diamond, pp. 85–88.

Leimer, Dean, and Selig Lesnoy, "Social Security and Private Saving: New Time Series Evidence," *Journal of Political Economy* 90, no. 3 (June 1982), pp. 606–642.

Pozen, Robert, Sylvester J. Schieber, and John Shoven, "Improving Social Security's Progressivity and Solvency with Hybrid Indexing," *American Economic Review* 94, no. 2.

Rosen, Harvey S. and Ted Gayer, *Public Finance* (New York, NY: McGraw-Hill/Irwin, 2010).

Steuerle, C. Eugene, and Jon M. Bakija, *Retooling Social Security for the 21st Century: Right and Wrong Approaches to Reform* (Washington, DC: Urban Institute, 1994).

Behind the Numbers

Social Security information.
  Components, taxes, and bankruptcy.
    Social Security Administration—
    www.socialsecurity.gov
History and projections.
  Social Security Administration; 2012 Trustees Report—www.ssa.gov/oact/tr/2012/tr2012.pdf

CHAPTER THIRTY-SEVEN

Personal Income Taxes

Learning Objectives

After reading this chapter you should be able to:

LO1   Explain the rudiments of federal income taxes.

LO2   Describe the concepts of horizontal and vertical equity and how they apply to the issue of taxation.

LO3   Summarize the trade-off that exists between simplicity and horizontal equity when people are making tax policy.

LO4   Describe how taxes can alter the incentives of people to work and save.

LO5   List examples of where taxes are used to motivate socially desirable outcomes.

LO6   Summarize the debates over taxes that took place during the 1990s and continue today.

Chapter Outline

How Income Taxes Work

Issues in Income Taxation

Incentives and the Tax Code

Who Pays Income Taxes?

The Tax Debates of the Last Decade

Summary

In 2013 income taxes accounted for $1,234 billion of the $2,712 billion that made up federal revenue. As Figure 37.1 suggests, the rest came from payroll (FICA), corporate, customs, excise, estate, and miscellaneous taxes. Personal income taxes make up almost a majority of the revenue government takes in. These taxes also provoke many of the disagreements between Republicans and Democrats. Each party fights for policies it believes are best for the nation and that help its constituencies.

Usually the political fights surrounding the personal income tax code boil down to whether the rich pay their "fair share." To look at these controversies with any insight, we will need to understand the way taxes work and who pays them before we get into which party has the better claim on taxes.

This chapter leads off with a discussion of how income taxes work in the United States. Following that, we discuss whether and how income taxes alter the willingness of people to work and save and how capital gains fit into this picture. We then introduce surprising news about who actually pays taxes. At the end we lay out some of the interesting tax debates of the last decades.

How Income Taxes Work

Federal income taxes in the United States are collected through a series of guesses that are corrected on April 15 of the year after the tax year. When you get a new job, you have to fill out a W-4 form on which you specify how many exemptions you are taking. Usually, your exemptions are you and the others in your household, but you can adjust the number by as many as necessary to improve the guess on the taxes you will owe. The number you provide is used by your employer to figure out how much tax should be withheld from each of your paychecks. **Withholding** is the deduction from your paycheck in which you and the government estimate how much tax you are going to owe during a year so you can pay it a little at a time rather than all at once. On April 15 you use the amount you actually earned, as reported to you on a W-2 or a 1099 form, to compute what you actually owe. People

withholding
Deduction from your paycheck to cover the estimated amount of taxes you are going to owe during a year.

FIGURE 37.1 Federal taxes and their sources in billions.

Source: Office of Management and Budget, www.whitehouse.gov/omb/budget/Historicals

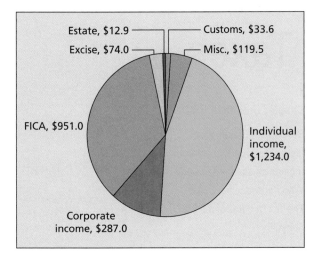

who have had too much withheld get a tax refund. If they have too little withheld, they have to make it up by April 15.

As you can see from Figure 37.2, the amount of tax you owe looks complicated. In reality tax computations are simple for most people because, thanks to a 1986 law, most people can skip the most complicated step, the deductions, and fill out as few as 10 lines on their tax forms. Still, for many others, tax forms, rules, and procedures are complicated and jargon-filled. To understand how taxes affect people, we must first take a crack at understanding those forms, rules, procedures and jargon.

The tax you owe is, of course, influenced by how much you earn. The **adjusted gross income (AGI)** is the total net income from all sources. To get that number, add together all of your income from the traditional sources (wages, salaries, tips, interest, and dividends). Then add in any net profit from businesses and rental apartments, any profit you have from asset sales (called **capital gains**), and, finally, adjust that for net alimony received. (If you paid alimony, this is a negative.)

To figure out how much of that adjusted gross income is taxable, you first have to

adjusted gross income (AGI)
Total net income from all sources.

capital gains
Any profit generated by selling an asset for more than was paid for it.

FIGURE 37.2 Federal income taxes, 2012.

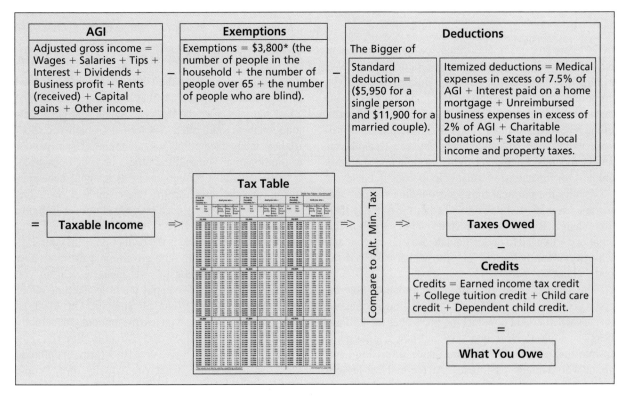

adjust that number by two other numbers. The first, **exemptions,** is an amount by which AGI is reduced that is determined by the size of your family. These exemptions are similar to, but not the same as, the exemptions you compute for form W-4. For that form you can essentially create fictitious people in order to make your withholding correct. Here, the exemptions have to be real. Each person in the household counts as one. Each person over 65 counts as one more, as does each blind person. For the 2012 tax year, each exemption reduced AGI by $3,800. For example, a married couple, both of whose members are old and blind, would have had six exemptions, whereas a husband and wife with two small children would have had four. In the first case the total exemption is 6 × $3,800, or $22,800. In the second example it is 4 × $3,800, or $15,200.

Deductions are also amounts by which AGI is reduced. These are complicated by the fact that they are the greater of either a minimum level or the sum of particular expenditures, the value of which is money that will not be taxed. The minimum level of deduction is called the **standard deduction,** and this is the amount that most people take. **Itemized deductions** are for particular expenses on which government does not want taxes paid. The reason most people can compute their taxes relatively easily is that they skip this complicated step. Rather than itemizing deductions, they accept the value of the standard deduction.

When people itemize (that is, "list"), they add up those things that are **deductible** (approved types of expenses) and instead of reducing their taxable income by a fixed amount, they reduce it by the sum of those expenses. For instance, when people buy homes, they typically have mortgage payments. In the early years of paying a mortgage, the payment is almost entirely interest. That interest is deductible. Other deductible items that are listed include state and local income and property taxes, charitable donations, certain employment expenses, and certain (usually very high) medical expenses.

exemptions
An amount by which AGI is reduced which is determined by the size of the family.

deductions
Amounts by which AGI is reduced; the greater of either the standard deduction or itemized deductions.

standard deduction
The minimum level of deduction.

itemized deductions
Deductions for particular expenses on which the government does not want taxes paid.

deductible
Approved types of expenses for income tax purposes.

Most people do not itemize their deductions because if they did, the total would not equal the standard deduction. This is especially true for those who rent their residences, because renters cannot deduct mortgage interest and property taxes. Only those who own the properties are entitled to take these deductions.

The standard deduction simplifies taxes for most people, and it reduces the amount of tax that they owe. Those people who itemize have at least one, if not many, more forms than the people who take the standard deduction. In addition, since the standard deduction gives the people who take it a larger reduction off income than they would otherwise get, it reduces their tax burden.

Taxable income is therefore adjusted gross income minus personal exemptions minus (the greater of either the standard or itemized) deductions.

Another thing people must know in order to compute the tax they owe is their **filing status.** A person's filing status can be one of four things: single, married filing jointly, married filing separately, and single head of household. Single people without children file as singles, whereas those singles with kids in the household file as a single head of household. Almost all married people file jointly, though those going through a separation or a divorce typically file separately. Most married couples pay less tax if they file jointly, though some couples file separately because they balk at sharing financial information with one another.

In the 2012 tax year, for married couples the standard deduction was $11,900; for single people it was $5,950. As a result, for those married couples with two children who took the standard deduction, the first $27,100 ($3,800 × 4 + $11,900) they earned was tax-free. For single people the first $9,750 was tax free.

The tax tables show the amount most people owe in tax. To read tax tables, find the column that contains the filing status. Then read the row to find the amount of taxable income. As an example, take a single person who does not own a home and whose only income is salary. The taxes she or he owes are very simple to compute. Say such a person earns $52,000 a year and takes the standard deduction. The taxable income is $52,000 − $5,950 (standard deduction) − $3,800 (personal exemption), or $42,050. A 2012 tax table is duplicated here in Figure 37.3, and circled on that form is the tax amount of $6,549.

taxable income
Adjusted gross income minus personal exemptions minus (the greater of either the standard or itemized) deductions.

filing status
Classification of taxpayers based on household; can be single, married filing jointly, married filing separately, and single head of household.

FIGURE 37.3 Tax table for 2012.

Source: www.irs.gov/pub/irs-pdf/i1040tt.pdf

2012 Tax Table

If line 43 (taxable income) is — At least	But less than	Single	Married filing jointly *	Married filing separately	Head of a house-hold
39,000					
39,000	39,050	5,786	4,984	5,786	5,234
39,050	39,100	5,799	4,991	5,799	5,241
39,100	39,150	5,811	4,999	5,811	5,249
39,150	39,200	5,824	5,006	5,824	5,256
39,200	39,250	5,836	5,014	5,836	5,264
39,250	39,300	5,849	5,021	5,849	5,271
39,300	39,350	5,861	5,029	5,861	5,279
39,350	39,400	5,874	5,036	5,874	5,286
39,400	39,450	5,886	5,044	5,886	5,294
39,450	39,500	5,899	5,051	5,899	5,301
39,500	39,550	5,911	5,059	5,911	5,309
39,550	39,600	5,924	5,066	5,924	5,316
39,600	39,650	5,936	5,074	5,936	5,324
39,650	39,700	5,949	5,081	5,949	5,331
39,700	39,750	5,961	5,089	5,961	5,339
39,750	39,800	5,974	5,096	5,974	5,346
39,800	39,850	5,986	5,104	5,986	5,354
39,850	39,900	5,999	5,111	5,999	5,361
39,900	39,950	6,011	5,119	6,011	5,369
39,950	40,000	6,024	5,126	6,024	5,376
40,000					
40,000	40,050	6,036	5,134	6,036	5,384
40,050	40,100	6,049	5,141	6,049	5,391
40,100	40,150	6,061	5,149	6,061	5,399
40,150	40,200	6,074	5,156	6,074	5,406
40,200	40,250	6,086	5,164	6,086	5,414
40,250	40,300	6,099	5,171	6,099	5,421
40,300	40,350	6,111	5,179	6,111	5,429
40,350	40,400	6,124	5,186	6,124	5,436
40,400	40,450	6,136	5,194	6,136	5,444
40,450	40,500	6,149	5,201	6,149	5,451
40,500	40,550	6,161	5,209	6,161	5,459
40,550	40,600	6,174	5,216	6,174	5,466
40,600	40,650	6,186	5,224	6,186	5,474
40,650	40,700	6,199	5,231	6,199	5,481
40,700	40,750	6,211	5,239	6,211	5,489
40,750	40,800	6,224	5,246	6,224	5,496
40,800	40,850	6,236	5,254	6,236	5,504
40,850	40,900	6,249	5,261	6,249	5,511
40,900	40,950	6,261	5,269	6,261	5,519
40,950	41,000	6,274	5,276	6,274	5,526
41,000					
41,000	41,050	6,286	5,284	6,286	5,534
41,050	41,100	6,299	5,291	6,299	5,541
41,100	41,150	6,311	5,299	6,311	5,549
41,150	41,200	6,324	5,306	6,324	5,556
41,200	41,250	6,336	5,314	6,336	5,564
41,250	41,300	6,349	5,321	6,349	5,571
41,300	41,350	6,361	5,329	6,361	5,579
41,350	41,400	6,374	5,336	6,374	5,586
41,400	41,450	6,386	5,344	6,386	5,594
41,450	41,500	6,399	5,351	6,399	5,601
41,500	41,550	6,411	5,359	6,411	5,609
41,550	41,600	6,424	5,366	6,424	5,616
41,600	41,650	6,436	5,374	6,436	5,624
41,650	41,700	6,449	5,381	6,449	5,631
41,700	41,750	6,461	5,389	6,461	5,639
41,750	41,800	6,474	5,396	6,474	5,646
41,800	41,850	6,486	5,404	6,486	5,654
41,850	41,900	6,499	5,411	6,499	5,661
41,900	41,950	6,511	5,419	6,511	5,669
41,950	42,000	6,524	5,426	6,524	5,676

If line 43 (taxable income) is — At least	But less than	Single	Married filing jointly *	Married filing separately	Head of a house-hold
42,000					
42,000	42,050	6,536	5,434	6,536	5,684
42,050	42,100	6,549	5,441	6,549	5,691
42,100	42,150	6,561	5,449	6,561	5,699
42,150	42,200	6,574	5,456	6,574	5,706
42,200	42,250	6,586	5,464	6,586	5,714
42,250	42,300	6,599	5,471	6,599	5,721
42,300	42,350	6,611	5,479	6,611	5,729
42,350	42,400	6,624	5,486	6,624	5,736
42,400	42,450	6,636	5,494	6,636	5,744
42,450	42,500	6,649	5,501	6,649	5,751
42,500	42,550	6,661	5,509	6,661	5,759
42,550	42,600	6,674	5,516	6,674	5,766
42,600	42,650	6,686	5,524	6,686	5,774
42,650	42,700	6,699	5,531	6,699	5,781
42,700	42,750	6,711	5,539	6,711	5,789
42,750	42,800	6,724	5,546	6,724	5,796
42,800	42,850	6,736	5,554	6,736	5,804
42,850	42,900	6,749	5,561	6,749	5,811
42,900	42,950	6,761	5,569	6,761	5,819
42,950	43,000	6,774	5,576	6,774	5,826
43,000					
43,000	43,050	6,786	5,584	6,786	5,834
43,050	43,100	6,799	5,591	6,799	5,841
43,100	43,150	6,811	5,599	6,811	5,849
43,150	43,200	6,824	5,606	6,824	5,856
43,200	43,250	6,836	5,614	6,836	5,864
43,250	43,300	6,849	5,621	6,849	5,871
43,300	43,350	6,861	5,629	6,861	5,879
43,350	43,400	6,874	5,636	6,874	5,886
43,400	43,450	6,886	5,644	6,886	5,894
43,450	43,500	6,899	5,651	6,899	5,901
43,500	43,550	6,911	5,659	6,911	5,909
43,550	43,600	6,924	5,666	6,924	5,916
43,600	43,650	6,936	5,674	6,936	5,924
43,650	43,700	6,949	5,681	6,949	5,931
43,700	43,750	6,961	5,689	6,961	5,939
43,750	43,800	6,974	5,696	6,974	5,946
43,800	43,850	6,986	5,704	6,986	5,954
43,850	43,900	6,999	5,711	6,999	5,961
43,900	43,950	7,011	5,719	7,011	5,969
43,950	44,000	7,024	5,726	7,024	5,976
44,000					
44,000	44,050	7,036	5,734	7,036	5,984
44,050	44,100	7,049	5,741	7,049	5,991
44,100	44,150	7,061	5,749	7,061	5,999
44,150	44,200	7,074	5,756	7,074	6,006
44,200	44,250	7,086	5,764	7,086	6,014
44,250	44,300	7,099	5,771	7,099	6,021
44,300	44,350	7,111	5,779	7,111	6,029
44,350	44,400	7,124	5,786	7,124	6,036
44,400	44,450	7,136	5,794	7,136	6,044
44,450	44,500	7,149	5,801	7,149	6,051
44,500	44,550	7,161	5,809	7,161	6,059
44,550	44,600	7,174	5,816	7,174	6,066
44,600	44,650	7,186	5,824	7,186	6,074
44,650	44,700	7,199	5,831	7,199	6,081
44,700	44,750	7,211	5,839	7,211	6,089
44,750	44,800	7,224	5,846	7,224	6,096
44,800	44,850	7,236	5,854	7,236	6,104
44,850	44,900	7,249	5,861	7,249	6,111
44,900	44,950	7,261	5,869	7,261	6,119
44,950	45,000	7,274	5,876	7,274	6,126

If line 43 (taxable income) is — At least	But less than	Single	Married filing jointly *	Married filing separately	Head of a house-hold
45,000					
45,000	45,050	7,286	5,884	7,286	6,134
45,050	45,100	7,299	5,891	7,299	6,141
45,100	45,150	7,311	5,899	7,311	6,149
45,150	45,200	7,324	5,906	7,324	6,156
45,200	45,250	7,336	5,914	7,336	6,164
45,250	45,300	7,349	5,921	7,349	6,171
45,300	45,350	7,361	5,929	7,361	6,179
45,350	45,400	7,374	5,936	7,374	6,186
45,400	45,450	7,386	5,944	7,386	6,194
45,450	45,500	7,399	5,951	7,399	6,201
45,500	45,550	7,411	5,959	7,411	6,209
45,550	45,600	7,424	5,966	7,424	6,216
45,600	45,650	7,436	5,974	7,436	6,224
45,650	45,700	7,449	5,981	7,449	6,231
45,700	45,750	7,461	5,989	7,461	6,239
45,750	45,800	7,474	5,996	7,474	6,246
45,800	45,850	7,486	6,004	7,486	6,254
45,850	45,900	7,499	6,011	7,499	6,261
45,900	45,950	7,511	6,019	7,511	6,269
45,950	46,000	7,524	6,026	7,524	6,276
46,000					
46,000	46,050	7,536	6,034	7,536	6,284
46,050	46,100	7,549	6,041	7,549	6,291
46,100	46,150	7,561	6,049	7,561	6,299
46,150	46,200	7,574	6,056	7,574	6,306
46,200	46,250	7,586	6,064	7,586	6,314
46,250	46,300	7,599	6,071	7,599	6,321
46,300	46,350	7,611	6,079	7,611	6,329
46,350	46,400	7,624	6,086	7,624	6,336
46,400	46,450	7,636	6,094	7,636	6,344
46,450	46,500	7,649	6,101	7,649	6,351
46,500	46,550	7,661	6,109	7,661	6,359
46,550	46,600	7,674	6,116	7,674	6,366
46,600	46,650	7,686	6,124	7,686	6,374
46,650	46,700	7,699	6,131	7,699	6,381
46,700	46,750	7,711	6,139	7,711	6,389
46,750	46,800	7,724	6,146	7,724	6,396
46,800	46,850	7,736	6,154	7,736	6,404
46,850	46,900	7,749	6,161	7,749	6,411
46,900	46,950	7,761	6,169	7,761	6,419
46,950	47,000	7,774	6,176	7,774	6,426
47,000					
47,000	47,050	7,786	6,184	7,786	6,434
47,050	47,100	7,799	6,191	7,799	6,441
47,100	47,150	7,811	6,199	7,811	6,449
47,150	47,200	7,824	6,206	7,824	6,456
47,200	47,250	7,836	6,214	7,836	6,464
47,250	47,300	7,849	6,221	7,849	6,471
47,300	47,350	7,861	6,229	7,861	6,479
47,350	47,400	7,874	6,236	7,874	6,489
47,400	47,450	7,886	6,244	7,886	6,501
47,450	47,500	7,899	6,251	7,899	6,514
47,500	47,550	7,911	6,259	7,911	6,526
47,550	47,600	7,924	6,266	7,924	6,539
47,600	47,650	7,936	6,274	7,936	6,551
47,650	47,700	7,949	6,281	7,949	6,564
47,700	47,750	7,961	6,289	7,961	6,576
47,750	47,800	7,974	6,296	7,974	6,589
47,800	47,850	7,986	6,304	7,986	6,601
47,850	47,900	7,999	6,311	7,999	6,614
47,900	47,950	8,011	6,319	8,011	6,626
47,950	48,000	8,024	6,326	8,024	6,639

*This column must also be used by a qualifying widow(er).

Take the amount of taxable income, $42,050, and find the column labeled single. The person with that taxable income owes $6,549.

TABLE 37.1   Marginal tax rate.

Status	10%	15%	25%	28%	33%	35%
Single	$0–8,700	$8,700–35,350	$35,350–85,650	$85,650–178,650	$178,650–388,350	$388,350–
Single head of household	$0–12,400	$12,400–47,350	$47,350–122,300	$122,300–198,050	$198,050–388,350	$388,350–
Married filing jointly	$0–17,400	$17,400–70,700	$70,700–142,700	$142,700–217,450	$217,450–388,350	$388,350–
Married filing separately	$0–8,700	$8,700–35,350	$35,350–71,350	$71,350–108,725	$108,725–194,175	$194,175–

An increasingly important part of the tax calculation process is the alternative minimum tax. This tax, invented in the 1960s to prevent the superrich from accumulating so many deductions that they could avoid taxes altogether, has begun to hit ordinary middle-class taxpayers. The alternative minimum tax is doubly frustrating for taxpayers who do their own taxes because after they have completed their federal return, if they come under its provisions, they have to refigure their taxes using its provisions. There is no obvious way to know this until you are almost entirely finished completing your 1040.

One positive result of the political turmoil of the 2012 election was that shortly after the election, the AMT was reformed to index its thresholds for inflation. That made it so that the annual exercise of passing a "patch" in December is no longer necessary.

The tax rates in the United States are **progressive** in that with higher income you pay a higher rate of tax. Table 37.1 shows the so-called tax brackets in the United States for 2012. One result of President Obama's reelection was the creation of a new 39.6 percent bracket in 2013 at the top end. The **marginal tax rate** is the percentage of each dollar in that bracket that must be paid in tax. This means that our single person making $52,000, with taxable income of $42,050, has a tax rate of zero on the first $9,750 of income, pays 10 percent on the next $8,700, and pays 15 percent on the next $22,650.

progressive taxation
Those with higher income pay a higher rate of tax.

marginal tax rate
The percentage of each dollar in a bracket that must be paid in tax.

Even after you have figured your tax, this is not what you actually owe. There are four important tax credits that now go into the computation. The first, the earned income tax credit, is designed for the working poor. This can be a substantial increase in your take-home pay if you have children and do not make a lot of money. For those with at least two children, the credit amounts to as much as $5,891. The second important credit is the child credit. For those married couples who make less than $110,000, this credit amounts to $1,000 per child. The

third major credit is the child (and elder) care tax credit. For the majority of families with child care expenses, this credit allows for between 20 percent and 30 percent (again, depending on AGI) of those expenses to come off the tax bill. The last of the major credits is a tuition tax credit (renamed the American Opportunity Credit). This allows for up to $2,400 of college-related expenses to come off the tax bill.

There is an important distinction between tax credits and deductions. A tax deduction comes off taxable income, so the savings to taxpayers are whatever their marginal tax rate is times the amount of the deduction. For example, if a person is in the 15 percent tax bracket, a $1,000 deduction is worth $150. A $1,000 credit, on the other hand, is $1,000 off the tax bill. Tax credits are therefore better than deductions if the two are in equal amounts.

There is another aspect of the distinction between credits and deductions that is important. During tax debates there is often a discussion of whether there should be a tax deduction for something or a tax credit for it. Since credits are more costly to the government than deductions, we can imagine that the choice facing policymakers for the tax cut would be a $2,500 deduction or a $500 credit. For people in the 15 percent tax bracket, a $2,500 tax deduction is worth between nothing (because they still end up with insufficient deductions to get over the standard deduction) and 15 percent of $2,500, or $375. For people in the 28 percent bracket, a $2,500 deduction is worth up to $700. The net result of this is that credits are better than deductions when they are in equal amounts and that for tax reductions of equal cost to the government, credits are better than deductions for the poor. For the rich the opposite is true: Tax deductions are preferred over tax credits.

For people with a variety of income sources and many deductions, the rules are very complicated. The vast majority of people are not in this predicament. You have to own a farm or business, have a significant and actively changing investment portfolio, have significant medical expenses that you have to pay yourself, work in an environment where you get high pay but have to pay for lots of work expenses (like a truck driver), or have some other strange source of income in order to have overly complicated income taxes.

Issues in Income Taxation

Horizontal and Vertical Equity

One question that always arises with regard to income taxes is whether they are fair. The very definition of "fair" requires some thought. To be fair, it seems clear that equal people should be treated equally. This concept, called **horizontal equity,** is not much disputed. People who make the same income, from the same sources, with the same family structure, and who are the same in every other dimension should pay the same taxes.

horizontal equity
Equal people should be treated equally.

vertical equity
People across the income scale are treated fairly with regard to ability to pay.

Where the controversy lies with most people is the issue of **vertical equity**. That is, are people across the income scale treated fairly with regard to their ability to pay? As you saw with Table 37.1, people at the upper end of the income scale pay much more in tax and much higher percentages of tax than people at the lower end.

Equity versus Simplicity

There is a distinct trade-off between horizontal equity and simplicity. This is because it is difficult to nail down the question of "sameness" that is at the heart of the definition of horizontal equity. Most economists who study the issue of taxation want the tax code to be **neutral**. For instance, to ensure neutrality, income earned from work must be treated the same as income made from investments. The problem is that in order to accomplish neutrality, the tax code would have to be very complicated. Consider capital gains income.

neutral
When applied to a tax code, the implication that it does not favor particular forms of income or expenditure.

When assets are bought and later sold at a profit, there is capital gain. Under the principles of neutrality that capital gain should be taxed—the question is how much? This question arises because there are problems with capital gains that do not affect earnings from work. First, much of the increase in the value of an asset is simply the compensation for inflation. We tax all gains rather than just the inflation-adjusted gains because this is easier. Second, some assets are difficult to evaluate, so capital gains are taxed only on realization (when you actually have the profit in hand) rather than accrual (when the asset price increase happened). This undertaxes capital gains by letting the holder of them defer the tax.

Taxing on realization rather than accrual is simple, but it creates a different problem whose solution only creates another problem. Because there is no tax until an asset is sold, when a person dies while in possession of an asset, there are capital gains. Perhaps there is no paperwork to find out when it was bought, so there is no way of finding out exactly how big the capital gain is. To solve this, all capital gains, and therefore all taxes owed on those gains, are forgiven at death. This creates yet another problem. There is an incentive for the elderly to hold assets with large capital gains rather than sell them, because doing so avoids the capital gains tax.

Thus the problem is that there is a trade-off between simplicity and equity. In order to be simple we will violate equity and in order to be fair, this will cost us simplicity.

Incentives and the Tax Code

There is an active debate among politicians and among economists about the effects of income taxes on the behavior of people. Two of the most interesting of these issues are how such taxes affect people's willingness to work and save. Republican politicians and conservative economists are convinced that income taxes cause people to work and save less. Democratic politicians and liberal economists are convinced that people do not work and save any less and may, in fact, work and save more.

substitution effect
Purchase of less of a product than originally wanted when its price is high because a lower-priced product is available.

income effect
An increase in price lowers spending power; if the good is normal, this further lowers consumption; if it is inferior, it can increase consumption back toward where it was (or even further). This effect works in either direction.

This is because there is a fundamental disagreement between economists concerning the relative importance of what economists call the **substitution effect** and the **income effect**. Any time you change the price of something, in this case either the take-home wage rate or the after-tax interest rate, you create these two effects. The substitution effect moves people toward the good that is now cheaper or away from the good that is now more expensive. As an example, if there are only two goods, apples and oranges, and the price of apples increases, you would move toward oranges. This is not the end of the story, though. There is also an income effect. This can go either direction and depends on the Chapter 2 concepts of normal and inferior. If a good is inferior, the increase in price lowers your real spending power and you would move back toward that good.

Do Taxes Alter Work Decisions?

One of the most well-researched questions in economics is the effect of take-home pay on the number of hours worked. To the untrained observer this may not seem like a very difficult question, but it actually is. The substitution effect is the more obviously seen effect. Since taxes reduce the take-home pay for every hour worked, the incentive to work, rather than stay home and relax, is lessened. Thus you reduce your work effort. The other side of the story, though, is the reduction in income. If you do the work that is necessary to generate a certain standard of living, then you will have to work more hours to have the income to sustain that standard of living. The empirical research suggests that if taxes do alter the work decision, it is only very slightly. Most estimates suggest that the substitution effect is exactly countered by the income effect. That is, an increase in taxes has no effect on work effort, though some have found the effect to be that it takes an 8 percent reduction in after-tax wage rates to generate a 1 percent reduction in work hours. Either way, taxes do not substantially alter the incentive to work.

Do Taxes Alter Savings Decisions?

A similar result has been found on after-tax interest rates. Though there is disagreement in methodology that generates a disagreement in the conclusion, many economists also believe that an increase in tax rates has little or no effect on saving behavior. This also suggests that the substitution effect and income effect completely counter each other. There are, though, estimates that suggest that the net is not zero. In particular, Michael Boskin estimated that a 2.5 percent decrease in the after-tax interest rates results in a 1 percent decrease in savings.

Taxes for Social Engineering

If taxes do not substantially alter the incentive of people to work or save, then you might think that policy makers would have given up on using taxes to get people to do other desirable things. If you thought that, you would be wrong. President Clinton proposed and Congress enacted a plan to use tax credits to provide an incentive to go to college. Tax deductions and credits for a variety of desirable outcomes have been tried at a variety of different times. Typically the breaks do not end up causing more of the desired outcome, but simply subsidize the people who were already engaging in it.[1]

President Bush was less fond of tax changes of this type, but President Obama jumped right in with billions of targeted tax deductions and credits in his 2009 Economic Recovery Act (i.e; his stimulus package). In that package there were tax credits for first-time home buyers, for buyers of hybrid cars, and even for buyers of energy-efficient water heaters. The belief that the federal income tax code can be used to motivate socially desirable activities is deeply held in the halls of the capital, yet there is little evidence that these tax credits have a significant impact.

Who Pays Income Taxes?

A vastly misunderstood concept of income taxation is who it is that pays. For years Republicans and Democrats alike have perpetuated the myth that middle Americans pay this tax and the rich do not pay their fair share. A look at Table 37.2 should begin to dispel that myth. The first column indicates the percentile of tax returns; the second and third columns indicate the percentage of income earned and taxes paid by everyone at or below that percentile.

TABLE 37.2 Distribution of taxes, 2010.

Source: Statistics of Income: Individual Income Tax Returns 2010, Internal Revenue Service, Washington, DC.

Percentile of Taxpayers, Bottom x% of Returns*	Cumulative Percentage of Adjusted Gross Income	Cumulative Percentage of Taxes Paid
10	<1	0
20	<1	0
30	1	0.1
40	2.5	0.3
50	5	0.85
60	12	2.2
70	21	5
80	31	9
90	43	18
100	100	35
		100

*Example: The bottom 40 percent of taxpayers earn 2.5 percent of adjusted gross income and pay 0.85 percent of all federal income taxes.

[1] If the research on college tax credits that is published in the next few years duplicates the results of the research on work and savings, the tax deductions and credits will probably not increase the number of people going to college but will merely be a special tax break to those who would have gone to college anyway. Another effect of this subsidy is that it gives colleges and universities an increased ability to raise tuition.

FIGURE 37.4   Income and tax distributions.

Source: Statistics of Income: Individual Income Tax Returns, Internal Revenue Service, Washington, DC., www.irs.gov/uac/SOI-Tax-Stats-Individual-Income-Tax-Returns.

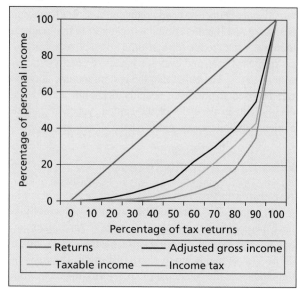

For instance, the bottom 40 percent of earners account for 2.5 percent of income and 0.85 percent of taxes paid.

From this table you can draw several myth-breaking conclusions. First, the bottom half of taxpayers pays only 2 percent of the income tax while the top half pays the remaining 98 percent. Second, the top 10 percent of taxpayers accounts for 65 percent of federal income taxes paid while the rest of us account for only 35 percent. Third, if it were true that the rich were not paying as much as the middle class, the second column would not always exceed the third. It does, and the rich pay far more tax than do the rest of us.

Figure 37.4 portrays the same information graphically. If all income and taxes were earned and paid equally, it would represent a straight line. The degree to which the income earned, shown as AGI, is bowed is the degree to which income earned is unequal. If taxes were paid mostly by the middle class, then the tax curve would be above the income curve. Since the opposite is true, it should be clear that there is significant effective progressivity in the tax code.

The Tax Debates of the Last Decade

One of the central themes of the political debates of the 1990s and 2000s was whether tax cuts should be across-the-board or targeted. Republican presidential

candidates offered across-the-board tax cuts, whereas Democratic presidential candidates offered tax cuts that were targeted to specific populations. The difference in philosophy boils down to essentially two differences of opinion: whether most of the tax cuts should go to the people who pay most of the tax or whether the tax code should be used to encourage particular behaviors and help people with the least income.

On the first difference of opinion, it is clear that any across-the-board tax cut must go mostly to the rich since it is they who pay the vast majority of income taxes. Thus an across-the-board tax cut by definition favors the rich. Whether this is fair criticism is relative. If you look at where most of the dollars go in such a cut, it is indisputable that the rich get most of the money. On the other hand, this is because they pay the most. Giving a tax cut to the poor gives a tax cut to people who do not pay any federal income taxes to begin with.[2]

Because of the progressivity of the tax code, simply reducing the tax rate by a fixed percentage not only gives more of a tax break to upper-income taxpayers, but it also changes the income distribution in a way that favors upper-income Americans. To see how, consider Table 37.3. The second column indicates before-tax income, showing a circumstance where the upper-income person makes 10 times what the lower-income person makes. The third column indicates the tax that would be paid under the simple hypothetical tax code where 10 percent of the first $50,000 and 20 percent of the rest is paid in tax. The progressivity of the income tax is displayed here in that the upper-income household makes 10 times as much as the lower-income household but pays 15 times as much tax. The fourth column shows the after-tax income. Again, note the effect of the progressive income tax is to reduce the ratio of spending power of the high-income to lower-income person from 10 to 1 to 9.44 to 1. The fifth and sixth columns show the effect of a 10 percent reduction in tax rates. The 10 percent tax rate becomes 9 percent and the 20 percent tax rate becomes 18 percent.

Republicans and Democrats will interpret Table 37.3 in two entirely different ways. The Republicans will say that under both tax codes the upper-income people are paying 15 times the taxes that the lower-income people are paying. Moreover, they will claim that any tax cut

---

[2] Tax cuts to the poor typically result from increasing the earned income tax credit. This credit often exceeds the amount of tax owed by a substantial amount. Many low-income families pay "negative taxes," so a tax cut to them simply makes this more negative.

TABLE 37.3 Hypothetical example of the effect of a 10 percent cut in tax rates on income distribution.

	Before Tax	Tax Code where Tax = 10% of the First $50,000 and 20% of the Rest		Tax Code after a 10% Cut in Tax Rates where Tax = 9% of the First $50,000 and 18% of the Rest	
	Before Tax	Tax	After Tax	Tax	After Tax
Lower-income person	$10,000	$1,000	$9,000	$900	$9,100
Upper-income person	$100,000	$15,000	$85,000	$13,500	$86,500
Ratio	10	15	9.44	15	9.51

that helps the poor will change the distribution of taxes to be even further slanted to upper-income people. Democrats will focus on the distribution of after-tax income figure and note that an across-the-board tax cut increases the ratio of an upper-income person's after-tax income to a lower-income person's after-tax income from 9.44 to 9.51. As a result, though an across-the-board tax cut keeps the percentage of government funded by each group the same, it changes the after-tax income distribution in favor of the rich.

Another great debate of the last decade centered on unraveling the 1986 tax reform law that eliminated most social engineering from the tax code. Prior to that year thousands of provisions were included to induce people to do a variety of things. The law passed in 1986 eliminated almost all of them. Slowly, but steadily, the Clinton administration sought provisions to again urge people in particular directions. For instance, they sought and got partial tax deductions and credits for higher education.

After his election in 2000, George W. Bush sought and got two substantial personal income tax cuts. The first, in 2001, cut marginal tax rates, phased in an increase in the dependent child credit, and phased out the estate (inheritance) tax. The second, in 2003, sped up the timetable on the 2001 tax cuts and reduced the tax rate on corporate dividends.

Taken together, the beneficiaries of these tax cuts were middle-income and higher-income families with children and the wealthy. Middle-income families with children saw dramatic declines in their effective rates as the per-child tax credit jumped from $200 per child to $1,000 per child. The wealthy saw a sizable reduction in their taxes as well with the reduction in marginal income tax rates by 3 to 5 percentage points (depending on bracket), the reduction in the rate at which dividends are taxed, and the phasing out of the estate tax.

One of the central questions of the 2008 presidential campaign was whether the 2003 tax cuts should be allowed to expire in 2011. President Bush repeatedly attempted to convince a skeptical Democratic Congress to make the cuts permanent. Senator McCain vowed to make them permanent were he elected. Then candidate and now President Obama argued that only those tax cuts that assisted those making less than $250,000 should be maintained. As if the point needed more emphasis, he had a ready response to Congressional Republican complaints that only those that paid federal income taxes should benefit from tax cuts: "I won." President Obama and Congressional Democrats argued for and ultimately passed the 2009 stimulus. In it were provisions cutting taxes for anyone who paid Social Security taxes. This included billions of dollars for millions of taxpayers whose federal income tax liability was zeroed out as part of the plan. The mid-term elections of 2010 constituted a significant shift in the other direction as Republicans made historic gains in both the House and Senate. One consequence of those changes was that the Bush tax cuts were extended through 2012, setting up an obvious election issue for both parties. In a democracy such as exists in the United States, elections have consequences and regardless of the politics of the time, taxes are always going to be a focal point for debate.

Summary

You now understand how taxes work and are able to apply that knowledge and the concepts of horizontal and vertical equity to the U.S. tax code. You understand the trade-off that exists between simplicity and horizontal equity and understand that in theory taxes can alter the incentives of people to work and save but that little effect has actually been shown. You know that this has not stopped policy makers from using taxes to motivate socially desirable outcomes. Last, you should be able to understand in a greater context the debates over taxes that began during the 1990s and continue today.

Key Terms

adjusted gross income (AGI), 394
capital gains, 394
deductible, 395
deductions, 395
exemptions, 395
filing status, 395

horizontal equity, 398
income effect, 398
itemized deductions, 395
marginal tax rate, 397
neutral, 398
progressive taxation, 397

standard deduction, 395
substitution effect, 398
taxable income, 395
vertical equity, 398
withholding, 393

Quiz Yourself

1. The tax brackets have higher tax rates for more taxable income. This makes the federal income tax
   a. proportional.
   b. regressive.
   c. progressive.
   d. integrative.

2. Because there are _____, adjusted gross income is always _____ taxable income.
   a. deductions and exemptions; less than
   b. deductions and exemptions; greater than
   c. credits; greater than
   d. credits; less than

3. The alternative minimum tax has the effect of limiting
   a. income.
   b. taxable income.
   c. deductions.
   d. exemptions.

4. If Congress wants to use $100 billion on tax cuts, the version that would help a family of four making $40,000 a year would
   a. lower marginal tax rates by one percentage point.
   b. increase the standard deduction by $2,000.
   c. increase the child credit by $1,000.
   d. index the alternative minimum tax to inflation.

5. If someone is in the 25 percent tax bracket, this means that _____ is owed in taxes.
   a. 25 percent of his or her salary
   b. 25 percent of his or her adjusted gross income
   c. 25 percent of his or her taxable income
   d. less than 25 percent of his or her taxable income

6. Which of the following would immediately be more valuable for most people?
   a. A $1,000 increase in the child credit.
   b. A decrease in the degree to which brackets are inflation-indexed.
   c. An indexing of the alternative minimum tax.
   d. A $2,500 increase in the standard deduction.

Short Answer Questions

1. Suppose someone were to say that they earned $100,000 per year, that they paid less than $10,000 in federal income taxes, but that their marginal tax rate was 25 percent. Could that be true?

2. Use the tax tables in the chapter to compute the taxes of someone taking the standard deduction, having a spouse, three children, and $80,000 in income.

3. Explain why someone who cared about the poor and energy savings would advocate for a tax credit rather than a tax deduction if $100 billion was going to be devoted to tax cuts to promote energy-saving changes to behavior.

4. Explain why an across-the-board tax cut would benefit those at the higher end of the income scale more than it would affect those at the bottom end.

Think about This

If current law is not changed, the alternative minimum tax will affect 30 percent of taxpayers. The problem with fixing it is that doing so only helps the top end of taxpayers. One solution would be to simply index the current point at which the AMT kicks in. The longer we wait, the greater the pressure will be to do something because the impact will start to affect people who are not that wealthy. This is what happens when you do not index brackets for inflation. When should they fix this?

Talk about This

The Democrats tend to work toward tax code adjustments that help those at the lowest end of the income scale; Republicans do the opposite. As a college graduate you are likely to start at the low end and become part of the high end. Are your attitudes about a political party going to stay the same or change as your income circumstances change?

For More Insight See

Boskin, Michael J., "Taxation, Saving and the Rate of Interest," *Journal of Political Economy,* vol. 86, no. 2, pt. 2 (April 1978).

Citizens for Tax Justice, *The Hidden Entitlements* (Washington, DC: Robert S. McIntyre, 1996).

Hyman, David, *Public Finance: A Contemporary Application of Theory to Policy,* 6th ed. (Fort Worth, TX: Dryden Press, 1999), esp. Chapters 13 and 14.

Slemrod, Joel, "Do We Know How Progressive the Income Tax Should Be?" *National Tax Journal* 36, no. 3 (September 1983), pp. 361–369.

Slemrod, Joel, *Do Taxes Matter? The Impact of the Tax Reform Act of 1986* (Cambridge, MA: MIT Press, 1991).

Behind the Numbers

Fiscal year
  Federal revenue and income taxes.
    Budget of the United States Government; historical tables—www.whitehouse.gov/omb/budget/Historicals
Federal tax data.
  Income and tax distribution.
    Statistics of income—www.irs.gov
Tax tables, rates, exemptions, and deductions.
  Internal Revenue Service; publications—www.irs.gov

CHAPTER THIRTY-EIGHT

Energy Prices

Learning Objectives

After reading this chapter you should be able to:

LO1 Define a cartel.

LO2 Model how a cartel can make its members large sums of money.

LO3 Show why cartels are not typically stable and describe the conditions necessary for creating cartel stability.

LO4 Evaluate whether OPEC qualifies as a cartel.

LO5 Summarize the history of inflation-adjusted oil and gasoline prices.

LO6 Model the role of expectations in determining gasoline prices and explain why events in the Middle East can cause prices at the pump to change in a matter of days.

Chapter Outline

The Historical View

OPEC

Why Do Prices Change So Fast?

Electric Utilities

What Will the Future Hold?

Kick It Up a Notch

Summary

The world runs on petroleum products. Whether it is gasoline for automobiles, diesel fuel for trains and trucks, or home heating oil, modern society could not survive without oil. With proven oil reserves at 1,470 billion barrels, roughly 500 billion barrels more believed to be yet undiscovered, and oil consumption running at a little over 89 million barrels a day, it is likely that oil reserves will run out in the second half of the 21st century.

This chapter reviews the history of oil and gasoline prices and discusses the causes and effects of significant changes. We consider the Organization of Petroleum Exporting Countries (OPEC) and how it developed and collapsed as an effective oil cartel. We also talk about why gasoline prices seem to rise and fall much more quickly than supplies would justify and use the 1999–2013 period as our primary focus. We look at electricity prices and why the industry lends itself to monopoly, why this has led to government price regulation, and why the California experience with deregulation was so problematic. Last, we look at the future and try to get an idea of where the oil industry might be 50 to 100 years from now.

The Historical View

Oil and Gasoline Price History

Gasoline prices, which were never stable, skyrocketed in the 1970s. Although several events coincided during that decade to increase prices, many politicians declared that this period was the beginning of a general long-term "energy crisis." A brief look at Figure 38.1 suggests that the crisis was actually short run in nature. As a matter of fact, by 1998, the prices of crude oil and gasoline had fallen to a point at or near their 30-year lows. Crude oil prices doubled in the 1999–2000 time frame, doubled again in the 2003–2005 time frame, and doubled once again from 2007 to July 2008. Non-inflation-adjusted gasoline prices reached all-time highs of above $4 per gallon during the July 4th weekend of 2008 and began a six-month plummet that ended with them dropping in some areas of the United States to below $1.30 per gallon by Christmas 2008. Crude oil prices fell nearly 75 percent during that same span. Prices climbed steadily back once the Great Recession ended and spiked in early 2011

FIGURE 38.1   Inflation-adjusted gasoline and domestic and imported crude oil prices, 2011 (2005 dollars).

Source: U.S. Energy Information Administration, www.eia.gov

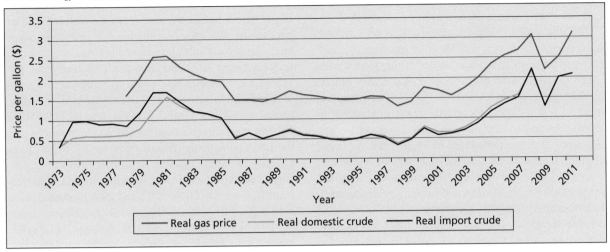

as turmoil in the Middle East created significant uncertainty about oil availability.

The top curve in Figure 38.1 shows the path of gasoline prices (GDP deflator adjusted for inflation) since the general conversion to unleaded fuel in 1978. The middle curve tracks the price of domestically produced crude oil, and the bottom curve shows the price of imported crude. Though oil prices are usually quoted in barrels, the prices have been converted to gallons for use here, and the prices have been adjusted for inflation.

Geopolitical History

Some geopolitical history here will provide insight into why oil prices changed as they did. As you can see from Table 38.1, oil is not evenly distributed throughout the world. You can surmise from this that the politics of the Middle East, and the Persian Gulf in particular, have been important in determining oil supplies.

TABLE 38.1   Global reserves by region.

Source: U.S. Energy Information Administration, www.eia.gov.

Group	Barrels in Reserve (in billions)	Percentage of World Reserves
Persian Gulf OPEC	799	54
Non-Persian Gulf OPEC	395	27
Rest of the world	279	19

The Arab–Israeli wars of 1967 and 1973 generated a great deal of animosity between Arab nations and the Western world. The United States in particular was castigated because it supported Israel. The United States provided both substantial intelligence and support in material that helped the Israelis to prevail in taking (in 1967) and then holding (in 1973) the West Bank of the Jordan River from Jordan, the Golan Heights from Syria, and the Gaza Strip and Sinai peninsula from Egypt.

After this, Arab nations, angered by U.S. aid to Israel, refused to sell oil to the United States and much of the rest of the Western world. Though this did not lead to the rationing of gasoline in the United States, it did in Great Britain. This embargo also resulted in marked increases in prices. Figure 38.1 indicates that these first jumps in oil prices occurred in 1973 and 1974.

The significant price increases that came about in the late 1970s resulted from the economic power that OPEC wielded as an oil cartel. How cartels come about and how they can raise prices substantially will be thoroughly explained later in this chapter; but suffice it to say, in inflation-adjusted terms, crude oil and gasoline prices reached record highs during this time. Gasoline hit $1.40 a gallon, the 2012 equivalent of $3.50, and crude oil hit $40 a barrel, the 2012 equivalent of $100.

During this time in Iran, the Ayatollah Khomeni took over from the deposed Shah, making neighbors such as Iraq, Kuwait, and Saudi Arabia very nervous. There is some dispute as to who the aggressor was, but these fears proved to be well founded, when in 1980 Iran and Iraq went to war. Although this war had many impacts more morally significant than its effect on the price of oil,[1] the impact on the price of oil changed the business of oil forever.

Because modern weapons are expensive, because both Iran and Iraq were strapped for cash, and because each country had only one realistic way of raising money, each began to sell as much oil as it could. While their official production figures do not show it, likely because they had to lie to fellow OPEC members, greater production allowed them to purchase more and better weapons.

As oil prices rose through the 1970s, Iran and Iraq began to pump more oil. Additionally, other nations engaged in efforts to find new sources of oil. New reserves were found in the North Sea, in Mexico, and in many other countries, and these reserves began to be exploited. In 1982 and 1983 a major recession rocked the United States and Europe, depressing demand for oil. As a result of these factors, the price of oil collapsed. Ultimately, by 1986 the price per barrel of oil fell to less than $10, and the average price of oil at the end of the year was $12.51.

When the Iran–Iraq war ended in 1988, oil prices began to recover but reached only the $15 level—a little more than 30 cents a gallon. At the end of the war, Iraq owed Saudi Arabia and Kuwait $40 billion each, as it had borrowed feverishly to buy weaponry. At $15 a barrel Iraq could not afford to both pay these debts and rebuild its war-torn country. Adding to the insult that Iraq felt, Kuwait and Saudi Arabia were not budging on OPEC production quotas, and Iraq felt that it had done Kuwait and Saudi Arabia a favor by fighting Iran in the first place. As we will see later when we discuss cartels, production quotas must be held down to keep prices high.

On August 2, 1990, Iraq invaded Kuwait, and the United States was convinced it was poised to continue the attack into Saudi Arabia. The fear of another war in the Persian Gulf sent oil prices to nearly $30 a barrel very quickly, which caused the average price for the year to be $20 per barrel. With the American- and British-led victory in the Gulf, prices calmed down and until 1998 fluctuated between $10 and $15 a barrel.

Since that time OPEC has reasserted itself with a series of production cuts that led the price of crude oil to top $30 a barrel in the spring of 2000. Another

politically inspired set of price swings occurred in the run-up to and aftermath of the Iraq war in 2003. Gas prices spiked at over $2 per gallon in many U.S. cities in the month before the war. Once the conventional aspect of the war ended without major petroleum shortages, the price of gasoline came back to a more normal level. Between 2003 and 2005 the Iraqi insurgency prevented a continuous flow of oil from that country and, coupled with increased worldwide demand for oil, prices spiked once again. Historical highs were set in 2004 and 2005 in nominal terms and for the first time in 25 years, the inflation-adjusted record price for oil began to be challenged. Inflation-adjusted gasoline prices briefly exceeded record levels in the weeks following Hurricane Katrina. Events in 2006, 2007, and 2008 propelled prices even higher. In 2006 the Bush administration was warning Iran against pursuing nuclear weapons. Oil markets reacted with significant concern that the administration was contemplating military action. At the same time, continued conflict in Nigeria and growing world demand from China and India were driving up prices. In 2007 and into 2008 investors looking for a place to make money started driving up world crude oil prices. Their bet was that the growth of China and India coupled with the flattening of world oil production would create a severe oil shortage. (Note in Figure 38.2 that at 84 million barrels per day, world oil production was stagnant from 2005 through 2012.)

The Middle East in general and the Persian Gulf in particular have proven that they can rival the Balkans in the old adage that "they produce more history than they can consume locally." The price of oil is inextricably tied to the political, military, and religious tensions of the region, tensions that are historically significant but would likely be dismissed in the West were it not for the oil.

OPEC

What OPEC Does

In the preceding historical survey of the price of oil, we alluded to the important part OPEC has played. OPEC is a **cartel** (an organization of individual competitors that join to form as a single monopolist) that is composed of Algeria, Indonesia, Iran, Iraq, Kuwait, Libya, Nigeria, Qatar, Saudi Arabia, United Arab Emirates, and Venezuela: countries that export oil. Taken

cartel
An organization of individual competitors that join to form a single monopolist.

---

[1] Iraq first used poison gas on Iranian soldiers and its own citizens, Iranians recruited children to serve as soldiers, the Reagan administration sold the Iranians weapons while using the profits to fund the Nicaraguan contras, and the CIA gave intelligence support to Iraq.

FIGURE 38.2   Worldwide oil production, 1970–2012.

Source: U.S. Energy Information Administration, www.eia.gov

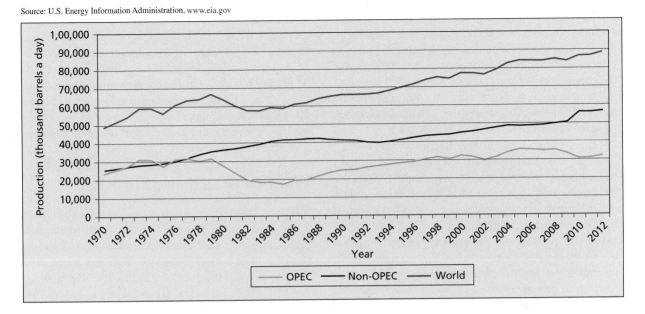

together, they have, as Table 38.1 shows, 81 percent of the proven oil reserves in the world. There was a time when this gave them enormous political power to wield. Through the 1990s, however, oil prices were such that the cartel seemed to be powerless, only to be revived in 1999 and 2000. How did all this happen?

When groups of people, firms, or countries have little power as individuals but perceive their joint power as great, they hypothesize themselves as a joint force. If something exists or arises that binds them together and there are not too many of them to organize, there is a chance they can pull it off. These ingredients were present when, in the late 1960s and early 1970s, Middle Eastern oil-exporting countries saw that together they could punish Israel's main supporters and make a profit at the same time.

This turned a loose organization, OPEC, into a powerful oil cartel. Cartels can exist in many different industries where a small number of competitors make up the vast majority of the suppliers of a commodity. The trouble is all cartels have a self-destructive tendency and OPEC was no different.

How Cartels Work

Cartels work because the individual perfect competitors join forces to act like a monopolist. In order to do this they must agree on a mechanism to withhold their goods from the market. In OPEC's case, that means they must, together, agree on a plan to reduce oil production. That plan usually means that each country must limit its production to a fraction of what it was producing before they formed the cartel. If they succeed in getting that agreement, prices will rise. Recall from Chapter 5 that in the long run and under perfect competition the price of a good will equal both the marginal cost and the average cost. If prices rise, profits rise and all of the members of the cartel are happy.

Why Cartels Are Not Stable

This is not the end of the story, though, because cartels such as these are not stable. Let's look at an intuitive reason why. Suppose your teacher in this class announced, at the beginning of the semester, that exams would be graded on a curve. This would mean that regardless of how well people did on exams, a predetermined percentage of students would be assigned As, Bs, Cs, Ds, and Fs. A clever class of students would band together to make a joint promise not to study. They would reason that if they all studied, they would end up ranking exactly the same (based on their aptitude for economics) as they would if they did not study at all.

Let's add here the outlandish assumption that students have no desire to study economics for fun and that they just want the grade for as little effort as possible. What would happen then? Would no students study? The scheme might work for the first quiz, but it would start falling apart as one or more students eventually sneaked off to study. They would see that it was in their interest to study because they could get better grades. Eventually, other students would notice that some were cheating. They would see their own grades drop in relation to those of their peers as the cheaters passed them by. Noncheaters would then start to cheat—that is to say, they would study. If, as we speculate, everyone ends up studying as they would without the prior agreement, then the agreement has become meaningless.

This is rather close to what happened with OPEC. Countries saw that they could make money by cheating even a little. A country committed to cheating would see that cheating paid because at their agreed-upon production their marginal revenue (the new high cartel price) was greater than the marginal cost so the country could make a profit. That profit would greatly exceed the profit previously received at the cartel's imposed quota. As in our previous example, using grading on a curve where everyone schemed together, individual greed induced cheating on the collective and this caused all gains to evaporate. Cheating by OPEC members led not only to the disappearance of the large profits, but also to the evaporation of all economic profits.

Putting another nail in the coffin of OPEC was the introduction of other, non-OPEC countries into the mix. A large importer, Great Britain, motivated by high prices to find its own sources, found oil in the North Sea. Moreover, it found enough to both solve its own problems and become an exporter. Mexico and other countries also found oil and began selling it in large quantities. Although OPEC tried to persuade these countries to join in a larger, more powerful cartel, none agreed. They reasoned that they could still sell at or slightly below the cartel price, and they could do so without any production quotas. Figure 38.2 highlights this fact by showing that, as a percentage of total world production, OPEC is no longer the biggest producer. Other nations are producing oil and taking market share from OPEC.

Back from the Dead

The 1990s saw oil prices fall dramatically and remain below historical averages until 1999, when prices took a sudden jump higher. How did OPEC, which seemed dead, come back to life? In fact, the potential profitability of OPEC never disappeared. It was only the behavior of the individual countries that dissipated potential profits. Throughout 1998 and 1999, OPEC began a series of production cuts that eventually totaled 4.3 million barrels a day. They thus drove up world prices. Unlike previous oil price spikes, they chose to let up before a major inflation episode struck the United States. Thus OPEC seems back in the saddle again, controlling world oil prices. Will it last? It might, but only if OPEC learns from its past mistakes. In the long run, after all the political issues in Iraq are settled, if OPEC is to maintain its pricing power, it must settle on a price that does not motivate non-OPEC countries to explore for additional oil. Even if it accomplishes this, there will still be the tendency for self-interest on the part of OPEC members to exceed their quotas.

Why Do Prices Change So Fast?

It takes months for an empty tanker to leave the United States, arrive in the Persian Gulf, be loaded with crude oil, arrive back in the United States, be offloaded, and the crude oil to be refined into gasoline. If that is true, how is it possible that the price of gasoline at a neighborhood gas station can change by 20 percent in a week? The answer takes us back to Chapter 2 and the determinants of supply and demand. Remember that the expectations of the future price of a good affect both the current supply curve and the current demand curve.

Remember, too, that if the price is expected to rise, then on our supply and demand diagram there will be little to no delay in the demand curve's moving to the right and the supply curve's moving to the left. This is because consumers will want to stock up before any price increase fully takes effect and producers will want to hang on to what they have in hopes of being able to sell it for more later. The impact of this is that prices will rise now in anticipation of price increases later.

To see how this works in the oil industry, recall the reaction in the United States to Iraq's invasion of Kuwait. Within days gasoline prices went up by as much as 25 cents per gallon. How did this happen? Starting with the oil-importing companies and ending with the gas stations, each wanted to buy and store all the product it could before the prices went up. Normally, no one in gasoline production keeps significant quantities in storage. It costs money to store oil and other petroleum products.

The oil companies thus hurried to fill their tankers before the price went up too far. Refineries got in the act by rushing to get tankers lined up to sell them their crude before the price went up too far; distributors did the same thing, and so did gas stations. At every stage, the demand for product rose because firms wanted to put as much cheap input in storage as possible. They would then have more when the prices rose.

Also true in such circumstances is that at every stage, firms do not want to sell out of their storage to provide someone down the line with product to store—that is, unless the buyer is willing to pay more. Prices rise and storage tanks fill up. If there were an actual gasoline shortage, this would not be bad: It would be beneficial to have the extra oil in storage.

When prices are anticipated to fall, the opposite happens: Firms attempt to get rid of product. Because firms will want to get as much as possible for the gasoline that is in storage and will empty storage tanks only when it is clear that prices will in fact fall, prices decrease more slowly than they increase. Prices did fall after the Gulf War, and they fell by more than the 25 cents they had increased, but the decrease took much longer than the increase had taken.

The ultimate example of rapid price swings based on price expectations occurred the afternoon and evening of September 11, 2001. In response to concerns, both real and imagined, over the availability of gasoline, prices at some stations tripled. Some stations, particularly in the Midwest, were charging $1.40 per gallon in the morning hours prior to the terrorist attacks and were charging more than $4.00 per gallon later that day. While some price increase could be explained by changes in wholesale prices (they increased between 5 and 10 cents per gallon that day), the bulk of the price jump occurred because of a rumor-fed fear that prices would dramatically rise if refineries were shut down or oil imports stopped. While consumer advocates and attorney generals were upset, consumers in particular were not blameless. Two-hour gas lines were not uncommon that afternoon and evening fueled by the same rumor-fed fear that if they did not fill up then, the price would be higher the next day. But by morning it became apparent that refineries were not in jeopardy, and prices fell to previous levels.

Is It All a Conspiracy?

There is a common view in the general public that gasoline prices are all a conspiracy and that deals are cut in backrooms to set the price of gasoline. Were that true it would be against the law both federally and in every state in which it occurred. Absent an explicit conspiracy, what would explain the fact that prices increase not just rapidly (which is explained by the "expected price" phenomenon from Chapter 2) but at almost exactly the same time from gas station to gas station?

When a station gets its supply, the price it pays changes to reflect changing wholesale prices. Were that the end of the story, then prices would change only when stations got a new supply. The twist is that the cost of the gasoline in the ground is quite literally "sunk" and therefore ignored. Remember from Chapter 5 that fixed/sunk costs are ignored when setting the profit-maximizing price. It is only the cost of replacing that gasoline, its opportunity cost, that concerns the profit-maximizing gas station. Since that price changes daily, even if the gasoline in the underground tank is a week old, gas stations will adjust their price daily to reflect the cost of replacing it.

Why would the prices at neighboring gas stations change within minutes of one another, and why would it take only hours for price increases to be reflected across town? The answer to these questions revolves around the fact that the industry is governed by oligopoly. The neighboring stations must keep their prices at or below one another so when wholesale prices change there is a natural tendency for the resulting retail prices to come out close. In most communities, though there are many gas stations, there are but a few wholesale suppliers. The wholesale suppliers face rapidly changing national spot markets for gasoline and keep their prices in line with their competitors (few as they may be) in order to maintain their gas station customer base. Since only a few wholesalers are selling to the same set of retailers at the same wholesale price, and since those retailers are pricing according to the replacement cost of the gasoline, it should not be surprising that gas prices seem to change at the same time across a community.

From $1 to $4 per Gallon in 10 Years?

We need to take a step back to understand something about the "price" of oil. As Table 38.2 shows, there is not one price. Every grade and type of crude oil has a price based on the ease with which you can refine it into saleable products like gasoline. As a result there can be a 25 percent difference in the crude oil price between the output of countries and even within countries. When oil prices are referred to on the news, they typically choose

TABLE 38.2 Crude oil prices, various types.

Source: U.S. Energy Information Administration, www.eia.gov

Variety of Oil	Price of Oil				
	Apr-07	Jul-08	Jan-09	Apr-11	May-13
West Texas Intermediate	$64.10	$133.60	$31.76	107.55	96.29
Brent Sea (U.K.)	66.78	142.45	34.33	115.09	104.55
Saudi Light	62.34	136.02	35.21	106.93	110.97

FIGURE 38.3   Refiner acquisition cost, December 1998–January 2009.

Source: U.S. Energy Information Administration, www.eia.gov

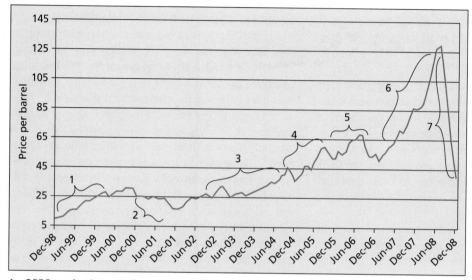

1—OPEC production cuts; low stocks of oil; bad weather.
2—Release of oil from the Strategic Petroleum Reserve; recession.
3—Political unrest in oil-producing Venezuela and Nigeria; war in Iraq.
4—Hurricanes damage platforms in the Gulf of Mexico.
5—Threatened conflict between the U.S. and Iran. Nigerian civil war heats up.
6—Global commodity speculation given increases in Chinese and Indian demand and
     stagnant production.
7—Global financial crisis and recession.

a representative type. The most often-quoted oil prices are Brent Sea, Saudi Light, and West Texas Intermediate.

Still, by whatever measure, the price of oil skyrocketed between December 1998 and 2008. For data consistency purposes the U.S. Department of Energy produces a weighted average of imported oil prices that it calls the Refiner Acquisition Cost of Imported Oil. Figure 38.3 shows how that measure increased over the 10-year period from late 1998 to 2008.

What caused this rapid increase in prices? The short answer is increased world demand coupled with problems in the world oil supply chain brought about by increased OPEC discipline, political unrest in oil-producing countries, and the U.S.-led war in Iraq. Gasoline prices, which tend to closely follow crude oil prices, were also impacted by limited U.S. refining capacity.

The main factors in increasing demand between 2002 and 2008 were the global economic expansion coming out of the 2001 recession; the significant increase in miles driven by the typical American; the substitution by Americans from more fuel-efficient cars to less fuel-efficient vans, pickups, and SUVs; and the long-term expansion of demand in India and China.

Americans have steadily migrated to less fuel-efficient vehicles. Whereas cars made up 70 percent of the U.S. fleet in the late 1990s, they now make up 60 percent. Though the fuel efficiency of cars has increased and the fuel efficiency of vans, pickups, and SUVs has increased, the impact of moving to the larger vehicle has totally eliminated the benefit of greater gas mileage. As you can see from Figure 38.4, this increase in demand, combined with a variety of supply issues, caused gasoline prices to spike.

Chinese demand for petroleum has increased markedly as well. Once a net exporter of fuels, China is now a leading importer. Over the last 10 years while global petroleum demand has increased 16 percent, China's petroleum demand increased 94 percent. Over the next 10 years China is expected to account for 40 percent of the increase in world oil demand.

Just as there is more than one variety of oil, there is also more than one variety of gasoline. Gasoline is not simply "regular," "plus," or "premium." For environmental reasons gasoline is formulated for the particular climate and environmental conditions of local areas as well as state and local law. Gasoline prices are also impacted by state and local taxes. These taxes average 27.4 cents per gallon,

FIGURE 38.4   Gasoline prices, December 1998–January 2009.

Source: U.S. Energy Information Administration, www.eia.gov

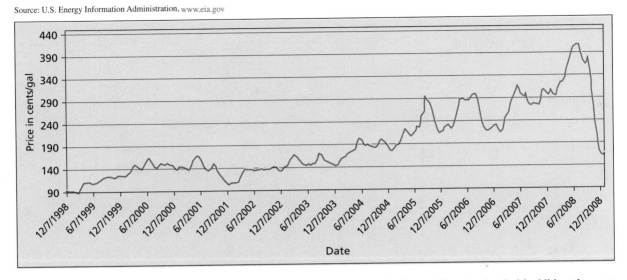

with New York, Hawaii, and Connecticut topping the charts at 42.4, 42, and 37 cents, respectively, and Alaska, New Jersey, and South Carolina having the lowest taxes, at 8, 14.5, and 16.8 cents, respectively.

Though gasoline can be imported directly, more than 90 percent of gasoline is produced by a limited number of refineries in the United States from crude oil that is increasingly imported. Figure 38.5 shows the location and capacity of refineries in the United States. Of significant note is that the refineries along the Gulf Coast of the United States are susceptible to hurricanes. The four hurricanes that hit the area in the summer and fall of 2004, and five more in 2005, highlighted this particular bottleneck. In 2004, with the hurricanes coming in one after the other, ships carrying crude oil from Venezuela and Africa could not make it to port, thereby constraining U.S. supplies of gasoline. Hurricane Katrina decimated the Port of New Orleans and in the process dramatically affected gasoline prices in the late summer and early fall of 2005.

Who is to blame for all this? Mostly ourselves. The United States government has chosen to limit new exploration and the creation of more refining capacity, largely for environmental reasons. The BP spill in the Gulf of Mexico only underscored the doubt many Americans had regarding the potentially enormous consequences of drilling in environmentally sensitive locations. It also doesn't help the situation that Americans generally are to blame for driving more miles and driving less fuel-efficient cars. The war in Iraq cut supplies coming from that country with Iraqi oil production still not back to pre-invasion levels. Blaming the Chinese for increasing their appetite for

driving is the "pot calling the kettle black" but they are, so we can blame them too. Finally, OPEC has become far more disciplined in its management of cartel prices. In the end, we are running on a global energy system where, if anything goes wrong, prices escalate rapidly, and for 10 years many things have gone wrong.

Electric Utilities

Electricity Production

While it took more than a century for Edison to capitalize effectively on Benjamin Franklin's dreams for electricity with his lightbulb, it did not take that long for the United States to become dependent on it. Similarly, while the motivation for building the Hoover Dam may have been economic stimulation, flood control, and irrigation, the by-product of cheap electricity was credited with allowing millions to live and find work in southern California.

For the most part, electricity is produced by regulated utility companies. These companies incur substantial fixed costs that present nearly insurmountable barriers to entry. These fixed costs include the power plant itself as well as the transmission lines and transformers that get the electricity into homes so that consumers can use it.

Their variable inputs are sometimes nearly free, as is the case with hydroelectric, wind, and solar power; but more typically, oil, natural gas, coal, or nuclear fuel must be purchased. Where you live often determines how your electricity is produced. Nationally, burning coal to produce electricity through steam turbines accounts

FIGURE 38.5   Refinery locations and capacity in the United States.

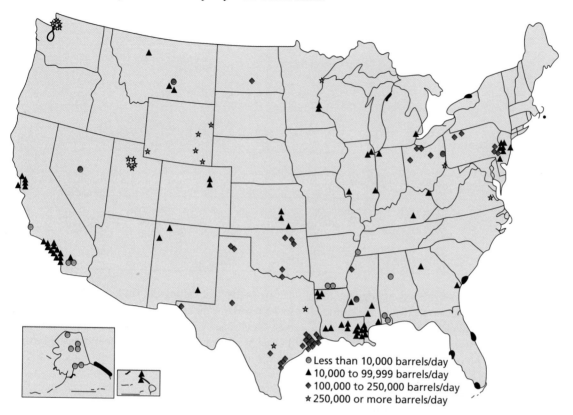

○ Less than 10,000 barrels/day
▲ 10,000 to 99,999 barrels/day
◆ 100,000 to 250,000 barrels/day
★ 250,000 or more barrels/day

for 40 percent of electricity produced. Nuclear power accounts for 20 percent of electricity production, while natural gas accounts for as much as a third of electricity production during the summer months and as little as 20 percent during winter months. Hydroelectric power and other renewables account the remainder.

The distribution of that reliance varies substantially across the country. The Pacific and Mountain West regions produce 15 to 20 times the amount of electricity through the turbines of their dams than does New England. Nuclear power provides almost 70 percent of the electricity usage in Connecticut, but nothing in Washington State and less than 10 percent in Maine. Not surprisingly, burning coal is a main source of electricity where coal is abundant.

Why Are Electric Utilities a Regulated Monopoly?

Because of the high fixed costs of production, the residential electricity market is characterized by monopoly because these costs tend to deter entry. Whether or not the proper model for this market is that of a natural monopoly or a simple monopoly depends on the type of electricity produced and the distance of transmission.

A **natural monopoly** exists when there are high fixed costs and diminishing marginal costs. In nuclear and hydroelectric power the variable costs are low. In nuclear power the rods themselves are cheap, relative to the amount of coal that would have to be purchased to produce the same electricity. On the other hand, the personnel that are required at a nuclear facility are highly trained and compensated, on top of which when things go wrong at a nuclear facility, they can go terribly wrong. In hydroelectric power, the variable input is free since the water that drives the turbines does so because of gravity. In both cases the cost of the facility is enormous relative to the costs of the variable inputs. Even when coal, oil, or natural gas are burned to generate electricity, the market tends toward monopoly because of the high fixed costs of the transmission network.

natural monopoly
Exists when there are high fixed costs and diminishing marginal costs.

Figure 38.6 shows what the price-output combination would be in an unregulated market for electricity in the case of a simple monopoly while Figure 38.7 shows the price-output combination for an unregulated natural monopoly. In either case the price is substantially above the marginal cost. This, combined with the fact that

FIGURE 38.6   A simple monopoly.

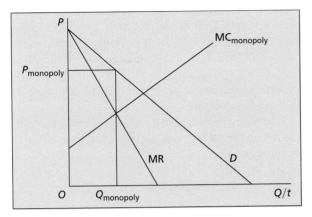

FIGURE 38.7   A natural monopoly.

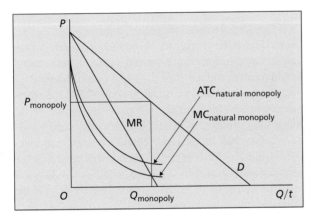

FIGURE 38.8   A regulated simple monopoly.

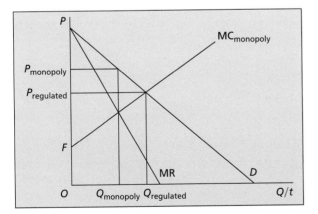

people need electricity to live a modern life, led to the widespread regulation of prices for electric utilities.

Figures 38.8 and 38.9 show the likely regulated prices that would exist if the regulators sought to allow the electric companies normal profits.

FIGURE 38.9   A regulated natural monopoly.

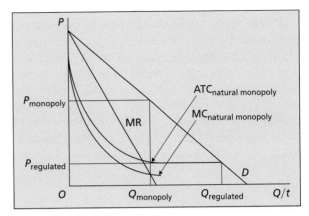

What Will the Future Hold?

Oil reserves are likely to be almost entirely depleted before the end of the 21st century. What will happen? Will we revert to the Stone Age once all the oil is gone? No. There are no perfect substitutes for oil and gas today, but there are some serviceable ones. We already use vegetation-based fuels; and we produce electricity with geo-thermal and solar power and with wind. As supplies decrease, more efficient uses of petroleum will be invented. Why are economists less worried about the end of fossil fuels than are people in other fields? Economists, who are not usually accused of making Pollyanna-ish predictions, are convinced that normal human self-interest will be more than adequate to spur on the important innovations that will be needed.

A lot of money will be made as we find substitutes for fossil fuels. As these fuels become more scarce and we exhaust all sources of them, they will become more and more expensive. Moreover, prices will not fall in the latter half of the 21st century. This will spur investment and investment will spur innovation. It always has and it always will.

Consider this: If you were an oil company, and you anticipated the end of your current form of business, you would spend as much money as it took to figure out a way to continue to sell fuels to your current customers. You would spend money on a variety of promising leads. You would try, for example, to figure out how to use renewable corn or soybeans to fuel existing cars, and, if that did not work, you would experiment with high-power, quick-charge batteries that you could sell so cars could run on electricity without the current problems of slow acceleration and long recharge times.

Evidence of the power of the profit motive is all around us. It has been known for nearly a half century that there was thick oil in relatively thin layers of rock in the Bakken formation, a deposit of oil shale that runs from North Dakota through eastern Montana and into southern Canada. It was simply too expensive to exploit using conventional vertical drilling. because if you drilled down and hit the oil, only a small portion would be recoverable with that method. The oil was too thick to flow toward the well. In the last 10 years, horizontal drilling and hydraulic fracturing (dubbed "fracking") has unleashed three or more decades' worth of natural gas in Pennsylvania, and the same

process is just now beginning to be exploited in North Dakota. The potential is now that this oil could completely supply U.S. needs that have heretofore come only from imported oil. It is only because oil prices rose during the last decade that anyone bothered to consider this possibility. At $100 per barrel, interesting drilling tactics are profitable that are not so profitable at $40 per barrel.

Nearly any problem can be solved with the proper incentive, and profit is one of the oldest and most effective incentives of all.

Kick It Up a Notch

Going back to the question of how cartels work, consider Figure 38.10. On the left panel is the market for oil. If the market were governed by perfect competition, then the price–quantity combination would be P_{comp}, Q_{comp}. This price would be carried over to the right panel, which would show the cost functions of a representative oil-producing country. Recall from Chapter 5 that the long-run equilibrium in such a market would mean that the price line would come tangent at the bottom of the average total cost (ATC) curve, where it would also intersect marginal cost (MC). Thus the representative oil-producing country would sell q_{comp}, because this is where marginal revenue (MR) intersects marginal cost (MC). At this level of production, they would make only normal profit, that is, the profit consistent with the return expected in other industries.

If they joined a cartel with other, similar countries, then the model for the market would be monopoly rather than perfect competition. If that were the case, then the cartel would jointly produce only Q_{cartel} and would charge P_{cartel} because that's where marginal revenue (MR) intersects marginal cost (MC) on the left panel of Figure 38.10. Since total production of all countries combined would be less than before, the representative country's production would also have to be less than it was before. Some negotiations between the member countries would result in each one being allocated a quota, labeled q_{quota}. If the representative country produced q_{quota} and received P_{cartel} per barrel, it would make an economic profit, that is, profit above normal, in the amount of *abcd*.

Cartels are not stable because cheating pays. The right-hand panel of Figure 38.10 shows this; see that

FIGURE 38.10 A model of a cartel.

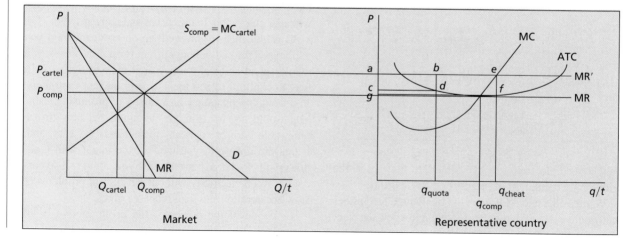

q_{quota} marginal revenue MR′ was greater than the marginal cost MC. Countries that cheated did so hoping that no one would notice. A country committed to cheating would see that cheating paid. Looking again at Figure 38.10, you see that at the new high cartel price P_{cartel} the country would maximize profit at q_{cheat}. This is where MR′ equals MC. That profit, *gaef*, would greatly exceed the profit previously received at the cartel's imposed quota. As in our previous example, using grading on a curve where everyone schemed together, individual greed induced cheating on the collective and this caused all gains to evaporate. Cheating by OPEC members led not only to the disappearance of the large profits (*gaef*), but also to the evaporation of all economic profits.

Summary

Now that you have completed this chapter, you know what a cartel is, that OPEC is a major oil-producing cartel, why it is that cartels work to make their members large sums of money, why it is that they are not stable, and that they seem to be able to rise again from the dead. You know that, inflation adjusted, the price of oil and the price of gasoline have been historically unstable and that this instability has been a consequence of geopolitics and the inherent instability of cartels. You understand why it is that events in the Middle East can alter prices at the pump within a few days.

Key Terms

cartel, 406

natural monopoly, 412

Quiz Yourself

1. In order to compare the price of gasoline in the 1970s with the price in 2007, you have to adjust for
   a. the availability of oil.
   b. the price of oil.
   c. overall inflation.
   d. unemployment.

2. The heaviest concentration of proven oil reserves is found in
   a. Alaska.
   b. the North Sea.
   c. the Persian Gulf.
   d. Texas.

3. When a group of competitors joins together to form a monopoly, they are forming a
   a. cartel.
   b. coalition.
   c. union.
   d. trust.

4. Cartels are considered _____ because each participant is motivated to _____.
   a. stable; work with each other cooperatively
   b. stable; work in their own interest to produce more
   c. unstable; work with each other cooperatively
   d. unstable; work in their own interest to produce more

5. Gasoline prices in early 2007 were above $2.25. They were
   a. the highest nominal prices and highest inflation-adjusted prices in American history.
   b. the highest nominal prices but were not the highest inflation-adjusted prices in American history.
   c. neither the highest nominal prices nor the highest inflation-adjusted prices in American history.
   d. the highest inflation-adjusted prices but were not the highest nominal prices in American history.

6. California electricity deregulation involved deregulating _____ prices while regulating _____ prices.
   a. wholesale; retail
   b. retail; wholesale
   c. real; nominal
   d. nominal; real

Short Answer Questions

1. There have been other cartels through history: most notably drug cartels in the 1980s in Colombia and during more recent times in Mexico. They never suffered from cheating. Why?

2. At the height of the 2008 financial crisis, in the time it took a completely full oil tanker to travel from Saudi Arabia to the United States, the price of oil fell nearly $50 per barrel. Use the expected price formulation to explain how that could happen.

3. What would be the principal obstacle preventing a cartel from emerging in the production of beef?

4. Why might the cartel model still make sense even when OPEC produces less than half of the world's oil?

Think about This

All energy consumption involves externalities that are recognized. Given that we have spent billions of dollars militarily defending access to oil, should we consider that an externality too? Aren't the consumers of energy indirectly compelling increased spending on the military?

Talk about This

Oil prices are highly sensitive to output changes. Hurricanes, terrorist acts, and other unexpected occurrences regularly cause the price of oil to increase by 10 percent within the course of a month, only to fall again when the trouble subsides. Should the federal government use its strategic petroleum reserve to counter these effects or should it use the reserve only in a true emergency?

For More Insight See

Adelman, Morris, *Genie Out of the Bottle: World Oil Since 1970* (Cambridge, MA: MIT Press, 1995).

Behind the Numbers

Global energy resource data, 2001.
Oil consumption per day.
Global oil reserves by region.
World crude oil production.
Energy prices.
   Oil and gasoline prices—www.eia.gov

CHAPTER THIRTY-NINE

If We Build It, Will They Come? And Other Sports Questions

Learning Objectives

After reading this chapter you should be able to:

LO1 Apply economic principles to issues of sports.

LO2 Conclude that despite the obvious attempts of cities to acquire sports franchises through league expansion and by other means, no economic evidence suggests that having a franchise enhances a city's economic stature.

LO4 Analyze how owners decide, when negotiating with players, whether they wish to make more money or win championships, since it is clear that teams in small markets cannot do both.

LO5 Summarize the basics of sports labor economics history and the vocabulary that is central to it.

LO6 Apply the concept of monopoly to motorsports.

Chapter Outline

The Problem for Cities

The Problem for Owners

The Sports Labor Market

The Vocabulary of Sports Economics

Summary

Sports offers an interesting venue in which to ask economic questions. For instance, if you are the mayor of a city whose citizens want a sports franchise, are you better off if you get one from another city, or do you mount a campaign to garner an expansion franchise? If it will enhance the chances of getting a franchise, do you build a multimillion-dollar stadium and hope you get a team to put in it? Now suppose you are a mayor of a city that already has a franchise whose owner is threatening to leave. Do you build the franchise owner a stadium, even though the one the team is in is only 25 years old? The question that underlies all these decisions is whether a sports franchise is an important economic attraction for a city. Mayors make deals all the time to attract other kinds of major employers. Why not a sports franchise?

To change perspective, suppose now that you are an owner of a franchise. What would make you want to move your team to a different city or to hold your own city hostage to build you a stadium? How do you decide whether to bid for high-priced talent? Can you compete in the financial arena if you do? Can you compete on the field, the pitch, the ice, or the court if you do not?

These are all questions that arise in all sports, and they are all economic in their nature. We answer each by looking at them from two perspectives: the city's and the team owner's. Since no discussion of the economics of sports today would be complete without a discussion of labor, we include that, too. We try to figure out how we went from sports as games to sports as business.

The Problem for Cities

Expansion versus Luring a Team

One of the emerging trends of the 1990s, like the 1950s, was the sudden increase in the desire among owners of sports franchises to move their teams from one city to another. Compared to other sports, baseball has been relatively stable. It has increased in numbers of teams, but existing teams have tended not to move. Other sports, however, have seen teams move all over the place. Some of that movement, such as baseball's movement west, occurred with the Dodgers and Giants relocating from New York to California during the 1950s. That made good economic sense for the sport at the time. The movement of the Rams and Raiders out of Los Angeles, on the other hand, made little economic sense for the National Football League.[1] In nearly all of the recent franchise shifts, movement has resulted from a city's offering enticements to owners. In each case, the franchise owner has made millions.

A city has to decide on its strategy when it seeks to attract a team. While each sport has added new teams in the last several years, such expansion is not always the surest way for a particular city to get a team. In part, this is because there's no guarantee that a given sport will expand or will choose that city. Football and baseball added only two teams each between 1970 and 1990. Though the 1990s have seen increased expansion in both sports, many cities have waited in line for an expansion franchise, only to be spurned. When cities lose patience, they may turn their attention to finding teams that are in financial trouble and offering their owners the lure of millions of dollars as well as profit guarantees.

Cities that have been spurned in the expansion process and have subsequently sought out financially troubled teams have succeeded in getting them, but at a high cost. After St. Louis lost the football Cardinals to Arizona, it sought, but was denied, an expansion team while franchises were granted to Jacksonville and Charlotte instead. It turned, then, to luring an existing team. The Los Angeles Rams wanted a stadium built in Los Angeles containing revenue-producing luxury boxes,

---

[1]The only economic aspect of the decision not to have a team in the second largest city in the United States that makes sense is that the Rams and Raiders rarely sold out the Los Angeles Coliseum. This meant that not only were their games blacked out during that time, but also the network slated to cover the game could not cover any other game during that time. With no team in Los Angeles, there are no game blackouts and that means more ad revenue to the networks, which could potentially mean a higher bid for broadcast rights.

and the owner threatened to move if demands were not met. As part of its expansion bid, St. Louis was already in the process of building such a stadium. When Los Angeles refused to build one, the Rams moved to St. Louis. Before their Super Bowl year, the team drew fewer fans than it had drawn in Los Angeles. Nevertheless, the owner made more money because corporations paid hundreds of thousands of dollars for luxury boxes. Nashville has the same story to tell as the Oilers moved from Houston. In each case, a city stood in line, was denied a place at the table, and managed to buy its way in anyway.

In its pursuit of a team, a city has to decide whether it should build a stadium in hopes that a team and a franchise will come. This "if you build it, they will come" strategy is fraught with uncertain payoffs. St. Louis built it, and the Rams did come. St. Petersburg built it, and no one came. In hopes that the Chicago White Sox would move, the Tampa–St. Petersburg area built a new stadium, but, at the last minute, the city of Chicago and the state of Illinois agreed to build the White Sox a new stadium. The White Sox are still in Chicago. Though the Tampa Bay area ultimately got an expansion franchise, the wait lasted 10 years, and the city may have to build another new stadium because the facility in which the team plays is considered one of the worst places to see a baseball game in the major leagues. Building in hopes of getting a franchise sometimes works and sometimes does not. Since it rarely happens that a city gets a franchise without either a good stadium or one that is already under construction, building a new facility may be the only chance a city has, even though it may not be a very good bet.

While these lessons regarding expansion apply to the American sports world of the NFL, NBA, MLB, and NHL, they don't apply to soccer. Quite literally, a city in England could get its local club team into the Premier League, England's top league, in just a few seasons. Unlike American sports, where the franchises are in the league as long as they wish to be and expansion is quite limited, in European soccer, the teams have to stay out of the cellar in order to stay in their respective leagues. At the conclusion of each season, three soccer clubs are "relegated." That means they are dropped from the Premier League down to a lower league, and the three top lower league teams are promoted to the Premier League for the next season. A city desiring a place in the Premier League could, theoretically, purchase enough talent on the open market for soccer players to win enough games over enough seasons to go from being a local soccer club to playing Manchester United (the Yankees of the Premier League). This also leads to the odd result that in England in 2012–2013, there were six London-area teams in the Premier League and sizable cities with no teams.

Does a Team Enhance the Local Economy?

From a rational perspective, a city needs more reasons for having a franchise than just wanting to have one. To this end, the justification that most proponents give for getting a team is that doing so is an investment in the city's future. If that were true, the jobs gained, the tax income generated, and the prestige gained from having a team would genuinely be enough to pay for the costs of building the stadium. Because most mayors consider economic development a vital responsibility of their terms in office, you might think that enticing a team to move in would be the same as enticing any other major employer to move in. Does it not make sense for a mayor who seeks to draw a major employer to an area to also seek out a sports franchise that will employ many people?

While the reasoning sounds good, sports franchises simply do not generate very good jobs for people other than the athletes. Whether the jobs are created in the facility or are in surrounding restaurants, their pay scale is relatively low, and they provide few benefits. Moreover, though each baseball team has 81 home dates, in basketball the number is 41, and in football it is a mere 8. You cannot build a local economy with only a few workdays a year.

It turns out that whether a sports franchise can be an economic cornerstone is a well-researched question. You may be surprised to know, though, that in nearly every study on the subject, economists have concluded that sports teams do next to nothing to improve economic activity in a city. The research has focused on whether cities that have lost franchises did any worse economically than they would have had they not lost the team. Research also questioned whether cities that were granted a franchise did any better than they would have without one. The conclusion that was consistently drawn was that a city's economic activity was almost totally unrelated to whether it had a franchise.

The reason that sports teams do not add much to a local economy is that money spent on tickets, parking, and memorabilia is mostly local. This is referred to as

local substitution
The effect of the substitution of one economic activity for another within a community, so the net effect is zero.

local substitution, and it means that local people are going to games instead of eating out or going to movies or other things they would have done locally with their money. In the larger picture, sports is just a branch of the entertainment industry. Having a team changes how entertainment dollars are spent, but it does not change the amount that is spent. To make a somewhat exaggerated point, the Queens Park Rangers from the Premier League were a relegated team in 2013. As such, their fans had five other London-area Premier League teams to see when they were relegated. There was no loss of economic activity,

SPRING TRAINING AND THE NCAA

The competition for teams is not confined to the big-time professional leagues, nor even professional team sports. Beginning in the 1990s, first in Florida and then years later in Arizona, cities began attempting to lure Major League Baseball teams and their spring training sites. The threats made by teams became far more real in the 2000s as many threatened to move to Arizona for their annual training during the months of February and March. In fact, while at one time there were fewer than 10 teams in Arizona during spring training, half the league now trains there. It can be argued that the cities in the competition to be spring training sites are more rational because a very high percentage of the people watching spring training games come from outside the area. Some people choose their spring break vacation site based on where their favorite team locates. If this is the case, the local substitution effect can be said to be minor.

It is also worth noting that, although college teams do not threaten to move, the NCAA has. It was once located in Overland Park, Kansas (a Kansas City suburb), and that city benefited from garnering a disproportionate number of NCAA men's basketball tournaments. In 1999, the NCAA garnered many concessions from the city of Indianapolis and moved to that city. With it they brought the ability to locate major tournaments in the city and state. The men's Final Four is in that city in every fifth year. In the other years they get an opening weekend set of games, or a second weekend round, or get the women's Final Four. Again, because the vast majority of the people in attendance are from out of town, the local substitution argument is negated, and because it is on a repeating basis, the city's reasoning is somewhat more defensible.

even soccer-related economic activity, in London as a result of their relegation. In this sense, arguing whether a city should attract a sports team is like arguing whether a city should fight to attract a Super Walmart. Both produce about the same gross revenue and employ large numbers of people at low wages. The difference is that for a Walmart, much of the money leaves the local area in payment for the store's goods, and for a team, huge amounts of money go to a few rich stars.

Although some cities may not feel they have "arrived" or are "major league" until they have at least one baseball, basketball, hockey, or football team, they pay a very high price for that honor. Some cities grow in population to the point where a team is justified, but they have none. The Norfolk–Virginia Beach area of Virginia is now the largest Standard Metropolitan Statistical Area without any major league football, basketball, hockey, or baseball franchise. When people in Norfolk–Virginia Beach look at the attention that a small city of less than 100,000 gets each year with the Packers in Green Bay, they may conclude that they will not be living in an important area until they have one. If image is everything, then it may be worth it to assess citizens millions in taxes to get a franchise. Otherwise such outlays of money are highly questionable.

Why Are Stadiums Publicly Funded?

That outlays for stadiums are questionable as a means of creating economic growth does not prevent the issue from coming up. Public funding of stadiums can be explained in terms of **positive externalities** and bargaining power.

The positive externalities here are the benefits to the fans of having a team in the city which are in excess of what they get from going to the games. There are millions of sports fans who enjoy having a team in their city whether or not they ever go to a game or watch it on television. They enjoy following the team in the newspaper and talking about the team with their friends. Because they value that experience, voters, having decided that they want to keep a team, are willing to pay taxes to keep the team. This is similar to their willingness to pay taxes to support the arts when they do not attend concerts or museums.

positive externalities
The benefit that a person other than the buyer or seller receives as a result of a transaction.

Having seen why voters may be willing to pay taxes to keep a team, we need to look at why they end up having

to pay to keep a team. Because teams have demonstrated a willingness to move, and cities have demonstrated a willingness to lure the teams of other cities, all of the bargaining power belongs to the team owner. One of the things that we assumed in Chapter 5 when we discussed perfect competition was that there were many buyers and many sellers and that none had any market power. Here the market power is concentrated with the owner, who can move the team if voters do not pay for the stadium.

The Problem for Owners

To Move or to Stay

Owners are the big winners in sports when teams play musical chairs with their locations. Owners understand that an individual team's worth is based on how much it can rake in from memorabilia sales, luxury boxes, and, in the case of baseball, local TV revenue. They also know that it is to their advantage to have many suitors for their teams and to do little to discourage talk of moving.

Unfortunately, owners are often at cross-purposes with their leagues since it may be in the best interests of the leagues to have stable teams. Each owner knows that the sport is harmed by movement. Each owner knows that the owner of the team that is moving makes a great deal of money. As a result, it is in the communal best interests of sports that teams do not move around too much. However, it is in every individual owner's best interests to consider moving, to threaten to move, and sometimes to actually move. This is why baseball and football have ownership rules that require agreement of two-thirds to three-quarters of the other owners for a team to move or be sold. Though the owners of the Minnesota Twins, the Pittsburgh Pirates, and the Chicago White Sox threatened to move their baseball teams, none have. In football, the owners have seen the money that others have made in moving. To keep the option open for themselves they have routinely approved other owners' moves.[2]

When teams relocate, it is because the owners want to make more money. Some relocations lead to the need for new team mascots; new mascots mean vast increases in sales of shirts, hats, and other memorabilia. The Browns reaped such benefits when they moved to Baltimore and became the Ravens; and the Oilers did also when they

---

[2]An exception to this was the refusal of the NFL to let the Seahawks move from Seattle to Los Angeles. This location was too lucrative to just let someone have. It will likely be the location of an expansion franchise, and all owners will get a cut of the franchise fee.

moved to Nashville and became the Titans. Even teams that should have changed their mascots but did not reaped revenue from the sales of memorabilia. For instance, the Jazz moved from New Orleans to Utah, and the Lakers moved from Minneapolis to Los Angeles. Each move meant sales to a whole new set of fans in the new city.

Football teams usually move to gain stadiums with luxury boxes. Such boxes provide a significant source of extra revenue for a team. Though television contracts for football are admittedly large, the NFL spreads the revenue equally among the teams. The teams therefore get the same amount, whether they are in New York or Green Bay. Since the league's contract with the players dictates salary costs for all the teams, owners are left with small margins of profitability and a motivation to look for alternative sources of revenue. Luxury boxes make the difference. Because luxury box revenue is not shared between the teams the way ticket revenue is, potential revenue from such boxes has been enough of an incentive for the Rams to move from Los Angeles to St. Louis, enough for the Oilers to move from Houston to Nashville, enough for the Browns to move from Cleveland to Baltimore, and enough for the New England Patriots to nearly move from the Boston area to Hartford, Connecticut. Oddly enough, in each case, luxury boxes improved team finances enough to warrant movement from a larger metropolitan area to a smaller one.

To Win or to Profit

Some teams are worth very little where they are and would be worth much more if they moved. The Kansas City Royals and Minnesota Twins are two baseball teams that cannot simultaneously field consistently competitive clubs and make a profit. In baseball, team revenues are largely affected by local television deals. The Yankees' TV deal, for example, dwarfs that of the combined size of the Royals, the Twins, the Mariners, and a number of other "small-market" teams. The Royals were sold for $96 million in 1996 on the condition that the team not leave Kansas City for at least 10 years. Had the owners been able to at least threaten to move to another city, chances are good that they would have sold for many times $96 million. A move to someplace like Charlotte, Orlando, or another large, growing city would generate a lucrative local TV deal. It may be, however, that the only owner with sensitivity toward his city and the team's fans was the late Ewing Kaufman, whose will required that anyone who bought the team be required to keep it in Kansas City for a decade. For a prospective owner, nothing can be better than to be able to buy a struggling team

for under $100 million and to sell it 10 years later for a half billion. This is probably a temptation that a living owner will not pass up, and, unless things change, the Kansas City Royals will go down in history with the Washington Senators, who moved and became the Texas Rangers, and the Seattle Pilots, who moved and became the Milwaukee Brewers.

This is not to say a small-market team cannot win. Some such teams will win if they construct a superior farm system and are lucky enough to see their players all mature at exactly the right time. This happened with the Royals in the late 1970s, with the Twins in the middle 1980s, with the Mariners in the middle 1990s, and most recently with the Rays in 2008 through 2010. Unfortunately, if a team is that lucky, free agency will limit the time that the team can win and remain profitable. The Braves, Yankees, and Dodgers will always be ready to buy up the talent as soon as the players are eligible for free agency. As further evidence of this problem, a special committee appointed by the commissioner of baseball noted that, from 1994 to 1999, no team whose payroll was in the bottom half of major league baseball won a playoff game. Though the Rays bucked the trend for three years, their roster was raided prior to the 2011 season.

In early 2009, the NBA, as quietly as possible, borrowed $132 million to help its struggling franchises make payroll. Though their short-term troubles could be tied to the state of the economy in late 2008 and early 2009, it is a long-term challenge for all sports leagues when there is a marked imbalance in team revenues. Owners face the "win or make money, but you can't do both" challenge when they are at the bottom of the league in team revenues.

Similarly, in NASCAR, the top teams with the top names and millions in sponsorship money can field teams that win 90 percent of races. In 2008, the teams fielded by Joe Gibbs Racing, Hendrick Motorsports, Roush Racing, and Richard Childress Racing won all but three of the 36 races and the top 13 spots in the Sprint Cup championship standings.

The ultimate example of this phenomenon occurred with the Premier League's Manchester City. Purchased in 2008 by a group from Abu Dhabi who invested millions in garnering worldwide talent, they were sold in 2009 to Sheikh Mansour, an individual estimated to be worth $30 billion from a family estimated to be worth a trillion dollars. With massive investments, the team won Britain's FA Cup in 2011 and won the 2012 Premier

TABLE 39.1 Purchase prices, current values, and rates of return on selected Major League Baseball franchises.

Source: *Forbes*, www.forbes.com

Team	Purchase Price (Year)	*Forbes* Magazine 2012 Estimate of Value (millions)	Real Annual Rate of Return
New York Yankees	$10 million (1973)	$2,300	10%
St. Louis Cardinals	$3.75 million (1953)	$716	5%
Los Angeles Dodgers	$347,000 (1944)	$1,615	9%
Kansas City Royals	$96 million (1996)	$457	7%
Montreal Expos	$50 million (1999)*	$631	17%

*In 2003 MLB purchased the Expos for $120 million so as to be able to contract or move them. This was part of an agreement that allowed the former owner to buy the Florida Marlins. The Expos bcame the Washington Nationals.

League for the first time in 44 years, all while losing nearly $200 million a year.

Don't Feel Sorry for Them Just Yet

While it may be tempting to feel sorry for the "poor" owners who lose money each and every year on their franchises, you can probably leave the Kleenex in your pocket. As Tables 39.1 and 39.2 indicate, even though baseball and football franchises may claim to lose money each year, the return on their investment is still substantial. How? Because history suggests that the team will sell for substantially more than the owner paid for it. Economist Rodney D. Fort specializes in sports economics, even writing a textbook devoted to

it. Having collected financial data on NFL and MLB franchises over the years, he has come to the conclusion that it is the capital gain that makes these investments truly valuable.

You might expect there to be high real rates of return on owning powerhouse franchises like the Yankees, Cardinals, and Dodgers in baseball and the Cowboys and Steelers in football. On the other hand, even baseball's lowly Royals and Expos/Nationals and football's historic futility champions, the Arizona Cardinals, earned substantial profits for their owners. For comparison, it should be noted that these real rates of return are better than typical alternatives. Specifically, real stock market returns average between 5 and 8 percent.

TABLE 39.2 Purchase prices, current values, and rates of return on selected National Football League franchises.

Source: *Forbes*, www.forbes.com

Team	Purchase Price on Most Recent Sale	*Forbes* Magazine 2012 Estimate of Value (millions)	Real Annual Rate of Return
Pittsburgh Steelers	$2,500 (1933)	$1,100	18%
Dallas Cowboys	$150 million (1989)	$2,100	9%
Oakland Raiders	$180,000 (1972)	$750	18%
Phoenix Cardinals	$50,000 (1932)	$922	13%
New Orleans Saints	$71 million (1985)	$971	7%

The Sports Labor Market

What Owners Will Pay

When we think about the market for talent in any sport, we have to recognize that it is fundamentally no different from any other labor market. Firms will hire the marginal laborer as long as the contribution of the employee to revenue equals or exceeds the money that must be paid to that employee. This concept, called the **marginal revenue product of labor**, is important in any firm. In sports, the marginal revenue product of labor is the money that the team generates in revenue because a particular player is on the team. It would include any increase in revenue that results directly from their performance as well as all that revenue that results indirectly, say in the form of memorabilia sales, from the player being on the team. So a star may make a team win, which causes it to draw more fans. But the star's presence may also cause sales of team logo jerseys to increase. In deciding whether to sign a player to a large contract, therefore, an owner must decide whether the player is worth the money. If the player brings in at least as much in revenue to the team as the salary that the player commands, then the player is worth it.

marginal revenue product of labor
The additional revenue generated from hiring an additional worker.

What Players Will Accept

The issue for players is whether the pay they are offered to play for a team exceeds their next best offer. This next best offer is a player's **reservation wage**. It is the least that the player will sign for, because anything less makes an offer from some other team or some other job more desirable. Before the days of lucrative sports contracts, players quit their sports before they otherwise would have because their outside offers were better. Depending on the institutional structure of the sport, a player's reservation wage can be very high because he[3] will have offers from other teams, or it can be very low because the player is able to offer his services to only one team. In the latter case, the reservation wage is the next best job, but outside of the sport.

The pay that a player will end up getting will thus be between the most it can be, the marginal revenue

reservation wage
The least amount that a player will accept because it is the next best offer.

product, and the least it can be, the reservation wage. This gap can be enormous.

The Vocabulary of Sports Economics

Franchise owners, of course, spend their time attempting to increase revenues and fighting increases in expenditures. We have dealt with the revenue side and the luxury-box solution, but the expenditure side is stickier. The problem owners face is players who are **free agents**. It is increasingly difficult to compete in the major sports without an ability to buy talent. Total revenue for the average "small-market" major league baseball team is between $30 million and $40 million. No team with a payroll under $48 million, however, was in the playoffs in 1998. The 1997 Florida Marlins lost millions winning the World Series, and the owner proceeded to sell all of the team's high-salaried players the following year. Though this practice occurs most often in baseball, it is done in other sports as well. In basketball, for example, once Michael left the Bulls, the owner of the now Jordanless team traded, sold, or decided not to renew contracts on Pippen, Rodman, and a host of others. As a result, the Bulls became the first team to win a championship in basketball and follow that with a season in which they were eligible for the **draft** lottery.

free agent
A player who is able to offer services to the highest bidder.

draft
The process by which new talent is assigned to teams.

The draft is a mechanism designed to provide competitive balance. By allowing teams that finished poorly to draft first, the leagues infuse the poorer teams with the best of the young talent. One problem with such a draft is that it motivates teams to play badly to vie for the first pick. This was the accusation in the NBA when, in hopes of getting Ralph Sampson with the first pick in the 1983 draft, the Houston Rockets played very badly. While never proven conclusively, the concern was they were playing badly intentionally. In 1985 the NBA created a system whereby the teams that did not make the playoffs were entered into a lottery. In 1990 the system was changed so that the chance of winning was higher for the poorer performing teams.[4]

---

[3]"He" is appropriate here as long as big money is associated only with men's professional team sports.

[4]Specifically, of the 29 teams in the NBA, 13 do not make the playoffs and are in the lottery as a result. Like the lotto, each team's logo is printed on Ping-Pong balls. A team has one ball plus one for each team they were behind in the race to the playoffs. Thus the worst team in the league has 13 of the 91 balls in the hopper. As a result, their probability of getting the first pick is 14.3 out of 100.

It is difficult, if not impossible, for a team to win without great talent; and unless it manages to find that talent through the draft, it must bid for the talent of players who are free agents. With the single exception of the 1998 NBA lockout, the ultimate winners in labor negotiations during the last several years have been the players. Athletes have successfully negotiated for greater access to free markets for their talent. Free agency has driven average salaries up faster than revenues from TV or ticket sales so that today, a single player can make more in a year (though only in nominal terms) than it cost to build Yankee Stadium in 1923.

Quite often today's owners must decide whether to make money or to win games. It is unfortunate that for more than a few teams, in more than a few sports, these are conflicting goals. Owners within each of the major sports have complained about their inability to turn a profit or to at least break even. Because only a few players are on the free agent market each year and because many teams consider themselves just a few wins short of either contending for the playoffs, or better, winning a championship, the price that players are able to command is quite high.

Sports franchise owners have attempted to institute **salary caps**, in order to protect themselves from themselves. That is, they want to

salary cap
The maximum in total payroll that a team can pay its players.

protect themselves from being tempted to bid against one another. Other than baseball, each major professional team sport has some form of salary cap in place. The owners hope to lessen their costs at the expense of players by limiting the amount of money they can bid against each other for talent. Sometimes it is not in the best interests of the owners to have strict salary caps. During the 1980s the NBA allowed teams to have one player's salary not count against the cap as long as any further signings were done at the minimum. This rule, called the Larry Bird exemption, was instituted so that teams could keep a marquee player.

Another avenue for allowing small-market teams to succeed is to put into place a general sharing of revenues, or at least a sharing of the television revenues. Since

revenue sharing
The process by which some revenues are distributed to all teams rather than simply the teams that generate them.

football does **revenue sharing** well and baseball does not, you would expect a more fluid mix of winners and losers in football than in baseball. That is, in fact, what we saw in the 1990s. Two baseball teams dominated the decade, the Atlanta Braves and the New York Yankees, both of which had a "local"

television market via cable that was, in fact, thoroughly national. Neither, of course, shared the revenue it got with the other baseball teams, and this gave them an absurd advantage in bidding for high-priced talent.

In a simpler time sports were games played by men who were happy to be paid at all. Owners were happy to oblige them by hardly paying them at all. There were no women's professional leagues and no laws requiring high schools and colleges to fund women's athletics. Without a doubt there was grumbling among players about their pay, but not until 1977 did business considerations come into play. In that year baseball had an epiphany. An arbitrator declared two players free agents and the sport was forever changed. Within a few years other sports also gained forms of free agency and players who had had virtually no right to the economic benefits of the free competitive market began to get rich.

Prior to 1977 all players in all team sports were bound to the team they played for the previous year. Having

reserve clause
A contract clause that requires that players re-sign with the team to which they belonged the previous year.

this so-called **reserve clause** in contracts meant that the only choice players had was to either play for what the owner offered or retire. Whereas star players in their later years had the sort of leverage that was afforded by the support of public opinion, lesser players did not. Even when Joe DiMaggio, considered by many the best right-handed hitter of all time, held out for a better contract by going home to San Francisco to open a restaurant, he ultimately came back to the Yankees for much less than he was worth. Going back to our discussion on the reservation wage, with the reserve clause in place, the reservation wage for players bound by it was very low.

From 1977 on, each sport has engaged in collective bargaining agreements that have given players more and more freedom of movement and contracts that are much more lucrative in terms of salaries and incentives. These agreements usually require teams to pay a minimum salary. Baseball's minimum salary was set at $300,000 in 2004 and adjusted for inflation thereafter. Hockey's minimum salary had been the lowest of the majors sports and is now the highest, at $450,000. The NBA has a minimum salary chart that is based on years of service. For a rookie, the minimum salary for the 2006–2007 season was $412,718 while for a 10-year veteran it was $1,138,500. The interesting thing about the NBA system is that it works against veterans who wish to finish their careers as role players. If you refer to Chapter 31's discussion of the minimum wage, this is an example of how

THE NATIONAL HOCKEY LEAGUE'S 2004–2005 LOCKOUT

In 2004–2005 the National Hockey League became the first sports league to lose an entire season to a work stoppage. The NHL owners chose to lock out the players after negotiations failed to produce an agreement to lower salaries. The players refused an owner demand that the league adopt a salary cap that would have cut players' salaries by 30 percent. In the end, after a completely lost season, the owners got almost exactly what they wanted. This stands with a football strike in the 1980s and a basketball strike in the 1990s as the only cases in sports history in which owners unambiguously won a labor dispute. Because the owners won, they tried it again in 2012–2013. In that dispute, however, the season wasn't lost, but both sides did. The sport's following dropped significantly.

this type of minimum wage can actually hurt someone it was intended to help.

In each sport players are bound to the team they played for the previous year for a period of time that ranges from four to six years, depending on the sport. These collective bargaining agreements have decidedly raised the reservation wage of players with the requisite experience to have earned free agency. For free agents, the reservation wage is the next best offer from another team. That is usually very close to their marginal revenue product.

Thus free agency and other aspects of collective bargaining agreements have raised average salaries in all sports far faster than inflation. Though there is dispute among economists as to how much credit for this change goes to free agency, in some sports, average salaries have increased more than tenfold in 20 years. This increase may be attributed to an increase in the marginal revenue product of players, which has come about in part because the sports are more popular, they draw larger gates and television audiences, and sales of memorabilia have grown. For whatever reason, consider this: In the 1920s Babe Ruth became the first player to earn more than the president. In 2008 the minimum major league salary was only $10,000 less than the president's.

Of course when you change a system, good and bad outcomes ensue. Along with higher pay and benefits for players arrived at through collective bargaining agreements, professional sports has had to endure **strikes** and **lockouts**. Each sport has lost at least part of a season to this sort of work stoppage. A strike, a refusal by the players to work, is usually

strike
An action by labor to deny employers the services of the employees.

lockout
An action by employers to deny employees access to their jobs.

THE NFL LOCKOUT

At the completion of the February 2011 Super Bowl, the NFL owners locked out its players. The dispute, like nearly every labor-management dispute before or after it, was about compensation. The previous contract gave the owners the right to the first $1 billion in revenues and 40 percent of the remaining (approximately) $8 billion. The players got 60 percent of the revenues after the first $1 billion. Because revenues to the sport grew so rapidly during the previous contract, the owners felt the old agreement unfairly enriched the players and wanted the first $2 billion in revenues and a larger share of the remainder. Although there were other issues, such as long-term health benefits for players and the potential for an 18-game schedule, the real issue was money.

What warrants a side explanation is that the players tried an interesting tactic: decertification. When a union and an employer come to loggerheads in a dispute, the players can strike or the owners can lock out the workers (players). When there is no union, a lockout constitutes a violation of antitrust law. Shortly after talks broke down, the union decertified. Because it was a transparent attempt by the players to short-circuit the lockout, the owners sued. A lower court ruling in favor of the players was overturned on appeal and the two sides worked out a deal.

voted for when the players want something in a new contract that is quite different from the status quo. A lockout, a refusal by the owners to let the players work, is usually instituted when the owners want to make extensive changes in existing contracts.

Baseball owners have tried other avenues to get around the competitive nature of bidding on free agents. After 1986, baseball free agents found that owners were no longer willing to bid on their services. The change was so abrupt that it caught many off-guard. Subsequently, players began to suspect that it could only have resulted from the collusion of the owners not to bid on each other's players. In 1987 the first case went to an arbitrator. The owners offered the "How could we possibly collude?" defense, arguing that such an arrangement would have been impossible to enforce among themselves. It was not lost on millions of baseball fans or the arbitrator that, in a different era, a different set of owners had managed to collude to keep blacks and Hispanics from the game until 1946. Various arbitrators found that baseball owners had in fact colluded and were ordered to pay $280 million in damages.

To illustrate how much, or how little, power each side has, consider the alternatives a player has. If a league has a structure that prevents owners in the league from bidding against one another, then players have little choice but to accept what the team offers—that is, unless the player has value in another league. For most athletes, this power only exists for two-sport stars. For soccer players, however, there are myriad other leagues in other countries willing to pay players. A player on a Premier League team doesn't just have options to move to another team; he has options to move to another league. The Spanish and German leagues, for instance, regularly sign players who have played in the Premier League.

What differentiates team sports like baseball, football, hockey, and basketball from individual sports like golf and tennis is that individual sports have no "owners" with whom to negotiate. Players can make as much as they want. They just have to win.

One problem with team sports is that it is under the control of a small number of self-serving owners. They pay the talented players. Unfortunately, anytime only a few bosses bid on talent, the bosses are usually satisfied, and the talent usually grumbles. In golf and tennis there are no owners, so golfers and tennis players never grumble. They accept the direct relationship that exists between winning and income. While I am a fan of many sports, auto racing, and, in particular, National Association of Stock Car Auto Racing (NASCAR),[5] is interesting to me as an economist. It is something like golf and tennis in that individual achievement is vital. It is also something like team sports in that an individual driver must rely on a host of others doing their jobs. In auto racing there are so many different owners and so many different drivers that something like perfect competition exists. Moreover, there is easy entrance and exit from the market because anybody with sufficient capital can start a new team and attempt to qualify for major events like the Daytona 500 or Indianapolis 500. Additionally, there are enough buyers and sellers of talent that the prices arrived at for talent seem fair to all concerned. The only issue that could upset this balance would be if NASCAR, Indy Racing League (IRL) or Formula 1 got so lax with safety that drivers were forced to band together to fix a problem. Thus they would become adversaries instead of partners with the owners and sponsors. Unless something like this happens, racing will probably remain an example of how, under perfect competition, all parties get what they are worth and are worth what they get.

What a Monopoly Will Do for You

Motor sports offers an interesting lesson in the power of monopoly. Three of the major series (NASCAR, the IRL, and Formula 1) are owned by a single person or family. The France family, the Hulman-George family, and Bernie Ecclestone control their respective series with iron fists. Moreover, many of the venues in which the series operate are owned by these people as well. To the never-ending frustration of the track owners who attempt to host races at other sites, these series owners control the destiny of their sport to a degree that no baseball or football owner can imagine.

The IRL, which drove its principal competitor (CART) out of business, is owned by the family that controls the Indianapolis Motor Speedway. In 2002, excepting a race in Denver, CART's total attendance was less than that of the Indy 500. From the time when the two series split in 1996, the IRL was able to use the family-owned Indy 500 to bully CART and television networks.

The France family, which owns a controlling interest in International Speedway Corporation (ISC, a holding company for many tracks where NASCAR runs) and the track in Daytona, was hounded in court by the owner of the Texas Motor Speedway until it acquiesced to

---

[5]NASCAR is the governing body of the most notable of several stock car racing circuits. Stock cars are called "stock" because they look vaguely like regular passenger cars that you can buy at your local dealer.

give that track a second race. In 2007, Kentucky Motor Speedway's owners sued NASCAR, attempting to get a race at their track near Cincinnati. Their legal argument was based on the assertion that because the France family owned NASCAR and ISC, they were in violation of the Sherman Anti-Trust Act. They bolstered this argument with the fact that an ISC track, the California Motor Speedway, received a second race starting in 2004 though it has yet to sell out a race. In 2008, a federal judge dismissed the suit and upheld the authority of NASCAR to set its dates and tracks, thereby solidifying this family business's stranglehold on the sport.

Formula 1 racing has rarely been able to maintain the same race schedule two years in a row. The problem here is that the owner, Bernie Ecclestone, requires such a high advance fee to hold a race in a particular location that promoters cannot afford to build a fan base for this worldwide form of racing.

As in all economics, market power, and especially monopoly power, determines who the winners and losers are.

Summary

You now understand how economic principles can be applied to the issues of sports. In particular you understand that, despite the obvious attempts of cities to acquire franchises through expansion and by luring others, there is no economic evidence to suggest that having a franchise enhances a city's economic stature. You understand that owners are not only on the opposite side of this particular bargain, but they also face a problem of their own. They must negotiate with players; if they are doing so in a small market, they must often decide whether they wish to make money or win. Last, you now understand the basics of sports labor economics history and the vocabulary that is central to it.

Key Terms

draft, 423
free agent, 423
local substitution, 419
lockout, 425

marginal revenue product of
  labor, 423
positive externalities, 420
reservation wage, 423

reserve clause, 424
revenue sharing, 424
salary cap, 424
strike, 425

Quiz Yourself

1. The value of a sports franchise to a city's economy depends greatly on
   a. the sale of memorabilia to citizens.
   b. the degree to which non-ticket-based sales increase.
   c. the degree to which restaurant revenues rise.
   d. the degree to which noncitizens spend money in the city.

2. Most baseball franchises have _____ over the years while the sale price of the typical team has _____.
   a. made a profit; fallen
   b. lost money; fallen
   c. made a profit; risen
   d. lost money; risen

3. The typical problem for generating parity in sports leagues is that
   a. there is no mechanism for bringing in new talent in a way that helps the bad teams.
   b. there is no means by which players on one team can move to another.

   c. with no salary cap and with unlimited free agency, big city, high-revenue teams have an advantage.
   d. no one wants it.

4. The motorsports industry is dominated by independent teams running in series operated as
   a. monopolies.
   b. oligopolies.
   c. monopolistic competitors.
   d. perfect competitors.

5. Economists note that a reason exists for policy makers to subsidize sports stadiums and it is that
   a. they bring in billions of dollars to their communities.
   b. they result in large increases in city payrolls.
   c. they result in enormous increases in taxes.
   d. the teams make people happy—even those who don't go to the games.

6. When the National Hockey League had its 2004–2005 work stoppage, it was
   a. a player strike over salaries that were too low.
   b. a player strike over a limited ability to move to another team.
   c. an owner lockout over reducing salaries.
   d. an owner lockout over union work rules.

Short Answer Questions

1. How did the reserve clause serve to allow owners to pay something close to the players' reservation wage rather than their marginal revenue product of labor?
2. Use the local substitution argument to consider what the economic value of your college's basketball team truly is.
3. If someone from the arts community were to argue for a subsidy to garner an arts festival, how would the local substitution argument apply and how might the external benefits argument apply?

Think about This

Formula 1 may never compete again in the United States as a result of a problem with tires at the Indianapolis Motor Speedway. Michelin's tire was simply too dangerous for the teams to safely run the 2005 U.S. Grand Prix. Because there are two competing tire companies supplying tires to competitor teams, neither would agree to the other's posed solutions. This would never happen in NASCAR or the IRL because they use only one tire manufacturer. Once a problem was identified, it would have been in everyone's interest to find a solution. What does this tell you about the benefits and costs of oligopoly over monopoly?

Talk about This

The Indianapolis Colts used an implied threat to move as a means by which to induce the state of Indiana and the city of Indianapolis to build them a new stadium. This is somewhat ironic since the same family used the fact that Indianapolis built them a stadium in the 1980s to leave Baltimore. To what degree are the combined threats by owners to leave their respective cities a conspiracy?

For More Insight See

Kahn, Lawrence M., "The Sports Business as a Labor Market Laboratory," *Journal of Economic Perspectives* 14, no. 3 (Summer 2000).

Sheehan, Richard, *Keeping Score: The Economics of Big-Time Sports* (South Bend, IN: Diamond Communications, 1996).

Siegfried, John, and Andrew Zimbalist, "The Economics of Sports Facilities and Their Communities," *Journal of Economic Perspectives* 14, no. 3 (Summer 2000).

CHAPTER FORTY

The Stock Market and Crashes

Learning Objectives

After reading this chapter you should be able to:

LO1 Describe how stock prices are determined and what stock markets do.

LO2 Apply the concept of present value to the fundamental elements of stock prices and describe how prices can get out of line with their fundamental value.

LO3 Explain that bankruptcy is an important feature in corporate business but that many of the bankruptcies of 2001 and 2002 involved a level of deception on the part of their accountants that was potentially quite damaging.

Chapter Outline

Stock Prices

Efficient Markets

Stock Market Crashes

The Accounting Scandals of 2001 and 2002

Rebound of 2006–2007 and the Drop of 2008–2009

Summary

Even to many of the people who invest in it, the stock market is a mystery. Investors buy stocks, that is, shares of the value of a company. As stockholders they have the right to vote in shareholders' meetings and a right to a prorated share of dividends. The questions of what makes the prices of stocks go up and down in general and why prices actually soar or plummet on any particular day have perplexed both stockholders and economists for many years.

Figures 40.1, 40.2, and 40.3 show the values of three important measures of the stock market. In each, the level of each of these indices is in black and the common logarithm (the log base 10) is in blue. You can see that the level of each has grown over time, and though each saw a major dip in 2000 and 2001, that dip was small, given the substantial runs of the previous 20 years. You can also see that the plunge in late 2008 brought each index back to a level that was similar to its 2001 low. Graphs such as these are deceiving though, if you just look at the level, which is why the logarithmic scale is useful. For instance, when looking at historic swings

from 25 or even 70 years ago, what is imperceptible on the level scale is quite noticeable on the logarithmic scale. So you probably know that the Dow Jones and S&P 500 each grew rapidly in the 1920s and then plunged in the 1930s. It is impossible to see that on the level scale but much easier to see it on the logarithmic scale.

What could cause stocks to go up by more than 50 percent in four months, as they did in 1982? What could cause a stock market to lose 20 percent of its value on a single day, as it did in October 1987? Assuming that the price of a share of stock does, in fact, represent the value of that share of the company in question, how can the value of anything change so fast?

The ultimate question of what actually determines stock market prices is the focus of this chapter. We explore what traditional economic theory has to say on the subject of how stock prices are determined. We discuss how a stock market can advance economic growth by helping to transfer financial capital into the hands of the people who can use it best. We show that if a stock

FIGURE 40.1 The Dow Jones Industrial Average, 1896–2012.

Source: Yahoo! Finance, http://finance.yahoo.com

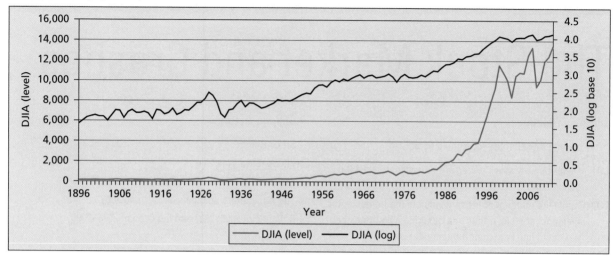

FIGURE 40.2 Standard and Poor's 500, 1870–2012.

Source: Yahoo! Finance, http://finance.yahoo.com

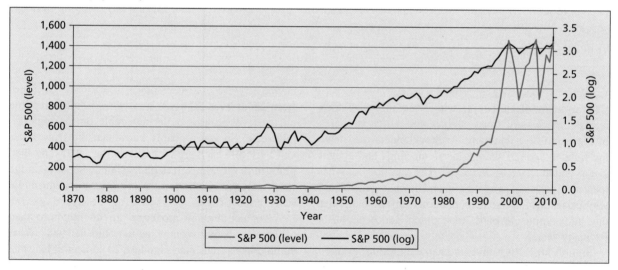

market is "efficient," small investors—investors who invest relatively small amounts of money—do not need to take a lot of time thinking about their investments because it will not do them much good. We move to a discussion of the causes and effects of some of history's stock market crashes and what might be done to prevent them. We finish with a discussion of bankruptcy and the accounting scandals of 2001 and 2002.

Stock Prices

How Stock Prices Are Determined

Traditional economic analysis has always suggested that the value of any asset is based on three things: the flow of returns that come from the asset, the amount that the asset is expected to sell for when it is sold, and the rate at which the future flow of those returns is "discounted." To

FIGURE 40.3   NASDAQ Composite Index, 2012.

Source: Yahoo! Finance, http://finance.yahoo.com

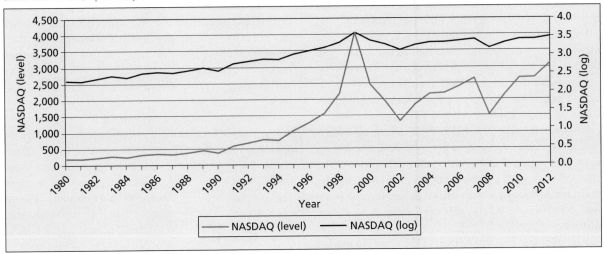

compute the value of a stock, we add up payments that come in at different times. To put those payments on an even playing field, we use the concept of present value that we introduced in Chapter 7.

Although the math for computing present value is somewhat complicated, the concept is not hard to understand. If there are 1 million shares of a company and the company profits are exactly $1 million, then the earnings per share is exactly $1. How much would you pay for a share of stock that would yield earnings of $1/year forever? What it is worth is the present value of that $1 each year. Recall that you learned in Chapter 7 that one of the components of present value is the interest rate. Sometimes we change the jargon a bit and refer to it as the discount rate, but it is the same concept: the amount by which future payments are discounted. In the previous example, if you are confident of being paid $1/year/share forever, the present value is the reciprocal of the interest rate. If the interest rate is 5 percent, then the present value is $20. If it is 10 percent, the present value is $10.

Since we rarely act as if companies will last forever, we usually judge the value of a stock to be the present value of its expected dividend payments plus the present value of its expected final sales price. Both of these present values are greatly determined by the discount rate, the interest rate that is used to translate future payments into present value. As the discount rate rises, the present value of the payments falls.

You can see from everything we have said so far that the price of a share of stock can move as a result of a change in any of the three variables. A change in

the profit expectations will change both dividend expectations and final sale price expectations. These in turn will change the price of the stock. A change in interest rates will also change the stock price. In the end, though, the ultimate long-term value of a stock is determined by its profit expectations and the interest rate. These are known as **fundamentals**, elements that go into a stock's price that make long-term economic sense.

fundamentals
Elements that determine stock prices that make long-term economic sense—profit expectations and interest rates.

What Stock Markets Do

Stock markets exist as an efficient way of getting available financial capital to whichever investors can make the best use of that financial capital. Stock markets set share prices, thereby providing investors information about which companies are doing well and which are not. Stock markets allow firms that need new influxes of money to get what they need, and they allow investors to invest their money in places that provide good returns.

Though most of the shares traded on any particular day are stock issued many years before, an important function of a stock market is to support new companies with investors' funds. When a company sells stock for the first time in an attempt to raise money for expansion, this **initial public offering (IPO)** turns what is typically a small, privately

initial public offering (IPO)
A company's first sale of stock to the public in an attempt to raise money for expansion.

held firm into one that now has stockholders, issues dividends, and has a board of directors.[1] It allows companies to grow far beyond what owners can borrow or otherwise raise themselves. Though such firms can incorporate and sell stock among a limited number of people,[2] an IPO opens up the possibility that an unlimited number of people, or even other corporations, can become its investors.

For stocks that are not IPOs, the market has two effects. First, it has the effect of spreading risk equally across all stocks to all stockholders. In economic terms, it equalizes the risk-adjusted rates of return across investments. If one company is going to yield a return on equity that is greater than another, the market price of the share of stock of the better company will rise until the return is equal to any new investors. In this way the stock market provides a way of signaling value to all future investors.

An additional important effect of the non-IPO market is that it provides liquidity to those shares of stock that were previously issued. IPOs only have value when their owners know that they can sell them if they wish to turn their investments into cash. Without a market for previously issued securities, it would be overly costly to issue new ones.

Efficient Markets

A market is labeled **efficient** by economists if all available information is accounted for in the market. For in-

efficient market
All information is taken into account by participants in a market.

stance, if markets are efficient, the price of a share of stock will encapsulate everything that investors know about that stock. If investors are concerned that a product that a company sells is likely to generate cumbersome lawsuits, for example, the market price will fall by the value that the market places on the uncertainty it is feeling about the company and on the expected legal exposure.

What this "efficient market hypothesis" means for everyday investors is that they do not have to worry about outsmarting the market. The Wall Street gurus who spend every waking minute looking for new information on the market will bid prices up and down in appropriate ways as new information on profits, risks,

and interest rates comes in. Since all of that information will be absorbed into the market long before most other investors find out about it, most other investors cannot take advantage of it. As unlikely as it may seem, new investors can simply invest in whatever they like, knowing that the chances are good that anything they pick will have the same chances of doing as well as anything else a professional outside Wall Street might pick.

While maintaining a diverse portfolio of investments is less risky than picking a specific stock, investors do not always have enough money to buy a variety of different stocks. Such investors can avail themselves of index funds, which buy stocks in exact proportion to their

stock index
A weighted average of stock prices in a particular group.

value in a commonly known **stock index**, like the Dow Jones Industrial, Standard and Poor's, and NASDAQ (see Figures 40.1 to 40.3). Since a stock index is simply a weighted average of stock prices in a particular group, buying shares of an index fund provides diversity and an expected return that is on a par with any other investment involving similar risk.

The best evidence that markets are efficient is the stories you hear about how well monkeys do when picking stocks. Newspapers often compare the hypothetical monetary returns earned from a monkey's random choices with the returns generated by professional investors. Unhappily for the professionals, monkeys have been known to hold their own.

Stock Market Crashes

The American stock market "crashed" twice in the 20th century, once in October 1929 and again in October 1987. In both cases a loss of at least 25 percent of the stock market's total value was experienced in a matter of days. The real question that economists who believe that stock markets are rational have to answer is this: Is it possible that expectations of things that are fundamental can change for everyone simultaneously and by amounts necessary to change stock prices that much?

If the answer to that question is "no," that things that are fundamental cannot change that much or that fast, then the stock market is not much more socially useful than a casino. On the other hand, if you can explain everything that goes on in a stock market in terms of changes in fundamental economic variables, then, as we explained before, the stock market is socially useful.

---

[1] Sometimes IPOs are not so small. When AT&T spun off its hardware division, Lucent, that IPO was very large.

[2] Such an entity is called an S-corporation.

Bubbles

It is crucial for us to know how a stock market, or how any market for anything else, crashes. If people invest their savings for retirement, college, or anything else, and their investments are going to be subject to wild swings, then it is important to know whether increases in stock prices happen because of increases in value or because of what economists call **bubbles**. A bubble of any kind grows slowly and looks very nice while it exists, but, when bubbles break, they break fast and ugly. The metaphor of a bubble is often used to describe an asset market that grows beyond all economic reason.

bubble
The state of a market where the current price is far above its value determined by fundamentals.

The two fundamentals that go into the formula for the value of an asset are the flow of payments it produces and the interest rate. The price of a stock can change a great deal if either of these changes a great deal. Economists are not overly concerned about this, and their lack of concern becomes justified when the stock prices of companies that are believed to generate losses in the short run and great profits in later years vary quite a bit with a change in interest rates. This variability does not bother economists much even if the stock price can change by a large percentage in a short time. The expected flow of payments, or profits, also is not likely to change quickly enough to change the price of the stock greatly or quickly.

The main source of crashes and the bursting bubbles is more likely to be abrupt changes in the sale price that is projected for the future. This is especially true if our expectations of future prices are based, at least in part, on current prices. For instance, because today's price is $90, you may think the price next year will be $100. If the price today were $80, you might expect that the future price might be $90, and so on.

The bubble bursts when a stock price falls and you think this indicates that it will be worth less next year. That makes you think that its value today is lessened. Now you start thinking that its value will be even less next year, and its current value becomes even less in your mind. This vicious cycle spirals the value of the stock down, and it can all happen very fast. As we discussed earlier, nearly every stock in the world lost in the neighborhood of 25 percent of its value within hours of the start of the October 1987 crash.

If stock market crashes had no impacts other than hurting some of the investors who hung on too long, there would be no issue of concern. The problem is that stock market crashes have real impacts on average families. When stocks are doing very well, people feel richer, and they are richer. They do not have to save as much because their previous savings are doing so well. As a result, they feel comfortable buying new homes, cars, major appliances, and furniture that they would not have purchased if things were not as good.

Homes, cars, appliances, and furniture are all goods that have to be made by industry, and industry runs on its workers. When the demand for their labor is high, workers get more hours, better pay, and a host of other benefits. With better pay, workers are richer, and they buy more and more. This is an economically virtuous cycle in which good times create more good times. A good stock market causes a good economy, and a good economy fosters an even better stock market. Unfortunately, we cannot avoid the reality that what goes up can also come down. When the stock market falls, people lose wealth, and they then buy fewer goods. Stock values fall even lower; consumption drops even further.

The doldrums within Japan's stock market lasted for all of the decade of the 1990s. Japan's equivalent to the Dow Jones Industrial Average, the Nikkei Index, remained depressed during a time in which the American stock market values tripled. The virtuous cycle that existed in the United States during the 1990s and the vicious cycle that existed in Japan during the same period give testimony to two important conclusions: (1) A stock market's health influences the rest of the economy and (2) stock prices can rise and fall very quickly.

Example of a Crash: NASDAQ 2000

In 1999 the NASDAQ (National Association of Securities Dealers Automated Quotations) increased 84 percent from 2,208 to 4,069 on the back of a technology sector that seemed to grow without bound. By March 10, 2000, the NASDAQ was above 5,000. The NASDAQ did not finally bottom out until October of 2002 when it reached a low of 1,114. What could have happened that an entire market index would lose 78 percent of its value in 31 months (see Figure 40.4)?

There are a number of explanations. Some of them revolve around our notion of the bubble while others are more fundamental. The technology sector in general, and some of the hottest companies in particular, were operating with staggering losses while being touted as leaders of the "new economy." As a matter of fact, for the dot-coms, making a profit was a sign of "stagnant thinking." New-economy thinking led firms to plow everything they made into improving name recognition and

FIGURE 40.4 NASDAQ Composite Index, 1999–2003.

Source: MSN Money, http://money.msn.com

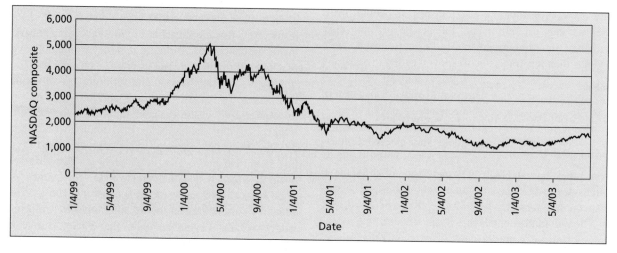

market share. To this end, the 1999 and 2000 Super Bowl broadcasts were filled with elaborate multimillion-dollar-per-minute dot-com ads.

Expectations for these companies were that losses now would be more than made up for with massive profits later. If you do the math, and we will avoid that here, you will see that anytime you have losses early on and profits much later, the net present value of this investment can change quite rapidly with reasonably small changes in interest rates or profit expectations.

To see this, take a hypothetical dot-com that is expected to lose $1 per share for 10 years and then make $5 per share thereafter. If the appropriate interest rate on a comparably risky investment is 10 percent, then, using the fundamentals, the stock would be worth $14.44. If you increase the interest rate to 11 percent, the stock's value would drop to $11.23. A 10 percent increase (1 percentage point) in the interest rate would translate to a 22 percent drop in the value of the stock. If the expected profit to the company had been spread out evenly throughout the lifetime of a company of equal value, an increase in the interest rate of 1 percentage point would only decrease the value of the stock to $13.13. Thus, one explanation of the drop in the NASDAQ is that interest rates rose during the period.

A second explanation of the drop in the NASDAQ is diminished profit expectations. Again, because the profits were expected to come much later in the process, small changes had large effects. Continuing with our hypothetical dot-com, a drop in profit expectations to $4 per share, even keeping interest rates constant at

10 percent, would drop the value of the share of stock to $10.22. Thus, a 20 percent drop in profit expectations drops the share price 29 percent.

The final explanation for the 1999 run-up and the 2000–2001 tumble is the bubble explanation. Recall that a bubble is the metaphor for an asset whose value has stretched far beyond its fundamental value, based on the notion that expected increases in the asset price are self-fulfilling. Whether the NASDAQ in March 2000 was in a bubble state is in some dispute because of the aforementioned changes in fundamentals that occurred during the period. On the other hand, there is little doubt that the buying frenzy among investors in 1999 and early 2000 was fed by the desire by many not to be left out of "the next Microsoft" or "the next Intel." Thus, if people buy without regard to the fundamentals, a bubble is created, and when fundamentals are reexamined, bubbles burst.

The Accounting Scandals of 2001 and 2002

In the aftermath of the September 11, 2001, attacks on New York City's World Trade Center buildings and the recession of 2001, the Enron Corporation declared bankruptcy. Enron, the United States' seventh-largest corporation in terms of revenue, declared **bankruptcy**, owing more than $5 billion and lacking the

bankruptcy
A legal status entered into when a company or individual cannot pay its debt.

creditors
The people or institutions to which a company or individual owes money.

ability to pay the interest on that debt. Companies or individuals declare bankruptcy when they lack the necessary funds to pay their **creditors**. While Kmart and Global Crossing also declared bankruptcy during the same period of time, the Enron bankruptcy made far more news. Why? Kmart served many more customers, and Global Crossing was more in debt ($12 billion), but Enron's demise was potentially far more damaging.

Bankruptcy

When a corporation cannot pay its creditors, it must either renegotiate the repayment schedule that it has with its creditors or it must declare bankruptcy. When a company declares bankruptcy, it has two choices: It can try to reorganize and go forward or it can simply give up. The former, called *Chapter 11* bankruptcy, protects a company from its creditors so as to give the company time to get its financial affairs back on track. The latter, called *Chapter 13* bankruptcy, lets the company sell off its assets in an orderly fashion so as to preserve as much value as possible for the last-in-line stockholders. Nearly every case of corporate bankruptcy you hear on the news is of the Chapter 11 variety.

When a company declares bankruptcy, a judge is appointed to oversee its financial affairs. Major financial decisions, such as the sale of assets, must first be approved by the judge.

Why Capitalism Needs Bankruptcy Laws

While on the surface it may seem strange that the ability to avoid debts would be viewed as a "good" thing, under capitalism bankruptcy laws actually aid economic efficiency. Without the ability to seek protection from your creditors, even a temporary inability to pay your debts would make it so that any one of them could foreclose on the business. This could reduce or even eliminate the business's ability to turn things around. It would happen because, while it would be in the collective interest of the creditors for the company to get back on its feet, it would be in their individual interest to be the first in line to get their money back.

Suppose, for example, that a company owes money to three different banks. Suppose, too, that the company has insufficient funds to pay these creditors this year but that, given the chance, it can probably make enough money over the next few years to pay them what it owes. Further suppose that if the company sells its assets, it can

pay what it owes to only two of the three banks. Without the protection of Chapter 11 bankruptcy, it would be in the interests of each of the banks individually to foreclose because each would not want to be the one bank that wasn't paid. In an apparent contradiction, it might easily also be in the banks' interests for the company to be allowed to continue without anyone foreclosing. Bankruptcy laws enable firms to continue under judicial supervision and afford all concerned the hope that they will pay off their debts.

The Kmart and Global Crossing Cases

When Kmart and Global Crossing filed for Chapter 11 bankruptcy in 2002, economists found the reasons to be familiar and not all that troubling. Kmart, in the middle of a discount store sandwich with Walmart and Target, went bankrupt because it was not able to discount as deeply as Walmart, nor was it able to market to upscale consumers as effectively as Target. Global Crossing took a gigantic gamble borrowing billions to string fiber-optic cable under the oceans, connecting Europe, Asia, and North America with Internet-friendly broadband connections.

Bankruptcies like these do not trouble economists in the way they appear to disturb people in the press, bankers, and shareholders. Economists hold that when companies get outcompeted, it's right that they lose money. Further, when they do it long enough, they should go out of business. They maintain that capitalism works only when the promise of profit is countered by the threat of bankruptcy. Incompetence and risky business decisions that turn out badly must have consequences, and in the cases of Kmart and Global Crossing this is exactly what happened. Kmart suffered from management and marketing strategies that were not up to those of the competition. Global Crossing operated on the premise that intercontinental bandwidth would be a hot commodity, and it used debt to finance its decision. AT&T, which is in the same market and raised its money with sales of stock and reinvested profits, also made little money in this market. It survived because its losses resulted only in disappointing earnings to stockholders. Global Crossing, on the other hand, could not generate enough profit to pay the interest on its $12 billion debt.

Both Kmart and Global Crossing declared bankruptcy even though they possessed more in assets than they owed their creditors. Kmart had $16 billion in assets and $2 billion in debts while Global Crossing had $22 billion in assets and $12 billion in debts. There were two problems, though: The assets were listed at book value rather than market value, and the assets were not such that they were producing revenue.

Two examples may illustrate the problem. When Kmart builds a store and outfits it with the Kmart logo and colors, it may cost $10 million, but there is no one who will pay $10 million for it after it is built. Similarly, it may have cost Global Crossing $20 billion to lay fiber-optic cable from one end of the ocean to another, but that by no means suggests that anyone will buy it from Global Crossing for that amount of money.

To illustrate further the circumstance in which there are many assets and no revenue from those assets with which to pay creditors, suppose someone is worth $5 billion and borrows $10 billion to buy gold coins. The person has an asset worth $10 billion but has no revenue coming in to pay the interest on the debt. Now suppose the person takes those coins and drops them one by one in the ocean between New York and London. Our hypothetical person now has $15 billion in assets on his or her books, but the coins that are apparently worth $10 billion may actually be worth next to nothing. There is genuinely $10 billion worth of debt with no revenue in sight to pay for the interest that is accruing on it.

What Happened in the Enron Case

Usually it is not that difficult to say what a business does. Walmart, for example, is a discount retailer; GM makes cars; and State Farm sells insurance. To get a handle on what happened in the Enron case, you have to understand Enron's actual business activities. What did Enron do to make money? It was an energy trading company. It bought electricity, oil, natural gas, gasoline, and other energy sources from producers, with the intent of reselling them to industrial companies and utilities. It made money by "buying low and selling high." It did this rather well for several years during the 1990s. Later it started getting into sideline businesses such as the buying and selling of bandwidth for the Internet.

"Buying low and selling high" is always good business practice, but it is hard to sustain because economic profit always induces entry (i.e., new competition), especially when there are few barriers. Enron had few competitors in this industry in the early 1990s, but when other companies saw that profits were achievable in this arena, they jumped in. With no barriers against getting into the arena, Dynegy Inc., Reliant Energy, El Paso Energy, Duke Energy North American, and Calpine Corp. joined the competition, and they raided Enron for valued employees who knew the game. Had this been the end

of the story, there would not have been much of a story at all. It would have been the typical "company has idea, milks it for as long as it can, and then settles in for a run of normal profits."

What happened with Enron was that its management wanted to keep things going and its executives were paid almost exclusively in stock and stock options. One of the classic problems in corporate capitalism is called the **principal–agent problem,** a problem that occurs when the owners of the company (the shareholders) are motivated by long-term profitability for the company and the managers are motivated by monetary gain for themselves. When chief executive officers (CEOs) are paid high salaries, they may avoid potentially lucrative business avenues that might be accompanied by some level of risk. The problem is that the agent, in this case the CEO, is not making decisions consistent with the principals' (in this case the stockholders') wishes. The primary concern in this example of the principal–agent problem is that salaried CEOs will avoid risking their jobs and will err on the side of caution.

principal–agent problem
The problem that occurs when the owner of an asset and the manager of that asset are different and have different preferences.

For years it has been taken on faith that the best way for stockholders to get the CEO to do their bidding was to tie the CEO's compensation to stock performance. One version of this has the CEO paid only in stock. Thus, when stock prices are low the CEO is paid less than when the stock price is high.

An extreme version of this scheme is in place when management is paid in stock options. Stock options are authorizations that allow those who hold them to buy a specific number of shares of stock at the price stated on the option. They are enormously valuable when the stock price is above the option price but have no value when the underlying stock price is below the option price. Enron's compensation package for its managers was a combination of stocks and options.

Enron's management compensation was thus tied to stock performance, and in the eyes of Enron shareholders, this was good. Their perception was that management decisions that affected the company in good ways were rewarded while those that affected the company in bad ways were punished. It unfortunately also put management in a position such that if it could deceive the *markets* into thinking that it was doing better than it actually was, then management could enrich itself. This is not new. This is the primary reason why accounting firms exist. They are supposed to guard against such deception by going over the corporate financial statements of the companies they audit so as to certify to the public that when a company says it earned $1 billion, it actually did.

Enron's deception took the form of high-debt, off-the-books gambles. Enron created several subsidiaries, named, for whatever reason, for "Star Wars" characters, and it saddled each with millions in debt. Each subsidiary had a high-risk, high-return niche market. None of this would be interesting except for the fact that the debt of these firms was secured by assets of the larger corporation. That in turn would not be interesting except that this debt was deceptively noted in Enron financial statements.

Enron would state that it was owed money by other companies; it would report this as an asset but would not mention that it was also a debt. Even more troubling, the smaller subsidiaries would borrow from banks to pay Enron the interest, thus raising Enron's reported profits. In the final analysis, Enron was overstating its profits by $1.2 billion and its assets by even more.

When the whole thing collapsed in the fall of 2001, there were two fatally wounded companies: Enron and its accounting firm, Arthur Andersen. Andersen had certified Enron's books to be accurate when they demonstrably were not. It had participated in the creation of the subsidiaries and had gone along with the attempt to cover things up by issuing a reminder to employees working on the Enron account to shred "unneeded" documents. Though this "reminder" was technically a simple restatement of company policy, everyone at Andersen who worked on the Enron case knew that it meant to shred the evidence. Why would an accounting firm participate in such fraud? It again boils down to the principal–agent problem. The lead accountant in any firm wants to please his or her clients. The clients pay the firms millions in fees per year for which the lead accountants are handsomely rewarded. The *principal,* the accounting firm, must trust the action of its *agent,* the lead accountant. Their interests are sometimes at odds because the accounting firm is worthless without a reputation for honesty. That reputation was effectively sold by the lead accountant, without Andersen's knowledge or consent. The upshot of all this was that Andersen was destroyed by the actions of its lead accountant in the Enron case.

Why the Enron Case Matters More Than the Others

The Kmart and Global Crossing cases really do not have much influence on the economy as a whole, but the Enron debacle is an ominous sign of a systemic problem.

Economically speaking, Kmart's loss is Walmart's and Target's gain. Global Crossing rolled the dice and it came up "snake-eyes." The risk associated with buying Global Crossing stock was pretty well understood, and if international bandwidth markets had taken off, Global Crossing stockholders would have made a fortune. Because they did not, and because the firm was very much in debt, the stockholders were left with nearly worthless stock. Enron stockholders were simply lied to. Investors must be able to rely on the veracity of financial statements.

Investors take calculated risks. They assemble the information and make decisions based on that information. The area of uncertainty that investors expect is that of the return to be received from their investments. Some companies make a profit and others do not. They seek to avoid the uncertainty over the veracity of financial reports by insisting on independent audits. If accounting firms aid the company's deceptive tactics rather than uncover them, then investors are left with two areas of uncertainty: (1) Will the company make money? and (2) Will the financial statements tell me the truth? The additional uncertainty about the accuracy of audits raises the required rate of return on stocks and results in inhibiting some profitable business avenues.

As a direct result of problems evidenced by Enron and Andersen, other companies began to reveal their own "overstatements" of profits. One by one, Xerox, World-Com, and other corporate giants came out with earnings "corrections." As a result, investors continued to lose confidence through 2002, and stock values dropped an additional 20 percent from levels that were already 20 percent to 60 percent below the levels of March 2000. It was not until the early spring of 2003 that the markets began to shake off the effects of these scandals.

Rebound of 2006–2007 and the Drop of 2008–2009

As the economy grew out of the 2001 recession, stocks were slow to recover. By mid-2008, however, the DJIA and S&P500 had reached or exceeded their March 2000 levels (though the NASDAQ stood at barely half its all-time high). What was behind this resurgence? Profits and persistently low long-term interest rates, fundamental determinants of stock market value, reasserted themselves during 2006 through early 2008.

It was another bubble, the housing bubble, described in Chapter 11, that then came crashing down on the heads of investors in 2008. Companies, especially financial services companies, with significant exposure to housing finance were the first to drop. By Labor Day 2008, it was clear that the problems of the housing and financial services industry would not be confined to just those industries.

Not all drops in the stock market result from bursting bubbles. When the automakers and their parts suppliers experienced a dramatic drop in sales and losses topped $10 billion per quarter at General Motors, few economists were calling it a bubble in this area. These changes were part of the fundamental aspect of what stock markets do. When profit expectations fall because of poor sales, stock prices fall.

Bank and insurance stocks were hit by a very high level of uncertainty. The across-the-board drop in these stocks was due to investor concern about their ability to distinguish between healthy and vulnerable financial institutions. The concern was magnified by the fact that the rating agencies, Standard and Poor's and Moody's, had failed to forecast the problems with housing generally and AIG in particular.

As 2009 was moving into 2010 and beyond and the economy began to recover (albeit at a painfully slow pace), the stock market made handsome gains. These gains, it must be said, were driven by the two fundamentals: profit expectations and interest rates. Corporate profits increased much faster during this period than did any other economic measure. The reason was that employers of all varieties found that once they got past the recession's bottom and had made adjustments to their labor force, the remaining workers were quite productive. Sales increased while, for the most part, costs did not. The result was higher profits and those higher profits created expectations of higher future profits. Combined with low interest rates, the result was a 134 percent rise in the Dow Jones Industrial Average from its March 2009 lows to its level in June 2013.

Summary

You now understand how stock prices are determined and what stock markets do. You should understand the fundamental elements of stock prices and understand how prices can get out of line with their fundamental value. You were able to see these concepts at work as you read about the Asian financial crisis of the late 1990s and the NASDAQ of 2000. You understand the economic need for bankruptcy law and the consequences of the accounting scandals and bankruptcies of 2001 and 2002. Finally, you understand that the drop in stock market prices during 2008 and 2009 resulted from fundamental changes to profitability.

Key Terms

bankruptcy, 434
bubble, 433
creditors, 435

efficient market, 432
fundamentals, 431
initial public offering (IPO), 431

principal–agent problem, 436
stock index, 432

Quiz Yourself

1. The fundamental value of a share of stock is based on the present value of expected future
   a. dividends.
   b. revenues.
   c. profits.
   d. costs.

2. A stock index is
   a. essentially the weighted sum of stock prices.
   b. the simple sum of stock prices.
   c. the geometric average of stock prices.
   d. the consensus view of professional economists.

3. If you invested in 20 different companies and chose those companies at random, you would be counting on the _____ market hypothesis and its implication that you would do as well as you would with any other investment strategy.
   a. random
   b. complete
   c. stock
   d. efficient

4. Stock market crashes tend to result when stocks get _____ their fundamental values.
   a. too far below
   b. too close to
   c. too far above
   d. confused with

5. A stock market exists
   a. only to service the sale of new issues, called IPOs.
   b. to provide liquidity to all stocks, including recent IPOs.
   c. to help policy makers predict the future.
   d. to make the rich richer.

6. The principal–agent problem centers on the separation of
   a. supply and demand.
   b. investors and savers.
   c. owners and managers.
   d. interest and dividends.

Short Answer Questions

1. Explain why the announcement of higher interest rate targets by the Federal Reserve (if they were at least somewhat of a surprise) would likely result in lower stock prices.

2. Explain why, if a company's profits are growing at rates greater than the current interest rates and have been expected to continue doing so for several more years, a stock price can greatly exceed what might otherwise seem reasonable for the sum of the assets of that company.

3. Explain why a stock market must exist for the re-sale of stock first issued many years ago for newly issued stock (an IPO) to garner significant interest among investors.

4. Explain how the "bubble" process, in which expectations get way out in front of reality on the upside, can be duplicated on the downside, causing a stock to fall below a reasonable level.

Think about This

Not all asset bubbles are related to stocks. In 2005 there was a concern about housing prices on the coasts exceeding all rational prices. One of history's bubbles involved tulip bulbs. The problem is that bubbles are easier to recognize in retrospect. Are there any assets you can think of that currently look like a bubble?

Talk about This

Stock markets are designed to allow corporations to raise initial capital. In providing liquidity to previously issued securities, they enhance that function. For these benefits we devote some of our best and brightest financial minds. Is that a good use of resources?

For More Insight See

Journal of Economic Perspectives 4, no. 2 (Spring 1990). See articles by Joseph E. Stiglitz; Andrei Schliefer and Lawrence H. Summers; Peter M. Garber; Robert J. Schiller; Eugene N. White; and Robert P. Flood and Robert J. Hodrick.

Behind the Numbers

Historical data.
   Dow Jones Industrial Average; S&P 500; Nasdaq; http://finance.yahoo.com

CHAPTER FORTY-ONE

Unions

Learning Objectives

After reading this chapter you should be able to:

LO1 Describe why labor unions exist and model how they alter the bargaining relationship between employers and employees.

LO2 Distinguish between a competitive labor market and one where there is market power only with the employer, only with the employee, and when both have power.

LO3 Differentiate between labor unions that seek to raise wages by reducing supply and those that seek to raise wages by using collective bargaining as a monopolist.

LO4 Use knowledge of the history of unions in the United States to predict the future of unionization in the United States.

Chapter Outline

Why Unions Exist

A Union as a Monopolist

The History of Labor Unions

Where Unions Go from Here

Kick It Up a Notch

Summary

The role of labor unions in the United States has been the subject of some controversy for more than 100 years. As the economy developed from agriculture to industrial manufacturing, labor issues came to the forefront. Although the struggle to organize labor to demand better treatment began much earlier, it was not until the 1930s that legislation was enacted giving workers the right to bargain collectively and to join unions. Unions grew in influence and membership, with their representation in the work force peaking at nearly 30 percent in 1975. That year saw the beginning of a long and rapid decline, and unions now represent less than 15 percent of the total work force and less than 10 percent of the private work force.

On a theoretical level, we discuss here why unions are usually desirable in a manufacturing economy, and we show how they can serve the best interests of both laborers and the economy as a whole. We then survey the early struggles, the pertinent laws, and the successes and failures of unions. We use two measures of union power to illustrate the health of labor in the United States, and

we conclude with some insights into the ways unions are making the transition to the 21st century.

Why Unions Exist

The Perfectly Competitive Labor Market

When the United States was almost entirely agrarian in nature, aside from those who were enslaved, indentured, or otherwise beholden to masters of one sort or another, people worked mainly for themselves. Obviously, if you work for yourself, and outside influences are not at work, your pay and working conditions cannot be unfair since your own productivity determines your own wealth. As the United States grew throughout the 19th century, however, it evolved into an economy where fewer and fewer people worked for themselves. The industrial revolution came to the fore, and more and more people began to work for companies that manufactured goods. The supply and demand model of the economy supports us in

FIGURE 41.1 A labor market under perfect competition.

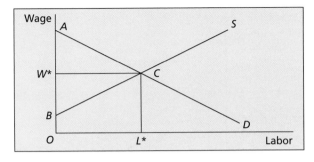

concluding that any time one person buys something from another person, there are gains to both sides. This applies to labor as well.

Figure 41.1 indicates that if the good being sold is labor, and the price at which it is sold is the wage, then, like any market in perfect competition, there is an equilibrium wage and an equilibrium amount sold that makes both parties better off than they were before the transaction took place. In Figure 41.1, at equilibrium the wage paid is W^* for L^* labor. The firm that hires the labor pays it OW^*CL^*, values it at (i.e., generates revenue from the sales of output from it of) $OACL^*$, and therefore gets the difference that is its consumer surplus (or profit) of W^*AC. The workers get paid OW^*CL^* when it costs them only $OBCL^*$ in opportunity cost to provide their efforts. As a result, they get producer surplus of BW^*C. There is no other wage–labor combination that provides as much surplus to the combination of both workers and firms as this one.

In a fairly subtle way, we conditioned all this on the assumption that there was perfect competition in the labor market. This means that there are many independent firms and many independent—that is, nonunion—workers, so that neither buyers nor sellers of labor have any control over the wage. Perfect competition also requires that all parties involved have good information about their alternatives.

A Reaction to Monopsony

We can safely assume that there is perfect competition if we are talking about a very large city and a field that is not particularly specialized. For instance, there are many carpenters in large cities, and there are many contractors who hire them. On the other hand, competition can be a lot less than perfect for two reasons, which both boil down to whether the number of firms buying labor is limited. The most extreme example of this would be a so-called company town, where only one firm buys labor in a particular area. Though company towns tend to be rare today, towns like Redmond, Washington, with Microsoft, and State College, Pennsylvania, with Penn State University, are close. On the other hand, history is replete with companies that literally owned entire towns. Mining towns were especially likely to be company towns, with all the problems of paternalistic control and subjugation of workers with which they have been associated.

The case where the specialization is so narrow that there are at most only a few potential buyers of that skill is one that is somewhat different in cause but similar in effect. This is fairly common in high-skill specialties where there is only one employer in a large area. You may be actually sitting at a chair in such a location. While assistant, associate, and full professors in colleges earn pretty good salaries, adjunct professors at colleges and universities are paid very little. Faculty at midlevel universities often earn in the neighborhood of $70,000 and teach four to six courses per year. Though there are research and service obligations to their jobs, their salaries translate to between $12,000 and $17,500 per course. Adjuncts are often paid less than $3,000 for a semester-long course. Many colleges are in towns where they are the only employer of people with masters and doctoral degrees (especially in the arts and humanities). For that reason, for people who are in the college town as a result of their spouse's work, a college can offer to pay them very little and still get relatively high-quality instruction.

Regardless of the reason, if it is the case that there is only one employer in an area, that employer has power that is very similar to the monopoly power enjoyed by utilities. Recall that under monopoly there is only one seller of a good and that seller can charge very high prices.

monopsony
A market with only one buyer.

When the market has only one buyer, a **monopsony** exists. In a monopsony the seller rather than the buyer is exploited.

Figure 41.2 shows how monopsony alters the perfectly competitive markets depicted in Figure 41.2. Before going into the detail of the graph, though, we need to step back and deal with a little labor vocabulary. As we mentioned briefly in the explanation of Figure 41.2, the demand curve for labor represents how much money an additional worker can generate for the firm as that worker increases production and therefore sales revenue. This is called the **marginal revenue product of labor,** and it is equal to the demand curve, because

marginal revenue product of labor
The additional revenue generated from hiring an additional worker.

FIGURE 41.2   A company town and a monopsony market for labor.

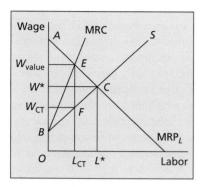

FIGURE 41.3   The impact of licensing.

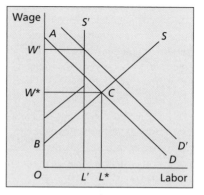

the firm will be willing to pay up to the amount of money it can make from its workers' efforts in order to squeeze all possible profit out of its labor force.

In addition, since there is only one buyer of labor, the firm is not looking at an equilibrium wage that it must pay its employees. The firm decides how much labor it wants, and it pays the minimum required to get that labor. To get more workers, it not only has to pay the new workers more; it also has to pay all workers more. Thus if the firm wants to hire more workers, its costs do not rise along the supply curve; they rise faster. The cost of increasing hiring is therefore not the supply curve but the curve that is labeled the **marginal resource cost (MRC)** in Figure 41.2. This shows the increase in total labor costs to the firm of buying increasing amounts of labor.

marginal resource cost (MRC)
The increase in total labor costs to the firm of buying increasing amounts of labor.

To solidify this in your mind, consider Table 41.1. The first column represents the wage that is paid. The second is the quantity supplied. The third, the total cost to the employer, is the product of the first and second. The final column is the difference in the total cost from one worker to the next. Notice that it rises substantially faster than the first column.

The monopsonist firm maximizes profit when it hires at the point where the marginal revenue product of labor

TABLE 41.1   Relationship between supply and marginal resource cost.

Wage	Quantity Supplied	Total Cost to the Employer	Marginal Resource Cost
5	1	5	
6	2	12	7
7	3	21	9
8	4	32	11
9	5	45	13

equals the marginal resource cost. In Figure 41.2 this is L_{CT} (i.e., in a company town) rather than L^* workers. To find what these workers are paid, we take L_{CT} up to the supply curve to get W_{CT}. If we want to know what these workers are worth, we go up to the demand curve to find that the amount of money they are making for the company is W_{value}. It should be clear that under monopsony workers do not earn what they are worth. As a check, note that under perfect competition, at L^*, workers earn their marginal revenue product; that is, they earn exactly what they are worth.

A Way to Restrict Competition and Improve Quality

Some unions and professional organizations enhance the pay of their members by restricting the supply of workers and by increasing the value of their members. Thus Figure 41.3 alters Figure 41.1 by reflecting the reduction in potential workers as a changing of the shape of the supply curve. First, the supply curve moves to the left because there is a cost to the employee of learning how to become skilled in this area. The costs to the newly licensed employees are reflected in the general movement of the supply curve to the left. Since the number of openings for training in the field, here noted as L', is limited, the supply curve is perfectly inelastic at that point. Because there is an improvement in skills of the workers and the quality of their work, there is a movement of the demand curve to the right. This raises the wage to those who ultimately work in the field. Among others, the American Medical Association, the American Bar Association, the International Brotherhood of Electrical Workers, and the Plumbers and Steamfitters[1] all follow this pattern.

By restricting the ability of people to become workers in a particular field, these types of unions keep the

[1]The United Association of Journeymen and Apprentices of the Plumbing and Pipe Fitting Industry of the United States and Canada.

supply of workers down. You cannot practice medicine or law without a license, and that license serves as a mechanism to restrict competition. While you can wire your own house or do your own plumbing, in many communities you cannot sell these services to others without a license.

The other side of Figure 41.3 is the increase in demand. Because of the training that union plumbers and electricians get, we can model their increased productivity and quality as an increase in the demand for their services. Thus, having a certification process also increases the pay of these workers, because an increase in the demand occurs for their services. As you can see, the net result is an increase in the price of these services and an uncertain effect on the numbers of these services that are provided.

If, on the other hand, the net effect of unionization of this form is that the labor sold is reduced, then unionization of this type detracts from economic efficiency. Otherwise, unionization is neutral or good for it. Though there is considerable debate among labor economists on this point, they tend to suggest that the net impact of licensing is generally negative.

A Reaction to Information Issues

Another reason that the actual market for labor may not be the perfectly competitive version is that workers may not have good information about other positions they might fill. Workers who explore other prospects tend to be viewed as disloyal by their bosses and co-workers. To avoid this perception as well as the effort of looking for a new job, people may not know what they are worth elsewhere. Though it was not stated above, one of the things that makes the perfectly competitive labor market perfect—workers earn what they are worth—is that workers who are paid less than market wages know it and will move on to other, better-paying jobs. If they do not know about the other jobs, they are not likely to move even when they are poorly paid or poorly treated.

There are a couple of ways that this works to hurt workers. The first, as stated above, is that there is a tendency for employers and co-workers to distrust people seeking better jobs, especially when those better jobs are with the competition. Therefore, there is sociological "peer pressure" that stands in the way of workers finding out what they are worth. Second, employers are not above conspiring with one another to strike fear into workers. This works when there is a limited number of firms and they collude in agreeing not to bid against one another for workers. When this works, each of the firms can threaten "disloyal" workers with statements like "you will never work in this town again."

A Union as a Monopolist

Unions exist to ensure that workers get at least what they are worth in a perfectly competitive market and possibly more. In economic speak, laborers band together in unions so they can force employers to provide them with wages that are equal to their marginal revenue product. They do this by countering the market power that firms have with market power of their own. Unions are most effective when they are the single seller to a firm's single buyer. Sometimes unions such as the United Auto Workers, the United Mine Workers, and the Teamsters[2] provide labor to many different buyers of labor. In such cases, it is the union that possesses the sole market power.

The formal model of unions is the same as the model of monopolies. In Figure 41.4 you see the impact of having a union control all labor. The marginal revenue to the union is set equal to the supply curve to find the amount of labor the union wishes to provide. This occurs at L_{union}. That means that wages are higher than before, as W_{union} exceeds W^*. If we look at unions as if they existed in a vacuum, it would appear they are bad for the economy, since the consumer surplus falls by less than producer surplus grows, so unions appear to hurt the economy.

Unions did not arise and they do not exist in a vacuum. In some cases, poor treatment, poor pay, or both poor pay and poor treatment encouraged workers to organize. For others, Figure 41.4 depicts the end of the story. When unions simply use their monopoly power to sell labor to different competitive firms, then the existence of the union detracts from economic efficiency. We can see,

FIGURE 41.4 A union's effect on wages in a perfectly competitive labor market.

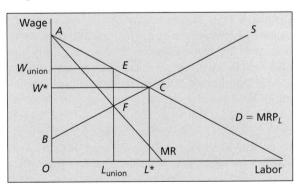

[2]The United Automobile, Aerospace, and Agricultural Implement Workers of America; the United Mine Workers of America; and the International Brotherhood of Teamsters, Chauffeurs, Warehousemen and Helpers of America, respectively.

FIGURE 41.5 The union fights the one-company town, or monopoly versus monopsony.

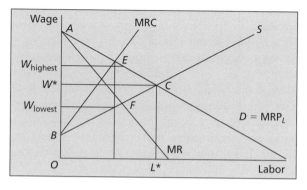

though, that some workers lose opportunities to work, because L_{union} is less than L^*. We also see that the gain to those who keep their jobs is greater than the loss to those who lose theirs, because the producer surplus increases. Clearly the firms that do the hiring are worse off as their consumer surplus is reduced. The net effect is that unions reduce the total amount of the surplus.

To compare those unions that exist as a reaction to monopsony power to the case without the union, we need to combine Figures 41.2 and 41.4. In Figure 41.5 we can find out where the battle lines are drawn. In its monopolistic form the union will want to set the wages at $W_{highest}$. This is what the union would demand if it was bargaining with many different employers. The "company" that rules the company town will want to pay what it would have paid if it were bargaining with many independent workers, W_{lowest}. There are some sophisticated economic models that are designed to predict the outcome of bargaining between unions and firms, but at this point we have difficulty making good predictions about where within the range the wages will ultimately settle.

Once a wage has been agreed on in this range, the number of workers the employer will hire depends on the supply and demand curves. To find out exactly how many will be hired, remember that since we are not going to be at equilibrium, it will be the lower of quantity demanded and quantity supplied at that wage. To find quantity demanded at that wage, take that wage to the demand curve. Similarly, to find quantity supplied, go over to the supply curve. As long as the bargaining process works out between what unions want and what firms are willing to pay, the economy is better with a union in a company town than it is without a union in a company town. The result of the bargain is that the loss of consumer plus producer surplus is limited.

The History of Labor Unions

Labor organizations have existed in the United States since shoemakers banded together near the end of the American Revolutionary War. Labor's battle was largely unsuccessful until the beginning of the 20th century, though, because courts saw their actions as restraint of trade or conspiracy. Thus any union that organized and struck an employer for better conditions or better wages had these actions stopped by the courts.[3]

Before laws began to support laborers' attempts to form unions, and before unions had any rights under the law, there were court rulings that were decidedly anti-union. At one point, in a dispute between workers and a company that made railroad cars, sympathetic railroad workers refused to handle cars made by that particular company. The company retaliated by having U.S. mail cars attached to the "offending" company's cars. When railroad workers then uncoupled the mail cars from the company's cars in sympathy for the company's workers, they were jailed for conspiracy to tamper with the U.S. mail. From the end of the Civil War to 1914, the courts, Congress, and most presidents were beholden to large corporate interests, interests that saw that union members were fired, jailed, beaten, and killed. Seldom were they successful in getting pay increases.

All that began to change in 1914 when President Woodrow Wilson, a Democrat, was able to work with a Congress controlled by the Democrats. In that year, laws were enacted to grant labor rights. Although one of these laws, the Clayton Act, was overturned by the Supreme Court, its passage marked a clear dividing line between the political parties. Republicans sided with management and Democrats with organized labor.

Through the 1920s Republicans held both the presidency and Congress and nearly no headway was allowed for labor unions. The Great Depression, which started in 1929, changed the economic and political landscape. As millions of workers lost their jobs, Democrats were voted into office; and, under the presidency of Franklin Roosevelt, Congress enacted the Norris–La Guardia Act, the National Industrial Recovery Act, and the Wagner Act, among others. These laws reestablished labor rights that had been granted under the Clayton Act, and they created new ones. Under these acts, workers were given the right to organize

[3]See Campbell R. McConnell, Stanley L. Brue, and David A. MacPherson, *Contemporary Labor Economics*, 8th ed. (New York: Irwin/McGraw-Hill, 2008), Chapter 10.

and to bargain collectively. Additionally, they stipulated that exercising these rights could no longer be construed as conspiracy to restrain trade. The law now stated that whenever a majority of workers voted for union representation, the union was held to represent all workers, whether non-union workers wanted to be represented or not. In actuality, it was often the case that when a firm's workers were represented by a union, membership in that union was required as a condition of employment for all the employees.

These rights did not apply to everyone. Most notably, government employees were still forbidden from striking, but the new laws did give labor a great deal of muscle. As the economy surged out of the depression and into World War II, strikes were becoming commonplace. Strikes were considered serious enough that, during World War II, Congress temporarily gave the president power to seize control of industries in which strikes were considered to be jeopardizing the production of war material.

In the year following Japan's surrender in World War II, nearly 120 million workdays, 1.9 percent of all potential work time, were lost to strikes. In part, this was because a wide disparity existed between where wages were going before the war and where they were as a result of a wartime freeze. Since wages were frozen for much of the war, workers wanted to at least be paid what they would have been paid had the freeze not been in place. Management liked the low current wages and argued that the health insurance

benefits that were put in place to balance the wage freeze were sufficient to make up for the freeze.

As a result of depression-era laws, labor was still holding nearly all of the cards and was quite successful in achieving its aims. Organized labor was so successful that to keep its power in check, a Republican Congress passed the Taft–Hartley Act over President Harry Truman's veto.

The Taft–Hartley Act amended the Wagner Act in ways that gave management back some of the cards it had held in previous years. It allowed states to determine whether they would allow workers who did not want union representation to work for a company for whom a majority wanted union representation. It also allowed the president to order a cooling-off period, temporarily ending any strike that threatened the economic health of the nation.

In 1962 President John Kennedy issued an executive order that gave federal employees the right to unionize and to bargain collectively in ways they had not been able to do under the Wagner Act. Though still unable to strike, they were granted grievance procedures. Other protections were instituted that led greater numbers of public employees to form and to join unions.

A look at Figures 41.6 and 41.7 shows that since the time of President Kennedy, there has been a general decline in the number of workers who belong to unions. Though union power peaked in the middle 1970s, the decline has been long and consistent. The exception

FIGURE 41.6 Union membership as a percentage of the work force.

Source: Bureau of Labor and Statistics, www.bls.gov/news.release/union2.toc.htm

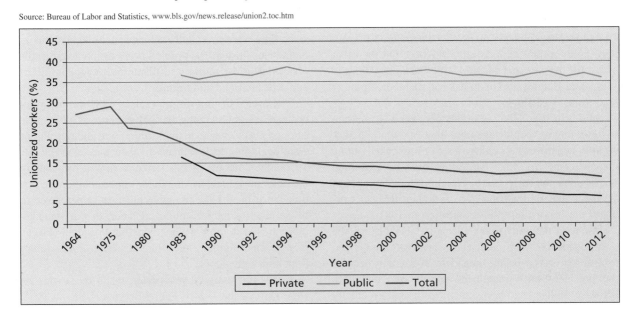

FIGURE 41.7   Lost time from strikes and lockouts.

Source: Bureau of Labor and Statistics, www.bls.gov/wsp

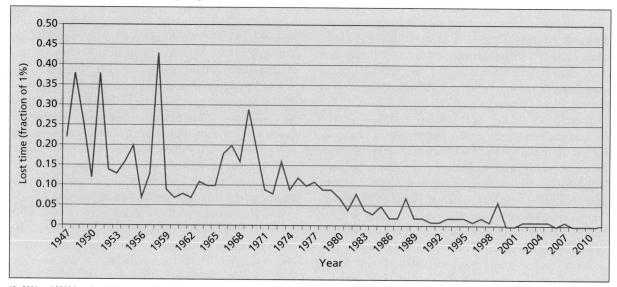

*In 2001 and 2002 less than 0.05 percent of work time was lost to strikes or lockouts.

has been the relative health of public employee unions. Figure 41.6 shows that the percentage of all workers who are unionized and the percentage of private-sector employees who are unionized have fallen dramatically since the 1980s. It further shows that the percentage of public employees who are unionized has stayed at a relatively constant 35 percent to 40 percent.

This difference between the health of public and private employees' unions is most clearly seen in just a few unions. The United Auto Workers lost nearly half of its 1.5 million members between 1978 and 1995. The United Steelworkers of America once numbered 1.3 million; today membership is only 400,000. On the other hand, the American Federation of State, County, and Municipal Employees Union has had membership more than triple since 1968.

Similarly, if you look at work stoppages as a measure of labor unions' confidence (that they can win in a situation in which workers either strike or are locked out by management), you find that unions have been running scared since the early 1980s. The drop in the number of strikes is generally attributed to President Reagan's firing of the striking air traffic controllers in 1981.

In one of the more ironic events in labor history, the only president of the United States who had ever belonged to a union or had been a president of a union became the president most identified with labor's downfall. President Reagan had been a member of, and eventually

president of, the Screen Actors' Guild. When the Professional Air Traffic Controllers Organization (PATCO), the union representing the air traffic controllers, struck in the summer of 1981, President Reagan followed the law, which unambiguously stated that public employees who engaged in strikes were to be terminated. At the time, hardly anyone thought he would actually follow through and fire the controllers, and virtually everyone thought he would hire them back after the strike was settled. When they struck, he fired them. He then ordered his secretary of transportation not to negotiate with them, since they were fired and no longer held legal status as employees. Instead, he ordered every available air traffic controller in the military to fill in until new controllers could be recruited and trained.

The events of this single week in 1981 are given inordinate weight by many, but it does serve as a timepost. Though PATCO was a small union and though unions were beginning to lose many of their battles in the late 1970s, the outcome of this strike is viewed by many in the labor movement as singularly important. For the first time since the 1930s, the government was perceived to be as much a foe of unionized labor as was management. It is even more ironic, then, that President Reagan garnered more union votes than any other 20th-century Republican president.

It was not until 17 years later, when the Teamsters Union struck the United Parcel Service (UPS) in 1998, that a major union won major concessions from an employer. Whether this strike serves as another turning point or simply magnifies labor's difficulties by serving as the exception that proves the rule will not be known for several years. For more than 15 years nearly every major strike left workers worse off than they had been when the strike started. The only exception to this generalization is strikes by already highly paid professional athletes, which succeeded in making them even more highly paid. Less than one-tenth of 1 percent of all work time was lost to strikes over the late 1990s, a consequence that can be attributed to the realization on the part of labor that they would lose any confrontation.

The ultimate reasons that organized labor won the UPS strike are the same as the reasons that any union wins a strike. The workers were not easily replaceable and the company that employed them had competitors that were taking its market share. The labor market of the late 1990s was such that finding dependable workers was difficult. This contrasts with strikes such as the strike by Caterpillar's Peoria, Illinois, workers in the early 1990s. In that period of time dependable workers willing to take jobs at $15 to $25 an hour were not difficult to find. In 1998 such workers were much more difficult to find. Thus, the Teamsters would demand higher wages. Another difference was that UPS saw its market share in the overnight delivery business disappear. The fear that customers would not return after the strike induced the company to settle. Conversely, Caterpillar had less of a concern that competitors would or could take market share for long because of Caterpillar's dominance in the heavy construction equipment industry.

In July 2005, the AFL-CIO had its most significant defections in decades as the Teamsters and other unions abandoned the umbrella organization. The dispute centered on whether the financial resources of the unions should be devoted to electing politicians sympathetic to union concerns or whether they should be devoted to increasing union membership by unionizing previously unorganized industries.

Where Unions Go from Here

Unions composed of men and women who work in the public sector will likely survive long into the future, as there are far fewer pressures on them than there are on unions in the private sector. For instance, if a car company decides it can no longer afford its union's pay demands, it can move its production facilities to a location where the workers are only too happy to take the jobs at whatever the company is offering. On the other hand, if a city cannot afford its firefighters' wage demands, it must negotiate. It cannot move to a location where it can hire other firefighters and pay lower wages.

Unions in the private sector are likely to have continuing difficulty for three basic reasons. First, because employment growth has been most evident in service and retail industries where many employers hire only a few employees each, unions have found it much more difficult to organize these workers. Second, since old-line manufacturing in areas like automobiles and steel is susceptible to international trade pressures to keep costs down, unions will have a hard time winning concessions even in industries in which they are still strong. Third, the impact of Walmart and other major retailers on consumer good manufacturers has been enormous. When firms are faced with a specific retailer that is responsible for nearly half their sales, and that retailer demands significant cost concessions, unions representing the employees of those manufacturing firms are faced with a tough choice. Either they give in to wage reductions or they risk having their jobs leave for foreign lower-cost venues. For these reasons the picture for private-sector unions is rather bleak.

In general, the health of private-sector unions will depend greatly on whether we return to the days when only a few major employers hired most workers. The information age has seen many start-up companies lure workers away from larger companies. The wages of computer engineers, programmers, and the employees who actually make computers are pretty close to what these workers are worth. If, on the other hand, the computer industry begins to centralize around only a few major employers and start-ups become rare, unions may finally make inroads into information-age industries. Unless that happens, public-sector unions may dominate the labor movement by the end of the 21st century.

Public-sector unions play an increasing role in our economy and in our politics. The tension between the Wisconsin governor and the public employees of that state in 2011 show why this is the case. Public employees are attached to their employer for a much longer period of time than private-sector employees. This is largely the case because public-sector employees remain on defined-benefit pension plans that reward longevity with one employer. Those pensions pay off very well for those people who join the police force, or the firefighters, or the school system when they are young and stay with them until retirement. None of these professions pay well in terms of salaries, but they all have benefit packages that well exceed what is typical for private-sector workers in that salary range. This is especially true when you count the near certainty of continued employment and the very low employee contribution rates for those benefits. The future for public-sector employees likely will continue

or fall on the basis of these public-sector unions' ability to retain that benefits advantage. They understand this very well, which is why public-sector employee unions are some of the most prolific contributors to politicians who protect their interests.

Kick It Up a Notch

Referring back to Figure 41.2 and using the notions of consumer and producer surplus introduced in Chapter 3, we can see that monopsony is worse than perfect competition. Firms do better because they pay less, and workers do worse because they make less. The net to society is reduced by EFC because the consumer surplus to firms is $W_{CT}AEF$ while the producer surplus to workers shrinks to $BW_{CT}F$. That combined area is less than the optimal level by EFC. We can conclude from the preceding that if the problem that

unions combat is monopsony, then unions can make things better by moving the market toward its original equilibrium.

In Figure 41.4 we see that the fall in consumer surplus is $W_{union}AE$ and the increase in producer surplus is $BW_{union}EF$. As a result, in combination there is a net reduction, and unions appear to hurt the economy. Remember from the body of the chapter, unions do not exist in a vacuum and are typically a reaction to something operating against workers.

Summary

You now understand why labor unions exist and how they alter the bargaining relationship between employers and employees. You understand how a competitive labor market differs from one where there is market power with only the employer, with only the employee, and when both have power. You understand that labor unions differ

in that some seek to raise wages by reducing supply, whereas others seek to raise wages by using collective bargaining as a monopolist. Last, you now understand how unions came about in the United States, and you have enough knowledge of recent history to be able to project where unionization is going in the United States.

Key Terms

marginal resource cost (MRC), 442   marginal revenue product of labor, 441   monopsony, 441

Quiz Yourself

1. When there is only one employer in a city, the model that economists use is one for
   a. monopoly.
   b. monopsony.
   c. perfect competition.
   d. monopolistic competition.
2. When there are many employers in a city and one union, the model that economists use is one for
   a. monopoly.
   b. monopsony.
   c. perfect competition.
   d. monopolistic competition.
3. Under perfect competition marginal resource cost _____ supply; under monopsony marginal resource cost _____ supply.
   a. equals; equals
   b. equals; is greater than
   c. equals; is less than
   d. is greater than; is less than

4. A union that trains and restricts supply has an effect on the supply curve that moves it to the _____ and, at a point, makes it _____.
   a. left; vertical
   b. left; horizontal
   c. right; vertical
   d. right; horizontal

5. Labor unions have greater representation in _____ employees.
   a. public
   b. service
   c. manufacturing
   d. retail

6. In the past 30 years work stoppages have
   a. plummeted.
   b. remained constant.
   c. increased slowly.
   d. increased rapidly.

Short Answer Questions

1. Explain why the marginal resource cost rises faster than the supply curve for labor.

2. Explain why, in a negotiation between a monopolistic union and a monopsonistic company in a town, there would not be a single outcome of wage and quantity like there is if only one of those two conditions hold.

3. Explain why there has been such a reduction in the number of work stoppages.

4. Use the context of the monopoly-monopsony tension to explain why public employees are so heavily unionized.

Think about This

The ability of unions to have their demands met has decreased markedly since the 1981 PATCO strike. Work stoppages have also decreased since that time. Are unions just not trying to make their influence known or do they not strike knowing they have little chance of winning?

For More Insight See

McConnell, Campbell R., Stanley L. Brue, and David A. MacPherson, *Contemporary Labor Economics,* 10th ed. (New York: Irwin/McGraw-Hill, 2013), esp. Chapters 10, 11, and 13.

Behind the Numbers

Union and private work force information.
Statistical Abstract of the United States; labor—www.census.gov/compendia/statab/cats/labor_force_employment_earnings/work_stoppages_and_unions.html

CHAPTER FORTY-TWO

Walmart: Always Low Prices (and Low Wages)—Always

Learning Objectives

After reading this chapter you should be able to:

LO1 Describe the importance of Walmart in the U.S. economy.

LO2 Demonstrate that the grocery sector continues to have a variety of competitors with monopolist competition being an adequate model to explain it.

LO3 Show that consumers tend to benefit when Walmart enters a community but that labor may win or lose, that other businesses may win or lose, and that the net impact is not always easy to compute.

Chapter Outline

The Market Form

Who Is Affected?

Summary

Depending on whom you talk to, Walmart is either one of the great American success stories and the driving force behind the upsurge in American productivity, or it is the emblem for low-wage, no-benefit, dead-end jobs, and the destroyer of small business. The reality is that it is all of that. Begun by Sam Walton as a small discount store in Bentonville, Arkansas, it has grown over the last 30 years to become the largest nongovernmental employer in the United States, responsible for more than 2 percent of U.S. GDP. With nearly every new store there is a debate about whether a new Walmart is good or bad for the community. Several communities, and one state, Vermont, have banned large discount stores on the argument that what Walmart brings, low-priced merchandise and low-wage jobs, is not worth the cost in terms of other lost jobs and lost local character. This chapter explores the pros and cons of "big-box stores" in general and Walmart in particular.

The Market Form

Most communities that have Walmart Supercenters have other large grocery-chain–affiliated stores as well. Also in the mix are individually owned stores, some of which are affiliated with what was once called the International Grocers Association but is now known as the familiar IGA. Your prototypical community will have stores of all varieties. From warehouse stores like Sam's and Costco to the "supers" (Kmart, Walmart, and Target), to the national chains (Kroger, Safeway, etc.), to the national holding companies (for example, Ahold is a holding company with regional stores like Stop & Shop and Giant), to the regional chains (Wegmans, Winn-Dixie, and Publix, etc.) to the IGA-affiliated stores, the grocery business is large and diverse. The market form that best describes this set of conditions is monopolistic competition. Though very small towns may have only one grocery store (monopoly) and small cities may have just two or three (oligopoly), the vast majority of Americans live in a community in which three of the four types of stores are present.

Every grocery store has a monopoly of sorts based on its location but is faced with competition from other stores as consumers are willing to travel short distances past one store to go to another. Many people have a preference for stores that include or do not include some goods. While some are intimidated by a "super" store, others are attracted to them because they can do grocery shopping, have their pharmacy needs met, and pick up a power tool and a new-release DVD all in one location. Some consumers want the "hometown proud" feeling of an IGA affiliate because they want to be on a first-name basis with their meat cutter and appreciate the fact that the owner sponsors a local Little League team. Monopolistic competition fits this market quite well.

A look at Figure 42.1 clearly shows that the top 10 grocery store companies and holding companies are widely dispersed throughout the United States with little likelihood that any one firm could gain a monopoly in any but the smallest of communities. Table 42.1 shows the percentage of total grocery sales by the top 10 firms. These top 10 grocery chains (and holding companies) account for three-quarters of all such sales. However you slice the data, the concern that Walmart is establishing a monopoly is not supported.

A similar concern is the degree to which Walmart affects its suppliers. To many firms, large and small, Walmart is their largest buyer. Were Walmart to become its only potential buyer, the problem of monopsony would occur. In that circumstance, companies are forced to reduce the prices to Walmart for fear that Walmart will shut them out. Just as Walmart can "make" a company by vastly expanding the market for a company's products, it can just as easily break it by compelling the firm to produce goods more cheaply. This can, and often does, result in the company outsourcing production to another country, reducing wages and benefits at its U.S. production facilities, or making products from less expensive and less durable materials.

FIGURE 42.1 Store locations of the top 10 grocery store outlets in the United States.

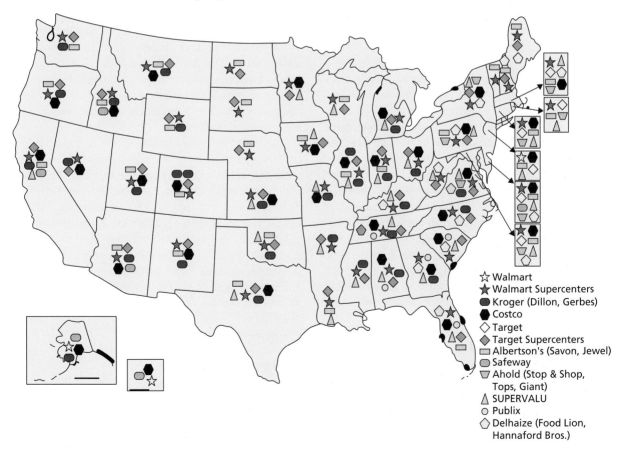

TABLE 42.1   Top 10 grocery store chain sales in the United States.

Source: www.stores.org/2012/Top-100-Retailers

Rank	Company	Annual Sales (billions)	% of Total Grocery Sales ($985b)	% of Top 10 Grocery Sales ($634b)
1	Walmart	$316	32.09%	49.86%
2	Kroger	$85	8.68	13.49
3	Target	$68	6.95	10.80
4	Safeway	$37	3.75	5.82
5	SUPERVALU	$29	2.97	4.62
6	Publix	$27	2.74	4.25
7	Ahold USA / Royal Ahold	$25	2.55	3.96
8	Delhaize America	$19	1.95	3.03
9	Meijer	$17	1.69	2.62
10	Whole Foods Market	$10	0.99	1.54

Who Is Affected?

There are many stakeholders when any "super" comes to town and, especially in the Northeast and West, local city and county authorities have developed zoning laws that are clearly aimed at keeping "supers" at bay. In examining why some object to the introduction of a Walmart Supercenter into a community, it helps to look at who wins and who loses. First, as a group, consumers unambiguously win because Walmarts tend to charge substantially less for identical items when comparisons are made between its prices and those of other big national or regional grocery stores like Kroger, Safeway, Food Lion, or Albertsons. Often Walmart can sell its staple items (like milk and bread) for less than IGA affiliates pay their suppliers. Second, workers may win or lose depending on two things: (1) whether there is a net increase in jobs or whether the jobs gained at the Walmart are countered by lost jobs at competitors, and, (2) what Walmart pays its employees. Third, taxpayers may win or lose depending on whether or not there is a net addition to sales in the community that results in a net increase in sales taxes. Finally, some of the owners of small businesses and other existing corporate retailers may be affected negatively, while others may benefit from such an endeavour. Let's examine some data.

Most Consumers Stand to Gain—Some Lose Options

We'll take each set of stakeholders in turn, starting with the buying public. The gain to consumers from paying less for their groceries is substantial. The average Walmart Supercenter sells between $100 and $150 million worth of goods in a year. Estimates vary considerably, but a trade association of mass marketers suggests that Walmart's prices are 15 percent to 22 percent lower than national averages. Suppose the average consumer saves 15 percent. The gain to the consumers who voluntarily switch from an average store to a Super Walmart is (per store) between $15 and $33 million annually.

Whatever these consumers do with the saved money, it is clear that they benefit from this perspective. Whether or not the local economy benefits depends on what consumers do with the saved money. If they consume more locally produced goods and services, then the local community benefits. If they put the money in their Wall Street managed investment accounts, the local community does not benefit as much.

There may be some locations where a "super" drives an IGA-type store out of business and in so doing makes some consumers worse off because they now have their optimal grocery option removed from their set of choices. To ballpark that loss, suppose a family used to pay $1,000 more a year on groceries at an IGA than they would have at a Walmart and did so because they liked the personalized service available at the IGA store. They have shown through their "revealed preferences" that this option is worth at least $1,000. For every 1,000 consumers so affected, the loss would be $1,000,000. What seems likely is that consumers as an aggregate are better off though some may be worse off.

Workers Probably Lose

It's hard to tell what the impact will be on workers because it is unclear whether there will be any net addition (or net loss) to the work force. If there is a net addition, it may not be great enough to offset the loss associated with the fact that, nationally, Walmart's pay is $5 to $10 less per hour (including benefits) than the typically unionized grocery store it is challenging. Nearly every supercenter that has opened in the last two years has employed approximately 450 people. However, there are problems with that number: First, about a third of the jobs are part-time, and second, the literature on displacements suggests that between 75 percent and 133 percent of such jobs will be displaced elsewhere in the community.[1] If we assume that a work year contains 2,080 hours, and, further, if we assume Walmart pays its employees $8 per hour and its competitors pay $18 per hour, there will be a loss to the community of workers that is somewhere between $4 million and $10 million per store.

Sales Tax Revenues Won't Be Affected Much

The question of whether taxpayers will gain or lose depends on whether the net sales in the state increase. The literature on the degree to which new supercenters increase total sales in a community suggests that between 70 percent and 80 percent of their sales displace sales that would have taken place in that community anyway. The problem with saying that sales taxes would therefore increase is that (1) a sizable portion of the sales are for tax-exempt items like food and (2) very little of the taxable sales would go to people who would have spent their money outside the state.

The latter point is important because sales taxes in many states go directly to the state. Therefore, whether the sales are in the particular community or in one of the neighboring counties, the sales taxes collected are the same. So, though more sales taxes would be collected in the community, there would be little effect on total sales tax collections.

[1] One nonacademic source suggests that Walmart gets so much more work out of an employee that the total number of workers falls when a Walmart comes to town.

Some Businesses Will Get Hurt; Others Will Be Helped

The impact of Walmart and other "supers" on other stores in the area is not clear. IGA affiliates follow a strategy of not trying to "out-Walmart" Walmart. They "believe that a good grocery store isn't a sprawling, impersonal example of cookie-cutter commerce, but a community hub owned and operated by the very people who know the area best—the citizens." As a result they support local charities, sponsor many local children's athletic teams, stock food products not often stocked at a "super," happily take special orders for meats not typically carried by the "supers," cut meat on-site rather than having it delivered already packaged, and their owners are on-site and part of their communities. At least some of Walmart's growth has been at the expense of these stores.

What is also important in the mix is that Walmarts tend to lead to the creation of complementary businesses. This "pull-factor" has been estimated to increase the creation of other retail business and other economic activity. A new Walmart is likely to "pull" retail sales from neighboring counties. That also leads to new fast-food and chain sit-down restaurants and other "big-box" retailers like Home Depot, Best Buy, and Staples that often follow "supers." Walmart can be the instant critical mass for an undeveloped or depressed area to become economically vibrant.

Community Effects

Sociologists have entered the Walmart discussion by pointing out that the introduction of "supers" has the impact of displacing stores that are owned by people who are also community leaders. This suggests that there is a further external cost to Walmarts in that they damage a community's noneconomic fabric. They also argue that after controlling for a host of other variables, shortly after a Walmart enters a market, local rates of poverty rise.

Summary

The net result of any new Walmart is what you would expect. Consumers mostly win and workers mostly lose; some businesses win and others lose, with the net being somewhat positive depending on the particulars of the community. If the new store simply replaces sales that would have occurred in the town anyway and the gain in employment is offset completely by the closing of other businesses, then what consumers gain is approximately equal to what workers lose. If, as is more likely, there is some net addition to employment and complementary businesses grow alongside the Walmart, then it is a net addition to the community. The local business leaders will gain or lose depending on whether they try to go head-to-head with Walmart (a suicidal venture) or they attempt to complement the Walmart by selling what Walmart does not, service.

Quiz Yourself

1. The impact of a new Walmart on a community's consumers is
   a. significantly positive for those that get lower prices.
   b. somewhat negative for those that prefer a personal touch (if stores offering it close).
   c. substantially negative in all aspects.
   d. a combination of *a* and *b*.

2. The impact of a new Walmart on a community's workers is
   a. only positive in that new jobs are created.
   b. only negative because better-paying jobs at competitors are lost.
   c. positive and negative because new jobs are created, but they often displace better-paying ones.
   d. only positive because Walmart pays better than their competitors.

3. We can measure how much someone values the personal touch of a small grocery store by using the amount extra they pay at that store even when there is a Walmart in town. Economists call that
   a. revealed demand.
   b. revealed preference.
   c. parsing the preference.
   d. noting the demand.

4. The impact of Walmart on its suppliers is
   a. unambiguously positive.
   b. unambiguously negative.
   c. positive and negative in that Walmart enlarges the market for their products but demands a much lower price than they typically receive.
   d. negligible.

5. The predominant market form for the grocery business in the majority of U.S. cities is one of
   a. monopoly.
   b. oligopoly.
   c. monopolistic competition.
   d. perfect competition.

6. Walmart's entry into the grocery business in the 1990s
   a. turned it into a monopoly.
   b. had no impact on the market form; it remained perfectly competitive.
   c. had no impact on the market form; it remained monopolistically competitive.
   d. had no impact on the market form; it remained an oligopoly.

Short Answer Questions

1. Theory suggests that Walmart might be able to come in, drive out competitors, and then raise prices. Data suggest that it doesn't happen. What would explain why Walmart doesn't do this?

2. Give an example of a "pull effect" that you have seen with a new large retail operation in your city or town, and explain whether this is simply an example of local substitution.

3. What are the strategies that grocery stores use to survive when a new Walmart locates in their area?

4. What is the gain to consumer surplus associated with a new large retailer, and why might that not be enough to overcome the losses associated with it?

Think about This

Walmart's entry into the grocery business in the 1990s had an important effect in lowering the price of groceries to poor people. Should this be taken into account when establishing the poverty line?

Talk about This

Major American companies that used to manufacture their goods in the United States are now manufacturing their goods in China because Walmart puts enormous pressure on the company to lower prices. This is because its practice is to tell a manufacturer what it will pay for a good. If the company wishes to sell its goods in a Walmart, it will lower prices. This is good for you in that you get goods at a lower cost. It is bad for the U.S. employees of the business because they lose their jobs. What is the net good/bad in your mind?

For More Insight See

Boyina, Manjula, "An Examination of Pull Factor Change in Non-Metro Counties in Kansas: A Study of the Economic Impact of Walmart Construction," *Kansas Policy Review* 26, no. 2.

Franklin, Andrew W., "The Impact of Walmart Supercenter Food Store Sales on Supermarket Concentration in U.S. Metropolitan Areas." Paper presented at the USDA conference, "The American Consumer and the Changing Structure of the Food System," Arlington, Virginia, May 3–5, 2000.

Stone, Kenneth E., Georgeanne Artz, and Albert Myles, *The Economic Impact of Walmart Supercenters on Existing Businesses in Mississippi:* www2.econ.iastate.edu/faculty/stone/mssupercenterstudy.pdf

Hicks, Michael J., *The Local Economic Impact of Walmart* (New York: Cambria Press).

CHAPTER FORTY-THREE

The Economic Impact of Casino Gambling

Learning Objectives

After reading this chapter you should be able to:

LO1 Describe the potential economic impact of casino gambling in the context of the local substitution problem.

LO2 Apply the concept of externalities to casino gambling.

LO3 Summarize the local economic impact of casino gambling while noting that it depends greatly on where the casino is located.

Chapter Outline

The Perceived Impact of Casino Gambling

Local Substitution

The "Modest" Upside of Casino Gambling

The Economic Reasons for Opposing Casino Gambling

Summary

When state and local governments run into financial difficulties, one of the first solutions brought to the table is casino gambling. Whether it be the introduction of gambling to the state or its expansion to a new part of the state, the argument goes something like this: "If we open a new casino, gaming companies will hire people to build it, more people to run it, and in the end they will all be paying more in taxes." This "everyone wins" scenario is plagued with the same logical flaw as the "if we build it they will come" argument for publicly funding the construction of a new sports stadium. This is in addition to the negative externality that is created for casino communities.

The Perceived Impact of Casino Gambling

The perception that gambling has an enormous economic impact on a community is understandable. More than 76 million Americans set foot in a casino each year, leaving nearly $37 billion. The casinos themselves employ 339,098 people while paying more than $7.9 billion in taxes. That, in a nutshell, is why gambling became one of the "answers" to state budget crises that stemmed from the 2001 recession and were once again turned to by states looking to close budget gaps in 2009 through 2011.

Local Substitution

The problem with the argument that a casino is an economic boon to its host community is that the money that goes into the casino came out of the pockets of some other businesses and therefore does not increase total economic activity in the community. To explain why, I will use my hometown as an example.

Terre Haute, Indiana, is known for two things: It was the college town for Larry Bird, and it is the home of the U.S. penitentiary that housed and then executed Timothy McVeigh. It is also home to economic and population decline. Once considered a major city in the state, it currently struggles to be noticed by the state's leaders. Some local leaders proposed that the solution to Terre

Haute's economic woes included a riverboat on the Wabash River that defines the city's western edge.

It is unambiguously true that such a facility would have cost in the neighborhood of $100 million to construct and that many of those construction jobs would have gone to citizens of the city. It is also true that once operational, a casino in Terre Haute would employ hundreds of workers at all levels of pay and responsibility. The problem is that money would have, in large part, come from people who already spend their entertainment dollars in the city.

The confusion over whether casinos are an economic answer to a community's problems results from the fact that the thing right in front of you often masks the equally sized but more dispersed negative impacts. This is true even if there are not the negative social consequences associated with gambling.

When properly examined, the bulk of the money that is spent on gaming in a community is money that usually comes from inside the community. The only substantial impact comes when a casino is located in a relatively rural area with a major market unserved by an existing casino. Thus residents of Cincinnati will drive to Indiana's neighboring Aurora to gamble when they otherwise would not have gone across the Ohio River to spend their entertainment dollars. Chicago, Illinois, is on the Illinois and Indiana border. Three cities on the Indiana side of the border, Gary, Michigan City, and Hammond, all have casinos but these mostly serve the Chicago metropolitan area.

A Terre Haute casino might draw Indianapolis residents, but it is not close enough to make it a slam-dunk success. The other problem with relying on the Indianapolis market is that if the issue of casinos is opened up again in the Indiana legislature, other towns much closer to Indianapolis will certainly want in on the game. In the end, the people most likely to patronize a Terre Haute casino are people who already spend their entertainment dollars in Terre Haute. We know that this is exactly what will happen because it is exactly what happened to the people of eastern Indiana in 2011 when ground was broken on a new casino in Cincinnati. The two casinos in eastern Indiana faced significant competition in late 2012 and suffered from the fact that their main customer base now has a newer casino much closer to home.

This Indiana example is playing out in many states. Whether it be gambling in Wisconsin, Missouri, or anywhere else, the names change but the idea stays the same.

The "Modest" Upside of Casino Gambling

Senior Economist Thomas A. Garrett of the St. Louis Federal Reserve notes that, "Although economic development is used by the casino industry and local governments to sell the idea of casino gambling to the citizenry, the degree to which the introduction and growth of commercial casinos in an area lead to increased economic development remains unclear." The evidence, as Dr. Garrett puts it, favors a "modest impact." In particular, the impact depends on where the casino is (rural or urban) and whether there is a large unserved market nearby.

Were there no externalities associated with casino gambling, the Garrett data would suggest that it is no different from any other recreational activity. That it is no ticket to an economic panacea would not preclude it from being part of the larger solution of economic growth. Again, looking at my state's experience shows that the impact of casino gambling is quite modest. From 1991 to 2001, the period of significant casino growth in the state of Indiana, the annual growth rate in personal income in counties with a casino was 5.3 percent, whereas in counties without a casino that annual growth rate was 5.2 percent.

Further, the notion that casinos are a boon to community tax coffers is partly wrong and partly deceiving. Much of the revenue that gets attributed to the casino would have been paid by other entertainment operators were there no casino. Concentrating the dollars paid into one source doesn't make them any greater. The real increase in tax revenue attributable to casinos exists because the effective tax rate on a gambled (and lost) dollar is substantially higher than the effective tax rate on a dollar spent at a restaurant or a dollar spent at a bowling alley. It is a tax increase that brings in the revenue to local governments, not an increase in economic activity. No wonder politicians fall for casino industry promises of money; they offer the possibility of raising taxes without the negative political consequence.

The Economic Reasons for Opposing Casino Gambling

The economic reasons to oppose this modest economic growth opportunity are the same as the reasons to oppose or limit the sale of tobacco, alcohol, drugs, and prostitution. Gambling is quite clearly addictive. Addicts of all varieties will do anything to satisfy their desires.

Gambling addicts will run up credit card debt, mortgage their homes, and put their families in terrible financial condition before seeking help. This leads to another problem: Gambling is associated with costs borne by someone other than the gambler or the casino. In the presence of **externalities,** free markets produce more of the good or service (including gambling entertainment) than is consistent with economic efficiency.

externalities
Effects of a transaction that hurts or helps people who are not part of that transaction.

Psychologists who study gambling addicts contend that most inveterate gamblers became attracted to it because they won significant sums of money their first time. This creates an emotional high in the same centers of the brain that drug addiction affects and, like drug addicts, gamblers continually try to repeat that high. Of course, they can't win over the long run. Casinos make money, money that used to belong to gamblers. To a statistician, gambling has a negative "expected value." That means that the average person who brings in $100 to a casino will leave with less than $100. This is because the gambles themselves are never "fair." Whether it's craps, poker, blackjack, or any other game, the "house" has a *"vig,"* or percentage of the average gamble that is its take. The "vig" is what pays for the employees, the facility, and the profits to the casino company. This is why there are few gamblers who make their money gambling.

vig
The expected percentage of any gamble that a casino will keep.

This, of course, is no different from any other form of entertainment. You never leave a movie theater with more money than you went in with. Assuming the movie was good, you do not complain because you got to see the movie. The allure of gambling is that you will win. When your first experience with gambling is like mine (I fed $40 in quarters into a slot machine in 20 minutes and won nothing), casino gambling has no appeal. On the other hand, psychologists insist that when you win big your first time out, there is a "high." It is a high that could potentially lead to addiction. As a result, you can make an economic argument against casinos on the same grounds you argue that cocaine or methamphetamine should be illegal.

That addiction can also create other negative behaviors by the gambler, and those behaviors can affect innocent third parties. When gamblers borrow extensively to support their addiction to gambling, the result can be high rates of bankruptcy. Higher bankruptcy rates lead to higher interest rates for the rest of us because credit card companies cannot distinguish people using their credit cards to buy food, clothing, or pay hotel bills from those who use their cards to support a gambling addiction. In addition, the money that gamblers use to support their habit could have been put to better use on food, clothing, or other goods for their family. When gamblers divorce, leaving spouses and their children on public assistance, those consequences are an external cost of gambling. Left unregulated or untaxed, any such market that produces external costs will produce too much.

Summary

You now understand that it is easy to overstate the impact of a new casino on the economy of a community. The impact is "modest" because of the degree of local substitution. There is no panacea of better jobs, higher incomes, and greater tax revenues. You also understand that gambling is addictive and that economists consider addictive goods worthy of regulation. Finally, you understand that a casino produces external costs and, like any good where that happens, an unregulated, untaxed market will produce too much gambling.

Key Terms

externalities, 457

vig, 457

Quiz Yourself

1. The argument that casinos have little economic impact on a community is based on the notion of
   a. supply.
   b. demand.
   c. opportunity cost.
   d. local substitution.

2. Economists generally believe that a new casino in a city that already has them would likely have —————— economic impact.
   a. an enormously negative
   b. a modestly negative
   c. an enormously positive
   d. a modestly positive

3. Which one of the following communities would likely see the greatest economic impact from a new casino?
   a. Plainfield, IN (just outside Indianapolis).
   b. Gary, IN (outside Chicago and already has one).
   c. Terre Haute, IN (Indianapolis is 70 miles away; no other population center is closer than 180 miles).
   d. Las Vegas, NV.

4. The percentage that casinos make on the average bet is called the
   a. vig.
   b. rip.
   c. take.
   d. rob.

5. The argument that increasing the number of casinos in a state will increase overall tax revenue in the state is
   a. substantially correct, because they pay substantial taxes.
   b. overstated but still partially correct, because there is tax substitution, but gambling profits are taxed more heavily than other profits.
   c. understated because they pay more taxes than is generally known.
   d. wrong because casino profits are not taxed.

6. The concern that gambling affects not only the gambler and casino but others is called a ————— and suggests that there would be too ————— production in an unregulated or untaxed market.
   a. positive externality; much
   b. negative externality; much
   c. positive externality; little
   d. negative externality; little

Short Answer Questions

1. If you were in a political argument with someone taking the side of the casino industry and she pointed out that casinos pay significant taxes, how would you (being on the other side) respond?

2. Suppose you were in a political argument with someone who wanted to locate a casino in your city (supposing that it had none), because there was a large city across the river in another state (also without one), and he pointed out that you could lure all those people in that large city to spend their money in your city. Supposing that you were against it, how would you counter that particular point?

3. What externalities exist when there is a casino, and how might those externalities be dealt with in a way that would allow a casino while also mitigating the externalities?

Think about This

Casino companies, Walmart, and sports teams make the same case with regard to economic development, and they are mostly wrong for the same reasons: local substitution. Why do they still succeed in overstating their economic impact?

Talk about This

The effect of gambling addiction is similar to the effect of other addictions though it is less apparent to others. Alcoholics, drug addicts, and so on, are easier to spot. Part of the problem is that inveterate gamblers can be successful at their addiction (winning a televised poker championship) or unsuccessful (and losing everything), while no one becomes a successful meth addict. Is gambling a problem only for the losers? Should casinos allow people to lose only a particular amount of money?

For More Insight See

Evans, W. N., and J. Topoleski, "The Social and Economic Impact of Native American Casinos," NBER Working Paper No. 9198: http://papers.nber.org/papers/w9198

Garrett, Thomas A., *Casino Gambling in America and Its Economic Impacts,* Federal Reserve Bank of St. Louis: http://research.stlouisfed.org

Garrett, Thomas A., and Mark W. Nichols, *Do Casinos Export Bankruptcy?* Federal Reserve Bank of St. Louis: http://research.stlouisfed.org/wp/2005/2005-019.pdf

Behind the Numbers

Taxes, wages, revenue, and visitations.
   American Gaming Association— www.americangaming.org; Center for Gaming Rese- http://arch gaming.unlv.edu

INDEX

A

Aaron, Henry, 392
Abortions, under Medicaid, 270
Absolute advantage (trade), 200–202
Acceptable deaths, 239
Accounting, generational, 155
Accounting costs, 54
   defined, 55
Accounting scandals (2001–2002), 434–437
Acid rain, 249–250
AD (*see* Aggregate demand)
Adams, Scott, 342
Addictions:
   to gambling, 456–457
   to substances, 235–236
Adelman, Morris, 416
Adjusted gross income (AGI), 395
Administrative lag (fiscal policy), 119
Advances (to authors), 365
Adverse impact discrimination, 308
Adverse selection, 263
Advertising:
   for prescription drugs, 283
   for tobacco and alcohol, 235–236
AFC (*see* Average fixed cost)
AFDC (Aid to Families with Dependent
      Children), 377–379
Affirmative action, 313–314
AFL-CIO, 447
Africa, trade with, 199
African Americans:
   and crime statistics, 294–295
   discrimination against, 305–314
   high school graduation by, 353–354
   poverty among, 373
Aggregate demand (AD), 103–104
   and austerity, 224
   determinants of, 107
   increases in, 227–228
   and interest rates, 129
   shifts in, 105–107
   unexpected movement in, 116–117
Aggregate demand shocks, 116–117
Aggregate supply (AS), 104–105
   classical and Keynesian views of, 104–105
   determinants of, 109
   and economic growth, 228
   increases in, 227–228
   shifts in, 107

Aggregate supply and aggregate demand model, 109
Aggregate supply shocks, 117–118
AGI (adjusted gross income), 395
Ahold, 450–452
Aid to Families with Dependent Children (AFDC), 377–379
AIDS (acquired immunodeficiency syndrome), 261
AIDS drugs, 283, 286–288
AIG, 167, 168, 186, 438
AIME (average index of monthly earnings), 383
Air pollution, 249–252
Air Tran, 70
Albertson's, 451, 452
Alcohol, 234–239
Alesina, Alberto, 125
Allied Chemical, 250
Alternative minimum tax (AMT), 396, 398
American Bar Association, 442
American Civil War, 150
American Federation of State, County, and Municipal
      Employees Union, 446
American Federation of Teachers, 357
American Indians, poverty among, 373
American Medical Association, 442
American Revolutionary War, 150
Americans with Disabilities Act, 356
Amortization of mortgages, 164–165
AMT (*see* Alternative minimum tax)
Anderson, Richard, 242
Anheuser-Busch, 236
Antidumping, 204
Apple Inc., 212
Arab–Israeli wars (1967–1973), 405
Arrow, Kenneth J., 316
Arthur Andersen, 437
Articles of Confederation, 150
Artz, Georgeanne, 454
AS (*see* Aggregate supply)
Asian Americans, poverty among, 373
Asian financial crisis, 133–134
Asset substitution effect, 385
Assets, value of, 433
ATC (*see* Average total cost)
AT&T, 432n, 435
Attainable production level, 5
Auditors, approach, in measuring discrimination, 310
Auerbach, Alan, 161, 155, 161
Austerity, 223–225
Automobile sales, discrimination in, 312
Automobiles, fuel efficiency of, 410–411
AVC (*see* Average variable cost)

Average fixed cost (AFC), 57–59
Average index of monthly earnings (AIME), 383
Average total cost (ATC), 57–59, 60
Average variable cost (AVC), 57–59, 60

B

Bailey, Elizabeth M., 256
Bakija, Jon, 386, 392
Balance of payments, 210
Balanced-budget amendment, 157–159
Bankruptcy, 292, 434–437
   among gamblers, 457
   gender differences in, 306
   of Social Security, potential, 388–389
   types of, 435
Barriers to entry, 68
Base year, 80
Baseball teams, 418–421, 423–425
Baseline budgeting, 145–146
Basketball teams, 419–420, 424–425
Becker, Gary, 294–211, 311
Bequest effect, 386
Bernanke, Ben, 127–132
Bernheim, Douglas, 161
Bertrand, Marianne, 310, 316
Best Buy, 453
"Big-box" stores (*see also* Walmart), 450
Bird, Larry, 455
Blank, Rebecca, 379, 381
Blau, Francine, 316
Blockbuster, 291
Blood, sale of, 265
BLS (Bureau of Labor Statistics)
Boeger, Leesa, 360
Bonds, 155–156
Boskin, Michael, 399, 402
Boyina, Manjula, 454
Bracket creep, 151n
Brokering tickets, 343–348
Brown, Charles, 342
Brown, Gardner M., Jr., 256
Brue, Stanley L., 449
Bubbles (*see also* Housing bubble),
   166, 182–185, 433–435
Buchanan, James, 120
Budget:
   and elasticity, 43
   federal (*see* Federal budget)
Buffett, Warren, 159
Buildable land, 157
Built-in stabilizers, 115, 157
Bureau of Labor Statistics (BLS), 79–82
Burger King, 69

Bush, George H. W. and administration,
   133, 140, 148
Bush, George W. and administration:
   congressional disagreements with, 141
   energy strategy of, 327
   and Kyoto Protocol, 253–254
   and oil prices, 406
   and recession of 2007–2009, 167–168
   and Social Security reform, 389–390
   tax cuts by, 110–111, 123, 157, 152, 153, 401
   and tax incentives, 399
   and war in Iraq, 152–153
Business confidence, 106
Business cycles, 87–89, 119, 120
Buying power, 24

C

California, 253
California Motor Speedway, 427
Calpine Corp., 436
Canada:
   cigarette tax in, 239–240
   debt-to-GDP ratio for, 154
   drug prices in, 287
   health care system in, 265–266
   trade with, 199
Cap and trade, 252–253
Capital account, 210
Capital budget, 153
Capital gains, 152, 395
Capital gains taxes, 319, 322, 395, 399
Capital market, 229
Capitalism, 20, 203, 435
Card, David, 340–342
CART, 427
Cartels, 405–408, 411, 414–415
Cartesian coordinates, 14
Case-Shiller home price index,
   154–155, 162–163
Cash benefit poverty programs, 375
Casino gambling, 455–457
Castro, Fidel, 205
Caterpillar, 447
Causation, 9
Central banks (*see also* Federal Reserve), 132, 232
CEO salaries, 436
CEOs (chief executive officers), 436
Ceteris paribus, 21
Chain-based index, 82
Chapter 11 bankruptcy, 435
Chapter 13 bankruptcy, 435
Charter schools, 358

Chicago, Illinois, 418
Chichilinsky, Gacielka, 256
Chief executive officers (CEOs), 436
Child (elder) care tax credit, 398
Child credit (income tax), 318, 398
Child Health Insurance Program, 280
Child labor, 204
China:
    copyright infringement in, 295
    currency manipulation by, 214
    economic growth in, 232
    and Kyoto Protocol, 253–254
    manufacturing in, 454
    petroleum demand in, 410–411
    policy disputes with, 161, 214
    trade deficit with, 216
    trade with, 198–199
    U.S. debt to, 156
Chrysler, 168, 181
CIA Factbook, 233
Cingular/AT&T, 69
Circular flow model, 6–7
Cities:
    minimum wages set by, 337
    sports teams based in, 418–419
Civil liability, 292–294
Clark, Robert, 392
Class action lawsuits, 294
Classical economics, 104–105
Clayton Act, 444, 445
Clean Air Act (1970), 249
Clean Air Act (1990), 250, 252
Clean Water Act (1972), 249, 251
Climate change, 250–251
Clinton, Bill and administration:
    congressional disagreements with, 141
    discretionary fiscal policy of, 119
    and EITC, 339
    federal deficit under, 158
    health care plan of, 257–258
    and Kyoto Protocol, 253–254
    on mandatory spending, 142–143
    and Medicare cuts, 146
    and student loans, 367–368
    and tax credits for college, 399
    tax-related social engineering by, 399
    welfare reforms by, 371
Coal, for electricity production, 412
Coase, Ronald, 248–249, 251
Coca-Cola, 69
Cogan, John F., 120, 392
Cohen, Mark, 304
COLA (cost-of-living adjustment), 80
Colander, David, 138

Cold War, 152
Collective bargaining (*see also* Unions), 425, 445
    and public school reform, 357
College education, 361–370
College tax credits, 399
College textbooks market, 364–366
Commercial banks, 131
Common property, 248
Commonwealth Edison, 67–68
Communism, 20
Community policing, 298
Company towns, 441, 444
Comparative advantage (trade), 200, 203
Competition, 67–70
    monopolistic, 68–70, 440, 443, 450, 452
    perfect, 62, 67–74, 287, 440–443
    and profit maximization, 62–63
    and unions/professional organizations, 442–443
Complements, 26–27
Concentration ratio, 70
Confidence:
    business/consumer, 106
    and recession of 2007–2009, 168–169
Congestible public goods, 49
Congress, federal spending and, 140–141
Congressional Budget Office, 158–159
Consolidated Edison, 68
Constant opportunity cost, 6, 10
Constitution:
    balanced-budget amendment to, 157–158
    government spending under, 140–141
Consumer confidence, 106
Consumer price index (CPI), 85
    core, 83
    degree of error in, 80–82
    and inflation, 80–82
    for medical care, 261
    and poverty line, 374
    and Social Security, 80n
Consumer surplus, 47–48
    and farm price floors, 329–330, 338
    with illegal goods/services, 235
    and minimum wage, 337
    and prescription drugs, 284
Consumers, 19
Consumption, discrimination in, 311–313
Contingency attorneys, 294
Continuing resolutions, 141
Contractionary fiscal policy, 115–116
Contracts, 291–292, 424, 425
Co-payment (insurance), 259
Copyrights, 68, 291, 295, 364–366
Core CPI, 83
Core PCE, 83

Corn prices, 327–328
Corporate paper, 131
Correlation, 9
Corruption:
  in developing countries, 231
Cost(s), 54, 57–59
  of crime, 296–297
  of education, 352–355, 361–368
  of government health insurance programs
      (*see also* specific programs), 274
  of research, 362–363
Cost function, 55
Cost of living, 374–375
Costco, 450–452
Cost-of-living adjustment (COLA), 80
Cost-push inflation, 110
Covered Bond, 219, 222
CPI (*see* Consumer price index)
Credit card debt, 155
Credit default swaps, 167
Creditors, 435
Credits (income tax), 394, 397, 399
Crime, 296–301
  and abortion, 300
  and atmospheric lead, 300
  costs of, 296–297
  and educational level, 352
  optimal sentencing for, 302
  optimal spending on control of, 300–302
  perpetrators of, 294–295
  racial differences in, 294–295, 308
  rational criminal model (*see also* Illegal goods and
      services), 295–296
Cross-price elasticity of demand, 40
Crowding out, 142
C&S Wholesale Grocers, 452
Cuba, 205
Currencies:
  foreign exchange markets, 6–7, 211–212
  international financial transactions, 209–211
  and shift in aggregate demand, 110–111
  (*see also* Exchange rates)
Current account, 211–212
Current-services budgeting, 145–146
Curry, George E., 316
Cyclical deficit, 153
Cyclical unemployment, 86–87

D

Darity, William A., Jr., 316
Deadweight loss, 49–50, 284
Death penalty, 302
Deaths, acceptable, 239

Debt:
  economists' view of, 153–155
  European, crisis of, 106, 216
  national, 150, 153–155
Deductible, insurance, 258–259
Deductions (income tax), 395–396, 398
Default risk, 99
Defense spending, 142–145, 146, 152
Deficit:
  budget (*see also* Federal budget), 150
  economists' view of, 153–155
Deflation, 88, 134, 186, 228
Delhaize, 451
Delta airlines, 70
Demand, 21–22
  aggregate (*see* Aggregate demand)
  cross-price elasticity of, 40
  determinants of, 26–28
  elasticity of, 40–44
  excess, 24
  income elasticity of, 40
  law of, 24–25
  price elasticity of, 40
  quantity demanded vs., 19–20
Demand curve, 19–22
  and decriminalization, 240–241
  and elasticity, 43–44
  for health care services, 271–272
  and law of demand, 24–25
  movements in, 28–29
  with private health insurance, 262–263
  for ticket scalping, 346–347
Demand schedule, 21–22
Demand-pull inflation, 110
Demand-side macroeconomics, 110–111
Dependency ratio, 192–193
Depression, 89
Descartes, René, 14
Desertification, 251
Developed countries, 227–231
Developing countries, 229–232
DFP (*see* Discretionary fiscal policy)
Diamond, Peter, 389, 392
DiIulio, John J., 304
DiMaggio, Joe, 425
Diminishing marginal utility, law of, 24–25
Diminishing returns, 56
Direct correlation, 9
Disability insurance (Social Security), 383–384
Discount rate, 128n, 421
Discount window, 131
Discouraged-worker effect, 86
Discretionary fiscal policy (DFP), 114, 185–187
  and aggregate supply and aggregate
      demand model, 115–116

in counteracting shocks, 116–118
history of, 118–119
mistiming of, 118–119
in Obama stimulus plan, 177
political use of, 119–120
Discretionary spending (federal), 142–144
Discrimination, 305–315
and affirmative action, 313–314
in consumption and lending markets, 311–313
definitions related to, 308–309
detection and measurement of, 310
economic status of minorities, 307–308
economic status of women, 305–306
in labor market, 310–311
Disparate treatment discrimination, 308
Division of labor, 56
DJIA (*see* Dow Jones Industrial Average)
Dollar, U.S., 106–107, 212–216
Dot-com bubble, 433–434
Dow Jones Industrial Average (DJIA), 432, 437, 430–432, 437
Draft (sports), 424
Drug companies, 283–284
Drug price indexes, 286
Drugs:
illegal (*see* Illegal goods and services)
over-the-counter, 239
prescription, 282–288
Drunk driving, 238
Du, Jiangtao, 361
Duke Energy North American, 436
Dumping, 204
Durable goods, 104
Dynegy Inc., 436

E

Earned Income Tax Credit (EITC), 318, 339, 376, 398, 400n
Eau Claire Rule, 330
Ecclestone, Bernie, 427
Economic costs:
defined
(*see also* Cost[s]), 54–55
Economic Freedom, Index of, 20
Economic growth and development, 227–233
in already developed countries, 227–229
with casino gambling, 456
with city sports franchises, 418–419
in developed vs. developing countries, 229–231
fostering/inhibiting development, 230–234
Economic profit, 70–74
Economic Recovery Act (2009), 399
Economics, defined, 1, 2
Economy, measuring, 78–82
Education, 350–370

college and university, 361–370
and income, 308
as investment in human capital, 351–352
and poverty, 373
racial inequalities in, 308
school reform issues, 356–359
spending on, 142–144, 350, 352–355, 361–367
Efficient markets, 432
Effluent permits, 252–253
Ehrlich, Isaac, 304
EITC (*see* Earned Income Tax Credit)
El Paso Energy, 436
Elastic demand, 41, 44
Elastic supply, 45–46
Elasticity, 40–46
of demand, 40–44
and demand curve, 43–44
determinants of, 43
formula for, 40
graphical explanation of, 41–42
health, 262–263
and minimum wage, 338, 340
of supply, 45–46
and taxes on tobacco/alcohol, 239–240
and total expenditure rule, 43
unitary, 41
verbal explanation of, 42–44
Electric utilities, 411, 412–413
Ellerman, A. Denny, 256
Elmendorf, Douglas, 125
Employment:
and aggregate supply, 104
in casinos, 455
classical and Keynesian views of, 104–105
in recession of 2007–2009, 168–169
by Wal-Mart, 450
Encouraged-worker effect, 86
Endangered Species Act (1973), 250–251
Energy prices, 404–415
electric utilities, 411, 412–413
future of, 413–414
historical view of, 404–406
and OPEC, 406–408
reasons for rapid changes in, 408–412
Energy sources, environmental consequences of, 245, 248–249
England, health care in, 265–266
Enron Corporation, 434, 437–438
Entitlements, 142–144
Entry barriers, 67–68
Environmental problems, 244–254
economic solutions to, 249–253
externalities approach to, 251–252
and Kyoto GHG reduction process, 253–254
with lower production costs, 203–204

Environmental problems *(Continued)*
    property rights approach to, 252–253
    types of, 253–255
Environmental Protection Agency, 253
Environmental quality of life, 84–85
Equilibrium, 23, 33–35
Equilibrium price, 19
Equilibrium quantity, 19
Equilibrium wage, 338, 441
Ethanol, corn-based, 327–328
Ethics *(see also* Morality issues), 292
Euro, 219–225
Europe:
    antipoverty programs in, 377
    health care system in, 265–266
    poverty in, 375
    trade with, 199
European Central Bank, 127, 219, 223–225
European Economic Community, 219
European Union, 219
    and Article 123, 219, 223–224
    and Article 125, 219, 224
    and Article 126, 219
    and the Maastrict Treaty, 219
    and the United Kingdom, 219
Excess demand, 24
Excess supply, 24
Exchange rates, 106–107, 212–216
    determinants of, 215–216
    and international trade, 211–216
    and shift in aggregate demand, 106–107
    and "strong dollar, " *(see also* Foreign exchange markets),
        105–107
Excise taxes, 26, 28–29, 30–32
Excludable public goods, 49
Exclusivity, 49
Exemptions (income tax), 394–396
Expansion (business cycle), 87
Expansionary fiscal policy, 115–116
Expected future price, 26, 28–29, 30, 31, 32–33
Expenditures approach (GDP computation), 79
External benefits, 351–352, 362–363
External costs, 236–239
Externalities, 244–246
    with casino gambling, 456
    for city sports teams, 420
    with environmental problems, 244–246
    positive, 420
    and Social Security, 384–385
Exxon Valdez disaster, 247

F

Factor markets, 6–7
Fallacy of composition, 9

Fannie Mae *(see* Federal National Mortgage
        Association)
Farm policy, 326–328
FDA *(see* Food and Drug Administration)
Fed *(see* Federal Reserve)
Federal budget, 149–159
    and balanced-budget amendment, 157–159
    deficits, 150
    economists' view of deficit and debt,
        153–155
    history of, 150–153
    owners of federal debt, 155–157
    projections of surplus/deficit, 158–159
    surpluses, 150
Federal debt *(see* National debt)
Federal funds rate, 127, 156–157
Federal Home Loan Mortgage Corporation
        (Freddie Mac), 158, 166, 168, 187
Federal justice system, 142–144
Federal National Mortgage Association
        (Fannie Mae), 158, 166, 168, 188
Federal Reserve (Fed):
    chairs of, 126–138
    goals of, 127
    inflation regulated by, 83
    influence of, 126
    ownership of national debt by, 155–156
    policies of *(see* Monetary policy)
    in recession of 2007–2009, 155–156
Federal revenue, 394
Federal spending, 139–148
    and aggregate demand, 107
    budgeting for, 145–146
    constitutional provisions for, 140–141
    disagreements over, 140–141
    distribution of, 145
    on education, 142–144, 352, 367–368
    on health care, 257–258
    and inflation, 110
    marginal analysis of, 145
    in Obama stimulus plan, 158–159
    and opportunity cost, 143
    shenanigans with, 140–141
    and shift in aggregate demand, 110–111
    sources of money for *(see also*
        Federal budget), 116
Fee-for-service health care plans,
        259–260, 262–263
Feenberg, Daniel, 125
Feenstra, Robert C., 208
Feiner, Susan F., 316
Feldstein, Martin, 386, 392
Ferber, Marianne, 316
FICA withholding, 259, 383
Filing status (income tax), 396

Financial crisis of 2008, 158
  and budget deficit, 153
  and housing bubble, 168, 437–438
  monetary policy tools created
        for, 131–132
Financial transactions, international, 209–211
Fiscal policy, 114–124
  aggregate supply and aggregate demand
        model of, 115–116
  to counteract shocks, 116–117
  discretionary, 114–124, 159
  evaluating, 118–123
  nondiscretionary, 114–124, 159
  Obama stimulus plan, 120–123
Fixed costs, 57–59
Fixed exchange rate system, 214
Fixed inputs, 55
Floating exchange rate
        system, 213–215
Flood, Robert P., 439
Florida, prisons in, 301
Food and Drug Administration (FDA),
        287–288, 293
Food Lion, 451–452
Food Stamps, 376–377
Football teams, 418–423, 423–425
Ford, Gerald, 115
Ford Motor Company, 181
Foreclosures, home, 168
Foreign aid, spending on, 143
Foreign exchange markets, 6–7, 211–212
Foreign exchange rates
        (*see* Exchange rates)
Foreign purchases effect, 103–104
Formula 1, 426–427
Fort, Rodney D., 423
Fortin, Nicole, 381
Fossil fuels, 245, 247, 251, 412
Foxconn, 212
Fracking , 84, 414
France:
  assistance to Greece, Spain, Ireland,
        Italy, 224
  and the European Central Bank, 223
  franc, 219
  and GDP growth, 220
  and long term interest rates, 221
  and per capita GDP, 220
France family, 427
Franchises, sports, 417–427
Franklin, Andrew W., 454
Frazier, Curtis L., 362
Freddie Mac (*see* Federal Home Loan Mortgage
        Corporation)
Free agents (sports), 424

Free markets, 20
Freeman, Richard B., 304
Frictional unemployment, 87
Fryer, Roland, 314, 316
Full employment, 104–105
Fully funded pensions, 383
Functional finance, 153–154
Fundamentals (stock price), 431
Future value, 97–99

G

Gambling, 455–457
Garber, Peter M., 439
Gardner, Bruce L., 329
Garrett, Major, 281
Garrett, Thomas A., 456
Gasoline prices (*see* Energy prices)
Gasoline–corn price relationship,
        327–328
Gates, Bill, 380
GDP (*see* Gross domestic product)
GDP deflator (GDPDEF), 82–84
GEDs (*see* General Equivalency Degrees)
Geithner, Timothy, 132
General Equivalency Degrees
        (GEDs), 308, 354–355
General Motors, 168, 181, 436, 438
Generational accounting, 155
Germany:
  assistance to Greece, Spain, Ireland,
        Italy, 224
    and debt-to-GDP ratio of, 154
  and deficits, 223
  and the European Central Bank, 223
  and GDP growth, 220
  and long-term interest rates, 221
    mark, 219
  and per capita GDP, 219–220
GI Bill, 368
Gilroy, Curtis, 342
Gini index, 229
GlaxoSmithKline, 287
Global Crossing, 435–437
Global warming, 250–253
Globalization, 88–89, 211
GNI (*see* Gross national income)
Gold standard, 214
Goldman Sachs, 131
Goods, 5, 49
Goods and services markets (*see also* illegal goods and
        services), 7, 311–313
Goodstein, Eban, 256
Gottschalk, Peter, 381

Government:
  accounting used by, 150
  economic influence vs. economic control by, 110–111
  farm policy of, 328–332
  justifications for interventions by, 384–385
  as owner of national debt, 155
  size of, 145
  structure of, and fiscal policy, 118–119
  subsidies from
  (*see also specific topics*, e.g.: Monetary policy),
    26, 28, 29, 30, 32–33
Government regulation:
  of environmental problems, 246–254
  of illegal or addictive goods/services, 235–238
  and shift in aggregate supply, 109
  and supply-side economics, 111
Gramlich, Edward M., 392
Graphing, 14–17
Great Britain, oil reserves in, 408
  farm prices in, 330
  and labor unions, 444
  and origin of Social Security, 382–383
Greece:
  debt crisis, 106, 216
  and debt to GDP, 222
  drachma, 219
  and the euro, 219, 225
  GDP growth, 219
  and long term interest rates, 221
  per capita GDP, 221
  and tax evasion, 222
Grexit, 225
Greene, P., 363
Greenhouse gases, 247, 252–254
Greenspan, Alan, 133–134
Grocery stores, 450–452
Gross domestic product
    (GDP), 78
  computation of, 79, 90
  deficits as percentage of, 161–162
  federal spending as percentage of, 140
  and foreign trade, 210
  national debt as percentage of, 154
  and official poverty numbers, 375
  post-World War II, 84
  and price changes, 82
  problems with, 84–85
  and recognition lag, 118–119
  spent on health care, 257
  Walmart's contribution to, 450
Gross national income (GNI), 229–230
Grossman, Michael, 242
Groundwater contamination, 256
Gulf of Mexico oil spill, 247, 411
Gulf War, 406

H

Hanushek, Eric, 356, 360
Happel, Stephen, 349
Hausman, Jerry, 92
Head Start, 376
Heal, Geoffrey, 256
Health care, 257–267
Child Health Insurance Program (CHIP), 280
  economic models of, 261–262
  federal spending on, 145–146
  government-provided, 269
  insurance for, 260
Medicaid, 270–273, 279, 280
Medicare, 273–279
  money spent on, 257–258
  in Obama stimulus plan, 146
  in U.S. vs. other countries, 265–266
Health insurance, 258–265, 273
Health maintenance organizations (HMOs), 259–260,
    273–275
Heckman, James J., 316
Hedonic price, 80n
Herfindahl-Hirschman Index (HHI), 70
Heritage Foundation, 20, 229, 374
Higher education, 361–368
Highway construction, 142
Hirschman, Ira, 53
Hispanic Americans, 354, 373
HMOs (*see* Health maintenance organizations)
Hockey teams, 425–426
Hodrick, Robert J., 439
Home building, 155
Home Depot, 453
Home equity lines of credit, 155
Home ownership, poverty and, 374
Home prices, 162–164
Honda, 181, 294
Honda Civic, 412
Horizontal equity (income taxes), 398–399
Housing Authority Apartments, 376
Housing bubble, 162–169
  creation of, 166–167
  economic effects of, 168–169
  and factors in home prices, 162–164
  and financial crisis of 2008, 437–438
  individual effects of, 167–169
  and liquidity trap, 131
  and recession of 2007–2009, 89, 154–155
  and short sale, 169
  and types of mortgages, 163–166
Hoxby, Caroline, 357, 360
Hufbauer, Gary, 2, 169
Hulman-George family, 427
Human capital, 351–352

Human life, value of, 292–293
Hurricanes, 251, 411
Hydroelectric power, 247, 254, 412
Hyman, David, 392, 403

I

IBM, 68
IGA affiliates, 450–453
Illegal goods and services, 234–243
  and computation of GDP, 84–85
  ticket scalping, 347
Incentives, 8
  to control health care costs, 274–275
  and supply-side economics, 111
  and tax code, 398–399
  of welfare programs, 377–381
Income, 26, 27, 29
  and college education, 366–367
  and crime rates, 295–296
  inequalities of, 306, 307, 309, 317–323, 380
  mobility, 322–323
  and poverty line (*see also* Poverty), 372, 377–378
Income approach (GDP computation), 79
Income effect, 398
Income elasticity of demand, 40
Income Inequality, 317–323
  causes of, 321–322
  costs and benefits of, 322–323
  international comparisons of, 323
  measurements of, 317–319
Income taxes (*see* Personal income taxes)
Increasing opportunity cost, 5–6, 10
Index of Economic Freedom, 20, 229
India, 410
Indiana, casinos in, 456
Indianapolis Motor Speedway, 427
Induced retirement effect, 385
Indy Racing League (IRL), 426–427
Inelastic demand, 41, 43–44
Inelastic supply, 46
Inelasticity, 41, 42–44
Inferior goods, 26, 27
Inflation:
  causes of, 109–110
  in developing countries, 231–232
  and federal funds rate, 127
  historic, 88
  interest rate effect on, 96
  during last 30 years, 132–135
  measuring, 80–82
  and monetary policy, 110–111, 132
  and real interest rate, 95
  and recession of 2007–2009, 155–156
  winners and losers from, 82

Inflation rate, 80–81
Inflation targeting, 127
Infrastructure:
  in developing countries, 231
  politically motivated projects, 119–120
  trust funds for, 155
Initial public offerings (IPOs), 431–432
In-kind subsidies, 375
Innes, Robert, 256
Input costs, 110
Inputs, 30, 32–33, 55
Insurance, 258–265
  consumption of insured activity, 262–263
  health, 258–265, 273
  retirement annuities, 312–313
  social, 387
Intangible losses (crime), 297
Intellectual property, 291, 366
Interest rate effect, 104
Interest rates, 93–99
  and federal borrowing, 158
  and inflation, 132–134
  in monetary policy, 129
  and recessions, 132–135
  and shift in aggregate demand, 106–109
  and shift in aggregate supply, 109
Interest-only mortgages, 165–166
Intergenerational Income Elasticity, 323
Internal rate of return, 96–97
Internal Revenue Service (IRS), Statistics of Income, 317–319
International Brotherhood of Electrical Workers, 442
International Brotherhood of Teamsters, Chauffeurs, Warehousemen and Helpers of America, 443n
International financial transactions, 209–211
International Grocers Association, 450
International policy, federal spending and, 143
International Speedway Corporation (ISC), 427
International trade, 197–206
  barriers to, 205–206
  benefits of, 199–203
  demonstrating gains from, 200–202
  as diplomatic weapon, 205
  and exchange rates, 211–216
  financial transactions in, 209–211
  foreign exchange markets, 211–212
  limiting, 203–205
  opposition to, 202
  and outsourcing, 202–203
  with South Korea, 216
  terms of, 202
  and U.S. as debtor nation, 209
Inverse correlation, 9
Investment banks, 131
Investments, risk and reward with, 95
IPOs (initial public offerings), 431–432

Iran, 205, 405–406
Iraq, 205, 292, 406
Ireland:
    and debt to GDP, 222
    and the euro, 219, 225
    GDP growth, 219
    and housing bubble, 219, 221–224
    and long term interest rates, 221
    per capita GDP, 221
IRL (Indy Racing League), 426–427
ISC (International Speedway Corporation), 427
Italy, 154
Itemized deduction (income tax), 396

J

Jackson, Andrew, 150
Jail costs, 300–301
Japan:
    debt-to-GDP ratio for, 154–155
    deflation in, 88, 134, 183–186
    earthquake, tsunami, and nuclear crisis of 2011, 180
    economic growth in, 181–182, 232
    and lost decade, 180–187
    policy mistakes, 183–185
    real estate, value of, 183
    rice industry in, 203
    stock market of, 181, 182–183, 184, 433
    trade with, 181, 199
    U.S. debt to, 156
    and World War II, 180, 184, 185
Jennings, Marianne, 349
Johnson, George, 381
Johnson, Lyndon and administration, 110, 115n, 374
Jordan, Michael, 424
Jorgenson, Dale, 381
Joskow, Paul L., 256

K

Kahn, Lawrence M., 428
Kaufman, Ewing, 421–423
Kennedy, John F., 374, 445
Kentucky Motor Speedway, 427
Keynes, John Maynard, 104–105
Keynesian economics, 104–105, 224
KFC, 69
Kmart, 435–438, 450
Kohen, Andrew, 342
Kotlikoff, Laurence, 155
Kroger, 450–452
Krueger, Alan, 342
Krueger, Andrew, 340–341

Krugman, Paul, 120, 158, 161, 186, 207
Kuwait, 232, 406
Kyoto Protocol, 253–254

L

Labor, marginal revenue product of, 423
Labor costs, 285
Labor markets:
    discrimination in, 310–311
    and minimum wage, 336, 337
    under perfect competition, 440–441, 443
    for sports, 423–427
Labor rights, 444–445
Labor unions (*see* Unions)
Labor-force participation rate, 305–306
Ladd, Helen F., 316
Landfills, 250
Larry Bird exemption, 424
Law(s), 290–294
    bankruptcy, 292, 435
    civil liability, 292–294
    priorities in enforcing, 290–292, 301, 302
    property rights, 292–294
    unions' rights under, 294, 444–445
Lawsuits:
    for civil liability, 292–294
    class action, 294
    against drug companies, 285–286
Lebow, David, 82, 92
Lee, Ronald, 148, 160, 281
Lehman Brothers, 131, 158
Leigh, Andrew, 357, 360
Leimer, Dean, 386, 392
Lemieux, Thomas, 381
Lending discrimination, 311–313
Lesnoy, Selig, 386, 392
Levitt, Steven, 300–303, 304
Liability, civil, 292–294
Liar loans, 167
Libya, 205
Licensing, 331, 442–443
Lines, graphing, 15–17
Linux, 68
Liquidity trap, 131
Literacy, 231
Living wage, 335
Loans:
    car, 96–97, 155
    default on home loans, 309
    liar, 167
    money created by, 128
    student, 101, 292, 367–368

Loblaw Cos., 452
Local substitution, 419
Lochner, Lance, 352, 360
Lockouts, 425, 446
Logrolling, 141
Long run, 71, 340
Los Angeles, California, 418
Loury, Glenn, 314, 316
Luxury box revenue (sports), 420
Lynch, Thomas, 148

M

M1, 127–128
M2, 127–128
M3, 127n
Maastrict Treaty, 219
MacPherson, David A., 448
Macroeconomics, 77–90
    business cycles, 87–89
    demand-side, 110–111
    measuring the economy, 83, 87
    and minimum wage, 339
    and national income, 90
    real gross domestic product, 82–85
    supply-side, 111
    unemployment, 85–87
Major League Baseball (MLB), 421–423
Managed float exchange system, 214–215
Mandation, 263
Mandatory spending (federal), 142–144
Marginal analysis, 7–8
    of costs of crime, 301–302
    of drug approval process, 288
    of federal spending, 145
Marginal benefit, 8, 57–59
Marginal cost (MC), 8, 57–59, 60
    of cleaner environment, 245–246
    under perfect competition, 71–74
    of tickets, 344
Marginal resource cost (MRC), 442
Marginal revenue (MR), 61
Marginal revenue curve, 67
Marginal revenue product of labor,
    423, 441–442
Marginal tax rate, 398
Marginal utility, 24–25
Market(s), 8, 19
    efficient, 432
    for money, 94
    (*see also* Stock market)
Market basket, 79–82
Market failure, 48–49

Market forms, 66–70, 364–366, 450
Market power, 443
Market risk, 99
Marketing, 19
Mason, Patrick L., 316
Maximizing profit, 62–63
Maximum out of pocket expense, 259
Maximum taxable earnings, 383–384
MC (*see* Marginal cost)
McCain, John, 111, 401
McConnell, Campbell R., 449
McDonald's, 67, 69
McGraw-Hill, 364–366
McGwire, Mark, 343
McKnight, Claire, 53
McVeigh, Timothy, 456
Means test (Social Security), 390
Measuring the economy, 78–82
Medicaid, 144–145, 147, 259–260, 264, 269–279
    characteristics of, 376
    costs for elderly under, 272–273
    costs of, 271–272
    cost-saving measures in, 273
    eligibility for, 270–271
    for foster families, 378
    payments under, 271
    provisions of, 259–260, 270
    recipients of, 269–270
    relationship of Medicare and, 279–280
    smokers on, 239, 241
    spending on, 270–272
Medicare, 270
    cost control provisions in, 275–276
    costs of, 270, 274–275
    diagnosis-related groups under, 275–276
    federal spending on, 144, 145
    funding for, 156, 189–195
    origin of, 383–384
    Part A, 275
    Part B, 275–276
    prescription drug coverage (Part D), 148, 276
    and private insurance for the elderly, 273–274
    provider types, 275
    provisions of, 259–260
    relationship of Medicaid and, 279–280
    smokers vs. nonsmokers on, 238
    spending on, 152, 270
    tax rate for, 384
    trust fund for, 155
Medicare Trust Fund, 270, 274, 277–279
Medications (*see* Prescription drugs)
Merit pay, for teachers, 357
Metrick, Andrew, 256
Mexico, 199, 287, 408

Michelin, 428
Microeconomics, 78
Microsoft, 67, 68, 441
Middle East revolutions, impact of,
    110, 117–118, 405
Miller, Matthew, 281
Milwaukee school voucher program, 358
Minimum wage, 296, 335–341
    alternatives to, 339
    economic analysis of, 335–338
    elasticity argument against, 340
    macroeconomics argument
        against, 339
    as price floor, 330
    real-world implications of, 338–339
    for sports players, 425
    work effort argument against, 340
Minorities:
    economic status of, 307–308
    high school graduation rates for (*see also* Racial
        inequalities), 354
Mitchell, Olivia S., 392
MLB (*see* Major League Baseball)
Model (*see also specific models*), 2, 3
Monetary aggregate, 127–128
Monetary authority, 132
Monetary policy, 126–136
    and central bank independence, 132
    goals of, 127
    and inflation, 110
    during last 30 years, 132–135
    modeling, 128–129
    and monetary transmission mechanism, 129–131
    tools created in 2008 for, 131–132
    traditional and ordinary tools of
        (*see also* Recession of 2007–2009), 127–128
Monetary transmission, 128–131
Money (*see also* Currencies),
    128, 131–132
Money creation, 128
Monopolistic competition, 68–70
    by grocery stores, 450–451
    other market forms vs., 69–70
    in textbook market, 364
Monopoly(-ies), 68
    cartels as, 407
    drug industry as, 283–284
    electric utilities as, 412–413
    event promoters as, 344–345
    grocery stores as, 450–451
    and maximization of profit, 62
    natural, 412–413
    other market forms vs., 69–70
    public schools as, 356–357

    simple, 412–413
    unions as, 443–444
Monopsonies, 441–442, 444, 447–448
Montero, Juan Pablo, 256
Moody's, 438
Moral hazard, 263
Morality issues:
    with blood and organ sales, 265
    for government regulation, 238
Moretti, E., 352, 360
Morgan Stanley, 131
Mortgage lending discrimination, 314
Mortgage-backed securities, 131–132, 166,
    186, 219
Mortgages, 96–97, 101, 155, 163–164, 167
    selling of, 167–168
    30-percent guideline for, 164–167, 168
    traditional, 164–165
    types of, 163–166
MR (marginal revenue), 61
MRC (marginal resource cost), 442
Mullahy, John, 242
Mullainathan, Sendhil, 310, 316
Munnell, Alicia, 386
Myles, Albert, 454

N

NASCAR teams, 421, 426
NASDAQ bubble, 166–167, 434
NASDAQ Composite Index, 431–434, 437
Nashville, Tennessee, 418
National Basketball Association
    (NBA), 421, 424–425
National (federal) debt, 150, 153–158
National Education Association, 357
National Football League (NFL), 420–423
    and lockout, 426
National Hockey League, 426
National Income, 79, 90
National Industrial Recovery Act, 444–445
Natural gas, for electricity production, 412
Natural monopolies, 412–413
Natural resources, 244–0
    limited, 245
    renewable, 245
    sustainablility of, 245
    stewardship of, 245
NBA (*see* National Basketball Association)
NDFP (*see* Nondiscretionary fiscal policy)
Neal, Derek, 358, 360
Negative-amortization mortgages, 165–167
Net benefit, 8

Net interest, federal spending on, 142, 144
Net present value, 366–367
Net tax rate, 155
Neumark, David, 342
Neutral tax code, 398
Newhouse, Joseph, 281
NFL (National Football League),
          420–423
Nigeria, 231
Nikkei 225, 88
Nikkei Index, 433
Nominal interest rate, 94–95
Nominal output, 78–79
Nondiscretionary fiscal policy (NDFP),
          114, 185–187
    and aggregate supply and aggregate
          demand model, 115–116
    as built-in stabilizer, 115
    in counteracting shocks, 117–118
    evaluating, 118
    and Obama stimulus plan, 159
Nontariff trade barriers, 205
Nordhaus, William, 256
Norfolk–Virginia Beach area, Virginia, 419
Normal goods, 26, 27
Normal profit, 70–71
Normative analysis, 8
Norris–La Guardia Act, 444–445
Novy-Marx, Robert, 193–194, 196
Nuclear power, 247, 254, 412
Number of sellers, 30, 31
Nursing home care, 272–273

O

Oates, Wallace E., 256
Obama, Barack and administration, 120
    and alternative minimum tax, 398
    energy strategy of, 327
    and greenhouse emissions, 253–254
    initial budget of, 158
    and Social Security reform, 390
    and tax cuts, 111, 115, 401
    and tax incentives, 399
    Obama stimulus plan, 111, 115, 169
    and budget deficits, 153
    congressional deliberation of, 119–120
    congressional votes for, 141
    criticism's of, 120
    discretionary and nondiscretionary
          aspects of, 123
    federal spending under, 140–146, 159–160
    infrastructure projects in, 119–120

    and recession of 2007–2009, 158–159
    tax cuts in, 399, 401
    tax incentives in, 399
Obamacare (*see* Patient Protection and Affordable Care Act)
Obstfeld, Maurice, 207
Occupy Wall Street, 317
Off-budget, 150–151
Office of Management and Budget, 158–159
Off-shoring, 203
Oil prices (*see* Energy prices)
Oil reserves, 404, 406, 408, 413–414
Oligopolies, 69
    gasoline industry as, 409
    other market forms vs., 69–70
    and textbook market, 364
Oligopolistic markets, 69
On-budget, 150
OPEC (*see* Organization of Petroleum
          Exporting Countries)
Open-market operations, 127–128, 155
Operating budget, 153
Operational lag (fiscal policy), 119
Opportunity cost, 2
    and absolute advantage, 200
    of cleaner environment,
          245–246
    constant, 5–6, 10
    and federal spending, 143
    increasing, 5–6, 10
    made in developing countries, 232
    production possibilities frontier model
          of, 5, 6, 10
    and retirement savings, 385
Optimization assumption, 8
Option ARMs, 168
Organization of Petroleum Exporting Countries,
          (OPEC), 199, 405–408, 411
Organs, sale of, 265
Origin, 14
Orphan drugs, 283
Output, 19
    and diminishing returns, 56
    measuring, 78–79
    potential, price of, 30, 31, 32
Outsourcing, 202–203, 451

P

Pacific Islander Americans, poverty among, 373
Palmer, Karen, 256
PATCO (*see* Professional Air Traffic Controllers
          Organization)
Patents, 68, 283, 291

Patient Protection and Affordable Care Act (PPACA),
   257–266, 270, 276, 279
   and adverse selection, 261, 263
   assorted provisions of, 263–265
   and employers, 263–265
   and exchanges, 261
   and mandation, 263–265
   and Medicaid, 261
   and minimized insurance, 259
   and private health insurance, 261–263–265
   and taxes, 261, 263
Paulson, Henry, 132, 158
Pay option adjustable rate mortgages, 166
Pay-as-you-go pensions, 383
Payroll taxes, 383
PCPs (primary care physicians), 259
Peace dividend, 152
Peak (business cycle), 87
Pelaez, Rolando F., 53
Penn State University, 441
Pensions, 306, 390
   Chicago, 194
   county and municipal liabilities, 193–195
   defined benefit, 189–195, 357, 447
   defined contributions, 190
   Employee Retirement Income Security Act of 1974
      (ERISA), 190
   Pension Guaranty Trust Corporation, 190
   state and local government, 189–195
   state liabilities, 193–195
Pepsi, 69
Per capita real GDP, 84
Perfect competition, 67–68
   in labor market, 430–431, 443
   markets meeting criteria for, 69–70
   and maximization of profit, 62
   monopoly vs., 284
   and monopsony, 431–432
   other market forms vs., 69–70
   supply under, 70–74
Perfectly elastic demand, 44
Perfectly elastic supply, 46
Perfectly inelastic demand, 44
Perfectly inelastic supply, 46
Personal Consumption Expenditures deflator, 83
Personal income taxes, 115, 151n, 394–401
   alternative minimum tax, 398
   calculating, 395–398
   debates over, 399–401
   distribution of, 399–400
   issues with, 398–399
   payers of, 399–400
   rates for, 397–399
   and stock market gains, 152

   and willingness to work and save, 398–399
   withholding of, 394–395
Peterson, Paul E., 360
Phelps, Charles, 268
Phillips, 181
Philip Morris, 70
Pick-a-pay mortgages, 166
Pippen, Scott, 424
Plants, extinction of, 250–251
Plumbers and steamfitters, 432
Points, graphing, 15
Polasky, Stephen, 256
Political business cycle, 119–120
Political instability, 231
Politics:
   in federal spending, 141–142, 146
   and fiscal policy, 119–120
   of income taxes, 394, 398–401
Pollution, 244–254
Population, home prices and, 163
Population of potential buyers, 26, 28, 29
Porter, Michael E., 256
Portney, Paul R., 256
Positive analysis, 8
Positive externalities, 420
Poteba, James M., 256
Poverty, 371–372
   as "bad," 379
   gender differences in, 306
   through history, 373–374
   and living wage, 335–336
   measuring, 372–375
   and minimum wage, 335, 336
   programs related to (*see also* Welfare), 272–275
   in the U.S. vs. Europe, 375
   wealth vs., 374
Poverty gap, 372
Poverty line, 372–374
Poverty rate, 372–375, 390
Power sources:
   environmental consequences of, 244, 247, 250–254
   fixed and variable costs of, 412
Pozen, Robert, 390, 392
PPACA (*see* Patient Protection and Affordable Care Act)
Preferred provider organizations (PPOs), 259–260
Prescription drugs, 282–288
   and drug industry as monopoly, 283–284
FDA approval of, 283, 287–288
   liability for ill effects linked to, 293–294
   under Medicare, 148, 276
   and perceptions of drug companies, 283
   prices of, 285–287
Present value, 95–97
   and car fuel efficiency, 412

and costs of prescription drugs, 285
  of death penalty, 302
  of education spending, 366–367
  of human life, 292–293
  of natural resources, 245
  of Social Security, 386–387
  of stock, 431
Price(s), 19
  classical and Keynesian views of, 104–105
  of college textbooks, 364–366
  and elasticity, 41–42
  energy, 404–415
  farm, 326–329
  of gasoline, 253–254
  measuring, 79–80
  of prescription drugs, 285–287
  setting, 61
  stock, 430–431
  of substitute/complement goods, 26, 27, 28
Price ceiling, 34, 35
Price elasticity of demand, 40
Price elasticity of supply, 39, 45–46
Price expectations:
  changes in, 33
  as determinant of demand, 26, 29
  as determinant of supply, 30, 31, 32
Price floors, 34–35, 329–330
Price gouging, 34–35
Price index, 80
Price indexes:
  chain-based index, 82
  consumer price index, 80–83
  GDP deflator, 83–84
  Producer Price Index, 83
Price of inputs, 30, 32
Price of other potential output, 30, 31, 32
Price of the market basket in the base year, 80
Price supports, for farm products, 328–332
Primary care physicians (PCPs), 259
Primary credit rate or discount rate, 128
Principal–agent problem, 436, 437
Prison costs, 300–301
Private property, 290–291
Private schools, 357–358
Private-sector unions, 445–446
Procyclical (budget amendment), 157–158
Producer Price Index, 83
Producer surplus, 47, 246–247
  and farm price floors, 329–330, 338
  with illegal goods/services, 235
  and minimum wage, 337
  and prescription drugs, 284
Producers, 19
Product Accounts, 79, 90
Production, 55–57

Production costs, 109, 203–204
Production function, 55–56
Production possibilities frontier, 2–6
  for international trade, 201–202
  opportunity cost on, 10
Production rules, 63
Professional Air Traffic Controllers Organization (PATCO), 446–448
Profit, 54
  by industry type, 71
  made in developing countries, 233
  maximizing, 62–63
  normal vs. economic, 70–74
Progressive taxation, 398, 398–401
Property rights, 290–292
  enforcing, 291–292
  and environmental problems, 248–249
  intellectual property, 291
  and natural resources, 248–249
  negative consequences of, 292
  to solve environmental problems, 252–253
Prospective payments, 275
Prostitution, 236, 240–241, 296
  and sexual slavery, 236
Public employees, unionization of, 445, 447
Public goods, 49
Public schools, 350–358
Publishing process, 364–365
Publix, 450–452
Pucher, John, 53
Pull factor, Walmart and, 453
Purchasing power parity, 230
Purely private goods, 49
Purely public goods, 49

Q

Quantitative easing (QE2), 88, 131–132, 169
Quantity demanded, 19, 21, 22, 23
Quantity supplied, 19, 21, 22, 23
Quotas:
  for affirmative action, 314
  trade, 204–205

R

R. J. Reynolds, 235–236
Racial inequalities, 309
  and affirmative action, 313–314
  in automobile sales, 312
  in crime statistics, 294–295, 308
  in default on home loans, 309
  in education, 308

Racial inequalities, *(Continued)*
  in high school graduation rates, 354
  in labor market, 310–311
  in real estate market, 311–312
  in wages, 310–311
Ramo, Joshua Cooper, 138
Rational criminal model, 295–296
Rational discrimination, 309
Rauh, Joshua, 193–194, 196
RCA, 181
Reagan, Ronald and administration:
  and agriculture subsidies, 332
  and budget of 1984, 141
  and deficits of 1980s, 151–152
  EITC during, 339
  federal spending during, 140
  and labor unions, 446
  and student loans, 368
  supply-side actions of, 111
Real estate market, discrimination in, 311–312
Real estate values, 88–89
Real gross domestic product (RGDP), 82–85
  and aggregate demand, 103–104
  and aggregate supply, 104
  in business cycle, 87
  and recession of 2007–2009, 153–154
Real-balances effect, 24–25, 103
Real interest rate, 94–95, 216
Recession(s), 87
  fiscal policy counteracting, 118–119
  historic, 87–89, 118
  and monetary policy, 132–135
Recession of 2007–2009, 118, 153–160
  and African Americans, 307, 308
  beginning of, 87, 118–119
  crisis of confidence in, 158–159
  Fed's role in, 126
  and housing bubble (*see also* Housing bubble), 154–155
  and increased inflation, 155–156
  initial policy reactions to, 156–157
  and Obama stimulus package, 158–160
  role of Federal Reserve in, 126
  trade, impact on, 197
Recognition lag (fiscal policy), 118–119
Recovery (business cycle), 87
Rector, Robert, 374, 381
Redmond, Washington, 441
Refiner Acquisition Cost of Imported Oil, 409, 410
Refundable Tax Credits, 318–319
Regressions, in measuring discrimination, 310, 311
Regulated monopolies, 413
Reliant Energy, 436
Renminbi, 212
Reservation wages, 423–424
Reserve clause (sports contracts), 425

Reserve ratio, 128
Resources, 2
Restless legs syndrome, 287
Retirement, 382–390
Retirement age (Social Security), 383–384
Retirement annuities, 312–313
Retrospective payment, 274–275
Revenue, 54, 59–62
  from casino gambling, 456
  federal, 394, 395
Revenue sharing, 424–425
Revolving credit, 155–156
Reyes, Jessica, 300, 304
RGDP (*see* Real gross domestic product)
Richardson, J. David, 207
Risk, 99, 432
Risk aversion, 258
Risk neutrality, 258
Risk premium, 99
Rivalry, 49
Rodman, Dennis, 424
Rodrik, Dani, 207
Roosevelt, Franklin, 444
Rosen, Harvey, 392
Royalties (to authors), 365–366
Rudd, Jeremy, 82, 92
Rule of 72, 99
Rules of thumb, in hiring, 309
Russia, trade with, 205
Ruth, Babe, 425

S

Safeway, 450–452
Salary caps (sports), 424
Sales taxes, 453
Sampson, Ralph, 424
Sam's Club, 450
SAT scores, 353–355
Saudi Arabia, 232, 406
Saving:
  for retirement, 385–386
  and tax rates, 399
Scalping tickets, 343–348
Scarce resources, 2
Schaller, Bruce, 53
Scherer, F. M., 289
Schieber, Sylvester J., 390, 392
Schiller, Robert J., 439
SCHIPs (*see* State Child Health
      Insurance Programs)
Schliefer, Andrei, 439
Schmalensee, Richard, 256
School Lunch program, 376

School reform issues, 356–359
School vouchers, 358
Schumpeter, Joseph, 92
Scientific method, 21
S-corporations, 432n
Screen Actors' Guild, 446
Seasonal unemployment, 86
Section 8 apartments, 376
Securitization, 164–165
Sellers, number of, 30, 33
September 2001 attacks, 134
    oil price swings following, 409
    and spending increases, 152
Sex discrimination, 309, 312–314
Sex tours, 242
Sheehan, Richard, 428
Sheiner, Louise, 125
Shocks, 116
    aggregate demand, 116–117
    aggregate supply, 117–118
Shogren, Jason F., 256
Short run, 71, 340
Short sale, 169
Shortages, 24, 33–34
Shoven, John, 390, 392
Siegfried, John, 428
Simple monopolies, 412, 413
Simplifying assumption, 3
Sindelar, Jody, 242
Single-payer system, 265–266
Skinner, Jonathan, 148, 161, 281
Slave labor, 204
Slemrod, Joel, 403
Slope, 14, 41–42
Smeeding, Timothy, 375, 377, 381
Social cost, 247
Social engineering, taxes for, 399, 400
Social insurance, 387
Social Security, 144–145, 270, 382–390
    benefits under, 383–384
    cost of living adjustment (COLA), 80n
    economic effects of, 385–386
    fixing, 389–390
    funding for, 388–390, 189–195
    history of, 382–384
    need for, 384–385
    spending on, 152
    taxes for, 150–151, 384
    temporary tax cut for, 383
    value of, 386–387
Social Security Act (1935),
    382
Social Security Trust Fund,
    155, 277, 388–390
Socialism, 20

Solar power, 247, 254
Solow Growth Model, 230–231
Somalia, lawlessness in, 292
Sony, 181
South Korea, 231
Sowell, Thomas, 316
Soybean prices, 327
S&P 500, 429, 430, 432, 437
Spain:
    and debt to GDP, 222
    and the euro, 219, 225
    GDP growth, 219
    and housing bubble, 219, 221–224
    and long term interest rates, 221
    per capita GDP, 221
Spending:
    on crime control, 300–301
    on education, 142–144, 352–355, 363, 367–368
    by federal government
        (*see* Federal spending),
    on sports stadiums, 420
    on welfare, 377
Sports, 417–427
    city-based teams, 418–423
    economics of, 424–427
    labor market for, 423–427
    relocation of NCAA, 419
    relocation of teams, 419–420
    return on investment in, 421–423
    spending on stadiums, 420
    winning vs. profiting of teams,
        421–423
Sprint/Nextel, 69
SSI (*see* Supplemental Security Income),
St. Louis, Missouri, 418
St. Petersburg, Florida, 418
Standard and Poor's (*see also* S&P 500), 430
Standard deduction (income tax), 396
Staples, 453
State budgets, 158
State Child Health Insurance Programs (SCHIPs), 144–145,
    269, 271
State College, Pennsylvania, 441
State Farm, 436
States:
    education spending by, 351
Medicaid programs of, 270–271
    minimum wages set by, 337, 342
Statistical discrimination, 309
Steiger, Douglas, 138
Steuerle, C. Eugene, 386, 392
Stevens, Ted, 141
Stiglitz, Joseph, 439
Stock, James H., 138
Stock indexes, 432

Stock market, 429–438
  in 2006–2007, 437
  in 2008–2009, 437–438
  and accounting scandals, 434–437
  crashes of, 432–434
  efficient, 432
  function of, 431–432
  stock price determination, 430–431
Stock options, 436
Stock prices, 430–431
Stone, Kenneth E., 454
Strikes:
  in history of unions, 445–447
  in sports, 425–426
"Strong dollar," 113–114
Structural deficit, 153–154
Structural unemployment, 87
Student loans, 101, 292, 367
Subsidies:
  government, 26, 28–29, 30, 32–33
  in-kind, 375
  of nonsmokers by smokers, 238
  for public universities (*see also* Price supports), 362–363
Substitutes, 26, 27, 29
  with casinos, 455–456
  number and closeness of, 43
  and price changes, 80–81
  with sports events, 419
  with super stores, 453
Substitution effect, 24, 398
  and income taxes, 398
Summers, Lawrence H., 439
"Super" stores, 452, 453
Supervalu, 451, 452
Supplemental Security Income (SSI), 270, 376
Supply, 21
  aggregate, 104–111
  determinants of, 29–33
  elasticity of, 45–46
  excess, 24
  law of, 25–26
  under perfect competition, 70–74
  price elasticity of, 40
  quantity supplied vs., 19–20, 21
Supply and demand model, 18, 37
  and ceteris paribus, 21
  and changes in oil prices, 408–409
  and changes in price expectations, 33
  demand schedule, 21–22
  determinants of demand, 26–29
  determinants of supply, 29–33
  equilibrium, 23
  and equilibrium changes, 33–35

  for health care, 261–262
  for international trade, 202
  law of demand, 24–25
  law of supply, 25–26
  markets, 19
  quantity demanded and quantity supplied, 19–20
  shortages and surpluses, 24, 33–34
  supply schedule, 23
Supply curve, 19, 25–26, 29–33
  decriminalization of illegal goods/services, 240–241
  and law of supply, 25–26
  movements in, 32–33
  for ticket scalping, 347
Supply schedule, 23
Supply-side economics, 111
Supply-side macroeconomics, 111
Surpluses, 24, 33–34
  budget (*see also* Federal budget), 150
  consumer (*see also* Consumer surplus), 47–48
  producer (*see also* Producer surplus), 48
Survivor benefits (Social Security), 383–384
Swartz, Katherine, 260

T

Taco Bell, 69
Taft-Hartley Act, 445
Tampa Bay area, Florida, 418
TANF (*see* Temporary Assistance to Needy Families)
Target, 435, 450, 451
Target Supercenters, 451
Tariffs, 204
TARP (*see* Troubled Assets Rescue Plan)
Taste, 26, 27, 28
Tax cuts, 110–111, 114–115
  by Bush, 123, 157, 152, 401
  impacts of, 119–120
  in Obama stimulus plan, 146, 169–170
  political debates on, 111, 146, 399–401
  sources of money for, 117
Tax tables, 397
Taxable income, 396
Taxes, 9
  and casino gambling, 456
  for education, 352, 356–359
  EITC, 339, 376, 398, 400n
  on emissions, 253–254
  excise, 26, 28–33
  federal revenue from, 394, 395
  and fiscal policy lags, 118–119
  on gasoline, 411
  income, 111, 115, 151n, 152, 394, 401
  and inflation, 110

Medicare/Medicaid, 258–266, 269–279
  in Obama stimulus plan, 111, 115
  under Reagan, 151, 152
  during Revolutionary War, 180
  sales, 453
  and shift in aggregate demand, 106–109
  for Social Security, 150–151, 384, 386, 388–390
  supply-side impact of, 111
  tariffs, 204
  on tobacco and alcohol, 239
Taylor, John B., 120, 125, 158
Teachers, 350–358, 361–363, 441
Teamsters Union, 443, 446, 447
Technology:
  as determinant of supply, 30–31
  and used textbook sales, 367
Temporary Assistance to Needy Families
        (TANF), 270, 376, 397
Tenure, for teachers, 357
Term papers, sale of, 30–31
Terms of trade, 202
Terre Haute, Indiana, 455–456
Texas, prisons in, 301
Texas Motor Speedway, 427
Textbooks
  electronic, 366–367
  market of, 364–366
  renting, 364–366, 367
Third-party payers, 262–263
Thorton, Mark, 242
Ticket brokers/scalping, 343–348
Time, elasticity and, 43
Tobacco, 234–239
Topel, Robert, 381
Total cost, 57–59
Total cost function, 58
Total expenditure rule, 43
Total revenue (TR), 61–62
Toyota, 181
TR (total revenue), 61–62
Trade (*see* International trade)
Trade barriers, 203–204
Trade protection, 206–207
Trademarks, 291
Traditional mortgages, 164–165
Training, federal spending on, 142
Triest, Robert, 381
Troubled Assets Rescue Program (TARP), 9, 119,
        140, 153, 169, 177, 223–224
Trough (business cycle), 87
Truman, Harry, 113, 445
Trust funds, 150, 155
  Medicare, 270, 273–280
  Social Security, 155, 277, 388–390

Tschirhart, John, 256
Tuition tax credit, 398

U

Unattainable production level, 5
Underemployment, 85–86
Underground economy, 228, 230
Unemployment, 85–87
  and aggregate supply, 104–105
  classical and Keynesian views of, 104–105
  measuring, 85–87
  in Obama stimulus plan, 146
  and production possibilities frontier, 5
  in recession of 2007–2009, 158, 310
  types of, 86–87
Unemployment rates, 85–86
  during depressions, 89
  post-World War II, 86
  during recessions, 88
Uninsured persons, 260
Unions, 440–448
  future of, 447
  history of, 444–447
  as monopolies, 443–444
  public vs. private employees in, 445, 446
  reasons for, 440–443
  in sports, 425–426
  for teachers, 357
Unitary elasticity, 41
United Association of Journeymen and Apprentices of the
        Plumbing and Pipe Fitting Industry of the United
        States and Canada, 442n
United Auto Workers, 443, 446
United Automobile, Aerospace, and Agricultural
        Workers of America, 443n
United Kingdom, (*see also* Great Britain) 154, 265–266
United Mine Workers of America, 443
United Nations Intergovernmental Panel on
        Climate Change, 247
United Parcel Service (UPS), 446, 447
United States:
  antipoverty spending in, 377
  and Arab–Israeli wars, 405
  balance of payments for, 210
  as debtor nation, 209
  debt-to-GDP ratio for, 154
  drug prices in, 287
  health care compared to other countries, 265–266
  poverty in, 375
United Steelworkers of America, 446
University education, 361–368
UPS (*see* United Parcel Service)

V

Van der Linde, Claas, 256
Variable costs, 57–59
Variable inputs, 55
Verizon Wireless, 69
Vermont, 450
Vertical equity (income taxes), 398
Veterans' benefits, federal spending on, 142
Vig, 457

W

Wachovia, 158
Wages:
   in developed vs. developing countries, 231
   gender differences in, 306
   living, 335
   minimum wage, 296, 330, 335–341
   under monopsony, 442
   and perfect competition, 441, 443
   racial inequalities in, 310–311
   reservation, 423–424
   for sports players, 425–426
   union control of, 443
   at Walmart, 453
   Wagner Act, 444–445
Waldfogel, Jane, 316
The Wall Street Journal, 20
Walmart Supercenters, 450–452
Walton, Sam, 452
War, costs of veteran's benefits, 143
Wastewater treatment, 250
Water pollution, 250
Watson, Mark W., 138
Wealth:
   gender differences in, 306
   and home ownership, 374
Wealth inequality, 292, 317–323
   causes of, 321–322
   measurements of , 320–321
Weather, changes in, 250–251
Wegmans, 452
Weitzman, Martin, 256
Welfare, 371, 375–379
   federal spending on, 143–145
   in Obama stimulus plan, 159–160
   reform of, 378–379
   results of, 377–379
   spending on, 377
   types of programs, 375–376
   Welfare dependency, 379, 379

Wells Fargo, 158
Wendy's, 69
Weyant, John P., 256
White, Eugene N., 439
WIC (*see* Women, Infants and Children)
Wildlife, extinction of, 244, 250–251
Williamson, Jeffrey G., 207
Wilson, Woodrow, 444
Wind power, 247, 254
Winkler, Anne, 316
Winn-Dixie, 450
Wisconsin, 193, 358, 447
Withholding, tax, 394–395
Wolff, Edward, 381
Women:
   and affirmative action, 313–314
   economic status of, 305–306
   poverty among, 373
   sex discrimination, 309, 312–314
   in teaching, 357
Women, Infants and Children (WIC), 376–377
Wood, Adrian, 207
Work effort:
   effect of Social Security on, 385
   and minimum wage, 340
   tax incentives for, 398
Work force:
   for economic growth, 229
   effect of Wal-Mart on, 452–453
Work stoppages, 446
Worker productivity, economic growth
     and, 228–229
WorldCom, 437

X

X-axis, 14
Xerox, 437
X-intercept, 14

Y

Y-axis, 14
Yield curve, 99
Yinger, John, 316
Y-intercept, 14

Z

Zimbalist, Andrew